We dedicate this work to the memory of two colleagues who participated in the early planning of this research project, Howard Palmer and Shankar Yelaja.

ETHNICITY AND CULTURE IN CANADA

The Research Landscape
Edited by J.W. Berry and J.A. Laponce

Ethnicity, write J.W. Berry and J.A. Laponce in their introduction to this volume, is likely to be to the twenty-first century what class was to the twentieth; that is, a major source of tension and political conflict. However, ethnicity is also increasingly likely to be a source of inspiration and diversification within society.

Because of the rapidly developing importance of ethnicity and culture in Canada, the Social Sciences and Humanities Research Council and the Ministry of Multiculturalism and Citizenship undertook in 1991 a project to review research on the subject. This volume, in nineteen chapters, is the record of the findings. The papers cover such topics as demography, political philosophy, history, anthropology, sociology, media studies, literature, language learning, education, and ethnic and multicultural attitudes.

Looking back to the Commission on Bilingualism and Biculturalism, mandated in 1963, the editors point out that the terminology has changed radically, and that the evolution from biculturalism to multiculturalism has clarified not only the political agenda but the research agenda as well. An insistent theme recurs throughout this volume: multiculturalism is taken increasingly as being a characteristic of Canadian society as a whole, rather than a concept focused exclusively on new Canadians.

While the Canadian population has always been ethnically diverse, only recently has the diversity been systematically analysed. Ethnic and multicultural studies are remarkably well developed in Canada, the editors conclude. However, they point out one shortcoming more apparent in some fields than others: we often know quite well how the dominant group views a minority, but we often lack knowledge of the reverse attitudes and opinions. Berry and Laponce recommend that we replace one-way mirrors with windows, preferably open windows.

J.W. Berry is a professor in the Department of Psychology, Queen's University.

J.A. Laponce is a professor in the Department of Political Science, University of British Columbia, and the Institute of Interethnic Relations, University of Ottawa.

Ethnicity and Culture in Canada: The Research Landscape

EDITED BY J.W. BERRY
AND J.A. LAPONCE

UNIVERSITY OF TORONTO PRESS
Toronto Buffalo London

© University of Toronto Press Incorporated 1994
Toronto Buffalo London
Printed in Canada

ISBN 0-8020-2897-7 (cloth)
ISBN 0-8020-7759-5 (paper)

Printed on acid-free paper

Canadian Cataloguing in Publication Data

Main entry under title:

Ethnicity and culture in Canada: the research
landscape

Includes index.
ISBN 0-8020-2897-7 (bound) ISBN 0-8020-7759-5 (pbk.)

1. Multiculturalism – Canada. 2. Ethnology –
Canada – Research. I. Berry, John. II. Laponce,
J.A., 1925–

FC104.E85 1994   305.8′00971   C93-094628-6
FI035.A1E85 1994

Contents

viii   Contents

Acknowledgments

This book is the outcome of the project 'State of the Art Review of Research on Canada's Multicultural Society' carried out by John Berry, Jean Burnet, Rudolf Kalin, Jean Laponce, John Meisel, and Gilles Paquet. The project was jointly funded by the Social Sciences and Humanities Research Council of Canada, and by Multiculturalism and Citizenship Canada. The project consisted of a report, a bibliography, and a register of researchers on multiculturalism, which were submitted in 1992.

The two editors of this volume thank the other four members of the research group for their continuing support and guidance during the conversion of the report into book form. We are grateful to Perry Millar for indexing the English chapters and to Guylaine Daoust for indexing the French text. We, editors and authors, very much appreciated that Jean Wilson, who did the copy editing, had such sharp eyes and such a mean hand; and we appreciated equally that Anne Forte and Virgil Duff could steer the book so carefully and so quickly to publication at the University of Toronto Press. We also thank the Social Sciences and Humanities Research Council and Multiculturalism and Citizenship for their original support, and the Council for a supplementary grant for the preparation of the manuscript.

John Berry and Jean Laponce

Contributors

Dagmar Berndorff

Department of Psychology, Ontario Institute for Studies in Education

John W. Berry

Department of Psychology, Queen's University

Richard Y. Bourhis

Département de psychologie, Université du Québec à Montréal

Norman Buchignani

Department of Anthropology, University of Lethbridge

Richard Clément

École de psychologie, Université d'Ottawa

Jim Cummins

Modern Language Centre, Ontario Institute for Studies in Education

Kim Demetriou

Department of Applied Psychology, Ontario Institute for Studies in Education

Augie Fleras

Department of Sociology, University of Waterloo

Peter J. Gamlin

Department of Applied Psychology, Ontario Institute for Studies in Education

Denise Helly

Institut québécois de recherche sur la culture

Rudolf Kalin

Department of Psychology, Queen's University

Karol J. Krótki

Department of Sociology, University of Alberta

Iza Laponce

Main Library, University of British Columbia

Jean Laponce

Department of Political Science, University of British Columbia and Institute of Interethnic Relations, Department of Political Science, University of Ottawa

David Leahy

Department of French, Concordia University

Paul Letkemann

Department of Anthropology, University of Lethbridge

Anna Mitsopulos

Department of Applied Psychology, Ontario Institute for Studies in Education

Brian J. O'Neill

Faculty of Social Work, Wilfrid Laurier University

Enoch Padolsky

Department of English, Carleton University

Gilles Paquet

Faculté d'administration, Université d'Ottawa

E. Diane Pask

Faculty of Law, University of Calgary

Anthony W. Rasporich

Department of History, University of Calgary

Colin Reid

Department of Sociology, University of Alberta

Sherry Simon

Department of French, Concordia University

Elliot Tepper

Department of Political Science, Carleton University

Morton Weinfeld   Department of Sociology, University of
                       Waterloo

Shankar A. Yelaja   Faculty of Social Work, Wilfrid Laurier
                       University

ETHNICITY AND CULTURE IN CANADA

J.W. BERRY AND J.A. LAPONCE

Evaluating Research on Canada's Multiethnic and Multicultural Society: An Introduction

Ethnicity is likely to be to the twenty-first century what class was to the twentieth – a major source of social tensions and political conflicts; hence it will be a major focus of attention for an academia that will be asked to provide facts, explanations, and theories. But ethnicity is also likely to be, increasingly, a source of creation and diversification – from life-styles to constitutions to literature – that will sustain the interest of the social sciences and the humanities alike.

Less than 20 years ago, it was widely assumed that ethnicity was a source of old and disappearing cleavages, at least in industrialized and democratic societies (Glazer & Moynihan 1963; Porter 1972; Fishman 1985; van den Berghe 1981). This assumption has been defeated by facts. Ethnicity has not weakened; on the contrary it has reasserted itself as one of the major factors challenging and shaping modern societies. Why this revival? One cannot point to a single cause. The search for an explanation leads to a varied set of fundamental structural factors that reinforce one another. The globalization of the economy has produced, as a counterpoint, the desire to surround oneself with familiar, smaller, and more 'meaningful' communities; the weakening of the nation state, at a time when security and prosperity call for the formation of supranational markets and alliances, gives subnational regions a chance to assert their autonomy; the wide difference in population growth between a prosperous but demographically declining North and a poor but overpopulated South produces population migrations that keep diversifying the industrialized countries, both culturally and physically; and the very fact that modern societies have learned to moderate their class conflicts has opened the stage for the mobilization of people around ethnic interests.

Modern industrial states will keep being reshaped through the mixing, within their borders, of different races, religions, languages, and nations;

thus they will have to keep finding solutions to the ever new problems created by the clash of cultures. That will not be an easy task since, unlike economic interests, ethnic and cultural demands are not easily divisible, hence difficult to solve by compromise.

The reaction of the social sciences and humanities to the revival of ethnicity has been slow, but Canadian scholars were among the first to redirect their research and take into account an ethnic phenomenon that would not vanish from modern conditions and become a field reserved for anthropologists and historians. That leading role has been taken by institutions such as the Centre international de recherche sur le bilinguisme (founded in 1967), the Canadian Ethnic Studies Association (created in 1977), the Institut québécois de recherche sur la culture (1979), and the Laurier Institute (1983); it is measured also by the quality of journals such as *Canadian Ethnic Studies* (started in 1969), and *Canadian Review of Studies in Nationalism* (started in 1974). The increased attention paid to ethnicity is also visible at the level of university curricula, largely because, in the past 15 years, the federal government has funded over 20 chairs and institutes devoted to the study either of specific minorities (the first three chairs were chairs of Hungarian, Ukrainian, and Mennonite studies) or of interethnic relations in general (the three most recent chairs are concerned with Intercultural, Ethnic, and Race relations, Ethnic studies, and Multiethnic studies).

Other countries have followed the same road, notably the United States and Great Britain, with institutes such as the Centre for Research on Ethnic Relations (UK), the Institute of Race Relations (UK), the Center for Migration Studies (US), the Center for Research in International Migrations and Ethnicity (Sweden), the Institute for Migrations and Nationalities (Croatia) and Journals such as *Ethnic and Racial Studies* (UK), *Immigrants and Minorities* (UK), *Journal of Ethnic Studies* (US), *Explorations in Ethnic Studies* (US), *Plural Societies* (Netherlands), and *Journal of Intercultural Studies* (Australia). All major publishers in North America now have sections or divisions that deal with multiculturalism, thus reflecting the growing popularity of a subject that extends to disciplines other than anthropology. That publishing move was anticipated by book series of long standing such as those of Sage on Cross-Cultural Psychology and of Multilingual Matters on Multilingual and Multicultural Societies.

WHAT WE MEAN BY ETHNICITY AND CULTURE

The terms 'ethnicity' and 'culture' are among the least stable in the academic vocabulary. It is thus essential that we clarify at the outset what the editors and the authors of this volume mean by multicultural and by multiethnic.

Consider first the word 'ethnic.' Its recent history offers an excellent example of the difficulties faced by a term employed by academics whose specific intention was to escape the ambiguities of ordinary language. In 1896, Vacher de Lapouge, in *Les sélections sociales*, noted, quite rightly, that the term 'race' had become most confusing since it referred not only to the transmission of biological characteristics (as in *White race*) but also to the transmission of cultural values (as in *peasant race*). Let us, said de Lapouge, keep *race* for genetic inheritance and let us use either *ethne* or *ethnie* to refer to the transmission of cultural traits and values. That was more easily said than implemented at a time when ethnic and ethnos had already a variety of meanings that ranged from *nation* to *heathen* to *primitive*. His suggestion was nevertheless taken up by subsequent writers, but only very slowly. In 1906, André Siegfried still refers to English Protestants and to French Catholics as the 'two races of Canada,' and the Canadian census, up to the 1950s, used 'race' to refer to national origin. The term 'ethnic,' used in a sense that would be closer to nation than to race and applied to what was then called 'civilized' populations, did not gain wide currency until after the Second World War, but for reasons that had not been anticipated by de Lapouge and that defeated, by and large, the purpose he had in mind. 'Ethnic' was still, after the war, in the shadow of 'race,' but race had become so loaded with negative political associations that it became an irresistible temptation to use 'ethnic' as a euphemism and as a dilutant. As a result, ethnic now sometimes means race, and sometimes it does not; sometimes it covers religion and sometimes it does not. One needs the context to be able to make sense of the term. In his *Thesaurus of Ethnicity*, Fred Riggs (1985) spends over 50 pages describing the uses and misuses of the word and proposing a whole set of specialized terms that would avoid confusion; but thus far he has been even less successful than Vacher de Lapouge.

The word 'culture' is not any clearer. It was first used by Tylor (1871) to refer to 'that complex whole which includes knowledge, belief, art, morals, laws, customs, and any other capabilities and habits acquired by man as a member of society.' A comprehensive survey by Kroeber and Kluckhohn (1952) identified over 200 formal definitions of the term. Their contribution has been to categorize these definitions into six groups: *descriptive* (lists of what is included); *historical* (emphasizing heritage and descent); *normative* (emphasizing shared rules); *psychological* (emphasizing the processes of adaptation and learning); *structural* (emphasizing organization and pattern), and *genetic* (emphasizing the origin or genesis of ɪre). No single definition appears to have general acceptance at the present time.

It should thus be expected that, in the papers to follow, the usage of the terms multiethnic and multicultural will not be systematic. The organizers of the conference where these papers were first discussed did not impose their own definitions of the terms on the authors, not only because they did not share one among themselves and knew that semantic diktats are pointless anyway, but also because they recognized that the various disciplines involved had different needs.

The meanings of our two key terms will be found to range from the wide definitions of Laponce and Berry and Kalin to the narrower definitions of Simon and Padolsky. Laponce takes the position that, from a research point of view, it is advantageous to consider that everyone in Canada is ethnic, whether the term is used to describe – to take only one example – someone describing himself or herself as simply 'German' or 'German-Canadian' or simply 'Canadian.' Kalin and Berry's position is very close, although they are more reluctant than Laponce to apply the term 'ethnic' to people who consider themselves to be simply Canadians. Narrower definitions, such as those used by Simon and Padolsky, are more common and more useful in the fields of language and literature where one needs to restrict the corpus to minority cultures; in that case the definition excludes dominant groups. But, whatever definition they use, the authors are in agreement in thinking that it would be a mistake to study these minority groups or cultures out of context, out of the complex set of minority-dominant group relations[1].

Why use the twin concepts of multicultural and multiethnic? Would not one have been sufficient? If we include ethnicity and culture in our title, it is not only because they recur in the book; but because, while often synonymous when they are preceded by the qualifier 'multi,' they capture, at times, significant differences. Consider, for example, the following classification problem: if we have the choice of taking Blacks, Catholics, and Hutterites as examples of groups belonging either to a multicultural or to a multiethnic society, would we not, in certain contexts, say Canada at large, be reluctant to use the cultural definer for Blacks, and the ethnic definer for Catholics, while Hutterites could fit into either category?

If so, why? Because ethnic is more likely to refer to the primordial group into which one is born, while cultural refers to the primordial set of behaviours and attitudes that one experiences or displays? If that is the case we should find a frequent lack of congruence between the ways individuals and groups perceive themselves and the way they are perceived by others, and we should be able to trace the effects of policies that make a group become or appear to be more cultural than ethnic or vice versa. The controversy over the enumeration of Métis as proposed by the Charlottetown Agreement reflects this tension between the two terms. If the boundaries of a group are made more rigid and a function of inheritance criteria, one risks shifting the perception of that group away from the cultural towards the racial.

Even the academics who often use the terms multicultural and multiethnic interchangeably would probably not rank the two terms in the same semantic space on the Osgood dimensions that differentiate meaning.[2] How much simpler if one had followed Vacher de Lapouge's recommendation. That would have avoided much confusion.

That confusion is unlikely to diminish. Linguistics tells us that the life expectancy of words varies according to whether they are positively or negatively loaded. Words with negative loadings die sooner than those with a positive charge and are replaced by euphemisms. We should thus expect that, one of our two key concepts, multiculturalism, will, at least in the ordinary language, push multiethnic aside since ethnic is partly used to mean race. That is indeed what seems to be happening. For example, a recent booklet published by Multicultural Studies to advertise video cassettes intended to be used for instruction in the humanities and social sciences covers exclusively racial minorities. That shift in language occurs also at the academic level. An on-line search of the computerized UBC card catalogue indicates that out of 398 books entered since 1978 with either 'multiethnic' or 'multicultural' in their titles, multicultural accounted for 90 per cent of the total.[3] We are close to having come full circle. In the nineteenth century, race was used to mean culture as well as race. The twentieth may well end with culture meaning race as well as culture.

THE RISE OF MULTICULTURALISM

Let us pursue our semantic discussion and use it to describe the evolution of Canadian government policy concerning what we now call multiculturalism. Let us start by recalling the very words of the Commission on Bilingualism and Biculturalism mandate of 1963 (the so-called B & B Commission). That Commission was instructed to 'make recommendations designed to ensure the bilingual and basically bicultural character of the federal administration' and to report on the role of private and public organizations 'in promoting bilingualism, better cultural relations and a more wide-spread appreciation of the basically bicultural character of our country and of the subsequent contribution made by the other cultures' (1969). The other cultures are presented here as a historical appendage that does not affect the *basically bicultural* character of Canada. Today, the language of the document appears very dated. Irrespective of whether that original position was and remains sociologically and politically right – a point discussed by Gilles Paquet in his paper – one cannot but be struck by the magnitude of the shift in language when comparing the mandate of the B & B Commission to recent documents such as the Charter of Rights and Freedoms or the Canada Clause of the Charlottetown Agreement. The shift was initiated by the B & B commissioners themselves in Volume 4 of their report, a volume that recommended enhancing the 'other cultures.' One of the non-French and non-English commissioners, Professor Rudnyckyj, in his minority report, suggested going even further and promoting regional languages. The federal government did not go that far when it introduced, in 1971, its policy of multiculturalism, a policy intended to reduce levels of prejudice, to support and encourage heritage cultural maintenance, to reduce pressures towards assimilation, and to promote intergroup contact and sharing in order to avoid ethnocultural group isolation. But that policy statement, by stating that there were 'no official cultures,' gave status to cultures other than French and English. Section 27 of the 1982 Charter of Rights had the same effect and opened the possibility, discussed by Pask in her paper, that the promotion of culture eventually would be extended to cover language. The federal Multiculturalism Act of 1988 reaffirmed a policy promoting the freedom of all to 'preserve, enhance and share their cultural heritage,' stated that the promotion of multiculturalism was 'a fundamental characteristic of Canadian heritage and identity,' and encouraged Canadian institutions to be 'both respectful and inclusive of Canada's multicultural character.' The ill-fated Canada Clause of the 1992 Charlottetown Agreement (ill-fated for reasons other than its provisions concerning multiculturalism) proposed reinforcing the status of the cultures other than those of anglophones and francophones. Since the 1960s the official ground has been shifting in the direction of multiculturalism.

There are two major reasons for that evolution, one demographic, the other political. The demographic studies surveyed in the papers by Tepper and by Krótki and Reid measure a considerable shift in the composition of the Canadian population. Among immigrants, the third pillar, that consisting of settlers of non-British non-French origin, keeps growing and is already the largest. To ignore that fact is no longer politically possible.

The policy of protecting and increasing the status of minority groups is also a strategy of nation-building (Wilson, 1991). Such policy is similar to that of the European kings who formed alliances with the lower orders against the feudal barons, the Canadian barons being the provinces.

More fundamentally, we may also see at work here an expansion mechanism particular to democratic systems. Schattschnieder (1960) identified that mechanism when studying the expansion of the franchise from the eighteenth century onward. In an adversarial system, he says, it will normally be to the advantage of either the government or the opposition that some new groups be brought into the electorate. Promises will be made to that effect, and the groups eventually will be enfranchised. Similarly, when one defines the political coalition 'game' in terms of groups rather than individuals, the logic of democratic expansion calls for more and more such groups appearing on the scene, particularly ethnic groups that will use envy as an emotion and equality as a principle to enhance their relative position. There is thus, as noted by Rocher (1973), an inherent contradiction between the principles of bilingualism and multiculturalism.

The number of ethnic groups that have become major players in the constitutional, and more generally in the whole political field, has increased significantly in the last decade. Whether these groups are 'Children of the Charter' (Cairns 1992) or groups that claim a similar status, the political process has become markedly more complicated. Gone are the days of classical British parliamentary democracy. The representatives are no longer trusted to represent. Canada has become a kind of *Landsgemeinde* writ large, a huge town hall meeting, but one that would not trust the elders. Has that development been functional for the ethnic minorities? Probably not for Quebec, since the political system has lost much of the flexibility it needs to accommodate the changing relations of its two major ethnic communities. However, functional or not, the evolution from *bi* to *multi* is in the logic of nation-building by a dominant ethnic group that rests its legitimacy, in part, on its ability to arbitrate the often divergent claims of the less powerful ethnic communities.

But is the dominant ethnic group still capable of arbitrating? Increasingly one hears it queried whether there is anyone who can speak for English Canada. That the latter's head be no more visible than the hand of Adam Smith may be unsettling, but that does not necessarily imply ineffectiveness. Invisible as it may be, the government of English Canada is probably much more effective than it might appear to be, at least at the level of ethnic goal setting. However, we lack, as noted by Jean Laponce in his paper, studies of the interaction between ethnicity and politics, notably electoral politics for groups other than anglophones and franco-phones.

While complicating the political 'game,' hence making Quebec's cards more difficult to play, the evolution from *bi* to *multi* has helped bring to the fore and one hopes put on the road to resolution an issue not surveyed in this book, the long sidetracked Aboriginal question. Has that same policy of multiculturalism been equally favourable to the newcomers? The opinions range from strong hostility to strong endorsement, but often the positions taken on the issue derive from general political preferences and assumptions rather than from observed effects on the groups concerned. To measure these effects we need more studies of the kind done in Toronto by Raymond Breton and his colleagues (Breton et al. 1990).

It is likely that the effects of the policy of multiculturalism will be positive for the individuals who want to maintain some level of ethnic distinctiveness, but dysfunctional for those who want to lose it. Imagine three new immigrants from a non-French, non-English background: one wants to retain culture and language, the second wants to retain culture but not language, and the third wants to retain neither. At first, all three will be pleased by a multicultural policy that is the equivalent of a smile and a welcome, the equivalent of opening a door and paying a compli-ment to the guest. However, the immigrant who wants to assimilate and cross the threshold only once will become annoyed if the host keeps smiling and saying something nice and opening the door again and again; that forces one into the minority frame of mind that one either never had or wanted to leave behind.[4] Our second hypothetical newcomer will keep being pleased, but not the first when he or she realizes that keeping one's culture does not imply keeping also one's language. A less welcoming policy might not have created expectations that were not or could not be met. For a proper policy assessment, we need many more measures than those now available of the frequency of these three types and of their actual perceptions and reactions.

OVERVIEW OF THE VOLUME

This volume grew out of the 'State of the Art Review of Research on Canada's Multicultural Society' commissioned by the department of Multiculturalism and Citizenship and the SSHRCC in 1991. It attends to four specific features of Canada's multicultural society: *ethnocultural groups* (their demography, immigrant history, settlement patterns, language, and cultural maintenance or loss), *Canadian society and its institutions* (national policies and programs, immigration, preferential status, employment equity), *social relationships* between ethnocultural groups and the society at large (conflict, prejudice, ethnic and racial attitudes, discrimination, equality of access), and finally *integration and acculturation* (social and economic adaptation, separation, marginalization, official language learning, and citizenship).

Unable to survey the whole field covered by Canadian ethnic and cultural studies, the conveners of the conference at which these papers were first presented asked each author to survey the fields within his or her area of specialization. We are thus proceeding by depth probes rather than by extensive coverage. If that results in regrettable gaps and shortcomings, the fault is not with the authors. It is entirely with the editors and organizers of the project.

The authors were asked not only to survey their field but also to end their paper with specific recommendations. For these field-by-field, subfield-by-subfield recommendations, the reader should turn to the relevant papers. Here, let us simply highlight some of these observations and recommendations.

We are in general agreement in our overall assessment: ethnic and multicultural studies are remarkably well developed in Canada. A large number of academics in university and other settings, and a sizeable group of private sector experts, consider multiculturalism to be part of their core interests. We identified about 400 of them in 32 disciplines in the Social Science Register produced by the University of Western Ontario; and the bibliography prepared by Iza Laponce for the period 1970–90 lists nearly 5000 entries under the headings of multiethnic and multicultural in fields other than education and literature.

The first six papers – those by Karol Krótki and Colin Reid, Gilles Paquet, Denise Helly, Elliot Tepper, Diane Pask, and Anthony Rasporich – document substantial knowledge about the fundamental character of Canada's multiethnic society. They do identify, however, a number of shortcomings.

First, while the Canadian population has always been ethnically diverse, only recently has that diversity been analyzed systematically. In part, that has been because the diversity has increased; in part it has been because some hitherto excluded groups in the population, notably the First Nations, have begun to be considered as full partners, thus expanding the focus of attention beyond French-English relations. That so many of us are recent converts to such globalization will explain an insistent theme that recurs throughout this volume, as it recurs throughout this introduction: that multiculturalism be taken, increasingly, as a characteristic of Canadian society as a whole, rather than be focused exclusively on New Canadians. With this change in definition academia went through an evolution similar to that of the Department of Multiculturalism and Citizenship.

Second, we recognize that ethnic demographers, using as their chief source the Canadian census, have made available a great deal of information about the diversity of the population. They have examined immigration, ethnic origin, ethnic intermarriage, language knowledge and language retention, and educational levels. The Canadian census is one of the very best for the study of multiculturalism, but it has serious limitations. It does not allow the analyst to distinguish between ethnic origin and ethnic identity. When using census data, it is thus easy to slip into making the assumption that those of neither British, French, nor First Nations origin are New Canadians, not only by their origins, but in their present identification as well. It is also easy to assume that ethnic origin is fixed, although researchers have found that some individuals report different ethnic origin from one census to another. This may be because of changes in national and political divisions, or changes in psychological attachment to multiple ethnic realities. Ethnic origin data indicate the potential strength of ethnic categories, but the origin reported to the census may never have explained much of a person's behaviour patterns and values or may have ceased to be relevant because of assimilation that for long was public policy, and may still remain, as indicated earlier, the newcomers' preferred outcome. We hope that the census-takers will devise the appropriate questions for distinguishing between origin and identity. We hope also that the census will refine its categories to describe more precisely the immigrants from non-traditional sources that continue to be grouped into vague categories such as Black.

Third, broad philosophical questions arising out of Canada's diversity are at last receiving the attention they deserve (see notably Charles Taylor 1992). The referendum on the Charlottetown Agreement invited a public debate over the notions of citizenship and of individual and collective rights. The call for such a debate, made in the pages that follow, notably by Gilles Paquet, has thus been satisfied in part by recent events and publications; but the recommendation that the philosophical debate be enlightened by the sociology and the demography of the Canadian case remains valid. The debate over individual and collective rights is in part clouded by semantic confusion, a confusion that comes often from not distinguishing two very distinct types of so-called collective rights, those given to certain categories of individuals and those given to collectivities.

The four sociopolitical papers – those by Jean Laponce, Norman Buchignani and Paul Letkemann, Morton Weinfeld, and Augie Fleras – are able to deal with only some aspects of a huge field. Most notably absent are treatments of the workplace in a multicultural setting, of pressure group activities of ethnocultural communities and organizations, and of the economic integration and impact of immigrant and ethnocultural groups. But, limited as they are, our depth probes enable us to identify some research gaps and to make specific recommendations.

Understandably, political studies of ethnicity have focused on the francophone-anglophone and more recently on the Native/non-Native cleavage. The 'others' are too often lumped into vague aggregates. We lack studies of the linkage between the political system and specific collective identities by means of electoral participation, party support, political culture, and interest group. We need many more studies of the kind done by Daiva Stasiulis (1991), Alain Pelletier (1991), and Jerome Black (1991), among too few others. There is also a need for surveys on ethnic participation in the political and economic life of Canada to be carried out at regular intervals, ideally with a repeated core of basic questions.

The two papers by Richard Bourhis and by Rudolph Kalin and John Berry, which are concerned with interethnic relations, reveal some important attitudinal and behavioural characteristics of individuals and groups. There appears to be general support among Canadians for the idea of Canada as a multicultural society. However, this support is likely to be more passive and permissive than active, and is accompanied by a desire for, and commitment to, a common Canadian identity. Unfortunately, there is only minimal continuity or compatibility between studies over time, or across regions. This makes it difficult to gain a general understanding and interpretation of the state of ethnocultural and linguistic group relations or to monitor changes over time. If multiculturalism, as many believe, is a major social experiment, then monitoring and evaluating the effects of the experiment are essential. This means that national surveys of ethnic and racial attitudes should be carried out at regular intervals.

The reviews of the ethnic (taken here in the restrictive sense of the term) and of the minority literature by Enoch Padolsky as well as by Sherry Simon and David Leahy show that a remarkable variety of groups have shared in the vast development of Canadian literature that has occurred in recent decades. The policy of multiculturalism is not the sole cause of the flowering of writing by authors of other than British or French origins: the high education level of immigrants in recent decades has increased the numbers both of readers and of writers in many ethnic groups. And the aid to writers made available through the publication program of Multiculturalism Canada has played a significant part. It is apparent, however, that obstacles still impede minority writers and critics. We need more studies on a subject that requires the joint efforts of sociology and literary criticism.

The papers by Richard Clément, Jim Cummins, Peter Gamlin and his colleagues, and Brian O'Neill and Shankar Yelaja attend to two particularly controversial aspects of multiculturalism: the respective status of official and heritage languages; and the balance between extant educational institutions and the need for institutional changes that will meet the needs of a multicultural population. The time has come for a systematic study of the effectiveness of second-language teaching and learning in Canada. The literature that we surveyed indicates a great deal of conflicting evidence, often based on shaky foundations. It is thus important that a comprehensive interdisciplinary study be carried out on language teaching and learning in Canada.

The chapter by Iza Laponce, as well as the bibliography she prepared for this review of research, reveals the large number and diversity of studies published in the past 20 years, but they also identify a problem that affects all fields concerned, one not specific to ethnic studies: Canada has not adapted sufficiently well to the needs of the electronic age in the field of information retrieval. There is a risk that we may become dependent on large commercial bibliographic servers that are not sensitive to the needs of Canadian researchers since they are located outside Canada. The electronic bibliography of more than 4500 items mentioned above, a bibliography that can be searched electronically by author's name, by index categories, and by combinations of words in title, is hardly being used for lack of a proper distribution system. We hope that Iza Laponce's proposal for the creation of a Canadian consortium of machine retrieval bibliographies or some other institution serving the community of Canadian researchers will be considered and implemented.

Finally, let us stress the need to correct a shortcoming more apparent in some fields than others, more apparent in political science, for example, than in literature or cross-cultural psychology, a shortcoming that results from spyglass and one-way mirror effects: we often know quite well how the dominant group views a minority but lack knowledge of the reverse attitudes and opinions. Here, the recommendation is that we replace the one-way mirrors with windows, preferably open windows.

NOTES

1 For the problems posed to bibliographers by the enlargement of the definition of the field of multicultural studies, see Judy Young (1992). The definition one uses has considerable research consequences. The use of a broad
definition led Berry, Kalin, and Taylor (1977) to survey *all* Canadians; while
a narrow definition led O'Bryan, Reitz, and Kuplowska (1976) to survey
only minority groups.

2 Osgood (1957) asks his subjects to locate words between the extremes of
polar dimensions such as good-bad, active-passive, dangerous-useful, and
many others. If two terms are located at the same point of such a multidi-
mentional space, they can be treated as synonymous, irrespective of what
the dictionary has to say about their respective meanings.

3 The *Psychological Abstracts* contain, in the titles listed between 1980 and
1992, the following words at the indicated frequency : ethnic+ 1442; mino-
rit+ 954, multicul+ 200; multiethnic+ 17 (the + is used to indicate that the
search includes any expansion of the word, such as minority or minorities
in the case of minorit+). In the *Current Index of Journals in Education (CIJE)*
the scores were as follows: minorit+ 1611, ethnic+ 1240, multicul+ 613,
multiethnic+ 85.

4 For the distinction between minorities by will and minorities by force, see
J.A. Laponce (1960).

REFERENCES

Berry, J.W., Kalin, R., and Taylor, D.M. (1977). *Multiculturalism and ethnic
    attitudes in Canada*. Ottawa: Ministry of Supply and Services
Black, Jerome (1991, spring). Ethnic minorities and mass politics: Some observa-
    tions in the Toronto setting. *International Journal of Canadian Studies*, 3:129–51
Breton, Raymond, Isajiw, Wsevolod, Kalbach, Warren, and Reitz, Jeffrey (1990).
    Ethnic identity and equality: Varieties of experience in a Canadian city. Toronto:
    Toronto University Press
Cairns, Alan (1992). *Charter versus federalism: The dilemmas of constitutional
    reform*. Montreal: McGill-Queen's University Press
Fishman, J. (1985). *The rise and fall of ethnic revival*. Berlin: Walter de Gruyter

Glazer, N. and Moynihan, D. (eds) (1963). *Beyond the melting pot.* Cambridge, MA: Peabody Museum

Kroeber, A. and Kluckhohn, E. (1952). *Culture: A critical review of concepts and definitions.* Cambridge, MA: Peabody Museum

Laponce, J.A. (1960). *The protection of minorities.* Berkeley & Los Angeles: University of California Press

O'Bryan, K.G., Reitz, J.G., and Kuplowska, O.M. (1976). *Non-official languages: A study in Canadian federalism.* Ottawa: Ministry of Supply and Services

Osgood, Charles, et al. (1957). *The measurement of meaning.* Urbana: University of Illinois Press

Pelletier, Alain (1991). Ethnie et politique: La représentation des groupes ethniques et des minorités visibles à la chambre des communes. In K. Megyerry (ed.), *Minorités visibles, communautés ethnoculturelles, et politique canadienne* (pp 101–59). Toronto: Dundurn Press

Porter, John (1972). Dilemmas and contradiction of a multiethnic society. *Transactions of the Royal Society of Canada.* 10:183–205n

Riggs, Fred W. (1985). *Ethnicity.* Paris: International Social Science Council

Rocher, Guy (1973). *Les ambiguités d'un Canada bilingue et multiculturel: le Québec en mutation.* Montréal: Hurtubise

Royal Commission on Bilingualism and Biculturalism (1969). *Report.* 4 books. Ottawa: Queen's Printer

Schasttschneider, E.E. (1960). *The semi-sovereign people.* New York: Holt, Rinehart & Winston

Siegfried, André (1906). *Le Canada, les deux races: problèmes politiques contemporains.* Paris: Rivière

Stasiulis, Daiva K. (1991). Partis et parti pris: la représentation des groupes ethniques en politique canadienne. In K. Megyerry (ed.), *Minorités visibles, communautés ethno-culturelles et politique canadienne* (pp 3–99). Toronto: Dundurn Press

Taylor, Charles (1992). *The politics of recognition.* Princeton: Princeton University Press

Tylor, E.B. (1871). *Primitive culture.* London: Murray

Vacher de Lapouge, G. (1896). *Les sélections sociales.* Paris: Fontemoing

Van den Berghe, Pierre (1981). *The ethnic phenomenon.* New York: Elsevier

Wilson, V. Seymour (1991). The Evolving Policy of Multiculturalism in Canada. Paper presented at the Conference on Research on Multiculturalism, Queen's University

Young, Judy (1992). Bibliographic challenges in the study of multiculturalism in the 1990s. Paper presented at the 1992 Learned Societies meetings in Charlottetown.

KAROL J. KRÓTKI AND COLIN REID

Demography of Canadian Population by Ethnic Group

DEMOGRAPHY BY ETHNIC GROUP

Data available in Canada on ethnicity are rich, pertain to a long period of time, and are of high quality – of very high quality when compared internationally. In Table 1 the ten types of census data with significance for ethnic studies and analyses are listed with their census dates: mother tongue, home language, official languages, place of birth or nativity, place of birth of parents, period of immigration, citizenship, ethnic origin, Aboriginal status, religion.[1] Apart from census data, there are data with some ethnic content in the realm of vital statistics, more generously in the summary reports of immigration authorities, and more recently through the General Social Survey (GSS) conducted by Statistics Canada in five-year cycles. For an assessment of the ethno-cultural questions in GSS see Boyd (1990). For examples of various periodic and ad hoc surveys carrying ethnic questions (literacy, alcohol and drug use, graduates in the labour market, and the like) see Goldmann (1992). Social surveys of ethnicities as such are a rare event in Canada and their numerical results unimportant in comparison with the mass of data arising out of routine sources, but there are often – almost invariably – questions on aspects of ethnicities in sampling and non-sampling surveys on other topics such as fertility. The three regional and two national fertility surveys included some ethnic questions (Krótki 1989).

Collectors and producers of Canadian data have been remarkably successful in this difficult area in terms of securing comparability over time (numerous and frequent complaints to the contrary notwithstanding, e.g., White 1990), and somewhat slow in reflecting societal changes in their statistics. Table 1 summarizes such changes as have been taking place in

TABLE 1
Ethno-cultural and language questions in Canadian censuses since Confederation

	First	1961	1966	1971	1976	1981	1986	1991
	1							4
Mother tongue	1901	x	–	x	x	x	x	x
Home language	2	–	–	x	–	x	x	x
Official languages	1901	x	–	x	–	x	x	x
Place of birth	1871	x	–	x	–	x	x	x
Place of birth of parents	1891	–	–	x	–	–	–	–
Period/year of immigratation	1901	x	–	x	–	x	–	x
Citizenship	1901	x	–	x	–	x	x	x
Ethnic origin	1871	x	–	x	–	x	x	x
Aboriginal status	3	–	–	–	–	–	x	x
Religion	1871	x	–	x	–	x	–	x

1 Census year in which asked first time before 1961
2 There is some evidence that home language was asked in 1891.
3 The Métis were recorded as such (actually as halfbreed) in 1941. Does that constitute 'aboriginal status'?
4 There was a fourth language question in the 1991 census (see note 2, Table 4)
Extracted from Census Handbook 99–104: Fig. 1, and suitably augmented with respect to 1991

census definitions. The United States tended to introduce changes in definitions and practices of data collection more rapidly and more frequently. For a summary of the significant departures among practices and consequent changes in results see Farley (1991). Race tends to be the primary focus south of the border, ethnic ancestry in Canada.

Social scientists have made frequent and imaginative use of these data, but the task is unfinished and mountains of data await attention. In the history of analysis of ethnic data two periods can be distinguished: ethnic origin until about 1965, and language thereafter. Both waves were motivated by political powers and discussions. It remains for subsequent analysis to determine why the two waves were fed so differentially.

The decisive watershed here must have been the enquiries carried out and reports made available under the auspices of the Royal Commission on Bilingualism and Biculturalism (e.g., Innis 1973), hereafter B & B.[2] The reports from this largest and most expensive social science enquiry ever conducted for Canadian society are peppered with materials relevant to multiculturalism, though the concept itself is not yet much evident.

In response to recommendations in B & B Book IV then Prime Minister Pierre Elliott Trudeau announced in 1971 a 'policy of multiculturalism within a bilingual framework.' For the reception it received among members of the public see Berry et al. (1980). It is noticeable that in those days immigrants who were 'coloured' were found to be acceptable (ibid.:264). Demographic building blocks for the discussion, such as race, people, ethnic group, language, sex differentials, and immigration received much attention. For example, B & B book 3A contains data and analyses on labour force and ethnic origin (15), income and language groups (20), mutuality of influences (78), anglophone head start (81), poverty and ethnic origin (84), individual and institutional bilingualism (90, 113), language of work (139), and so on.

Subsequently, the Employment Equity Act, the Multiculturalism Act, and the Constitution itself added to the legal and policy imperatives which drive much of the data collected and analysis conducted. Methods of data collection on visible minorities (one of the four groups singled out for attention on grounds of equity) still suffer from inadequate standardization (Boxhill 1991).

Canada has grown through immigration of different ethnic origins. The 300,000 Aboriginals (guesstimated by Charbonneau 1984:32) at the time of the Europeans' arrival experienced three centuries of depopulation (Normandeau & Piché 1984) reaching their nadir of hardly more than 100,000 in 1921 (to some writers, in 1911). The decline in the case of Indians alone took them from 128 ths (2.4 per cent of the total population of Canada) in 1901 to 106 ths (1.3 per cent; Canada DBS 1924). The Aboriginals have since grown to over 700,000 in the 1986 census or close to 3 per cent (Norris 1990:37). The peak in their growth was in the 1960s, but it still remains rapid (Robitaille & Choinière 1987), with an increasing relevance to multiculturalism (1,145,000 by 2001 according to Hagey et al. 1989) and increasing proportions outside the reserves (16 per cent in 1966, 29 per cent in 1984 – Siggner 1986). The demographic history of Aboriginals can be traced only with difficulty. In addition to the ever-present issues of coverage and completeness (two different concepts not always understood by analysts), as well as differential attitudes to self-reporting by Aboriginal respondents, resulting in such manifestations as the boycotting of enumerations, the various administrations disclosed in the past varying attitudes to the inclusion and exclusion of Aboriginals (e.g., Kuczynski 1930).

Table 2 shows the proportion of Canadian-born in the first five population censuses by province. As noted by Beaujot & McQuillan (1982: 87) although 'the eastern provinces welcomed the majority of immigrants into the country, they were not able to retain many of them as permanent residents. Indeed the Ontario-Quebec border constitutes a dividing line

TABLE 2
Proportion of population born in Canada by province 1871–1911

| Province | 1871[1] | Per cent Canadian-born | | | |
		1881	1891	1901	1911
Prince Edward Island		91.3	94.1	95.6	97.3
Nova Scotia	91.6	93.6	94.1	94.7	92.3
New Brunswick	86.3	90.3	93.1	94.6	94.8
Quebec	93.3	94.3	94.5	94.6	92.7
Ontario	72.6	77.7	80.8	85.2	79.9
Manitoba		74.3	70.8	70.1	58.1
Saskatchewan			80.9	57.6	50.5
Alberta					43.3
British Columbia		70.7	57.9	55.8	43.1
CANADA	83.0	85.9	86.6	87.0	78.0

SOURCE: Census of Canada, 1871–1911
Adapted from Beaujot & McQuillan 1982
1 Most of them born in British (and French) territories that became Canada in 1867

between favoured and unfavoured destinations.' We split the table into two parts to show this dividing line in proportions born. The lower part of the table shows proportions, which public opinion would have found excessive today. Admittedly, the numbers were small and the society lived in ignorance. Yet, its mild disquiet gave rise to the cry about 'Sifton's folly' and to the quinquennial census.[3]

There were significant differences among ethnic groups in their preferences for given regions. British and German immigrants were more likely to be attracted to Ontario than other European groups, while American immigrants were particularly attracted to the wide-open western regions. In 1911, 22 per cent of Alberta's population and 14 per cent of Saskatchewan's was born in the United States ... [G]roups of immigrants often came from quite restricted areas in their countries of origin. Interestingly, when we look closely at their destinations we frequently find a quite localized pattern of settlement as well. This is typical of what demographers term 'chain migration,' a pattern whereby migrants are aided by friends and relatives already established in the new homeland. (Beaujot & McQuillan 1982:87)

Two more comments need to be made before this introduction is concluded. Over time, the source of immigrants changed radically. The category 'other,' which accounted for 7 per cent of immigrants before the First World War, grew to 66 per cent some years after the Second World War. Ethnically important, this change is linguistically much less important, as will be shown in the section on languages. It will be recalled that since 1965 it is languages that matter.

The second comment is that early immigrants brought with them healthy reproductive habits: the six children with the homely wife advocated by Sir Clifford, while still plain Mr Sifton, federal minister of interior; not so more recent immigrants. Fertility rates by ethnicity (e.g., George 1978:47; Basavarajappa & Halli 1987) show that nontraditional immigrants known for their high fertility in their countries of origin started adjusting to Canada's low fertility before they migrated (see section on the overriding influence of low fertility). Even before the nontraditional immigrants became important, the foreign-born already by 1971 had on the average irrespective of their period of immigration, and for all age groups, fertility lower than Canadian-born (e.g., ibid.:44).

ENDOGAMY/EXOGAMY

Ethnic intermarriage is the route to the melting pot and assimilation, in the sense that it is through intermarriage that assimilation is both begun and completed. For a somewhat less apocalyptic assessment of intermarriage, see Lachapelle and Henripin (1982:149). For a discussion of ethnic identity and ethnic intermarriage see Goldstein and Segall (1985). For a theoretical exercise on the effect of intermarriage in the disappearance of mother tongues in Canada see Laponce (1987: Table 20).

Intermarriage has been studied in Canada whenever suitable data have become available. The works *are* numerous, some being general, some dealing with one ethnic group, some concerned with the effect of intermarriage on the ethnic composition/identity, some tracing genetic composition (e.g., Brym et al. 1985; Castonguay 1979, 1983; De Braekeleer 1990; Goldstein & Segall 1985). Basavarajappa (1978) reported on proportions married by sex, by ethnic group and birthplace, as well as by religious group and birthplace. He found high proportions married among the foreign-born for each ethnic and religious group, or most of the groups, but ignored intermarriage. Veevers (1977:19) reported a very slight decline in ethnic endogamy between 1961 and 1971 from 78 per cent to 77 per cent, all ten ethnic groups taking part in it except Jews. The support given to endogamy by some religions (Jews, Hindus, Moslems) is not studied much in Canada. De Vries and Vallee (1980) reported on the basis of ethnicity in the 1971 census that the French had the highest endogamy, next to the British and the native Indian/Inuit, and the Scandinavians and Poles the lowest (p 155). Needless to say, for the same ethnicities but foreign-born the endogamy is much higher (p 161). For mother-tongue endogamy, the pecking order is the same, but understandably again at a higher level (p 164). Since the emergence of multiethnicities in the population censuses of 1981 and 1986 we have indirect data on the eventual outcome of intermarriage. These are discussed below in the section on multiethnicities, multilanguages, and measurements of the future.

The census provides data on intermarriage, but vital statistics do not, at least not since one large province removed ethnic origin from its registration certificates (probably without notifying the National Vital Statistics Council). As an example, the vital statistics report for 1946 (Canada DBS 1949) contains tables on births by racial origin of parents (pp 106 & 124) and birthplaces of parents (pp 126 & 146), tables on mortality by racial origin (pp 165 & 212) and birthplaces of parents (pp 166 & 226), tables on nuptiality by birthplaces of bridegrooms and brides (p 658), and religious denominations of bridegrooms and brides (p 674), but apparently no nuptiality by racial origin. These analytic riches are no longer available. What can still be obtained is the birthplace of father and mother on birth certificates in machine readable form and on CANSIM (the StatCan data bank); also birthplace and religion of bridegroom and bride (Canada 1980:44, 45). These items would enable one to study intermarriage of immigrants by birthplace and intermarriage between religions. We have not come across analytic studies relying on this information.

Demographers advising statisticians more recently noticed that mother tongue of parents and home language are missing from the birth certificate (surely ethnic origin and religion as well, Veevers 1983:29, 56) and from death and marriage certificates. These concerns percolated to the formal recommendations that ethnicity, [home?] language, and mother tongue be included on the birth certificate (but not religion? ibid.:56, 71), also presumably on the death certificate and the marriage certificate, though the committee of demographers (ibid.) dealt with fertility only.

Much of the literature on nuptiality does not deal with ethnic intermarriage (e.g., Grindstaff 1990), but the content is usually stated clearly in the title. Some monographic treatments of, say, marriage and divorce contain extensive presentations of issues in ethnic intermarriage. Kalbach (1983) gives demographic data on the propensities for ethnic intermarriage in Canada, as reflected in the ethnic origins of husbands and wives. Driedger (1983) uses demographic data on intermarriage in connection with student dating and mating. Chimbos and Agocs (1983) report on a survey, with no demographic data, of immigrants' attitudes towards their children's interethnic marriages.

Richard (1991a and 1991b) went back to intermarriages reported in the 1871 census and compared them with 1971. Ethnicities were less varied a century ago and the analysis concentrates on respondent determinants of intermarriage. Apparently, urban residence, and being native-born and literate, increased a husband's ethno-religious exogamy in 1871.

Studies of intermarriage depend on the data available. Canadian data are rich in ethnicity and languages; hence intermarriage studies focus on the two. The study of intermarriage *between* religions is also possible when the religions of the two partners have been recorded on the same document or can be record-linked. In the 1971 report on Canada's religious composition no attempt was made to assess religious intermarriage, although the data for both partners were recorded on the census document (Scott 1976). For the period 1963–72 religion endogamy declined from 84 per cent to 75 per cent (Veevers 1977:19). All 11 religions took part in it without exception, the highest endogamy remaining among Jews (86), the lowest to be found among Presbyterians (27).

In due course, as things develop in the stability or non-stability of married or common-law unions, studies of intermarriage *among* religions will become possible, provided the religions involved in sequential partnering have been recorded.[4] For remarks on serial monogamy, probably unrelated to multiculturalism, see Veevers (1977:51). As far as it has been possible to establish, intercohabitation (in the meaning of intermarriage from the perspective of endogamy/exogamy) by ethnicity, language, and religion has not been studied in Canada. For 1986, data on cohabitation by ethnicity are available (top French 12 per cent, bottom Chinese 1 per cent – Burch 1990:30); also for religion: top Catholics (yes!) 6 per cent, bottom Eastern churches 1 per cent (ibid.:32).[5]

Endogamy and exogamy can also be studied by country of origin (including various combinations with the period of immigration), the sometimes available country of last residence, by the various kinds of languages available in the basic documents (not only mother tongue, but also home language and official languages), and for that matter any variable that has been recorded for both partners in the union, such as indicators of socio-economic status (e.g., occupations), the latter conceivably of increasing importance with couples of the DINK-type (double income, no kids). Termote and Gavreau (1988) looked into the links between linguistic mobility and bilingualism and found it different for men

and women (136). Echo of the long-standing concern among some Quebecers that bilingualism is the thin edge of assimilation? In the third
release from the 1991 census (Canada 1992) it is reported that intermarry-
ing francophone mothers are more successful (56 per cent) in passing on
their French to their children than francophone fathers (44 per cent). We
did not come across a similar interest for anglophones. Termote and
Gavreau (1988) also concluded that any comparative measurement should
incorporate the size of the group (167).

IMMIGRATION/NATIVITY/CITIZENSHIP

The proportion of foreign-born was always high in Canada; say, five times
higher than in other countries that think they have a problem with
foreigners flooding in. Social scientists keep reporting on the Canadian
proportion (e.g., George 1978:11). During the three census years 1911,
1921, and 1931 it was 22 per cent, and indicators in the 1990s suggest a
long-term proportion of no less than 17 per cent. The population growth
during the last quinquennial (1986–91) was almost twice (8 per cent) that
of the previous quinquennium, largely due to increased immigration. It
has been shown that annual immigration equal to long-term declines due
to natural decrease would result in a permanent proportion of 20 per cent
foreign-born (Ryder 1990; on somewhat different assumptions, the proportion is projected to be some 24 per cent – Mitra 1992), reinforced
annually, no doubt a continuing demographic base for multiculturalism.

It is illustrative to compare the foreign-born population in Canada in
1981 with the same countries of birth in the United States in 1980 (Dumas
1990:Table 8). Europe is still important for Canada (67 per cent), twice as
important as for the US (with 34 per cent of immigrants born in Europe),
though data on arrivals in Canada since 1981 show that the Canadian dependence on Europe will lessen. For the US it is the countries of Central
and South America that are, proportionately speaking, more than twice as
important as for Canada (33 and 13 per cent); from Asia 18 per cent in the
US and 14 per cent in Canada. The US apparently has been ready to take in
for quite some time immigrants from nontraditional sources. (Are social
scientists and policy makers ignorant of this situation?) However, the
proportions from nontraditional sources have to be put against absolute
numbers: almost 4 million foreign-born in Canada and 14 million in the
US, instead of 40 million in the US, if the tenfold principle is applied to
such a comparison.

Changes in immigration sources are reflected in the proportion of foreign-born by ethnicity. For example, the proportion of Ukrainians among foreign-born declined in four periods, starting 'before 1946' from 6.6 per cent through 2.9, and 0.7 to 0.4. The percentage of Asian groups changed from 1.6 through 2.4, and 7.5 to 14.4 (George 1978:48).

Yet the overriding importance of immigration for Canada has to be qualified. Canada, the country of immigration, experienced two, possibly three, important periods of net negative immigration: 1861–91, in the 1930s (George 1978:32; Kalbach 1970:26), and possibly in some years of the 1980s considering how unreliable emigration data are. During these periods, and throughout its history, Canada acted as a sieve for immigrants to the United States. Thus, the net effect of immigration on Canada was modest: 22 per cent of the growth in 1841–1940, compared with 41 in the United States (and 58 for Argentina, 19 for Brazil – Petersen 1980:240). The power of a nation's demography provides the wherewithal with which countries send out their multitudes, but economics temper or accelerate these forces. Canadian social scientists could pay attention to the interplay of these forces in Canada, among both traditional and nontraditional sources of immigrants (Krótki 1992).

The 1971 census was a boon to analytic endeavours inasmuch as it asked for the nativity of parents (Kalbach & McVey 1979:179) for the first time since 1931. By and large, it appears that being of foreign parentage, even if only one parent was foreign-born, gives income advantages over native-born (Richmond & Kalbach 1980).

The *Demographic Review* (1989) envisages the following scenario: in a few years the natural increase will become negative, the population size will start declining, at some stage the decline will be equal to the additions by immigration, and the combination of subtraction by natural increase and additions by immigration will result in zero growth. Under assumptions used by the *Demographic Review* stabilization would take place at 18 million (the same population size as in the late 1950s) in some 200 years. Students of multiculturalism need to provide alternatives on updated assumptions: e.g., when at what level will annual immigration of 250,000 stop the decline in population size?

Since the *Demographic Review* calculations, both the Canada wiggle and the Quebec wiggle on the fertility chart turned slightly upwards: Dumas (1991:41) reports a 5 per cent increase for Canada to 1.82 children and a 12 per cent increase for Quebec to 1.60. For Canada it is the increase in first children that made the main contribution, for Quebec the increase in second children. It is not possible to say which, if any, is a stronger indicator of a long-term change. What is reasonably certain, and of greater relevance from the perspective of multiculturalism, is that the 'make-up' immigration will be largely from nontraditional sources. Dumas (1990:81) shows that in 1969 the countries sending the largest numbers to Canada were Great Britain, the United States, and Italy; in 1988: Hong Kong, India, Poland (a temporary hangover from the communist regime?), and the Philippines. Here lies the interest and topicality of long-term multiculturalism!

Not much is made by Canadian social scientists out of data on citizenship, possibly because not taking out citizenship was and still is not particularly disadvantaging to the immigrant. Until recently, one could become a federal civil servant without being a citizen of the country (a unique case in the world?). Kalbach wrote about the time lag between immigration and citizenship on the basis of the 1961 census (1970:348). In 1972–4 out of the immigrants in the five years preceding the 1971 census, 60 per cent of Czechoslovakians and Poles became Canadians, but only 5 per cent of American citizens, 7 per cent of Scandinavians, and less than 10 per cent of the Irish and British West Indians (strangely enough, 19 per cent for Britishers – George 1978:67). For all foreign-born and for the categories shown in 1971, Poles have the highest proportion, with 88 per cent Canadian citizens, Spain and Portugal the lowest with 23 per cent (George 1978:60). By 1981 the highest proportions of citizens were among those born in the USSR, Africa, and Asia (Canada 1984c: Chart 17).

The proportion taking out Canadian citizenship early could be a reflection not only of the inconvenience of holding previously issued passports, but also of ethnically varying respect for orderliness of arrangements. Will the Czechoslovakian and Polish tendency to take out Canadian citizenship early lessen with the onset of democracy in their home countries (with apparent implications for multiculturalism)?

LANGUAGE RETENTION

Much of the writing on language retention in Canada treats it as a monolithic problem. In fact, the degree of language retention varies greatly among regions, leading to polarization, with only Ottawa, like Brussels, eventually remaining bilingual. Furthermore, language retention subsumes three distinct problems: transfer to English, transfer from (rarely, to) French, and allophone retention. These problems can be illustrated with the use of an index of retention, where 100 means that the population size of the ethnic group is equal to the population speaking the appropriate mother tongue. The three problems can be summarized as follows: English 110, French 90, heritage languages 30.[6]

The same index of retention can be applied to the home language or a still more message-conveying index can be used of home language over mother tongue. We would then have three indices: mother-tongue retention, home-language retention, and linguistic continuity index. The last name comes from Lachapelle and Henripin (1982:162). The two authors find it convenient to break up the allophones into endophones (Amerindian and Inuit) and exophones (heritage languages of immigrants; ibid.:4). They then ask what fertility would be necessary to ensure the replacement of language groups, demographic replacement requiring 2.1 children per woman. The answer is 1.9 for anglophones, 2.2 for francophones, 4.0 for endophones, and 10.5 for exophones (the last one almost a biological impossibility; ibid.:164). Their conclusion is that we must again conclude that the exogenous-language group has no specifically Canadian existence: its strength can only be kept up with the help of massive and regular input from other countries (ibid.:164).

What Lachapelle and Henripin (1982) have done for official languages O'Bryan et al. (1976) have done for non-official, or heritage, languages. This was a brave effort and a necessary one, but in the long run we must agree, however regretfully, with the Lachapelle and Henripin assessment of the role of heritage languages in Canadian multiculturalism.

The historical losses of francophonie in Canada are greater than the index of mother-tongue retention of 90 would suggest. There are and have been over the historical periods French losses from the denominator of the index, that is from the ethnicity, leaving the French index deceptively high. There were emigrants to foreign lands and in the case of Quebec out-migrants to other provinces. For the emigration before 1930 see Lavoie (1972). There are immigrants from abroad and in-migrants from other provinces (the latter is a rare phenomenon) who tend to opt in favour of English rather than French, even when living in Quebec (hence the need for law 178). Their numbers swell the English numerator, rather than the French one. There were losses through what has been called euphemistically 'language mobility' (e.g., Henripin 1974, 1985; Castonguay 1979)[7] or ethnic slippage of members of the French ethnic group towards the English group. Caldwell is one of the few anglophones who treat the matter with sympathy and understanding (e.g., 1984; Caldwell & Waddell 1985).

Language mobility is a movement between the numerators and typically lowers the French numerator. Some writers use 'language transfer' in place of language mobility (e.g., Kralt 1977:35). The 1971 census provided data on gains by the English mother tongue (de Vries & Vallee 1980:107, 109) from ethnic groups other than English, and gains by the English home language from mother tongues other than English (ibid.:122, 123), staggering losses to the other groups whichever way one would count, reinforcing the Lachapelle-Henripin conclusion cited above.[8]

To complete the scheme of presentation, one should mention a fourth problem, or at least a subproblem: that of the French of the Acadians in New Brunswick, the only officially bilingual province in Canada, somewhat dramatically compared with Northern Ireland in Aunger (1981). The linguistic vulnerability of the Acadians may have made their capital, Moncton, too bilingual, too marginal to continue as their centre of vitality (Laponce 1987:134), an example of incomplete systems analysis at the planning bench.

In Table 3 the linguistic continuity index (Lachapelle & Henripin 1982:163) is shown. It compares the home language with the mother tongue. Only English is viable with an index higher than 100 (and French in Quebec with 100, not shown in the table). It is clear, once again, that in the long run the heritage languages (those spoken by exophones) shown in Table 2, and even more so languages not shown in Table 2, have no future. Heritage language programs are important morally, psychologically, and ethically, but numerically only parents speaking to their offspring can be effective. The 1991 census has shown the Ukrainian-speaking population to have the most unusual age pyramid of all populations of the world. In fact it is not a pyramid, but a vase with the narrowest bottom (2 per cent) and the largest top (45 per cent). And only 30 years earlier there were more Ukrainian-speaking women than Ukrainian ethnics (Krótki 1978; Polish women married to Ukrainian men? children fathered by Poles, and classified as Polish ethnics in accordance with the Canadian definition of ethnicity, but speaking the Ukrainian of their mothers?).

The linguistic continuity indices for the country as a whole remained the same between 1981 and 1986: English 111, French 96, exophones 55 (Bourbeau 1989:26), but English gained even in Quebec City (119 on 116) and Montreal (122 on 119). For 'the rest of Canada' English declined from 112 to 111 and 'endophones' increased from 45 to 46. There is little doubt about the ultimate victory of English, but it is instructive to note the subtle changes on the way.

The current and future situations of the two official languages are likely to be affected by the conflicting influences of the Canadian Charter of Rights and Freedoms and the Charter of the French language in Quebec

TABLE 3
Single and multiple responses on mother tongue and home language, Canada 1986

Single responses	Mother tongue[1]	Home language[2]	[3]
English	15,334,085	16,595,535	108
French	6,159,740	5,798,470	94
Italian	453,820	271,835	62
German	438,675	112,550	26
Chinese	266,560	230,480	86
Ukrainian	298,410	46,150	22
Aboriginals	138,060	97,280	70
Other languages	1,263,040	710,030	52
	24,354,390	23,862,230	
Multiple responses			
English and French	332,610	351,900	106
Other multiples	622,335	807,770	130
	954,940[4]	1,158,670[5]	
	25,309,330	25,020,900[6]	

1 Calculated from Canada 1987: Table 1; 1989: Table 1
2 Calculated from Canada 1991:47
3 = home language as a percentage of mother tongue, called linguistic continuity index
   by Lachapelle & Henripin 1982
4 = 3.8% of total population in the case of mother tongue
5 = 4.6% of total population in the case of home language
6 Mother tongue was a 100% question, home language was a 20% question; the latter
   excluded some 288 ths, just over 1%, in institutions, etc.; to that extent the percentages
   speaking home language are underestimates.

(Paillé 1991). Not for the first time will ethnic demographics be affected by politics. A study has been undertaken to show what numbers are coming out of the concept of the 'right to receive education in one's language.' It has been found that the numbers having the 'right' to French in all provinces outside Quebec, except one, will decrease between 1986 and 1992. The exception is Alberta (and the two territories). On the other hand, those entertaining the 'right' to receive education in English in Quebec will increase in the same period by 3 per cent (ibid.:42). Once more the anglophones 'cried wolf' prematurely. The finding also provides a new twist on the generally reported and accepted decline in the linguistic minorities in Quebec and outside Quebec (e.g., Beaujot 1982).

For the nature of the various language questions asked at census see Table 4. Mother tongue is a slow witness to the disappearance of heritage

TABLE 4
Language questions in Canadian censuses since 1901

Year	Official language	Mother tongue	Home language
1901	Ability to speak English, French, or both well enough to carry on a conversation (English only, French only, both, neither)	Mother tongue is one's native language, the language of his race; but not necessarily the language in which he thinks or which he speaks most fluently, or uses chiefly in conversation	Not asked
1911	Same	Not asked	Language spoken most often at home
1921	Same	Language of customary speech employed by the person	Not asked
1931	Same	Language learned by children and still spoken or the language of the home whether the person has learned it or not (eg, infants)	Not asked
1941	Same	First language learned in childhood if still understood by the person	Not asked
1951	Same	Same	Not asked
1961	Same	Same	Not asked
1971	Same	Same	Language spoken most often by the person at home
1976	Not asked	Same	Not asked
1981	Same (as in 1971 and as defined in 1901)	Same	Same (as in 1971 and as defined in 1911)[1]
1986	Same	Same	Same
1991	Same[2]	Same	Same

Adapted from and extended: Kralt (1976:5; 1980:18, 19)

1 'What language do you yourself speak at home? and 'If more than one language, which language do you speak most often?'

2 A fourth language question, asked for the first time in 1991, was: 'What language(s), other than English and French, can this person speak well enough to conduct a conversation?' Four language questions, winning against all other claims on the census questionnaire space, are an objective indication of the increasing interest in language retention, including the 'non-official languages.'

languages, and the home language performs this function more directly (e.g., Beaujot & McQuillan 1982:190). Social scientists have not explained why the break between 1961 and 1971 was so radical. That *was* before the coming of multiethnicities (see the section on multiethnicities below). For a different conceptualization of the inevitable disaster, but the same pictorial impression see Reitz (1980: Figures I, II). A table has been produced in a manner suggesting a figure with the same message: disastrous disappearance of mother tongues (Laponce 1987). By and large it can be said that heritage languages survive through immigration (Kralt 1976:16) and not through multicultural interests of the ethnic groups concerned.

There was a minor, but possibly significant, change in the home language between 1981 and 1986 (Bourbeau 1989:27). Of the eleven most frequently spoken languages, Ukrainian dropped out (fading away after a glorious history?) and Spanish moved in (the new boy on the block? though not quite yet the masses from across the Rio Grande). The 700,000 Aboriginals reported in 1986 that only 100,000 of them speak one of their eleven languages at home (Beaujot 1991:285). Even if they lose their languages entirely it is unlikely that they will assimilate into the majority society (Beaujot 1991:288), thus remaining a continuing element in multiculturalism. One runs the risk of reading too much into these marginal changes, but following the participating languages closely (with such controls as may be required by social science methodology) is essential for understanding multiculturalism.

From the perspective of multiculturalism the retention of heritage languages is a fundamental consideration. Where will multiculturalism be without multilanguages? Cultureless nationalism or even racism? Meaningless power base for local politics? For the racism dimension affecting aboriginals see Frideres (1988). Demographers need not engage in speculations. Models exist for objective pursuits in up to five analysis stages: period of immigration; ethnicity and ethnic transfers; mother-tongue retention; home-language retention; linguistic continuity. At each of the five stages models are expected to produce very different results for each of the four language groups: anglophones, francophones, exophones, endophones.

The experience of ethnic groups with respect to the preservation of their ethnicity and language retention varies greatly. In 1971 native Indians and Eskimos were the only ethnic group whose 'new ethnics' (roughly post–Second World War) had a markedly lower language retention (13 per cent) than their 'old ethnics' (roughly pre-Second World War

55 per cent), with probably grievous reflections on the cultural content of this ethnic group (Kralt 1977:34). A later result for 1981–6 is reported without reference to the earlier result (Maslove & Hawkes 1990:23, 24). The mother-tongue retention rates for the main groups of Aboriginals are high (85 and 73), though for the smaller and mixed groups they are very low (between 2 and 24). The linguistic continuity index has actually increased slightly for all five groups shown. Are these inconsistencies between 1971 and 1986 genuine reflections of the social situation or the result of the measurement process?[9]

In the monumental work by Lachapelle and Henripin (1982) we are confronted with 19 conclusions. They represent the state of the art in this all-important area of multiculturalism. Four examples of these conclusions based on demographic analysis follow. First, there is a strong probability that, in Canada as a whole, the proportion of francophones will decrease during the next few decades, while that of anglophones will increase (xxxi). Second, in Canada less Quebec, it is highly probable that the proportion of anglophones will increase during the next few decades, while that of francophones will decrease (xxxiii). Third, the French group always shows appreciable losses in its linguistic exchanges with the English group, except in regions of Quebec where anglophones are only a small minority (xxxv). Fourth, proportionately to the other official language group in a given region, the bilingualism rate of the French group is much higher than that of the English group (xxxvi). The polarization implied in these conclusions continued, according to the 1986 data (Bourbeau 1989). The index of dissimilarity shows a monotonic climb since 1961 from 63.4 to 69.5 in 1981 (Canada 1984b).

For a broad view of the place of the language for an individual and his or her society, neuropsychological and geopolitical, see Laponce (1987).

The topic of language in Canada must not be left without a note on bilingualism. Since the bilingualism policy was redefined and reinforced in the late 1960s after prodding from the B & B Commission, the advance in bilingualism continues (more than 4 million were bilingual in 1986, Bourbeau 1989), particularly among the young (Ross 1989:26), but rather among the English, while among the French bilingualism is slightly more common among the older age groups (Canada 1985). Quebec, Ontario, and New Brunswick with 65 per cent of the population account for 86 per cent of bilinguals. The number of bilinguals among the French, not to mention the proportion, is much higher than among the English. The French outside Quebec are the most bilingual group in Canada. Among the anglophones and allophones (presumably, exophones) those in

Quebec are the most bilingual, and so on (Bourbeau 1989). Each one of these features is loaded with demographic and constitutional material.

For a peep into the future, current school enrolments should be analysed to determine the number of francophones and allophones attending English schools, and of francophones and allophones attending French schools. These are often available in massive public reports (see Canada 1978) with summaries provided in research reports, predominantly emanating from Quebec. Paillé is a prolific writer in this area (e.g., 1991).

ETHNICITY AND EDUCATIONAL ATTAINMENT

A reasonably thorough search of the literature for demographically based studies addressing ethnicity and education produced few references. It is, therefore, not surprising that the Macdonald Commission concluded: 'Given the importance of this sector [education] to Canada's future, relevant data and analyses are very scarce' (1985, Vol. 2:735, in Corrigan & Shamai 1986:1). Furthermore, 'studies which trace student performance over time are virtually non-existent in Canada' (1985, Vol. 2:740, in Corrigan & Shamai 1986:1). The following studies remedy this situation and provide some insight into ethnicity and education from the demographic perspective. An elaborate census monograph by Richmond and Kalbach (1980) deals with the influence of nativity on material well-being. Foreign-born males are better off than native-born; for females the advantage is slighter. Much of the explanation of the differentials lies in education. When 'like' with 'like' in education are compared, much of the advantage of the foreign-born disappears.

Beaujot et al. (1988, 32–5) analyze the 1981 census data on educational attainment of Canadian-born and foreign-born (population aged 15+). When all foreign-born are put together and compared with all native-born, the foreign-born have at the same time more less-educated and more more-educated. However, the U-shaped situation does not affect the same ethnic groups: south and east Europeans come to Canada with elementary education, Africans and South Asians with university education. Together they produce the U-shape.

It appears that much of the difference in proportions at various levels of schooling for various immigrant groups is the outcome of implementation of the point system in 1968. The proportion of immigrants affected by this system varies, as family immigrants and refugees are not assessed under it. In some years markedly less than half the immigrants come in with points, and Beaujot et al. (1988) argued persuasively that '[t]he level of education of immigrants is related to their period of immigration' (ibid.:34). Those arriving in Canada before 1960 generally had 'lower education attainments when compared with those who arrived in the 1970s' (ibid.:34). Still, it appears that length of stay in the country has overridden even the disadvantages of low education of immigrants admitted in the pre–'point system' era.[10] Social scientists could temper their work on discrimination with qualifications of that kind.

It has been suggested that only 'ethnics' born in Canada could be fairly compared with native-born Canadians, as both would then have been exposed to similar schooling. This argument would be relevant if the purpose was the detection of psychological or genetic differences. Demographers limit themselves in the first instance to determination of independent demographic and socio-economic variables.

Richmond (1986) takes the analyses a step further, although writing earlier than Beaujot et al. (1988). He has the benefit of the 1971 data with the place of births of parents, on which we commented above in citing Richmond and Kalbach (1980). Richmond compares educational achievement and qualifications of the Canadian-born of Canadian parentage with the Canadian-born of foreign parentage, and with foreign-born, for Metropolitan Toronto, 1982 (ages 20+). He found that Canadian-born children of foreign parentage did not experience an educational handicap as a result of either 'their ethnic ancestry or generational position' (Richmond 1986:87). In fact, these second-generation Canadians experienced both educational mobility (when compared to the educational achievements of same-sex parents) and equalled or surpassed the educational attainments of the second generation of part British, Irish, or American ancestry. Thus Richmond takes issue with Porter's (1965) notion of the 'vertical mosaic,' which sees an individual's or group's educational opportunity primarily as the outcome of ethnic origin. Non-British ancestry, argues Richmond, is not an obstacle to be overcome, but is rather an advantage (or at least not a disadvantage) when it comes to educational opportunity and the consequent social mobility in Canada.[11]

Corrigan and Shamai (1986), using Canadian census data for the period 1921–81, also studied the effect of ethnic origin on educational attainment. They found an 'almost *constant* educational achievement rank in Canada since 1921' (ibid.:7). This ranking shows Jews and Asian groups at the top, the British near or above the average ('in a *declining* trend,' ibid.:7), the French below the average, and Aboriginals mired at the bottom. Between 1981 and 1986 the proportion with less than Grade 9 declined by a few percentage points for each of the four groups shown, as did that of university degree holders (Maslove & Hawkes 1990: Table 2).[12]

The two largest ethnic groups, the British and the French, compose two-thirds of the population. They occupy the middle range of the educational attainment rankings over time, while other ethnic groups, such as the Chinese and the Blacks, remain more polarized (Corrigan & Shamai 1986:15). To a great degree, then, the effect of ethnic origin on educational attainment has been and continues to be governed by the factors which maintain the historically consistent rankings mentioned above. It remains for others to extend the analysis, utilizing the demographic facts uncovered in studies summarized here.

For the educational attainments of the immigrant and non-immigrant populations according to the 1986 census, see Mori and Burke (1989: Table 1); for Aboriginals and non-Aboriginals in Canada and the northern regions according to the 1981 and 1986 censuses see Maslove and Hawkes (1990: Table 6).

ECONOMIC SUCCESS

Data on income and professional qualifications were collected during censuses long before multiculturalism became topical. The 1961 census variables were cross-classified by ethnicity and period of immigration. Postwar immigrants had the largest proportion with low income, then native-born, then prewar immigrants. The contrary was true for high incomes: postwar immigrants had the lowest proportion, then native-born, then prewar immigrants (Kalbach 1970:285). These were the days before the influence of the point system, so the favourable position of prewar immigrants surprised the analyst. George (1978:60) in a straightforward profile study, that is without the elaborations available in a census monograph, reports the mean and median income of foreign-born as 8 and 9 per cent above that of native-born. Within the foreign-born males and since the Second World War, the earlier the period of immigration the higher the income. Thus, it appears that the point system is less important than the tolerance and long-term lack of discrimination in Canadian society and the ability of the foreign-born to adjust. If these conclusions seem too far-fetched based on available evidence, they should be treated as an invitation to social scientists to take them up as testable hypotheses.

As in the case of other characteristics, the Aboriginals in terms of economic success are in a category of their own: their reported income does not include income in kind. Those in the North receive slightly higher incomes than Aboriginals elsewhere, though not by as much as the non-Aboriginals. They are dependent for a much higher proportion of their income on transfer payments (Maslove & Hawkes 1990:29). It is probably meaningless to cite the mean incomes of Aboriginals (non-Aboriginals); $8600 ($13,100, Canada 1985) in 1981 and $10,678 ($18,272, Maslove & Hawkes 1990:30) in 1986 in the absence of a thorough analysis. Complete understanding of these and other demographic features is still necessary. This task is not facilitated by the varying degrees, incidence, and effectiveness with which population censuses were carried out in the past and have been boycotted by groups of respondents more recently. The allegedly high-income Kahnawake have been 'refuseniks' since 1971, for example.

Professional distribution has been assessed through indices of relative concentration of postwar immigrants by ethnicity: 100 meaning a 'fair' or proportionate share of the given occupation. Data were arranged in three five-year periods. Generally and before the impact of the point system, eastern Europeans had a high share of low income and low prestige occupations, and a low share of high occupations (Kalbach 1970:277–81), consistent with their low educational attainments. For analysis of that kind to be meaningful, education and period of immigration (any other relevant and available variable?) must be held constant. Only then can the influence of ethnicity be isolated. For another example of a discussion of occupational attainments by immigrants see Boyd (1985). By and large the Jewish group had the highest indices of relative concentration in the managerial and related occupations, whatever the period of immigration (Kalbach 1970).

Similar findings on Jews were reported in the numerous reports of the B & B Commission. This came about somewhat serendipituously and outside the central interest of the commission on English-French differentials. The 1971 census data became available after the bulk of the B & B reports came out. These data already contained information from respondent immigrants who came in under the point system two or three years before the census. This was also the census when the rarely asked question on the nativity of parents was posed. We commented already on the good use made of these data by Richmond and Kalbach (1980). However, their sensational findings were deflated (the income differentials narrowed considerably) when proper controls on education and size of town were imposed. In other words, immigrants experienced advantages not as immigrants, but as better educated arrivals in towns with higher incomes. For a discussion of the role of immigrant culture in influencing fertility and income see Krishnan (1987).

By the time 1981 census data were analysed the immigrants' advantages narrowed (family immigrants following the earliest and pure high points immigrants?) or even disappeared altogether for more recent immigrants (Beaujot et al. 1988). Specifically, immigrants from southern Europe and from nontraditional sources took longer to reach parity or exceed the level of native-born (up to 20 years) than immigrants from northern and western Europe. Contrary to this evidence, it has been stated that '[i]mmigrants with foreign qualifications, from any origin, earn somewhat less than those qualifications apparently warrant' (Economic Council of Canada 1991:133).

The treatment of economic success is often difficult because available data refer to the year just before the field enumeration carried out for the purposes of the census, while the characteristics cross-classified may be steeped in the distant past. Nevertheless, the area has been fortunate in having been treated by a high level of research with all possible controls applied and modern techniques of analysis used.

For the type of data available and the economic position of native-born and foreign-born, see Beaujot et al. (1988: Tables 14, 15, 18, and 32). The individual successes of the foreign-born (the micro level) should be interpreted societally (the macro level), seeing that their labour-force participation is higher than that of native-born (George 1978:55), both for males and for females.[13] This is probably another area where much additional understanding relevant to multiculturalism could be gained.

There is considerable literature in Canada on the impact of immigration on the economy at the macro level. It deals with the fundamentals of Canada's origin, history, and development. It concerns such typically economic subjects as government spending, investment, balance of payments, efficient allocation of resources, unemployment, economic growth (e.g., Parai 1974). The Economic Council of Canada (defunct by the time this report is published) has a long series of works on immigration to its credit (e.g., Parai 1965). They are probably no more than tangential to multiculturalism, and, in any case, are not suitable for brief summary. Nevertheless, it is probably important to say that they are innocent of demography and of the understanding of the demographic potential building up in countries of nontraditional sourcing of immigrants. Canada with limited demographic potential (low fertility) cannot exercise much

influence over the building up of such demographic potential elsewhere.
More about this later in the section on low fertility.

MULTIETHNICITIES, MULTILANGUAGES, AND MEASUREMENTS OF
THE FUTURE

The permissive arrangement in 1981 enticed 8 per cent of Canadians to
report multiethnic origins (Krótki & Odynak 1990:428; 1839 ths for a
population of 24,083 ths). The requirement to make as many entries as
relevant in 1986 resulted in close to seven million multiethnics or 28 per
cent (Krótki & Odynak 1990:433; 6986 ths for a population of 25,022 ths).
Krótki and Odynak (1990) suggest a new method of dealing with
multiethnicities for analytic purposes (applicable also to multilanguages).
Other writers prefer to count each ethnicity in multireporting as one (e.g.,
White 1990:48, 54). The new world of multiethnicities is shown in Tables
3, 5, and 6. These tables summarize the new challenges facing social
scientists working in Canada on multiculturalism. The need for new
hypotheses and theory construction is shown in Tables 7 and 8. It is clear
from the tables that the longer an ethnic group has been in the country, the
greater its intermarriage, and consequently the more numerous its
multiethnicities. It remains to be seen whether nontraditional immigrants
will be subject to the same experience. Residential segregation on grounds
of ethnicity is less important in Canada than elsewhere and it remains to
be seen whether it can be separated from intermarriage in the emergence
of multiethnicities (religion and religiosity could probably be left if
subsumed as another feature of ethnicity). The eventual study of multiethnicities will be expensive because it will require holding constant
periods of immigration (recording, record linking, drawing generous
samples, and analyzing).

    For the problems created by the phenomenon of multilanguages, but
also for the research opportunities arising therein, see, for example,
Castonguay (1991) and White (1990: Ch 4).

    These developments are a sign that Canadian statisticians and census/
survey takers feel dutybound to be in step with changing social reality.
When employment equity legislation was passed, as already indicated, to
make arrangements for four groups (women, disabled, visible minorities,
Aboriginals), steps have been taken to provide or tighten up the provision
of denominators. Social scientists must now ensure that good use is made
of these new items of information and that the weaknesses of the data -
(and there are many!) are corrected. The problems are severe, as the

TABLE 5
Intercensal change in single origins of selected ethnic groups, Canada and Alberta,
1971–81 and 1981–6

| | Percentage of change | | | |
| | Canada | | Alberta | |
	1971–81	1981–6	1971–81	1981–6
British	0.52	−34.54	26.41	−38.48
French	4.19	−5.37	18.17	−30.64
Austrian	−3.54	−38.72	1.51	−50.51
German	−13.27	−21.50	0.94	−21.58
Scandinavian	−26.51	−39.28	−20.18	−40.78
Czechoslovakian	−17.31	−17.97	−13.69	−26.44
Polish	−19.57	−12.66	−15.04	−24.32
Romanian	−17.86	−16.63	−18.63	−26.58
Russian	−23.33	−35.10	−24.62	−45.76
Ukrainian	−8.79	−20.66	0.89	−21.91
Greek	24.01	−6.85	48.15	−16.30
Italian	2.35	−5.13	7.28	−11.18
Portuguese	94.17	6.11	156.81	2.53
Jewish	−11.09	−3.47	29.33	−16.01
Chinese	143.44	24.57	184.93	33.83
Japanese	10.02	−1.83	17.26	1.24

Adapted from Halli et al. (1990:427, 431). Any intercensal comparisons must be qualified
because of changes in the wording of the questions, in collection methodology, and in
processing methodology

definitions of visible minorities are extremely subjective. They are policy-
and legally-driven (see Goldmann 1992) rather than placed within
traditional sociological and anthropological frameworks. So far, Canada
has avoided most of the excesses of the United States.[14]

On the other hand, a census that reports the race and nationality of
every individual in the society leaves no room for miscellany (Petersen
1980:237). Is it likely that the new categories will develop into groups and
eventually into communities? More likely such a development will be
'blocked and reversed by the contrary process of assimilation' (ibid.:241).
The task of measuring these subtle developments and changes is
formidable, but it is recommended as good social science. To contribute
to the discussion about who has a deeper melting pot is probably futile,
if the discussion cannot be supported by objective data. To quote the
desire of third-generation immigrants to return to their ethnicity, but
without paying the price of language acquisition, is cheap social policy.

TABLE 6
Multiple origins as a percentage of single origins,
Canada and Alberta 1986

	Canada	Alberta
English	96	129
Irish	418	580
Scottish	353	443
Welsh	542	586
French	33	282
Austrian	200	290
German	175	163
Scandinavian	157	158
Czechoslovakian	131	165
Polish	175	269
Romanian	174	248
Russian	223	363
Ukrainian	129	124
Greek	23	70
Italian	42	112
Portuguese	19	40
Jewish	40	90
Chinese	15	15
Japanese	35	51

Adapted from Halli et al. (1990:419, 423, 424);
and from Krótki & Odynak (1990)

If the policy of multiculturalism creates resentment among the receiving groups (Economic Council of Canada 1991:136), enforced assimilation would only increase social friction.

CLUSTERING (ETHNIC SEGREGATION)

In the absence of segregation, the proportionate ethnic composition of each area would be an image of the ethnic distribution prevailing in the entire country. Clearly this is not the case. Ethnic groups select certain areas and avoid others, similarly to poorer people aggregating in less expensive areas and richer people tending to reside in more expensive areas. On the whole, ethnic segregation tends to be less pervasive than in the United States. Analysis is difficult because of the confounding elements of ethnic flavour, population density, population size, existence of community services and facilities (so-called ethnic completeness), and

TABLE 7
Hypotheses for emergence of multiethnicities

The purely arithmetical exercises that can be carried out with the new data provide
considerable insight into the differential behaviour of ethnic groups in response to the
new census definition inviting respondents to record their ethnicity in terms of multiples.
These exercises also suggest the working of various influences that could be isolated with
suitable research designs. The following hypotheses are offered for consideration by
researchers:
1 the larger the ethnic group the less intermarriage experience, if only for arithmetic or
  geometric reasons;
2 the longer the ethnic group had been in Canada, on average, the more intermarriage
  experience there is;
3 the less dispersion or the more concentration, the less intermarriage experience there is;
4 in-groups, because of their supreme confidence, have less intermarriage than out-
  groups with their anxiety to conform (is that because in-groups are more desirable and
  out-groups are good at seducing?);
5 current age distribution (mean age, proportion of young, etc.) is irrelevant to past
  experience of intermarriage and interethnic differences are too small to affect the
  measurements that can be developed, which are currently rather crude;
6 the search for independent variables needs to be intensified as most hypotheses are
  currently left with 40 or 50 (or even 70?) per cent unexplained variability. In fact,
  practising sociologists begin to talk in terms of multicollinearity, when the proportion
  explained becomes too high. Adapted from Halli et al. (1990:437)

subjective preferences. For writings on residential segregation see, for
example, Balakrishnan and Selvanathan (1990).

By 1986 the Canadian inner city was displaying a number of distinctive
characteristics: since 1981 it had experienced population growth for the
first time since 1951, had more elderly than outlying areas, had more
unmarried and living alone, more childless families, more immigrants,
more 'ethnics,' more university-educated, more managers and professionals, lower mean income (drop from 70 per cent to 62), fewer
homeowners, and higher dwelling values. These differences though, were
probably less marked than in the US. The 12 largest metropolitan areas
were inhabited by 30 per cent foreign-born, twice as many as in the
country as a whole (Ram et al. 1989:25). Ethnic concentrations, though
noticeable, were mild again, 110 in 1981, in Saskatoon and Edmonton 92
and 98 respectively (ibid.:27).

From the perspective of multiculturalism the topical question is at what
degree of concentration does the risk of race riots or ethnic riots become
a realistic possibility. Given some such proportion, can multiculturalism
affect the majority and susceptible minorities to the extent that such a tendency is avoided through a process of explanation, education, spread of

TABLE 8
Endogamy, exogamy, and time of immigration, Canada and Alberta 1986

		Immigration				
		Early			Recent	
		Ca	Al(1)		Ca	Al
	English	96	129	Portuguese	19	40
				Spanish	98	113
				Chinese	15	15
	Amerindian	92	100			
	Inuit	34	281	Iranian	18	25
				Korean	7	9
Endogamy						
	French	33	282	Croatian	26	37
				Japanese	35	51
				Greek	23	70
	Scottish	353	443	Czechoslovakian (2)	131	185
	Irish	418	580	Yugoslavian (3)	65	88
	Welsh	542	586			
Exogamy						
				Polish	175	269
	Métis	154	138	Russian	223	363
	Armenian	22	186	Ukrainian	129	124

Ca = Canada
   multiple origins as a percentage of single origins 1986
Al = Alberta
   multiple origins as a percentage of single origins 1986
1 The Alberta behaviour belongs more logically to the sw quarter, rather than the nw
   quarter where Canadian behaviour finds itself.
2 Czech 94 130
   Slovak 70   94
   These two categories gave rise to hostile comments. Respondents' entries were coded in
   line with entries made.
3 Macedonian 52 114
source: Adapted from Halli et al. (1990:425)

knowledge, and introduction of mere familiarity? There appear to be no
analyses and writings which address this question though, of course, the
very idea of multiculturalism is aiming at the avoidance of possible
developments implied in the question. The proportion suggested above
cannot be easily calculated because it is confounded by the influence of
density, concentration, proximity, and size of the groups, competition for
scarce resources (such as recreational space), economic opportunities,
confusion with violence directed economically and criminally.

Another geographical concern arises in connection with so-called contact regions (Lachapelle 1990:25). These are the regions around Quebec, both inside Quebec and inside the provinces surrounding Quebec. Until recently, French was losing in the contact regions, but some gains have also been recorded. Some gains might be due to the spread of official bilingualism, not necessarily the kind of gain which appeals to Quebec nationalists. The contact regions are called by other writers 'border counties' (e.g., Kralt 1976:29), and both give substance to the concept' of the Soo-Moncton Line (Joy 1967:23–9). Much of Canadian politics and history and of Canada's future plays itself out on this demographic concept.

In this section on geography, the phenomenon of polarization must be mentioned: Quebec becomes more French, the rest of Canada becomes more English (for details see the section on economic success, above). To watch and measure this development is probably the saddest duty of social scientists, especially of demographers. Constitutional implications should be seen in the steady decline of Quebec's share in the total population of the country from 29 per cent after the Second World War to just above 25 per cent in 1991. Since 1901 only British Columbia has increased its share consistently, census after census.

THE OVERRIDING INFLUENCE OF LOW FERTILITY

The quiet revolution of the 1960s in Quebec was followed, and even accompanied, by a decline in fertility below Canadian levels, from previous levels which were above those in the rest of Canada. Along with a turn against the influence of the Roman Catholic Church came a decline in nuptiality and an increase in informal cohabitation. We will never know the extent of the demographic element in fuelling separatist inclinations towards political separation as a self-defence mechanism in view of dwindling numbers. There is no doubt about political concerns arising out of insufficient numbers. Public debates are shot through with them. Political decisions to increase fertility were reported in the first section of this paper, where reference was made to Sifton's recruitment of high fertility, nontraditional immigrants. In the final section of this paper, the Quebec baby bonus is discussed. The most profound, almost philosophical, but policy-inclined study is probably Henripin (1989). To him there is something 'morbid' ('sickening' – 'maladif,' 116) in a living organism not reproducing itself.

In the not so distant past, the various populations of Canada behaved 'as expected' in traditional sociological theory. French mother-tongue mothers reported in 1941 higher fertility than English mother-tongue Catholics, who in turn had higher fertility than Protestant English mother tongues (Charles 1948:72). One might add, though it is not immediately relevant to multiculturalism, that other characteristics behaved 'as expected'; rural had higher fertility than urban, farm higher than nonfarm, lower education had higher fertility than higher education (ibid.:73, 74), higher income more (yes!) than lower income (ibid.:77). The life of the social analyst was easy in those days. Only European mother-tongue mothers had fertility patterns of their own (ibid.:77) and there were interesting differences between Quebec and Ontario (ibid.:126, 127). Data on age at marriage by mother tongue and religion are given in totals participating (ibid.:208), presumably because in those days the method of estimating singulate age at marriage had not yet been elaborated, but even from the crude data it appears that Jews (by religion) tended to marry late. Earnings of husband by ethnic group are also given in totals participating (ibid.:220). Relevant analyses of variance are given in separate appendices (e.g., ibid.:303) and are not integrated with the text.

Twenty years later Henripin compared the Charles study and her conclusion that Catholic fertility is 40 per cent higher than that of Protestants (Henripin says less dramatically that Protestants are 28 per cent lower than Catholics – Charles 1948:68; Henripin 1972:211) with more recent data. 'The persistence of such a difference is remarkable and this finding is similar to findings by other authors ... Even if ... [Church imposed] prohibitions disappear from the scene, it is not certain that the difference in fertility levels between Catholics and Protestant would vanish. This is probably not just a question of family planning methods, but also a philosophy of life that will long remain influenced by religious affiliation' (Henripin 1972:211, 212). As the book was being printed, at least in its English version, the fertility revolution in Quebec was taking place!

Chapter 6 in Henripin (1972) deals with Canadian fertility according to country of origin and period of immigration, and according to ethnic origin, mother tongue, and religion. In Table 6.16 a comparison is offered of Catholic fertility for French mother-tongue mothers with their English counterparts. For those aged 45–49 almost all the 16 socio-economic groups show higher French fertility than English. For mothers aged 35–39 only six French groups are higher, a change that passed at the time unnoticed.

There is a popular belief in Canada that immigrants from nontraditional sources and their offspring are flooding the country. In fact, as pointed out above, immigrants from countries of high fertility adjusted to

Canadian low fertility mores before they came to Canada.[15] As early as 1971 (just before Canadian fertility dipped below replacement levels), Asian women had fertility as low as Jewish women, while their older sisters still had high fertility, as high as the Quebecers, though still lower than Indians (Balakrishnan et al. 1979). Thus, the immigrants, now in their majority from nontraditional sources, make up the Canadian deficiency in natural increase, but do it somewhat inefficiently with low fertility (Krótki 1990).

The awareness of fertility differentials among ethnic groups, particularly low fertility among nontraditional sources, is established (e.g., Basavarajappa & Halli 1987; Krishnan & Krótki 1992). The 1971 monograph on fertility (Balakrishnan et al. 1979) shows fertility on all five topics of interest to us: religion (57), nativity (66), mother tongue (95), home language (107), ethnicity (109). For the 12 ethnic groups given in Table 2.29 (11), all show marked declines in fertility for women aged up to 44 in comparison with women aged 45 and over, three groups being in 1971 already below replacement (Jewish, Asian, 'other, and unknown'). There is one continuing exception, at least for the time being, to the prevailing low fertility – the Aboriginal peoples – but even their period total fertility rate declined from 6.16 to 3.96, lessening to that extent the size of the issue for multiculturalism. Still, although their growth rate is declining, it continues to be high enough to increase their share in the total population, though there were very recent reports of 2.6, just about their replacement level. Their demographic situation has been well documented (e.g., Romaniuc 1981, 1987). Less so, the preservation of their languages. Few writers face the fact that there is no cultural or multicultural future for them (e.g., Laponce 1987). At the advisory seminar for demographers mentioned above, the challenge was issued for cultural variables (non-quantifiable?) to be employed in explanation of fertility differentials (discussion participants Lux and Krishnan in Veevers 1983:29).

As recently as 1968 Canada's leading metropolis had these expected features (Balakrishnan et al. 1975): Protestants stronger users of contraceptives (60) than Catholics, the latter approving much less of abortion than Protestants (132, 133). One reads the 1971 report on fertility differentials by religion in the country as a whole as ancient history (Scott 1976:38); Catholics are behind Mormons, Hutterites, and the Salvation Army in the number of children per married woman, but well ahead of Anglicans and Lutherans. By 1984, the year of the Canadian Fertility Survey, the religious differentials disappeared, though persistent differences by religiosity, irrespective of religion, have been reported

(Balakrishnan et al. 1993). As shown elsewhere in this report, the visible minority dozen of children must be put among fables.

However, even if religion ceased being an important variable in determining fertility, might it have retained an influence in the society of interest to multiculturalism? Did it retain its early characteristics as social glue? The answer is no (e.g., Baril & Mori 1991): formal religious affiliations dropped, church attendance declined, objective measures of religiosity weakened (though they still break the society more meaningfully than religion; Balakrishnan et al. 1993).

It is not unreasonable to suggest that a country with low fertility, in particular with fertility below replacement, cannot restrict effectively and for any length of time immigration from populations with an appropriate demographic potential, though there is no awareness of this fact or logical hypothesis in Canadian literature on immigration policies and practices. Simmons (1988; Simmons & Keohane 1992) is a rare exception; see also Krótki (1992). Ebanks (1990) and the Economic Council of Canada (1991: 133) says 'there is some question whether the amount of immigration can be controlled at all ... recommendations about levels might turn out to be purely academic.'

Some demographers working with Canadian data have thrown light onto inter-ethnic fertility differentials through application of the minority status hypothesis (e.g., Halli 1989; Trovato 1981; Trovato & Burch 1980), but a special taste is required for forcing one's data into a somewhat artificial framework.

POPULATION POLICIES AND THEIR ETHNIC IMPACT

While the ramifications of population policies are very wide (e.g., public intervention in housing is a population policy), it is convenient to think of population policies *in sensu stricto* as being of two kinds: those concerned with immigration and those with fertility.

Literature on population policies in Canada is rather modest (Krótki & Termote 1990), though richer in the case of immigration than in the case of fertility. However, even the richer immigration literature is further limited from the perspective of this paper by the restrained interest of such policy literature in multiculturalism and ethnic issues, and languages and religion. For a discussion by demographers of antinatalist and pronatalist policies at the invitation of statisticians see Veevers (1983:81–5).

In the case of fertility, most Canadian governments and much public opinion see no role for governments and public power in this area ('in the bedrooms of the nation'). Quebec is an important exception in this regard with the baby bonus introduced in 1988 (Rochon 1990, cited in Romaniuc 1991:71), which increases every few months and reaches $7,500 for the third and each subsequent child.[16] It is also Quebec that gave rise to a brave engagement in a political discussion of demographic features (Henripin 1989). It was brave because it exposed the demographic analyst to complaints from some of his reviewers. He was accused of entering a discussion that is unsuited to tools of objective, demographic methodology. Another example of political suggestions taking demography into account with respect to the preservation of the French language in North America can be found in Laponce (1988).

At the other end of the scale, among the elderly, public opinion sees a genuine role for governments and public interventions. It is also there that ethnicity is a strong intervening factor (Driedger & Chappell 1987). Endogamy is still stronger than among the younger generations (55), as is the tendency of the elderly to stick together. Porter's perspective of the vertical mosaic and ethnicity impeding social mobility is truer than among the young (28). The proportions of the elderly vary greatly among ethnic groups (Canada 1984a), and consequently the 'burden' on society varies: above the mean are Jews, Poles, Ukrainians, British, and Germans; below the mean are French, Dutch, Chinese, Italians, and Aboriginals. Demographic theory teaches us that this placement of ethnic groups is mainly the outcome of the period of immigration. Whether ethnicity-selective mortality could have some impact requires investigation. For a discussion of ethnic mortality differentials see Trovato (1988).

CONCLUSION

In this section we have extracted such recommendations as have arisen during the discussions offered throughout the other sections of the paper. Some recommendations not specifically arising in the previous sections are also offered.

In the introductory section it became apparent that a number of infrastructural elements are needed: a register of sampling and non-sampling surveys with ethnic and multicultural questions, documentation of the switch in research interests from ethnicity to languages around 1965 and its political and sociocultural significance, standardization in the methodology of data collection, particularly with regard to visible minorities, and research contributions to the prevention of census boycotts by some Aboriginal groups. Further light on two demographic questions would be useful: the prevalence of 'chain-migration' and the early adjustment of immigrants to Canadian fertility norms.

Infrastructural needs arising in the case of intermarriage are vital statistics registration documents to include such multicultural variables as ethnicity, mother tongue, home language, religion (the latter *is* given on the marriage certificate); the study of the potential impact in Canada of the Swiss model (protection of language to have priority over protection of ethnicity; minority populations to control their linguistic-territorial boundaries). Specific research studies would include the pace of intermarriage as an indicator of assimilation; the incidence of intermarriage by place of birth and religion; exogamous unions by variables other than ethnicity and the two types of languages such as religion, nativity, education, and occupation (social mobility).

The infrastructures required by the discussion on immigration are immigration size and age-sex composition to turn a declining population into a stationary one; a 'futures' study to assess the acceptable impact of maximum nontraditional insertions into the society (ripe candidates are Toronto and Vancouver); the American and Canadian experience with 'melting pot' policies vs pluralisms; estimates of emigration from Canada by ethnicity. Among specific questions would be time-lags between immigration and citizenship; and Canada's influence over the interplay of demography, economy, society, and politics in countries of emigration.

Our section on language retention is probably the most important section of this paper because of the importance of the language question for the development of the constitutional situation. We need continuing fundamental inputs on the four language problems summarized as anglophones 110, francophones 90, endophones 30 (same 30 for exophones?, can endophones survive at all without immigration inputs?), and the linguistic survival of Acadians. The 19 conclusions in Lachapelle and Henripin (1982) provide a framework to monitor these problems. A protocol of specific research topics would include: data quality used for estimates of language mobility and ethnic slippage, the differential pace of language losses, home language in comparison with mother tongue as an indicator of what will happen to the ethnic group (the usefulness of the three indices and the associated replacement levels), demography of language education, the progress of linguistic polarization and the role of the contact regions.

The education system should be the great equalizer, so much so that a truly eugenic study of ethnicity would look at the ethnic groups only after they all went through the Canadian system of education (genuine 'holding constant'). There are no minor studies here. Problems emerging are all infrastructures. The effectiveness of the point system is watered down through family immigrants and refugees, but prevails in spite of alleged anti-immigrant discrimination prevalent in the society and in the economy, judging from objective indicators such as financial well-being. The assessment of the vertical mosaic hypothesis in light of objectively measured experiences of immigrants is probably a mere academic refinement, but the hypothesis has dominated Canadian sociological thinking for such a long time that it ought to be treated as an infrastructure item (use parental place of birth, if data allow, as was done in 1971). Other matters that should be studied include school participation of Aboriginals as against the national drop-out experience; the logistics of Aboriginal language preservation; problems in literacy and numeracy by ethnicity, especially due to the ahistorical and aliterary introduction of the Inuit script; and social mobility in and among cultural groups and the importance of educational attainments.

Infrastructures required for the assessment of economic success include the validity and availability of controls for the study of economic success; economic impact of immigrants on the society in general (labour force participation, dependency ratio) and their individual successes (lower claims on social services, higher tax contributions). Minor questions are the reciprocal issues in the adjustment process, the demographic meaning of income differentials affecting Aboriginals, and the conflicting conclusions of Kalbach (1970) and George (1978) (mere methodology?).

The Canadian melting pot, never admitted as a matter of policy, came to the demographic surface with the emergence of multiethnicities and multilanguages: what is needed is a discussion of the merits of the melting pot against multiculturalism, based on objective evidence and not on conjecture. These new types of data need to be studied both separately and jointly. Statistics Canada should be encouraged to develop ways of measuring (increasingly multiple) ethnic origin. A minor concern should be watching and measuring the pace of intermarriage of nontraditional immigrants; is there a need to measure ethnic identity? Why are there no problems in residential segregation?

It goes without saying that Canada's attitude to immigration (and that of the sending countries to their corresponding emigration) would be very different in conditions of high Canadian fertility, notwithstanding the similarity of experiences in the first century. Subjects to be studied are the demography, sociology, and economy of below replacement fertility in the development of multiculturalism; the generality of below replacement fertility among ethnicities and the fate of the one exception; the cultural explanation in such fertility differentials as exist among ethnic groups (the challenge in Veevers 1983).

Such population policies as are discernible (family allowances, old age pensions, a tax system that is unfriendly to married couples, anti-discriminatory policies and practices related to gender and age) have hardly any ethnic dimension, except possibly in the long run the baby bonus in Quebec. What has an ethnic dimension are developments in Canadian immigration policies shaped by the fertility differential in Canada and in sending countries. Authors, publishers, text writers, and course-givers should be fed information on multiculturalism and its place in the society in the hope that they will regurgitate it. Minor matters to be studied are variations in the proportion of the elderly (immigration or fertility or internal migration) among ethnic groups, and studies of ethnic-selective mortality.

NOTES

1 Religion no longer breaks up modern societies into significant societal sub-groups. Religiosity does, but religiosity, according to general agreement, is not a proper subject for public enquiries based on public funds. For an example of the use of religiosity see Balakrishnan et al. (1993).
2 Conceivably the appearance of the voluminous reports by the B & B Com-mission (six main volumes, some in more than one part, and some 146 research reports) might have influenced the reporting of languages spoken and understood in the 1971 census, even if it could not affect actual ability and practice.
3 In the circumstances prevailing in communication in the early years, Ot-tawa administrators became apprehensive about what might be happening in the distant west with its vast, open spaces. A census might give them a grip on the teeming masses of nontraditional immigrants, strange peasants from the distant land of Galicia, with furs turned inside out, homely wives, and six children. Thus, a census, even if in the wrong year, was soon con-verted into a legislative requirement, by 1956 covering the whole country.
4 Canada ignored the requirement to separate state and church in the religion question on the census questionnaire. Researchers at the Jewish-Canadian Congress always made good use of it, unlike their counterparts in the US (Petersen 1980:237).
5 The Roman Catholic pride of place probably would have been yielded if the exercise were controlled for provinces to remove the effect of the anti-Church 'quiet revolution' in Quebec.

6 If 110 for English was better and more widely understood, then the existence of 'The Society for the Preservation of the English Language in Canada' would be unnecessary. If the 90 for French was better and more widely understood among anglophones (and allophones for that matter) then the reason, actually the necessity, for laws 22, 101, and 178 in Quebec would be viewed with the kind of sympathy that is lacking when consideration is based on individual rights, rather than societal or community needs.

7 Castonguay is an interesting case. He is deeply involved in estimation of the French ethnicity and language. One must hope that, although a professor of mathematics, he is given academic credit for his important concerns and writings in language retention (e.g., Castonguay 1985, 1988).

8 As indicated in the first section of this paper, the interest in languages was slow to develop compared to the much older concern with ethnicities, so much so that when a civil engineer wrote the first book on 'languages in conflict' he could not find a publisher. He had to issue the book at his own expense (Joy 1967). Since then, publishers have woken up to the topic.

9 Actually Maslove and Hawkes (1990: Table 5) leave calculation of the retention ratio to the reader and what they call the retention rate (Table 4; it is a ratio in any case) is the linguistic continuity index.

10 The authors of the study (Beaujot et al. 1988) recognize that some immigrants, if they arrived as young children, will have received all of their formal education in Canada. Apparently this was not enough to destroy their background characteristics and equalize their attainments with those of the native-born.

11 The same thought can be expressed 'the other way round' beginning with the apparently uplifting background influences overwhelming the downgrading influences of Canadian schools, shall we say to dilute the societal responsibility, that is, the Canadian school system.

12 Although the component parts all show declines, Aboriginals for the country as a whole show a slight increase. Apparently Aboriginals outside the North must have done even worse.

13 It probably would be excessive to extend the argument to the dependency ratio of foreign-born being markedly lower than that of native-born (0.39 against 0.65; George 1978:41). In fact, the calculations are nonsensical, most of the age group 0–14 of the foreign-born having become native-born.

14 'The subsequent change to new imperatives came so quickly that universities, for example, were for a time 'simultaneously forbidden to record the race of their faculty and students and required to report what proportions of each were of specified minorities' (Petersen 1980:238).

15 This is less unusual than it may appear. 'Free migrants [that is distinct from slaves] ... are generally already half-assimilated even before leaving home'

(Petersen 1980:240). Thus, social scientists of receiving countries need to study the anthropological (multi)cultures of sending countries only when they have time to spare.

16 *Globe and Mail*, 13 Apr. 1992, 'Quebec bucks trend to decline in birth rate,' Patricia Poirier of the Quebec Bureau; an example of good journalistic reporting of short-term trends.

REFERENCES

Aunger, E.A. (1981). *In search of political stability: A comparative study of New Brunswick and Northern Ireland*. Montreal/Kingston: McGill-Queen's University Press

Balakrishnan, T.R., Ebanks, G.E., and Grindstaff, C.F. (1979). *Patterns of fertility in Canada, 1971*. Ottawa: Statistics Canada; French editions also in print

– , Kantner, J.R., and Allingham, J.D. (1975). *Fertility and family planning in a Canadian metropolis*. Montreal/Kingston: McGill-Queen's University Press

– , Lapierre-Adamcyk, E., and Krótki, K.J. (1993). *Family and childbearing in Canada: A demographic analysis*. Toronto: University of Toronto Press

– , and Selvanathan, K. (1990). Ethnic residential segregation in metropolitan Canada. In S.S. Halli, F. Trovato, and L. Driedger (eds), *Ethnic demography: Canadian immigrant, racial and cultural variations* (pp 399–414). Ottawa: Carleton University Press

Baril, A., and Mori, G.A. (1991). Leaving the fold: Declining church attendance. *Canadian Social Trends*, 22:21–4

Basavarajappa, K.G. (1978). *Marital status and nuptiality in Canada* 1971 Census of Canada Profile Study. Ottawa: Minister of Supply and Services. Includes French version.

– , and Halli, S.S. (1987). Fertility of Asian ethnic groups in Canada, 1971–81. In P. Krishnan, F. Trovato, and G. Fearn (eds), *Contributions to demography: Methodological and substantive* (pp 311–22). Edmonton: Dept of Sociology, University of Alberta

Beaujot, R.P. (1982). The decline of official language minorities in Quebec and English Canada. *Canadian Journal of Sociology, 7*:367–89

– (1991). *Population change in Canada: The challenges of policy and adaptation*. Toronto: McClelland & Stewart

– , Basavarajappa, K.G., and Verma, R.B.P. (1988). *Income of immigrants in Canada: A census data analysis*. (Current Demographic Analysis Series). Ottawa: Supply and Services Canada. French edition also in print

– , and McQuillan, K. (1982). *Growth and dualism: The demographic development of Canadian society*. Agincourt, ON: Gage Educational Publishing

Berry, J.W., Kalin, R., and Taylor, D.M. (1980). Multiculturalism and ethnic attitudes in Canada. In J.E. Goldstein and R.M. Bienvenue (eds), *Ethnicity and Ethnic Relations in Canada* (pp 259–78). Toronto: Butterworths

Bourbeau, R. (1989). *Canada, a linguistic profile.* 1986 Census of Canada. Focus on Canada Series. Includes French version. Ottawa: Statistics Canada

Boxhill, W. (1991). Approaches to the collection of data on visible minorities in Canada: A review and commentary. Ottawa: Statistics Canada

Boyd, M. (1985). Immigration and occupational attainment in Canada. In M. Boyd, J. Goyder, F.E. Jones, H.A. McRoberts, P.C. Pineo, and J. Porter (eds), *Ascription and achievement: Studies in mobility and status attainment in Canada* (pp 393–446). Ottawa: Carleton University Press

– (1990). *Ethno-cultural questions on the General Social Survey: An assessment.* Ottawa: Statistics Canada, Centre for Ethnic Measurement

Brym, R.J., Gillespie, M.W., and Gillis, A.R. (1985). Anomie, opportunity, and the density of ethnic ties: Another view of Jewish outmarriage in Canada. *Canadian Review of Sociology and Anthropology,* 22:102–12

Burch, T.K. (1990). *Families in Canada.* 1986 Census of Canada. Focus on Canada series. Includes French version. Ottawa: Statistics Canada

Caldwell, G. (1984). Anglo-Quebec: Demographic realities and options for the future. In R.Y. Bourhis (ed.), *Conflict and language planning in Quebec* (pp 205–22). Clevedon, Avon, Eng.: Multilingual Matters

– , and Waddell, E. (eds) (1985). *The English of Quebec: From majority to minority status.* Quebec: Institut québécois de recherche sur la culture

Canada, Dominion Bureau of Statistics (1924). *Census of Canada 1921, Vol. 1, Population: Number, sex and age distribution – racial origins – religions.* Ottawa: F.A. Acland

– (1949). *Vital statistics 1946.* Ottawa: Dominion Bureau of Statistics

– (1978). *Minority and second languge education, elementary and secondary levels.* 1975–76 and 1976–77. (First in a series.) Ottawa: Minister of Industry, Trade and Commerce

– (1980). *Directory of Health Division information.* Ottawa: Minister of Supply and Services

– (1984a). *Census of Canada 1981. The elderly of Canada.* Ottawa: Statistics Canada

– (1984b). *Census of Canada 1981. Canada: Changing population distribution.* Ottawa: Statistics Canada

– (1984c). *Census of Canada 1981. Canada's immigrants.* Ottawa: Statistics Canada

– (1985). *Language in Canada.* Ottawa: Statistics Canada

– (1987). *Language: Part 1. The Nation.* Ottawa: Minister of Supply and Services

– (1989). *Language: Part 2. The Nation.* Ottawa: Minister of Supply and Services

– CEM (1991). *Canadian census ethnocultural questions 1871–1991.* Ottawa: Statistics Canada, Centre for Ethnic Measurement

- *Mother tongue: The Nation* (1992). Ottawa: Statistics Canada, Cat. No. 93–313
Castonguay, C. (1979). Exogamie et anglicization chez les minorités cana-diennes-françaises. *Revue canadienne de sociologie et d'anthropologie,* 16:21–31
- (1983). Exogamie et transferts linguistiques chez les populations de langue maternelle français au Canada. In Association Internationale des Démographes de Langue Française, *Demographie et destin des sous-populations: Colloque de Liége* (pp 209–15). Paris: Ouvrage Subventionné par le Conseil de la Langue Française du Québec et l'institut National d'Études Démographiques
- (1985). Transferts et semi-transferts linguistiques au Québec d'après le recensement de 1981. *Cahiers québécois de démographie,* 14(1):241–257
- (1988). Virage démographique et Québec français. *Cahiers québécois de démographie,* 17(1):49–60
- (1991). Incidence des réponses multiples sur la mesure de la composition et de l'assimilation linguistiques aux derniers recensements. Communications libres. Section démographie. Congrès de l'ACFAS, Sherbrooke, 22 et 23 mai 1991. Montreal: Presses de l'Université de Montréal
Charbonneau, H. (1984). Trois siècles de dépopulation amérindienne. In L. Normandeau and V. Piché (eds), *Les populations amérindiennes et inuit du Canada: Aperçu démographique* (pp 28–48). Montreal: Presses de l'Université de Montréal
Charles, E. (1948). *The changing size of the Canadian family.* Ottawa: Dominion Bureau of Statistics
Chimbos, P., and Agocs, C. (1983). Kin and hometown network as support systems for the immigration and settlement of Greek Canadians. *Canadian Ethnic Studies,* 15(2):42–56
Corrigan, P., and Shamai, S. (1986). *Ethnicity, gender and educational achievement in Canada: An historical-statistical analysis, based on Censal data, 1921–1981.* Toronto: Ontario Institute for Studies in Education
De Braekeleer, M. (1990). Homogeneité genetique des Canadiens français du Québec: Mythe ou realité? *Cahiers québécois de démographie,* 19(1):29–48
Demographic Review (1989). *Charting Canada's future.* Ottawa: Health and Welfare Canada. Includes French version
De Vries, J., and Vallee, F.G. (1980). *Language use in Canada.* Ottawa: Statistics Canada
Driedger, L. (1983). Ethnic intermarriage: Student dating and mating. In K. Ishwaran (ed.), *Marriage and divorce in Canada* (pp 213–31). Toronto: Methuen
- , and Chappell, N. (1987). *Aging and ethnicity: Toward an interface.* Toronto: Butterworths

Dumas, J. (1990). *Report on the demographic situation in Canada 1988.* (Current Demographic Analysis Series. Ottawa: Minister of Supply and Services Canada

– (1991). *Report on the demographic situation in Canada 1991.* (Current Demographic Analysis Series, Statistics Canada Cat. No. 91-209E Annual). Ottawa: Minister of Supply and Services Canada

Ebanks, G.E. (1990). Immigration: Its nature and impact. *Canadian Studies in Population* 17(2):13–17

Economic Council of Canada (1991). *Economic and social impacts of immigration.* Ottawa: Minister of Supply and Services Canada

Farley, R. (1991). The new census question about ancestry: What did it tell us? *Demography,* 28:411–30

Frideres, J.S. (1988). *Native peoples in Canada: Contemporary conflicts.* Scarborough: Prentice-Hall Canada

George, M.V. (1978). *Place of birth and citizenship of Canada's population* Includes French version. (1971 Census of Canada, Profile Study). Ottawa: Statistics Canada

Goldmann, G. (1992). Canadian data on ethnic origin: Who needs it and why? Paper prepared for the joint Canada/United States conference on the measurement of ethnicity, 1–3 Apr. 1992

Goldstein, J., and Segall, A. (1985). Ethnic intermarriage and ethnic identity. *Canadian Ethnic Studies,* 17(3):60–90

Grindstaff, C.F. (1990). Ethnic, marital and economic status of women. In S.S. Halli, F. Trovato, and L. Driedger (eds), *Ethnic demography: Canadian immigrant, racial and cultural variations* (pp 315–42). Ottawa: Carleton University Press

Hagey, N.J., Larocque, G., and McBride, C. (1989). Faits saillants des conditions des autochtones 1981–2001. Ottawa: Indian and Northern Affairs

Halli, S.S. (1989). Toward a re-conceptualization of minority group status and fertility hypothesis: The case of orientals in Canada. *Journal of Comparative Family Studies,* 20(1):21–45

– , Trovato, F., and Driedger, L. (1990). *Ethnic demography: Canadian immigrant, racial and cultural variations.* Ottawa: Carleton University Press

Henripin, J. (1972). *Trends and factors of fertility in Canada.* Ottawa: Statistics Canada. French edition published in 1968

– (1974). *Immigration and language imbalance.* (A report commissioned by the Canadian Immigration and Population Study). Ottawa: Manpower and Immigration Canada. French version also in print

– (1985). Le Québécois dont la langue est flottante et la mobilité linguistique. *Cahiers québécois de démographie,* 14(1):87–98

– (1989). *Naître ou ne pas être*. Québec: Institut québécois de recherche sur la culture

Innis, H.R. (1973). *Bilingualism and biculturalism* (Abridged version of the Royal Commission Report). Toronto: McClelland & Stewart

Joy, R. (1967). *Languages in conflict*. Ottawa: Self-published

Kalbach, W.E. (1970). *The impact of immigration on Canada's population*. Ottawa: Dominion Bureau of Statistics

– (1983). Propensities of intermarriage in Canada, as reflected in ethnic origins of husbands and their wives. In K. Ishwaran (ed.), *Marriage and divorce in Canada* (pp 196–212). Toronto: Methuen

– , and McVey, W., Jr (1979). *The demographic bases of Canadian society*, 2nd ed. Toronto: McGraw-Hill Ryerson

Kralt, J. (1976). *Language in Canada* 1971 Census of Canada, Profile Study. Ottawa: Statistics Canada. The publication is undated, but from the external evidence it appears that it was published in 1976. Includes French version.

– (1977). *Ethnic origins of Canadians*. 1971 Census of Canada, Profile Study. Includes French version. Ottawa: Statistics Canada

– (1980). *A user's guide to 1976 census data on mother tongue*. (Working Paper No. 3-DSC 79). Ottawa: Minister of Supply and Services Canada

Krishnan, V. (1987). The relationship between income and fertility: The role of immigrant culture. In P. Krishnan, F. Trovato, and G. Fearn (eds), *Contributions to demography: Methodological and substantive* (pp 483–504). Edmonton: Dept of Sociology, University of Alberta

– , and Krótki, K.J. (1992). Immigrant fertility: An examination of social characteristics and assimilation. *Sociological Focus* 25(1):37–8, Feb. 1992

Krótki, K.J. (1978). Linguistic assimilation in Canada by age and sex: An objective estimate through life table techniques. In *Second Banff Conference on Central and Eastern European Studies, 1978*. Vol. 3 (pp 54–88). Edmonton, Alberta: The University of Alberta, CEESSA. Also appeared as Research Discussion Paper Nr 23 (1980), Population Research Laboratory, University of Alberta

– (1989). The history and methodology of the Canadian Fertility Survey of 1984. In J. Legare, T.R, Balakrishnan, and R. Beaujot (eds), *The family in crisis?/Crise de famille? A population crisis?/Crise démographique?* (pp 17–51). Ottawa: Royal Society of Canada. Also in Population Reprints, Nr 98(1989), Population Research Laboratory, University of Alberta

– (1990). Why are Canadians dying out? *Transactions of the Royal Society of Canada*, 4(series 5):115–39

– (1992). 'East-west or south-north immigration into Europe.' Paper presented to IAS-IIASA-IF conference on *Mass migration in Europe: Implications in East and West*. Vienna, 7 Mar. 1992

– , and Odynak D. (1990). The emergence of multiethnicities in the eighties. In S.S. Halli, F. Trovato, and L. Driedger, (eds) *Ethnic demography: Immigrant, racial and cultural variations* (pp 415–57). Ottawa: Carleton University Press. Also in Population Reprints (1992) Nr 106. Population Research Laboratory, University of Alberta

– , and Termote, M. (eds). (1990). Towards a population policy for Canada: Migration, ethnicity, regions and social concerns. Special issue of *Canadian Studies in Population, 17*(2)

Kuczynski, R.R. (1930). *Birth registration and birth statistics in Canada*. Washington, DC: Brookings Institution

Lachapelle, R. (1990). Evolution of language groups and the official language situation in Canada. In *Demolinguistic trends and the evolution of Canadian institutions* (pp 7–33). Published by the Association for Canadian Studies, the Dept. of the Secretary of State, and the Office of the Commissioner for Official Languages

– , and Henripin, J. (1982). *The demolinguistic situation in Canada: Past trends and future prospects.* (D.A. Mark, trans.). Montreal: Institute for Research on Public Policy. French edition published 1980

Laponce, J.A. (1987). *Languages and their territories* (2nd ed). (A. Martin-Sperry, trans.). Toronto: University of Toronto Press. French edition published 1984

– (1988). Conseil au Prince qui voudrait assurer la survie du français en Amérique du Nord. *Cahiers québécois de démographie, 17*(1):35–48

Lavoie, Y. (1972). *L'émigration des Canadiens aux États-Unis avant 1930*. Montréal: Les Presses de l'Université de Montréal

Maslove, A., and Hawkes, D.C. (1990). *Canada's north: A profile.* 1986 Census of Canada, Focus on Canada Series. Ottawa: Statistics Canada. Includes French version.

Mitra, S. (1992). Below replacement fertility: Net international migration and Canada's future population. *Canadian Studies in Population, 19*(1):27–46

Mori, G.A., and Burke, B. (1989). *Educational attainments of Canadians.* 1986 Census of Canada, Focus on Canada Series. Ottawa: Statistics Canada. Includes French version.

Normandeau, L., and Piché, V. (eds) (1984). *Les populations amérindiennes et inuit du Canada: Aperçu démographique.* Montreal: Presses de l'Université de Montréal

Norris, M.J. (1990). The demography of aboriginal people in Canada. In S. Halli, F. Trovato, and L. Driedger (eds), *Ethnic demography: Immigrant, racial and cultural variations* (pp 33–59). Ottawa: Carleton University Press

O'Bryan, K.G., Reitz, J.G., and Kuplowska, D.M. (1976). *Non-official languages: A study of Canadian multiculturalism.* Ottawa: Minister Responsible for Multiculturalism. French version also in print

Paillé, M. (1991). *Les écoliers du Canada admissibles à recevoir leur instruction en français ou en anglais.* Québec: Conseil de la Langue Française

Parai, L. (1965). *Immigration and emigration of professional and skilled manpower during the postwar period.* Special Study Nr 1. Ottawa: Economic Council of Canada

– (1974). *The economic impact of immigration.* Canadian immigration and population study. Ottawa: Manpower and Immigration. French edition also in print

Peterson, W. (1980). Concepts of ethnicity. In S. Thernstrom (ed.), *Harvard encyclopedia of American ethnic groups* (pp 234–42). Cambridge, MA: Harvard University Press

Porter, J. (1965). *The vertical mosaic: An analysis of social class and power in Canada.* Toronto: University of Toronto Press

Ram, B., Norris, M.J., and Skof, K. (1989). *The inner city in transition.* 1986 Census of Canada, Focus on Canada Series. Ottawa: Statistics Canada. Includes French version.

Reitz, J.G. (1980). Language and community survival. In J.E. Goldstein and R.M. Bienvenue (eds), *Ethnicity and ethnic relations in Canada* (pp 111–29). Toronto: Butterworths

Richard, M.A. (1991a). *Ethnic groups and marital choices: Ethnic history and marital assimilation, Canada 1871 and 1971.* Vancouver: UBC Press

– (1991b). Factors in the assimilation of ethno-religious populations in Canada, 1871 and 1971. *Canadian Review of Sociology and Anthropology, 28*:99–111

Richmond, A.H. (1986). Ethnogenerational variation in educational achievement. *Canadian Ethnic Studies, 18*(3):75–89

– , and Kalbach, W. (1980). *Factors in the adjustment of immigrants and their descendents.* Ottawa: Statistics Canada

Robitaille, N., and Choiniere, R. (1987). L'acroissement démographique des groupes autochtones au Canada au xxe siècle. *Cahiers québécois de démographie, 16*(1):3–35

Romaniuc, A. (1981). Increase in natural fertility during the early stages of modernization: Canadian Indians case study. *Demography, 18*(2):157–72

– (1987). Transition from traditional high to modern low fertility: Canadian aboriginals. *Canadian Studies in Population, 14*:69–88

Romaniuc, A. (1991). Fertility in Canada: Retrospective and prospective. *Canadian Studies in Population, 18*(2):56–77

Ross, L. (1989). *Canada's youth.* 1986 Census of Canada, Focus on Canada Series. Ottawa: Statistics Canada. Includes French version.

Royal Commission on Bilingualism and Biculturalism (1969a). *Report of the Royal Commission on Bilingualism and Biculturalism.* Book III: The work world. Ottawa: Queen's Printer

– (1969b). *Report of the Royal Commission on Bilingualism and Biculturalism*. Book IV: The cultural contribution of the other ethnic groups. Ottawa: Queen's Printer

Ryder, N. (1990). *Cohort fertility over time: Canada and the US*. (Paper presented at the Annual Meeting of the PAA, Toronto, 1990).

Scott, J. (1976). *Canada's religious composition*. 1971 Census of Canada, Profile Study. Ottawa: Statistics Canada. Includes French version.

Siggner, A.J. (1986). The socio-demographic conditions of registered Indians. *Canadian Social Trends*, 3:2–9. French version available.

Simmons, A.B. (1988). *The political economy of Canadian immigration: International and internal forces affecting the national origins of immigrants to Canada in the 1980s*. (Report prepared for the Review of Demography and its Implications for Economic and Social Policy). Ottawa: Health and Welfare Canada

Simmons, A.B., and Keohane K. (1992). Canadian immigration policy: State strategies and the quest for legitimacy. *The Canadian Review of Sociology and Anthropology*, 29: 421–52

Termote, M., and Gauvreau, D. (1988). *La situation démolinguistique du Québec*. Dossiers du Conseil de la Langue Française, No. 30. Québec: Conseil de la Langue Française

Trovato, F. (1981). Canadian ethnic fertility. *Sociological Focus, 14*: 57–77

– (1988). Mortality differentials in Canada, 1951–1971: French, British, and Indians. *Culture, Medicine and Psychiatry, 12*: 219–37

– , and Burch, T.K. (1980). Minority group status and fertility in Canada. *Canadian Ethnic Studies, 12*(3): 1–18

Veevers, J.E. (1977). *The family in Canada*. 1971 Census of Canada, Profile Study. Ottawa: Statistics Canada. Includes French version.

– (1983). *Demographic aspects of vital statistics: Fertility*. Ottawa: Statistics Canada

White, P.M. (1990). *Ethnic diversity in Canada* (1986 Census of Canada, Focus on Canada Series. Ottawa: Statistics Canada. Includes French version.

GILLES PAQUET

Political Philosophy
of Multiculturalism

FRAMEWORK FOR STRATEGIC ANALYSIS

In the multiculturalism debate, there are two playing fields. The first-order reality (what we call the 'terrain of realities') is the 'material order': it connotes the flows of material resources generated under different technical, legal, social, political or economic arrangements. While there are no simple and unambiguous indicators of the ensuing welfare levels for the different communities, or of the economic surplus generated by certain agreed arrangements, the debates, speculations and discords in the market are mainly about the production, allocation and distribution of material and financial resources. Analysts are mainly searching for technical-legal arrangements or re-arrangements likely to maximize the overall welfare level or the economic or financial surplus.

The second-order reality (what we call the 'theatre of representations' or the 'symbolic order') connotes the images of and the conversations about material order or some features derived more or less clearly from it. It underpins decisions by different social actors not only to act in certain ways but to value goods or agency differently. Myths, values, symbolic resources play an important role in shaping the representations and perceptions of social actors. While the theatre of representations may be boldly presumed by some to be a simple mirror image of the terrain of realities, this is a most unlikely scenario. Assumptions are made, distortions, generalizations, focalizations, and sheer fantasizing are omnipresent in the construction of these representations.

Action by the different stakeholders is often triggered by imperatives emanating from the material order; much more often, however, action is generated by second-order reality, by representations, (i.e., the framing of first-order reality) (Tersky & Kahneman 1981).

The Terrain of Realities

There are a number of demographic, socio-economic, political, geographic, and historical dimensions defining the material order. Some of these have been analyzed by the Economic Council of Canada in *New Faces in the Crowd*. For instance, the historical context of Canada had prepared the ground for multiculturalism. As Hugh Thorburn explains, the existence of two linguistic and ethnic groups since the eighteenth century in semi-separate portions of the Canadian space had made more or less unthinkable the simple assimilationist dream that underpinned the American melting pot. In that sense, multiculturalism may simply be regarded (and is regarded by some) as an extension of an already existing Canadian arrangement (Thorburn in Dwivedi 1989).

As a more significant portion of the Canadian population came to be drawn from other sources than the charter groups, and as the two charter groups were seeing their privileges confirmed somewhat by the Royal Commission on Bilinguism and Biculturalism, it was normal for opinion-moulders in the rest of the Canadian constituency to press government and to alert citizens to the need for some clarification in their status as *other* Canadians. In this context, multiculturalism was a modest symbolic gesture offering heightened respect to the other Canadians. It served also the Trudeau government in providing a 'liberal' alternative to the two-nation policy of Stanfield: a policy attractive to Québécois but in no way serving other Canadians.

No single pattern has materialized in the ethnocultural field. In the continuum between Franco/Anglo conformity/assimilationism *and* segragated enclavic ethnic identity proposed by Leo Driedger, for instance, (Driedger in Dwivedi 1989), various groups are voluntarily or involuntarily led to different patterns of adjustment.

Theatre of Representations

The approach developed in the material order makes little allowance for the echo box of representations. Yet this constructed second-order reality or symbolic order influences dramatically, though indirectly, the allocation of material and financial resources. The symbolic order shapes the forum. 'The construction of a symbolic order ... entails the shaping of cultural traditions: values and norms on the one hand; customs and ways of doing things on the other. Perhaps the most important component of this cultural way of life is that embedded in the forms and styles of public institutions ... [that] become incorporated in systems of ideas that are symbolically reinforced in laws, official speeches and documents, constitutional provisions and their public discussion, advertisements, and other public relations behaviours' (Breton 1984).

The construction of second-order reality in the theater of representations is collectively arrived at. As a collective decision, it may be viewed as a process of conflict resolution, as the interplay of different games being played by the different social actors. Trebilcock et al. have identified a number of games being played out at the same time (the electoral game, the political game, the bureaucratic game, the special-interest-group game, the media game, etc.), but they have emphasized almost exclusively the interactions among these games on the terrain of the material economy (Trebilcock et al. 1982). What must be added to this material and financial playing field is the fact that since none of the groups involved are really capable of apprehending any 'so-called objective reality,' these groups construct their own 'second-order realities' (Watzlawick 1988).

Two central elements are at the core of the construction of representations by the different groups involved in public issues: the vision-distorting glasses everyone wears because of the experience into which they anchor their perceptions (Kahneman & Tersky 1979); and the attentional deployment of the group: 'the structure of attention forms the network of communication between individuals and lies at the heart of the system of resource deployment' (Berger 1989). The attention of the citizenry is the scarce resource that opinion-moulders compete for: mobilizing the attention of the public is the way to frame and reframe problems and issues.

The dynamics of communication in the forum centres on the problem of attention deployment: far from being the locus of perfect competition between ideas and attention-grabbing issues, the forum is pregnant with important synergies. The media play on those and tend to dramatize issues to ensure that they remain in the forefront of the collective psyche. To do so, they draw on the socio-cultural background of the citizens, on their myths, on the sensitivities and propensities and fears, to ensure that the citizens are mobilized (Hilgartner & Bosk 1988). In pressure times or crisis situations, a sort of *groupthink* might even develop – a tendency for social actors to echo each other's views and to accept such echoes as confirmation that proves both reassuring and comforting (Janis 1982). The media play a central role in this process.

These representations have a determining impact on the socio-political multilogue and, in the case of issues as complex and contentious as multiculturalism, the perversion of the languages of problem definition has often fed a cumulative process of discord under a veneer of mutual understanding (Laurent & Paquet 1991; Nielsen 1991).

Dynamics of Multiculturalism

Polyethnicity has become a reality in Canada: there are now some ten million Canadians who are not from the two charter groups. Multiculturalism as an idea and a policy has also caught on and has been evolving: from its origin as an innocuous symbolic gesture, it has grown into a nation-building public philosophy (Thorburn). The media and the clerisy of opinion-moulders in ethnic groups played a key role in this process. The 'other ethnic' Canadians who do not find their roots with the 'peuples fondateurs' have been bombarded with rhetoric exalting the irreducible differences between the points of view of the 'peuples fondateurs' and their own.

Non-charter Canadians have heard from Quebec affirmations of the right to secede for fear of cultural cross-breeding, *and* from English Canada a statement of the 'devoir d'ingérence' commanding centralization in the name of egalitarianism and some fraternal duty to protect individual rights in threatened minority groups in Quebec (Robin 1989; Buchanan 1991). These Manichean representations orchestrated by the media and the clerisies have occupied centre stage and shaped public opinion. The ten million 'autres Canadiens,' having no real power in the media, have been unable to have a real impact on the representations or to reframe them so as to give the transcultural or evolving cultural identity point of view they defend any opportunity to be aired and to affect the outcome of the constitutional debate. This failure has generated much unease.

Yet with the Charter of Rights and the entrenchment in the new constitution of the 'multicultural' nature of Canada, the expectations of 'other' Canadians have been heightened and the belief that they do *not* have to adapt their mores has been nurtured, while the 'dominant cultures' have remained dominant. The gap between expectations and realities has generated much *ressentiment* and frustration: many Canadians (new and old) have come to argue that the multiculturalism policy may have degenerated unwittingly or not into a containment policy (Paquet 1989); that 'intentionally or not, the multicultural policy preserves the reality of Canadian ethnic hierarchy' (Kallen 1982); that as a result of the new ethnocentrism generated by the policy, and the new rhetoric of rights that has been carpentered to underpin it, there has been a dangerous drift from unhyphenated Canadianism into ethnic particularism (Kallen 1982) or as others would put it toward a 'tribalization' of Canadian society (Spicer 1988).

A recent wide-ranging survey of the literature (Thomas 1990) has even acknowledged 'a growing intolerance among Canadians about ... the survival of the Canadian identity,' a certain degree of xenophobia and racism, and the 'need to develop a national inclusive identity.' While these tensions remain somewhat benign at this time, there is also much complacency due to the fact that these tensions, while they exist, have not yet materialized into overt conflicts as they have elsewhere. These tensions have not generated yet anything more than an ill-defined malaise about the need to 'specify limits in the expression of multiculturalism' (Cameron 1990), or about 'les dangers d'un Canada insoucieux d'intégrer ses immigrants' for it might fall into a form of 'Babelization,' or the need to foster the development of a 'métaculture,' 'une psyché commune authentiquement canadienne.'

Fundamentally, this malaise remains very much unspoken and underexpressed even if it is strongly felt, which is largely ascribable to the fact that any statement about the importance of constructing a 'national' culture or metaculture or about 'national' preferences or 'dominant cultures' is interpreted as essentially racist. Cosmopolitanism has come to be regarded as the only attitude that is *morally and politically correct*. In this context, establishing a hierarchy between the positive commitment to Canadian dualism in the 1982 Constitution and the 'rhetorical flourish' (Peter Hogg) about multiculturalism in Article 27 of the Charter of Rights and Freedoms poses quite a challenge: it appears difficult to deny that a hierarchy exists between the realities that these statements underpin, yet it also appears to be politically incorrect to discuss such a hierarchy openly (Bastarache 1988).

CURRENT SOCIAL LEARNING AND ALTERNATIVE SCENARIOS

It is difficult to anticipate what will percolate in time from the extensive research undertaken by colleagues in a large number of specialized areas both about the terrain of realities and the theater of representations. This section of the paper is therefore conjectural and adventurous. Yet, some preliminary glimpses at current social learning and at some alternative approaches for the next decade are possible.

Current Social Learning

On the terrain of realities, it has become clear that Canada is facing some reduction in the pace of natural increase that will need to be compensated by a net immigration balance, that is, if immigration is regarded as desirable, as providing benefits that outweigh the costs. A recent report from the Economic Council of Canada (1991) argue that what Canadians will gain economically from more immigration is very small. As for the social impact of such increase in immigration levels, the Council can only suggest that it is 'cautiously optimistic that the risk is acceptable,' but there are risks of social friction.

This cautious optimism has led the Council to argue that government policy has to address potential social costs through adjustments in the current multiculturalism policy that 'would pay handsome dividends.' The nature of these adjustments has been only obliquely hinted at. It would shift the policy from its present stance, where 'multiculturalism demands too much adjustment by Canadians and too little by immigrants,' to one where adjustment responsibilities might be more balanced. The idea that a 'moral contract' might embody such an arrangement has been proposed. A variety of measures to ease the incorporation of immigrants into Canadian society (combatting prejudice, more information and training, etc.) were also proposed.

This evaluation of the situation would not appear to have triggered a modification in the somewhat kaleidoscopic nature of the policy stand that exists in Canada in connection with multiculturalism. Clearly the Canadian federal government does not speak with one voice on this issue, which appears to be the result more of a certain 'confusion' and of concern to be 'politically correct' than the result of deeply rooted philosophical differences. There are also important differences among regions and groups as to what is the appropriate policy for Canada, though maybe less than has been suggested.

The federal government and many groups in English Canada outside Quebec have not veered away yet from staunch support of the 1971 Trudeau statement, however difficult it is to defend. However, there is profound malaise about policies in most federal departments polled (apart from Secretary of State and the Department of Multiculturalism). The conclusions of the Economic Council of Canada about the need to adjust the policy appear to be widely supported in those agencies, but without a clear *projet alternatif* beyond robust promotion of Canadian citizenship. This promotion was echoed officially very clearly for the first time in the federal government's September 1991 constitutional proposals (Canada 1991).

The unease of the Quebec government about the multiculturalism policy has remained strong ever since its inception, which has translated into support for a more *integrationist* model than in the rest of the country.

Canadians have retained a certain diffidence about multiculturalism. The clerisies were no more vehement in Quebec than in the rest of the country in denouncing abandonment of the dominant culture concept. In English Canada, however, critical comments about multiculturalism were more strident on both sides of the argument, some demanding a more vibrant and decisive delivery of the promises made in the Trudeau statement (Kallen) and others denouncing the debilitating effect of the policy on the national ethos (Brotz).

In the last decade especially, there has been concern on all sides about the erosion of national symbols, which seems to have captured the attention of Canadians as an indication of the adjustments required from a host society to accommodate newcomers. While much has been made of the Quebec/rest of Canada (ROC) differences in attitudes towards xenocultures, some have argued that these differences are much less sharp and significant between French and English Quebeckers than has been assumed (Bolduc & Fortin 1990). The central issue seems to be concern for French as a dominant language (and therefore dominant culture) rather than xenophobia. Recent ethnographic writings have challenged this view (Richler 1991).

Perceptions and representations have evolved in Canada in recent years, and not in the direction that multiculturalism suggests. While the evidence has bearing on ethnic tolerance only obliquely the proportion of Canadians who feel that 'there are too many immigrants coming to Canada' has grown from around 30 per cent in 1988-early 1989 to some 43 per cent later in 1989 (Palmer 1991). Moreover, the perceptions of the cultural minorities are clearly registering that prejudice, xenophobic attitudes, and discriminatory practices are still important in Quebec, especially in the work place (Langlais, Laplante & Levy 1990).

The sense of unease associated with the fragmentation of the Canadian social fabric is quite prevalent. It exists clearly in the ROC, where excessive individualism and relativism has generated some erosion of the sense of community and has triggered an emphasis on mere 'co-existence' thereby generating a 'mosaic madness' (Bibby 1990). A quick review of the press over the recent past also reveals that there are numerous new Canadians who denounce the 'serial monoculturalism' that has resulted from the multiculturalism policy. They do so because as a result 'minority ethnics lose the opportunity to develop into their full citizenship as Canadians' (Sugunasiri 1990). For other members of the 'minority ethnic groups', 'multiculturalism as a response to the concerns of ethnic Canadians is illusory and gives false hope to those ethnic Canadians who seek to be part of the country ... [and] is insulting because it tends to denigrate the individuality of ethnic Canadians and instead defines them as members of "different" groups'; as a result 'it pays them to remain peripheral' (Meghji 1990). There is a large number of comments along the same line from both minority ethnics and mainstream Canadians leading to a call for reframing the policy (*Winnipeg Free Press*, 12 Jan. 1990; *Calgary Herald*, 27 Mar. 1990; *Globe & Mail*, 17 Nov. 1990; *Le Devoir*, 10 Nov. 1990.

Intellectuals have also contributed much to the philosophical and critical evaluation of the multiculturalism policy. Robert Harney has reviewed this variegated literature in a recent interpretative essay that has been very widely read and quoted (Harney 1988). He suggests four interpretations of the public policy of multiculturalism: (1) as a product of the postwar arrival of nationalist intellectuals (Poles, Balts, and Ukrainians especially) at a time when there was a failure of will to assimilate newcomers by Anglo-Canadians; (2) as 'an innovative and altruistic civic philosophy of democratic pluralism to replace loyalty to the British Empire as a legitimizing principle for the Canadian state'; (3) as an anglophone device to minimize the valence of the French minority, and (4) as a tactic of politicians to control the new ethnic and immigrant vote.

None of these narratives (or any mixture of them) has become the canonical one. One reason for this lack of clear diagnosis is the terminological confusion that has plagued the debate. Québécois, for instance, have underlined the sharp distinction between *ethnie* and *nation*: ethnie 'renvoie à un ensemble de caractéristiques et de traditions dont l'existence ou la persistance peuvent se vérifier au niveau des individus et des familles,' while nation connotes 'une société complète, qui possède ses caractéristiques propres en tant que société, qui a son mode d'organisation et de fonctionnement' (Camille Laurin quoted by Harney 1988: 76–7). This was a fundamental tenet in Québécois' claim for their collective rights but not for those of new Canadians. An alternative set of definitions would lead the Ukrainians to argue conversely. One senses that the looseness in the use of those words allowed a certain Babelian quality to develop in the debates.

In this context it became quite easy for some groups to fantasize: from census ethnic membership, one could be led to presume ethnocultural sentiments, and from those to forge collective ethno-national rights for new Canadians 'as if traces of the failed Hapsburg monarchy had crossed the sea with them' (Harney 1988:66). It is also in this context that the deliberate funding of institutions of ethnic maintenance has been perceived as a policy, that has blocked the natural integrating forces at work on the arriving ethnics *and* as a process of 'ethnicization of the immigrants.' Such a policy, which continues to declare that there is no official culture in Canada and to promise that new immigrants could carry on living with all their customs in Canada, could only be interpreted as using the *concept-bateau* of culture as a way to help ethnic entrepreneurs turn ethnic identity into institutionalized ethnies or to pay people to 'create institutions of otherness' (Harney 1988:85).

This is the basis for some to fear that *ressentiment* might ensue as the stark contrast between the egalitarian promises made to new Canadians and the realities of the fairly resilient hegemonies of the Anglo and French establishments will begin to reveal itself in allowing new immigrants to proceed only so far so fast (Paquet 1989b).

Indeed, recognizing the cultural identity of a minority group and promoting its maintenance through official financial support may well be an indirect and Machiavellian technique to consecrate exclusion of the minority group, or more appropriately to continue to dominate it. In that sense, the relationship between national identity and cultural identity is clear: the definition of a de facto dominant national culture can only amount to marginalization of the group with a different ethnocultural identity. In that context, the National identity then becomes the foundation of a hierarchy (Oriol 1979), and this underlines the unhealthy rapports between ethnic and national culture and the disingenuity of a policy that thrives on ambiguities and confusions. There are no real ethnic rights or multicultural obligations, as some ethnic critics like Kallen have clearly seen; so the affirmation and celebration of polyethnicity and the promotion of the multicultural ethos without any real ressources to back it up can only fabricate explosive cleavages between expectations and realities.

Alternative Scenarios

There are a variety of ways in which one might harness both the transformed socio-demographic fabric of Canada and the expectations manufactured by a generation of multiculturalism policy as we know it. The *first* family of such scenarios is built around the notion that the present policy is adequate and needs no substantial change. This scenario suggests that the evidence in support of multiculturalism working well is sufficient to support the present policy. At best such a scenario would call for cosmetic changes in programs. The word *integration* has been used to refer to this scenario together with maintenance of relationships with other groups (Berry 1991). The label, while most accurate in psychological terms, may be misleading for it connotes a degree of intermingling and abolition of differences which may not recognize the extent of the maintenance of otherness. Integration is used here in the sense of 'rapprochement,' though in the late sixties it clearly had the sense of 'acculturation' (Morissette 1991). The term *incorporation* used by Breton et al. in 1990 is also ambiguous, but it certainly also connotes the sense that the integrity of the incorporated is to be maintained. The approach based on 'rapprochement' regards the possibilities of separation and assimilation (the two polar cases) as sufficiently abhorrent to bet on the present middle-of-the-road strategy.

A *second* family of scenarios, while still 'cautiously optimistic,' calls for 'adjustment' to the present multiculturalism policy and proposes that such adjustments be negotiated as part of a *moral contract* between charter and non-charter Canadians (Economic Council of Canada 1991; Gagnon-Tremblay 1990). This approach calls for mutual adjustment between the two groups and suggests implicitly that all cultures are not on a par, and that there are 'official cultures' in Canada. Dominant or older cultures might have to accommodate the newly arrived, but there is no more possibility that the newly arrived can be told that they would not have to adjust and modify their 'manières de vivre.' The moral contract is a negotiated agreement or convention about the nature of the mutual adjustment compatible with the maintenance of a certain Canadianness defined *ex ante*; it would call for ongoing negotiations and definition of a new set of social armistices between cultures and ethnies, but it shifts considerably the burden of adjustment to newcomers and therefore contrasts with the present arrangement.

A *third* way has been called *interculturalisme* and has become the brand of pluralism Quebec has adopted to distinguish its policy from the present multiculturalism policy. The main difference between the two is the dual constraint of a hierarchy of cultures and a recognition that the process would require a certain degree of asymmetry. While multiculturalism has been defined by Lise Bissonnette as 'a simple collage,' she has defined interculturalism as 'a gentle ecumenical embrace' (Bissonnette 1988). The degree of osmosis is much greater but the asymmetric nature of this osmosis is clearly understood.

Such an approach emphasizes the integrative capacity of the official cultures (integration here has a sense much closer to gentle acculturation): for 'Québec "s'intégrer," c'est devenir *partie intégrante* d'une collectivité' (Morissette 1991). Other words used in connection with this family of scenarios are useful guideposts: 'tronc commun,' 'priorité au centre de gravité' give a clear sense of hierarchy of cultures and the idea of the necessity of both 'une culture publique commune' and 'un nationalisme territorial québécois' that transcend the simple anthropological sense of identity and ethnie and suggest an asymmetric moral contract (Harvey 1990).

A *fourth* scenario gambles on a fusion of cultures to 'actively create a new culture': this is *transculturalism* (Caccia 1984; Robin 1989; Tassinari 1989; Van Schendel 1989; *Vice Versa* passim). This experiment wants to break the equation langue=culture=nation and urges a coalition around a symbol like language, allowing the identity to be dominated neither by a nationality nor by culture but rather allowing it to be *created* by a multilogue among all those groups that have a contribution to make. The 'migrant identity' evolves as a sort of 'métissage culturel ... transnationa-litaire et transculturel.'

This fourth scenario is an optimistic gamble on change and creativity which redefines membership (10,000 appartenances), ethnicity ('ethnicité migrante'), culture ('la transculture signifie assumer sa culture d'origine, et, sans la nier, la traverser pour accéder et participer à la culture des autres'), nation ('attitude d'affirmation et de dépassement'), and asserts 'une conception dynamique du cosmopolitisme, par opposition au statisme de la société multiculturelle, à la mosaique canadienne comme politique officielle ... ou au patchwork ethnique .. au melting pot américain.' On the basis of a 'langue dominante,' it is 'une plate-forme très osée': it is not the end of nationalism but rather the beginning of a new form of territorial nationalism based on a renewal of the civil society designed to replace the old ethnic nationalism based on ethnicity and state (Harvey 1990b).

It is unclear which scenario will prevail: despite mounting critical literature on assimilation and absorption, there is also a strong sense that a high degree of integration is desirable and a growing conviction that multiculturalism can only lead to an impasse (Spicer 1988; Paquet 1989b; *Globe & Mail* 1991; Corbo 1991). Consequently, the current malaise is likely to generate greater efforts to integrate all ethnocultural groups more firmly into some Canadian/Quebec civil society. The fact that this integration will occur within the present language terrains (serving as rallying points) seems fairly certain; the extent to which the new emergent metaculture to be constructed will metamorphose the old and preserve the new remains to be determined.

CITIZENSHIP AS AN UMBRELLA STRATEGY

Resolution of the present difficulties might come about through debate on the restorative qualities of citizenship as a way of life aiming at redefining Canadian citizenship. The argument has been promoted from a variety of quarters (Paquet 1989b; Kaplan 1991) in the recent past and has been propelled to centre stage by the federal constitutional documents issued in September 1991, and the declared intention of the Canadian government to put forward a new Citizenship Act in 1992.

Citizenship would manage the multiplicity of conflicting roles individuals are asked to shoulder and provide a public political sphere in which to do it. The idea of an umbrella strategy is derived from management literature and pertains to strategies that set out broad guidelines and leave the specifics to be worked out in practice (Mintzberg & Jorgensen 1987).

Citizenship as Practice

There are two fairly distinct traditions in the literature on citizenship: one emphasizes a conception of citizenship as status and is couched in a language of entitlements; the other emphasizes citizenship as practice and gives rise to a language of duties. The former tradition (liberal individualism) has been dominant in the Anglo-American world, where citizenship has been regarded as a status which 'inheres in individuals but requires the endorsement of civil law for its protection ... from the predatoriness of other individuals and from the arbitrariness of governments.' Individuals born in this world acquire the *status as of right* and 'do not have to do anything to become or remain citizens, unless they feel the status threatened' (Oldfield 1990).

In the latter tradition (civic republicanism), 'it is by acting that, by public service of fairly specific kinds, that individuals demonstrate that they are citizens. This public service relates to what it is necessary for citizens to do in order to define, establish, and sustain a political community of fellow-citizens ... It is action ... which is both constitutive of citizenship, and constitutive and sustaining of the community of which the citizen is member' (Oldfield 1990).

While many have celebrated the 'restorative qualities of citizenship' (Dimock 1990), others have defamed it as myth and as a 'rhetoric of complacency whose result is to reassure those who cannot bear the moral complexity of a market society that they are sensitive and superior beings,' and therefore as a form of 'moral narcissism' (Ignatieff 1989). At the core of this conflict is a crucial disagreement about the dynamics of participation. For some, it is the desire to engage in the practice of citizenship that is crucial, and citizens have to be inculcated with an 'attitude of mind,' 'moeurs ... codes of moral and civil conduct' so that a virtuous circle may be created where participation breeds participation; others believe that such a circle cannot be created.

The refurbished notion of citizenship envisaged here is clearly more active than passive, and directed towards the public arenas, not only to private ones. As such it focuses on the problem of *community membership,* and tries to construct conditions of active membership based less on ethnic or national ascription than on commitment and achievement. As such, it should take precedence over all other charters or sets of rules since it addresses the very admissibility and admission of the member into the community.

Identity defined on that basis does not stem from national or ethnic roots which are communitarian but exclusive, nor from a liberal pluralism that verges on atomism; it is based rather on a notion of 'positive freedom' and on a loyalty to a negotiated notion that 'if we may ... conceive of a liberal polity not as a neutral umpire for subjectively valued pursuits, but as a shared endeavor to create institutions and policies that will increase all citizens' personal and collective capacities for deliberative self-governance, we may better support feelings of meaningful community membership' (Smith 1988). As such, it can accommodate any mix of communitarianism and liberalism negotiated in a social contract.

Citizenship in a Polyethnic and Bi-National Society

There has been a recognition that citizenship in a polyethnic and bi-national society is not easy to develop. Besides simplistic ministerial references to 'linking citizenship to cultural diversity,' little has been done to determine what this sort of citizenship might be. We already know that active citizenship in contemporary liberal democracies is at a low ebb (Parry 1989). To develop it in a fractured context can only be more difficult, which is exactly the challenge faced by the European Community (Aron 1974).

Yet, the concept of citizenship is far from clear (Barbalet 1988; Oliver 1991). It has been regarded as a *concept-bateau* by many observers and interpreted very diversely according to ideology. But the very malleability of the concept makes it attractive as a *negotiated* ensemble of rights and obligations. Citizenship creates a 'community under law' : it is not a 'goal in itself but a means toward enlarging the life chances of men' (Dahrendorf 1974). It is a central concept of political democracy that has escaped from the shackles of ethnie and nation and has led to a balance of rights and obligations on a commitment to a political society (Kelly 1979; Janowitz 1980).

The construction of 'citizenship' has been a bizarre story in Canadian history. The term does not appear in the 1867 Constitution. In the Charter of 1982, the notion of citizenship has been trivialized; it has become clear that through the Supreme Court interpretations the notion of *person* has been interpreted as applying to any person happening to be in Canada or subject to Canadian laws (Garant in Colas 1991). This has meant that any notion of 'moral contract' between the new Canadian and the host society has been shortcircuited by the decision that anybody happening to be in Canada was de facto a Canadian citizen.

In that context, it is sufficient to sneak in to become a citizen, a most bizarre extension of the 'esprit de la loi.' It may be necessary to redefine what is meant by a Canadian citizen.

In Quebec, the notion of citizenship has been a matter of some debate for years. There has been an oscillation between *jus soli* (à la française) and *jus sanguini* (à l'allemande). The refusal to credit any notion of nation or ethnie has led Pierre Trudeau to suggest a notion of citizenship entirely based on a certaine 'volonté,' 'sens civique' or 'civisme' and therefore quite compatible with the Supreme Court definition. This definition was quite different from the communitarian notion of citizenship coinciding with ethnicity that emerged from the nationalist movement (Beaudry in Colas 1991) and maybe too close to the atomism pole.

Citizenship has become a crucible in which a *new identity* is always in the process of being forged, when it becomes understood that any identity or citizenship is always in transition, and therefore *intégration sans assimilation* becomes a concept that is not an oxymoron. Citizenship as an inclusive concept may be constructed politically in the same manner as 'communautés culturelles,' as an exclusive concept, has been constructed (Fontaine & Shiose in Colas 1991).

In that sense, citizenship conditions may be negotiated in a manner that would recognize both the *diversity* of the social fabric and the need for some *unifying* concept to provide a linking force. Up to now, multiculturalism as a national policy has emphasized the pluralist forces at the cost of minimizing the centripetal bond. The notion of citizenship would recognize the patchwork quilt social fabric without losing sight of the need to channel the energy of this varied group into a well-defined direction. Whether or not Canadianism can mobilize the 'limited identities' that characterize people all over Canada is unclear, but negotiating 'moral' or 'social' contracts about what binds us together and keeps us going may be neither impossible nor unhelpful.

Civic Inclusion and Unintended Consequences

The tendency for citizenship to be inclusive has meant that any need to ration citizenship rights has been perceived as a form of racism. Yet indiscriminate civic inclusion can only translate into a form of anomie that destroys any possibility of identity, culture, and effective collective action. The revolutionary character of citizenship is ascribable to the possibility of generalized inclusion; it does not mean that generalized inclusion is desirable, or that lack of screening is going to translate into a better society. Indiscriminate civic inclusion may not be without its discontents (Eckstein 1984). Often this translates into unreasonable expectations and disillusions, resentment and violence (Paquet 1989).

Whether or not a new notion of citizenship might generate a workable social contract may depend on the possibility of recognizing that citizenship need not connote egalitarianism. In a multi-ethnic and binational society, meaningful membership may not develop without a sense of hierarchy. Different but equal is an impossible gambit: this antinomy is at the core of a most important double bind plaguing intercultural relations. Equality denies differences (Laurent & Paquet 1991). Already, such a hierarchy has been institutionalized imperfectly by creating political categories of people 'communautés culturelles' who are neither fully citizens not really aliens. This is a case where 'le politique ... a produit des catégories politiques devenant des catégories sociales de référence dans l'environnement' (Fontaine & Shiose in Colas 1991). There is no reason to believe that citizenship might not become such a negotiated political category.

If Ralf Dahrendorf's diagnosis of the 1990s is accurate (and much of the current transformation in the world would appear to support it):

more and more people (it appears) do not want to live in a multiracial or even a multicultural society. Further this applies not only to cosy majorities but to the affected minorities as well. They demand their own niche if not their own region or country. Separate but equal was a slogan much scorned by liberals in the 1960s; in the 1980s it has become very topical, and often separateness is stressed more than equality. There is a clamour for homogeneity which rejects all attemps to build civilized societies by having civil societies first and cultural differences within them second. (Dahrendorf 1988:156)

Yet this gamble on 'le sens civique' was what the Trudeau policy was attempting to realize (Beaudry in Colas 1991). However, the strategy has been effected in a manner that has not succeeded in eradicating the 'identités multiples' in Canada because of its failure to generate a cohesive Canadian identity. Such an identity may not be easy to develop and would probably have to be built around a priority language (French in Quebec, English in the rest of Canada) and therefore would effectively generate a hierarchy between the groups that speak those languages *and* the others. It can only be built around those two axes via a negotiated citizenship spelling out the rights and obligations of all citizens, but also the conditions of membership and the exact nature of the adaptation expected both from new members and from the host society. The foundations on which one might be able to develop this Canadian notion of active citizenship are discussed at length in the theoretical literature (Kelly 1979; Janowitz 1980; Colas et al. 1991). The process of negotiation may even have begun with the September 1991 federal constitutional proposals.

The idea that separateness is becoming the dominant value, that loss of identity is the central fear of most human beings, and that one cannot have equality and differences (for in fact equality denies differences) have generated a solution that entails differences and separateness (and therefore hierarchy) (Dumont 1983; Laurent & Paquet 1991). This in turn raises the questions of the rights and duties of minorities or other groups that are not assigned a place at the top of the pyramid.

Citizenship and 'Communautés Culturelles'

Even if the new 'moral contract' that underpins the notion of citizenship does not confirm generalized egalitarianism, it also cannot legitimize any type of hierarchy. Separation may call for social distance and hierarchy within bounds. Membership does not necessarily entitle all members to the same life chances, but different entitlements or obligations cannot be so wide-ranging that these tear the social fabric.

What is necessary is evolution of a sort of *civil theology* embodied in a number of standards, guidelines, and agreements designed to ensure the protection of minorities and 'communautés culturelles' through political means complementary to the Charter (Leslie 1986). A Citizenship Act designed to limit or develop what for the time being is implicit in Article 27 of the Charter about minority rights and the rights of 'communautés culturelles' might be beneficial.

CONCLUSION

Whatever the drift in the multiculturalism policy, and whether it is reshaped by a large number of limited but complementary agreements embodied in a Citizenship Act may not be the essential issue. The central problem is that the debate about multiculturalism has revealed some problems with the underlying Canadian social contract.

The bond between generations, between social groups, between regions, and instituted in a variety of programs embodying this solidarity has shown signs of strains. The multicultural fabric of the country is only one dimension where such strains materialize. Everyone is conscious that without cooperation little possibility exists of developing a successful socio-economy, yet, for want of glue, the country shows signs of tearing at the seams (Valaskakis 1990; Grimond 1991).

Rethinking citizenship has already begun in polyethnic and pluricultural societies as a way of bringing about a solution to the generalized prisoner's dilemma that plagues our societies (Wihtol de Wenden 1989). Whether it succeeds in bringing about a social optimum is not the issue. What is at stake is public management of the transformation of modern communities into post-modern societies.

For the time being no public philosophy appears capable of providing the necessary inspiration for the reconstruction of new solidarities. There is a crisis of nationalities, of social programs, of regions and territories within national boundaries, and extreme tensions among generations. Unless a new notion of citizenship can bring about new principles on which to rebuild our community, anomie will continue to run amok and what took a few generations to build in terms of trust and social capital will be quickly dissipated. In this reconstruction, the multiculturalism debate is, in a sense, exemplary, and its solution may also hold the key to many other crises plaguing Canada and other pluralist societies.

But the difficulty in conducting an honest debate about these issues may be more acute with respect to multiculturalism than elsewhere. Any questioning of the wisdom of the policy is branded so quickly as racist that many have simply abandoned the forum. The result is not less *ressentiment* but less open airing of deeply felt concerns. This is probably the most important impediment to revision of a policy broadly regarded as unfortunate in some of its consequences and impact despite the generous spirit from which it blossomed.

Removing the taboos attached to the critical evaluation of multiculturalism, and accepting that many sacred cows (including egalitarianism) may have to be slaughtered in the process, may be a useful first step.

NOTE

Anne Burgess, Linda Cardinal, Marise Guindon, Jak Jabes, Paul Laurent, Joseph Pestieau and Marc Racette have been of help in many different and complementary ways and I am grateful for their assistance. The comments from the participants at the October conference, in particular those of Jean Burnet and Rudy Kalin, have been most helpful. As will become obvious, I may not always have been able or willing to meet all the criticisms I have received to the satisfaction of all these expert colleagues; consequently, I must claim sole responsibility for the final text, if only to avoid any possibility of guilt by association.

REFERENCES

Aron, R. (1974). Is multinational citizenship possible?. *Social Research*, 41:638–56
Barbalet, J.M. (1988). *Citizenship*. Minneapolis: University of Minnesota Press
Bastarache, M. (1988). Dualité et multiculturalisme. *Revue de l'association canadienne d'éducation de langue*, 16:36–40
Berger, L.A. (1989). Economics and hermeneutics. *Economics and Philosophy*, 5:209–33
Berry, J.W. (1991). *Sociopsychological costs and benefits of multiculturalism*. Working Paper No. 24. Ottawa: Economic Council of Canada
Bibby, R.W. (1990). *Mosaic madness*. Toronto: Stoddart
Bissonnette, L. (1988). Vice Versa targets transcultural society. *Globe & Mail*, 30 July D-2
Bolduc, D., and Fortin, P. (1990). Les francophones sont-ils plus xénophobes que les anglophones au Québec? Une analyse quantitative exploratoire. *Canadian Ethnic Studies*, 22:54–77
Breton, R. (1984). The production and allocation of symbolic resources: An analysis of the linguistic and ethnocultural fields in Canada.' *Canadian Review of Sociology and Anthropology*, 21:123–44
– et al.(1990). *Ethnic identity and equality*. Toronto: University of Toronto Press
Brotz, H. (1980). Multiculturalism in Canada: Muddle. *Canadian Public Policy*, 6:41–6
Buchanan, A. (1991). Toward a theory of secession. *Ethics*, 101:322–42
Caccia, F. (1984). L'ethnicité comme post-modernité. *Vice Versa*, 2(1):12–13, 22
Cameron, D.R. (1990). Lord Durham then and now. *Journal of Canadian Studies*, 25:5–23
Colas, D., Emeri, C., and Zylberberg, J. (1991). *Citoyenneté et nationalité*. Paris: Presses Universitaires de France
Corbo, C. (1991). Contre le multiculturalisme, pour l'intégration. *Le Devoir*, 21 sept.
Dahrendorf, R. (1988). *The modern social conflict*. New York: Weidenfeld & Nicolson
Dimock, M. (1990, Jan.–Feb.). The restorative qualities of citizenship. *Public Administration Review*, 50:21–5
Dumont, L. (1983). *Essais sur l'individualisme*. Paris: Le Seuil
Dwivedi, O.P. (ed.) (1989). *Canada 2000: Race relations and public policy*. Guelph, ON: University of Guelph, Dept of Political Studies
Eckstein, H. (1984). Civic inclusion and its discontents. *Daedalus*, 113:107–60

Economic Council of Canada (1991). *New faces in the crowd.* Ottawa: Supply & Services Canada

Gagnon-Tremblay, M. (1990). *Au Québec, pour bâtir ensemble.* Québec: Gouvernement du Québec

Globe & Mail (1991). Misgivings about Canada's multiculturalism policy. 8 May, A-14

Grimond, J. (1991). For want of glue: A survey of Canada. *The Economist,* 29 June

Harney, R.F. (1988). 'So great a heritage as ours': Immigration and the survival of the Canadian polity. *Daedalus,* 117:51–97

Harvey, J. (1990). Vouloir l'identité québécoise. *Relations,* nov. 266–9

Hilgartner, S., and Bosk, C.L. (1988). The rise and fall of social problems: A public arenas model. *American Journal of Sociology,* 94:53–78

Ignatieff, M. (1989). Citizenship and moral narcissism. *The Political Quarterly,* 60:63–74

Janis, I.L. (1982). *Groupthink: Psychological studies of policy decisions and fiascoes.* Boston: Houghton-Mifflin

Janowitz, M. (1980). Observations on the sociology of citizenship: Obligations and rights. *Social Forces,* 59:1–24

Kahneman, D., and Tersky, A. (1979). Prospect theory: An analysis of decision under risk. *Econometrica,* 47:263–91

Kallen, E. (1982). *Ethnicity and human rights in Canada.* Toronto: Gage Publishing Ltd

Kaplan, W. (1991). About Canadian citizenship. Mimeo, 10p.

Kelly, G.A. (1979). Who needs a theory of citizenship?. *Daedalus,* 108:21–36

Langlais, J., Laplante, P., and Levy, J. (1990). *Le Québec de demain et les communautés culturelles.* Montréal: Éditions du Méridien

Laurent, P., and Paquet, G. (1991). Intercultural relations: A Myrdal-Tocqueville-Girard interpretative scheme. *International Political Science Review,* 12:173–85

Leslie, P.M. (1986). L'aspect politique et collectif. *Les Cahiers de Droit,* 27:161–70

Meghji, A. (1990). Keeping 'ethnics' at the periphery. *Toronto Star,* 15 May, A-23

Mintzberg, H., and Jorgensen, J. (1987). Emergent strategy for public policy. *Canadian Public Administration,* 30:214–29

Morissette, D. (1991). *Multiculturalisme versus interculturalisme: Une autre facette du débat sur la sécurité culturelle du Québec.* Montréal: Bureau des relations fédérales provinciales

Nielsen, R. (1991). How we got where we are. *The Idler,* 32:15–19

Oldfield, A. (1990). Citizenship: An unnatural practice? *The Political Quarterly,* 61:177–87

Oliver, D. (1991). Active citizenship in the 1990s. *Parliamentary Affairs, 44*: 157–71

Oriol, M. (1979). Identité produite, identitée instituée, identitée exprimée: Confusions des théories de l'identité nationale et culturelle. *Cahiers internationaux de sociologie, 66*:19–28

Palmer, D.L. (1991). *Contact effects and changing levels of prejudice in Canada.* Mimeo

Paquet, G. (1989a). Multiculturalism as national policy. *Journal of Cultural Economics, 13*:17–34

– (1989b). Pour une notion renouvelée de citoyenneté. *Transactions of the Royal Society of Canada*, Fifth Series, Tome IV, 83–100

Parry, G. (1989). Democracy and Amateurism: The informed citizen. *Government and Opposition, 24*:489–502

Richler, M. (1991). Inside/outside – Quebec. *The New Yorker*, 23 Sept. Pp 40–92

Robin, R. (1989). La langue entre l'idéologie et l'utopie. *Vice Versa, 27*:28–32

Smith, R.M. (1988). The American creed and American identity: The limits of liberal citizenship in the United States. *Western Political Quarterly, 41*:225–51

Spicer, K. (1988). The best and worst of multiculturalism. *Ottawa Citizen*, 13 July

Sugunasiri, S. (1990). 'Minority ethnics' build walls of seclusion. *Toronto Star*, 29 Oct., A-21

Tassinari L. (1989). La ville continue: Montréal et l'expérience transculturelle de *Vice Versa*. *Revue international d'action communautaire, 21*(61):57–62

Thomas, D. (1990). *Immigrant integration and the Canadian identity*, Ottawa: Employment and Immigration Canada

Trebilcock, M.J. et al. (1982). *The choice of governing instrument*. Ottawa: Economic Council of Canada

Tersky, A., and Kahneman, D. (1981). The framing of decisions and the psychology of choice. *Science, 211*, 30 Jan. 1981, 453–8

Valaskakis, K. (1990). *Canada in the nineties*. Montreal: Gamma Institute Press

Van Schendel, N. (1989). Nationalité, langue et transculture. *Vice Versa, 27*:22–5

Watzlawick, P. (ed.) (1988). *L'invention de la réalité*. Paris: Seuil

Wihtol de Wenden, C. (1989). Citoyenneté, nationalité et immigration. *Revue internationale d'action communautaire, 21*(61):43–8.

DENISE HELLY

Politique québécoise face au 'pluralisme culturel' et pistes de recherche: 1977–1990

LE MULTICULTURALISME FRANCOPHONE 1977–1985

Durant la Révolution tranquille, une nouvelle classe de technocrates francophones accède aux leviers de décision dont ceux du champ de l'immigration.[1] Cette consolidation de l'État provincial aux mains de francophones induit une nouvelle représentation du Québec comme territoire premier de l'affirmation du fait français au Canada. Dès lors, l'insertion des immigrés à la communauté francophone va devenir un objet d'intervention et de débat public au Québec. Le ministère de l'Immigration du Québec sera d'ailleurs fondé en 1968.

Selon les articles 3 et 4 de la loi de création du ministère, sa fonction est double: établissement d'immigrants utiles au développement du Québec et adaptation de ces derniers au milieu québécois, au travers, entre autres aspects, de 'la conservation des coutumes ethniques.' Des Centres d'Orientation et de Formation des Immigrants (COFI) sont mis en place afin de permettre l'apprentissage des deux langues officielles. Ils sont de juridiction partagée, fédérale et provinciale, et offrent des cours aux immigrants se destinant au marché du travail. Ils passent sous seule responsabilité provinciale en 1970 et comportent par la suite uniquement des classes de français. Selon l'esprit de la loi de fondation du ministère de l'Immigration, des subventions sont aussi rendues disponibles aux associations ethniques aidant à l'établissement des immigrants. Une autre mesure législative concerne cet établissement. En 1975, la Charte des droits et libertés de la personne du Québec inscrit le droit au respect des cultures d'origine.

Mais le débat politique et les mesures adoptées jusqu'en 1977 se centrent sur les choix linguistiques des immigrés et non sur la notion de différence culturelle. Pour exemples de cet intérêt de l'opinion publique, des partis politiques et des instances gouvernementales à la question linguistique: la crise de Saint-Léonard (1967–1969), la création de la notion d'allophone (1972),[2] la loi 22 (1974) et l'accent mis sur le volet linguistique dans la Charte de la langue française (1977).

Néanmoins la loi 101 amorce une nouvelle période. Concernant les immigrés, elle comprend deux volets. Elle oblige les enfants d'immigrés éduqués à l'étranger à fréquenter les écoles francophones et, au nom de l'article 43 de la Charte des droits et libertés de la personne, elle crée à leur intention un programme visant l'enseignement de la langue et de l'histoire du pays d'origine de leurs parents (PELO). Elle amorce une mutation radicale du statut des immigrés au sein de la société québécoise mettant en valeur la présence historique des populations immigrées établies au Québec depuis plusieurs siècles, ainsi que leurs héritages linguistiques et culturels. Ce faisant, elle ouvre la voie à une transformation de la représentation de l'identité québécoise: les référents linguistique et culturel de la communauté canadienne-française ne constituent plus les bases de la collectivité territoriale francophone du Québec. Par sa valorisation et sa reconnaissance des cultures immigrées, la loi 101 sape les bases de l'équivalence faite jusqu'alors entre la langue française et la spécificité culturelle des colons fondateurs. Par son projet de voir les immigrés parler le français, elle soulève en effet une question: quel est le lien entre la culture des descendants des colons fondateurs et la langue française si celle-ci est parlée par des personnes socialisées dans d'autres cultures? Selon l'esprit de la loi 101, les deux référents de l'identification canadienne-française, langue et culture, doivent être dissociés afin d'inclure les immigrés et leurs descendants dans la collectivité territoriale francophone. D'éléments amalgamés, perçus comme étrangers aux francophones de souche ou comme excroissances de la communauté anglo-britannique, les immigrés deviennent, par la loi 101, des locuteurs de langues spécifiques et des porteurs d'héritages divers inclus dans une collectivité québécoise francophone en expansion.

Cette reconnaissance par la loi 101 de la diversité historique de la francophonie québécoise est suivie, en 1981, par un texte du gouvernement péquiste affirmant le 'pluralisme culturel' de la société québécoise et visant une participation égalitaire des immigrés et de leurs descendants. Il s'agit du Plan d'Action à l'intention des Communautés Culturelles[3] qui met de l'avant le respect de la différence culturelle, le droit au maintien de leurs cultures d'origine par les immigrés et la richesse de leur apport au patrimoine culturel québécois. À la même date, le ministère de l'Immigration est renommé ministère des Communautés culturelles et de l'Immigration (MCCI). Le terme de 'communauté culturelle' désigne un groupe de personnes ayant pour langue d'usage ou maternelle une langue autre que le français ou l'anglais et disposant d'institutions (associations, journaux, services commerciaux, par ex.) (PACC 1981: 18–20). Le terme de minorité culturelle ou ethnique est totalement rejeté du vocabulaire politique québécois.

L'objectif à long terme de ce plan d'action est le 'redressement énergique d'une situation anormale de marginalisation des communautés culturelles.' Cette marginalisation réfère essentiellement à une faible présence des immigrés au sein du personnel et des instances décisionnelles des institutions publiques. Un virage politique est ainsi amorcé par le Parti Québécois en vue de consolider la francophonie québécoise, et une alliance avec les groupes immigrés, souvent partisans du statu quo ou de la primauté du pouvoir fédéral, est tentée. Cette alliance exige de nouvelles prises de position et mesures des institutions publiques; elle enclenche aussi un débat à propos de la place des groupes immigrés au sein de la société québécoise et des modalités de leur intégration égalitaire.

De nouvelles situations vont alimenter largement le débat. À partir de 1984–1985, les projections d'une éventuelle baisse de la population provinciale sont divulguées par les médias. De plus, les sources du flux migratoire québécois se diversifient et la part des immigrants provenant du Tiers Monde augmente. Le 'pluralisme culturel' est dit s'accentuer et le nombre d'immigrants allophones devant être francisés croît. D'autre part, l'application de la loi 101 se heurte à des obstacles de taille du fait de la concentration d'enfants de milieux immigrés défavorisés dans certaines écoles de Montréal. Enfin, la conjoncture économique du début des années 1980 ne facilite pas l'insertion sur le marché du travail des nouveaux arrivants, car elle engendre un recul du secteur manufacturier grand employeur d'immigrés peu qualifiés. Les difficultés d'insertion des immigrés sont souvent pointées, ainsi que des attitudes d'intervenants publics et privés pouvant handicaper leur insertion. Sont particulièrement pointés des problèmes d'adaptation psycho-sociale et familiale de certains milieux et clientèles scolaires d'origine immigrée. Ces problèmes d'insertion sociale alimentent d'autant plus le débat en cause que des incidents racistes ou perçus comme tels surviennent à Montréal entre des élèves d'écoles à forte concentration ethnique et entre le corps policier et des jeunes gens d'origine immigrée. Enfin, élément non moindre, la politisation du pluralisme culturel par le Plan d'action favorise la formation et la contestation de nouvelles élites ethniques venant pointer l'insertion inégalitaire de fractions de la population immigrée.

Entre 1977 et 1985, des instances publiques et para-publiques dessinent des lignes d'orientation nouvelle et implantent quelques programmes. L'accent est essentiellement mis sur l'importance de la différence culturelle et linguistique et peu sur les situations socio-économiques des clientèles ethniques non rejointes par les organismes publics et para-publics. Sensibilisation au 'pluralisme culturel' de la société québécoise, séances d'information des clientèles et du personnel des agences, recours à des interprètes sont les principales mesures adoptées. Ainsi, les Centres locaux de santé communautaire (CLSC) tentent de répondre aux besoins de clientèles ethniques en créant des postes d'agents de liaison affectés au service de celles-ci. Mais ces nouveaux employés, peu nombreux de surcroît, ne peuvent résoudre des difficultés créées par des situations de pauvreté des clientèles et le manque de ressources disponibles des CLSC. Ces difficultés sont particulièrement visibles lors d'interventions visant à aider des familles connaissant des difficultés d'emploi ou des situations de violence familiale. Quant aux Centres de services sociaux (CSS), ils mettent en place des programmes de sensibilisation de leur personnel au 'pluralisme culturel.' Par exemple, un Comité de travail sur l'accessibilité des services sociaux aux communautés culturelles, formé en 1984 par le Centre régional des services sociaux et de santé du Montréal métropolitain (CSSMM), pointe les défaillances multiples de l'offre des services sociaux et de santé aux groupes ethniques mais ses seules actions consistent en la commande d'études statistiques sur les groupes ethnolinguistiques de sa région de juridiction.

La même année 1984, la Communauté Urbaine de Montréal met sur pied un Comité consultatif sur les relations interculturelles et interraciales, comprenant seize membres dont douze provenant des communautés ethnoculturelles. Le but de cette intervention est le même que dans le cas des agences citées précédemment: promouvoir la tolérance et l'égalité entre tous les citoyens, refléter le caractère multiculturel et multiracial de la région de Montréal. Ainsi, de 1981 à 1985, en dépit du Plan d'action, les mesures adoptées sont le plus souvent symboliques.

LA RÉPARATION HISTORIQUE

À la suite de l'arrivée au pouvoir du Parti libéral à la fin de 1985, s'amorce une autre période. Le gouvernement libéral prend position dès

1986, prônant le principe du respect des droits individuels et sociaux des immigrés. Par une déclaration publique, il réaffirme le respect dû aux diverses cultures et races présentes sur le territoire provincial (Déclaration sur les relations interethniques et interraciales), et il adopte un règlement marquant l'entrée en vigueur de programmes d'accès à l'égalité.

Il montre, par contre, un moindre intérêt pour des mesures étatiques favorisant la reproduction des cultures immigrées. Le PELO est transformé et perd son but premier d'aide à la reproduction des cultures d'origine et à l'adaptation des enfants immigrés, pour devenir un programme facultatif d'enseignement de langues secondaires ouvert à l'ensemble de la clientèle scolaire. Les élèves francophones de souche peuvent désormais côtoyer des enfants d'immigrés dans les classes d'apprentissage des langues dites d'origine. Ce sera là, en fait, la seule mesure touchant la sphère éducative car le ministère de l'Éducation ne formule aucune politique d'ensemble de 1986 à 1991 en dépit des multiples aspects le concernant et sans cesse invoqués par les comités aviseurs, aspects tels que la croissance de la clientèle scolaire allophone, les modifications de curriculum, la formation des maîtres et surtout l'adoption d'un programme d'éducation interculturelle. Aussi peu présents demeureront les ministères des Communications et des Affaires culturelles.

D'autre part, de 1986 à 1991, déclarations, consultations, colloques, avis et rapports d'étude abordant selon divers angles le thème de l'intégration abondent. La Commission des droits de la personne du Québec et le Conseil des Communautés culturelles et de l'Immigration apportent de nombreux constats et avis. Des organismes para-publics, des commissions scolaires de l'île de Montréal, la Ville de Montréal et des agences para-municipales de la région montréalaise (STCUM, SPCUM) créent des programmes visant des populations immigrées, implantant, dans le cas des agences municipales, des programmes d'accès à l'égalité en emploi. Trois institutions gouvernementales adoptent une politique d'ensemble dont la portée est limitée cependant. Ce sont le ministère des Services Sociaux et de la Santé entre 1986 et 1989, le Conseil du Trésor et le ministère de l'Immigration et des Communautés culturelles en 1990.

En 1986, le gouvernement amende la loi de 1971 sur les services sociaux et de santé en adoptant la loi 142. Celle-ci vise à améliorer l'accès des communautés d'expression anglaise à ces services. Puis, en juin 1986, est créé un Comité consultatif sur l'accessibilité des services de santé et des services sociaux aux communautés culturelles (Comité Sirros), lequel dépose son rapport en novembre 1987. Les orientations d'une politique générale sont alors rendues publiques en un document intitulé *Pour améliorer la santé et le bien-être au Québec* où l'on trouve trois éléments fondamentaux: adaptation de l'information aux clientèles visées; sensibilisation du personnel; implantation d'un programme d'accès à l'égalité. En pratique, le Ministère se propose d'implanter un programme d'information à l'intention des communautés culturelles et un programme d'accès à l'égalité en emploi pour les membres de celles-ci. Il oblige par ailleurs les établissements (en particulier ceux de l'île de Montréal) à favoriser l'embauche de personnel issu des communautés culturelles, à constituer une banque d'interprètes qualifiés et à sensibiliser leur personnel aux diverses cultures présentes au sein de leur région et, le cas échéant, à proposer les programmes de perfectionnement appropriés.

Suite à une recommandation du Comité Sirros, un Bureau des services aux communautés culturelles est mis sur pied au Ministère. Il élabore un Plan d'action à l'intention des communautés culturelles, et, en janvier 1989, organise une journée de consultation auprès d'organismes ethniques en vue de recueillir leurs réactions et de discuter des formes de collaboration possibles. Les représentants d'une quarantaine d'organismes oeuvrant bénévolement dans le domaine de la santé et des services sociaux auprès d'une clientèle issue des communautés culturelles participent à cette consultation. Ils accueillent favorablement le Plan d'action bien que voulant être assurés de l'implantation de programmes d'accès à l'égalité en emploi et de la reconnaissance de leurs organismes comme partenaires du réseau.

Au mois de mars 1989, le Ministère rend public le Plan d'action, lequel révisé en février 1990, dévoile six objectifs, chacun d'entre eux assorti de moyens d'action, de modalités d'implantation, d'un échéancier et de critères d'évaluation. Le Plan vise la prise en compte de la 'dimension interculturelle' et identifie trois principaux domaines d'intervention: la communication avec la clientèle tant au plan linguistique que culturel, l'information adéquate des communautés culturelles sur le système socio-sanitaire du Québec et la représentation des 'Québécois issus des diverses communautés ethnoculturelles minoritaires' à tous les niveaux du réseau de la santé et des services sociaux. Deux autres objectifs correspondent à la reconnaissance des organismes communautaires comme partenaires du réseau et à la promotion de la recherche. L'accroissement du financement des organismes communautaires et l'amélioration de l'accessibilité des services aux communautés culturelles semblent montrer que le Ministère a effectué des changements réels depuis 1986.

Deux autres institutions majeures interviennent dans le champ. En mars 1990, le Conseil du Trésor crée, pour la fonction publique, un programme d'égalité en emploi à l'intention des minorités visibles et des allophones. Enfin, en décembre 1990, le ministère des Communautés culturelles et de l'Immigration dépose une nouvelle politique d'immigration mettant l'accent sur la francisation et l'intégration sociale des immigrants, et non, comme le faisait le Plan d'action de 1981, sur la promotion du 'pluralisme culturel.' Au titre de la francisation, ce ministère a créé depuis 1988 de nouveaux programmes visant à étendre la clientèle des COFI. Des cours de français sont désormais disponibles pour les revendicateurs de statut de réfugié et pour les femmes immigrées ne participant pas au marché du travail.

L'adoption de cette nouvelle politique d'immigration et d'intégration est prolongée par des négociations sur le partage des sphères de juridiction fédérale et provinciale en la matière. En 1991, l'entente Gagnon-Tremblay/McDougall confère au Québec la responsabilité de l'accueil et de l'intégration linguistique et culturelle des immigrants sur son territoire. Cependant, le ministère fédéral de la Citoyenneté et du Multiculturalisme détient le droit d'offrir des services aux groupes ethnoculturels de la province. Similairement, le Québec obtient la gestion des services d'intégration économique des immigrants et le gouvernement fédéral garde le droit d'intervenir en la matière. Ces transferts de pouvoir s'accompagnent de compensations financières.

La politique québécoise montre depuis 1990 une nouvelle inflexion. Les interventions étatiques doivent désormais viser une insertion des immigrés basée sur le partage de quelques principes politiques fondateurs (démocratie, droits individuels, francophonie) alors que l'épanouissement de la diversité culturelle de la société québécoise, par ailleurs nullement refusé, est dit le fait de la société civile. Suivant une orientation prise par le Parti Québécois en 1981, le gouvernement libéral met l'accent sur une politique de réparation de situations de mise en tutelle des immigrés et de leurs descendants, et illustre le type de politique de l'État-providence visant une réparation historique et systémique.

Par contre, le gouvernement libéral ne suit nullement l'autre versant de la politique péquiste qui tendait à établir un multiculturalisme francophone et dont un des buts était la reproduction des communautés ethniques comme instances d'identification et d'intégration. Ainsi, la politique du PLQ ne se rapproche nullement à l'heure actuelle des politiques multi-

culturalistes des années 1970 mais plutôt de celle suivie par le gouvernement canadien depuis 1983, laquelle met de plus en plus l'accent sur
l'intégration égalitaire des immigrés et de leurs descendants. Une
convergence est apparue entre les perspectives adoptées à Québec et à
Ottawa qui les porte vers une intervention et un discours insistant sur les
droits des immigrés, l'intégration sociale et économique et la lutte contre
toute forme de discrimination dont le racisme. Un changement radical
s'est opéré par rapport à la politique canadienne des années 1970 et
québécoise de 1977 à 1985. Il tient à la nature de l'immigration depuis
une dizaine d'années, composée d'individus de plus en plus éduqués et
intéressés à l'égalité de leurs droits socio-économiques, tendance qui ne
pourra que s'accentuer enraisonde la fonction assignée à l'immigration
comme bassin de main-d'oeuvre experte utile à la compétitivité de
l'économie. On pourrait aussi avancer que cette convergence tient à la
nécessité de cimenter l'unité nationale que ce soit au Québec ou au
Canada anglais, face à l'influence culturelle américaine, la fragmentation
ethnique qu'induirait une politique insistant sur la reproduction d'une
société mosaïque, et au débat constitutionnel.

APPRÉCIATION DE LA POLITIQUE QUÉBÉCOISE ET PISTES DE
RECHERCHE

Près de quinze ans après la loi 101, le bilan des interventions gouvernementales face au 'pluralisme culturel' est inégal et les quelques gestes
marquants posés l'ont été récemment et demeureront limités dans leurs
effets.

Parailleurs, un premier constat sur l'état de la recherche sur cette
politique québécoise étonne. Dix ans après le Plan d'action de 1981 et de
multiples déclarations et mesures gouvernementales, l'esprit et l'évolution de cette politique ne sont nullement analysés par les chercheurs québécois alors que le sujet du 'pluralisme culturel' a provoqué de nombreux débats et recherches sur l'insertion des immigrés et de leurs descendants. Rares sont en effet les études sur ce sujet et n'existe, à notre
connaissance, qu'un article de Daniel Gay.[4] Par contre, des analyses
d'interventions particulières ont été réalisées par des chercheurs, souvent rattachés aux organismes publics intervenant dans le domaine des
relations ethniques et raciales (Commission des Droits de la personne
notamment). Quelques observations peuvent être faites, qui montrent
quatre pistes d'examen de cette politique par des chercheurs.

Francisation

Le but premier de la politisation du thème du 'pluralisme culturel' tel que posé depuis l'adoption de la loi 101, est l'affirmation d'une francophonie pluraliste. Mais ce projet francophone comporte d'importantes failles en dépit des récentes tentatives du MCCI d'étendre les programmes de francisation des immigrants sous sa juridiction. Il demeure une difficulté des COFI à répondre à la demande des immigrants, un man-que de moyens alloués pour combler les besoins des clientèles allophones ayant des difficultés d'apprentissage, une précarité de statut du personnel servant ces clientèles et une absence de programmes de formation de la main-d'oeuvre permettant aux PME de franciser leur main-d'oeuvre. Ainsi l'insertion sur le marché du travail de certaines catégories d'immigrés, leur intégration dans des réseaux de sociabilité francophones et leur participation à la vie politique, autant de buts du Plan d'Action de 1981 et de la nouvelle politique du MCCI de 1990, sont-elles encore hypothéquées. Rappelons que les allophones représentent quelque 50 pour cent du flux migratoire annuel, soit quelque 20 000 personnes ou plus et, vu les bassins d'émigrants francophones potentiels dans le monde, l'arrivée de nombreux nouveaux entrants ne parlant pas le français ne peut qu'augmenter si les niveaux d'entrées annuelles sont augmentés. Ce chiffre ne tient aucun compte de la population immigrée allophone établie au Québec.

Vu ces limites, l'affirmation d'une francophonie pluraliste et de l'inclusion des immigrés dans la société québécoise francophone ne s'accompagne nullement de programmes d'intervention efficaces comme le sont, par exemple, ceux mis en place en Suède et s'adressant à l'ensemble des nouveaux immmigrants, quel que soit leur statut à l'entrée dans le pays. Il apparaît que l'enseignement et l'expansion de la langue officielle sur le sol québécois ne sont pas conçus comme une nécessité et un droit des immigrants mais au contraire comme une obligation ou un privilège de ceux-ci.

Il existe un autre paradoxe. Alors que les adultes allophones ne sont pas suffisamment aidés dans leur apprentissage du français et les effets de leur différence linguistique sur leur intégration économique, politique et culturelle peu entrevus, les enfants de langue maternelle francophone sont encouragés à apprendre la langue de leurs compagnons de classe imigrés et le personnel des institutions publiques et para-publiques vivement invité à découvrir et respecter les cultures autres. Ces deux orientations apparaissent contradictoires, car elles enclenchent trois processus dont les effets à long terme ne convergent nullement: l'un de reproduction d'enclaves d'emploi et de sociabilité des immigrés anglophones, un second de marginalisation socio-économique et d'exposition à une acculturation difficile des immigrants défavorisés, généralement allophones, un troisième de transformation par des institutions publiques de référents identitaires de la communauté francophone en vue de créer une collectivité territoriale québécoise pluraliste et englobant tous les résidents.

Les fondements sociaux de ces orientations contradictoires ainsi que les dynamiques qu'elles enclenchent, composent des sujets de recherche non abordés au Québec. Il en est de même de dimensions plus limitées de la francisation des immigrés que, seuls, quelques chercheurs ont traitées, telles que les conditions et modalités d'apprentissage du français comme langue seconde par des individus provenant de familles linguistiques non indo-européennes.[5]

Programmes d'accès à l'égalité[6]

Le second volet le plus important de l'intervention gouvernementale concerne les programmes d'accès à l'égalité en emploi adoptés en 1989 et 1990 en vue du recrutement d'individus immigrés au sein des institutions publiques. Les modalités de définition des populations-cibles et d'application de ces programmes, ainsi que l'efficacité de ces derniers demeurent encore à étudier. Ces programmes tentent de modifier les règles du recrutement d'individus supposés discriminés car se trouvant très peu présents au sein du personnel de ces organismes. L'effet de ces programmes ne pourra cependant qu'être symbolique, car ils semblent, ne pouvoir donner lieu à l'embauche que de quelques centaines de personnes des groupes-cibles, vu les restrictions budgétaires et les critères d'éligibilité existants. Dans le cas du programme adopté en 1990 par le Conseil du Trésor et concernant directement la fonction publique, un contrôle de la connaissance du français doit intervenir six mois après l'embauche d'une personne d'un groupe-cible, défini comme allophone ou racial. Cette procédure laisse supposer le recrutement de personnes quelque peu francisées puisqu'elles sont supposées parfaire leur connaissance parlée et écrite de la langue en six mois. Sinon, cette procédure laisse supputer l'ouverture de postes de travail peu qualifiés, ne demandant qu'une très faible maîtrise de la langue française.

Postulats des interventions contre la discrimination

De multiples interventions ont été mises en oeuvre en vue d'éviter la discrimination raciale et culturelle que ce soit lors du recrutement de personnel ou d'offre de services à des populations immigrées. Leur efficacité semble limitée car, afin d'atteindre cet objectif, ministères, agences para-publiques, municipalités, services municipaux et institutions privées, notamment des entreprises de communication, ont adopté des mesures basées sur un postulat: la discrimination serait le produit d'une orientation de valeurs individuelle. Aussi faut-il transformer mentalités et orientations qui donnent lieu à des pratiques hostiles, discriminatoires, lors de l'embauche de personnes ou lors de contacts avec une clientèles d'origines autres que francophone de souche. L'intervention suit alors deux versants: sensibilisation ou campagnes d'information visant une valorisation de la tolérance; formation ou apprentissage de connaissances relatives aux populations immigrées telles que leur histoire, valeurs, modes de vie quotidiens, etc. Il est supputé, semble-t-il, que stéréotypes et attitudes discriminatoires sont le fruit de l'ignorance et d'une mauvaise information et non de situations sociales, notamment de restructuration socio-économique. La vision selon laquelle la 'population d'accueil' doit apprendre à côtoyer des cultures autres repose sur le postulat de la nature purement cognitive des stéréotypes.

Une étude et une mise à jour plus analytique de ces postulat sur lesquel reposent ces divers modes d'intervention restent à faire. Un autre postulat dont l'analyse serait possible consiste en l'affirmation de la primauté des relations individuelles sur les relations sociales lors de l'exposition à d'autres cultures.

Culture d'origine, acculturation et différence culturelle

Il est encore un postulat jamais formulé et analysé par les chercheurs qui sous-tend les interventions en vue de transformer les mentalités et attitudes des francophones de souche et de valoriser les apports culturels des néo-Québécois et immigrés. Il s'agit d'une vision statique et positiviste de la transformation des pratiques culturelles, i.e., du processus de l'acculturation. Des cultures d'origine sont dites exister et la réinterprétation culturelle qu'opèrent les immigrants lors de leur établissement dans une nouvelle société ne constitue nullement un objet d'attention et de valorisation. Les cultures d'origine toujours en transformation sur le sol du pays d'immigration sont hypostasiées sous la forme de pratiques populaires les plus visibles ou exotiques, c.a.d. contrevenant, de manière agréable ou non, aux codes culturels du groupe majoritaire. Un folklore ethnique est ainsi créé qui s'attache à la nourriture, aux fêtes, aux relations entre sexes, au vêtement, etc. Ce folklore devient signe d'une différence à valoriser et respecter. Pourtant une culture n'est nullement un univers de signes portés par une population circonscrite géographiquement. Elle est une articulation de schémas d'interprétation laissant place à une plasticité permanente. Plasticité et différenciation qu'illustrent les adaptations multiples qu'opèrent des populations dites de même origine. Il faut penser aux diasporas juive, chinoise, libanaise, haïtienne qui ont connu des contextes d'immigration divers (Europe, Antilles, Amérique du nord, Afrique noire) et évolué différemment.

NOTES

1   Une subvention du ministère de la Citoyenneté et du Multiculturalisme, octroyée en 1990, a permis la réalisation de la recherche dont quelques conclusions sont reproduites dans ce texte. Le rapport de cette recherche a été remis en février 1991 sous le titre: Denise Helly et Francine Bernèche, *Le Québec face au 'pluralisme culturel,' 1977–1990: Un premier bilan.* 342 pages, plus 80 pages de bibliographie.
2   Commission d'enquête sur la situation de la langue française et les droits linguistiques au Québec, étude 3. Commission dite Gendron.
3   Gouvernement du Québec (1981). *Programme d'action à l'intention des communautés culturelles.* Québec: Éditeur officiel.
4   Gay, Daniel (1985, automne). 'Réflexions critiques sur les politiques ethniques du gouvernement fédéral canadien et du gouvernement du Québec,' *Revue Internationale d'Action Communautaire,* 14\54:79–96.
5   Les principales études existantes sont:
Anglejan, Alison D' et al. (1978). *Les difficultés d'apprentissage dans les COFIS.* Rapport de recherche. Montréal: Université de Montréal. 277 p.
– (1981). *Difficultés d'apprentissage de la langue seconde chez l'immigrant adulte en situation scolaire: une étude dans le contexte québécois.* Québec: Centre international de recherche sur le bilinguisme, Université Laval. 127 p.
Archambault, Ariane, et Jean-Claude Corbeil (1982). *L'enseignement du français, langue seconde, aux adultes.* Québec: Conseil de la langue française. 141 p.

Larivée, Yves (1989). *Immigration et langue de travail*. Rapport synthèse, Table ronde. Québec: Office de la langue française. 31 p.

Ouellet, Alfred (1978). *Compte-rendu et réflexions critiques du rapport de recherche sur les difficultés d'apprentissage dans les COFI*. Québec: ministère de l'Immigration. 26 p.

Painchaud, Gisèle, Alison D'anglejan, et Claude Renaud (1984a). *L'acquisition du français par un groupe d'immigrants asiatiques clients de COFI*. Faculté des sciences de l'éducation, Section d'andragogie. Montréal: Université de Montréal. 75 p.

– (1984b). *Acquisition du français par des immigrants adultes au Québec*. Québec: Centre international de recherche sur le bilinguisme, Université Laval. 86 p.

6 Les principales études dans le domaine de l'égalité des droits sont: Commission des droits de la personne du Québec (1988). *Bilan de la recherche sur la situation des minorités ethniques et visibles dans le logement et pistes d'intervention*. Montréal: Commission des droits de la personne du Québec. 25 p.

Conseil de la langue française (1982). *Les communautés culturelles et la fonction publique québécoise*. Rapport du groupe de travail interministériel formé par le CIPDC. Québec: Conseil de la langue française. 88 p. (Coll. Notes et documents, no 16)

Centre de recherche-action sur les relations raciales (1987). *Les droits à l'égalité, la discrimination raciale et la communauté asiatique de Montréal*. Montréal

– (1990). *L'équité dans l'emploi pour les minorités visibles dans les Centres d'emploi du Canada à Montréal*. Montréal: Centre de recherche-action sur les relations raciales

Grist, Mary-Ann (1983). *La participation des communautés culturelles aux concours de recrutement de la Fonction publique*. Rapport de stage. Québec: Commission de la fonction publique, Direction de la recherche et de l'évaluation. 39 p.

Le Borgne, Louis (1988). *Le bureaucrate et le métèque: les programmes de discrimination positive au Québec*. Communication présentée au colloque 'Les étrangers dans la ville,' Rennes, les 14, 15 et 16 décembre, 25 p.

Lescop, Renée (1988). *Politiques et programmes dans le domaine du logement: leurs effets sur l'exercice du droit au logement pour les minorités ethnoculturelles du Québec*. Annexe III. Montréal: Commission des droits de la personne du Québec, Direction de la recherche, mai 1988

Pycock, Jane, et Lise Legault (1980). *La sous-représentation des minorités dans la fonction publique du Québec: rapport sur les causes et solutions*. Montréal: l'auteur. 18 p.

Simard, C., et M.B. Tahon (1987). *Programme d'accès à l'égalité: analyse et impacts*. Note de recherche no 33, Université du Québec à Montréal, Science politique, 47 p.

ELLIOT L. TEPPER

Immigration Policy and Multiculturalism

INTRODUCTION

Immigration and multiculturalism are inextricably linked. Together they are integral to the identity and evolution of the Canadian polity. Immigration policy, of course, is the originating source of Canada's ethnic, religious, and racial diversity. Because of settlement patterns, it contributes to regional diversity as well.

Multiculturalism policy, in turn, facilitates the management of diversity. It is an expression of the practice of integration, retention of personal elements of identity, instead of a policy of assimilation, the requirement of total disappearance, or subordination of identity in an effort to gain societal acceptance. Multiculturalism also legitimizes the self-conception of the state as resting on pluralist foundations. It fosters acceptance of the reality that Canada is a nation of immigrants. In doing so, maintenance of group as well as individual association is sanctioned as an integral component of national identity.

Immigration and multiculturalism are important elements in Canada's approach to nation-building (see Breton 1986). Recurrent waves of migrants replenish the population base. Multiculturalism provides the ideological construct for accommodating diversity. Legitimacy is sustained for individuals as members of groups, for groups as well as individuals as constituent elements of the polity, and for Canada as distinct from its melting-pot neighbour to the south.[1]

Boundary maintenance is difficult in demarcating a separate field for the study of the relationship between immigration policy and multiculturalism. Immigration is in some sense the mother of multiculturalism.

Without immigration there would be no policy of multiculturalism, nor the various subdivisions of the Multiculturalism Review Project, which have led to this volume.

Here I will focus on literature which traces the thread between immigration and the ethno-demographic transformation of the country. Special emphasis is given to the search for academic literature which dwells on the *implication* rather than description, support or denunciation of the impact of immigration on demographic change. The analysis is divided into several parts. Initially a broadly chronological approach is employed, tying in lengthy time periods with thematic highlights. Then a discussion of Canada's present situation is given. Finally, some suggestions for the future are presented, a future which will see the dimensions of diversity deepen and the demands for scholarly analysis increase.

The first part of the paper will deal with the causal relationship between immigration policy and the emergence of multiculturalism as a social reality and a government policy. It examines the issues raised – or neglected – by academics who study the relationship between immigration-related pluralism and societal transformation. The second part deals with some especially important themes relating to the current Canadian situation within a national and global context. It discusses some issues regarding the nature of the research enterprise in this area of central importance. Recommendations are made throughout the text for the next stage in the development of the field.

Even this somewhat demarcated field yields an unwieldy quantity of literature. However the primary message of this paper is not about the fuzziness of definitional boundaries and the vastness of the field. Rather the leitmotifs are the centrality of race, the permanence of ethnicity, the relative paucity of material, and the lack of access to much of the rather limited material which exists.

Further, as a study originating in a cooperative venture (stimulated by a government department and a research council), there is a suggestion that government and academe explore new ways of interacting in order to ensure higher quality and increased research in forms which are more widely available to the research community.

As Canada restructures itself for the next century, immigration policy increasingly will play a role in determining what the country is, and multiculturalism policy will bear the weight of assisting the transition to what the country wishes to become. Academe's role is to perform its pedagogical task of analysis and communication of research findings.

IMMIGRATION LITERATURE THEN AND NOW

Racial arithmetic has always been a concern for students of immigration. What has changed is the definition of race. The link between newcomers and societal change has been clear in the minds of policymakers and students from the dawn of European competition for the land and resources of the territory presently known as Canada. Yet scholarly analysis remains surprisingly sparse and has limited impact on the general perceptions and self-definitions of the state.

One important task of scholarship is to fill in the blanks much more emphatically about the nature of diversity in Canada. The concomitant requirement is to 'mainstream' the literature on diversity, to present a more complete picture of the country, by integrating the enhanced scope of analysis into the central story of what the country was, is, and will be.

First Nations and Early Settlement

Immigration policy had little to do with Canada's earliest beginnings and the creation of diversity. But that is no reason to ignore the existence of a de facto multicultural reality. Canada has always been more ethnically diverse than is generally realized. The First Nations – Native peoples who live in what is now Canada – are internally diversified and have played a limited role in the minds of those who control Canada's search for self-definition or of those who write about it. They infrequently figure in academic work about early settlement, as if Europeans were moving into more or less empty lands.

The building blocs of a more accurate self-perception of the state are becoming more widely available. Expansion of research on the first inhabitants of the continent is well under way, in forms available beyond the confines of obscure libraries. See, for example, the 500-page study by Olive P. Dickason, *Canada's First Nations*, which contains 38 pages of bibliography (Dickason 1992).

Still, the process of integrating a more complete history of Canada into public consciousness is at its earliest stages:

Canada, it used to be said by non-Indians ... is a country of much geography and little history ... How can such a thing be said, much less believed, when people have been living here for thousands of years? As [Amerindians] see it, Canada has fifty-five founding nations rather than the two that have been officially acknowledged ... Canada's history has usually been presented not [even] as beginning with the first Europeans, the Norse, who arrived here in about AD 1000, but with the French, who came ... in the sixteenth century. (Dickason 1992:11)

The lacunae have been noted by others and at least partially corrected. A history text published recently notes: 'The structures of European society were built atop the ruins of native society. But native people did not cease to exist; they were simply ignored by historians.' The new text makes frequent reference to Natives, women, and to diversity in its retelling of history (Bercuson et al. 1992). However, as we will see, the 'discovery' of diversity is recent and its incorporation into mainstream thinking is more the exception than the rule.

With regard to the United Empire Loyalists who settled Upper Canada we know from the little-recognized work of McGee (*Loyalist Mosaic*, 1984) that they were drawn from the most ethnically diverse areas in the American colonies. In the original Loyalist movement, people of German background outnumbered English settlers and were just part of a great mixture of Europe's migrants to the New World.

As for the much earlier French settlement, even less information has entered the common picture of who lived where, when, and why. Settlement history in general seems to plod methodically, and haphazardly, from 'European' to French to British to Other, an enduring image which has been politically useful but empirically incomplete.

Immigration as a policy tool has been consciously used over time to create new ethnodemographic balances. We are reminded by Bell and Tepperman (1979) that the British became numerically predominant in the colonial era only through a deliberate immigration program in the 1800s, an early example of using immigration policy to create desired racial demographic results.

Movement of people, whether by policy or other imperatives, transformed the demographic map. The role of racial, religious and ethnic minorities in the early period of European colonial settlement is too little known. Wink's (1971) and Walker's work on the Black community (1978) or various recent publications on the Chinese, among others (Li 1988; Wickberg 1978) are samples of the research which is possible. Numerous studies and monographs on the Jews and Ukrainians, for example, can be used as starting points to help fill in *regional* as well as general histories about the reality of ethnicity in earlier periods of Canadian history. (See Anctil 1986; Weinfeld et al. 1981; Lupol 1978, and other studies from the Canadian Institute of Ukrainian Studies.) The notion of 'two founding races,' whatever its political accuracy, is historically a partial view at best, and one which requires revision based on an expanded research enterprise.

Colony to Non-Nationhood in the Second World War

Immigration policy led to huge migration inflows around the turn of this century. There was a clear policy choice to settle rather than lose parts of the West. Immigration policy transformed the make-up of the nascent state. The largest number of immigrants *ever* admitted to Canada was in 1913. Over 400,000 people moved here in that year, at a time when the existing population was less than a third its current size.

Studies of immigration early in the century such as J.S. Woodsworth's classic *Strangers Within Our Gates* (1909), W.G. Smith (1920), and the redoubtable Leacock always connected immigration to demographic change. (See Leacock and other valuable historical extracts in the collection by Palmer 1975).

One of the recurring themes from the start – long before the concept of multiculturalism appeared – is the tension between fear of the foreigner and the imperative need for labour and population. Defence concerns and economic compulsions repeatedly have won out over fear, but not without controversy and policies of racial selectivity that subsequent generations repudiate.

A quote from Leacock reminds us that immigrants were habitually viewed as racial groups, and that almost none but those presently here are viewed as suitable:

Still more important [than the increased volume of immigration] is the economic and racial character of the immigrants of the twentieth century. They no longer consist of the strenuous, the enterprising; they are not except in minor degree political or religious refugees ... They are, in great measure, mere herds of the proletariat of Europe, the lowest classes of industrial society, without home and work, fit objects indeed for philanthropic pity but indifferent material from which to build the commonwealth of the future. ('Canada and the Immigration Problem.' In *National and English Review*, Apr. 1911, pp 316–27. Cited in Palmer 1975:48)

Debate at the start of the century was remarkably similar to that of the present. Leacock worried about the ability 'to assimilate this enormous influx of alien elements,' wanted a policy of 'going slow,' and was quite willing to allow the West to remain unpopulated rather than settle it with people 'who stand in no hereditary relation with the rest of Canada.' Canada's all-time high point in immigration came two years after Leacock's plea to leave the West unpopulated rather than import people to fill the space.

The twenties and thirties brought many newcomers (until the Depression hit), but little change in the discourse. Historical literature of the interwar years, reviewed in a book on 'war, ethnicity and the Canadian state' (Hillmer et al. 1988) reveals continuity of perspective. 'Critics of the "new immigration" abounded in the universities and the public service,' notes Hillmer. The criticism was familiar: 'They worried about the displacement of "good" Canadians by strangers ... the capacity of the land to absorb new immigration ... The foreign looking and the foreign sounding were on the rise, concentrated and unassimilable. Argument along these lines were heard in the economic good times of the 1920's and more understandably, during the Depression' (Hillmer 1988:xiv–xv). Restriction on Asian immigration was obtained by means of Oriental Exclusion Acts enacted in 1923 and 1930.

Out of the crucible of war a new nation could have been forged. Instead, widespread suspicion of diversity persisted. Pre-war attitudes came to fruition in wartime conditions: 'The presence in Canada of groups so diverse in racial origin, language religion, political and economic backgrounds ... is a grave obstacle to development of national solidarity and common culture.' (Kemp 1932, in Hillmer 1988: xv–xvi).

When war came, minorities paid a steep price. Italian, German, and especially Japanese minorities suffered the worst effects domestically (Adachi 1976; Sunahara 1981). Immigration from abroad was brought to a standstill. Even a boatload of Jewish refugee children was sent back to Nazi Germany (Abella & Troper 1982).

Accordingly, a rare opportunity was squandered. An occasion to create a sense of nationhood from the great struggle against tyranny was lost, not just in renewal of French-English tensions over conscription, but also in failure to create unity out of diversity, in a time of extreme adversity. The problem of national identity was not the foreigner but fear of the foreigner.[2]

Postwar to the 1960s

Depression and war virtually halted immigration for a decade and a half. A new era was launched immediately after the war. Pent-up demand at home and abroad, a broadened horizon nurtured in wartime international cooperation, the presence of thousands of 'Displaced Persons' in chaotic and wartime Europe all contributed to a transformed immigration policy.

The policy was expressed cautiously, even negatively. In May 1947, the long-reigning prime minister, William Lyon Mackenzie King, rose in the House of Commons and announced that Canada needed population, but immigrants would be selected with great care, that numbers would not be allowed to exceed absorptive capacity or to fundamentally alter the character of the country. Restrictions on Asian immigration would remain on the books.

Research material is certainly available for the post-Second World War period. Freda Hawkins has produced book-length studies of immigration policy related directly to public concern (Hawkins 1972, 1988). Anthony Richmond has done so as well from the point of view of the immigrants themselves (Richmond 1967). Both have numerous articles to augment their larger studies, as do many other authors. Full-length scholarly treatment of many groups arriving in the postwar wave are available in the Generations series funded by Multiculturalism Canada, including an overview provided by Burnet and Palmer (1988).

Research clearly has not changed public perception even regarding this more recent period. After the colonial settlement period, after depression and war, but long before multiculturalism became a government policy, or even a term in the public discourse, diversity was a well-established empirical reality. Despite the cautious tone of government policy, thousands and then millions came to Canada over the next fifteen years. From that period until now, Canada remains approximately 15 per cent foreign-born.

Even now it is probably not well known that numerical predominance of a single group in Canada ended over half a century ago. The proportion of the population of British-only descent slipped below the 50 per cent mark in about 1940. The component of French-only descent fell below 30 per cent in the 1960s, and is now below the 25 per cent mark. Neither Charter population ranks high in recent immigration patterns, which have shifted strongly to Asia, Latin America, and Africa. Canada is a country of minorities. It has no majority population.

Yet perception still seems to persist that the change in Canada's demography is a product of very recent changes in immigration patterns. Charter group numerical predominance may still be perceived by many, especially outside Canada's three largest cities, to be a matter of imminent loss rather than a half-century old fact.[3]

The failure to dent public perception about demographic reality may lie outside the realm of scholarship. The staying power of myth may relate to power relations, schooling practices, simple inertia, or to broader patterns of misperception regarding aspects of Canadian life. What does appear to be the case is that relatively few academics were writing about postwar changes until recently; that the material currently available is still confined to a small portion of producing academics; and that the relationship between historic patterns of immigration and the demographic situation in Canada is still not well understood. The research agenda for the future should include significant inducement to better understand the past.

1960s to the 1980s

Canada's immigration laws became more open and less racially determined. Oriental Exclusion Acts were removed from the statute books in 1949. Reforms begun in the 1950s culminated in the late 1960s with passage of new legislation, eliminating de facto racial and religious barriers to admission. The new openness, and shifting global trends in availability of migrants, have led to dramatic changes in the ethnic, religious and racial characteristics of newcomers. (See Krótki elsewhere in this volume, and below.)

In turn there has been a change in the literature relating to immigration and multiculturalism. For a country based on considerable diversity, discovery of pluralism seems to have come rather slowly. The term mosaic may have first appeared in 1938 (see Gibbon 1938). It did not become entrenched as a term or as a concept until after publication of John Porter's *Vertical Mosaic* in 1965. As recently as Canada's centennial, in a volume written by the most senior historians in the country, 'racial conflict' refers to French-English relations (*The Canadians: 1867–1967* [1967]).

Addition of pluralism to significant public discourse did not occur until 1970, with the release of Book 4 of the Royal Commission on Bilingualism and Biculturalism. The term 'multiculturalism' as a concept and policy came the following year. Book 4, a byproduct of the effort to resolve issues relating to dualism, pointed to the existence of *The Contributions of the Other Ethnic Groups*. In 1971 Prime Minister Trudeau rose in the House to reformulate the definition of the polity: that Canada is a multicultural society within a bilingual framework. In 1988 Parliament passed the Multiculturalism Act. In 1991, the Department of Multiculturalism and Citizenship was created as a full-fledged entity, separate from the Department of the Secretary of State. Then in 1993, it was abruptly merged – and submerged – into the amorphous new department called Heritage Canada.

Multiculturalism and the image of a mosaic are closely associated in time and concept. However, most academic literature continues to relate multiculturalism to 'the Other,' a legacy into the 1990s of the old notion of 'strangers within our gates.' Government policy and this study's definition are both inclusive: 'multiculturalism is a characteristic of Canadian society in general, and of its whole population, rather than pertaining only to non-charter groups.' However this view is not part of the dialogue. Multiculturalism is not often seen as a mosaic encompassing the totality of the population.

On the contrary, literature about multiculturalism and immigration continues to be preoccupied with 'absorptive capacity,' the ability of the country to adjust to the presence of 'the Other' (see, for example, Thomas 1991). What has changed from earlier times is that there is now more concern for equality; the relationship of immigration and pluralism are now more widely recognized; overt racism and religious discrimination is not legitimised; and considerable educational material is emerging regarding preparation for a more diverse future.

Expansion of the literature is also noticeable. As the country has become more diverse, scholarly interest has differentiated into the various areas covered by the other contributions to this multiculturalism review. Some of the milestones of the era are the works of Richmond (1967), Palmer (1975), and Breton et al. (1980). Palmer may have been the first to link immigration to the new phrase 'multiculturalism.' Jeffrey Reitz in Breton et al. discusses themes reminiscent of much earlier times: 'Immigrants, Their Descendants, and the Cohesion of Canada.' The enduring concern of this society of immigrants remains the potential for societal disruption by new immigrants.

1980s and into the 1990s

Immigration policy has become rationalized, resting on clearer and more objective criteria, including elimination of racial and geographic criteria. Practice, however, has gyrated erratically in the past few years. Steady rationalization of policy has not led to steady increase in immigration flows. Recession in 1980–1 led to sudden restriction of economic migration in 1982. Levels of intake drift downward throughout the middle years, reaching historic postwar lows in 1985 (see Figure 4).

After extensive public consultations, a five-year plan for immigration levels was introduced for the first time, setting slowly expanding levels of intake into the 1990s. Something on the order of a million people will be added to the population by the movement of people across borders. Numbers are in fact imprecise, as targets may be exceeded or under-filled; emergency refugee flows occur; and people emigrate as well as immigrate, in uneven and undocumented quantities. Moreover, the policy changes are accompanied by cautious and even negative and controversial regulatory practices, an eerie replay of the postwar pro-nouncements.

What is clear is that Canada will continue to be transformed by immigration. Literature on the subject also continues to evolve. Some of these changes relate to the consequences of higher levels of ethnic diversity. Themes explored by others in this series are likely to find that much of their source material has been written since the revisions in immigration policy. This is especially so for ethnic histories, ethnic literature, and multicultural education (a substantial body of material).

Research specifically on immigration and multiculturalism also undergoes some changes. As immigrants in the past two decades come increasingly from what are currently considered non-traditional sources, immigration policy once again becomes openly controversial. There are surprisingly few book-length attacks on the policy shift from the right (Collins 1979; Campbell 1988). Some searching studies from various perspectives appear (Malerak 1987; Whitaker 1991, 1987). Multicultur-alism as a philosophy and policy, of course, also receives academic scrutiny (for example, Roberts & Clifton 1982; Stasiulus 1988; Paquet 1988 and elsewhere in this volume; Harney 1988; Bibby 1990).

Research *linking* immigration and multiculturalism is more difficult to categorize. There has been an explosion of material but also differentia-tion into numerous subfields. Strictly within immigration research, there has been lively debate on the economic, reproductive, and migratory behaviour of immigrants, along with assessment of settlement patterns, adaptive behaviour and strategies, aging, and other elements of standard demographic analysis (for a review of this literature see the contributions of Weinfeld and Krótki in this volume).

Students of these subjects may track their evolution in such journals as *International Migration Review, Canadian Studies in Population, Canadian Social Trends*, and *Current Demographic Analysis*. A recent addition is *Infoshare/Infopartage*, the journal of the Canadian Ethnocultural Council. A few authors have covered a broad range of topics relating immigration and multiculturalism (see, for example, the breadth of the contributions of T. John Samuel listed in the bibliography for this chapter).

There is even the emergence of a small and underdeveloped field of refugee studies. Given the magnitude of the flow to Canada, surprisingly few studies focus on refugee *policy*. Apart from the pioneering work of Dirks (1978, 1984, 1985) there are only scattered examinations of policy per se (e.g., Somerset 1982; Hathaway 1986; Matas 1989).

Not surprisingly, most of the limited number of academic studies which do exist examine the origin, settlement, and adaptation of large and recent refugee movements to Canada, especially the peoples of Indochina (see, for example, Adelman 1982; Dorais, Chan & Indra 1987; Lanphier 1981; Neuwirth 1989; Tepper 1980, 1981). Societal implications of the refugee situation receive occasional mention (see Buchignani 1989). Asylum and repatriation are likely soon to receive additional research attention.

However, here as in other areas, public concern and even government curiosity seem to be greater than strictly academic research in an area of growing importance to Canada. One of the largest refugee studies so far, for instance, is a government inquiry into the mental health of refugees and immigrants ('After the Door Is Opened'). Its accompanying bibliographic publication is the most complete in the field (Beiser 1988; Wood 1988). Refugee studies is another field which would benefit from a directed research agenda.

Overlapping these areas are studies of 'new Canadians' or first-generation Canadians, a domain of multiculturalism. They also gain in specificity over time. There are increasingly detailed studies of particular communities, subdivided into areas such as gender, age, and language retention.

In this field, publications of the Canadian Ethnic Studies Association, including its journal *Canadian Ethnic Studies* and its book series, provide a reliable guide to the deepening maturation and sophistication of research interests. Other more specialized fora provide the same function. The Canadian-Asian Symposium, for example, holds annual meetings with the Canadian Asian Studies Association and produces proceedings on a regular basis. Its first is titled *Visible Minorities and Multiculturalism* (Ujimoto & Hirabayashi 1980).

For our purposes the latter serves to remind us that there is even the promulgation of new policy and research vocabulary during this period such as 'visible minority' and 'employment equity.' The two terms also introduce the second major component of this paper, and a series of observations regarding the current state of the art.

IMMIGRATION, RACE, AND THE NEW DEMOGRAPHIC TRANSITION

Race relations is one of the most dynamic fields of research to emerge as a result of immigration policies and societal response. Most studies are not directly devoted to examining the linkage between race, immigration and multiculturalism. They are thus beyond the mandate of this paper. Some do so, of course (for example, see the two publications by Elliott & Fleras 1992; Dwivedi et al. 1989; Taylor 1991). Race relations literature has been given a separate state of the art review, a half a decade prior to this review of multiculturalism (see Henry 1986). However, there is little doubt about the implicit connection. There is even less doubt that they are salient in the public consciousness.

National interest in multiculturalism will swing sharply in the direction of linkage between immigration, race relations, and ethnocultural change in the years just ahead. Multiculturalism, as noted above, remains fixed in the public mind and research agendas as a policy directed to newcomers, at 'the Others.' The newcomers, whatever their numbers, increasingly will be culturally, religiously, and racially different from much of the present population base.

At the end of the twentieth century the country's immigration policy raises no less concern about race and ethnocultural transformation than at the turn of the last century. Accordingly, race relations and immigration should be an area of research priority. Informed debate rather than inflamed debate is a legitimate contribution of the academic community. (For consistent focus on the subject over time see the journal *Currents: Readings in Race Relations*.)

The likelihood that Canada is in for substantial transformation rests in the simple facts of domestic and international demography. Canada's birthrates are well below replacement levels and world supply of newcomers is not what it used to be. A mediating ideology, such as multiculturalism, will allow Canada (or its successor states) to assist the transformation to a much more multiracial, culturally, and religiously diverse social reality.

Demographically, there are two worlds: the few states which are facing population decline and the many which we think of as facing a population explosion. Canada is in the select category of the former group of states. The industrialized developed states form an ever-diminishing proportion of the world's population. Conversely, the less developed parts of the world – non-European and non-industrialized – form an ever-increasing percentage of the world's peoples.[4]

Figure 1 provides a view of the two primary groups, more and less developed, and the anticipated course of their population levels until 2025. The very significant gap between the two suggests that even with an accelerating trend towards lower birth rates in the second category, the less-developed regions, there will be a significant global population imbalance for the foreseeable future. The world will have to cope with a situation of increasing disparity between the sizes of the two broad categories of global citizens.

The dimensions of the growing disparity are highlighted in Figure 2. By the year 2025, the world could have a population base 'which is half Asian, one-fifth African, one-tenth Latin American and slightly less than one-fifth from the present industrialized countries.'[5] Put another way, 'Today's developed countries, including Japan, the Soviet Union and all of Europe, are home to roughly a quarter of mankind; by 2025 they will have barely one person in six. By then the combined populations of North America, Europe, Oceania, Japan, and the Soviet Union will be outnumbered by Africa's.'[6]

One implication in the imbalance is that there will be at least some population transfer between the two demographic universes. No matter what the scale of such movement it will not seriously relieve the sheer demographic weight of numbers in the aggregate known as the 'less developed' (although it could assist in some isolated or particular circumstances).

However, given the present and foreseeable demographic circumstances, there will be one inevitable result. If the world *is* to become interdependent and at peace, over time there will be a massive movement of people from the high pressure to the low pressure global demographic zones. Much more research is needed to place Canada in its international dimensions as a player in the voluntary and involuntary global movement of peoples.

Canada views itself as in need of people for demographic, economic, and humanitarian reasons. In this sense it is competing for the type of immigrants that it deems desirable. The citizenry is not reproducing itself, and so far the country has chosen to continue to expand rather than decline in population. That means attracting and maintaining people in substantial enough numbers to continue to grow.

Perhaps additional charts and graphs will make the relationship between immigration and multiculturalism clearer. Figure 3 indicates that the country is already very diverse in its ethno-demographic make-up, probably much more so than is commonly perceived. The 1986 Census

FIGURE 1
Average Annual Rate of Population Growth
More- and Less-Developed Regions
Medium-Range Projection
1950–2025

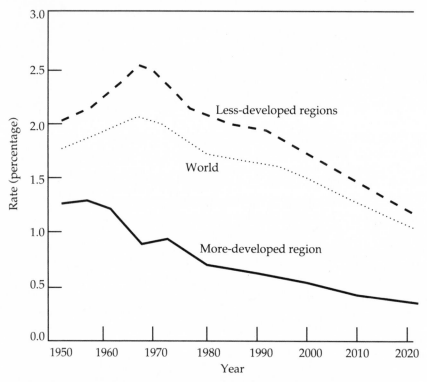

SOURCE: United Nations, Review of Recent National Demographic Target
Setting, Population Studies Number 108, New York, 1989

provides a snapshot of the population at that time. As noted earlier, the
country has no majority population. Still it might come as a surprise that
'the Other' is already the largest slice of the Canadian demographic pie.
The 1991 Census shows an accentuation of the trend, with increasing
proportions of the population being of neither British nor French only
descent nor a mixture of the two. While that does not imply homogeneity of perspective or opinion among the groups and individuals called

FIGURE 2
Proportion of Global Population
Developed and Developing Countries, 1950–2025

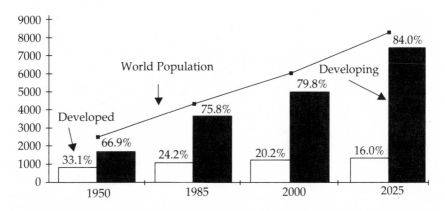

SOURCE: Data from United Nations. World Population Chart 1988. Tabah, Strasbourg

'Other,' it does imply a dramatically different set of national building blocs for the next century. (For additional interpretation see Tepper 1987.)

Figure 5 provides a view of what diversity means, in regard to Canada's future. While only two decades ago Canada drew on a few countries for a high proportion of its migrants, today world-sourcing is the norm. The pattern of intake may shift from year to year, but the trend to diversity is likely to remain. In turn, the requirement for a mediating construct, such as multiculturalism, is imperative. Research relating to Canada's future is research devoted to exploration of the conceptual and practical dimensions of constructing a polity resting on diversity.

ACCESS TO RESEARCH

Before closing there is one other aspect of the topic that requires mentioning. Scholarly investigation relating immigration to multiculturalism is indeed curiosity-based, as our paradigms suggest it should be. However, to a disproportionate degree it has been government which has had the curiosity, and academe which has provided the research response. There are probably few instances of a field of research being willed into

FIGURE 3
Ethnic Origins, Canada, 1991

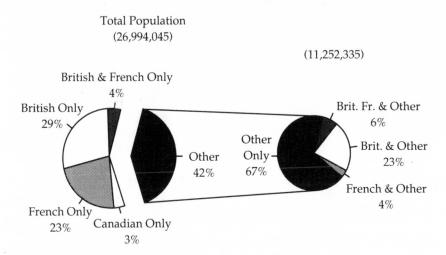

Total Population
(26,994,045)

(11,252,335)

British & French Only
4%

British Only
29%

Brit. Fr. & Other
6%

Other
42%

Other
Only
67%

Brit. & Other
23%

Brit. & Other
23%

French & Other
4%

French Only
23%   Canadian Only
3%

Prepared by Policy & Research, Multiculturalism Sector
SOURCE: Census of Canada, 1991

existence to the degree that this one has. For excellent policy reasons, various levels of government have taken an interest in the subject-matter of immigration and multiculturalism and have called upon the country's scholarly community for assistance. The academic response is no less (or more) excellent for its origins.

Royal commissions in the past offered a way to place academic research on the public record. The Macdonald Commission (Royal Commission on the Economic Union and Development: Prospects for Canada 1985) was a model of its kind. Numerous academic volumes emanated from its deliberations (including the relevant edited collection by Cairns & Williams 1986). The Commission itself, in the body of its report included specific examination of immigration policy (Volume 2, Ch. 16). Clearly based on extensive scholarly research, it directly related immigration to the ethno-demographic transformation of Canada.

However, the substitution of task forces for royal commissions, and the growth of sponsored research from many sources, leads to the continuing production, but not to the circulation, of academic research

FIGURE 4
Immigration, 1860–1988

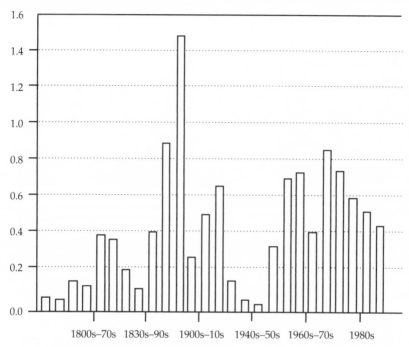

1800s–70s   1830s–90s   1900s–10s   1940s–50s   1960s–70s   1980s

Note: Each bar represents a five-year period

SOURCE: Employment and Immigration Canada, 'Immigration to Canada: A Statistical Overview,' 1989

on topics of interest to the academic community. One scholar speculates that the change in format is deliberate: 'It would appear that governments now prefer internally handled task forces because they are not bound to make the ... findings public, as in the case of royal commissions. This effectively removes task force findings and recommendations from the public discourse ...' (McFarlane 1992:293). In other cases the primary locus of responsibility rests in the natural division of labour. Agencies of government are simply better designed to initiate research than they are at tapping into normal academic distribution channels.

Maturation of the field requires a new relationship. Governments have little capacity for circulation of research but still require the best

FIGURE 5

The 15 major countries of immigration
to Canada, by country, 1987–90

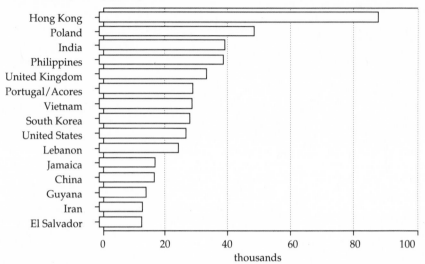

that the country has to offer. Academe would benefit from much better
access to government-sponsored research, and also from alternative
sources of funding. The country would benefit from a much higher level
of quality research, in circulation, accessible both to students and to the
interested reading public.

The end of the logical chain are funds to stimulate research apart from
direct government initiative, access to research which is government-
initiated, and systematic planning to circulate completed university- and
government-initiated research.

CONCLUSION

Immigration and multiculturalism are central to Canada's future. Given
the significance of the topic there has been surprisingly limited involvement of the academic community in joining the two fields of inquiry.
There has been even less incorporation of research findings into mainstream literature. Perhaps the multidisciplinary nature of the both fields
reduces academe's capacity for adequately treating the subject-matter.

Much of what has been produced has been stimulated by various
branches of government. Research findings often remain beyond the

purview of the reading public, although scholars may stay in the research area after initial invitation by government sources.

The salience of the issue will increase in the short term. Steps to increase the quantity, quality, and access to research are a priority. So, too, are steps needed to bring the entire field to the next stage in maturation – integration of the reality of diversity into the central perspectives of the state. Sustaining a humane and progressive social order will require the best conceptual preparation that Canada's academic community can produce. If academe is to play its role effectively, measures are needed to deepen our understanding of a world growing more interdependent and which is empirically multicultural.

NOTES

1 For a recent discussion see Lipset (1990). Chapter 10 opens with the observation: 'One of Canadians' important self images is that their society is a "mosaic," one that gives diverse ethnic groups the right to cultural survival. It contrasts with the once-traditional American emphasis on assimilation into the "melting pot." Canadian ethnocultural groups have a more protective environment than American ones because of the official acceptance of multiculturalism stemming from the need to conciliate French Canadians' (pp 173, 179).

2 Hillmer's contribution is titled 'The Second World War as an (Un)National Experience.' Another study of minorities during wartime starts with the observation: 'Far from multiculturalism ... the goal of English-speaking Canadians was Anglo-conformity: that immigrants to Canada should be forced to assimilate to the language and customs of the majority.' Hillmer refers to the dominant attitude of the period as nativism, 'opposition to an internal minority on the grounds that it posed a threat to Canadian national life.' See Thompson (1991: pp 3–4). For a study of nativism directed against Asians on the west coast, see Ward (1978).

3 Rejean Lachapelle suggests that 'Canada has been a country of minorities for over a century ... if we divide British origin into its English, Scottish and Irish components ...' (in Breton et al. 1980:21).

4 In fact, there are many worlds of demographic change. The states of the worlds array themselves all along the spectrum of growth and decline in birth and death rates. Almost the entire Third World has begun to embark on the transition curve of a decline in death rates, followed by a decline in birth rates, seeking an eventual new equilibrium at a much lower level than

before. The *rate* of decline has been much faster in developing than industrialized countries.

5 Based on long-term projections and on data to be treated with some caution. The author notes that Europe would be about one-twentieth of the
world's population (6.4 per cent) by 2025. Africa, half of Europe's size in
1950, would be almost four times larger than Europe at 2 per cent growth
rate (Tabah 1988:27-28).

6 *The Economist*, 20 January 1990. Of course, such projections do not take into
account the potentially devastating affect of the AIDS epidemic in Africa,
which could be so severe that it could actually significantly reduce the
population.

BIBLIOGRAPHY

Note: the bibliography presented here is indicative, not exhaustive

Adelman, H. (1982). *Canada and the Indochinese Refugees*. Regina: L.A. Weigle
Educational Associates

Abella, I., and Troper, H. (1982). *None is too many: Canada and the Jews of Europe,
1933–1948*. Toronto: Lester & Orpen Dennys

Adachi, K. (1976). *The Japanese: The enemy that never was*. Toronto: McClelland
and Stewart

Adelman, H. (1982). *Canada and the Indochinese refugees*. Regina: Weigle Educational Associates

Anderson, Alan B., and Frideres, James S. (1981). Ethnicity in Canada: Theoretical perspectives. Toronto: Butterworths

Anctil, P. (ed.) (1986). Le pluralisme au Québec/Ethnicity in Quebec. Special
issue. *Canadian Ethnic Studies, 18*

Akoodie, M.A. (1980). *Immigrant students: A comparative assessment of ethnic
identity, self-concept and locus of control amongst West Indian, East Indian and
Canadian students*. Unpublished doctoral thesis, University of Toronto

Atkey, R.G. (1990). Canadian immigration law and policy: A study in politics,
demographics and economics. *Canada–United States Law Journal, 16*:59–81

Avery, D.H. (1973). *Canadian immigration policy and the alien question, 1896–1918:
The Anglo-Canadian perspective*. London, ON: University of Western Ontario

Badets, J. (1989,Fall). Canada's immigrant population. *Canadian Social Trends*,
14:2–6

Balakrishnan, T.R. (1988, Oct.). Immigration and the changing ethnic mosaic of
Canadian cities. Report submitted to the Review of Demography and Its
Implications for Economic and Social Policy

Basavarajappa, K.G., and Ravi, V. (1985, Mar.) Asian immigrants in Canada: Some findings from the 1981 census, *International Migration*, 23(1):97–121

Beach, C.M., and Green, A.G. (1989). Policy forum on the role of immigration in Canada's future. Kingston: John Deutsch Institute for the Study of Economic Policy

Beaujot, R. (1989, Nov.) Immigration and the population of Canada. Report for Employment and Immigration Canada

– (1990). The challenge of changing demographics: A declining, and aging population will mean, among other things, paying more to encourage and support children. *Policy Options*, 11:19–22

Behiels, M.D. (1991). *Quebec and the question of emigration: From ethnocentrism to ethnic pluralism, 1900–1985.* Ottawa: Canadian Historical Association

Beiser, M. (1988). After the door is opened: The Canadian task force on mental health issues affecting immigrants and refugees. Ottawa: Health and Welfare Canada

Bell, David, and Tepperman, Lorne (1979). *The roots of disunity: A look at Canadian political culture.* Toronto: McClelland & Stewart

Bercuson, David J., Abel, Kerry, Akenson, Donald, Baskerville, Peter A., Bumsted, J.M., and Reid, John G. (1992). *Colonies: Canada to 1867.* Toronto: McGraw-Hill Ryerson

Berry, J. et al. (1977). Multiculturalism and ethnic attitudes in Canada. Ottawa: Minister of State for Multiculturalism

Bibby, R.W. (1978, Apr.). The delicate mosaic: A national examination of intergroup relations in Canada. *Social Indicators Research: An International and Interdisciplinary Journal for Quality-of-life Measurement*, 5:169–79

– (1990). *Mosaic madness.* Toronto: Stoddart

Bienvenue, R.M., and Goldstein, J. (eds) (1985). *Ethnicity and ethnic relations in Canada.* Toronto and Boston: Butterworths

Breton, R. (1986). Multiculturalism and Canadian nation-building. In A. Cairns and C. Williams (eds), *The Politics of gender, ethnicity, and language in Canada.* Toronto: University of Toronto Press

Breton, R., Reitz, J.G., and Valentine, V. (1980). *Cultural boundaries and the cohesion of Canada.* Montreal: Institute for Research on Public Policy

Buchignani, N. (1989, Jan.) Refugees and race relations in Canada. Paper presented at an International Symposium, The Refugee Crisis: British and Canadian Responses, Oxford University

– (1990). Contemporary race relations in the prairie provinces. Canada Council on Community and Race Relations Seminar, 22 Mar.

– Canadian ethnic research and multiculturalism. *Journal of Canadian Studies*, 17(1)

Buchignani, N., and Engel, J. (1983). *Cultures in Canada: Strength in diversity.* Regina: Weigl Educational Publishers

Burnet, J.R., with Palmer, Howard (1988). Coming Canadians. Ottawa: Ministry of Supply and Services

– (1990). State of the art. *Canadian Ethnic Studies,* Special Issue, 22(1)

Cairns, A., and Williams, C. (eds) (1986). *The politics of gender, ethnicity, and language in Canada* . Toronto: University of Toronto Press

Cairns, A. et al. (1987, Fall). The politics of gender, ethnicity and language in Canada. *Canadian Journal of Sociology,* 12(3):297–9

Campbell, C.M. (1988). *A time bomb ticking: Canadian immigration in crisis.* Toronto: Mackenzie Institute for the Study of Terrorism

Canada, Employment and Immigration (1989, Mar.) Attitudes and perceptions of selected dimensions of refugee and immigration policy in Canada: Final report. Report prepared by Angus Reid Associates Inc.

– (1989, Oct.) Immigration to Canada: Aspects of public opinion. Report prepared for Employment and Immigration Canada by Angus Reid Group Inc.

Canada's Immigrants (1984). Ottawa: Ministry of Supply and Services

Careless, J.M.S., and Brown, R. Craig (1967). *The Canadians: 1867–1967.* Toronto: Macmillan

Chan, K.B., and Indra, D. M. (1987). *Uprooting, loss and adaptation: The resettlement of Indo-Chinese refugees in Canada.* Ottawa: Canadian Public Health Association

Collins, D. (1979). *Immigration: The destruction of English Canada.* Richmond Hill: BMG Publications

Corbett, D. (1957). *Canada's immigration policy: A critique.* Toronto: Canadian Institute of International Affairs

– (1963, Spring). Canada's immigration policy, 1957–1962. *International Journal,* 18:166–80

D'Costa, R. (1989). Canadian immigration policy: A chronological review with particular reference to discrimination in O.P. Dwivedi et al. (eds), *Canada 2000; Race relations and public policy.* Guelph, ON: University of Guelph

Demographic considerations in determining future levels of immigration to Canada. Report prepared for the Experts' Meeting on Demography and Migration, OECD, Paris, 3–4 October 1988

Devoretz, D., and Maki, D. (1983, Jan.). The Immigration of Third World Professionals to Canada: 1968–1973. *World Development,* 11(1):55–64

Dickason, Olive Patricia (1992). *Canada's First Nations: A history of founding peoples from earliest times.* Toronto: McClelland & Stewart

Dirks, G. (1978). *Canada's refugee policy: Indifference or opportunism?.* Montreal/Kingston: McGill-Queen's University Press

- (1984, June). A policy within a policy: The identification and admission of refugees in Canada. *Canadian Journal of Political Science*, 17(2)
- (1985). Canadian refugee policy: Humanitarian and political determinants. In E. Colson and G. Ferris (eds), *Refugees and world politics*. New York: Praeger
Dorais, L.J., Chan, K., and Indra, D. (eds). (1988). *Ten years later: Indochinese communities in Canada*. Ottawa: Canadian Asian Studies Association
Dreidger, L. (ed.) (1978). *The Canadian ethnic mosaic*. Toronto: Canadian Ethnic Studies Association
- (ed.) (1987). *Ethnic Canada: Identities and inequalities*. Toronto: Copp Clark Pitman
- (1989). *The ethnic factor: Identity in diversity*. Toronto: McGraw-Hill Ryerson
Dwivedi, O.P. et al. (eds) (1989). *Canada 2000: Race relations and public policy*. Proceedings of the conference held at Carleton University, 30 October–1 November 1987. Ottawa. Guelph, Ont.: University of Guelph
Elliott, J.L. and Fleras, A. (1992). *Unequal Relations: An introduction to race and ethnic dynamics in Canada*. Scarborough: Prentice-Hall
Fleras, A., and Elliott, J. (1992). *Multiculturalism in Canada: The challenge of diversity*. Scarborough: Nelson
Foster, Kate (1926). *Our Canadian Mosaic*. Toronto: Dominion Council, YWCA
Gagné, M. (1989, Spring). L'insertion de la population immigrée sur le marché du travail au Québec. *Revue internationale d'action communautaire*, 21:153–63
Gibbon, J.M. (1938). *Canadian mosaic: The making of a northern nation*. Toronto: McClelland & Stewart
Government of Canada (1973). Canada's immigrants 1971. Ottawa: Statistics Canada
- (1984a). Royal Commission on Equality in Employment. Ottawa: Minister of Supply and Services
- (1984b). Report of Proceedings of the Symposium on Policing in Multicultural/Multiracial Urban Communities. Ottawa: Canadian Association of Chiefs of Police and Multiculturalism Canada
- (1985). Royal Commission on the Economic Union and Development Prospects for Canada. Ottawa: Minister of Supply and Services
- (1987). Institutional change strategies in response to multiculturalism. Ottawa: Dept of Secretary of State
Government of Quebec (1988). Avis: Relatif au project de loi C-93 sur le maintien et la valorisation du multiculturalisme au Québec. Montreal: Conseil des Communautés culturelles et de l'Immigration du Quebec
- (1988). Table municipale de concertation des communautés culturelles. Montreal: Conseil des Communautés culturelles et de l'Immigration du Québec et Union des Municipalités du Québec

Halli, S.S., Trovato, F., and Dreidger, L. (eds) (1990). *Ethnic demography. Canadian immigrant, racial and cultural variations.* Ottawa: Carleton University Press

Harney, R. (1988). So great a heritage as ours: Immigration and the survival of the Canadian polity. *Daedalus, 117*(4)

Hathaway, J. (1986). An Overview of Canadian refugee policy as it relates to Africa. Paper, Queen Elizabeth House, Oxford

Hawkins, F. (1988). *Canada and Immigration.* Montreal/Kingston: McGill-Queen's University Press

– (1989, 1991). *Critical years in immigration: Canada and Australia compared.* Montreal/Kingston: McGill-Queen's University Press

Hebert, R.M. (1991). Francophone perspectives on multiculturalism. Paper presented at Canadian Studies Conference, Twenty Years of Multiculturalism: Success and Failures, University of Manitoba, 1–2 Feb.

Henry, F. (1986). Literature review of race relations in Canada. Ottawa: Canadian Human Rights Commission

Herberg, E.N. (1989). *Ethnic groups in Canada: Adaptations and transitions.* Toronto: Nelson

Hillmer, Norman, Kordan, Bohdan, and Luciuk, Lubomyr (1988). *On guard for thee: War, ethnicity and the Canadian state, 1939–1945.* Canadian Committee for the History of the Second World War. Ottawa: Dept of Supply and Services

Isajiw, W. (1977). *Identities.* Toronto: Canadian Ethnic Studies Association

Jain, H. (1988, Sept.). Employment discrimination against visible minorities and employment equity. Report for the Secretary of State, Multiculturalism

Johnston, T. (1978). Canadian Black population and migration.' *Anthropos, 73*(3):588–92

Juteau, D. (ed.) (1979). *Frontières ethniques en devenir.* Otttawa: Éditions de l'Université d'Ottawa

Keenleyside, H.L. (1948). *Canadian immigration policy.* Vancouver: University of British Columbia

Knowles, Valerie (1992). *Strangers at our gates: Canadian immigration and immigration policy 1540–1990.* Toronto: Dundurn Press

Krishnan, P. (1980). Toward a prediction of third-world immigrants into Canada, 1973–1985. *International Migration, 18*:34–9

Lam, L. and Richmond, A.H. (1987, Autumn). A decade in Canada: Immigration, human rights and racism, 1978–87. *New Community, 14*(1–2):234–40

Lanphier, C.M. (1981). Canada's response to refugees. *International Migration Review, 15*(1)

Lawrence, R.B. (1973). *Canadian immigration policy and practice.* Hamilton: R.B. Lawrence

Li, P.S. (1980). Immigration laws and family patterns: Some demographic changes among Chinese families in Canada, 1885–1971. *Canadian Ethnic Studies*, 12(1):58–73

– (ed.) 1990. *Race and ethnic relations in Canada*. Toronto: Oxford University Press

Lipset, S.M. (1990). *Continental divide*. New York: Routledge

Logan, R. (1991, Spring). Immigration during the 1980s. *Canadian Social Trends*, 10–13

Lupul, M. (ed.) (1988). *Continuity and change: The cultural life of Alberta's first Ukrainians*. Edmonton: Canadian Institute of Ukrainian Studies

McDade, K. (1988, Apr.). Barriers to recognition of the credentials of immigrants in Canada. Ottawa: Studies in Social Policy

McFarlane, Bruce (1992). Anthropologists and sociologists and their contribution to policy in Canada. In William G. Carroll et al. (eds), *Fragile Truths: Twenty-five years of sociology and anthropology in Canada*. Ottawa: Carleton University Press

McGee, J. (1984). *Loyalist mosaic*. Toronto and Charlottetown: Dundurn Press

McNeill, W.H. (1986). *Polyethnicity and national unity in world history*. Toronto: University of Toronto Press

Malarek, V. (1987). *Haven's gate: Canada's immigration fiasco*. Toronto: Macmillan

Matas, D., and Simon, Ilana (1989). *Closing the doors: The failure of refugee protection*. Toronto: Summerhill Press

Moore, E.G., Ray, B.K., and Rosenberg, M.W. (1990, May). The redistribution of immigrants in Canada. Report prepared for Employment and Immigration Canada

Nagata, J. (1987). Is multiculturalism sacred? The power behind the pulpit in the religious congregations of Southeast Asian Christians in Canada. *Canadian Ethnic Studies*, 19(2):26–43

Nash, A. (1987, Oct.). *The economic impact of the entrepreneur immigrant program*. Ottawa: Studies in Social Policy

Neuwirth, Gertrud (1983). Southeast Asian refugee study: A report on the social and economic adaptation to life in Canada. Ottawa: Employment and Immigration Canada

– (1989). The settlement of Ethiopian refugees in Toronto. Ottawa: Employment and Immigration Canada

Ossenberg, R.J. (1966). Ideology in a plural society: Canadian dualism and the issue of immigration. Unpublished doctoral thesis, State University of New York at Buffalo

Palmer, H. (1975). *Immigration and the rise of multiculturalism*. Toronto: Copp Clark

- (1981, Fall). Canadian immigration and ethnic history in the 1970s and 1980s. *International Migration Review, 15*(3)
- (1981, Fall). Canadian immigration and ethnic hsitory in the 1970's and 1980's. *International Migration Review, 15*:3
- and Palmer, T. (eds) (1988). *Peoples of Alberta: Portraits of cultural diversity.* Saskatoon: Western Producer Prairie Books
Paquet, G. (1988). Multiculturalism as national policy. Paper presented at the Fifth International Conference on Cultural Economics, Ottawa
Parekh, N. (1989, Spring). Multiculturalism: Immigration and race relations. *Perception, 12*(2):46–7
Passaris, C. (1987, Dec.). Canada's demographic outlook and multicultural immigration. *International Migration, 25*(4):361–84
Patterson, G.J. (1985, Winter). The persistence of white ethnicity in Canada: The case of the Romanians. *East European Quarterly, 19*:493–500
Porter, John (1965). *The vertical mosaic.* Toronto: University of Toronto Press
- (1979). Ethnic pluralism in Canadian perspective. In John Porter, *The measure of Canadian society: Education, equality and opportunity.* Toronto: Gage Publications
Ram, B. (1985, Jan.). Regional distribution of India's immigrant community in Canada. *Population Review, 29*:80–94
Rappak, J.P., Rappak, M., and Beaujot, R. (1989, Mar.). The demographic implications of varying immigration levels and the age structure of immigration. Report for Employment and Immigration Canada
Reitz, J.G. (1988, Spring). The institutional structure of immigration as a determinant of racial competition: A comparison of Britain and Canada. *International Migration Review, 22*(1):117–46
Richard, M.A. (1989). Immigration policy, ethnic history and intermarriage, Canada 1871 and 1971. Unpublished doctoral thesis, York University
Richmond, A.H. (1967). *Post-war immigrants in Canada.* Toronto: University of Toronto Press
- (1976, Apr.). Immigration, population and the Canadian future. *Sociological Focus, 9*(2):125–36
- (1988). *Immigration and ethnic conflict.* London: St Martin's Press
Roberts, L.W., and Clifton, R.A. (1982). Exploring the ideology of Canadian multiculturalism. *Canadian Public Policy, 8*(1)
Royal Commission on Bilingualism and Biculturalism, Bk 4 (1969). *The contributions of the other ethnic groups.* Ottawa: Queen's Printer
Samuel, J. (1977, Oct.). Third World immigration, multiculturalism and education. Paper presented at the Conference on Canadian Immigration Policy and the Third World Community, Regina

– (1984). Economic adaptation of refugees in Canada: Experience of a quarter century. *International Migration Review, 17*

– (1987). Immigration and visible minorities in the year 2001: A projection. Working Paper No. 1 on Immigration and Ethno-Cultural Studies, Carleton University, published in *Canadian Ethnic Studes, 20*(2)

– (1988, May). Third World immigration and multiculturalism in Canada. Paper presented at joint meetings of Canadian Ethnology and other societies, University of Saskatoon, Saskaton, 11–15 May

– (1988, Aug.). Third World immigration, multiculturalism and ethnicity in Canada. Paper presented at National Symposium on the Demography of Immigrant, Racial and Ethnic Groups in Canada, University of Manitoba, Winnipeg, 26–7 Aug.

– (1989). Factors influencing the acceptance of immigrants. Unpublished paper

– (1990). Canadian immigrants and criminality. *International Migration*

– (1990). Immigrant children in Canda (with R. Verma). Paper presented at the Symposium on Immigrant Settlement and Integration, Toronto

– (1991). Immigration of children as an element of immigration policy. Paper presented at the Canadian Population Society, Victoria

– (1991, Apr.) Immigration and ethnicity in Toronto, Montreal and Vancouver (with Pamela White). *International Journal of Canadian Studies*

Satzewich, V. (1988). Modes of incorporation and racializatioin: The Canadian case. Unpublished doctoral thesis, University of Glasgow

– (1989). Racism and Canadian immigration policy: The government's view of Caribbean migration, 1962–1966. *Canadian Ethnic Studies, 21*(1):77–97

Schissel, B. et al. (1989, Summer). Social and economic content and attitudes toward immigrants in Canadian cities. *International Migration Review,* 23:289–308

Schroeter, G. (1978, Spring). In search of ethnicity: Multiculturalism in Canada. *Journal of Ethnic Studies, 6*(1):98–107

Sheridan, W. (1986). *Immigrant integration into Canadian society.* Ottawa: Library of Parliament, Research Branch

Smith, W.G. (1920). *A study in Canadian immigration.* Toronto: Ryerson

Somerset, F. (1982). Indochinese Refugees in Canada: Government Policy and Public Response. *New Community.* X:1

Stark, T. (1973). Impact of immigration on Canada's population. *International Migration Review, 7*(3):347–9

Stasiulus, D. (1988). The symbolic mosaic reaffirmed: Multiculturalism policy. In K.A. Graham (ed.), *How Ottawa Spends.* Ottawa: Carleton University Press

Sunahara, A.H. (1981). *The politics of racism: The uprooting of Japanese Canadian during the Second World War.* Toronto: James Lorimer

Tabah, S. World Population Chart, 1988. Strasbourg: United Nations

Taylor, K.W. (1991). Racism in Canadian immigration policy. *Canadian Ethnic Studies,* 23(1):1–21

Tepper, E.L. (1980). *Southeast Asian exodus: From tradition to settlement.* Ottawa: Canadian Asian Studies Association; Chicago: University of Chicago Press

– (1981). D'un continent à un autre: Les réfugiés du Sud-Est asiatique. Ottawa: Association canadienne des études asiatiques

– (1982). Is Ottawa different: Perceptions of discrimination and race relations in the nation's capital. Ottawa: Multiculturalism Directorate, Dept. of Secretary of State

– (1984). Racism and racial discrimination in Canada: A selective and interpretive bibliography. Ottawa Multiculturalism Directorate, Dept. of the Secretary of State

– (1987). Demographic change and pluralism. *Canadian Studies in Population,* 14(2):223–36

– (1988). *Self-employment in Canada among immigrants of different ethno-cultural background.* Ottawa: Employment and Immigration Canada

– (1988, Dec.). *Changing Canada: The institutional response to polyethnicity.* Ottawa: Health and Welfare Canada

Thomas, D. (1991, Jan.). The social integration of immigrants in Canada. Report prepared for Employment and Immigration Canada

Thompson, J.H. (1991). *Ethnic minorities during two world wars.* Ottawa: Canadian Historical Association

Ujimoti, K.V., and Hirabayashi, G. (1980). *Visible minorities and multiculturalism: Asians in Canada.* Toronto: Butterworths

Ujimoto, K.V., and Naidoo, J. (eds) (1987). *Asian Canadians: Contemporary issues.* Selections from proceedings of 7th Asian Canadian Symposium, University of Manitoba, Winnipeg, Manitoba, 4–7 June 1986. Guelph, ON: University of Guelph

Walker, J. (1978). *The Black loyalists.* London: Longman

Ward, P. (1978, 1991). *White Canada forever: Popular attitudes and public policy towards Orientals in British Columbia.* Montreal/Kingston: McGill-Queen's University Press

Weinfeld, M., Shafir, W., and Cotler, I. (eds) (1981). *The Canadian Jewish mosaic.* Toronto: John Wiley & Sons

Weiner, G. (1987, Spring). Immigration to the year 2000: A Canadian perspective. *Atlantic Community Quarterly,* 25:83–9

Whitaker, R. (1987). *Double standard: The secret history of Canadian immigration.* Toronto: Lester & Orpen Dennys

– (1989, Mar.). Double standard: The secret history of Canadian immigration. *Canadian Journal of Political Science*, 22(1):179–80

– (1991). *Canadian immigration policy since Confederation*. Ottawa: Canadian Historical Association

White, P.M. (1981, Spring). Immigration and ethnic diversity in urban Canada. *International Journal of Canadian Studies*, 3:69–85

– (1990). *Ethnic diversity in Canada*. Ottawa: Statistics Canada

Wickberg, E.B. (1980). Chinese associations in Canada. In V. Ujimoto, and G. Hirabayashi (eds), *Visible minorities and multiculturalism: Asians in Canada*. Toronto: Butterworths

– et al. (1982). *From China to Canada: A history of Chinese communities in Canada*. Toronto: McClelland & Stewart

Winks, R. (1971). *The Blacks in Canada*. Montreal/Kingston: McGill-Queen's University Press

Wojciechowski, J. (1986). Cultural pluralism and national identity in Canada. Report for the International Sociological Association

Wood, M. (1988). Review of literature on migrant mental health: The Canadian task force on mental health issues affecting immigrants and refugees. Ottawa: Health and Welfare Canda

Woodsworth, J.S. (1909, 1972). *Strangers within our gates*. Toronto: University of Toronto Press

Young, Judy (1992, May). Bibliographic challenges in the study of multiculturalism in the 1990's. Paper presented at the Learned Societies, University of Prince Edward Island

Ziegler, E. (1988). *Refugee movements and policy in Canada*. Review of demography and its implications for economic and social policy. Ottawa: Health and Welfare Canada

E. DIANE PASK

The Charter, Human Rights, and Multiculturalism in Common-Law Canada

INTRODUCTION

The objective of this paper is to survey current, common-law, anglophone legal research analyzing the impact in Canadian law of multiculturalism. References to case law will be limited. A major difficulty in this area is the lack of consistent terminology. There is general agreement that, in the context of the Canadian Charter of Rights and Freedoms[1] and section 27, the challenge for the courts is balancing individual rights with collective interests or group rights (as they may be called). There is no agreement on the meaning of 'multiculturalism,' on the distinction, if any, between 'civil liberties' and 'human rights,' or as to the basis for characterizing rights as either 'individual,' 'group,' or 'collective.'

This lack of agreement on terminology reflects a continuing debate on the meaning and objectives of multiculturalism in Canada. This flows from the inherent conflict between the concept of cultural pluralism and the theoretical and practical difficulties of shaping that concept in a framework of official French-English bilingualism and biculturalism. The various multiculturalism interest groups also do not agree on the objectives of any public policy on multiculturalism: should policies focus on the retention of culture and dominant society accommodation to cultural minorities or on anti-racism and other equality issues? This difference has been analyzed in terms of constituencies: visible minorities have been seen as focusing on equality issues of racial discrimination whereas immigrants and other ethnocultural minorities have been seen as perhaps placing greater importance on culture retention and related issues of minority language and education rights. Courts have little guidance in making these choices.

METHODOLOGY

A search has been undertaken of Canadian anglophone legal literature over the past twenty years to identify research and writing on legal issues and multiculturalism. Interdisciplinary literature has not been searched as that material is reflected in the bibliographies of other disciplines contained in this project. Such a search would also be repetitive of the excellent 2600-item interdisciplinary bibliography developed by the *Report on Multiculturalism and Access to Justice* prepared for the Department of Justice, Canada (Etherington et al. 1991). The University of British Columbia database 'Canadian Politics: Thesaurus' was searched, but its classification system does not easily provide access to legal research in this area. An effort has been made to include in the bibliography to this paper, research which has been circulated at conferences and is not easily referenced through traditional search methods. It has not been possible to include material arising out of the constitutional discussions surrounding the 'Consensus Report on the Constitution.'[2]

Legal research on topics in the area of law and multiculturalism is of comparatively recent origin. There has been, in many cases, insufficient time for the overall value and usefulness of the research to the Bench, Bar, and professoriate to become apparent. For that reason as well as because of the limitations of space and the number of publications available, textual reference has been made to only a relatively few pieces of research.

THE CHARTER

Section 27

Section 27 of the *Charter* states:

This *Charter* shall be interpreted in a manner consistent with the preservation and enhancement of the multicultural heritage of Canadians.

The first major Canadian legal study examining section 27 of the Charter was funded in 1985 by the Multiculturalism Directorate of the Department of the Secretary of State and coordinated by the Canadian Human Rights Foundation (*Multiculturalism and the Charter: A Legal Perspective* 1987). This study provides one of the foremost legal examinations of section 27.

Section 27, modelled on article 27 of the 1966 International Covenant on Civil and Political Rights, is seen as constitutionally unique and, therefore, as exceptionally difficult to interpret and apply (Magnet 1989). Most current writers see section 27 as an interpretive section (Gibson 1990; Magnet 1989; Gall 1987; Hogg 1982). It contains no positive guarantees and, therefore, early authorities found it impossible to visualize what a court could grant pursuant to section 27 alone (Tarnopolsky 1982). The concept of multiculturalism has been used in Canada as a legal tool in two broad contexts: (1) to obtain equality of opportunity based on social integration, and (2) to enhance a collective ethnic identity (Hudson 1987). However, the scope of section 27 remains to be determined, particularly in the context of other sections of the Charter, for example, the official languages sections.

Professor Magnet's work in interpreting the meaning of section 27 has been judicially referred to on many occasions as being of great assistance. It was expressly adopted by the Supreme Court of Canada in *R. v Keegstra*[3] with respect to the principle of non-discrimination and the need to prevent attacks on the individual's connection with his or her culture and hence upon the process of self-development. *Keegstra* stated that the section 27 commitment to a multicultural vision of Canada is worthy of notice in emphasizing the legislative objective of eradicating hate propaganda from society.

Fundamental Freedoms: Section 2

Section 2 is concerned with the assertion of individual rights by a person who is, nonetheless, a member of a group (Tarnopolsky 1982). Since section 27 contains no positive guarantees, it is seen as having impact on section 2 is two ways: (1) adjectival relevance for questions of interpretation; (2) by providing meaning and scope to a determination of what are 'reasonable limits prescribed by law as can be demonstrably justified in a free and democratic society' in the context of section 2 rights (Hogg 1982). For example, section 27 has been relied upon by the Supreme Court of Canada in finding uniform Sunday closing legislation to contravene the freedoms of conscience and religion[4] and in shielding minority interests from provincial Sunday closing legislation[5] and, by the Ontario Court of Appeal, in striking down provincial regulations providing for religious exercises in public schools.[6] A risk of physical injury to persons outside the faith has been seen as constituting a reasonable limit under section 1 of the Charter to the exercise of the Sikh religious practice of carrying kirpans.[7] The latter issue, of kirpans in courtrooms or schools, is one on which cases have gone both ways.

A large number of Charter challenges have been based upon the guarantee of freedom of expression in section 2(b). Those challenges most relevant to multiculturalism may be those concerned with hate propaganda or provincial language laws. Thus, freedom of expression in section 2(b) formed the basis of the unsuccessful challenge to the Criminal Code hate propaganda offences in *Keegstra*.[8] Canada's international obligations to prohibit hate propaganda (specifically, the International Convention on the Elimination of All Forms of Racial Discrimination),[9] and sections 27 and 15 of the Charter were found relevant in *Keegstra* to the validation of the hate propaganda offence under section 1 of the Charter. The balancing of freedom of expression with other fundamental values is receiving attention in current research.

Conflict between Individual Rights under Section 15 and Group Values

Section 15 of the Charter contains the guarantees of equality, non-discrimination and affirmative action with which the Charter is largely associated in the minds of many members of the public. An overview of the current state of the law concerning the basic concepts of equality contained in section 15 of the Charter can be found in Professor Gibson's excellent and thorough textbook, *The Law of the Charter: Equality Rights* (1990). Two of the first initiatives examining the equality section provide the theoretical foundation and context necessary in order to appreciate the importance of the section (Smith 1986; Bayefsky & Eberts 1985).

The main feature of the caselaw and research around equality issues is the number of conflicts that have arisen and will continue to arise between two very different approaches to equality, i.e. the individualistic thrust of s.15 and the pluralistic approach to equality of section 27 (Gibson 1990; Beckton 1987; Woehrling 1985). In the context of issues pertinent to multiculturalism, there are individual and collective aspects to a variety of linguistic, religious, and cultural issues.

It is not clear just how the balancing of these interests is to occur. For example, adoption agencies may have a policy of only permitting adoption of a child by parents with similar religious beliefs or a similar cultural or ethnic background. Does this deny the section 15 equality guarantees of the adopting parents? If section 27 is applicable in order to retain a multicultural heritage, is the 'best interests of the child' test still applicable? Overall, is this characterizable as denial of equality or preservation of cultural values or neither? (Beckton 1987).

Conflict between section 27 and sex-based equality stipulated under sections 15 and 28 is also possible. Religious rules or cultural norms may be both explicit and provide for sexual inequality. It is conceivable that religious or cultural groups could argue for the non-applicability of the federal Divorce Act or other relevant statutes and of section 15 of the Charter on the grounds that section 27 of the Charter mandates a different interpretation in the case of their members. The arguments from the group could be expected to focus on the ways in which the rules or norms reinforce cultural identity and the ways in which the particular statute and section 15 are seen as having the opposite effect.

Section 15 of the Charter provides a basis for legal recourse against sex-based inequality. This is a positive guarantee. It is difficult to see how positive rights could be justifiably denied to an individual claimant on the basis of interpretation. However, it has been suggested that the collective autonomy of semi-autonomous groups would base a claim to priority (Magnet 1989). A similar challenge arises in the context of criminal law. A 'cultural defence' to criminal charges of assault or civil allegations of child abuse has been posited. Such a defence must not undermine the fundamental norms of society concerning violence to women or children (Etherington et al. 1991).

The decision of the Supreme Court of Canada in *Andrews* v *Law Society of BC* is the leading case on the interpretation of section 15. Although the impact of *Andrews* in the area of multiculturalism has yet to be explored, the case strongly connects the purpose of section 15 with the development of a society which recognizes all persons at law as equally deserving of concern, respect, and consideration.

A reconciliation of section 15 with section 27 could mean that equality means something other than uniformity and, on the other hand, that discriminatory behaviour cannot be justified on the basis of preserving cultural values (Beckton 1987). Section 15(2), which allows affirmative action programs as a way to offset previous systemic discrimination, may be intended to offer such a reconciliation by justifying programs directed towards the preservation of multicultural values (Beckton 1987). On the other hand, it is argued that section 15(2) is 'not sufficient to guarantee the long-term protection of minority group rights' (Kallen 1987).

Issues in Education and Language

Linguistic and educational rights are seen as important social and collective rights which are strongly linked to culture (Foucher 1987). However, the guaranteed rights are those respecting the official language rights in ss.16–20 of the Charter which encompass instruction, facilities, and management of the education system (Foucher 1987). Section 22 of the Charter merely provides that official language rights do not abrogate or derogate from any customary right or privilege required or enjoyed either before or after coming into force of the Charter with respect to non-official languages.

Equal Access to Education

Multiculturalism in education concerns teaching of other languages, religion, the requirement of religious and patriotic exercises, observing religious holidays, the nature and extent of compulsory education, the position and funding of private schools, curriculum selection, physical appearance, and corporal punishment (Schmeiser 1987.) Indeed, the issue of education arises in the context of each of the key multicultural issues: (1) linguistic rights (includes the right to be educated in one's mother tongue); (2) minority religious rights (religious and denominational schools); (3) alternate cultural designs for living (state prescribed curricula vs cultural survival). Section 23, headed 'Minority Language Educational Rights,' has been seen as 'a unique set of constitutional provisions, quite peculiar to Canada.'[10] It has been argued that this section must be seen as granting a real collective right to the French or English linguistic minority in the province (Bastarache 1989). Questions to be explored concern the geographical area and the minimum number of children contemplated by section 23 as necessary to warrant the provision of minority language instruction.

It is argued that the link between education and culture is so close that bilingual education leads to assimilation (Foucher 1987). However, while some have argued that the right of parents to determine the education of their children should extend to all religious or linguistic groups (Kallen 1987), the Charter has not been interpreted to guarantee collective religious or cultural rights for minority groups. From a practical perspective, the key issue in this area in the future may well centre around access to government funding for a range of programs.

Language Rights

Sections 16–22 of the Charter are grouped under the heading 'Official Languages of Canada.' These sections have been analyzed in numerous cases which have considered the rights contained in those sections and their applications. A recent thorough examination concluded that the Supreme Court has signalled that a restrained approach is to be taken judicially towards them in order that the character of language guarantees develop through the political and social process (Tremblay & Bastarache 1989). A recent, excellent work can be recommended for its overall examination of the jurisprudence and existing research in the area of language rights (Schneiderman 1991).

Language rights must also be analyzed in light of the phenomenon of heterogeneity. It is impossible to grant official status to all the languages spoken by citizens of a state (Braën 1987). The general view is that while section 27 may support measures enhancing Canada's cultural diversity, it will not be effective to replace or restrict the position under the Charter of English and French, Protestantism and Roman Catholicism (Gibson 1990; Tremblay & Bastarache 1989).

Section 22 is called into play in the sense that it provides for the preservation of all vested rights (past and future) with respect to any of the unofficial languages (e.g., aboriginal languages of the Northwest Territories) (Didier 1987). Most recognition given to unofficial languages tends to be passive in character, that is, tolerance rather than promotion (Didier 1987), although the Northwest Territories has made provision for recognition of several Aboriginal languages.

The authorities in this area agree that the only language guarantees are those given to the two official languages. Section 27 gives the impression that all languages and cultures may be equal but sections 16–23 place two cultures on a privileged position with respect to language (Tremblay & Bastarache 1989). Rather, section 27 is a tool which may force governments to take positive action so that linguistic minorities can obtain access to an educational system which *respects* their language and culture (Anand 1987). Thus, section 27 has been applied to section 23 minority educational language guarantees to construe them to yield as much cultural advantage as possible (Gibson 1990). A recent, excellent work can be recommended for its overall examination of the jurisprudence and existing research in the area of language rights (Schneiderman 1991).

UNOFFICIAL LANGUAGES; THE DEVELOPMENT OF A RIGHT
TO BE HEARD AND UNDERSTOOD

Section 14 of the Charter does not guarantee a right to use a specific language. It merely facilitates the understanding of a person who does not speak or comprehend the official language in which the proceedings are occurring. This distinction, as between language rights and comprehension safeguards or legal rights, is set out lucidly in the work of several authorities (Newman 1989; Schneiderman 1991).

The areas of immigration and refugee law and of criminal law are, through statute and jurisprudence, recognizing that the rights of fair procedure under section 7 of the Charter or of fairness and natural justice, may be breached if the state does not assume some responsibility for assisting individuals to be heard and to be understood. This means that interpreters and translators must be provided. This does not answer the question of the extent and meaning of fairness in this context. Can it be argued that the use of interpreters is, in itself, essentially inequitable in that members of a minority language community using interpreters do not have an equal opportunity to be heard and understood?

It is said that courts have been reluctant to enhance language rights at the expense of the development of legal rights and due process perhaps for this reason (Newman 1989). The Official Languages Act[11] greatly facilitates the use of official languages. It remains to be seen where fairness and equity will take the unofficial languages.

Rights of Aboriginal Peoples

The claims of Aboriginal peoples are quite different from those of various racial and ethnic minorities and the aboriginal peoples object to discussion of their issues in the context of multiculturalism. It is not only inappropriate to integrate the two areas here, but the plethora of legal research addressing such Aboriginal issues as land claims, self-government, constitutional recognition, and access to justice would require a further paper to do justice to the area.

In summary, however, there has been an historical lack of contact between multicultural groups and Aboriginals. There are arguments pro and con with respect to the application of section 27 to Aboriginal people. For example, multiculturalism does not address Aboriginals as a 'people' but rather as a 'minority,' ignoring the issues of self-determination. Although section 27 has been referred to as a useful support to claims for promotion of self-governing structures, strategists for Aboriginal groups have raised concerns about the inherent conflict in Aboriginal groups placing reliance upon the Charter. Yet, a policy of multiculturalism supports the aboriginals' goals in relation to culture, land, and self-government (Sanders 1985, 1987; Magnet 1989).

Many questions concerning Aboriginal rights have arisen in the context of the various judicial inquiries concerning access to justice as well as in the context of the current constitutional discussions. Research assessing the results of these events is anticipated.

Reasonable Limits under Section 1

Section 1 requires that limitations imposed upon rights must be justifiable limits. The Supreme Court of Canada in *R. v Oakes*[12] set out the criteria to be used in assessing the validity of a limitation under section 1. First, the objective of the limitation must be of sufficient importance to override a constitutionally protected right or freedom; second, the means chosen must be reasonable and demonstrably justifiable. This establishes a proportionality test containing three components. The measure must be rationally connected to the objective; the means should impair the right or freedom as little as possible; and, there must be some proportionality between the objective and the effects of the limitation.

In *R. v Keegstra*[13] section 1 was described as having a dual function – the guarantee of rights and the placing of limits upon them – which have in common the underlying values of a free and democratic society. Some of these values were described in *Oakes*[14] as respect for the inherent dignity of the human person, commitment to social justice and equality, accommodation of a wide variety of beliefs, respect for cultural and group identity, and faith in social and political institutions which enhance the participation of individuals and groups in society.

It has been argued that section 27, in conjunction with section 1, might justify a limitation on a constitutional right in order to permit the protection or enhancement of the multiculturalism nature of our society (Magnet 1989; Gibson 1990). It could also be argued that section 27 could affect section 1 limits in preventing the imposition of limitations adversely affecting Canada's multicultural character (Gibson 1990). The problem is that collective rights, in the case of groups exercising semi-autonomous power, could alter the minimum standards of respect for individual rights in order to preserve the special characteristics of the group. Whether this is to be done, how and in what circumstances is, as yet, an unconfronted challenge.

ACCESS TO JUSTICE

A recent report and bibliography prepared for the Department of Justice, Canada provides a major contribution to Canadian legal research on multiculturalism (Etherington 1991). That report examined the range of issues connected with access to justice and multiculturalism in order to identify existing research, issues on which research is required, possible research methodologies and issues on which research is sufficient to warrant policy development, and implementation or institution of pilot projects.

That report remarked upon the general lack of legal research and, in particular, empirical research exploring multiculturalism and access to justice issues. It defines access to justice as going beyond procedural access to encompass a more fundamental analysis of the barriers to access created by the substance of laws, policies, and their relationships with social and political forces, in the context of race, gender, and ethnicity. It sees a growing concern developing with respect to access to justice issues because of a modern shift in focus from an interest in retention of cultural difference to an interest in equality and rights to full participation in Canadian society and institutions. That report suggested that cultural differences may operate as a factor to be considered in criminal cases in strengthening a traditional defence or excuse or may be recognized as a substantive defence in itself. Thus, the idea that cultural differences may affect criminal responsibility in a way somewhat analogous to the effect of the battered wife syndrome was raised in relation to the application of objective assessments of the reasonableness of an accused's conduct (Etherington 1991). However, the report urges that cultural differences must not be used to excuse violence against women and children. This issue also arises in the context of defences to civil law actions. The question of the significance which minority cultural differences or values should receive when they conflict with constitutional or majority values embedded in our legal system is only beginning to be addressed either in research or in caselaw.

Access to Criminal Justice

Empirical research has not proven that racial discrimination is a significant factor in the over-representation of Aboriginal people and members of visible minorities in the corrections system (Etherington 1991; Archibald 1989a; Laprairie 1990). This appears to arise, at least in part, from a lack of empirical research and statistical data (Clark 1989; Clairmont 1989). However, there is also a developing focus on incidence of crime and offence patterns as well as on broader socio-economic and political structures to explain the overrepresentation (Archibald 1989a; Laprairie 1990).

Empirical research on policing issues is lacking although one study exists which examines police hiring practices for compliance with Charter and human rights statutes (Jain 1988). Recent judicial inquiries have recommended police training in cross-cultural or race relations issues and have made recommendations aimed at controlling the impact of prosecutorial discretion on racial and cultural minorities (Marshall Commission 1989). Empirical research, however, is not available (Etherington 1991).

The Law Reform Commission of Canada has reported on the extent to which criminal procedures ensure that Aboriginal persons or members of cultural or religious minorities have equal access to justice and are treated equitably and with respect (Law Reform Commission 1991). It is regrettable that the report of the study dealing with multicultural justice and the treatment of minorities was not released in spring 1992 as anticipated. Issues which could have been covered in that study remain, therefore, to be dealt with in the future.

Access to Civil Justice

Lack of research on the impact of cultural differences on access to justice in the civil law context has been noted (Etherington 1991). The area of family law is the area of civil law in which cultural differences and values may be expected to have the greatest impact precisely because this area deals with issues of great personal significance: adoption, child protection, custody and access, change of name, control and division of property, separation, spousal and child support, divorce, and nullity of marriage. The insensitivity with which child welfare laws have treated Aboriginal children and tribal entry into the field has been forcefully discussed (Carasco 1986; Monture 1986; MacDonald 1984, 1985). Issues arising out of cultural differences in minority communities in the areas of child protection (Pask & Jayne 1983, 1984a, b, c) and custody (Zemans 1983) have been reviewed with concern. The tension in this area lies between the recognition of a need for greater cultural sensitivity to cultural differences and the concern that some minority cultural values are in direct conflict with values already enshrined in human rights and Charter legislation (Etherington 1991).

It has been recognized by many immigrant and refugee aid groups that language and cultural differences can prevent minority group members from obtaining knowledge of their legal rights and obligations or from making efforts to enforce or to obtain legal protection from infringement of those rights (Bogart 1990). Although many specific instances exist in which public legal information is made available in non-official languages, no research has been found which surveys this across Canada. The extent or effectiveness of these efforts to provide minority language groups with access to legal information have not been studied.

There is much to be learned from the area of immigration and refugee law that is applicable to the general practice of law in a multicultural society. It is estimated that interpreters are used in 95 per cent of the hearings before the Convention Refugee Determination Division of the Immigration and Refugee Board of Canada. It is difficult to determine issues of credibility where the testimony is filtered through an interpreter and where meaning is dependent on cross-cultural understanding. The Board is in the process of developing a system of accreditation for interpreters; a training program in cross-cultural communication for members is under consideration (Law Reform Commission 1991). This experience can be helpful to other decision-makers in other fora.

HUMAN RIGHTS LEGISLATION:
MULTICULTURALISM AND THE WORKPLACE

An eminent authority in this area has described the fundamental transformation of human rights in Canada, since Confederation, as involving the recognition that the promotion of some human rights requires government intervention and not just government abstention; and that some freedoms must be restricted by increased responsibilities necessary to guarantee the rights of others (Tarnopolsky 1989). The meaning and long-term impact of these requirements is largely determined in the context of federal and provincial human rights statutes and the commissions which operate under them.

All human rights statutes in Canada prohibit discrimination on the basis of race (in the wide sense), colour, sex, marital status (or family status or civil status), and age. A variety of terms are used to refer to ancestry. Several provinces prohibit discrimination on the basis of political opinion or belief, disabilities or handicaps and Quebec has added sexual orientation to the list. The statutes all focus on public and private activities preventing equality of access to places, activities and opportunities (Tarnopolsky & Pentney 1985). Discrimination in the workplace, the concept of the employer's duty to reasonably accommodate the employee, are issues of importance in the area of multiculturalism (Ivankovitch 1987; Baker 1987; Woodward 1987; Etherington 1991).

The statutes and the commissions which operate under them have been forcefully criticized for politicization, lack of industry and lack of adequate remedies, among other things (Ruff 1989; Norman 1987). Concerns have been expressed about the difficulties of enforcing rights under human rights legislation because of cost, delays or power imbalances between employee and employer (Etherington 1991). The area of employment discrimination is one which many people see as of increasing importance and in which further analysis is required (Etherington 1991).

EMPLOYMENT AND PAY EQUITY

The federal Employment Equity Act[15] applies to all employers under federal jurisdiction with more than 100 employers. Employers are required to identify and eliminate employment practices not legally authorized which result in employment barriers against person in designated groups. They must set equity goals for the designated groups and report on their progress in achieving those goals. The Canadian Human Rights Commission reviews the reports and may initiate an investigation where there are reasonable grounds to believe that systemic discrimination exists. The Act has been strongly criticized in a number of quarters because of the limited coverage, lack of mandatory goals and timetables, and lack of standardized reporting requirements (National Association of Women and the Law 1991).

The concept of equal pay for work of equal value compares the 'value' of work as between dissimilar jobs. The Canadian Human Rights Act makes it a discriminatory practice to provide pay differentials between male and female employees performing work of equal value. Pay equity statutes in Manitoba, Ontario, Prince Edward Island and Nova Scotia prescribe technical standards to determine the methods of comparison of the value of work. A thoughtful analysis of the Ontario Pay Equity Act[16] provides one of the few works available in this area (McDermott 1990). It is recognized that immigrant women may be among the most disadvantaged groups in society where they are subject to double or triple discrimination on the basis of gender, race and ethnic origin (National Association of Women and the Law 1991). However, legal research dealing with the impact of these programs on visible minority women is not yet available.

There is tension between the perceived need to provide affirmative action through employment equity programs for disadvantaged groups and the concern that such programs may be unreasonable and unfair to others (Abella 1984). The statutory language establishing these programs and the defensive legal challenges which may be brought against them have been analyzed in detail (Juriansz 1989). Legislative change is necessary in order to remove the effectiveness of legal challenge to the progress of the program.

MULTICULTURALISM AND THE LEGAL PROFESSION

Issues in this area range from legal education to the practice of law. Law schools are concerned about the underrepresentation of Aboriginal people and other visible minorities in the student population, the profession, and the Bench (Mazer & Peeris 1990). Discussions have been ongoing within law schools concerning the need to integrate multicultural perspectives within the standard curriculum. Admissions policies have increased places available for Aboriginal or minority groups (Etherington 1991). Discussions concerning the need for similar approaches with regard to faculty recruitment are underway (Etherington 1991).

The Canadian Judicial Council and the Western Judicial Education Centre have been heightening judicial awareness of gender, minority, and aboriginal concerns. Some law schools and universities have been exploring the use of cross-cultural training for faculty and staff. Research on the value and impact of these programs is not yet available.

GENDER

Recent critiques of feminist thought have argued that feminist legal theory has focused on problems of White, middle-class women and has ignored the impact of laws and legal institutions on visible minority women. A recent excellent article by a law teacher at a Canadian law school argues that cultural diversity is a feminist issue and that feminist theories can be applied to issues of cultural diversity beyond the feminist movement (Duclos 1990). This article examines selected Canadian legal issues connecting feminism and culture.

These issues are just beginning to be examined in Canada; for example, the *Canadian Journal of Women and the Law* has devoted the first issue of 1993, 'Racism Talking Cult' to this discussion. This work has the potential to have a major impact in Canadian feminist legal theory. On the one hand, it asks us to consider the myriad of ways in which we all oppress each other (Duclos 1990; Monture 1986). On the other hand, feminism is directed towards exposing and reforming sexism. It does not necessarily or at all have an interest in preserving sexist cultural practices. Nonetheless, there is a connection which arises from the unifying commitment to ending oppression on the basis of difference. Research is only now addressing these exceedingly difficult questions.

FUTURE RESEARCH

The basic conflict inherent in the Charter has been defined as follows:

At the same time as the Canadian constitutional system recognizes a special need of Canadian minorities for group autonomy, commitment to a *Charter*-based system requires that groups exercising general governmental functions respect fundamental norms of due process, personal liberty and equality. Thus, the systems of individual and group rights in the *Charter* come squarely into conflict. There is no readily apparent doctrine to regulate this considerable difficulty.[17]

This challenge is the central focus of future research in the area of law and multiculturalism. Since many people have serious reservations about the notion of collective rights for minority groups, the question of the limits of multiculturalism permeates the area.

Although particular research questions have been raised under the topics dealt with in this paper, there are specific topics which deserve highlighting:
- What is the meaning of multiculturalism in section 27 of the Charter and with what rights does the section deal? Much work needs to be done on the development of consistent definitions.
- Where specific Charter rights exist, as with respect to language rights or aboriginal rights, will section 27 also apply?
- How will the equality guarantees in section 15 of the Charter interrelate with section 27? How will gender-based conflict be resolved: will the price of greater cultural autonomy for particular groups be adherence to externally imposed guarantees of gender equality and safety?
- What relationships between religion and multiculturalism and between religion and the state should exist, if any?
- How does the exercise of discretion in the criminal and civil justice systems affect members of racial and ethnic minorities?
- Pursuant to which laws and procedures does the state best make and enforce laws against racist incitement? Are current rules of evidence adequate? Does enforcement of such laws enhance the legitimacy of the groups against which the laws are enforced?

- What types, approaches and styles of cross-cultural training are most helpful to person in the Bar, Bench, professorate, and law enforcement areas?
- How shall particular attention be paid to the difficulties facing visible minority women in gaining access to Canadian institutions, employment and legal protections?
- What is the role of law reform in increasing or decreasing levels of tolerance and non-discrimination?
- What role should multiculturalism play in our education system?
- How shall the challenges between the concepts of employment equity and non-discrimination be resolved?

Finally, there is the challenge of the interdisciplinary nature of law and multiculturalism. Jurisprudence and research on many of the issues referred to throughout this paper is ultimately dependent upon the development of an evidential foundation. The challenge directed towards social scientists concerns their role in the development of that evidence. Lawyers, on the other hand, will have to develop a better understanding of the limitations of such evidence and the applications to which it can legitimately be put.

Canadian society is attempting to craft laws upholding the commitment of this society to tolerance and co-existence. The test of that commitment will ultimately be found in the role of law and legal institutions in making effective the notions of compromise and consensual change.

NOTES

This paper, prepared in the fall of 1991, has been, to the extent possible, brought up to date (fall 1993). Recent jurisprudential developments have not significantly affected the general discussion.

The author wishes to acknowledge the research assistance of Cheryl M. Hass, BA (Hons) RT, LLB, of the BC Bar, and of the following law students in the Faculty of Law, University of Calgary: R. Castis, J. Devlin, S. Hildebrandt.

1 *Canadian Charter of Rights and Freedoms*, Part I of the *Constitution Act*, 1982, being Schedule 6 of the Canada Act (UK), 1982, c.11
2 Charlottetown, 28 Aug. 1992
3 [1990] 3 SCR 697 at 757 per Dickson, CJ
4 *Big M Drug Mart*, [1985] 1 SCR 295 at 337–8
5 *Edwards Books*, [1986] 2 SCR 713 at 758

6 *Zylberberg et al.* v *Sudbury Board of Education* (1988), 29 OAC 23
7 *R.* v *Hothi et al.* (1985), 35 Man. R. (2d) 159 (CA) leave refused (1986) 43 Man. R. (2d) 240 (SCC).
8 *R.* v *Keegstra*, [1990] 3 SCR 697.
9 Can. T.S. 1970, No. 28, Art. 4
10 *A.G. Quebec* v *Quebec Association of Protestant School Boards* [1984] 2 SCR 66 at 79.
11 S.C. 1988, c. 38
12 [1986] 1 SCR 103
13 [1990] 3 SCR 697 per Dickson CJ, at 735–6
14 *Supra* note 10 at 136 per Dickson, CJ
15 R.S.C. 1985, (2nd Supp.), c.23
16 R.S.O. 1990, c. P.7.
17 J.E. Magnet, "Multiculturalism and Collective Rights: Approaches to s.27" in G.A. Beaudoin and E. Ratushny (eds), *The Canadian Charter of Rights and Freedoms* (Toronto: Carswell 1989), 739 at 774

BIBLIOGRAPHY

Abella, R. (1984). *Report of the Commission on Equality in Employment*. Ottawa: Supply and Services
– (1991). Equality and human rights In Canada: Coping with the new isms. University Affairs (June 1991)
Agarwal, N.C. (1990). Pay equity in Canada: Current developments. *Canadian Labour Law Journal*, 41:518
Anand, R. (1985). Ethnic equality. In A.F. Bayefsky and M. Eberts (eds), *Equality rights and the Canadian Charter of Rights and Freedoms* (p 81). Toronto: Carswell
André, I. (1990). The genesis and persistence of the Commonwealth Caribbean Seasonal Agricultural Workers Program in Canada. *Osgoode Hall Law Journal*, 28:243
Archibald, B.P. (1989a). Prosecuting officers and the administration of justice in Nova Scotia. Research Volume 6. Nova Scotia: Royal Commission on the Donald Marshall Prosecution
– (1989b). Sentencing visible minorities: Equality and affirmative action in the criminal justice system. *Dalhousie Law Journal*, 12:371–411
Asch, M. (1984). *Home and native land: Aboriginal rights and the Canadian Constitution*. Toronto: Methuen
Baker, G.B. (1987). The changing norms of equality in the Supreme Court of Canada. *Supreme Ct. Law Rev.*, 9:497

Barry, J.P. (1983). The integration of the French and English languages into the justice system in New Brunswick. *Revue Generale de Droit*, 14:253–63

Bartlett, R.H. (1978). The Indian Act of Canada. *Buffalo Law Review*, 27:581

– (1983). Survey of Canadian law: Indian and Native law. *Ottawa Law Review*, 15:431–502

Bastarache, M. (ed.) (1987). *Language rights in Canada*. Translated by Translation Devirat. Montreal: Editions Yvon Blais

– (1989). Education rights of provincial official language minorities. In G.A. Beaudoin and E. Ratushny (eds), *The Canadian Charter of Rights and Freedoms* (pp 687–705). Toronto: Carswell

Bayefsky, A. (1980). *The Jamaican Women* case and the Canada Human Rights Act: Is government subject to the principle of equal opportunity? *UWOL Rev.*, 18:461–92

– , and Eberts, M. (eds) (1985). *Equality rights and the Canadian Charter of Rights and Freedoms*. Toronto: Carswell

Beatty, D., and Kennett, S. (1988). Striking back: Fighting words, social protest and political participation in free and democratic societies. *Canadian Bar Review*, 67:573–621

Beaudoin, G.A. (1979). Linguistic rights in Canada. *Freedom*, 197–207

– , and Ratushny, E. (eds) (1989). *The Canadian Charter of Rights and Freedoms*, 2nd ed. Toronto: Carswell

Beckton, C. (1987). Section 27 and Section 15 of the Charter. In Canadian Human Rights Foundation (ed.) *Multiculturalism and the Charter: A legal perspective* (p 1). Toronto: Carswell

– (1989). Freedom of expression. In G.A. Beaudoin and E. Ratushny (eds), *The Canadian Charter of Rights and Freedoms* (pp 195–225). Toronto: Carswell

Berger, T.R. (1985). The Charter and Canadian identity. *UWOL Rev.*, 23:1

Berlin, M.L., and Pentney, W.F. (1987). *Human rights and freedoms in Canada, cases, notes and materials*. Toronto: Butterworths

Bershad, L. (1985). Discriminatory treatment of the female offender in the criminal justice system. *UBC Law Rev.*, 26,:389

Blache, P. (1986). Affirmative action: To equality through inequalities? In J.M. Weiler and R.M. Elliot (eds), *Litigating the values of a nation: The Canadian Charter of Rights and Freedoms*. Toronto: Carswell

Bogart, W.A. and Vidmar, N. (1990). Problems and experiences with the Ontario civil justice system: An empirical assessment. In A.C. Hutchinson (ed.), *Access to civil justice* (p 1). Toronto: Carswell

Bold, M. (1986). Some formative issues in litigating equality. In L. Smith (ed.), *Righting the balance: Canada's new equality rights* (pp 243–54). Saskatoon: Canadian Human Rights Reporter

Bowlby, J.D. (1981). Conference on the cost of justice. *Canada Legal Aid Bulletin*, 4:13–29

Braën, A. (1987). Language rights. In M. Bastarache (ed.), *Language rights in Canada* (pp 1–63). Montreal: Editions Yvon Blais

Braun, S. (1987). Social and racial tolerance and freedom of expression in a democratic society: Friends or foes? *Regina* v. *Zundel. Dalhousie Law Journal*, 11:471

Brantingham, P.L. (1985). Judicare counsel and public defenders: Case outcome differences. *Can. Jour. of Criminology*, 27:67–82

Brownlee, B. (1991). Law and the immigrant: Beyond misunderstanding. *Law Now*, 15(10):6–9

Burns, P., and Reid, R.S. (1981). Delivery of criminal legal aid services in Canada: An overview of the continuing 'judicare versus public defender' debate. *UBC Law Rev.*, 15:403–29

Canada (1982). *Race relations and the law – Report of a symposium held in Vancouver*. Vancouver: Ministry of State for Multiculturalism

Canadian Bar Association (1984). *Report of the Special Committee on Racial and Religious Hatred*. Toronto: Canadian Bar Association

Canadian Bar Association of Ontario (1987). Submission to the Standing Committee on the Administration of Justice of the Legislative Assembly of Ontario Re: Bill 42, An Act to Regulate the Activities of Paralegal Agents. Toronto: Canadian Bar Association of Ontario

Canadian Human Rights Commission (1982). *Canadians and discrimination: An analysis of the 1981 opinion poll*. Ottawa: Minister of Justice

Canadian Human Rights Foundation (ed.) (1987). *Multiculturalism and the Charter: A legal perspective*. Toronto: Carswell

Canadian Institute for the Administration of Justice (1989). *Discrimination in the law and the administration of justice*. Kananaskis, Alberta: Canadian Institute for the Administration of Justice

Carasco, E. (1986). Canadian native children: Have child welfare laws broken the circle? *Canadian Journal of Family Law*, 5:111–38

Carter, R. (1973). Legal studies for Native people. *Canadian Bar Journal (Nova Scotia)*, 4:6–8

Castel, J. (1988). *Conflict of laws*, 6th ed. Toronto: Butterworths
– (1990). Discerning justice for battered women who kill. *University of Toronto Faculty of Law Review*, 48:229

Cheung, Y.W. (1980). Explaining ethnic and racial variations in criminality rates. *Canadian Criminal Forum*, 3:1–14

Christopher, T.C. (1991). Multiculturalism. *Law Now*, 15(10):10, 15

Chunn, D.E. (1987). Regulating the poor In Ontario: From police courts to family courts. *Canadian Journal of Family Law*, 6:85–102

Clairmont, D., Barnwell, W., and O'Malley, A. (1989). Appendix 4. Sentencing disparity and race in the Nova Scotia criminal justice system. In W. Head and D. Claimont, *Discrimination against blacks in Nova Scotia: The criminal justice system*. Research Study Volume 4. Nova Scotia: Royal Commission on the Donald Marshall Prosecution

Clark, D.H. (1989). *Sentencing patterns and sentencing options relating to Aboriginal offenders*. Ottawa: Department of Justice

Continuing Legal Education Society of British Columbia (1989). *Immigration and Multiculturalism*. Materials prepared for a seminar, Vancouver: Continuing Legal Education Society of British Columbia

Cotler, I. (1985). Hate literature. In Abella, R.S., and Rothman, M.L. (eds), *Justice beyond Orwell* (p 117). Montreal: Éditions Yvon Blais

– (1989). Freedom of conscience and religion. In G.A. Beaudoin and E. Ratushney (eds) *The Canadian Charter of Rights and Freedoms* (pp 165–93). Toronto: Carswell

– , and Marx, H. (eds) (1977). *The law and the poor in Canada*. Montreal: Black Rose Books

Dandurand, Y. (1974). Ethnic group members and the correctional system: A question of human right. *Canadian Journal of Correction*, 22:35–52

Darville, R. and Hiebert, M. (1985). *Small claims court materials: Can they be read? Can they be understood?* Ottawa: Canadian Law Information Council

Deloria, S. (1974). Legal education and Native people. *Saskatchewan Law Review*, 38:22–39

Dickson, B. (1984). The path to improving the accessibility of the law in Canada. *Provincial Judges Journal No. 4, 8*:2–6

Didier, E. (1987). The private law of language. In M. Bastarache (ed.), *Language rights in Canada* (pp 317–443). Montreal: Éditions Yvon Blais

Douyon, E., and Normandeau, A. (1990). Justice and ethnic minorities: An international selective bibliography. *Can. Jour. of Criminology*, 32:661

Duclos, N. (1990). Lessons of difference and feminist theory on cultural diversity. *Buffalo Law Review, 38*:325

Duncan, G.A. (1979). Public access to law in the '80's: Current trends in broadening public access. *Saskatchewan Law Review, 44*:123–9

Duncanson, I., and Kernvish, V. (1986). The reclamation of civil liberty. *Windsor Yearbook of Access to Justice, 6*:3–35

Eberts, M. (1987). Risks of equality litigation. In S.L. Martin and K.E. Mahoney (eds), *Equality and judicial neutrality* (pp 89–105). Toronto: Carswell

Estey, W. (1981). Who needs court? *Windsor Yearbook of Access to Justice,* 1:263–80

Etherington, B. (1991a). Religion and the duty of accommodation. *Canadian Labour Law Journal,* 1:51

Etherington, B., Bogart, W.A., Irish, M., and Stewart, G. (1991). *Preserving
identity by having many identities: A report on multiculturalism and access to
justice.* Windsor: Faculty of Law, University of Windsor

Foucher, P. (1985). *Constitutional language rights of official language minorities in
Canada.* Ottawa: Canadian Law Information Council, Supply & Services

– (1987). Language rights and education. In M. Bastarache (ed.), *Language rights
in Canada.* Montreal: Éditions Yvon Blais

Friedmann, K.A. (1970). The Alberta ombudsman. *U of T Law Journal,* 20:48

– (1979). The ombudsman in Nova Scotia and Newfoundland. *Dalhousie Law
Journal,* 5:471–93

Gall, G.L. (1986). Some miscellaneous aspects of section 15 of the Canadian
Charter of Rights and Freedoms. *Alta. Law Rev.,* 24:462

– (1987). Multiculturalism and the fundamental freedoms: Section 27 and
section 2. In Canadian Human Rights Foundation (ed.) *Multiculturalism and
the Charter: A legal perspective* (p 29). Toronto: Carswell

Gavigan, S.A.M. (1989). Petit treason in eighteenth century England: Women's
inequality before the law. (Special Issue: Women and Crime). *Can. Jour. of
Women and the Law,* 3:335

Gibson, D. (1984). Legal procedure: Access to justice; 1883–1983. *Dalhousie Law
Journal,* 9:3–30

– (1985). Protection of minority rights under the Canadian Charter of Rights
and Freedoms: Can politicians and judges nring harmony? In N. Nevitte and
A. Kornberg (eds), *Minorities and the Canadian state* (p. 31). Oakville: Mosaic
Press

– (1990). *The law of the Charter: Equality rights.* Toronto: Carswell

Gold, N. (1979). Legal education, law and justice: The clinical experience.
Saskatchewan Law Review, 44:97–122

Greenawalt, K. (1986). A neighbor's reflections on equality rights. In L. Smith
(ed.), *Righting the balance: Canada's new equality rights* (pp 189–213). Saskatoon:
Canadian Human Rights Reporter

Harris, M. (1986) *Justice denied: The law vs Donald Marshall.* Toronto: Macmillan

Hathaway, J.C. (1989). Postscript: Selective concern: An overview of refugee
law in Canada. *McGill Law Journal,* 34:354–57

– (1991) *The law of refugee status.* Toronto: Butterworths

Head, I.L. (1964). The stranger in our midst: A sketch of the legal status of the
alien in Canada. *Canada Yearbook of International Law,* 2:107

Head, W., and Claimont, D. (1989). *Discrimination against blacks in Nova Scotia:
The Criminal Justice System.* Research Study Volume 4. Nova Scotia: Royal
Commission on the Donald Marshall Prosecution

Henkel, W. (1989). A commentary on French language rights in prosecution of
provincial offences in Alberta. *Alberta Law Review,* 27:302–8

Hogg, P.W. (1982). *Canada Act, 1982 Annotated*. Toronto: Carswell Co.

Hucker, J. (1975). Immigration, natural justice and the Bill of Rights. *Osgoode Hall Law Journal, 13*:649–92

Hudson, M.R. (1987). Multiculturalism, government policy and constitutional enshrinement: A comparative study. In Canadian Human Rights Foundation (ed.), *Multiculturalism and the Charter: A legal perspective* (pp 59–122). Toronto: Carswell

Hurwitz, P. (1989). The new detention provisions of the Immigration Act: Can they withstand a Charter challenge? *University of Toronto Faculty of Law Review, 47*:587–606

Ianni, R.W. (1983). Are lawyers failing to meet the existing demand for legal services? *Canada–United States Law Journal, 6*:152–60

Ivankovich, I.F. (1986). Prolonging the Sunday closing imbroglio: *Regina* v *Videoflicks Ltd. Alta. Law Rev.*, 24:334

Jackman, M. (1988). The protection of welfare rights under the Charter. *Ottawa Law Review, 20*:257–338

Jackson, E. (1973). *Visible minorities in Nova Scotia: A call for equality*. Halifax: Nova Scotia Human Rights Commission

Jackson, M. (1984). The articulation of Native rights in Canadian Law. *UBC Law Review, 18*:255–87

Jain, H.C. (1988). The recruitment and selection of visible minorities in Canadian police organizations, 1985 to 1987. *Canadian Public Administration, 31*:463

Janisch, H.N. (1981). Administrative tribunals in the 80's: Rights of access by groups and individuals. *Windsor Yearbook of Access to Justice, 1*:303–26

Juriansz, R.G. (1989). Employment equity and pay equity: A cursory review. In *Discrimination in the law and the administration of justice*. Kananskis, Alberta: Canadian Institute for the Administration of Justice

– (1989). Visible minorities and discrimination in Canada. In *Discrimination in the Law and the Administration of Justice*. Kananskis, Alberta: Canadian Institute for the Administration of Justice

Justice Reform Committee Report, The (1988). *Access to justice*. British Columbia: Queen's Printer for British Columbia

Kaiser, H.A. (1990). The aftermath of the Marshall Commission: A preliminary opinion. *Dalhousie Law Journal, 13*:364

Kallen, E. (1987). Multiculturalism, minorities and motherhood: A social scientific critique of section 27. In Canadian Human Rights Foundation (ed.), *Multiculturalism and the Charter* (pp 123–38). Toronto: Carswell

– (1989). *Label me human: Minority rights of stigmatized Canadians*. Toronto: University of Toronto Press

Keene, J. (1983). *Human rights in Ontario*. Toronto: Carswell

Kelly, I.F. (1974). The Bill of Rights, the Indian Act and equality before the law: The need for and the development of a 'reasonableness' test. *Queen's Law Journal*, 2:151–82

Knopff, R. (1985). Prohibiting systemic discrimination: Policy development of discontinuity? *Saskatchewan Law Review*, 50:121–40

Lange, D.J. (1981). Constitutional jurisprudence, politics and minority language rights. *Manitoba Law Journal*, 11:33–57

Laprairie, C.P. (1989). Some issues in Aboriginal justice research: The case of Aboriginal women in Canada. *Women and Criminal Justice*, 1:81–91

– (1990). The role of sentencing in over-representation of Aboriginal people in correctional institutions. *Canadian Journal of Criminology*, 32:429

Law Reform Commission of Canada (1987). Report No. 31, *Recodifying criminal law*. Ottawa: Law Reform Commission of Canada

– (1991). *The determination of refugee status in Canada: A review of the procedure (A preliminary study)*. Ottawa: Law Reform Commission of Canada

– (1991). Report No. 34, *Report on Aboriginal peoples and criminal justice: Equality, respect and the search for the justice*. Ottawa: Law Reform Commission of Canada

Lewis, C., and Clare, I. (1989). *Report of the Ontario Task Force on Race Relations and Policing*. Ontario: Solicitor General

Longstaffe, S.E., McRae, K.N., and Ferguson, C.A. (1987). Sexual abuse on Manitoba Indian reserves: Medical, social and legal issues and obstacles to resolution. *Health Law in Canada*, 8:52–7

Loree, D.J., and Murphy, C. (1987). *Community policing in the 1980's: Recent advances in police programs*. Ottawa: Solicitor General Canada

Lowry, D.R. (1972). A plea for clinical law. *Canadian Bar Review*, 50:183–212

Lyon, W. D. (1981). Bilingual trials in Ontario. *Provincial Judges Journal*, 12:261–70

MacBain, J. (1985). Reasonable apprehension of bias in statutory schemes: The case of the Canadian Human Rights Act. *Administrative Law Review*, 16:109

McCalla Vickers, J. (1987). In L. Smith (ed.), *Righting the balance: Canada's new equality rights* (pp 3–24). Saskatoon: Canadian Human Rights Reporter

McDermott, P.C. (1990). Pay equity in Ontario: A critical legal analysis. *Osgoode Hall Law Journal*, 28:381

MacDonald, J.A. (1983). The Spallumcheen Indian band by-law and its potential impact on Native child welfare policy in British Columbia. *Canadian Journal of Family Law*, 4:75–95

– (1985). Child welfare and the Native Indian peoples of Canada. *Windsor Yearbook of Access to Justice*, 5:285–305

MacDonald, R.A. (1976). The community law program at Windsor: An interim report. *Gazette*, 10:344–51

- (1979). Law schools and public legal education: The community law program at Windsor. *Dalhousie Law Journal*, 5:779–90
- (1988). *Legal bilingualism*. Toronto: Faculty of Law, University of Toronto
MacLeod Rogers, B. (1987). Access to administrative tribunals. In N.R. Finkelstein and B. MacLeod Rogers (eds), *Recent developments in administrative law.* Toronto: Carswell
McKenna, I. B. (1990). Pay equity and arbitral restrictions under the Public Service Employee Relations Act. *Alberta Law Review*, 28:690
MacPherson, J. (1986). Litigating equality rights. In L. Smith (ed.), *Righting the balance: Canada's new equality rights* (pp 231–41). Saskatoon: Canadian Human Rights Reporter
McSweeney, K. (1984). Ignorance is no excuse: The Ontario legal aid plans role in the delivery of public legal education and information through its clinic funding system. *Canadian Community Law Journal*, 7:115–27
Magnet, J.E. (1981). Language rights: Myth and reality. *Revue Générale de Droit*, 12:261–70
- (1981). Court-ordered bilingualism. *Revue Générale de Droit*, 12:237–44
- (1986). The future of official language minorities. *Les Cahiers de Droit*, 27:189–202
- (1986). Collective rights, cultural autonomy and the Canadian state. *McGill Law Journal*, 32:170
- (1987). Interpreting multiculturalism. In Canadian Human Rights Foundation (ed.), *Multiculturalism and the Charter: A legal perspective* (p 145). Toronto: Carswell
- (1989). Multiculturalism and collective rights: Approaches to s.27. In G.A. Beaudoin and E. Ratushny (eds), *The Canadian Charter of Rights and Freedoms* (pp 739–80). Toronto: Carswell
Mahoney, K., and Cameron, J. (1988). Language as violence v freedom of expression: Canadian and American perspectives on group defamation. *Buffalo Law Review*, 37:337
- , and Martin, S. (eds), *Equality and judicial neutrality* (pp 391–401). Toronto: Carswell
Maloney, A. (1979). The ombudsman idea. *UBC Law Review*, 13:380–400
Mandel, M. (1985). Democracy, class and the national parole board. *Crim. LQ*, 27:159
- (1989). *The Charter of Rights and the legalization of politics in Canada*. Toronto: Wall & Thompson
Marchessault, J.G. (1979). Constitutional aspects of legal services in Canada. *Canada Legal Aid Bulletin*, 3:282–98
Martinson, D. (1990). *Lavallee v R.* – The Supreme Court of Canada addresses gender bias in the courts. *UBC Law Rev.*, 24:381

Mazer, M., and Peeris, R. (1990). *Access to legal education in Canada*. A study prepared at the University of Windsor for presentation at the Conference on Minority Access to Legal Education, 8 Nov. 1990, Ottawa

Monture, P.A. (1986). Ka-Nin-Geh-Heh-Gah-G-Sa-Nonh-Yah-Gah. *Canadian Journal of Women and the Law*, 2:159

– (1989). A vicious circle: Child welfare and First Nations. *Canadian Journal of Women and the Law*, 3:1

Moodley, K.A. (1984). The predicament of racial affirmative action: A critical review of equality now. *Queen's Quarterly*, 91:795

Moon, D. (1988). Discrimination and its justification: Coping with equality rights under the Charter. *Osgoode Hall Law Journal*, 28:673–712

Morrison, I. (1988). Security of the person and the person in need: S. 7 of the Charter and the right to welfare. *Journal of Legal and Social Policy*, 4:1–324

Morse, B.W. (1976). Native people and legal services in Canada. *McGill Law Journal*, 22:504–40

Mossman, M. J. (1983). Community legal clinics in Ontario. *Windsor Yearbook of Access to Justice*, 3:375–402

– , and Lightman, E.S. (1986). Towards equality through legal aid in Canada. *Journal of Canadian Studies No. 2*, 21:96–110

Murray, P. (1969). The uses of the French language in criminal courts outside Quebec: S. 11 of Bill c-120. *University of Toronto Faculty of Law Review*, 27:87

National Association of Women and the Law (1991). *A brief on employment equity*. Ottawa: National Association of Women and the Law

Nevitte, N., and Kornberg, A. (eds) (1985). *Minorities and the Canadian state*. Oakville: Mosaic Press

Newman, W.J. (1989). Language difficulties facing tribunals and participants: The approach of the new Official Languages Act. In *Discrimination in the law and the administration of justice*. Kananskis, Alberta: Canadian Institute for the Administration of Justice

Norman, K. (1987). Problems in human rights legislation and administration. Incomplete

Normandeau, A. (1989). The myth of a racist criminal – Justice system – Special review. *Canadian Journal of Criminology*, 31:591

Odsen, B.V. (1987). The need for pro bono programs in Alberta. *Journal of Law and Social Policy*, 2:93–117

O'Toole, C., and Ifejika, S. (1986). The police officer and incidents of discrimination. In Cryderman, B.K. (ed.) *Police, race and ethnicity: A guide for law enforcement* (pp 97–104). Toronto: Butterworths

Owen, S. (1990). The expanding role of the ombudsman in the administrative state. *University of Toronto Law Jour.*, 40:670

Pask, E.D., and Jayne, A. (1984a). Child protection issues among the Indo-Chinese refugees. In Connell-Thouez, K. and Knoppers, B.M. (eds), *Contemporary trends in family law: A national perspective* (pp 167–88). Toronto: Carswell

– (1984b). Part Four: Legal issues. In *Unaccompanied children in emergencies: The Canadian experience* (pp 137–269). Downsview, ON: York University, Refugee Documentation Project, July 1984

– (1984c). Resettlement of minor refugees: Some interdisciplinary issues. *Canadian Journal of Family Law*, 4:275–92

Pay Equity Commission, (1988). *Pay equity implementation series.* Toronto: Pay Equity Commission

Pentney, W.F., and Tarnopolsky, W. (1985). *Discrimination and the law.* Ontario: Richard De Boo

Petter, A. (1985). Not 'never on a Sunday': R. v *Videoflicks Ltd. et al. Sask. Law Review*, 49:96

Phenix, M.A. (1965). The public defender. *Saskatchewan Bar Review*, 30:110

Poulantzas, N.M. (1985). Multiculturalism, affirmative action programs under the Canadian Charter of Rights and Freedoms and the protection of minorities. *Rev. de Droit International*, 73:309

Ratushney, E. (1987). The need for a common perception of human rights in a world of diversity: A Canadian perspective. *Les Cahiers de Droit*, 28: 487–500

Read, R.F. (1970). Bias and the tribunals. *University of Toronto Law Journal*, 20:119

Regel, A.R. (1984). Hate propaganda: A reason to limit freedom of speech. *Sask. Law Review*, 49:303

Renner, K.E., and Warner, A.H. (1981). The standard of social justice applied to an evaluation of criminal cases appearing before the Halifax courts. *Windsor Yearbook of Access to Justice*, 1:62

Royal Commission on the Donald Marshall Jr. Prosecution (8 volumes). Halifax, NS: Royal Commission

Ruff, K. (1989). Critical survey of human rights acts and commissions in Canada. In *Discrimination in the law and the administration of justice.* Kananskis, Alberta: Canadian Institute for the Administration of Justice

Ryan, J., and Ominayak, B. (1987). The cultural effects of judicial bias. In S. Martin and K. Mahoney (eds), *Equality and judicial neutrality* (pp 346–57). Toronto: Carswell

Sanders, D. (1964). The Hutterites: A case study of minority rights. *Canadian Bar Review*, 42:225

– (1987). Article 27b and the Aboriginal peoples of Canada. In Canadian

Human Rights Foundation (ed.), *Multiculturalism and the Charter: A legal perspective* (p 157). Toronto: Carswell
- The renewal of Indian special status. In A. Bayefsky and M. Eberts (eds), *Equality rights and the Canadian Charter of Rights and Freedoms* (pp 529–63). Toronto: Carswell
Savage, H. (1978). Towards bridging the gap between legal services and legal education: Model projects in Native communities. *Canadian Community Law Journal*, 2:46–53
Savage, I. (1985). Systemic discrimination and s.15 of the Charter. *Saskatchewan Law Review*, 50:141–68
Schmeiser, D.A. (1987). Multiculturalism in Canadian education. In Canadian Human Rights Foundation (ed.), *Multiculturalism and the Charter: A legal perspective* (p 167). Toronto: Carswell
Schneiderman, D. (ed.) (1991). *Freedom of expression and the Charter*. Toronto: Carswell
- (ed.) (1991). *Language and the state*. Edmonton: National Conference on Constitutional Affairs, 1989
Sellers, E.A. (1986). Constitutionally entrenched linguistic minority rights: The Forest and Blaikie decision. *Manitoba Law Journal*, 15:257–70
Seward, S.B. and McDade, K. (1988). *Immigrant women in Canada: A policy perspective*. Ottawa: Canadian Advisory Council on the Status of Women
Seydegart, M. (1986). Introduction. Activating the equality promise: An exercise in democracy. In L. Smith (ed.), *Righting the balance: Canada's new equality rights*. Saskatoon: Canadian Human Rights Reporter
Sheehy, E.S. (1989). Canadian judges and the law of rape: Should the Charter insulate bias? *Ottawa Law Review*, 21:741
Sheppard, C. (1971). *The law of languages in Canada*. Royal Commission on Bilingualism and Biculturalism
Shetreet, S. (1979). The administration of justice: Practical problems, value conflicts and changing concepts. *UBC Law Review*, 13:52–80
Slattery, B. (1984). The hidden constitution: Aboriginal rights in Canada. *American Journal of Comparative Law*, 32:361–91
Smandych, R.C., Matthews, C.J., and Cox, S.J. (1987). *Canadian criminal justice history: An annotated bibliography*. Toronto: University of Toronto Press
Smith, L., ed. (1986). *Righting the balance: Canada's new equality rights*. Saskatoon: Canadian Human Rights Reporter
Special Committee on Hate Propaganda in Canada (1966). *Report of the Special Committee on Hate Propaganda in Canada* (Cohen Committee Report). Ottawa: Queen's Printer
Special Committee on the Participation of Visible Minorities in Canadian Society (1984). *Equality now!*. Ottawa: Supply and Services

Special Parliamentary Committee on Visible Minorities in Canadian Society,
Report of the. (1985). *Response of the Government of Canada to equality now.*
Ottawa: Supply and Services

Tanny, L.M. (1967). Ethnocentric discrimination and freedom of contract in a
changing social climate. *McGill Law Journal, 13*:186

– (1983). The equality rights in the Canadian Charter of Rights and Freedoms.
Can. Bar Rev., 61:242

– (1985). The effect of section 27 on the interpretation of the Charter. In T.
Yedlin (ed.), *Central and East European ethnicity in Canada: Adaptation and
reservation* (p 1). Edmonton: Central and East European Studies Society of
Alberta

– (1985). Equality and discrimination. In R.S. Abella and M.L. Rothman (eds),
Justice beyond Orwell (p 267). Montreal: Yvon Blais

– (1986). Ways for insuring the protection of minorities. *Les Cahiers de Droit,*
27:155–60

– (1987). The evolution of judicial attitudes. In S. Martin and K. Mahoney,
Equality and judicial neutrality (pp 378–90). Toronto: Carswell

– (1989). Discrimination in Canada: Our history and our legacy. In *discrimination in the law and the administration of justice.* Kananaskis, Alberta: Canadian
Institute for the Administration of Justice

Tarnopolsky, W.S. and Beaudoin, G. (eds) (1982). *Canadian Charter of Rights and
Freedoms: Commentary.* Toronto: Carswell

Tarnopolsky, W.S., and Pentney, W.F., (1985). *Discrimination and the law.*
Toronto: Richard DeBoo

Tarnopolsky, W.S. (1982). The equality rights (ss. 15, 27 and 28). In W.S. Tarnopolsky and G.A. Beaudoin (eds), *The Canadian Charter of Rights and Freedoms:
Commentary* (p 395). Toronto: Carswell

Task Force on Access to the Professions and Trades in Ontario, Report of the.
(1989). *Access!* Ontario: Ministry of Citizenship and Culture

Thompson, R. (ed.) (1987). *The rights of indigenous peoples in international law:
Selected essays on self-government.* Saskatoon: University of Saskatchewan
Native Law Centre

Thornhill, E. (1985). Focus on black women! *Can. J. of Women and the Law, 1*:153

Tom, W.C.Y. (1990). Equality rights in the federal independent immigrant
selection criteria. *Les Cahiers de Droit, 31*:477

Trembray, A., and Bastarache, M. (1989). Language rights (Sections 16–22). In
G.A. Beaudoion and E. Ratushny (eds), *The Canadian Charter of Rights and
Freedoms* (pp 653–85). Toronto: Carswell

Turner, J.N. (1970). Justice for the poor; The courts, the poor and the administration of justice. *Canadian Journal of Corrections, 12*:1

Ungerleider, C.S. (1985). Police intercultural education: Promoting understanding and empathy between police and ethnic communities. *Canadian Ethnic Studies, 17,* 51–66

– , and McGregor, J. (1990). *Police and race relations literature review, Appendix 1 in Race Relations Training Review.* Ontario: Solicitor General

Van Horne, W.A., and Tonneson, T.V. (eds) (1983). *Ethnicity, law and the social good.* Milwaukee: UW System American Ethnic Studies Coordinating Committee

Vidmar, N., and Melnitzer, J. (1984). Juror prejudice: An empirical study of a challenge for cause. *Osgoode Hall Law Journal, 22:*487

Wakeling, T.W. (1976). A case for the neighbourhood legal assistance clinic. *Queen's Law Journal, 3:*99–125

Whyte, J.D. (1974). The *Lavell* case and equality in Canada. *Queen's Quarterly, 81:*28

Wilson, L.C., and Mazer, B.M. (1978). Prepaid legal services come to Canada. *Gazette, 12:*366–76

– , and Wydrzynski, C.J. (1978). Prepaid legal services: Legal representation for the Canadian middle class. *U of T Law Journal, 28:*25–74

Winter, F. (1980). Legalese, bafflegab and 'plain language' laws. *Canadian Community Law Journal, 4:*5–14

Woehring, J. (1985). Minority cultural and linguistic rights and equality rights in the Charter. *McGill Law Journal, 31:*50–92

Woloshyn, D.F. (1987). *Canadian compliance with international law respecting the right of asylum of refugees.* Ottawa: National Library of Canada

Woodward, M. (1987). A qualification on the duty of employers to accommodate religious practices: *Bhinder v CNR UBC Law Review, 21:*471

Wydrzynski, C.J. (1979). Access to the legal system: The emerging concept of prepaid legal services. *Canadian Community Law Journal, 3:*47–56

Zemans, F.H. (1979). Legal aid and legal advice in Canada: An overview of the last decade in Quebec, Saskatchewan and Ontario. *Canadian Legal Aid Bulletin, 3:*155–201

– (1983). The issue of cultural diversity in custody disputes. *Reports of Family Law* (2d) 32:50

Zlotkin, N.K. (1984). Judicial recognition of Aboriginal customary law in Canada: Selected marriage and adoption cases. *Canadian Native Law Reporter, 4:*1–17

ANTHONY W. RASPORICH

Ethnicity in Canadian Historical Writing 1970–1990

Ethnic historiography in Canada has come of age. Whether that age is one of bronze, silver, or gold is yet to be determined by posterity, but it is by now a prominent feature of our intellectual landscape in Canada. By inference it would be wrong to consider the period prior to it one of the Dark Ages, for that would be to fall again into the familiar Whig trap of liberal historiography and its progressivist fallacy – all darkness before and ever-increasing light thereafter. One must remember that there were scholars, both professional and amateur, who pioneered this enterprise well before it was officially blessed with the imprimatur of state.

The renaissance of Canadian ethnic historiography was also a cultural artifact of the yeasty environment of the late 1960s when scholarly concerns with the limited political mandate of Canadian history created a demand for a broadened rubric which would include social history – women, labour, and ethnic groups. The birth of Canadian social history was accompanied by another negation, both popular and scholarly, in the anti-establishment cry against WASP control of Canadian society, ably documented in the scholarly classic by John Porter, *The Vertical Mosaic*, and in the rise of early Marxian polemics. Positive affirmation for a new vision of Canada, both past and present, was provided at the top echelon of Canadian society, in the Bilingual and Bicultural Commission's recommendations, particularly Book IV, *The Cultural Contributions of Other Ethnic Groups* (1970), which legitimized the contributions of the 'third force' in Canadian politics and society. That felicitous conjuncture of pluralism with biculturalism was enunciated in the multiculturalism policy officially unveiled in 1971 by Pierre Elliott Trudeau. This official thrust towards a new series of ethnic histories sponsored by the federal government was accompanied by a groundswell of popular interest in 'roots' and genealogy. Pride in one's ethnic heritage, slave, pauper, or other, ran to unprecedented levels in Canada, prompted by Canada's centennial in 1967 and by influences from the United States.

The recruitment of young professional historians to the task of defining and amplifying on the theme of ethnicity in Canadian history was not difficult. Scholars with previous interests and commitments saw and welcomed a new and more democratic social history in the making, and younger graduate students welcomed the professional opportunity to work at the cutting edge of a new national historiography. The professionalization and nationalization of ethnic historiography in the early seventies marked a sharp break or divide from the local, regional, and amateur enclaves which had previously protected and nurtured ethnic group histories and their records. 'Filiopietism' as the unqualified ancestor worship of the ethnic group and its past traditions came into disrepute, visibly so in the launching of the new Generations series of national ethnic group histories, which promised a departure from the self-promotional excesses embedded in previous group histories, and even in such officially sponsored works as *The Canadian Family Tree* (1979).

The Generations series followed a long and honourable tradition in Canadian historiography described in Berger's *The Writing of Canadian History* (1986), that is, the collective historical series. Beginning with such enterprises as The Makers of Canada and Canada and Its Provinces, the historical series caught hold in Canada, combining the publishers' sense of marketing with support from granting agencies and governments. Thus, the Generations series sponsored by the Secretary of State promised, and soon delivered, under the aegis of its co-editors, Burnet and Palmer, three histories by the mid-seventies. The series encountered some heavy critical resistance from both traditional historians and an emergent cadre of ethnic historians, particularly towards sociologists and other social scientists working in the vineyard of history. Some critical disdain was heaped on the concepts of 'official' and 'national' history, while other critics saw distinct limits to the notion of pluralist historiography. Yet, the series gradually gained both momentum and critical acceptance among its historian peers as it expanded to fourteen in number, including the fine overview volume by Burnet and Palmer (1988). Several volumes in the series, such as those on the Hungarians, Croatians, Chinese, and Ukrainians, were lauded for providing 'a broad picture of immigrant life in Canada. Their subjects are not cardboard cutouts, but real people with an historical presence. They move on a

Canadian stage and interact with their Canadian environment' (Perin 1990:208). The legitimization of ethnic historiography and a pluralistic view of the Canadian past came only gradually, reaching a watershed of recognition and acceptance by the early eighties (Morton 1981).

This momentum was further recognized in the 1980s in the broader acceptance by scholarly journals of review articles on the field, and in the impact upon textual materials at both the university and secondary school levels (Perin 1990). A case in point was the pamphlet series launched by the Canadian Historical Association in the early eighties on various ethnic groups. Reaching some fourteen in number, this series did much to publicize the role of ethnic groups in Canadian history, and extended the bounds of ethnicity further by including more of the Anglo-Celtic group, when and where they were minorities. Also, such groups not featured in the Generations series such as the Jews, West Indians, Finns, Germans, Italians, and Belgians, were considered as a distinct historical group. Other textbook series aimed at secondary and even primary schools began to appear in various provincial jurisdictions, and occasional historical films appeared, for example in the shortlived Newcomers series sponsored by Imperial Oil in the 1970s. Also some titles appeared in the 1980s from the National Film Board and the provincial educational television channels such as TV Ontario and ACCESS in Alberta.

The further absorption of ethnicity into national historical conscious-ness was evident in the Canadian Social History Series, whose mandate was to explore 'neglected areas of the day-to-day existence of Cana-dians.' This series included several classics in ethnic historiography such as the doctoral theses of Avery (1979), on the European immigrant workers and labour radicalism from 1896 to 1912, and Howard Palmer's fine study of nativism in Alberta (1982). More recently, the comparative work by Ramirez (1991) discusses Italian immigrants and French Cana-dians as people on the move in the North Atlantic economy from 1860 to 1914. Similarly, Mariana Valeverde's discussion of moral reform (1991) explores the darker side of racism and its impact on Canadian immigra-tion policy in the early twentieth century.

Measured against the rapid and continuous output of ethnic histori-ography through collective series, the development of single scholarly books and monographs has been slower and less spectacular, although of high quality at its best. The latter half of the seventies appeared to favour more popular books such as Adachi's *The Enemy That Never Was* (1976). The early eighties proved to be a vital period of output, with the appearance of Abella and Troper's excellent volume on the exclusion of the European Jews (1982) and several others on specific groups. This rate of output continued into the latter half of the eighties with such books as Zucchi on Toronto (1988). Yet the total of singly published group histories still lagged behind the productivity of monographs published in national series noted above, or by provincially-based institutes noted below.

A classic example of the concentration of scholarly energy and prodigious output, fuelled by the talent and prodigious output of a single individual, can be seen in the accomplishments of the late Robert Harney of the Multicultural History Society of Ontario. His own high-quality essays on the subject of immigration history, urban history, and the history of Italians in Canada have sketched out a scholarly agenda that will stretch into the next century (Anctil & Ramirez 1991). Perhaps even more important than these contributions were the many monographs published by the MHSO, as well the many special issues of *Polyphony* edited by him (Perin 1990). These special issues devoted to Italians, Finns, Hungarians, Armenians, and Macedonians, and urban issues devoted to Thunder Bay, Sudbury, and Toronto were vital beginnings for further scholarship on ethnicity. Similarly, the conference series produced collections of essays such as *Little Italies in North America* (1981), on Toronto's ethnic neighbourhoods in the nineteenth and twentieth centuries (1986), and the two Finn Forum conferences which led to the *Finnish Diaspora I & II* volumes (1981). As noted above, Harney's guiding hand shaped a generation of young scholars on Italian-Canadian history such as Zucchi, Iacovetta, and Sturino, and several more on other ethnic groups as well, notably Patrias, Petroff, Lindstrom-Best, and Kaprelian. Indeed, the monograph series of the MHSO reflected this positive impact in the publication of fine microhistorical studies – such as Danys on postwar Lithuanian immigration (1986).

While Ontario and Toronto led the provinces in the historical definition and dissemination of ethnicity, other provincial and local initiatives were pursued, with varied results. In Quebec, the Institut Québécois de Recherche sur la Culture was established in 1977, and under the direction of Gary Caldwell in the eighties published several important research monographs, notably Anctil and Caldwell's monograph on the Jews in Quebec (1983). Anctil's presidency of the Canadian Ethnic Studies Association and hosting of the CESA biennial conference in Montreal in 1985 also resulted in a significant special issue of *Canadian Ethnic Studies/Études Ethniques au Canada* on ethnicity in Quebec (1986, no. 2). Other studies on Quebec have tended to concentrate on the phenomenon of anti-Semitism and the history of the Jews in Quebec. Similarly, other studies on ethnic groups in Montreal have gradually appeared, notably the Italians in the work of Ramirez (1981, 1984, 1990), Taschereau (1988), and the global work of Perin on the subject of church-state relations between the Vatican and Quebec, and the role of the church in immigrant life (Perin, 1984, 1990). Other groups which received greater attention were the Chinese of Montreal, Helly (1987), and a forthcoming study by Chan.

In Atlantic Canada, the field of ethnic history has been more fragmented, in part because of the relatively slower pace of urbanization and the dominance of Anglo-Celtic and Acadian populations. Certainly, very few historical monographs the equal of Bell's *Foreign Protestants of Nova Scotia* on the German population of Lunenburg and the South Shore have emerged in the seventies and eighties. The Blacks of Nova Scotia have received considerable analysis, but subsequently other groups such as the Syrians, Jews, Germans and Italians have received attention (Palmer 1990, Bumsted 1989). Other works appeared in the 1980s on various ethnic groups. Various ethnic groups and others such as the Irish of Halifax, the Scots and West Indians of Cape Breton, and the Greeks and South Asians of Halifax were featured in a special issue of *Canadian Ethnic Studies/Études Ethniques au Canada* (1988, no. 3). Other institutes and associations have sponsored the development of ethnic studies and history, notably the Beaton Institute in Cape Breton, which has conducted an intensive oral history program; the Society for the Study of Ethnicity in Nova Scotia (SSENS), and the International Education Centre, which publishes an 'Ethnic Heritage' series, ranging across Anglo-Celtic groups, but also including studies on Germans, East Indians, Vietnamese, and Italians. Also, the IEC conference proceedings of 1988 is a useful collection of papers on the connections between oral, labour, and ethnic history (Moore & Morrison 1988).

Western Canada has perhaps been the most fertile ground for the field of ethnic history, with various local and provincial institutes, museums, and organizations sponsoring programs from historic villages to archival and publications programs. This grass-roots phenomenon taken together promotes an historical self-consciousness among and across a wide variety of settler groups. History suffuses popular culture as amateur and professional historians meld together, not always harmoniously, in the promotion of their particular group, but also in the advancement of the pluralist ideal of shared power. Prominent among the promoters and builders of ethnicity and historical studies of ethnic groups have been Manoly Lupul, founder of the Canadian Institute of Ukrainian Studies in

Edmonton, and the late Howard Palmer, the inspirational builder of the Research Centre for Canadian Ethnic Studies at the University of Calgary and editor from 1974 to 1980 of the national journal, *Canadian Ethnic Studies/Études Ethniques au Canada* founded in 1968 (Palmer 1990) The many monographs sponsored by the Institute of Ukrainian Studies have etched that group's contributions into Canadian history, along with the Palmers' fine studies on Alberta ethnic groups (Palmers 1985). The jointly sponsored Alberta Oral History Project between the University of Calgary and the Glenbow Archives also promises to promote a greater level of understanding of ethnicity, labour history, and the history of settlement in Alberta. For many other generalists on western Canadian history, the concept of pluralism and ethnicity are now so ingrained that general historians like Gerald Friesen see ethnicity as inseparable from the fabric of western history itself. Perhaps more than in any other region of Canada, the interraction of rural, labour, and urban history work together to illumine common themes of rural-urban migration, spatial segregation, racism, and assimilation.

The collection of archival materials and oral histories has been one of the key achievements of the past two decades. As the stuff of history, such documentation forms the core of new interpretations and illumination of unknown aspects of ethnic groups' social history. The collection of a national archives of ethnic materials has not been without its critics, notably Harney's critique (1982) of a national 'skimming the cream' sources to Ottawa, which posited that, these 'highly perishable ethnocultural resources once at risk because of official neglect are now threatened by the chaos of competition between archives and other depositories,' and considered that they might be better left decentralized. Whatever the merits of his argument, organizations like the National Archives, the MHSO, the provincial archives, and various other specialized ethnic archives aggressively sought out the sources for ethnic history. At the national level, the impressive results of acquisition of Finnish, Ukrainian, Polish, German, and Jewish materials in particular is recorded in the finding aids prepared for these groups by Laine (1989), Momryk (1984), Grenke (1989), and Tapper (1987). These achievements have been paralleled by the acquisitions policy of various provincial archives and the MHSO, with the co-hosting in 1991 by the Archives of Ontario a state-of-the-art conference entitled, 'Preserving the Ethnic Record,' in three primary areas – women's history, labour history, and the media. Similar expansion of the ethnic archival record has been observed at the Provincial Archives of Nova Scotia and at several of the provincial archives in Ontario and the west (Haycock & Watson 1988; Szalasnyj 1986). The Glenbow Archives in particular co-sponsored the CESA conference at Calgary in 1989, and has been involved in the Alberta Oral History Project referred to above. Various special collections sections of university libraries have over the years acquired important collections of ethnic materials such as: the Doukhobor materials at UBC and Saskatchewan, the Finnish collection at Lakehead, and Icelandic materials at Manitoba.

Historical writing about ethnicity would not have rooted either without the rich interdisciplinary environment which nurtured it in the past two decades. The parallel growth of urban, labour, and feminist studies provided the context of scholarly linkages in the social sciences which elucidated the theme of ethnicity. The concurrent research pursued by political scientists, sociologists, anthropologists, psychologists, linguists, demographers, and others into ethnicity in a past context have deepened historians' understanding of such issues as class stratification, ethnography, demography, language retention, acculturation, and assimilation. In short, both historical questions and the intellectual tools required for their answers became more complex and sophisticated given the rich associations with other social science disciplines. Few historians of ethnicity can proceed with any confidence in the field without having read the work of other social scientists included in this volume.

The work of labour historians has been inextricably tied to ethnic history, as demonstrated in yeasty scholarship of the seventies on the subject of labour radicalism in western Canada (Bercuson 1978; Avery 1990). Much of this work culminated in the special issue on 'Labour Radicals' edited by Wilson and Dahlie, published by *Canadian Ethnic Studies* in 1978, and included articles on British, Norwegian, Croatian, Finnish, and Ukrainian labour radicals. As mainstream labour history turned leftwards with Marxian analysis of working-class culture, momentum on ethnic working-class history was lost for a brief period. But it picked up again shortly with work on Italian working-class activity in the work of Pucci and Potestio (1988), Ramirez (1986), and by mid-decade in the work of Radforth on the polyethnic workforce on the Ontario forest frontier (1987) and Seager on the mining frontier of the far west (1986). Microstudies by graduate students on mining communities in British Columbia and Alberta, as well as popular local histories such as Bowen's two local books on the Nanaimo coalfields (1982, 1988), all added to the complex mosaic of emerging ethno-labour studies in the eighties. Further work on the urban labouring class, such as Tulchinsky on the needle trades in Toronto (1990), and Robinson on the kosher meat wars in Montreal (1990) are evidence of a vital ethnic labour history in the making.

Perhaps the Italian worker has attracted more scholarly attention of late than other group with the work of Ramirez on Montreal (1980, 1986, 1991), Sturino on Italian rural migrant labour in the twenties (1985), Zucchi on the Italian working class of Toronto (1985, 1988), Iacovetta on postwar Italian working people in Toronto (1992), and Sestieri Lee on Yellowknife goldminers, *Canadian Ethnic Studies* (27, 1987). The other group to attract significant interest by labour and ethnic historians has been the Finns, whose various activities in left-wing political organizations and strike actions has been described in the Finn Forum conferences and volumes arising therefrom. Notably, articles by Krats and Jalava on the Sudbury mining community, and Eklund on the labour and cultural organizations of Finnish Canadians are featured in the most recent publication, *Finns in North America* (Karni 1988).

A similar rising wave of scholarship is apparent in women's history, although it has largely been confined to the last decade, since many works in the 1970s in women's history were devoted to Anglo-Canadian women. A special issue of *Canadian Ethnic Studies* 12(1), 1981) featured several new scholars, all of whom explored new dimensions of ethnicity and femininity in historical and contemporary contexts. Further collective efforts advanced the corpus of ethnic women's history, particularly the publication by the MHSO of Jean Burnet's edited collection (1986). Articles by Lindstrom-Best on Finnish domestics, and Iacovetta on the Italian *contadina* gave voice to previously muted women in the labour movement – in industry, in homes as domestics, and in the family. In a way, it crystallized work that had already been under way by such scholars as Barber on immigrant domestics in Ontario (1980), Jackel on British working women in the west (1982), and Silverman, who had interviewed many women of diverse ethnic origins and class backgrounds for her pioneering work on women in Alberta (1984, 1985).

The first book-length study to emerge on the subject of women in a single ethnic group was Lindstrom-Best's (1988), which carefully delineated the nature of Finnish women's work and their role in the radical movement. Other parallel studies on the radical movement as a whole by Sangster focused on Finnish, Jewish, and Ukrainian women and their role in the socialist and communist cause (1989). One of the key women's histories to be currently recorded is by Swyripa, whose research on the images, roles and myths in Ukrainian women's history has begun to appear in such articles on popular images of Ukrainian pioneer women (1989). Such studies on a wide range of women's ethnic groups, and their contributions to labour, family, education, and politics in Canada have firmly ensconced ethnic women in the scholarly agenda (Strong-Boag 1989; Iacovetta 1992).

The confluence of educational history with women's history and the history of the family has also produced some fruitful connections for mainstream Canadian social history (Wilson 1990). A similar conjuncture has existed between educational history and ethnicity since at least the early seventies. Once again, the leading edge in this field was provided by Palmer and Jaenen in a special issue of *Canadian Ethnic Studies* (VII, no. 1, 1986) devoted to education and ethnicity in Canada. Featuring articles on Hutterite, Doukhobor, and Jewish education, this issue also provided thoughtful articles on cultural pluralism and reflections on contemporary trends in the classroom. As Palmer observed (1982, 477–8), the tensions between majoritarian assimilation and minority cultural persistence meant that 'the educational history of western Canada is marked by sporadic conflict between minority groups, such as Doukhobors, Mennonites, Hutterites, Ukrainians and French Canadians, and Anglo-Canadian politicians, journalists and educators who were seeking to assimilate them to a new way of life.' Particular journals such as *Prairie Forum* also explored this bipolar tension in several articles, and in a special issue devoted to ethnicity on the prairies (*Prairie Forum*, Fall 1982). The same observation of majority-minority tensions in schooling may also be made of Quebec historiography on education in the eighties, particularly with reference to language policy. Works by Laferrière (1983) and Behiels (1986) explored the issue of minority group responses to schooling in the postwar era, and a wide range of specific group studies on the Italians, Jews, Haitians, Greeks, South Asians, and Vietnamese analyzed the responses of diverse groups to various language bills (see bibliography, Quebec special issue, *Etudes Éthniques au Canada* (*18*(2), 1986, 178–82). In short, western Canada and Quebec presented similar areas of historical and contemporary analysis of minority group responses to assimilationist thrusts by Anglo and French-Canadian majorities (Constantinides 1987; Rudin 1985; Behiels 1991).

The social forces which shaped the Canadian city from its inception also shaped ethnic groups, their families, their work, and their neighbourhoods. Once again, a collective publishing enterprise, The History of Canadian Cities, provided a common vehicle for discussion, however brief, on the role of ethnicity in the formation of the social character of the

Canadian city (Artibise). In the six cities covered in the series (Winnipeg, Calgary, Regina, Vancouver, Toronto, and Hamilton), the authors invariably included significant discussions of ethnic immigrant districts such as Winnipeg's north end, Regina's east end, Calgary's Bridgeland district, Toronto's Cabbagetown, Hamilton's Corktown, and Vancouver's Chinatown and east end. Similarly, other urban historians and geographers have explored the unique character of Chinese districts in Montreal (Helly 1987) and Victoria (Lai 1987).

Perhaps Toronto has received the greatest attention of all as an immigrant city, particularly after the popular volume by Harney and Troper (1975). Harney's edited volumes and occasional papers further developed his metier of urban ethnic historiography, culminating in his edited volume on ethnic neighbourhoods of Toronto (Harney 1986), and provided rich scholarly frescoes of Toronto's immigrant 'quarters' from the nineteenth century on. The authors featured in this volume (Speisman, Zucchi, Lindstrom-Best) either had written or would later write definitive single-volume studies on their groups in Toronto. Such studies ensure Toronto's dominance as a premier venue for urban ethnic studies, but other Ontario cities with large ethnic concentrations of population, such as Thunder Bay and Sudbury, were also drawn into the orbit of Harney and the MHSO, having special issues of *Polyphony* devoted to them. Subsequently a modest local output of scholarly and amateur scholarship has appeared elucidating the contributions of the Finnish-Canadians to these two cities and their regions (Metsaranta 1989; Harney 1981).

Other studies of urban racial incidents and racial prejudice have also forged a common bond between the urban and ethnic historian. Indeed, Camus' *The Stranger* and *The Plague* may be read as psychic beginnings to studying early Canadian responses to the cholera epidemic of 1832 and smallpox in 1847, as Irish plots upon native Canadian populations in Montreal and Toronto. Later responses, such as frontier Calgarians' riots against the Chinese as carriers of smallpox in 1892, were extensions of the same mentality (Bilson, Dawson). New variations appeared in the anti-Oriental riots of 1907 in Vancouver (Roy 1979), and in Vancouver's rejection of the *Komagata Maru* and its human cargo of 400 Sikhs in 1914 (Johnston 1979). These reactions set the pattern for later responses to East and South Asians, as has been so ably discussed in Ward (1978) and in an earlier work by Morton (1974). These works have led the way to a further discussion of the hostile response to the Japanese and their evacuation during the Second World War such as by Sunahara (1981).

The definition of racism has not, however, been exclusively urban, given the frontierist manifestations of anti-Semitism and anti-Chinese prejudice documented by Calderwood on the Ku Klux Klan on the Prairies in the twenties (1972, 1975) and more recently by Bercuson and Wertheimer on the Keegstra affair (1985). But the predominant flare-ups, particularly of anti-Semitism, have occurred in cities such as Toronto and Montreal (Levitt & Shaffir 1987; Rome 1977, 1986; Betcherman 1975; Anctil 1983). While the city has not been the cause it has often been the venue for the most severe expression of violent action against minorities, and confirms the existence of the darker side of violence in Canadian social history.

Another illuminating intersection of disciplines for the study of immigration and ethnicity in Canadian history has been history and political studies – from the formation of immigrant political communities, to the relationship of ethnic groups with the state and their participation in Canadian political parties and the electoral process. While some of these interrelationships have been touched upon elsewhere in this collection, it has been well covered in Howard Palmer's superb essay, 'Ethnicity and Politics in Canada, 1867–Present' (1990). In the area of immigration policy, several new studies served to update the overview of Canadian official policy by Freda Hawkins (1972, 1989), notably those on refugee policy by Dirks (1977), Adelman (1991), Abella and Troper (1982) on Jewish refugees in the thirties, and Chan and Indra on Vietnamese refugees (1987). The two most important books of the eighties to appear were by Barbara Roberts (1988) on the deportation of political radicals in the Great Depression and Reginald Whitaker's exposé of the exclusion of left-wing European immigrants and the admission of rightists and ex-Nazis in the postwar era (1987). Indeed, the entire area of ethnic historiography was massively affected by the left-right dualism imposed by the Second World War, as the postwar refugee movements dramatically altered the demography of Canada's European ethnic groups. The historical record of that tension can be seen in the recent histories of Baltic minorities such as the Lithuanians (Danys 1986) and the Estonians (Aun 1985), but also among the Ukrainians, where an entire generation of historiography was profoundly affected by the nationalist versus Communist debate. Similar tensions were observable among the Croatian, Serbian, and Yugoslav views (Rasporich, Skoric).

The impact of two world wars themselves on ethnic groups in Canada has raised the whole issue of the relationship between the state and suspect minorities within it well past the wars themselves. The watching of these groups by the state has been raised with reference to the Austro-

Hungarians, Germans, Finns, and Bolsheviks in the First World War (Avery, Morton, Swyripa, Thompson, Gerus). Particular objection was taken by the Ukrainians to their treatment during the war (Luciuk 1988). For the Italians and Germans, tensions among fascists and anti-fascists in the interwar years were well described in the historiography of the eighties (Wagner, McLaughlin, Perin, Liberati). But it is the Second World War that ignited the greatest discussion of the Canadian government's relations to minorities. The internment of minorities was detailed in an edited collection by Hillmer, Kordan, and Luciuk (1988), supplementing a series of books (Prymak 1988) and articles appearing during the eighties (Keyserlink 1984) and (Palmer 1982) on wartime treatment of Germans and Italians, and other detainees, such as the Communists (Swankey 1975). Among the latter, individuals like Repka (1982) and Krawchuk (1985) wrote memoirs about the internees and conditions in camps such as Kananaskis and Petawawa. Yet other studies focused on the plight of the Jewish refugees during the war (Draper 1983), buttressed by such personal memoirs as Eric Koch's (1980) reminiscence of the settlement via internment camps of 7000 Jewish refugees in Canada in 1940–1.

The group which elicited the greatest historiographical debate were the Japanese in the Second World War. Given the considerable historical sympathy with the Japanese because of their relocation, internment, and dispossession, it was a surprise to some to see senior historian Jack Granatstein enter the lists with a defence of Canada's relocation of the Japanese in 1942. Such disclaimers, however qualified, run against the grain of liberal orthodoxy, and for that matter, current government policy, which proffered an official apology and compensation for wartime treatment to the Japanese survivors. Lastly, a number of personal memoirs gave witness to the historians' accounts of their unfair and unjust treatment during the war (Ito, Nakano and Nakano, Nakayama, Broadfoot).

The other important dimension of ethnic groups' interrelation with politics and government was their political orientation and their participation in the Canadian political process. The common preference of pre-Second World War European immigrants for parties of the left has already been suggested in the discussion of labour radicalism above. Several political studies of the Canadian left appeared in the seventies and eighties, such as Avakumovic on the Communist party (1975), which discussed in considerable detail the party's ethnic composition. But other more recent accounts such as Angus (1981) on the early years of the party were less interested in the issue of ethnicity except as it directly affected party policy, as with the expulsion of the Finns and Ukrainians by the Buck-Smith Anglo-Canadian faction from 1929 to 1931. Other internal party histories (1982) were even less forthcoming, but there appeared in the late eighties a good concluding chapter by Penner (1988) entitled 'The Ethnic Question and the Communist Party' (pp 268–84). Further to this, there was significant debate, particularly within the Ukrainian group, between orthodox Communist interpretations of history in the Ukraine and Canada by Krawchuk (1979) and Kolasky's highly critical study of pro-Communist organizations (1979).

Entirely new perspectives were fortuitously brought to this debate in the eighties as the women of the Finnish and Ukrainian left were brought into the picture by Lindstrom-Best (1986, 1988) and by Sangster on women of the left (1989). These two authors also broadened the framework of the left to include socialism, particularly the latter, which examined the CCF's attempt to recruit among ethnic groups. Few other studies did, with the exception perhaps of Hoffman on the CCF in eastern Saskatchewan in 1934 (1982), and Milnor (1968) on the ethnic revolt in Saskatchewan from 1929 to 1938. Yet we know of the considerable involvement of the Jews on the left in the CCF, such as Louis Rosenberg of the CCF in Regina and of David Lewis, who noted in his memoir (1981) his constant search as national secretary of the CCF for organizers, who were 'fluent in French as well as English, and in German, Ukrainian, Polish, Russian, Yiddish,and other minority languages.' Among current political scientists who work on prairie socialism, only Nelson Wiseman appears to have paid much attention to ethnicity in his articles on Manitoba's Ukrainians between the wars (1987), and the strategy of the Manitoba CCF in the postwar period (1979), and more generally in his book on the Manitoba CCF/NDP (1985).

Curiously, the relationship of the two mainline Liberal and Conservative parties to ethnic power bases has almost escaped the notice of Canadian historians. With the exception of J.W. Brennan on the courting of the 'foreign vote' in Saskatchewan in the early twentieth century (1978), some acknowledgment in urban histories in the Canadian Cities series of the role of ethnicity in urban politics, and in occasional articles by Rasporich on Thunder Bay ethnopolitics (1990), and more recently, a book of popular political history on Canadian mayors, such as Stephen Juba of Winnipeg and 'Wild' Bill Hawrelak of Edmonton. Other works by political scientists Bohdan Harasymiw (1982) and Rose Harasym (1982) described well the partisan voting preferences of the Ukrainians in

Canada, as did Wickberg for the Chinese (1981, 1982), and Buchignani and Indra on South Asian political organizations (1981). Thus, without the considerable work of other social scientists on the past political behaviour and organization of ethnic groups, Canadian political history would be impoverished on the subject.

A final point to be made about the state of ethnic history has to do with the vastly expanded infrastructure supporting publications in the field. Not only have the university presses expanded the number of titles in the field, but the number of outlets for publication have increased markedly over the past two decades. In addition to the two main journals in the field, *Canadian Ethnic Studies/Études Ethniques au Canada* established in 1969 and *Polyphony* in 1978, and the MHSO occasional papers series also launched in that year, there have been several others added for individual groups such as *The Hungarian Studies Review, The Jewish Historical Society of Canada Journal, The Journal of Mennonite Studies, The South Asian Review, The Icelandic Canadian, Hellenic Studies, Forum:A Ukrainian Review, Ukrainian Canadian,*and *Multiculturalism Education Journal.* To these one might also add a variety of newsmagazines such as *Fuse* and *Northern Mosaic* which occasionally carry articles of popular historical interest and import. On the international level, there is also a variety of institutes and journals which carry material of scholarly interest to Canadians: *Studi Emigrazione/Études Migrations* (Rome); *Migracijske Teme* (Zagreb); *Sirtolaisuus/ Migration* (Helsinki); *Ethnic and Racial Studies* (London); *International Migration Review;* and *Ethnic Forum.* For example, a recent publication of the Canadian Academic Centre in Italy has assembled an excellent collection of papers edited by Matteo Sanfillippo, *Italy-Canada Research,* which features state-of-the-art papers on Italian-Canadian historical connections (1988). Such publications, including the recent *Finns in North America* volume published in Turku by the International Migration Institute (1988), indicate the Canadian ethnic studies has indeed come of age in both national and international context.

EVALUATION AND PROGNOSIS

Much of the literature review above has been evaluated internally in its presentation, and several previous state-of-the-art reviews have assessed and reassessed the field of ethnic history nationally, as have several regional reviews for Atlantic Canada and for Quebec. So also have Canadian historians like Berger (1986) in his recent reflections on the new historiography in Canada in the seventies and eighties, and Avery and Ramirez in their evaluation of interdisciplinary research in Canadian studies (1990). Thus, much has been done, and much said about what has been done and not done in this burgeoning field. In essence, the field has been criticized for the uneven quality of the work produced, especially in its earlier phase of the seventies, and for the gaps that had not been addressed, particularly in the areas of labour and social history. The areas of concern were various: the romanticization of labour radicals when they were discussed (Perin 1990); the excessive emphasis on national as opposed to local and regional studies (Harney 1982; Bumsted 1989); the excessive preoccupation with the theme of nativism among the host society (Perin 1990:222–3); and finally, an overemphasis upon a pluralist, consensual model of history and a whiggish record of ethnic triumph over racist adversity (Dahlie 1983).

To select the most recent attempt to gore the sacred cow of multicultural history, one might look with profit at J.M. Bumsted's critique (1989) of ethnic studies in Atlantic Canada, subtitled 'Or, Some Ethnics Are More Ethnic than Others.' After allowing several reasons for ethnic studies as 'a growth industry,' such as the maintenance of group identity, righting of past wrongs, and as 'consciousness raising,' Bumsted gets to the point of academic scholarship on ethnicity as a sort of affirmative action program. While many of his criticisms are flawed, the main burden of his argument in his review article, is on who are the more valid subjects of ethnic history, even if based only on crude numbers. In doing so, he compares the relative merits of such works by Jabbra and Weale on the Lebanese and Medjuck and Krahn on the Jews to other studies by Toner on the Irish of New Brunswick, Thomas on the Welsh of New Brunswick and Nova Scotia, and Arsenault on the Prince Edward Island Acadians. While his conclusion is ambivalent, it need not be, since all of his second group have been and are legitimately included under the rubric of ethnicity.

The rise in Anglo-Celtic studies in the past decade, particularly the history of the Irish, is living disproof of an exclusivist view of ethnicity. Perhaps the liveliest debates on the subject of ethnic historiography in the past decade have been generated by Donald Akenson's prolific output on the Ontario Irish (1984, 1985). His work effectively dispels the previous notions of the Irish as poor, urban, technological peasants as previously described in the work of H.C. Pentland and Kenneth Duncan. Akenson then went on to write about the Orange Order and the Ulster Irish, separating Irish Protestants and Catholics (1988). Ever iconoclastic, Akenson has challenged many of our historical assumptions about ethnicity, religion, demography, and gender during the last ten years. With his work and new studies by Elliott (1988), Fitzgerald and King (1990), MacKay (1990), and Houston and Smyth (1990), a virtual renaissance of Irish-Canadian studies is in the making at both the scholarly and popular levels.

From a critical perspective, the growth of historical writing about ethnicity has suffered in compressed fashion some of the growing pains of nationalist historiography in Canada as a whole. A recent study by Taylor (1989) on early English-Canadian historiography in the nineteenth century has demonstrated the various phases of history as it passed from amateur to professional historiography. In the first two phases, it passed through what one might call 'filiopietism,' through a self-promotional and then patriotic phase of elevating a region or colony into a nation. Then, in the third phase, an intensely partisan feud over the correct interpretation of history broke out, one which might be seen in the left-right dichotomy described above for various groups of pre- and post-war migrants from eastern Europe (Momryk 1991). While professional historians were by training less inclined to engage in polemical discourse, there was nevertheless a bias of selection which occasionally meant that certain immigrants, either pro- or anti-nationalist, or pro- or anti-Communist, who might be read out of the paradigm. In sum, scholarly historians had not completely escaped the innate partisanship of the groups under discussion, and the sources under their control, in attempting to write a balanced account.

Yet another characteristic of the historical overviews of immigration history has been the natural tendency of historians to the narrative mode and the description of 'waves' of migrants. Typically this applied to the more mature groups – pre-First World War, interwar, and post-Second World War migrants – and the ascription of certain characteristics to each wave. This tendency began at least as early as Kaye (Kysilewsky) in 1966, with his description of 'three phases' of Ukrainian immigration. Other historians freely employed this chronological approach particularly in compressed summaries, with some minor variations according to group (Tan & Roy 1985; Lindstrom-Best 1985; Gerus & Rea 1985; McLaughlin 1985). This crude historical matrix may have imposed an arbitrary set of characteristics to each generation of migrants, which will certainly be tested by future historians and social scientists. Some like Kelebay on the Ukrainians and later, Rasporich on the Croatians, also attempted to apply the 'fragment' theory of Louis Hartz to founding societies (Kelebay 1980; Rasporich 1987).

The tendency of this approach to oversimplify in the 'generational' narrative was matched by yet another potentially reductionist fallacy, the urban-rural social categorization of the immigrant, either by place of origin in the sending society, or by place of settlement in the new society. While many of the new social historians, particularly students of Italian history and the Irish, are sensitive to these distinctions, many others have been careless in their application of rural-urban descriptors to immigrant population groups. This issue becomes doubly complicated by the slowness of western Canadian social historians to come to grips, for example, with the concept of farm wage-labour on the prairies, that is, the hired hand and other aspects of single-male migrant labour (McGinnis 1977; Cherwinski 1985; Danysk 1985; Rasporich 1978). Many of these questions must be resolved by social historians in combination with ethnic historians, since it is very often the immigrant who is at the centre of the issue.

Yet another related issue raised by Harney in one of his posthumously published papers on the subject of Italian immigration, was the national (Italian) versus regional (Friuli, Molise, Abbruzzi, Calabria, etc.) and local loyalties of the peasant villagers – 'campanalismo.' This tension between 'high' and 'low' culture, also expressed in the work of Roberto Perin and Franc Sturino (1988) and Zucchi (1988) is also applicable to many other national groups of the Mediterranean whose identifications are more often local and regional, such as the Croatians, Macedonians, and others. Whether the construction of nationalism can hold up in the plunge towards the global village will be worked out in the next generation of historical scholarship.

The globalization of scholarly enquiry may in fact accelerate the impulse towards historical microstudies of regions, pioneered by the French *annales* school which currently holds sway among the avant-garde social historians of French and English Canada. Intensive longitudinal studies of ethnic concentrations of population require study, such as the rural communities currently being explored by Loewen on Kleine Gemeinde Mennonites over three generations in Manitoba and in Nebraska (1990). Similarly, internationalization of research will permit comparative analysis of the variety long popular among anthropologists and sociologists of comparative case studies. Research is in progress on Jewish rural communities in North and South America; Italian communities in Argentina and Canada; and comparative studies of ethnic urban communities in Australia and Canada (Platt, Hoerder, Ramirez). With an increasing number of research institutes such as the Immigration History Research Center in Minneapolis directed by Vecoli, and similar enterprises throughout Europe, with scholars such as Hoerder in Bremen, Cižmić in Zagreb, Puskas in Budapest, and Koivukangas in Turku, the prospect for comparative studies is excellent.

The future agenda for the study of Canadian ethnicity and social history has already been set in motion in the direction of comparative and specialized historical microstudies of Canada's rural and urban past. But it has to be pursued in several directions – for example, the history of women across a variety of ethnic groups needs analysis, much as Joy Parr has done for labouring women and men in two industrial towns of southern Ontario. And, as Parr's study suggests what Harney began in his pioneering article, 'Men Without Women' (1979), the study of men and masculine culture needs historical analysis as well. Currently it is being studied for single-male British immigrants to the West by Danysk, and Iacovetta, who has explored the dimensions of gender and work among Toronto's immigrants (1992).

The history of work, long pursued by labour historians, needs also to be supplemented by studies in leisure and sports, and once again leadership in this area was supplied by a special issue of Harney's *Polyphony* (1985), with further work following on Toronto, Hamilton, and Sudbury (Tester 1986). The recent and fairly rapid development of this field in the eighties is apparent in such work as Barman on the British ideals of sport and fair play, Dahlie on skiing as a pursuit of identity and ethnic tradition among the Scandinavians, and Kidd on proletarian sports activities in Ontario in the thirties. Also, a most impressive, comprehensive analysis of sport and leisure in Alberta by Wetherell and Kmet (1990), was published under the aegis of Alberta Culture and Multiculturalism). In sum, then, both the history of work and leisure are in the process of being developed, but need to be placed more squarely on the agenda by social and ethnic historians in Canada.

The gaps in the scholarly agenda of ethnic historiography are still considerable, despite what has been accomplished they can only be catalogued briefly here. In the realm of political history, there is no comprehensive inter-ethnic history at any level – federal, provincial, or urban – the field is wide open for development. We have no comprehensive understanding of the concept of entrepreneurship in ethnic groups, and despite a few biographies of businessmen like Thomas Bata, Sam Bronfman, Giovanni Veltri, and Benjamin Hart, there has been very little delineation of ethnicity as an important variant of ethnic achievement, except as an extension of intra-group achievement appended to the history of the group. Yet, apart from a few studies of Anglo-Canadian businessmen and their class origins in the nineteenth century, there have been few prosopographic analyses of the ethnic and class origins of ethnic entrepreneurs in the postwar era (Rudin 1985; Newman 1981; Bliss 1990; Potestio 1987).

On the other end of the scale, on the topic of disachievement and anomie, there are few studies which have elaborated on the subject of dislocation, insanity, and poverty among ethnic groups, since the story is supposed to go the other way. Stephan Thernstrom's seminal American work, *Progress and Poverty* (1964) notwithstanding, there has been little understanding or appreciation in Canada of the impact of poverty, for example on the unemployed male immigrants who drifted across Canada and towards the Spanish Civil War in 1936. Similarly, despite abundant statistics on insanity and availability of sanitoria and mental hospital records, there have been few studies on epidemics or mental illness among immigrant populations, with the exception of cholera and smallpox among the nineteenth-century Irish. These are neither popular nor desirable topics for among ethnic groups, and one can only admire the spiritual honesty of William Kurelek (1980), who told his very painful tale of struggle with mental illness in his autobiography, on the advice of his psychiatrist, who 'persuaded me I'd be doing more good to people if I told the story as it really was.'

To conclude, the gaps in our historical understanding of ethnicity are greater than the firm islands of knowledge which have been established in the past twenty years. In that sense, the field itself conforms to Canadian patterns of settlement, as an archipelago of land islands connected by narrow filaments of communication and transportation extending over vast landspaces. But these clusters of knowledge and the intellectual ties which bind them are firm ones, established by the arduous efforts of the builders and thinkers noted above. The idea of ethnicity, as essential to the imagery of national maintenance is as has been noted, in the ascendant in North America as elsewhere in the world (Smith 1981). It is an idea whose time has come, and those who have successfully conjured Clio as the muse of ethnic historiography in Canada, have ensured through their great imaginative efforts, that she remain a permanent house guest.

REFERENCES

Abella, Irving and Troper, Harold (1982). *None is too many: Canada and the Jews of Europe, 1933–48*. Toronto: Lester and Orpen Dennys
Abu-Laban, Baha (1980). *An olive branch on the family tree*. Toronto: McClelland & Stewart
Adachi, Ken (1976). *The enemy that never was*. Toronto: McClelland & Stewart
Adelman, H. (ed.) (1991). *Refugee policy: Canada and the U.S.* Toronto: York Lanes
Akenson, Donald (1984). *The Irish in Ontario: A study in rural history*. Montreal/ Kingston: McGill-Queen's University Press
– (1985). *Being had: Historians, evidence and the Irish in North America*. Don Mills: P.D. Meany

– (1988). *Small differences: Irish Catholics and Irish Protestants, 1815–1922: An international perspective*. Montreal/Kingston: McGill-Queen's University Press

Anctil, Pierre, and Caldwell, Gary (1984). *Juifs et réalités juives au Québec*. Montréal: Institut québécois de recherche sur la culture

– , and Ramirez, Bruno (eds) (1991). *If one were to write a history*. Montreal: MHSO

Angus, Ian (ed.) (1981). *Canadian Bolsheviks: The early years of the Communist Party of Canada*. Monteal: Vanguard Press

Aun, Karl (1985). *The political refugees: A history of the Estonians in Canada*. Toronto: McClelland & Stewart

Avery, Donald (1979). *'Dangerous foreigners.'* Toronto: McClelland & Stewart

– , and Ramirez, Bruno (1990). Immigration and ethnic studies. In Alan F.J. Artibise (ed.), *Interdisciplinary approaches to Canadian society: A guide to the literature* (pp 77–116). Montreal/Kingston: Association for Canadian Studies/McGill-Queen's University Press

Barber, Marilyn (Sept. 1980). The women Ontario welcomed: Immigrant domestics for Ontario homes, 1870–1930. *Ontario History, 62*(3):148–73

Barman, Jean (1984). *Growing up British in British Columbia: Boys in private school*. Vancouver: UBC Press

Behiels, Michael (1991). *Quebec and the question of immigration: From ethnocentrism to ethnic pluralism, 1900–85*. Ottawa: CHA

Bercuson, David, and Wertheimer, Douglas (1985). *A trust betrayed: The Keegstra affair*. Toronto: Doubleday

Berger, Carl (1986, 2nd ed.) *The writing of Canadian history*. Toronto: University of Toronto Press

Betcherman, Lita-Rose (1975). *The swastika and the maple leaf: Fascist movements in the thirties*. Don Mills: Fitzhenry & Whiteside

Bilson, Geoffrey (1980). *A darkened house: Cholera in nineteenth-century Canada*. Toronto: University of Toronto Press (pp 65–8)

Bliss, J. Michael (1990). *Northern enterprise: Five centuries of Canadian business*. Toronto: McClelland & Stewart (pp 109–26, 200, 501, 564)

Bowen, Lynne (1982, 1987). *Boss whistle. Three dollar dreams*. Lantzville, BC: Oolichan

Buchignani, Norman, and Indra, Doreen (1985). *Continuous journey*. Toronto: McClelland & Stewart

Bumsted, J.M. (1989, Fall). Ethnic studies in Atlantic Canada: Or, some ethnics are more ethnic than others. *Acadiensis, 19*(1):192–204

Burnet, Jean (1979). Separate or equal: A dilemma of multiculturalism. In A.W. Rasporich (ed.), *The social sciences and public policy in Canada* (pp 176–83). Calgary: University of Calgary

– (1981). Minorities I have belonged to. *Canadian Ethnic Studies/Études ethniques au Canada, 13*(1):34–5

– (1986). *Looking into my sister's eyes: An exploration in women's history.* Toronto: MHSO

– , and Palmer, Howard (1988). *Coming Canadians: An introduction to a history of Canada's peoples* (pp 1–11). Toronto: McClelland & Stewart

Calderwood, William W. (1972). Pulpit, press and political reactions to the Ku Klux Klan in Saskatchewan. In Susan M. Trofimenkoff (ed.), *The twenties in western Canada* (pp 191–229). Ottawa: National Museums of Canada

– (1975, Autumn). Religious reactions to the Ku Klux Klan in Saskatchewan. *Saskatchewan History,* 26:103–14

Chan, Kwok, and Indra, Doreen (eds) (1987). *Uprooting, loss and adaptation: The resettlement of Indochinese refugees in Canada.* Ottawa: Canadian Public Health Association

Cherwinski, W.J.C. (1985). In search of Jake Trumper: The farm hand and the prairie farm family. In David Jones and Ian MacPherson (eds), *Building beyond the homestead* (pp 111–35). Calgary: University of Calgary Press

Chimbos, Peter (1980). *The Canadian odyssey.* Toronto: McClelland & Stewart

Dahlie, Jorgen (1983, Fall) Writing ethnic history: The generations series and the limits of pluralism. *Canadian Review of Studies in Nationalism,* 299–303

– (1990). Skiing for identity and tradition: Scandinavian venture and adventure in the Pacific Northwest, 1900–60. In E.A. Corbet and A.W. Rasporich (eds), *Winter sports in the West* (pp 99–112). Calgary: Alberta Historical Society/ University of Calgary

Danys, Milada (1986). *DP: Lithuanian immigration to Canada after the Second World War.* Toronto: MHSO

Danysk, Cecilia (1985). Showing these slaves their class position: Barriers to organizing prairie farm workers. In David Jones and Ian MacPherson (eds), *Building beyond the homestead* (pp 163–79). Calgary: University of Calgary Press

Dawson, J. Brian (1975). The Chinese experience in frontier Calgary, 1885–1910. In A.W. Rasporich and H.C. Klassen (eds), *Frontier Calgary: Town, city and region, 1875–1914* (pp 124–41). Calgary: McClelland & Stewart West

Dirks, Gerald (1977). *Canada's refugee policy: Indifference or opportunism?* Montreal/Kingston: McGill-Queen's University Press

Draper, Paula (1983). Muses behind barbed wire: Canada and the interned refugees. In J. Jacman and C. Borden (eds), *The Muses flee Hitler: Cultural transfer and adaptation, 1930–45.* Washington: Smithsonian Institute

Elliott, Bruce S. (1988). *Irish migrants in the Canadas: A new approach.* Montreal/ Kingston: McGill-Queen's University Press

Fitzgerald, Margaret, and King, Joseph (1990). *The uncounted Irish in Canada and the United States.* Toronto: P.D. Meany [Dutch]

Gerus, O., and Rea, J.E. (1985). *The Ukrainians in Canada.* Ottawa: Canadian Historical Association

Grenke, Arthur (1989). *Archival sources for the study of German language groups in Canada*. Ottawa: Supply and Services, 70 pp

Harasymiw, Bohdan (1982). Political participation of Ukrainians since 1945. In Manoly Lupul (ed.), *Heritage in transition* (pp 122–42). Toronto: McClelland & Stewart

Harney, Robert (1979). Men without women: Italian migrants in Canada, 1885–1930. *Canadian Ethnic Studies*, 11(1):48–69

– (ed.) (1981, Fall). Finns in Ontario. Special issue, *Polyphony*, (3)1

– (1982, Fall). Ethnic archival and library materials in Canada: Problems of bibliographic control and preservation. *Ethnic Forum*, 2(2):3–32

– (ed.) (1986). *Gathering place: Peoples and neighbourhoods of Toronto, 1834–1945*. Toronto: MHSO

Haycock, Sandra, and Watson, Joann (1988). Ethnicity oral history and the Public Archives of Nova Scotia. In D. Moore and J.H. Morrison (eds), *Work ethnicity and oral history*, 133

Hawkins, Freda (1972). *Canada and immigration: Public policy and public concern*. Montreal/Kingston: McGill-Queen's University Press

– (1989). *Critical years in immigration: Canada and Australia compared*. Montreal/Kingston: McGill-Queen's University Press

Helly, Denise (1987). *Les Chinois à Montréal, 1877–1951*. Montréal: IQRC

Hillmer, Norman et al. (eds) (1988). *On guard for thee ...* Ottawa: Canadian Committee for the History of the Second World War

Hoerder, Dirk (ed.) (1986). *Struggle a hard battle: Essays on working class immigrants*. Dekalb: Northern Illinois University Press

Houston, C.J., and Smyth, W.J. (1990). *Irish emigration and Canadian settlement: Patterns, links and letters*. Toronto: University of Toronto Press

Iacovetta, Franca (1992). *Such hardworking people: Italian immigrants in postwar Toronto*. Montreal/Kingston: McGill-Queen's University Press

Indra, D., and Buchignani, N. (1981). The political organization of South Asians in Canada, 1904–20. In J. Dahlie and T. Fernando (eds), *Ethnicity, power and politics* (pp 202–33). Toronto: Methuen

Jackel, Susan (ed.) (1982). *British emigrant gentlewomen in the Canadian west, 1880–1914*. Vancouver: UBC Press

Johnston, Hugh (1979, 1990). *The voyage of the 'Komagata Maru': The Sikh challenge to Canada's colour bar*. Vancouver: UBC Press

Karni, M., Koivukangas, O., Laine, E. (1988). *Finns in North America*. Turku: Institute of Immigration

Kaye, Val (1966). Three phases of Ukrainian immigration. *Slavs in Canada* (1). Edmonton: Inter-University Committee on Canadian Slavs (pp 36–44)

Kelebay, Yarema (1980). Three fragments of the Ukrainian community in Montreal, 1899–1970: A Hartzian approach. *Canadian Ethnic Studies*, 12(2):74–88

Keyserlink, Robert (1984). The Canadian government's attitude towards Germans and German Canadians in World War Two. *Canadian Ethnic Studies,* 16(1):16–29

Kidd, Bruce (1982). We must maintain a balance between propaganda and serious athletics: The workers' sport movement in Canada. *Proceedings, 5th Canadian Symposium on the History of Sport and Physical Education.* Toronto: School of Physical and Health Education, University of Toronto (pp 330–9)

Koch, Erich (1980). *Deemed suspect: A wartime blunder.* Toronto: Methuen

Krawchuk, Peter (1985). *Interned without cause: The internment of Canadian antifascists during World War Two.* Toronto: Kobzar

Kurelek, William (1980). *Someone with me.* Toronto: McClelland & Stewart

Lai, David Chuen-Yan (1987, Fall). The Chinese cemetery in Victoria. BC *Studies,* 75:24–43

Laine, Edward (1989). *Archival sources for the study of Finnish Canadians.* Ottawa: Supply and Services

Levitt, Cyril, and Shaffir, William (1987). *The riot at Christie Pits.* Toronto: Lester & Orpen Dennys

Lindstrom-Best, Varpu (1985). *The Finns in Canada.* Ottawa: Canadian Historical Association

– (1988). *Defiant sisters: A social history of Finnish immigrant women in Canada.* Toronto: MHSO

Loewen, R. (1990). Ethnic farmers and the 'outside' world: Mennonites in Manitoba and Nebraska, 1874–1900. *Journal of the Canadian Historical Association,* 1:195–215

Luciuk, Lubomyr (1988). *A time for atonement: Canada's first national internment operations and the Ukrainian Canadians, 1914–20.* Kingston: Limestone Press

McGinnis, David P. (1977). Farm labour in transition: Occupational structure and economic dependency in Alberta. In Howard Palmer (ed.), *The settlement of the West* (pp 174–86). Calgary: Comprint/University of Calgary

MacKay, Donald (1990). *The flight from famine: The coming of the Irish to Canada.* Toronto: McClelland & Stewart (pp 243–310)

McLaughlin, K.M. (1985). *The Germans in Canada.* Ottawa: CHA

Metsaranta, Marc (ed.). (1989). *Project Bay Street: Activities of the Finnish Canadians in Thunder Bay before 1915.* Steinbach: Thunder Bay Finnish-Canadian Historical Society

Momryk, Myron (1984). *A guide to the sources for the study of Ukrainian Canadians.* Ottawa: Supply and Services, 39 pp

– (1991). The writing of Ukrainian Canadian history, unpublished ms

Moore, D.E., and Morrison, J.H. (1988). *Work, ethnicity and oral history.* International Education Centre

Morton, James (1974). *In a sea of sterile mountains: The Chinese in British Columbia.* Vancouver: J.J. Douglas

Morton, W.L. (1981). Historical phenomenon of minorities in Canada. *Canadian Ethnic Studies, 13*(3):1–40

Newman, Peter (1981). *The acquisitors: The Canadian establishment*, II. Toronto: McClelland & Stewart (pp 117–49, 160–209)

Palmer, Howard (1982a). Ethnic relations in wartime: Nationalism and European minorities in Alberta during the Second World War. *Canadian Ethnic Studies, 14*(3):1–24

– (1982b). *Patterns of prejudice: A history of nativism in Alberta.* Toronto: McClelland & Stewart

– (1990). Ethnicity and politics in Canada: 1867–present. In Valeria G. Lerda (ed.), *From 'melting pot' to multiculturalism: The evolution of ethnic relations in the United States and Canada* (pp 169–204). Rome: Bulzoni Editore

Palmer, Howard and Tamara (eds) (1985). *The peoples of Alberta: Portraits of cultural diversity.* Saskatoon: Western Producer

Perin, Roberto (1984). Making good fascists and good Canadians: Consular propaganda and the Italian community in Montreal in the 1930s. In Gerald Gold (ed.), *Minorities and the mother country imagery* (pp 136–58). St John's: Institute of Social and Economic Research

– (1990). Writing about ethnicity. In John Schultz (ed.), *Writing about Canada: A handbook for modern Canadian history* (p 208). Scarborough: Prentice-Hall

Perin, Roberto, and Sturino, Franc (eds) (1988). *Arrangiarsi: The Italian immigrant experience in Canada.* Montreal: Guernica

Platt, D.C.M. (ed.) (1989). *Social welfare, 1850–1950: Australia, Argentina and Canada compared.* London: Macmillan

Potestio, John (ed.) (1987). *The memoirs of Giovanni Veltri.* Toronto: MHSO

Prokop, Manfred (1989, Spring). Canadianization of immigrant children: Role of the rural elementary school in Alberta, 1900–30. *Alberta History*, (37)2:1–11

Prymak, Thomas (1988). *Maple leaf and trident: The Ukrainian Canadians during the Second World War.* Toronto: MHSO

Pucci, A., and Potestio, J. (eds) (1988). *The Italian immigrant experience.* Thunder Bay: Canadian Italian Historical Association

Radecki, Henry, and Heydenkorn, Benedykt (1976). *A member of a distinguished family.* Toronto: McClelland & Stewart

Radforth, Ian (1987). *Bushworkers and bosses: Logging in Northern Ontario 1900–80.* Toronto: University of Toronto Press

Ramirez, Bruno (1980). *The Italians of Montreal.* Montreal: Éditions des Courant

– (1986). Brief encounters: Italian emigrant workers and the CPR 1900–30. *Labour, 17*

– (1989). *The Italians in Canada.* Ottawa: CHA

– (1991). *On the move: French Canadian and Italian immigrants in the North Atlantic 1860–1914.* Toronto: McClelland & Stewart

Rasporich, A.W. (1978). South Slavs on a northern margin: The frontier experi-

ences of Croatian migrants during Canada's Great Depression. In M.L.
Kovacs (ed.), *Ethnic Canadians: Culture and education* (pp 399–410). Regina:
Canadian Plains Research Center, University of Regina

– (1987). Three generations of Croatian immigrants to Canada: A Hartzian
perspective. In Vladimir Markotic (ed.), *Emigrants from Croatia and their
achievements* (pp 101–11). Calgary: Western Publishers

– (1990, Feb.). Twin city ethnopolitics: Urban rivalry, ethnic radicalism and
assimilation in the Lakehead, 1900–70. *Urban History Review*, 18(3):210–31

Repka, William and Kathleen (1982). *Dangerous patriots*. Vancouver: New Star

Roberts, Barbara (1988). *Whence they came: Deportation from Canada, 1900–35*.
Ottawa: University of Ottawa Press

Robinson, Ira (1990). The kosher meat war and the Jewish Community Council
of Montreal, 1922–25. *Canadian Ethnic Studies*, 22(2):41–54

Rome, David (1977). *Clouds in the thirties: On antisemitism in Canada,1929–39*, 3
vols. Montreal: Canadian Jewish Archives

Roy, Patricia (1979) White Canada forever: Two generations of studies. *Canadian Ethnic Studies*, 11(2):89–97

Royal Commission on Bilingualism and Biculturalism (1970). *Report: Book IV,
The cultural contributions of other ethnic groups*. Ottawa: Queen's Printer

Rudin, Ronald (1985). *Banking en français: The French banks of Quebec, 1835–1925*.
Toronto: University of Toronto Press

Sanfillippo, Matteo (1985). Les études canadiennes en Italie: La recherche
historique, 1974–88. *Annali Accademici Canadesi*, 2:185–96. Ottawa: Canadian
Academic Centre in Italy

Sangster, Joan (1989). *Dreams of equality: Women on the Canadian left*. Toronto:
McClelland Stewart

Seager, Allen (1986). Class, ethnicity and politics in the Alberta coalfields,
1905–45. In Dirk Hoerder (ed.), *Struggle a hard battle: Essays on working class
immigrants* (pp 305–24). DeKalb: Northern Illinois University Press

Silverman, Eliane (1984). *The last best west: Women on the Alberta frontier,
1890–1929*. Montreal: Eden Press

– (1985). Women's perceptions of marriage on the Alberta frontier. In David
Jones and Ian MacPherson (eds), *Building beyond the homestead: Rural history on
the Canadian prairies* (pp 49–67). Calgary: University of Calgary Press

Skorie, Sofija and Tomaskevich (eds) (1988). *Serbs in Ontario: A Socio-Cultural
Description*. Toronto: Serbian Heritage Academy

Smith, Allan (1981, June). National images and national maintenance: The
ascendancy of the ethnic idea in North America. *Canadian Journal of Political
Science*, 14(2):230–57

Strong-Boag, Veronica (1988). *The new day recalled: Lives of girls and women in
English Canada, 1919–39*. Toronto: Copp Clark Pitman

Sunahara, Ann (1981). *The politics of racism*. Toronto: Lorimer

Swankey, Ben (1975). Reflections of an Alberta communist. *Alberta History*, 23(4):20

Swyripa, Frances (1989). Baba and the community heroine. *Alberta*, (2)1:59–80

Szalasznyj, Kathlyn (1986). Preserving ethnicity: Archives/community networks in Saskatchewan. *Canadian Ethnic Studies*, 18(3):110–15

Tan, Jin, and Roy, Patricia (1985). *The Chinese in Canada*. Ottawa: Canadian Historical Association

Tapper, Lawrence (1987). *Archival sources for the study of Canadian Jewry*. Ottawa: Supply and Services, 95 pp

Taschereau, Sylvie (1988, Printemps). L'histoire de l'immigration au Québec: Une invitation à fuir les ghettos. *Revue d'histoire de l'Amérique française*, 41(4)575–91

Taylor, M. Brook (1989). *Promoters, patriots, and partisans: Historiography in nineteenth-century English Canada*. Toronto: University of Toronto Press

Tester, J. (ed.) (1986). *Sports pioneers: A history of the Finnish Canadian Amateur Sports Federation, 1906–86*. Sudbury: AC Alerts Historical Committee

Thernstrom, Stephan (1964). *Progress and poverty: Social mobility in a nineteenth-century city*. Cambridge, MA: Harvard University Press

Tulchinsky, Gerald (1990). Hidden among the smokestacks: Toronto's clothing industry, 1871–1901. In David Keane and Colin Read (eds), *Old Ontario* (pp 257–85). Toronto: Dundurn Press

Valererde, M. (1991). *The age of light, soap and water*. Toronto: McClelland & Stewart

Ward, Peter (1978, 1991) *White Canada forever: Popular attitudes and public policy toward Orientals in British Columbia*. Montreal/Kingston: McGill-Queen's University Press

Wetherell, Donald G., and Kmet, Irene (1990). *Useful pleasures: The shaping of leisure in Alberta, 1896–1945*. Regina: Canadian Plains Research Center/Alberta Culture and Multiculturalism

Whitaker, Reg (1987). *Double standard: The secret history of Canadian immigration*. Toronto: Lester & Orpen Dennys

Wickberg, E. (1981). Chinese organization and the Canadian political process: Two case studies. In J. Dahlie and T. Fernando (eds), *Ethnicity, power and politics in Canada*, (pp 172–7). Toronto: Methuen

– (ed.) (1982). *From China to Canada*. Toronto: McClelland & Stewart

Wilson, Donald, and Dahlie, Jorgen (eds) (1978). Special issue, Ethnic radicals. *Canadian Ethnic Studies*, 10(2)

Zucchi, John (1985). Historical studies on Italian immigrants to Canada. *Annali Accademici Canadesi*, 2:39–49. Ottawa: Canadian Academic Centre in Italy

– (1988). *Italians in Toronto: Development of a national identity, 1875–1945*. Montreal/Kingston: McGill-Queen's University Press

J.A. LAPONCE

Ethnicity and Voting Studies in Canada: Primary and Secondary Sources 1970–1991

Following an introduction, the purpose of which is to clarify the terms and concepts I shall use, this paper will have two sections, one devoted to *primary* sources, the other to the *secondary* literature.

INTRODUCTION

Much confusion results from the unstable vocabulary that we use to describe ethnic phenomena – unstable within as well as across disciplines (Riggs 1985). Political scientists normally use the terms *multicultural* and *multiculturalism* to refer either to an ideology or to a set of governmental policies. Rather than speak of a multicultural society we more commonly speak of a multi ethnic polity. But even within the sole discipline of political science, there is no agreement on what we mean by ethnic. It is thus essential that I specify my preferred usage.

I use the term *ethnic* to refer to a community having a real or imaginary common origin that distinguishes it from other communities. Ethnic identity is thus a socially and culturally structured 'we' that gives meaning to the self.

Many, possibly all, the elements of an individual's personal identity are potential for group identity – being Black, being Catholic, having a German name, being short, being a cook – but only a few of these specific personal characteristics turn at a particular point in time into a group identity that cuts across social roles. The individual identities that most often become group identities are those of national and state origin, language, religion, and race.

Thus, under my definition of ethnic, all Canadians are ethnics, whether their ethnicity is defined by terms such as German-Canadian,

Jewish, European, or simply Canadian. Some people are mono-ethnic while others are bi- or multi-ethnic. In the latter case the operative ethnic identifier is triggered by circumstances, sometimes Jewish, sometimes German, sometimes German-Canadian, and sometimes simply Canadian.

The notion of multiculturalism, as used by the Secretariat of State and the SSHRCC, has a meaning that is thus both narrower and wider than my notion of ethnicity – narrower since it is limited to non-dominant groups and broader since its conceptual boundaries are not exclusively focused on the group, on the 'we within me.'

Rather than link these different concepts of ethnicity by means of Boolean logic and thus restrict my corpus of cases to those falling within the overlap (that restriction would lead us to concentrate our attention on minority communities), I shall take them as additive. Consequently, the corpus of cases to be considered in this paper will refer to both dominant groups and minorities, and to individual ethnic origin (as typically defined by the objective categories of the census) as well as to group ethnic identity (as defined by the subject's own perceptions and sense of belonging). However, to avoid repeating 'ethnic and multicultural' I shall, henceforth, simply say ethnic, unless the discussion requires a distinction between dominant groups and minorities or between individuals and groups.

PRIMARY SOURCES

To relate ethnicity to electoral participation and party preference, three major primary sources are commonly used: the census, the election returns, and public opinion surveys done by both academic and commercial institutions. Sources such as party documents and ethnic association records – sources that are less often used by political scientists – will not be considered here.

The Census

The ethnic questions used by the Canadian census are of unequal value but, compared to those of foreign censuses, they are among the very best; they still provide information that has ceased to be recorded in other multi-ethnic societies. Unlike the Belgian census, the Canadian gives information concerning language; and, unlike the American census it gives information concerning religious affiliation.

Let us evaluate the questions of the Canadian census according to their ability (a) to discriminate among ethnic groups and (b) to distinguish individual from group identity. To do so let us consider separately the questions dealing with language, religion, national/state origin, and race.[1]

The language questions distinguish the spoken language (the language or languages in which one can conduct a conversation, and the language spoken at home most often) from the language learned in childhood and still understood. The census could, at little cost, add a question concerning the language spoken at work.

Unlike the questions on language, that on religion fails to distinguish cultural inclination from practice, it even invites the respondent to disregard the difference by asking that a specific denomination be mentioned 'even if the person is not currently a practicing member of that group.' As it now reads, the question is good but incomplete; it should be followed by a question regarding practice. Would that be too personal a question? Survey research has not found it to be particularly sensitive.

The censuses of recent decades make it easy for the respondent to record a 'no religion' response, but they still force the respondent into a single denomination. If one thinks of church attendance, that restriction is already debatable; but it becomes difficult to justify if one thinks simply of cultural orientation. It would be worth testing a question allowing for bi- or multi-denominational orientations, a question that would be comparable to that on national origin. This could be done by removing the instruction restricting the answer to 'only one' denomination and, as in the case of national origin, by keeping the question wide open.

The questions on country of birth, citizenship, and date of immigration offer good discriminators. The question concerning the ethnic or cultural origins of one's ancestors is well worded (the origin is no longer traced exclusively through the male line) and makes it possible to indicate multiple origins (*group or groups* says the instruction to the open-ended part of the question). The itemization of the answers is a little bizarre because of its mixing of categories such as English, Jewish, and Black, but that is, I realize, a way of introducing questions on *race* without seeming to do so. That is a move in the direction of the American census that distinguishes whites from Blacks, Hispanics and native Indians.

But the main flaw of the census question on what it calls 'ethnicity' (what I call ethno-state or ethno-national identity) is in its failing to record the group identity of the respondent in addition to the origins of his or her ancestors. In short, the census questions, while good on language, are quite timid in their recording religion, nationality, and race. They fail to give us good measures of the identity of the self. They are too exclusively focused on the past and inherited individual characteristics.

Election Returns

The usefulness of the census for the study of ethnic voting patterns is constrained by the territorial level at which the matching of the votes and socio-demographic characteristics can be made. Reaching the smallest territorial units of the census and of the election returns – the census tract and the polling unit – will typically be necessary for the study of very small but concentrated minorities. That matching is not always feasible since the boundaries do not necessarily coincide and, whenever feasible, it is a formidable task if it is done over large geographical areas. The matching of polls and tracts, as in the studies of North Winnipeg (Peterson & Avakumovic 1964), St Boniface (Donnelly 1976), Edmonton (Baird 1966), and Montreal St. Louis (Jedwab 1986) is typically done by researchers who, because of the local case study nature of the research, do not deposit their data in data banks where they could be retrieved and re-analyzed.

Now that the census has developed a computer retrieval system that enables one to obtain census tract information by specifying either tract location or street intersection, it should be possible to obtain a nationwide match or a near match of tracts and polls provided the election returns and the census data are entered on the same file.[2]

In the meantime, studies done at the provincial or national level will continue in the tradition of Escott Reid (1933) and match ethnicity and vote at the level of the constituency (see for example Lipset 1950; Irvine 1964; Meisel 1964 for regional and provincial correlations; Laponce 1969 for a nation-wide coverage).

For the matching of census and election returns at the constituency level, the major database is in Donald Blake's nation-wide compilation, at the constituency level, of party support and socio-demographic characteristics, including language, religion, and national origin, for the period 1908 to 1984. This remarkable time series remains underused, probably for lack of it being known that the file, deposited at the UBC data library, is available for redistribution.

However, the aggregation of the data at the constituency level, with an average population of 80,000 people, is too high for the study of small dispersed minorities. Aggregate studies call for some of the units being near homogeneous on the independent variable or being at least markedly over the majority. But, to take only one example, no Canadian federal riding has a Jewish majority. Publicly accessible machine readable data recording the vote and ethnic characteristics at lower levels of aggregation than the riding are thus a necessity for the study of the election behaviour of small minorities.

The Surveys

The *academic* surveys of interest to us fall into two major groups, those the primary purpose of which was the study of elections and those intended primarily for the study of other phenomena, notably ethnicity. I shall limit my corpus to the surveys indexed by the UBC data library that contained information on the respondent's vote and ethnicity. I shall separate those studies into two groups – the national election studies on the one hand, the remainder on the other hand (see Table 1).

The national election study of 1965 by Converse and his colleagues, that of 1968 by Meisel, those of 1974 and 1979 by Clarke and his colleagues, that of 1984 by Lambert and his colleagues, and that of 1988 by Johnston and his colleagues offer a rich time series, with the unfortunate gap of 1972,[3] for the relating of ethnic characteristics to party preference.

The ethnic questions used in these surveys pass the test of specificity (they use detailed categories: Anglican, Baptist, United Church, rather than simply Protestant) and measure religious and linguistic practice as well as origin, knowledge, or vague cultural orientation, but they suffer from four major weaknesses (explainable largely by the fact that ethnicity was not their primary focus).
- Race is not better itemized, and sometimes less well categorized, than by an the already deficient census. We do not get from the surveys good measures of the so-called visible minorities;
- The questions on state and national origin are, like those of the census that served as a model, of only limited use because of the near exclusive focus on the parents and the ancestors rather than the self – the Meisel survey of 1968 stands as an exception for its asking the respondents to describe how they thought of themselves: 'People may think of themselves as English Canadians, French Canadians, German, Italian, or Irish Canadian or in some other way. How do you prefer to

TABLE 1
Ethnic variables appearing in the voting analyses published in the *Canadian Journal of Political Science* 1970–91†*

	1970	1970	1972	1973	1973	1974	1974	1974	1974	1976	1976
	1	2	3	4	5*	6*	7*	8	9	10	11
	LB	S	L	G	R	M	C	I	WT	PH	J
LANGUAGE											
English: At Home										X	
French: At Home										X	
English: Mother Tongue							X				X
French: Mother Tongue							X	X			X
Other than French or English (MT)							X				
Other than French								X			
English: Home L. '58/MT since '62			X								
French: Home L. '58/MT since '62			X								
English: not defined											
French: not defined											
Other than F or E: not defined											
French in Quebec											
Non-French in Quebec											
French outside Quebec											
Non-French outside Quebec											
French (MT) in Quebec											
Self-defined anglophone					X						
Self-defined francophone					X						
English decision-makers											
English 'citizens'											
French decision-makers											
French 'citizens'											
RELIGION											
Catholic	X	X	X	X		X		X			
Protestant		X	X	X		X					
Other than Catholic								X			
Other than Prot. or Cath.		X		X		X					
Anglican	X										
Baptist											
Lutheran											
Presbyterian											
United Church	X										
Other than U, A, RC											
Other than U, A, Presb., Bapt., Luth, RC, no Rel.											

1976	1977	1978	1978	1978	1978	1980	1980	1981	1982	1985	1987	1987	1988	1990	1990
12	13*	14*	15	16*	17	18	19	20	21	22	23	24	25	26	27*
CL	PH	R	B	L	PH	OSW	W	OS	B	J	A	B	L	SFRT	L
X															
X															
					X										
													X		
					X										
													X		
		X													
		X													
								X							
								X							
								X							
								X							
	X														
														X	
														X	
														X	
														X	
			X							X			X	X	
													X	X	
									X						
			X												
			X												
			X												
			X												
			X			X									
			X												

(TABLE 1 continued)

	1970 1 LB	1970 2 S	1972 3 L	1973 4 G	1973 5* R	1974 6* M	1974 7* C	1974 8 I	1974 9 WT	1976 10 PH	1976 11 J
Jewish											
No religion											
Religion (general; no definition)											
NATIONAL AND STATE ORIGIN											
United Kingdom	X	X		X							X
Northern Europe other than UK	X										
Other than UK									X	X	
Other than UK or Canada				X							
France		X									
Other than France		X									
Other than UK or France											
Eastern Europe	X										
South European											
Western Europe											
Other than Europe											
Canadian-born British											
Canadian-born French											
Canadian-born other than B											
Canadian-born other than B, F											
Foreign-born British											
Foreign-born non-British											
Anglo-Saxon									X		
Canada				X							
Dutch											
Icelandic									X		
Irish-French									X		
Jewish									X		
Native Indian											
Slavic											
European other than UK, Slavic											
Ukrainian									X		
West Indian											

1976	1977	1978	1978	1978	1978	1980	1980	1981	1982	1985	1987	1987	1988	1990	1990
12	13*	14*	15	16*	17	18	19	20	21	22	23	24	25	26	27*
CL	PH	R	B	L	PH	OSW	W	OS	B	J	A	B	L	SFRT	L
													X		
											X				
				X			X		X			X		X	
									X						
						X								X	
						X									
														X	
												X			
												X			
				X											
							X		X						
									X						
									X						
									X						
									X						
									X						
							X								
							X								X
			X												
				X											
												X			

think of yourself?' The Clarke 1979 survey offers also a more partial exception since it contains a 'Who I am?' question that recorded a number of ethnic identifiers, such as Canadian and Québécois.

A question or series of questions on the ethnic identity of the self has become a must even if the number of categories resulting from an open question risks being large. Meisel needed only 30 different codes in 1968. A 1984 test of 212 UBC students asked to indicate what term described best the ethnic group to which they felt they belonged resulted in 63 different answers – 29 subjects used single words and 34 needed hyphening – while at the University of Montreal 92 students produced 20 different answers – 11 in the form of single words and nine in that of hyphenated constructions (Laponce 1992). If an open question turns out to be too costly, either to administer or to code, then a closed question such as that used by Kalin and Berry in their national surveys of ethnic self-identification could be used as a very good substitute. Their 1991 survey used the categories *Canadian*, British Canadian, French Canadian, Provincial (Québécois, etc..), Other ethnic-Canadian, and *Other ethnic-national*. The authors find that, from 1974 to 1991, the percentage of respondents identifying as *Canadian* had risen from 59 to 64 per cent for the sample as a whole, and from 59 to 65 per cent for Canadians of origins other than French or British (Kalin & Berry 1992).

Knowing the ethnic identity of the self is to national election research in the 1990s as important, I would think, as knowing the occupation of the head of the household and, for many 'assimilated' subjects, more important than knowing the national origin of their ancestors (the implication is not that this last question should be abandoned but that it should be supplemented).

NOTES TO TABLE 1
† The first entry identifies the date of the issue, the second the issue number, and the third the initials of the author. The works included in the list are, in order of entry: Baird and Laskin (1970), Segal (1970), Laponce (1972), Grayson (1973), Richert (1973), Maghami (1974), Cuneo (1974), Irvine (1974), Wiseman and Taylor (1974), Hamilton and Pinard (1976), Jenson (1976), Curtis and Lambert (1976), Hamilton and Pinard (1977), Rayside (1978), Blake (1978), Lightbody (1978), Hamilton and Pinard (1978), Ornstein, Stevenson, and Williams (1980), Wilson (1980), Ornstein and Stevenson (1981), Black (1982), Johnston (1985), Archer (1987), Black (1987), Laponce (1988), Sniderman, Fletcher, Russell, and Tetlock (1990), Long (1990).
* The entries flagged by a star do not relate ethnicity to the vote or party preference but relate it to participation in voting or knowledge of politics. More specifically the flagged entries relate ethnicity to: 5: attitudes to authority; 6: knowledge of politics; 7: orientation to continentalism; 13: attitudes to the separation of Quebec; 14: attitudes to bilingualism; 16: civic candidature; 27: participation in band elections.

- Unlike their equivalent in the United States, the Canadian national election studies are not, election after election, conducted by the same institution. Thus far, continuity has been limited to two elections: Meisel 1965 and 1968, and Clarke 1974 and 1979. Varying researchers has some obvious advantages. That encourages innovation and renders more likely changes in research focus. But the downside is a lack of continuity in the questions used and in the wording of those that are included. Meisel's 1968 question on the language of work, Clarke's 1979 question on self-identity (Who am I?), and Lambert's 1986 many questions on the nuclear family have had no follow up. That is regrettable.

How much continuity should there be and how should it be obtained? The problem goes beyond the relating of ethnicity to the vote, it is a general problem that cannot easily be resolved, and cannot, that is obvious, be resolved by fiat. It might help that a conference of interested parties reflect on this subject and propose a list of core questions since the national election studies are intended to serve the whole research community.

- The attitudinal and policy questions relevant to the study of ethnicity have been overwhelmingly focused on French-English relations and on bilingualism. Questions concerning other ethnic groups and languages have been unsystematic even in the more 'ethnically' comprehensive of the surveys, those of Meisel 1968 and Johnston 1988. For example, only three social groups – English Canadians, Whites, and Jews – have been targeted by both of these last two studies for a measure of attitudes, typically by means of ranking on a preference scale.

Contrary to the impression this last example might give (two dominant groups, one minority) there is a tendency to formulate questions from the ethnically and numerically dominant groups. One is more likely to think of testing for the attitudes of Protestants vis-à-vis Jews, than vice versa. That is perfectly understandable if each survey is thought of in isolation from the others. In a sample of 3000 respondents there would not be enough Indians to warrant a study of their perceptions of French and English Canadians even if one thought that such information was necessary to understand their party preferences.

However, the national surveys can and have been merged into single files, thus making it possible to study, by collapsing time, groups not numerous enough to be studied in each election year separately. Such mergers require that the questions remain the same, or remain at least sufficiently similar to be merged (see notably the Elkins' merger of the 1965, 1968, and 1974 election surveys deposited at the UBC data library).[4]

The likelihood that more and more election surveys will be merged into single files in order to create time series as well as to increase the number of observations, makes it all the more important that there be continuity of questions and wording and that the answers be itemized in sociologically discrete categories (Polish or Russian rather than eastern European). The Clarke 1979 survey was right in separating the Hindus, Moslems, and Sikhs who had been included in the same category in the previous survey (Clarke 1974). It may not yet have made any difference to research, because of the small number of cases, but users of future time series will appreciate the distinction having been introduced.

If we now turn our attention to the 'other' surveys (other than the national election studies), surveys that were retrieved from the computer catalogue of the UBC data library by linking the key words 'vote' and 'ethnic' (Pinard 1965; Hoffman 1965; Elkins et al. 1980; Atkinson et al. 1981; Myles 1982; Sniderman et al. 1987), the picture does not change markedly even though the studies in this second category are much richer in their probing of ethnic identity and interethnic attitudes.[5] It remains that ethnicity is typically measured by means of objective criteria (such as the origin of the ancestors) rather than by the recording of attitudes; it is treated as an individual rather than as a group characteristic. Only in Quebec does Pinard (1965) allow his respondents to select contemporary definitions, while Elkins (1980) invites his subjects to describe the groups to which they feel they belong. True, Sniderman (1987) asks a straightforward question about the ethnic group of the subect, but unfortunately the precoded answers refer to the countries of origin before coming to North America.

Among *commercial* surveys, one database stands out – the Canadian Institute of Public Opinion (CIPO) – for both its long-time coverage and its accessibility. Together with the national election surveys, the CIPO has provided the bulk of the data used for Canadian election research. The limitations of the CIPO are in the roughness of its socio-demographic categories (language is defined in only three categories – English, French, and 'Other' – religion recognizes only Protestants, Catholics, Jews, Other, and None). Its great advantage is in offering a time series that goes back to 1945[6] and offering many in-between election measures of attitudes and opinions (in recent years, one per month). This long period is covered by a questionnaire the socio-demographic section of which has gone through remarkably few changes, hence offering the possibility of merging the existing studies to the point where one can analyze very small ethnic groups such as Jews (Laponce 1988) or Francophones outside Quebec (Laponce 1987). The largest single file of CIPO surveys is that created by Laponce and Ruus (1984) and deposited at the UBC and Toronto data libraries. It contains over a quarter million respondents and covers the period 1945–84 (the new surveys distributed by CIPO will be regularly added to the file if the funds can be found to do so). Having such mergers in mind, CIPO could refine its ethnic (and other) categories, at very little cost, to offer data, eventually, on communities that are now out of the reach of election research.

In short, two main recommendations stem from our study of primary sources: we need better measures of the ethnic group identity of the respondent (as distinct from the country of origin of his or her ancestors) and we need, when drafting our questionnaires, to keep in mind the likelihood that the data to be generated will be merged with other databases (hence the importance of refining the codes beyond the needs of a single survey).

This should enable us to go far beyond our present state of knowledge. We have abundantly demonstrated, with increasingly refined controls, that the 'Charter' minorities, Catholics and French Canadians, have, for the past two generations tended, until very recently, to concentrate their votes on the Liberal party, and we noted that the more the English and Protestants in Quebec tended to be put in the position of a minority the more they too tended to support the federal Liberals. We have also measured the near similarity of the Jewish and Catholic vote outside Quebec. What we lack are nation-wide studies of the vote of the smaller minorities. To study study them specifically, we need data that would enable us to dispense with aggregate, *fourre tout* categories such as 'New Canadian' and 'Other.'

SECONDARY SOURCES

Between defining subjectively one's corpus of cases, which means in effect being guided by one's past readings, and defining it objectively, I opted for the second strategy and decided to retain as secondary sources all the articles published in the *Canadian Journal of Political Science*, *Canadian Ethnic Studies*, the *Canadian Review of Sociology and Anthropology* and the *Canadian Review of Studies in Nationalism* for the period 1970–91, on the first condition that the articles to be considered would relate ethnicity to voting and party preference and on the second condition that the works so identified would relate dependent and independent variables by means of tables, graphs, or equations. That last condition eliminated all the articles in the *Canadian Review of Studies of Nationalism*, leaving us a total of 42 studies.

The amount of attention given to language, religion, and national or state origin by the *CJPS* and by the *CRSA* is in rough equilibrium: 13, 12, and 14 articles of the former refer respectively to language, religion, or national/state origin; while in the latter the statistics are 3, 2, and 3. The *CES* (that is a consequence of their very definition of ethnicity) gives far less attention to religion and language than to state and national origin.

Altogether, out of 42 articles, language and religion appear 16 and 15 times respectively, while national and state origin is used 25 times. I see nothing exceptional in these statistics except the lack of attention given to race. Only two studies of native Indians might possibly come under that heading.

Tables 2 and 3, which list the independent variables used by the studies we surveyed – are striking by the near absence of the smaller ethnic groups. The variables listed under *language* refer specifically only to French and English; all other languages are merged under the residual 'other.'

Religious denominations other than Catholics and Protestants appear rarely: Anglicans, United Church and Jews only twice, Baptists, Lutherans, Presbyterians, and Mennonites only once out of 42 studies.

Few are the studies of groups whose national origin is not either French or British. The only such groups to have been studied at least twice are the Ukrainians (five times), the native Indians (three times but only once by reference to a specific tribe), the West Indians (twice), the Japanese (twice), the Dutch (twice), the Icelandic (twice), and the Jews (twice).

A marked difference appears between the *CJPS* and the other two journals. The *CES* and *CRSA* articles are much more sensitive to the community aspects of ethnicity; they are much more likely than the *CJPS* articles to use discrete and anthropologically meaningful categories such as Cree, Japanese, or German. The *CJPS* is more likely to use catch all geographical classifications with little, if any, ethnic meaning, classifications such as Northern European, Southern European, Eastern European.

Note also (that is the consequence of the lack of attention given by survey research to the notion of group identity) how rarely the category 'Canadian' appears on Tables 2 and 3; it appears only twice. While focusing, that is understandable, on the French/English cleavage, the

TABLE 2

Ethnic variables appearing in the voting analyses published in *Canadian Ethnic Studies* 1970–91†*

	1971 F 1	1971 W,M,G 2	1971 Q 3	1971 F 4	1980 B 5*	1980 L 6*	1982 H 7*	1988 B,L 8
LANGUAGE								
English: At Home								
French: At Home								
English: Mother Tongue								
French: Mother Tongue								
English: Home L. '58/MT since '62		X						
French: Home L. '58/MT since '62		X						
RELIGION								
Mennonite	X							
Non-Mennonite	X							
NATIONAL AND STATE ORIGIN								
British, German, or Scandinavian				X				
Canadian			X					
Chinese	X							
Cree-Indian								
French				X				
German								
Italian								
Italian-Canadian								
Japanese			X			X		
Mixed								
Natives					X			
Non-Orientals			X					
Polish								
Scandinavian							X	
Ukrainian				X			X	
West Indian								X
South European								X
West European								X
East European								X

† The first entry identifies the date of the issue, the second the issue number, and the third the initials of the author. The works included in the list are, in order of entry: Friesen (1971), White, Millar, and Gagné (1971), Quo (1971), Flanagan (1971), Boldt (1980), Lam (1980), Hoffman (1982), and Black and Leithner (1988).

* The entries flagged by a star do not relate ethnicity to the vote or party preference but relate it to participation in voting or knowledge of politics. More specifically the flagged entries relate ethnicity to: 5: Native Indian leadership; 6: political efficacy; 7: political involvement.

TABLE 3

Ethnic variables appearing in the voting analyses published in the *Canadian Review of Sociology and Anthropology* 1970–91†*

	1977 T,W 1	1978 B,C,L 2*	1978 C 3	1979 S 4*	1979 G 5*	1980 K 6	1981 M 7
LANGUAGE							
English school system teachers in Quebec							X
French school system teachers in Quebec							X
English: Home				X			
French: Home				X			
Other than English or French: Home				X			
English speakers (self-defined)					X		
French speakers (self-defined)					X		
Other than English or French (self-defined)					X		
RELIGION							
Protestant			X				
Catholic			X	X			
Angl., United, Presb., or Luth.				X			
Jewish			.	X			
NATIONAL AND STATE ORIGIN							
Anglo-Saxon	X						
British						X	
British born	X						
Dutch						X	
European born	X						
French	X	X				X	
Other than French		X					
German						X	
Icelandic	X						
Italian						X	
Jewish	X						
Polish	X						
Ukrainian	X					X	
Other than Brit., Fre., Ita., Ger., Dut., Ukr.						X	

† The first entry identifies the date of the issue, the second the issue number, and the third the initials of the author. The works included in the list are, in order of entry: Taylor and Wiseman (1977), Burke, Clarke, and LeDuc (1978), Cheal (1978), Sinclair (1979), Grabb (1979), Keddie (1980), and Murphy (1981).

* The entries flagged by a star do not relate ethnicity to the vote or party preference but relate it to participation in voting or knowledge of politics. More specifically the flagged entries relate ethnicity to: 2: political participation; 4 and 5: powerlessness (ie, alienation from the political processes).

studies of election and party preference have tended to ignore not only the minorities but also the dominant ethnic group, which we often continue to define as English Canadian or Anglophone but is increasingly likely to define itself as 'Canadian.'

It could be objected that the way I defined my corpus introduced a bias against small minorities by excluding books that might give a more comprehensive view of the relationship between ethnicity and elections. To test than no such bias affected the analysis, I checked the publications retrieved from Iza Laponce's computerized bibliography of Canadian politics by linking the two descriptors 'vote' and 'ethnic.' The works in that set that were not already included in the original corpus (Pinard 1970; Meisel 1973; Schwartz 1974a; Schwartz 1974b; Wilson 1975; Jacek & Cunningham 1975; Meisel 1975; Donnelly 1976; Clarke 1978; Lijphart 1979; Flanagan 1979; Wood 1981; McMenemy 1989; Olzak 1982; Pammett et al. 1983; Gingras & Nevitte 1983; Kornberg & Stewart 1983; Blais & Nadeau 1984; Clarke, Kornberg & Stewart 1985) do not change the nature of our observations[7] (tabular details can be obtained from the author on request).

In short, political scientists and political sociologists, whether in books or articles, have given little attention not only to what is written small but also to what is written very large on the ethnic map of the country. In their studies of electoral participation and party preference they have too often ignored the smaller minorities and too often bypassed those who, ethnically, define themselves simply as 'Canadians.'[8]

CONCLUSION

This review of the research on ethnicity and voting led me to interspace my observations with recommendations addressed to the census bureau, to the drafters of election survey questionnaires, and more generally to the students of elections in multi-ethnic societies. Let me conclude by emphasizing two of these recommendations.

In common parlance, the term *multi* is used increasingly, in Canada, to characterize individuals as well as communities that are neither Native, nor French, nor British; and, in academic writings, the term *ethnic* is frequently used to refer to non-Charter minority groups. To follow the bend of the language and to isolate such *multis* and such *ethnics* within a specific field of research would be a fundamental mistake; hence the recommendation that we approach the study of multi-ethnic societies from the assumption that everybody is an ethnic, even those who reject the term in the name of an overarching national identification that is in fact an ethnic identification among others. We cannot understand the attitudes or behaviours of specific minorities unless we compare them to other minorities as well as to the dominant groups. We need to take a global view of multiculturalism.

A second, more specific recommendation, flows naturally from the first. I noted, in the election studies included above, a one-way mirror effect, a tendency to study the perceptions or attitudes of the dominant groups vis-à-vis the minorities much more frequently than studying the reverse. Such one-sided view, far more frequent in political than in psychological research, is no longer warranted when election surveys can be merged to the point where even very small groups can reach the appropriate number of sample cases. My conclusion is thus a plea to open wide the field of multicultural research in order that it can take a global view of Canadian society, and a plea for removing the one-way mirrors that deprive us of the full view needed to study a rich set of interactions.

NOTES

I am very much indebted to Wendy Bancroft and Jas Sekhon for their assistance in searching the literature and summarizing it in tabular form.

1 Unless otherwise indicated, the comments refer to the 1991 census.
2 I am unable to estimate the cost of such operation.
3 The year 1972 is covered by the pre- and post-election surveys done by Market Opinion Research and redistributed by the ICPR.
4 The merged file does not always retain the detailed categorization of the originals. It has 7 religious categories, while the survey of 1965 had 11, that of 1968 had 41, and that of 1974 had 36.
5 Pinard's survey (1965) has an interesting measure of the perceived link between specific professions and britishness, a good series of questions about the language and religion of one's friends and relatives, and data about the ethnicity of one's workmates; Atkinson (1981) has a rich series of questions testing respondents' desire to have more or less immigration from selected countries; and a very useful question about the kind of discrimination the respondent may have encountered. Myles has the most probing questions about languages known and used (up to *three* languages known, used at home, and used at work).
6 The first machine readable poll in the UBC data bank is CIPO number 142. The preceding polls could not be either retrieved or read by the computer.

7 Note, however, the detailed categories used by Schwartz in her chapter in Rose's book on electoral behavior.

8 Would the study of the relationship between politics and ethnicity under other aspects than voting and party preference have led us to different conclusions? What of representation and candidate support at party conventions? What of the articulation of ethnic pressure groups to the political system? Such questions would require specific studies that would lead us, most likely, to agree with Stasiulis and Abu-Laban (1990) who complain, in their description of selected contests of the 1988 party nominations: 'It is a measure of Canadian Social Science impoverished conception of "Ethnic politics" ... that so little literature exists on the contribution of ethnic minorities to Canadian political life.' They think that the election of 1988 may have been a watershed marking the greater involvement of non-charter groups in federal politics. Their series of well-documented vignettes of selected contests, mostly in Toronto, is an implicit call for more systematic data.

REFERENCES

Archer, Keith (1987). A simultaneous equation model of Canadian voting behaviour. *The Canadian Journal of Political Science*, 20(3):553–72

Atkinson, Tom, Blighen, B., Ornstein, M., and Stevenson, M. (1981). *Social change in Canada*. Machine readable survey deposited at York University

Baird, Richard (1966). The Slavic vote. In Yar Slavutych, R.C. Elwood, V.J. Kaye, and J.M. Kirschbaum (eds), *Slavs in Canada* (pp 154–65). Edmonton: La Survivance Printing

– , and Laskin, Richard (1970). Factors in voter turnout and party preference in a Saskatchewan town. *The Canadian Journal of Political Science*, 3(3):450–62

Black, Jerome H. (1982). Immigrant political adaptation in Canada: Some tentative findings. *The Canadian Journal of Political Science*, 15(1):3–28

– (1987). The practice of politics in two settings: Political transferability among recent immigrants to Canada. *The Canadian Journal of Political Science*, 20(4):731–54

Black, Jerome H., and Leithner, C. (1988). Immigrants and political involvement in Canada: The role of the ethnic media. *Canadian Ethnic Studies*, 20(1):1–20

Blake, Donald (1978). Constituency contexts and Canadian elections: An exploratory study. *Canadian Journal of Political Science*, 11(2): 279–306

Boldt, Menno (1980). Canadian Native Indian leadership: Context and composition. *Canadian Ethnic Studies*, 12(1)15–33

Burke, Mike, Clarke, Harold D., and LeDuc, Lawrence (1978). Federal and provincial political participation in Canada: Some methodological and substantive considerations. *The Canadian Review of Sociology and Anthropology*, 15 (1):61–75

Cheal, David (1978). Models of mass politics in Canada. *The Canadian Review of Sociology and Anthropology*, 15(3): 325–38

Clarke, H., Jenson, J., LeDuc, L., and Pammet, J. (1974). *The 1974 national election survey* (online readable data file deposited at Canadian University data centres including York and UBC)

– (1979). *The 1979 national election survey* (online readable data file deposited at Canadian university data centres including York and UBC)

Clarke, Harold D. (1978). Partisanship and the Parti Québécois: The impact of the independence issue. *The American Review of Canadian Studies*, 8(2):28–47

Converse, Philip, Meisel, J., Pinard, M., Regenstreif, P., and Schwarz, M. (1966). *The 1965 Canadian national election study*. Machine-readable survey deposited at the Interuniversity Consortium for Political Research, Ann Arbor

Cuneo, Carl J. (1974). Education, language, and multidimensional continentalism. *The Canadian Journal of Political Science*, 7(3):536–50

Curtis, James E., and Lambert, Ronald D. (1976). Voting, election interest, and age: National findings for English and French Canadians. *The Canadian Journal of Political Science*, 9(2):293–307

Donnelly, Murray Samuel (1976). Ethnic participation in municipal government: Winnipeg, St Boniface and the Metropolitan Corporation of Greater Winnipeg. In L.D. Feldmand and M.D. Goldrick (eds), *The politics and government of urban Canada: Selected readings* (pp 118–28). Toronto: Methuen

Elkins, David (1974). National elections 1965, 1968 1974: Merged data file. Machine-readable data deposited at the UBC data library

– , Blake, D., and Johnston, R. (1980). BC Election Study. Machine-readable survey deposited at the UBC data library

Flanagan, Thomas (1971). Ethnic voting in Alberta provincial elections 1921–1971. *Canadian Ethnic Studies*, 3(2):304–21

– (1979). Ethnic voting in Alberta provincial elections, 1921–1975. In Carlo Caldarola (ed.), *Society and politics in Alberta: Research papers* (pp 304–21). Toronto: Methuen

Friesen, John W. (1971). Characteristics of Mennonite identity: A survey of Mennonite and non-Mennonite views. *Canadian Ethnic Studies*, 3(1):25–41

Grabb, Edward G. (1979). Relative centrality and political isolation: Canadian dimensions. *The Canadian Review of Sociology and Anthropology*, 16(3):343–65

Grayson, Paul J. (1973). Social position and interest recognition: The voter in Broadview, or are voters fools? *The Canadian Journal of Political Science*, 6(1):131–9

Hamilton, Richard, and Pinard, Maurice (1976). The bases of Parti Québécois support in recent Quebec elections. *The Canadian Journal of Political Science*, 9(1):3–26

– (1977). The independence issue and the polarization of the electorate: The 1973 Quebec election. *The Canadian Journal of Political Science*, 10(2):215–59

– (1978). The Parti Québécois comes to power: An analysis of the 1976 Quebec election. *The Canadian Journal of Political Science*, 11(4):739–76

Hoffman, David, and Schindeler, Fred (1968). *Ontario Political Culture Study*. Toronto: York Survey Research Centre

Hoffman, George (1982). The new party and the old issues: The Saskatchewan farmer-labour party and the ethnic vote, 1934. *Canadian Ethnic Studies*, 14(2):1–30

Irvine, William (1964). An analysis of voting shifts in Quebec. In John Meisel (ed.), *Papers on the 1962 election* (pp 129–44). Toronto: University of Toronto Press

– (1974). Explaining the religious bases of the Canadian partisan identity: Success on the third try. *The Canadian Journal of Political Science*, 7(3):560–3

Jacek, Henry, and Cunningham, Robert (1975). Ethnic conflict and political action: Political parties and voters in urban Canada. *International Review of Modern Sociology*, 5(2):143–55

Jedwab, Jack (1986). Uniting uptown and downtown: The Jewish electorate and Quebec provincial politics, 1927–39. *Canadian Ethnic Studies*, 18(2):7–19

Jenson, Jane (1976). Some patterns of partisan allegiance. *The Canadian Journal of Political Science*, 9(1):27–48

Johnston, Richard (1985). The reproduction of the religious cleavage in Canadian elections. *The Canadian Journal of Political Science*, 18(1):99–113

– , Blais, André, Brady, Henry, and Crête, Jean (1988). The 1988 national election survey. Machine-readable survey deposited at the UBC data library

Kalin, Rudolph, and Berry, J.W. (1992) Ethnic, national and provincial self-identity in Canada. Paper presented at the June 1992 meeting of the Canadian Psychological Association

Keddie, Vincent (1980). Class identification and party preference among manual workers and the influence of community union membership and kinship. *The Canadian Review of Sociology and Anthropology*, 17(1):24–36

Lam, Lawrence (1980). The role of ethnic media for immigrants: A case study of Chinese immigrants and their media in Toronto. *Canadian Ethnic Studies*, 12(1):74–92

Lambert, Ronald, Brown, S., Curtis, J., Kay, B., and Wilson, J. (1986). The 1984 Canadian national election study. Machine-readable survey deposited at the University of Waterloo

Laponce, Jean A. (1969). Ethnicity, religion, and politics in Canada. In M. Dogan and S. Rohkan (eds), *Quantitative Analysis in the Social Sciences* (pp 187–216). Boston: MIT Press

– (1972). Post-dicting electoral cleavages in Canadian federal elections, 1949–68: Material for a footnote. *The Canadian Journal of Political Science*, 5(2):270–86

– (1987). Assessing the neighbour effect on the vote of francophone minorities in Canada. *Political Geography Quarterly* 6(1):77–89

– (1988). Left or centre? The Canadian Jewish electorate, 1953–83. *The Canadian Journal of Political Science*, 21(4):691–714

– (1990). L'identité ethnique du simple au composé: essai de typologie In William Lapierre, Vincent Lemieux et Jacques Zylbeberg (eds), *Être contemporain: Mélanges en l'honneur de Gérard Bergeron*. Québec: Presses de l'Université Laval

– , and Ruus, Laine (1984). Composite CIPO Data File 1954–. Machine-readable file deposited at the UBC and the University of Toronto data libraries

Lightbody, James (1978). Electoral reform in local government: The case of Winnipeg. *The Canadian Journal of Political Science*, 11(2):307–32

Lijphart, Arend (1979). Religion vs linguistic vs class voting: The 'crucial experiment' of comparing Belgium, Canada, South Africa, and Switzerland. *The American Political Science Review*, 73(2):442–58

Lipset, Seymour Martin (1950). *Agrarian socialism: The Cooperative Commonwealth Federation in Saskatchewan: A study in political sociology*. Toronto: Oxford University Press

Long, Anthony J. (1990). Political revitalization in Canadian Native Indian societies. *The Canadian Journal of Political Science*, 23(4):751–73

Maghami, Farhat Ghaem (1974). Political knowledge among youth: Some notes on public opinion formation. *The Canadian Journal of Political Science*, 7(2):334–40

Meisel, John (1964). *Papers on the 1962 election*. Toronto: University of Toronto Press

– (1968). The 1968 Canadian national election. Machine-readable survey deposited at the ICPR, Ann Arbor

– (1973). *Working papers on Canadian politics*. Montreal: McGill-Queen's University Press

– (1975). Political styles and language-use in Canada. In Jean-Guy Savard and Richard Vigneault (eds), *Multilingual political systems: Problems and solutions* (pp 317–66). Quebec: Presses de l'Université Laval

Murphy, Raymond (1981). Teachers and the evolving structural context of economic and political attitudes in Quebec society. *The Canadian Review of Sociology and Anthropology*, 13(2):157–82

Myles, John (1982). Comparative class structure project: Canada. Machine-readable survey deposited at Carleton University

Ornstein, Michael D., and Stevenson, Michael (1981). Elite and public opinion before the Quebec referendum: A commentary on the state in Canada. *The Canadian Journal of Political Science*, 14(4):745–74

– , Stevenson, Michael, and Williams, Paul (1980). Region, class and political culture in Canada. *The Canadian Journal of Political Science*, 13(2):227

Peterson, Thomas, and Avakumovic, Ivan (1964). A return to the status quo: The election in Winnipeg North Centre. In John Meisel (ed), *Papers on the 1962 election* (pp 91–106). Toronto: University of Toronto Press

Pinard, Maurice (1970). Working class politics: An interpretation of the Quebec case. *The Canadian Review of Sociology and Anthropology*, 7(2):87–109

Quo, F.Q. (1971). Ethnic origin and political attitudes: The case of Orientals. *Canadian Ethnic Studies*, 3(2):119–39

Rayside, David M. (1978). The impact of the linguistic cleavage on the 'governing' parties of Belgium and Canada. *The Canadian Journal of Political Science*, 11(1):61–97

Richert, Jean Pierre (1973). Political socialization in Quebec: Young people's attitudes toward government. *The Canadian Journal of Political Science*, 6(2):303–13

Riggs, Fred (1985). *Ethnicity*. Hawaii: Dept of Political Science, University of Hawaii

Schwartz, Mildred A. (1974a). *Politics and territory: The sociology of regional persistence in Canada*. Montreal: McGill-Queen's University Press

– (1974b). Canadian voting behaviour. In Richard Rose (ed.), *Electoral behaviour: A comparative handbook* (pp 543–618). New York: Macmillan

Segal, David R. (1970). Status inconsistency and party choice in Canada: An attempt to replicate *The Canadian Journal of Political Science*, 3(3):471–4

Sinclair, Peter R. (1979). Political powerlessness and sociodemographic status in Canada. *The Canadian Review of Sociology and Anthropology*, 16(2):125–35

Sniderman, Paul, Fletcher, J., Russell, P., and Tetlock, P. (1987). *Attitudes toward civil liberties and the Canadian Charter of Rights*. Machine-readable survey deposited at York University

Stasiulis, Daiva, and Abu-Laban, Yasmeen (1990). Ethnic activism and the politics of limited inclusion in Canada. In Alain Gagnon and James Bickerton (eds), *Canadian politics: An introduction to the discipline* (pp 580–608). Peterborough, ON: Broadview Press

Taylor, K. W., and Wiseman, Nelson (1977). Class and ethnic voting in Winnipeg: The case of 1941. *The Canadian Review of Sociology and Anthropology*, 14(2):174–87

White, Graham, Millar, Jack, and Gagné, Wallace (1971). Political integration in Quebec during the 1960's. *Canadian Ethnic Studies*, 3(2):55–84

Wilson, Jeremy R. (1980). Geography, politics and culture: Electoral insularity in British Columbia. *The Canadian Journal of Political Science*, 13(4):751–74

Wilson, John (1975). Decline of the Liberal party in Manitoba politics. *Journal of Canadian Studies*, 10(1):24–41

Wiseman, Nelson, and Taylor, K.W. (1974). Ethnic vs class voting: The case of Winnipeg, 1945. *The Canadian Journal of Political Science*, (7)(2):314–28

Wood, John R. (1981). A visible minority votes: East Indian electoral behaviour in the Vancouver South provincial and federal elections of 1979. In Jorgen Dahlie and Tissa Fernando (eds), *Ethnicity, power and politics in Canada* (pp 177–201). Toronto: Methuen

NORMAN BUCHIGNANI AND PAUL LETKEMANN

Ethnographic Research

INTRODUCTION

This paper surveys contemporary anglophone research on ethnicity in Canada using ethnographic methods.[1] In the first section we delimit the ethnic phenomena and study methodologies considered. This section is followed by a historical review. We then approach the contemporary material in two ways. The third section surveys the literature as a function of ethnic group, and the fourth and fifth sections in terms of phenomena of increasing scale. The fourth section accordingly deals with individual level phenomena, family and household, informal community organization and community institutions. The fifth section addresses inter-group relations. Recommendations for future research complete the paper.

Scope of the Paper

We restrict our attention to the English-language literature.[2] We also exclude consideration of social history, ethnic literature, 'researched' folk books using analogous methods, studies in education, and most applied research.[3] First Nations cultural maintenance and inter-group relations issues are now objectively significant and highly publicized, and more ethnographers research First Nations subjects than any other world cultural group. However, First Nations research has evolved separately from that on immigrant-origin groups, making comparison difficult; they do not use they same terms and metaphors, or frame similarly what might be seen as the same by those outside either tradition. Thus the subtextual ethnic studies' image is of recent urban immigrant *individuals* loosely formed into minority *ethnic* groups, facing personal challenges involving adaptation, acculturation, and individual human rights. The First Nations literature generally evokes an image of autochthonous, culturally linked *national* groups seeking group political and cultural rights. Thus, while ethnic theory is sometimes used to analyze American First Nations phenomena (Cornell 1988; Jarvenpa 1985; Muga 1988), in Canada this is rarely done. Likewise, most First Nations people are now at least temporarily urban, but there is a numbing silence about them in the urban-based ethnicity literature. Through necessity we concentrate on immigrant origin populations, including only those First Nations studies that explicitly use mainstream ethnic theory, address personal level inter-group relations, or consider urban First Nation people, communities, and institutions.

What Do We Mean by Ethnographic Approaches?

It is important to make clear our disciplinary, methodological, and discursive constraints, as some topics considered here are also addressed in other papers. As most of the ethnographic studies we wish to address were not done by anthropologists at all, we have not taken the easy route of reviewing work done only by them. We therefore have looked to methods, analytical goals and writing styles for our criteria of inclusion. Methodologically, we include research predominantly employing fieldwork-based, qualitative data collection dependent on some degree of cultural and language competency; methods that observe what people actually do, and culturally situate what they say they do. Analytically, we incorporate studies that attempt multidimensional, socially and culturally positioned description and explanation of phenomena involving socio-cultural difference. These include those that develop culturally grounded, insiders' views of individual experience, personal strategies and goals; personally held and interpersonally-negotiated cultural meanings and ideas about self and others; and social organization that is face-to-face or seen to be so. Our central criterion of inclusion is whether a study attempts to 'keep the people in,' as a continuing weakness of Canadian ethnic research is that it too often homogenizes and mutes ethnic people, speaking for them rather than allowing them to speak for themselves.

Bounding the Topical Frame

What ethnicity 'really is' is not a factual, but a definitional matter (Isajiw 1974). All such definitions are political, bringing certain things into relief and shading others. Rigorous contemporary academic definitions of ethnicity usually foreground certain inter-group aspects of human behaviour and consciousness. However, this is strongly at variance with the folk and social problems discourse and much research influenced by it that sees the ethnic group central, and intergroup phenomena as derivative (Hughes 1948:156). The latter practice is so prevalent that all ethnographic studies dealing with ethnic minority groups are considered here, even those that make little reference to inter-group issues.

HISTORICAL DEVELOPMENTS

1890 to the End of the Second World War

Canada was an early centre of ethnographic research on First Nations cultures (Boas 1884; Dawson 1887). Despite great social concern over the immigration of 'foreigners,' and the early evocation of the 'Canadian mosaic' metaphor (Foster 1924; Gibbon 1938), with the significant exception of a few affiliated with the Chicago School of sociology and anthropology, ethnographers evinced little interest. This tradition was deeply involved with contemporary issues of immigrant adaptation, community structure, and urban race relations (Shore, 1987; Kivisto 1990; Bulmer 1984). A central objective, often achieved through ethnographic methods, was to capture the flavour of the contemporary scene from the point of view of the many types of people contextually situated in it. Early Canadian examples include several dissertations (Che'ng 1931; Sumida 1935), Das's (1923) investigation of the BC South Asian community, and the first work done by established ethnographers (Miner 1938; Hughes 1943; Young and Reid 1938; Deets 1939). These studies are significant, partly because fewer than fifty ethnic and race relations studies of *any* kind were done before 1946; partly because their ethnographic orientation allows a textual richness through which now-historical ethnic people clearly speak.

From 1946 to the Rise of Multiculturalism in 1971

Canada experienced a great social and demographic transformation during 1946–71, in which millions of immigrants from an increasingly diverse range of cultural and national backgrounds played a central role. While the ranks of Canadian social scientists expanded significantly, this great phase of Canadian immigration and settlement went by largely unnoticed by researchers. The period added only about a hundred relevant studies, including about a dozen PH D dissertations and fifteen MA level theses. No coherent tradition existed, as typical publications were one-time efforts by individuals who never again wrote on ethnicity. Ethnographic research in sociology languished as a result of the rising hegemony of survey research methods. 'Professionalization' in anthropology manifested itself in attempts to further differentiate itself from sociology, leading it to remain oriented towards overseas research and conventional studies of Natives (McFeet 1980). There was some psychologically oriented (Honigmann 1965; Dunning 1964; Lubart 1970) and ethnic relations work (Dunning 1959; Parker 1964; Braroe 1965) done on First Nations peoples. Research output on Hutterites was considerable (Pitt 1949; Serl 1964; Bennett 1967; Hostetler & Huntington 1967), and Doukhobours also received some attention (Hirabayashi 1952; Hawthorn 1955). The pioneering work of Garique (1956) on French-Canadian kinship is still referenced, but French-English relations received virtually no notice at all (Jackson 1966). There were several preliminary forays on recent immigrant groups: Mayer (1959) on Sikhs, Nagata (1964) on Greeks, Boissevain (1970) and Jansen (1969) on Italians, Erickson (1966) and Wai (1970) on Chinese, and Khattab (1969) on Arabs. The long-term southwestern Saskatchewan research project of Bennett (1969), Braroe (1969, 1975) and Kohl (1976) also considered ethnic relations.

Thus, today we have little detailed information about any 1960s immigrant or First Nations group concerning the role of objective and symbolically significant cultural difference. Breton's work on community institutions and personal relations (1961, 1964) had not yet had much impact, and studies of community structure were few. Despite the high salience of American race relations, almost nothing was done on urban inter-group relations.

CONTEMPORARY RESEARCH: OUTPUT, THEORETICAL
ORIENTATIONS, AND ETHNIC GROUP CONCENTRATIONS

Research Output and Theoretical Orientations

Since 1971, ethnographically-oriented research output totals roughly 350 publications, reports and dissertations – an average of seventeen items per year, up from three to four during 1946–71. Professorial and graduate student interest in ethnicity increased, at least up to the early 1980s.[4] Several things caused this growth: the great expansion of the social sciences between 1965 and 1975; the financial and ideological support of federal multiculturalism;[5] a more diverse professoriate and graduate students (note that most cited names are neither Anglo nor French); in sociology, postmodernism fuelled more interest in culture and ethnographic methods; in anthropology, doing fieldwork in other countries became more difficult and its theoretical rationales less convincing, while research on urban and applied topics in one's own country became more broadly acceptable. Ethnographic research nevertheless remains a minority option, for this corpus represents approximately the average output of ten to fifteen university-based professionals – of whom there are approximately a thousand in Canada in sociology and anthropology alone.

Perhaps the single most important recent conceptual development concerns how ethnographers theoretically characterize ethnicity. Mapping an image of the isolate, rural, overseas village into ethnic studies, 1950s and 1960s anthropological works focused on the ethnic group as a culture-bearing minority. A paradigm shift marked by Fredrik Barth's (1969) elegant but theoretically incomplete (Buchignani 1982a) vanguard effort led to a worldwide (1970–early 1980s) fluorescence of ethnographic ethnic research. This new approach made central the analysis personal ethnic identity, inter-group personal social relations, and those cultural symbols used to signal or identify ethnic affiliation. It was highly dependent on individual-level models of choice and identity activation, which decreased earlier tendencies to overbound ethnic groups, insured more thorough group social, cultural, and political contextualization, and generated a much more dynamic approach for the analysis of consensus, dissensus, and individual variation. Now, postmodern influences are pushing the level of analysis lower still – to that of actual named individuals and their accounts of their lives.

Representing Particular Ethnic Groups

Public, government, media and NGO interest has always concentrated on groups that discourse has linked to social issues and social problems.[6] Research interest has slavishly followed suit, making research output on various groups extremely uneven. Thus there are many ethnographic studies of South Asians and Indochinese, these having been portrayed as the country's most culturally different and highest relief refugee populations, respectively.[7] More dissertations on South Asian groups were produced in the past two decades than on all ethnocultural groups before 1975.[8] In addition, a number of ethnographies (Buchignani 1992; Chadney 1984; Joy 1989) and edited books, and scores of articles and book chapters have seen print. This literature's strengths are its individual-centred accounts of family relations, settlement strategies, and informal community structure. Its weaknesses are lack of attention to individual-level ethnic relations and to peoples' articulation of ethnic with other identities and statuses such as gender, class, and occupation.

The Indochinese literature arose since the 1978–9 refugee exodus from Vietnam, but it now ranks second. It includes a monograph on Vietnamese in Quebec City (Dorais et al. 1987), two edited books containing ethnographic case studies (Chan & Indra 1987; Dorais, Chan & Indra 1988), a PHD dissertation on Vietnamese Chinese family structure (Lam 1983) and many articles by Kwok Chan, Louis-Jacques Dorais, Doreen Indra, U.-F. Woon, and others. Here, the strengths are psycho-social adaptation as linked to family and household and community structure, and the personal relations of individual refugees with helping organizations and individuals. Weaknesses include insufficient attention to individual-level cultural meanings and too much conceptual dependence on the refugee social problems discourse.

Chinese have been less actively researched. Several doctoral dissertations (Aiken, published in 1989; Fisher 1980; Hoe 1976) have been produced, as well as a number of other works (Kwong 1984; Lai 1988; Lam 1982; Yu 1987). There have been a couple of dissertations done on postwar Japanese (Makabe 1976; Ujimoto 1973), but little other commentary. Other Asian and Middle Eastern groups so rarely attract research attention that one cannot say that a literature on them exists at all.[9]

With two predictable exceptions (Mennonites: Appavoo 1978; Laurence 1980; Martine 1977; Young 1974; and Hutterites: Hamilton 1974; Heiken 1978; Clark 1974; Stephenson 1978, 1986), most other immigrant origin populations scarcely have been touched. We have found only one ethnographic study on Ukrainians (Matiasz, nd) and on Germans, just two articles on Russian Germans (Kloberdanz 1986, 1988). Save for the work of Jansen (1978, 1986) and a few others, the Italian saga has been told only by demographers, survey researchers, novelists, and poets. There is likewise little on Greeks (Herman 1978; Katma 1985; Chimbos & Agocs 1983; Thomas 1988; Vasiliadis 1989b), Portuguese (Anderson 1974; Fernandez 1978; Joy 1989), Latin Americans (Bishop-Bovell 1985), Dutch (Ishwaran 1977), other eastern Europeans (Baker 1989; Markus & Schwartz 1984; Watts 1976), English (Price 1980), Scots (Macdonald 1988), Irish (none at all), French (Maxwell 1971), or Jews (Kallen 1977; Shaffir 1974). Work on African Canadians dates primarily from the 1970s (Clairmont & Magill 1974; Henry 1973; Poole 1979; Rosenberg 1988;

Vuorinen 1974) and is insufficient to provide a deep sense of the richness and variability of this complex population.

There have been substantial developments in First Nations research. In fact, several works dealing with Native-'White' interpersonal relations addressed in subsequent sections (Braroe 1975; Brody 1975; Keho 1975; Kennedy 1982; Lithman 1986; Paine 1977; Hedican 1991; Henrikson 1971, 1978; Plaice 1990; Waldram 1987) demonstrate far more analytical sophistication than typical ethnic research. The political and institutional relations of Inuit and reserve-based Indians with the state and its representatives also has received considerable attention (Dyck 1985, 1991; Salisbury 1986; Asch 1984; Brody 1988; Culhane Speck 1987). Weaknesses are a continuing topical conservatism and widespread rejection of ethnic theory; and little interest in urban Native people (notwithstanding Brody 1971; Dosman 1972; Ryan 1978; Stymeist 1975; Krotz 1980; Morinis 1982; Waldram 1990) Métis, and non-status Indians.

IDENTITY AND THE MAINTENANCE OF SOCIOCULTURAL DIVERSITY IN A MINORITY CONTEXT[10]

Ethnic Identity and the Individual

Before 1971 few works dealt centrally with how ethnic individuals conceive of themselves. A couple (Dunning 1959; Parker 1964) portrayed Native people in marginal social situations. Two (Mayer 1959; Nagata 1964) initiated studies on the situational expression of ethnic identity. Two others (Bennett 1969; Hostetler & Huntington 1967) linked Hutterites community institutions and personal identity. Since then, roughly one-quarter of studies address some aspect of identity. However, very few works deeply investigate either what it personally means to be Italian, Greek, or Serbian (Scheffel 1991 is a notable exception), or the presentation and negotiation of such identities in interactional situations. Instead, most fall back on a simpler, more generalized model.[11] This literature has concentrated primarily upon South Asians (Buchignani 1979a, 1981, 1991; Chadney 1977; Dusenbery 1987; Subramanian 1977; Buchignani & Indra 1981) and Indochinese (K. Chan 1983a; Chan & Lam 1987a; Woon 1985; Dorais 1988). See also Vuorinen (1974), Henry (1973) and Poole (1979) on African Canadians, Baker (1989) on Poles, and Markus and Schwartz (1984) on Soviet Jews.

Of the many things that can influence ethnic identity, religion has been explored the most, primarily concerning ethno-religious groups:

Sikhs (Chadney 1977; Buchignani & Indra 1981, 1987; Mayer 1959; Dusenbery 1987; Buchignani 1987), Ismailis (Dossa 1985, 1988, 1991), Jews (Shaffir 1974; Kallen 1977), Old Believers (Scheffel 1991) and Hutterites (Heiken 1978; Stephenson 1978). Some work also has been done on the effects of religious practice on Tibetan (Dargyay 1988; McLellan 1987) and Vietnamese Buddhist (Dorais 1989) identity. Much of this research is narrowly functionalist and a bit mechanical (notably that on Hutterites), showing how religious practice and institutions support a rather static and generalized representation of self concept and ethnic identity. Those on Sikhs and some other groups more dynamically illustrate conflicting religious and ethnic claims, and how religion is used to bolster specific presentations of personal identity and status, and to advance social, political and economic goals.[12] The symbolic construction of public group identities (addressed generally by Breton 1984; Cohen 1985) is also considered by Macdonald (1988) on Cape Breton Scots, Price (1980) on English Montrealers, and Sorenson (1991) on contested presentations of Ethiopian identity.

Two rather pernicious assumptions pervade the literature: that ethnic identity is central to people identified as ethnic, and that it is relatively static and uniform with respect to the context of its activation and to people's other identities and statuses. Both profoundly limit our insights into ethnic identity and gender, which have so far principally been addressed concerning generic 'immigrant women' (Ng 1988) and South Asians (Dossa 1985, 1988; Ghosh 1981a, 1981b; Khosla 1980, 1981; Cunningham 1990). Otherwise, when gender is considered it is chiefly through an 'additive' analysis of how women constrained by source culture gender roles reconcile their personal identities under their changed circumstances as immigrants. More often, discussion of ethnic group identities is not disaggregated by gender at all, and little attention has been paid to how group ideologies, revisionist histories, and symbols of 'us' are gendered, legitimating some men at the expense of women; such discussion is generally found in analyses of family and community practice (see below). Similarly, linkages between ethnic identity and occupation, kinship and class are usually embedded in ethnographies of group social organization. Representative exceptions include Joy (1984, 1989), Cassin (1977), Cassin and Griffith (1981), Teal (1986), and Martine (1977) on ethnicity, occupation and class, and Indra (1988), Jabbra (1983), Kallen (1977), Makabe (1976, 1978) and Sugiman and Nishio (1983) on identity and kinship. Research on the activation of ethnic identities at the boundaries of groups sadly remains the exception (see the section below on inter-group relations).

In summary, ethnic identity studies remain less deeply analytical than the available theoretical tools allow. Facile generalizations about the identity of particular groups mask extensive individual and situational variation. Few authors deeply engage international theory, instead involving themselves centrally with the topical literature on particular ethnic or First Nations groups, or with that on immigrant settlement. Even so, such studies do present a rich cultural context of meaning for ethnic identity that nicely augments survey-based research on identity retention.

Family and Household

Much ethnographic research focuses upon family and household, which are the context for most gender analysis and the analytical starting point for studies of informal community structure. Again, research effort is concentrated on a few high relief immigrant populations stereotyped as being highly family oriented: one or another South Asian group (40 per cent of all citations) and Vietnamese, Vietnamese Chinese, Khmer, or Lao (15 per cent) predominates.[13] For no other immigrant origin population are there more than five or six studies centrally on these subjects.[14] Urban Natives are completely neglected.

Family and household research is highly focused on issues of initial settlement and change. A central goal is to show how women and men functionally use family and kin-based resources to achieve a 'successful' settlement; though unstated, this appears to be as much motivated by public concern over immigrant mal-integration as by any theoretical rationale. Some of functional analysis' weaknesses are seen here: a stress on consensus and co-operation rather than dissent and conflict, on benefits rather than costs, on those that succeed rather than those who do not, and on consequences for 'the family' rather than for particular individuals. The work illustrates a deep problem of comparison, as all immigrant groups 'succeed' eventually, as judged by conventional folk and government standards. This functional approach has its strengths too. Researchers have demonstrated that many people *do* make effective use of culturally based resources and strategies, gaining some things they want more easily than their immigrant status, class, occupations, and educational backgrounds would suggest. A case in point is how individuals gain entry to Canada and settle in specific parts of the country, communities, and households. It has been known for a century that many immigrant groups practise extensive chain migration, but only in the past twenty years have researchers paid it much attention.

Even now, only a couple of studies investigate the source country side of the equation (Buchignani 1979b; Johnson 1988). The rest are dependent on Canada-based data collection and analysis, much of it *ex post facto*, but have confirmed many earlier assumptions. Buchignani (1991, Chs 2–3), Chen (1981), Chimbos and Agocs (1983), Chadney (1977) and others demonstrate how relatives in Canada facilitate kin immigration through the provision of information, funds, sponsorship, and an inexpensive and psychologically supportive place to stay. They and others (Mayer 1959; Anderson 1974; Indra 1988; Herman 1978) have shown how prospective immigrant families lower risk by sending out pathfinders, typically younger men (earlier, among Italians, Greeks, and Portuguese, later among South Asians), but also women among Indochinese, Chinese, Filipinos, and Caribbean groups. Many studies of Asian and southern European groups indicate that recent immigrants rarely live alone if kin-based residence is available, and that partially extended or joint households are common during periods of high immigration. Some go deeply into the culturally grounded, individual reasons for such household arrangements, concentrating on economic and psychological factors. Considerable attention is paid to household economy, particularly to how certain practices reduce costs and facilitate savings among recently immigrated South Asian, Indochinese, Chinese, Greeks, Italians, and Portuguese.[15] Such strategies include the subordination of personal occupational goals in the interest of general family economic welfare, high family labour force participation rates, the partial pooling of incomes beyond those of husband and wife, and making buying a family home a central consumer goal.

It is uniformly claimed that family and household provide important psychological support for immigrant individuals. This is not altogether surprising, considering how firmly this notion is entrenched in the social problem and immigrant settlement discourse. Ethnographic studies that employ complementary formal psychological testing are rare (Indra 1988), and most psychological assessments are based on direct observation, informant claims, and the attribution of psychological motives to the enormous energy put into re-establishing and maintaining family structure (Chan 1983a; Chan & Lam 1987a, 1987b; Woon 1986; Buchignani 1983; Lam 1983; Quereshi 1980; Srivastava 1975; Buchignani & Indra 1985).

Perhaps the biggest accomplishment of the family and household literature is that it provides many personalized, factually rich, individual and small group-centred representations of acculturation, cultural maintenance, adaptation, and integration. In particular, it resoundingly challenges the practice of depending only on survey-derived indicators of acculturation. Valuable in their own right, such indicators when used alone strain out deeply divergent individual and group-specific meanings assigned to what nominally appears to be the same behaviour, including many which seem to indicate a dreary march towards full acculturation. It is true that upon such casual observation Sikh, Chinese, and Lebanese-Canadian family structures look much like all the rest. But such observations take little notice of culturally based *meanings* that individuals assign to family relations, and how such meanings are tied to what people actually do. Taking South Asian groups as an illustrative example, what comes out strongly is a tendency for individuals to identify certain practices, values, and beliefs as *symbolic* of the whole complex of ideal family structure and to work hard to maintain these; many such symbols become established as community values (Cohen 1985). By maintaining the maintainable, and by attaching strong but selective symbolic significance to some things, much of the meaning complex of family culture in first generation households is thus supported without the necessity of sustaining all its behavioural manifestations. Maintaining such things also empowers some individuals, and allows them a greater sense of cultural continuity.

Much contemporary family theory depends on a conflict-cooperation model of individuals equipped with specific resources, strategies, and goals daily negotiating their familial roles and statuses with each other, with the structure of particular families being one result. However, no ethnographic study has yet extensively employed this generative approach (save marginally for Buchignani 1992). Rather, primary uses of this model are to show how received family ideologies contain and subordinate resisting women (Ghosh 1981a, 1981b), how women interpret and reinterpret these ideologies (Khosla 1980), or how husband-wife and parent-child accommodation and consensus-building develop (Razaul 1978; M. Siddique 1974; 1983; C. Siddique 1977; Ames & Inglis 1973; Buchignani 1983; Chadney 1980; Dossa 1985; Khosla 1981b; Jabbra 1991; Thomas 1988; Indra 1988). Family and household studies still often partition sociocultural space into generic (supposedly genderless) ethnic group culture and practice, and 'women's problems and concerns'; it is as if while at home ethnic men have culture, but women have personal problems. Deeply embedded in larger studies is a considerable amount of information about the home-based symbolic maintenance of other things highly conserved in the immigrant generation, notably language, food, dress, and religion.

The elderly have received little ethnographic attention (Chan 1983b; Dossa 1991). That concerning the children of South Asian immigrants stresses tensions arising over parental expectations concerning dating and marriage, and the inability of parents to fully control their adult children. In many dimensions of life the children of immigrant South Asians (Kurian & Ghosh 1983; Wakil, Siddique & Wakil 1981; Chawla 1971; Sandhu 1980) and others (Makabe 1978 and Maykovich 1976 on Japanese; Park 1986 on Koreans; Jabbra 1983 on Lebanese) secure more independence and latitude than in the source country. Studies centring on the second generation are nevertheless rare (Makabe 1976, 1978; Chawla 1971; Kurian 1991; Kurian & Ghosh 1983; Wakil, Siddique & Wakil 1981; Sandhu 1980).

Informal Community: Kinship, Friendship, and Acquaintance

Despite the importance of formal community institutions to long-term ethnic group persistence (Breton 1964), the heart of ethnic communities is always their informal structure. In part this is simply because few ethnic communities achieve significant institutional completeness. But also it is because of the centrality of extra-familial kinship and friendship relations in immigrant source cultures, the role of chain migration in bringing together people already linked by kinship, friendship, and common circumstance, and the functional benefits sought for and often secured through community contacts.

From the beginning, community has been the primary frame empirically bounding ethnographic research. Canadian ethnic group ethnographies are almost all community-based, even through community is not usually the central focus. Methodically mining the many ethnographies found in the chapter bibliography would uncover enough information about informal community to generate a sociology of informal ethnic community structure, but no one has yet attempted this synthesis. Studies in all groups show that informal community social space is multiply divided by gender, kinship, generation, class, and sometimes religion, linguistic, and cultural difference. Moreover, they show systematic relationships between these sub-community breaks in social network space and personal and ethnic group identities, culture-specific notions of kinship obligations and appropriate interpersonal behaviour, and functional need. They also demonstrate that adult immigrant individuals from those groups that have either 'Mediterranean' or 'Asian' family structures are likely to have very extensive community contacts, typically numbering in the hundreds. Even so, surprisingly little research has focused specifically on informal community structure or on building up theoretical models of Canadian ethnic group informal community structure (Buchignani 1988). Monographs on informal community include Anderson's (1974) pioneering work on Portuguese community contacts, Husaini (1981) on South Asians, Clark (1974) on Hutterites, Davis (1985) on Acadians, and Braroe (1975), Brody (1975), Culhane Speck (1983), Driben (1985), Hedican (1987, 1991), and Henrikson (1978) on First Nations groups. Substantial empirical gaps remain in our knowledge of informal ethnic community. We almost totally lack studies of western European, North American, and Latin American immigrant community structure, and of all communities where the second and third generation predominate. Little attention has been paid to gender-specific social networks (Dossa 1988; Indra 1988), those of ethnic seniors (Dossa 1991; Chan 1983b) or the second generation (Sandhu 1980; Makabe 1978) in any population.

Formal Community Institutions

The 1970s rise of urban and applied anthropology initiated a substantial tradition of ethnographic research on home country formal institutions. Even so, ethnographic research specifically on community institutions remains sparse, the literature broadly following the same pattern as that concerning informal community. Most of these studies concern one focal institution or set of institutions rather than the total institutional panorama of particular communities. Those which follow the latter course tend to be on one or another ethno-religious group: Hutterites (Bennett 1967; Heiken 1978; Hostetler & Huntington 1967; Stephenson 1978), Old Believers (Scheffel 1991), and Ismailis (Dossa 1985). Exceptions include Gold's (1975) study of a Quebec town and Matiasz's (nd) look at the associations attached to three Edmonton Ukrainian cathedrals. Save for Hutterites and a few studies of other ethno-religious groups (Shaffir 1974), the focus is almost entirely on the institutions of immigrant adults.

Studies dealing with religious institutions are most numerous (Avapoo 1978; Dorais 1989; Dossa 1985, 1988; Dusenbery 1987; Martine 1977; Matiasz, nd; McLellan 1987; Nagata 1986, 1987; Shaffir 1974; Young 1974). Most stress how such institutions support ethnic identity and self-concept, maintain informal social networks, or develop and maintain ethnic group cultural values, symbols, and symbolic community. This reaches its apogee in Hutterite research on the role of school and church in perpetuating their way of life, which remains highly functionalist, literal, and rife with filial piety. Only a few (Dorais 1989; Dusenbery 1987; Matiasz, nd; Nagata 1986, 1987) investigate how these institutions create divergent sub-group identities and groups, or generate conflict over who will control these institutions and determine community symbols.

Ethnic group associations and their leadership structure have received some attention (Baker 1989; Chan 1988; Dorais et al. 1987; Fisher 1980; Indra 1987b; Jabbra 1984; Jansen 1969, 1978; Kwong 1984; Macdonald 1988; Sorenson 1991; Thompson 1989; Wai 1970; Cunningham 1990; Stasiulis 1980; Tarasoff 1989). While many such associations have a formal charter to perpetuate elements of source population culture, researchers tend to characterize them in primarily social, social-psychological and symbolic terms, as providing individuals with feelings of connectedness and continuity, and a rationale for social association. Leadership and spokesperson roles have been analyzed in terms of how they provide opportunities for individuals to renegotiate or maintain personal statuses, and the consequences of their brokerage between ethnic individuals and the 'outside' (chiefly the institutions of the state).

Some attention has been paid to economic entrepreneurs, though specific studies are rare (Aiken 1989; Gold 1975; Herman 1978; Lai 1988; Poole 1979). Taken together, research illustrates the important functional and cultural brokerage roles played by individuals providing goods and services in nearly all large, socially dense ethnic communities. In contrast, little research has focused on ethnic businesses (Herman 1978; Joy 1989). Gold's (1975) study of entrepreneurship in a Quebec town remains the most detailed ethnographic study of community-based business organization presently available.

INTER-GROUP RELATIONS[16]

Inter-Personal Relations

Discrimination against South Asians and African Canadians became a significant social issue in large cities as early as 1975. To it has been added concern over the treatment of urban Natives by their neighbours, and of First Nations people everywhere by representatives of state institutions. Fighting 'racism' (a term which Canadian social science has not well conceptualized) has been central to federal multiculturalism since 1981. Even earlier, anthropological ethnic theory and interest were

quickly shifting to the boundaries of ethnic groups, with symbolic inter-
actionism and exchange theory producing well-acknowledged results.
And yet ethnographic research on individual-level ethnic relations has
not increased since the 1970s. This is one of the most significant gaps in
the literature, as ultimately groups do not 'acculturate,' 'assimilate,'
'adapt,' or 'form relations with others.' Individual people do, yet we lack
basic information about the nature of such relations. By extension, we
know little about how ethnic individuals are tied into Canadian society,
economics, culture, and polity at the most basic level of their own direct
experience with their neighbours and workmates.

The analytically most sophisticated and most widely cited body of
such research concerns First Nations peoples (Braroe 1965, 1975; Brody
1975; Henrikson 1971, 1978; Kennedy 1982; Paine 1977; Plaice 1990; Smith
1975; Stymeist 1975; Waldram 1987; Hedican 1991). Four reasons for this
impact stand out, and provide guidance for future work on immigrant-
origin populations. First, the book-length studies of Braroe (1975), Brody
(1975), Henrikson (1978), Kennedy (1982), and Plaice (1990) are almost
symmetric with respect to the ethnic boundary. They are neither studies
only of one group's reactions to their treatment by others, nor just of
those others administering that treatment. Second, they systematically
investigate what actually happens when two kinds of people interact,
not simply peoples' assessment of that interaction. Third, they connect
this observed behaviour to how individuals in both groups perceive it,
and to the socio-economic and political settings of interaction. Fourth,
they ground their findings in theory that is explanatorily powerful,
easily understood, and extendable to other groups and situations.

Despite its importance, this literature has provided only a base
foundation for a truly rich understanding of personal relations between
Natives and others. Most studies have been done of comparatively
powerless Native people afflicted with many personal problems interacting with confident, middle-class 'Whites.' It is not therefore surprising
that such studies rather uniformly portray Native-'White' interaction as
extremely asymmetrical, with 'Whites' largely determining the interactional frame in their own image. There are, of course, many other less
asymmetrical possibilities. Research has concentrated primarily on male-
to-male relations, neglecting male-to-female and female-to-female ones.
Virtually all have portrayed 'others' to be ethnically undifferentiated,
empowered 'Whites,' which is a gross simplification. Almost all Native
people are involved with Natives from different cultural and linguistic
backgrounds, and urban Natives frequently interact with others who are

poor or visible minorities themselves. Many Natives are neither poor nor
powerless. Much is made of Native cultures and their persistence by the
same authors, yet little attention is paid to how specific Aboriginal
source cultures affect inter-group relations.

Individual-level inter-group relations research on South Asian groups
(mostly on Sikhs) runs a distant second to that on First Nations peoples
(Buchignani 1992: Ch. 8, 1981; Buchignani & Indra 1981, 1987b; Dusenbery 1987; Joy 1989). The only other population with an appreciable
literature are Indochinese, and this chiefly concerns relations between
refugees and those providing them with assistance (Indra 1987b, 1989,
1992; Woon 1984; van Esterik 1991). African Canadians may be at the
greatest risk of discrimination of any immigrant origin population, but
with two important exceptions (Henry & Ginzberg 1985; Moeno 1981)
have received virtually no attention. Studies of relations between
different minority group populations remain scarce (Vasiliadis 1989a;
Buchignani & Indra 1981; Joy 1989; Indra 1985; Woon 1985).

At the same time, there is extensive research on how members of
particular ethnic groups view such relations and how they *say* they
interact with 'the outside.' We now have several rich analyses of how
source cultural values and personal situation interact to generate a
panorama of preferences concerning the acceptance of 'mainstream'
social and cultural practice (eg, Scheffel, 1991). For all Asian and Mediterranean groups one of the important expressed tensions in inter-group
relations concerns the perceived disparity between source country and
Canadian 'family values' and gender-linked practices such as dating and
marriage (Cunningham 1990). Many works dealing with groups stereotyped as highly ethnocentric (Hutterites, Mennonites, Old Believers,
Chassidim, Sikhs, and other South Asians) go further, analyzing perceptions of religious and moral difference and their consequences.

Relations between Ethnic Individuals and 'Outside' Institutions

No ethnic community is institutionally complete. This dependency on
mainstream society is so profound that 'fair' institutional access has been
an important social issue for almost twenty years. However, both in
public debate and in research the treatment of institutionalized 'racism'
has been highly ideological and crudely categorical (Buchignani 1991).
An ethnographic approach offers considerable potential here, but with
the notable exception of the studies on Native-'White' relations mentioned above, little has been done. No study, for example, uses ethno-

graphic methods to investigate ethnicity and bias in hiring, workplace relations, job advancement, or housing. There is, however, a growing literature on links between individuals and institutions providing various services: social (Welin & Ervin 1991; Disman 1983), health (Culhane Speck 1987; Onell 1986), immigrant settlement (Indra 1987b, 1992; van Esterik 1991; Gilad 1990; Ng 1988; Woon 1984) and Native services (Ryan 1978; Culhane Speck 1987) in particular. One strong theme in these studies is how profound organizational and interpersonal barriers restrict the effective provision of services. Another theme is closely linked – how rigid bureaucratic grids revise and recast idiosyncratic and culturally different client statements and other personal data to fit an extant frame of institutional meaning (Indra 1987b, 1989), thus re-making clients into normative middle class persons.

Representing Culture in the Nation State

Postmodernism has produced greater reluctance among ethnographic researchers today to take conceptual categories as given, whether they be those of the state, popular culture, ethnic individuals, or their own. There is increased interest in such categories as representations, and in how such representations are connected to personal meanings and are used in public discourse to generate conceptions of types of individuals, groups and the state itself. In this way, research on minority groups increasingly has been tied to issues of nation state formation and change (Williams 1989; Bentley 1987). Thus, while the topic may seem rather far removed from ethnography's sterotypical 'micro' focus, the question of how cultural groups and the state are represented is now part of its agenda.

In few rich countries is public discourse is so heavily laced with talk about culture, multiculturalism, cultural group and nation as in Canada. So far, though, researchers have not systematically responded to this potential. Much micro-level work has been done on the impact of patrons and brokers on shared meanings (Henrikson 1971, 1978; Paine 1977; Dyck 1985, 1991; Jansen 1969, 1978; Nagata 1987), but few studies follow even a partial postmodernist agenda (Handler 1988; Macdonald 1988; Indra 1989). Of these, Handler's (1988) widely read book on the nationalist Parti Québécois' reformulation of Québécois 'traditional' culture provides a model for future research on analogous topics such as the discourse on federal Multiculturalism and 'racism,' on institutional worldview creation and maintenance, and on group cultural images as negotiated meanings.

RECOMMENDATIONS

Ethnographic research on cultural difference, ethnic group social organization, and inter-group relations complements alternative research
strategies in two important ways. First, it produces rich descriptions of
the heart of ethnic culture, and how the individuals who carry and
modify these cultural traditions understand and react to life's challenges.
Second, such work is part of a sophisticated tradition of writing ethnography to be widely accessible; ethnographic accounts (eg, Brody 1975)
can be a powerful means of informing Canadians at large about ethnicity
and cultural difference. However, its influence in both academic and folk
domains could be much greater than it has been. The reasons are demographic, methodological, conceptual, and topical.

Demographic Constraints

Comparatively few currently employ ethnographic methods in Canadian
ethnic studies, and fewer still make this their career. It is thus not that
ethnography has little impact, but that few people are doing the impact-
ing. This will not change quickly unless research funding priorities
radically change, or theoretical orientations shift to make such work
more fashionable. The former seems unlikely, but perhaps not the latter.
Greater concern with cultural issues in sociology and postmodernist
influences in anthropology have undoubtably fuelled increased interest
in recent years, and both movements are sufficiently broadly based that
this trend will persist for some time.

Methodological Constraints

Suggesting that any single social science method is intrinsically superior
to the rest is blindly chauvinistic and indicative of a truly outdated
notion of knowledge creation. Still, even now methodological chauvin-
ism is the rule in Canadian ethnic studies, partitioning it into a number
of camps that rarely speak to each other; while the field is becoming
more cross-disciplinary, such links rarely extend across methodological
divides. It remains standard practice for ethnographers to totally neglect
the findings of survey researchers, social historians, social psychologists,
demographers, or education researchers, even when the latter data are
on the same focal population. Indeed, other ethnographers are routinely
neglected when they are working with only marginally different popula-

tions. A devastating consequence is the systematic underutilization of all research findings and far less topical and group-specific literature integration than is possible. It is difficult to see how this practice will change except through some kind of imposed quality control at the review and granting level, which at present seems improbable.

Conceptual Constraints

At the same time, ethnographically-oriented researchers themselves have limited the impact of their work (especially upon policy and programming) by how they have bounded their conceptual universe. Critically, a greater degree of conceptual distinction between popular culture social issues and research frames of understanding is necessary. The lack of this separation has had many negative consequences mentioned previously: research has too little definitional or conceptual autonomy; research activity on particular groups and topics is driven chiefly by the current social problems/issue public salience of the groups and topics in question; topical areas are narrowly framed by social issues without researchers even being aware of it; comparative work and theoretical integration are made difficult; theoretically and conceptual integration of the now-distinct literatures on First Nations and immigrant-origin peoples proceeds slowly; thorough disaggregation of discussion by gender remains the exception.

Group and Topical Constraints

Greater topical diversity is necessary also. There is no good reason for the high concentration of research on a few ethnic populations at the expense of all the rest, on immigrants rather than urban Natives, or on the first generation rather than the second or third. The old and the young, the well-off, suburb dwellers, and almost everyone outside Toronto, Vancouver, and Montreal remain almost invisible. A wide range of important topics deserve greater attention: the direct, person- and context-specific study of ethnic identity and personal meanings; detailed analyses of informal community structure and individuals' ethnic and non-ethnic personal relations; mainstreamers as ethnics; entrepreneurship, brokerage, and patronage; interpersonal dynamics in community institutions; and the representation of ethnicity in public discourse. More ethnographic research is needed also at the boundaries of groups on ethnic identity activation, the transactional basis of such relations, and the contextual allocation of power, privilege, and prestige.

NOTES

1 For 1970-91 we reviewed every issue of *Canadian Ethnic Studies, Canadian Review of Sociology and Anthropology, Culture, Journal of Canadian Studies, American Anthropologist, American Ethnologist, Man, Current Anthropology, International Migration Review, Ethnic and Racial Studies, Ethnic Groups,* and the *Journal of Ethnic Studies.* PH D dissertations are well considered, but MA theses are not. One of us has done several relevant reviews (Buchignani 1977b, 1980b, 1982a, 1982b, 1987b, 1987c). Space constraints require our use of citations to be illustrative rather than exhaustive. A full bibliography is available on request.

2 See Helly, Bourhis, and Clément on Quebec (issues in this volume).

3 See Rasporich's chapter on historical studies, Paldolsky, and Simon and Leady on ethnic minority literature, and Gemlin, and Yelaja and O'Neill on education in this volume.

4 11.5% (31 of 269) of sociocultural anthropologists affiliated with anglo-phone Canadian universities listed in the American Anthropological Association's 1990-1 *Directory of Departments,* and 13.5% of those at francophone universities (9 of 67) claimed ethnicity as a specialization. The anglophone percentage is up marginally from its 10% level in 1978-9 Buchignani (1982b:21). During 1985-6 alone (the last years for which we have full figures) four PH D dissertations and at least eight MA theses on relevant subjects were produced in sociology or anthropology. These represent roughly 5% of all sociology and anthropology PH D and 2-3% of MA output in that year.

5 See Wilson (1991) on multiculturalism policy, and, in this volume, Helly on the policy towards cultural communities in Quebec, and Paquet on the philosophical basis for multiculturalism.

6 See Krótki and Reid on demographic studies of Canadian ethnic populations.

7 See Buchignani (1977b, 1980b, 1987b) for reviews of the South Asian literature, and Indra (1987a) and Veilleux (1991) on Indochinese.

8 Buchignani (1977a), Chadney (1976), Subramanian (1977), and Dossa (1985) are representative.

9 On Filipinos see (Chen 1981). Excepting Razaul (1978), only Lebanese have received attention among Middle Eastern groups (Barclay 1976; Jabbra 1984, 1991).

10 See Weinfield on cultural persistence and assimilation, and Kalin and Berry on social psychological studies of ethnic identity.

11 The model: immigrants' much changed circumstances generate marginality and question pre-migration identities. Demand for psychological consistency, conformity pressure, and functional demands lead individuals to reformulate their multiple identities, one or more of which are ethnic.

12 Katma (1985) on Greeks; Matiasz (nd) on Ukrainians; Martine (1977) and Laurence (1980) on Mennonites; Migliore (1988) on Sicilians; Dorais (1989) and Nagata (1986, 1987) on Southeast Asians.

13 On South Asians, see Ames and Inglis (1973), Buchignani (1983), Buchignani and Indra (1985), Chadney (1975, 1980), Chawla (1971), Dossa (1985), Khosla (1981), Kurian (1991), Quereshi (1980), C. Siddique (1977), M. Siddique (1974, 1983), Srivastava (1975), and Subramanian (1977). On Indochinese see Chan (1983a), Chan and Lam (1987b), Lam (1983), Indra (1985), Boyd (1981), Dorais et al. (1987), and Woon (1986, 1987).

14 On Arabs see Barclay (1976), Jabbra (1983, 1991); and Fisher (1980) on Chinese.

15 See Buchignani (1980a, 1991), Chadney (1984), Dorais et al. (1987), Dossa (1985), Fisher (1980), Lam (1983), Razaul (1978), C. Siddique (1977) and M. Siddique (1974, 1983).

16 See also the chapter by Kalin and Berry in this volume.

REFERENCES

Aiken, R. (1989). *Montreal Chinese, property ownership and occupational change, 1881–1891*. New York: AMS Press

American Anthropological Association (1991). *Directory of departments*. Washington, DC: American Anthropological Association

Ames, M.M., and Inglis, J. (1973). Conflict and change in British Columbia Sikh family life. *BC Studies, 20*:15–49

Anderson, G. (1974). *Networks of contact: The Portuguese and Toronto*. Waterloo: Wilfrid Laurier University

Appavoo, M.D. (1978). Religion and family among the Markham Mennonites. Unpublished doctoral dissertation, Yale University

Asch, M. (1984). *Home and Native land: Aboriginal rights and the Canadian constitution*. Toronto: Methuen

Baker, R.P. (1989). The adaptation of Polish immigrants to Toronto: The Solidarity wave. *Canadian Ethnic Studies, 21*(3):74–90

Barclay, H. (1976). The Lebanese Muslim family. In K. Ishwaran (ed.), *The Canadian family* (pp 92–104). Toronto: Holt, Rinehart and Winston

Barth, F. (1969). Introduction. In F. Barth (ed.), *Ethnic groups and boundaries: The social organization of cultural difference.* Boston: Little Brown and Co

Bennett, J. (1967). *Hutterian brethern: The agricultural economy of a communal people.* Stanford: Stanford University Press

– (1969). *Northern plainsmen: Adaptive strategy and agrarian life.* Arlington Heights, IL: AHM Publishing

Bentley, G.C. (1987). Ethnicity and practice. *Comparative Studies in Society and History, 29*(1):24–55

Bishop-Bovell, B. (1985). An ethnographic study of first generation Latin American immigrant couples resident in Ontario. Unpublished master's thesis, Dept of Sociology, Queen's University

Boas, F. (1884) A journey in Cumberland Strait and on the west shore of Davis Strait in 1883 and 1884. *Journal of the American Geographical Society, 16*:242–72

Boissevain, J. (1970). *Italians of Montreal.* Ottawa: Queen's Printer

Boyd, M. (1981). *The new pioneers: Ethnicity and the Vietnamese refugees in Nova Scotia.* Ethnic Heritage Series, Volume 3. Halifax: International Education Centre, Saint Mary's University

Braroe, N. (1965). Reciprocal exploitation in an Indian-White community. *Southwestern Journal of Anthropology, 21*:166–78

– (1975). *Indian and white: Self-image and interaction in a Canadian plains community.* Stanford: Stanford University Press

Breton, R. (1961). Ethnic communities and the personal relations of immigrants. Unpublished doctoral thesis. Baltimore: Johns Hopkins University Press

– (1964). Institutional completeness of ethnic communities and personal relations of immigrants. *American Journal of Sociology, 70*(2):193–205

– (1984). The production and allocation of symbolic resources: An analysis of the linguistic and ethnocultural fields in Canada. *Canadian Review of Sociology and Anthropology, 21*(2):123–44

Brody, H. (1971). *Indians on skid row.* Ottawa: Northern Science Research Group, Dept of Northern Development

– (1975). *The people's land: Whites and the eastern Arctic.* Harmondsworth, Eng.: Penguin Books

– (1988). *Maps and dreams: Indians and the British Columbia frontier.* Vancouver: Douglas & McIntyre

Buchignani, N. (1977a). Immigration, adaptation, and the management of ethnic identity. Unpublished doctoral thesis, Dept of Sociology and Anthropology. Vancouver: Simon Fraser University

– (1977b). A review of the historical and sociological literature on East Indians in Canada. *Canadian Ethnic Studies, 9*(1):86–108

– (1979a). Social identity formation and interpretation: Recent East Indian immigration to British Columbia. In J. Elliott (ed.), *Two nations, many cultures: Ethnic groups in Canada* (pp 325–37). Scarborough, ON: Prentice-Hall

– (1979b). The effect of Canadian immigration on the political economy of Fiji. In O. Mehmet (ed.), *Poverty and social change in Southeast Asia* (pp 265–83). Ottawa: University of Ottawa Press

– (1980a). The economic adaptation of Southeast Asian refugees in Canada. In E. L. Tepper (ed.), *Southeast Asian exodus: From tradition to resettlement* (pp 191–204). Ottawa: Canadian Asian Studies Association

– (1980b). South Asians and the ethnic mosaic: An overview. *Canadian Ethnic Studies,* 11(1):48–68

– (1981a). The social and self identities of Fijian Indians in Vancouver. *Urban Anthropology,* 9(1):75–98

– (1982a). *Anthropological approaches to the study of ethnicity.* Occasional Paper in Ethnic and Immigration Studies (OP 82-13). Toronto: Multicultural History Society of Ontario

– (1982b). Canadian ethnic research and multiculturalism. *Journal of Canadian Studies,* 17(1):16–34

– (1983). Determinants of Fijian Indian social organization in Canada. In G. Kurian and R. Srivastava (eds), *Overseas Indians: A study in adaptation* (pp 68–89). New Delhi: Vikas

– (1987a). Conceptions of Sikh culture in the development of a comparative analysis of the Sikh diaspora. In M. Israel and J. O'Connell (eds), *Sikh religion and history in the twentieth century* (pp 276–95). Toronto: University of Toronto Press

– (1987b). Social science research on South Asians and Canada: retrospect and prospect. In M. Israel (ed.), *The South Asian diaspora in Canada* (pp 113–41). Toronto: Multicultural History Society of Ontario

– (1987c). Contemporary Canadian research on ethnicity employing anthropological perspectives. Plenary Address, Biennial Meeting, Canadian Ethnic Studies Association, Halifax

– (1988). Toward a sociology of Indochinese Canadian social organization: A preliminary statement. In K. Chan, et al. (eds), *Ten years later: Indochinese communities in Canada* (pp 13–36). Ottawa: Canadian Asian Studies Association

– (1991). Some comments on the elimination of racism in Canada. In Ormond McKague (ed.), *Racism in Canada* (pp 199–206). Saskatoon: Fifth House Publishers

– (1992). *Fijians in Canada: The structural determinants of a new community.* New York: AMS Press

– , and Indra, D.M. (1981). Inter-group conflict and community solidarity: Sikhs and South Asian Fijians in Vancouver. *Canadian Journal of Anthropology,* 1(2):149–57

– (1985). *Continuous journey: A social history of South Asians in Canada.* Toronto: McClelland & Stewart

– (1987). Key issues in Canadian-Sikh ethnic and race relations, and their implications for the study of the Sikh diaspora. In G. Barrier and V. Dusenbery (eds.), *The Sikh diaspora* (pp 141–84). New Delhi: Manohar

Bulmer, M. (1984). The Chicago school of sociology: Institutionalization, diversity, and the rise of sociological research. Chicago: University of Chicago Press

Cassin, A.M. (1977). Class and ethnicity: The social organization of working class East Indian immigrants in Vancouver. Unpublished master's thesis, University of British Columbia

– , and Griffith, A. (1981). Class and ethnicity: Producing the difference that counts. *Canadian Ethnic Studies, 8*(1):109–30

Ch'eng, T-F. (1931). *Oriental immigration in Canada.* Shanghai: Commercial Press

Chadney, J. (1975). The joint family as a structure and process. *Journal of Social Thought, 1*(1):17–22

– (1976). The Vancouver Sikhs: An ethnic community in Canada. Unpublished doctoral thesis. Michigan State University

– (1977). Demography, ethnic identity and decision-making: The case of the Vancouver Sikhs. *Urban Anthropology, 6*(3):187–204

– (1980). Sikh family patterns and ethnic adaptation in Vancouver. *Amerasia Journal, 7*(1):30–50

– (1984). *The Sikhs of Vancouver.* New York: AMS Press

Chan, K.B. (1983a). Resettlement of Vietnamese Chinese refugees in Montreal Canada: Some socio-psychological problems and dilemmas. *Canadian Ethnic Studies, 15*(1):36–50

– (1983b). Coping with aging and managing self-identity: The social world of the elderly Chinese. *Canadian Ethnic Studies, 15*(3):36–50

– (1988). The Chinese from Indochina ten years later in Montreal (1975–1985): A study in ethnic voluntary associations, community organizing and ethnic boundaries. In L.J. Dorais, K. Chan, and D. Indra (eds), *Ten years later: Indochinese communities in Canada.* Ottawa: Canadian Asian Studies Association

– , and Indra, D.M. (eds) (1987). *Uprooting, loss and adaptation: The resettlement of Indochinese refugees in Canada.* Ottawa: Canadian Public Health Association

Chan, K.B., and Lam, L. (1987a). Psychological problems of Chinese Vietnamese refugees resettling in Quebec. In K. Chan and D. Indra (eds), *Uprooting, loss and adaptation: The resettlement of Indochinese refugees in Canada* (pp 27–41). Ottawa: Canadian Public Health Association

– (1987b). Community, kinship and family in the Chinese Vietnamese community: Some enduring values and patterns of interaction. In K. Chan and D. Indra (eds), *Uprooting, loss and adaptation: The resettlement of Indochinese refugees in Canada* (pp 15–26). Ottawa: Canadian Public Health Association

Chawla, S. (1971). Indian children in Toronto: A study of socialization. Unpublished master's thesis. Toronto: York University

Chen, A. (1981). Kinship system and chain migration: Filipinos in Thunder Bay. In K. Ujimoto and G. Hirabayashi (eds), *Asian Canadian Symposium #5* (pp 185–206). Halifax: Mount Saint Vincent University

Chimbos, P., and Agocs, C. (1983). Kin and hometown networks as support systems for the immigration and settlement of Greek Canadians. *Canadian Ethnic Studies, 15*(2):42–56

Clairmont, D.H., and Magill, D.W. (1974). *Africville: The life and death of a Canadian Black community.* Toronto: McClelland & Stewart

Clark, P.G. (1974). Dynasty foundation in the communal society of the Hutterites. Unpublished doctoral thesis, University of British Columbia

Cohen, A.P. (1985). *The symbolic construction of community.* London: Tavistock

Cornell, S. (1988). The transformations of tribe: Organization and self-concept in Native American ethnicities. *Ethnic and Racial Studies, 11*(1):27–47

Culhane Speck, D. (1987). *An error in judgment: The politics of medical care in an Indian/White community.* Vancouver: Talon Books

Cunningham, J.D. (1990). Classical dance of India in Canada: Issues of adaptation and play. Unpublished doctoral thesis. Los Angeles, CA: William Lyon University

Dargyay, L. (1988). Tibetans in Alberta and their cultural identity. *Canadian Ethnic Studies, 20*(2):114–23

Das, R.K. (1923). *Hindustanee workers on the Pacific coast.* Berlin: Walter de Gruyter

Davis, N. (1985). *Ethnicity and ethnic group persistence in an Acadian village in Maritime Canada.* New York: AMS Press

Dawson, G.M. (1887). *Notes and observations on the Kwakiuool people.* Royal Society of Canada Transactions, Vol. 5, Section 11

Deets, L.E. (1939). *The Hutterites: A study in social cohesion.* Gettysburg: Time and News Publishing

Disman, M. (1983). Immigrants and other grieving people: Anthropological insights for counselling practices and policy issues. *Canadian Ethnic Studies, 15*(3):106–18

Dorais, L-J. (1988). Cold solitude and snowy peace: The Indochinese in Quebec City. In L-J. Dorais, et al. (eds), *Ten years later: Indochinese communities in Canada* (pp 165–88). Ottawa: Canadian Asian Studies Association

- (1989). Religion and refugee adaptation: The Vietnamese in Montreal. *Canadian Ethnic Studies*, 21(1):19–29
Dorais, L-J., Pilon-Le, L., and Huy, N. (1987). *Exiles in a cold land: A Vietnamese community in Canada*. New Haven: Yale University, Southeast Asia Studies
Dosman, E.J. (1972). *Indians: The urban dilemma*. Toronto: McClelland & Stewart
Dossa, P. (1985). Ritual and daily life: Transmission and interpretation of the Ismaili tradition in Vancouver. Unpublished doctoral thesis, Dept of Sociology and Anthropology, University of British Columbia
- (1988). Women's space/time: An anthropological perspective on Ismaili immigrant women in Calgary. *Canadian Ethnic Studies*, 20(1):45–65
- (1991). Time, age and ritual: An anthropological perspective on elderly Ismailis. In S. Sharma, A. Ervin, and D. Meintel (eds), *Immigrants and refugees in Canada: A national perspective on ethnicity, multiculturalism, and cross-cultural adjustment* (pp 37–46). Saskatoon: University of Saskatchewan and Université de Montréal
Driben, P. (1985). *Aroland is our home: An incomplete victory in applied anthropology*. New York: AMS Press
Dunning, R.W. (1959). Ethnic relations and the marginal man in Canada. *Human Organization, 18*(3)
- (1964). Some problems of reserve Indian communities: A case study. *Anthropologica*, 6:3–39
Dusenbery, V.A. (1981). Canadian ideology and public policy: The impact on Vancouver Sikh ethnic and religious adaptation. *Canadian Ethnic Studies*, 8(3):101–20
- (1987). Punjabi Sikhs and Gora Sikhs: Conflicting assertions of Sikh identity in North America. In J. O'Connell, M. Israel, and W.H. McLeod (eds), *Sikh history and religion in the twentieth century* (pp 334–55). Toronto: Centre for South Asian Studies, University of Toronto
Dyck, N. (ed.) (1985). *Indigenous peoples and the nation state: 'Fourth world' politics in Canada, Australia and Norway*. St John's, NF: Institute of Social and Economic Research
- (1991). *What is the Indian 'problem'? Tutelage and resistance in the Canadian Indian administration*. St John's, NF: Institute of Social and Economic Research
Erickson, B.H. (1966). Prestige, power and the Chinese. Unpublished doctoral thesis, University of British Columbia
Fernandez, R.L. (1978). The logic of ethnicity: A study of the Montreal *Portuguese*. Unpublished doctoral thesis, McGill University
Fisher, S. (1980). Changing patterns in social organization among the Chinese in Ottawa: A study in internal and external determinants. Unpublished doctoral thesis, Dept of Sociology, Carleton University

Foster, K.A. (1924). *Our Canadian mosaic*. Toronto: Dominion Council of the YWCA

Garique, P. (1956). French Canadian kinship and urban life. *American Anthropologist, 58*:1090–1101

Ghosh, R. (1981a). Minority within a minority: On being South Asian and female in Canada. In G. Kurian and R. Ghosh (eds), *Women in the family and the economy* (pp 413–26). Westport, CN: Greenwood Press

– (1981b). Social and economic integration of South Asian women in Montreal, Canada. In G. Kurian & R. Ghosh (eds), *Women in the family and the economy*. 59–71. Westport CN: Greenwood Press

Gibbon, J.M. (1938). *Canadian mosaic: The making of a northern nation*. Toronto: McClelland & Stewart

Gilad, L. (1990). *The northern route: An ethnography of refugee experiences*. St John's, NF: Institute of Social and Economic Research

Gold, G. (1975). *St Pascal*. Toronto: Holt Rinehart & Winston

Hamilton, R.A. (1974). *A study of the material culture of the Hutterian Brethern of southern Alberta*. Utah: Utah State University

Handler, R. (1988). *Nationalism and the politics of culture in Quebec*. Madison: University of Wisconsin Press

Hawthorn, H.B. (1955). *The Doukhobors of British Columbia*. Vancouver, BC: UBC and J. M. Dent & Sons

Hedican, E.J. (1987). *The Ogoki River guides: Emergent leadership among the northern Ojibwa*. Waterloo: Wilfrid Laurier University Press

– (1991). On the ethnopolitics of Canadian native leadership and identity. *Ethnic Groups, 9*(1):1–16

Heiken, D.E. (1978). The Hutterites: A comparative analysis of viability. Unpublished doctoral thesis. Dept of Anthropology, University of California, Santa Barbara

Henrikson, G. (1971). The transactional basis of influence: White men among the Naskapi Indians. In R. Paine (ed.), *Patrons and brokers in the East Arctic*. St John's, NF: Memorial University

– (1978). *Hunters in the barrens*. St John's, NF: Memorial University Press

Henry, F. (1973). *Forgotten Canadians: The Blacks of Nova Scotia*. Don Mills, ON: Longmans Canada

– , and Ginzberg, E. (1985). *Who gets the work: A test of racial discrimination in employment*. Toronto: Urban Alliance on Race Relations

Herman, H.V. (1978). *Men in white aprons: A study of ethnicity and occupation*. Toronto: Peter Martin

Hirabayashi, G. (1952). The Russian Dukhobours of British Columbia. Unpublished doctoral thesis, Dept of Sociology, University of Washington

Hoe, B. (1976). *Structural changes of two Chinese communities in Alberta, Canada.* Ottawa: Museum of Man

Honigmann, J.J. (1965). Social disintegration in five northern Canadian communities. *Canadian Review of Sociology and Anthropology,* 2:199–214

Hostetler, J.A., and Huntington, G.E. (1967). *The Hutterites in North America.* Toronto: Holt Rinehart & Winston

Hughes, E.C. (1943). *French Canada in transition.* Chicago: Chicago University Press

– (1948). The study of ethnic relations. *Dalhousie Review,* 26(4):477–82

Husaini, Z. (1981). Social networks: A factor in immigrant economic success. Unpublished doctoral thesis, Dept of Sociology, University of Alberta

Indra, D.M. (1979). Ethnicity, social stratification and opinion formation: An analysis of ethnic portrayal in the Vancouver Newspaper Press, 1903–76. Unpublished doctoral dissertation, Simon Fraser University

– (1980). Community and inter-ethnic relations of Southeast Asian refugees in Canada. In E. Tepper (ed.), *Southeast Asian exodus: From tradition to resettlement* (pp 173–90). Toronto: Canadian Asian Studies Association

– (1985). Khmer, Lao, Vietnamese and Vietnamese Chinese in Alberta. In H. Palmer (ed.), *Peoples of Alberta: Portraits in cultural diversity* (pp 437–63). Calgary: Western Producer

– (1987a). Social science research on Indochinese refugees in Canada. In K.B. Chan and D.M. Indra (eds), *Uprooting, loss and adaptation: The resettlement of Indochinese refugees in Canada* (pp 5–14). Ottawa: Canadian Public Health Association

– (1987b). Bureaucratic constraints, middlemen and community organization: Aspects of the political incorporation of Southeast Asians in Canada. In K.B. Chan and D.M. Indra (eds), *Uprooting, loss and adaptation: The resettlement of Indochinese refugees in Canada* (pp 147–70). Ottawa: Canadian Public Health Association

– (1988). Self concept and settlement: Southeast Asians in a small prairie city. In L.J. Dorais, K.B. Chan, and D.M. Indra (eds), *Ten years later: Indochinese communities in Canada* (pp 69–94). Ottawa: Canadian Asian Studies Association

– (1989). Ethnic human rights and feminist theory: Gender implications for refugee studies and practice. *Journal of Refugee Studies,* 2(2):221–42

– (1992). The spirit of the gift and the politics of resettlement: Canadian private sponsorship of South East Asians. In. V. Robinson (ed.), *The international refugee crisis: British and Canadian responses.* London: Macmillan

Isajiw, W. (1974). Definitions of ethnicity. *Ethnicity,* 1:111–24

Ishwaran, K. (1977). *Family kinship and community*. Toronto: McGraw-Hill Ryerson

Jabbra, N. (1983). Assimilation and acculturation of Lebanese extended families in Nova Scotia. *Canadian Ethnic Studies*, 15(1):544–72

– (1984). Community politics and ethnicity among Lebanese in Nova Scotia. *Canadian Review of Sociology and Anthropology*, 21(4):449–65

– (1991). Household and family among Lebanese immigrants in Nova Scotia: Continuity, change and adaptation. *Journal of Comparative Family Studies*, 22(1):39–56

Jackson, J.D. (1966). French-English relations in an Ontario community. *Canadian Review of Sociology and Anthropology*, 3(3):117–31

Jansen, C. (1969). Leadership in the Toronto Italian ethnic group. *International Migration Review*, 4(1):25–40

– (1978). Community organization of Italians in Toronto. In L. Driedger (ed.), *The Canadian ethnic mosaic* (pp 310–26). Toronto: McClelland & Stewart

– (1986). *Italians in a multicultural Canada*. Queenston, ON: Mellen

Jarvenpa, R. (1985). The political economy and political ethnicity of American Indian adaptations and identities. *Ethnic and Racial Studies*, 8(1):29–48

Johnson, H. (1988). The development of the Punjabi community in Vancouver since 1961. *Canadian Ethnic Studies*, 20(2):1–19

Joy, A. (1984). Work and ethnicity: The case of the Sikhs in the Okanagan valley of British Columbia. In R. Kanungo (ed.), *South Asians in the Canadian mosaic*. Montreal: Kala Bharati

– (1989). *Ethnicity in Canada: Social accommodation and cultural persistence among the Sikhs and the Portuguese*. New York: AMS Press

Kallen, E. (1977). *Spanning the generations: A study of Jewish identity*. Don Mills, ON: Longmans Academic Press

Katma, F. (1985). The role of the Greek Orthodox church in the Greek community of Montreal. Unpublished master's thesis, Dept of Sociology and Anthropology, Concordia University

Keho, A.B. (1975). Dakota Indian ethnicity in Saskatchewan. *Journal of Ethnic Studies*, 3(2):37–43

Kennedy, J. (1982). *Holding the line: Ethnic boundaries in a Northern Labrador community*. St John's, NF: Institute of Social and Economic Research

Khattab, A.M. (1969). The assimilation of Arab Muslims in Alberta. Unpublished master's thesis, University of Alberta

Khosla, R. (1980). A Canadian perspective on the Hindu woman: A study of identity transformation. Unpublished master's thesis, Dept of Sociology, McMaster University

- (1981). The changing familial role of South-Asian women in Canada: A study in identity transformation. In K.V. Ujimoto and G. Hirabayashi (eds), *Asian Canadians: Regional perspectives* (pp 178–84), Guelph, ON: Prepared for the Multiculturalism Directorate by the University of Guelph

Kivisto, P. (1990). The transplanted then and now: The reorientation of immigration studies from the Chicago school to the new social history. *Ethnic and Racial Studies, 13*(4):455–81

Kloberdanz, T.J. (1986). Unsre un' Die Andre: In-group affiliation among the Volga Germans of Russia and the great plains. *Plains Anthropologist, 31*(114, Part 1):281–94

- (1988). Symbols of German-Russian ethnic identity on the northern plains. *Great Plains Quarterly, 8*(1):3–15

Kohl, S.B. (1976). *Working together: Women and family in southwestern Saskatchewan.* Toronto: Holt, Rinehart & Winston

Krotz, L. (1980). *Urban Indians: The strangers in Canada's cities.* Edmonton: Hurtig

Kurian, G. (1991). Socialization of South Asian immigrant youth. In S. Sharma, A. Ervin, and D. Meintel (eds), *Immigrants and refugees in Canada: A national perspective on ethnicity, multiculturalism, and cross-cultural adjustment* (pp 47–57). Saskatoon: University of Saskatchewan and Université de Montréal

-, and Ghosh, R. (1983). Child rearing in transition in Indian immigrant families in Canada. In G. Kurian and R. Srivastava (eds), *Overseas Indians: A study in adaptation* (pp 128–40). Vikas

Kwong, J. (1984). Ethnic organization and community transformation: The Chinese in Winnipeg. *Ethnic and Racial Studies, 12*(3):374–86

Lai, D.C. (1988). *Chinatowns: Towns within cities in Canada.* Vancouver: UBC Press

Lam, L. (1983). Vietnamese-Chinese refugees in Montreal. Unpublished doctoral thesis. Dept.of Sociology, York University

Laurence, H. (1980). Change in religion, economics, and boundary conditions *among Amish Mennonites in southwestern Ontario.* Unpublished doctoral thesis, Dept of Anthropology, McGill University

Lithman, Y. (1986). *The community apart: A case study of a Canadian Indian reserve community.* Winnipeg: University of Manitoba Press

Lubart, J. (1970). *Psychodynamic problems of adaptation: Mackenzie Delta Eskimos.* Ottawa: Queen's Printer

Macdonald, N. (1988). Putting on the kilt: The Scottish stereotype and ethnic community survival in Cape Breton. *Canadian Ethnic Studies, 20*(3):132–46

McFeet, T. (1980). *Three hundred years of anthropology in Canada.* Occasional Paper 7, Dept of Anthropology, St Mary's University

McLellan, J. (1987). Religion and ethnicity: The role of Buddhism in maintaining ethnic identity among Tibetans in Lindsay, Ontario. *Canadian Ethnic Studies* 19(1):63–76

Makabe, T. (1976). Ethnic group identity: Canadian-born Japanese in metropolitan Toronto. Unpublished doctoral thesis, Dept of Anthropology, University of Toronto

– (1978). Ethnic identity and social mobility: The case of the second generation Japanese in Metropolitan Toronto. *Canadian Ethnic Studies*, 10(1):106–23

Markus, R.L., and Schwartz, D.V. (1984). Soviet Jewish émigrés in Toronto: Ethnic self-identity and issues of integration. *Canadian Ethnic Studies*, 16(2):71–88

Martine, H.M. (1977). The relationship of religious to socio-economic divisions among the Mennonites of Dutch-Prussian-Russian descent in Canada. Unpublished doctoral thesis, Dept of Anthropology, University of Toronto

Matiasz, S. (nd). Catholic Ukrainians or Ukrainian Catholics: Ethnicity and religion in Canada. Unpublished doctoral thesis, Dept of Anthropology, University of Alberta (in progress)

Maxwell, T.R. (1971). The French population in Metro Toronto: A study of ethnic participation and ethnic identity. Unpublished doctoral thesis, University of Toronto

Mayer, A.C. (1959). *A report on the East Indian community in Vancouver*. Vancouver: University of British Columbia

Maykovich, M.K. (1976). The Japanese family in tradition and change. In K. Ishwaran (ed.), *The Canadian family* (pp 162–82). Toronto: Holt, Rinehart & Winston

Migliore, S. (1988). Religious symbols and cultural identity: A Sicilian-Canadian example. *Canadian Ethnic Studies*, 20(1):78–94

Miner, H. (1939). *St. Denis: A French-Canadian parish*. Chicago: University of Chicago Press

Moeno, S.N. (1981). The 'non-white' South Africans in Toronto: A study of the effects of institutionalized apartheid in a multicultural society. Unpublished doctoral thesis, Dept of Anthropology, York University

Morinis, E.A. (1982). Skid row Indians and the politics of self. *Culture*, 2(3):93–106

Muga, D. (1988). Native Americans and the nationalities question: Premises for a Marxist approach to ethnicity and self-determination. *The Journal of Ethnic Studies*, 16(1):31–52

Nagata, J. (1964). Adaptation and integration of Greek working class immigrants in the city of Toronto: A situational approach. *International Migration Review*, 4(1):44–68

- (1986). The role of religion and religious institutions in establishing status and leadership in three Southeast Asian communities in Toronto. Mimeo
- (1987). Is multiculturalism sacred? The power behind the pulpit in the religious conversion of Southeast Asian Christians in Canada. *Canadian Ethnic Studies, 19*(2):26–43

Ng, R. (1988). *The politics of community services: Immigrant women, class and state.* Toronto: Garamond Press

Onell, J.D. (1986). The politics of health in the 4th World: A northern Canadian example. *Human Organization, 45*(2):119–27

Paine, R. (1977). Tutelage and ethnicity: A variable relationship. In R. Paine (ed.), *The white arctic: Anthropological essays on tutelage and ethnicity* (pp 246–63). Toronto: University of Toronto Press

Park, J.S. (1986). Korean families in Saskatoon. Unpublished master's thesis, Dept of Sociology, University of Saskatchewan

Parker, S. (1964). Ethnic identity and acculturation in two Eskimo villages. *American Anthropologist, 66*:325–40

Pitt, E.L. (1949). The Hutterite Brethren in Alberta. MA thesis, University of Alberta

Plaice, E. (1990). *The Native game: Settler perceptions of Indian/settler relations in central Labrador.* St John's, NF: Institute of Social and Economic Research

Poole, G. (1979). Development in the West Indies and migration to Canada. Unpublished doctoral thesis, Dept of Anthropology, McGill University

Price, K.A. (1980). The social construction of ethnicity: The case of English Montrealers. Unpublished doctoral thesis, Dept. of Anthropology, York University

Quereshi, R.B. (1980). The family model as a blueprint for social interaction among Pakistani Canadians. In K.V. Ujimoto and G. Hirabayashi (eds), *Asian Canadians and multiculturalism* (pp 46–61). Guelph, ON: University of Guelph

Razaul, H.M. (1978). Cultural assimilation and consumer decision-making among Muslim couples in Windsor, Ontario. Unpublished doctoral thesis, Dept of Anthropology, Wayne State University

Rosenberg, N.V. (1988). Ethnicity and class: Black country musicians in the Maritimes. *Journal of Canadian Studies, 23*(1–2):138–57

Ryan, J. (1978). *Wall of Words: The betrayal of the urban Indian.* Toronto: Peter Martin

Salisbury, R. (1986). *A homeland for the Cree: Regional development in James Bay, 1971–1981.* Montreal/Kingston: McGill-Queen's University Press

Sandhu, S.S. (1980). *The second generation: Culture and the East Indian community in Nova Scotia.* Ethnic Heritage Series, Vol. 2. Halifax: International Education Centre

Scheffel, D. (1991). *In the shadow of the antichrist: The Old Believers of Alberta.*
Peterborough: Broadview Press

Serl, V. (1964). *Stability and change in Hutterite society.* Unpublished doctoral
thesis, Department of Anthropology, University of Oregon

Shaffir, W. (1974). *Life in a religious community: The Lubavitcher Chassidim in
Montreal.* Toronto: Holt, Rinehart

Shore, M. (1987). *The science of social redemption: McGill, the Chicago school, and the
origins of social research in Canada.* Toronto: University of Toronto Press

Siddique, C. (1977). Changing family patterns: A comparative analysis of
immigrant Indian and Pakistani families of Saskatoon. *Canadian Journal of
Comparative Family Studies* 8(2):179–200

Siddique, M. (1974). Patterns of familial decision making and division of
labour: A study of the immigrant Indian and Pakistani community of Saskatoon. Unpublished master's thesis, University of Saskatchewan

– (1983). Changing family patterns: A comparative analysis of immigrant
Indian and Pakistani families in Saskatoon, Canada. In G. Kurian and R.
Srivastava (eds), *Overseas Indians: A Study in Adaptation* (pp 100–27). Delhi:
Vikas

Smith, D. (1975). *Natives and outsiders.* Ottawa: Native Research Centre

Sorenson, J. (1991). Politics of social identity: 'Ethiopians' in Canada. *The Journal
of Ethnic Studies,* 19(1):67–86

Srivastava, R.P. (1975). Family organization and change among the overseas
Indians with special reference to Indian immigrant families of British Colum-
bia, Canada. In G. Kurian (ed.), *Family in India: A regional view* (pp 369–91).
The Hague: Mouton

– (1983). The evolution of adaptive strategies: East Indians in Canada. In G.
Kurian and R. Srivastava (eds), *Overseas Indians: A study in adaptation* (pp
30–40). Delhi: Vikas

Stasiulis, D. (1980). The political structuring of ethnic community action: A
reformation. *Canadian Ethnic Studies,* 12(3):18–44

Stephenson, P.H. (1978). A dying of the old man and a putting on of the new:
The cybernetics of ritual metanola in the life of the Hutterian commune.
Unpublished doctoral thesis, Dept of Anthropology, University of Toronto

– (1986). On ethnographic genre and the experience of communal work with
the Hutterian people. *Culture,* 6(2):93–100

Stymeist, D. (1975). *Ethnics and Indians: Social relations in a northwestern Ontario
town.* Toronto: Peter Martin

Subramanian, I.A. (1977). Identity shift: Post-migration changes in identity
among first-generation East Indian immigrants in Toronto. Unpublished
doctoral thesis, University of Toronto

Sugiman, P., and Nishio, H. (1983). Socialization and cultural duality among aging Japanese Canadians. *Canadian Ethnic Studies, 15*(3):1–16

Sumida, R. (1935). The Japanese in British Columbia. Unpublished master's thesis, Dept of History. Vancouver: University of British Columbia

Tarasoff, K. (1989). *Spells, splits, and survivals in a Russian Canadian community: A study of Russian organizations in the greater Vancouver area.* New York.: AMS Press

Teal, G. (1986). Ethnicity, gender and occupation in the formation of the industrial working class: The case of the garment industry in Quebec. Unpublished doctoral thesis, Dept of Anthropology, McGill University

Thomas, G. (1988). Women in the Greek community of Nova Scotia. *Canadian Ethnic Studies, 20*(3):84–93

Thompson, R.H. (1989). *Toronto's Chinatown: The changing social organization of an ethnic community.* New York: AMS Press

Ujimoto, K.V. (1973). Post-war Japanese immigrants in Canada. Unpublished doctoral thesis, University of British Columbia

van Esterik, J. (1991). Communication claims in a refugee program: A case study of an anthropologist working with immigrant and refugee settlement agencies. In S. Sharma, A. Ervin, and D. Meintel (eds), *Immigrants and refugees in Canada: A national perspective on ethnicity, multiculturalism, and cross-cultural adjustment* (pp 185–95). Saskatoon: University of Saskatchewan and Université de Montréal

Vasiliadis, P. (1989a). *Dangerous truth: Interethnic competition in a northeastern Ontario goldmining community.* New York: AMS Press

– (1989b). *Who are you? Identity and ethnicity among the Toronto Macedonians.* New York: AMS Press

Veilleux, C. (1991). Canadian research on Indochinese refugees. Mimeo

Vuorinen, S.S. (1974). Ethnic identification of Caribbean immigrants in the Kitchener-Waterloo area. Unpublished doctoral thesis, University of Waterloo

Wai, H.Y. (1970). The Chinese and their voluntary associations in British Columbia. Unpublished master's thesis, Queen's University

Wakil, S.P., Siddique, C.M., and Wakil, F.A. (1981). Between two cultures: A study of socialization of children of immigrants. *Journal of Marriage and the Family* (November):929–40

Waldram, J.B. (1987). Ethnostatus distinctions in the western Canadian subarctic: Implications for inter-ethnic and interpersonal relations. *Culture.* 7(1):29–38

– (1990). The persistence of traditional medicine in urban areas: The case of Canada's Indians. *American Indian and Alaska Native Mental Health Research,* 4(1):9–30

Watts, K.M. (1976). Calgary's Polish community. Unpublished master's thesis, Dept of Anthropology, University of Calgary

Welin, L., and Ervin, A. (1991). Refugee clients and social service agencies: some aspects of cross-cultural misunderstanding. In S. Sharma, A. Ervin, and D. Meintel (eds), *Immigrants and refugees in Canada: A national perspective on ethnicity, multiculturalism, and cross-cultural adjustment* (pp 178–84). Saskatoon: University of Saskatchewan and Université de Montréal

Williams, B. (1989). A class act: Anthropology and the race to nation across ethnic terrain. *Annual Review of Anthropology*, 18:401–44

Wilson, V. Seymour (1991). The evolving policy of multiculturalism in Canada. Paper presented at the Conference on Research on Multiculturalism, Queen's University

Woon, Y-F. (1984). Indochinese refugee sponsorship: The case of Victoria, 1979–1980. *Canadian Ethnic Studies, 16*(1)

– (1985). Ethnic identity and ethnic boundaries: The Sino-Vietnamese in Victoria, British Columbia. *Canadian Review of Sociology and Anthropology*, 22(4):534–58

– (1986). Some adjustment aspects of Vietnamese and Sino-Vietnamese families in Victoria, Canada. *Journal of Comparative Family Studies, 17*(3):349–70

– (1987). Vietnamese and Sino-Vietnamese households in Victoria, Canada: Some comparative remarks. *Journal of Comparative Family Studies*

Young, C., and Reid, H. (1938). *The Japanese Canadians*. Toronto: University of Toronto Press

Young, M.M. (1974). Boundary maintenance in a religious minority group in western Canada. Unpublished doctoral thesis, Dept of Anthropology, University of Alberta

Yu, M. (1987). Human rights, discrimination, and coping behavior of the Chinese in Canada. *Canadian Ethnic Studies, 19*(3):114–24

MORTON WEINFELD

Ethnic Assimilation and the Retention of Ethnic Cultures

This paper reviews the current state of knowledge concerning the cultural survival and maintenance of Canadian ethnic groups and presents some conclusions and interpretations of the available evidence, along with suggestions for further research. The evidence used comes from the census, large-scale sample surveys, and smaller quantitative and qualitative studies. This review is by no means exhaustive, but focuses rather on major studies, with a primarily sociological orientation. It will combine descriptive, analytical, and evaluative dimensions.

The primary emphasis in this review will be on those ethnic groups in Canada who are multigenerational, and thus mainly European or White. These are the groups in which the questions of cultural survival and retention are posed most starkly, given their distance from the immigrant generation. Moreover, these are the groups in which the extant studies have found sufficiently large sub-samples of native-born and later generations. To be sure, the more recent largely non-White immigrant groups also wrestle with dilemmas of cultural retention, particularly as these may affect their children. But for these groups, the issue is confounded by pressing problems of racism and poverty. What is unclear at this point is whether any conclusions reached for the older ethnic groups can be applied with confidence for the more recent, visible minority groups.

A word about the socio-political environment in which processes of assimilation or survival have been taking place is in order. The Canadian state of the 1990s presents two desirable outcomes to its ethnic groups, operationalized through a variety of laws, government departments, and agencies, notably that of Multiculturalism. The first outcome is the possible survival of ethnic groups and specifically their cultures, within a 'multicultural' society (eg, section 27 of the Charter, various funding programs). The second outcome is the promise of full and equal participation in Canadian society, without discrimination (eg, section 15 of the Charter, anti-racist programs and efforts).

Even assuming good faith by the Canadian polity in outlining these options, the sociological dilemma is that it is difficult to maximize both objectives simultaneously, for either individuals or groups. No wishful thinking or theoretical hocus-pocus can deny the reality that these two outcomes are in a very real sense zero-sum, or close to it. Thus individuals and groups are in a sense forced – or free – to make trade-offs, to choose an appropriate mix of both these objectives. This does not denote an evil on the part of our society, but on the contrary, a certain degree of freedom of choice available in a liberal-democratic society.

For example, it is difficult for a truly committed Hutterite, or Hasidic Jew, to become president of the Royal Bank or a university professor of theoretical physics, leaving aside issues of prejudice and discrimination. Less extreme, similar trade-offs describe the case for most other ethnic groups in Canada. Perhaps there exists a set of policies which can engineer a society in which maximal ethnic cultural and communal survival can co-exist with maximal participation in a post-industrial liberal-democratic society, but it has yet to be discovered.

The measurement of adherence to ethnic identities or cultures usually comprises several well-recognized components, accepted by the evolved consensus of practitioners. The concepts of ethnic cultures and ethnic identification are particularly wide and multidimensional. Rounding up and regrouping 'the usual gang of suspects,' I have divided this paper into the following thematic areas: language retention; ethnic in-marriage and social networks; participation in ethnic organizations; ethnic regional and intra-urban concentrations; and self-identification and the ethno-cultural repertoire.

Each section reviews and evaluates the relevant research, synthesizes and interprets where possible, and outlines areas for further research.

This paper focuses on the findings with regard to immigrant minority groups within English Canada, that is, outside Quebec. Social scientific research directed specifically at the processes of ethnic-cultural retention of immigrant minority groups within Quebec is more recent, and thus limited. Indeed, the Quebec research focus has been on issues relating to immigrant social, cultural, economic, and political integration *into* Quebec society. A few general works provide overviews of selected groups which include references to issues of retention of the ethnic culture: Italians (Painchaud & Poulin 1988); Greeks (Ioannou 1983); Portuguese (Alpalhao & Da Rosa 1978); and Jews (Lasry 1982; Weinfeld 1984). For a review of the sociology of ethnic relations generally in Quebec, see Juteau (1991), and for a general overview of the policy environment affecting immigrant groups in Quebec, see the paper by Helly in this volume.

All research on ethno-cultural assimilation can be seen as responding to two theoretical paradigms. The first is the classical model of immigrant assimilation developed and refined through the works of Park, Wirth, and Gordon. The second are theories which evolved over the past two decades as part of an intellectual post hoc scramble to explain the unexpected continued ethnic salience, and seeming revival, in North America and world-wide. These latter theories are based largely on elements of economic or political competition (see Glazer & Moynihan 1975). In the North American context they are rooted in the empirical contention that ethnicity, even among older groups, still is an important explanatory variable (Greeley 1974). This latter view found a warm reception on the part of proponents of Canadian multiculturalism, eager as well to accentuate the differences between the so-called Canadian mosaic and the American melting pot.

LANGUAGE RETENTION

An ethnic language in Canada can serve two functions. The first is as a means of communication, used in a variety of domains in the private and public sphere. The second would be more symbolic, in which select words and phrases may reinforce ethnic identity, without requiring high levels of linguistic competence.

Many Canadians, certainly among the foreign-born, claim a proficiency in a non-official language (NOL). To the extent that immigrants may be employed or live in ethnic enclaves, the language is reinforced. But the evidence is clear concerning the generational loss of the language regarding both knowledge and use, as can be seen from studies of the 1986 census, even though variations in the rate of loss exist for different ethnic groups (Kralt & Pendakur 1991; Pendakur 1990). O'Bryan et al. (1975) found that both knowledge and use declined dramatically from the first to the second and third generation, though even among the second generation 18 per cent reported using it every day. In a pattern which may not be unusual, far more ethnic respondents (even in the second and third generations) supported the *idea* of ethnic language maintenance than seemed actually able to operationalize this idea with their children.

The same pattern obtains among Ukrainians, Jews, Italians, and Germans in Toronto, regarding fluency and use, as well as ability to read and write the language (Breton et al. 1990:49–56). However, significant proportions claim to know 'at least some' of their ethnic language even in the third generation, ranging from 12 per cent for Germans to 69 per cent of Jews.

In this sense the addition of an extra language question in the 1991 census will provide extremely valuable information about passive language knowledge, outside of mother tongue or main home use. Respondents can identify up to three languages in which they can carry on a conversation, apart from English or French. As inter-ethnic marriages have increased, with more than one language spoken in the home, a portion of language knowledge was not being measured. Clearly, far more Canadians know ethnic languages than use them regularly at home.

Ethnic language loss is not surprising. There exist clear economic benefits which are associated with knowledge of English and/or French in Canada (Economic Council of Canada 1991) despite the existence of ethnically segregated work environments in which immigrants can earn a living working primarily in the ethnic language. Of course, immigrants who speak little or no English and/or French may also have little formal education, and thus be employed in occupations without stringent language requirements (Breton et al. 1990:156). Ironically, the overall pattern linking ethnic occupations or labour market concentration with outcomes like occupational status and income is varied. In some case effects are negative (mainly for immigrant groups in Toronto), in some cases nil or positive (Breton et al. 1990:175–95; Weinfeld 1988).

This pattern of linguistic attrition is found also for highly identified and perhaps distinct groups such as Mennonites. Driedger and Hengstenberg (1986) found that assimilationist forces were at work eroding the position of German among Mennonites, particularly within urban areas. Even the phenomena of newly created 'ethnolects' can be interpreted in the perspective of linguistic assimilation. Thus in the case of Italians, as fluency in Italian is lost, one finds among Italo-Canadians an emerging Italian ethnolect in which there is a substantial borrowing, and transformation, of English words into the spoken language. The older Italo-Canadians in time speak the ethnolect even as the younger generation is switching to English (Danesi 1985).

What, if anything, can be done to reverse the inexorable generational processes of language loss? Heritage language teaching and learning programs are analyzed by Cummins in another paper in this volume. Little is known in Canada about the *long-term* effects of second-language private or public educational programs in general on ethnic identification, and on NOL competence in particular. Reitz reports that in homes in which the ethnic language is used regularly, ethnic school attendance has little additional effect on language retention (Reitz 1985:121). The more intriguing question would be the measurement of the impact of such schooling on children from homes in which the ethnic language was *not* used.

Many public school systems in Canada today offer some elements of NOL instruction to students, and these options come in a variety of formats. Some amount to minimal efforts at maintenance of the ethnic language with the acquisition of English – or French – as the major goal. Heritage language programs in Ontario, Quebec, and elsewhere are examples of programs in which students may take up to two and a half hours of extra instruction after regular classes; in 1980 a total of 76,000 such children were enrolled (Mallea 1984). These programs are similar in many ways to the private supplementary programs traditionally run by churches, and which still exist.

More intensive bilingual programs are also available. These include bilingual schools, found in various provinces as either public, private, or mixed schools in which a dual linguistic cultural program is offered combining, for example, Ukrainian, Hebrew/Yiddish, German, Greek, or Armenian instruction with English or French. Other public school programs aimed more at immigrant children also place a high value on additive bilingualism, rather than a 'subtractive' form. Certainly, some studies report cognitive benefits for the students in bilingual, and even trilingual (English, French, Hebrew) education programs (Tucker 1980, Genessee and Lambert 1979, cited in Lambert and Taylor 1984. See the paper by Cummins in this volume).

One should note here that Canadian NOL language policy has to date escaped the tensions which have marked bilingual (mainly English-Spanish) education programs in the US (Hakuta 1986). Here our English-French historical dualism is advantageous, making Canadians generally less apprehensive about bilingualism or indeed multilingualism, compared to Americans.

In any event, it is unclear what the long-term impact of any type of such second language schooling is, net of family background and initial language knowledge factors. Short of definitive research, one presumes such experiences cannot hurt. Other avenues for ethnic language retention might also be studied, such as ethnic summer camps or prolonged visits to the ancestral homeland and immersion there in the NOL environment.

Can ethnic cultures survive in any meaningful way with a substantial generational decline in language knowledge and use? How important is it for the ethnic identity of a third generation Italian-Canadian to be able to speak fluent/some Italian? Reitz (1985) argues that language retention promotes ethnic group cohesion, agreeing with de Vries that 'language maintenance is a necessary condition for the maintenance of ethnic identity' (1990:248). Certainly, the French language has emerged in the post-war period as the foundation and indeed the essence of Québécois culture. Many ethnic communal leaders and educators would no doubt agree, perhaps arguing further that familiarity with the great works of Dante, Ibn Kaldun, Euripedes, Shalom Aleichem, Confucius, and Shevchenko – in the original if possible – is even more desirable. Certainly ethnic language knowledge is a sine qua non for readership of the NOL press in Canada.

Yet one ought to consider alternate causal paths and alternate models. Immigration serves as a systematic process for keeping ethnic languages alive, as do enhanced means of international travel and communication. Language loss may in any way reflect, rather than cause, a loss of ethnic ties and cohesion over the generations. On the other hand, the selective and symbolic use of language – curse words, foods, songs, first names and family names, jokes – may serve as signifiers and markers which reinforce identity, associated with important ritualistic or life cycle events. Moreover, ethnic and/or non-English words have been incorporated regularly into contemporary spoken English.

Is the language glass therefore half full or half empty? The central trend of generational loss of ethnolinguistic fluency is clear. Yet clear elements of language knowledge, if not fluency, do persist beyond the immigrant generation. I.B. Singer recounts the story of his arrival to New York in the mid-1930s, where the first question he was asked by journalists was for a comment on the imminent death of the Yiddish language. Reflecting on that moment in the mid-1980s he replied that: 'After fifty years, Yiddish is still alive and the journalists are all dead.' While such optimism is clearly heroic –Yiddish has given way to Hebrew as the ethnic language of choice among mainstream North American Jews – it does suggest caution in prematurely writing off the language component.

Research is needed on the following areas:
- What impacts are economic globalization and increased travel and communication possibilities having upon ethnic languages? Is there any economic advantage for multilingualism in areas such as international trade and investment opportunities, as asserted by Multiculturalism Canada?
- Can various forms of NOL education stem or reverse the process of linguistic assimilation? What impacts have such programs been having on the long-term linguistic abilities of participants? What impacts do or can other interventions, such as travel abroad, summer camps, youth groups, have on language maintenance?
- To what extent can ethnic cultures be transmitted without a fluent linguistic base? (Of course, ethnic groups and cultures will vary here.) To what extent can the symbolic uses of an ethnic language, far short of fluency, play a role in reinforcing group boundaries or enhancing identities?
- A great many studies can be undertaken with the new language question found on the 1991 census, to analyze the extent and correlates of NOL competence other than as mother tongue or language of home use.

ETHNIC INTERMARRIAGE AND SOCIAL NETWORKS

Ethnic intermarriage is usually seen as both a consequence of, and contributor to, the process of decreasing ethnic cohesion and ultimately, assimilation. For many analysts, it is 'the last straw.' It is related to ethnic social networks – variables like friendship choice – as it reflects a loosening of ethnic ties. The assumption is also that ethno-cultural transmission is more difficult, and cultures diluted, in intermarried families.

The broad trend in Canada has been for a secular decline in overall levels of endogamy, from 1931 to 1981, though the degree varies for different groups, and in some cases, such as Italians, higher levels obtained in 1981 than in the 50 years previously (Herberg 1989:185–94.) The most endogamous groups in 1981 Canada, based on available data, were Jews and Asians. It should be noted, however, that since the 1960s annual rates of intermarriage have been increasing for Jews, in both Canada and the United States. Thus, one assumes that if this is the case with a well-known endogamous group, it may have general application. Rates of exogamy will be lower among visible minority groups, both because they are of more recent origin and because they are more likely to face racism in the process of assortative mate selection.

More important is the fact that rates of intermarriage are far higher for native-born Canadians than for immigrants. This was clearly the case in 1961 and 1971, for all non-English and non-French groups in Canada, including Jews and Asians (Kalbach & McVey 1979:321). Census data on Canadians claiming multiple origin are another de facto data source on intermarriage. The percentage of Canadian born claiming multiple ethnic origin is substantially higher than among the foreign-born. For example, among those claiming an Eastern European origin, those claiming a multiple ethnic origin represent 17.5 per cent of the foreign-born and 61.5 per cent of the Canadian-born; for those claiming a 'South Asian' origin, the percentages are 5.6 per cent and 24.2 per cent (Canada 1989).

None of this is surprising, and the trend is found even among visible minority groups. There are still issues of interpretation since one would be interested to know the partners' origins of the out-marrying ethnics. Are they marrying far afield, or in groups fairly similar to their own?

While there are very few studies in which intermarriage – the act – is itself an outcome measure, we do have studies in which attitudes to intermarriage are examined. The assumption is that liberal attitudes on exogamy would translate into corresponding behaviour.

In general, survey evidence suggests increasing Canadian tolerance for Catholic-Protestant, Jew-Gentile, and Black-White intermarriage in Canada (Canadian Institute of Public Opinion 1983). Another indicator of acceptance is the finding that the percentages of Canadians between 1984 and 1986 who reported they would *not* vote for a candidate of Jewish, Italian, Polish, or Black descent never broke single digits for any group (Buckner 1987:9). Moreover, mixed parentage, or ethnic exogamy, is highly associated with lower levels of ethnic identity, for a sample of 524 Winnipeg adults (Goldstein & Segall 1985). And if lower levels of ethnic identity in turn lead to greater propensities for intermarriage, the cyclical pattern is repeated.

In general, native-born generations of Jews, Italians, and Slavs are more likely to display more heterogeneous friendship patterns and a greater propensity for intermarriage (Weinfeld 1981a). To be sure, groups differ in their sense of a group obligation to marry within the groups, with Jews professing high endogamy, Ukrainians and Italians, medium, and Germans lower levels. For third-generation Italians, Germans, and Ukrainians in Toronto, only single digit percentages accept an obligation to marry within the ethnic groups (Isajiw 1990:78). This compares with Alba's finding for White ethnics in Albany that only 12 per cent of all parents attach great importance to their children's ethnic identity (Alba 1990:190). Friendship patterns with the exception of Jews become substantially more diffuse by the third generation, though not necessarily with the British majority group.

Reitz finds that numbers of ethnic in-group friends is related to ethnic self-identification. In general, ethnic friendship networks, and indeed actual endogamy, as opposed to an attitudinal reaction, decline among all ethnic groups across Canada (1980:131). Among the foreign-born, a decisive break seems to be those raised in Canada, compared to those who immigrated as adults. Among the former, as might be expected, we find higher rates of heterogeneity of friendship networks and lower rates of endogamous marriage.

Yet even in this picture of likely increasing rates of exogamy, with negative effects on the possibilities of generational transmission of the elements of ethnic cultures and identities, we note again the persistence of non-randomness in mate selection. Even among third-generation Canadians one can find 10 per cent to 15 per cent committed to some measures of ethnic continuity (Reitz 1980:131), and such numbers would translate into hundreds of thousands of Canadian citizens. For these Canadians, therefore, their ethnic heritage and/or communities are matters which are taken seriously.

American data are revealing. The American general pattern approximates the Canadian, with higher intermarriage rates found among the native-born than among the foreign-born, and with a particularly higher level of intermarriage among the younger cohorts of American-born women (Lieberson & Waters 1987:171–7). Yet examination of marriage patterns for American White women themselves of mixed origin reveals the following: (1) those of mixed ancestry are more likely to be married to a mixed ancestry husband, compared to single ancestry women; (2) despite this finding, mixed ancestry women still marry in-group men at a far greater rate than random chance (Lieberson & Waters 1987:181–7). So some residual attachment must exist even with a portion of the offspring of mixed marriages. In the absence of definitive evidence, one can speculate that a similar pattern obtains in Canada. Additional research is needed on: (1) The dynamics of which ethnic culture, if any, becomes dominant in an intermarriage, notably regarding socialization of children. What is the ethno-cultural content found within intermarried households? (2) Closer attention must be paid to marriage and friendship patterns among the Canadian born visible minorities, to determine whether racism will produce different patterns of intermarriage and friendship networks.

ETHNIC REGIONAL AND INTRA-URBAN CONCENTRATIONS

Ethnic residential concentrations, whether as ghettos or neighbourhoods, have been linked to ethnic communal cohesion and to the preservation of communal and cultural ties. From a perspective which sees such concentrations as possibly voluntary, ethnic communities need some critical mass in order to meet needs of community members and make feasible certain collective endeavours. This has been true for regional concentrations involving larger units like provinces or states, as well as within urban areas.

The broad outlines of ethnic regional concentrations in Canada are well known. Atlantic Canada and Quebec have lower levels of non-charter groups. Ontario has a large proportion of immigrants, old wave and new. Chinese and East Asians are overrepresented in BC, Eastern Europeans in the Prairies. Selected subgroups exist in well-defined regions, such as the Black community in Nova Scotia, Hutterites in farm colonies on the Prairies. These concentrations mask a certain process of change. Thus all immigrants tend now to flow to major centres in Ontario including Asian immigrants. In 1921 the largest proportion of Portuguese was found in the Atlantic provinces! And while 88 per cent of Canadian Asians lived in BC in 1901, 29 per cent were there in 1981 (Herberg 1989:127).

Specifically, Toronto, Vancouver, and Montreal have become dominant centres of contemporary ethnic life in Canada, with specific reference to newer immigrant waves. These cities, along with Winnipeg, Edmonton, and Calgary, are also centres of the major concentrations of older ethnic groups. It is important to note that this concentration, especially in Toronto, which has recently lost its WASP majority, means that the salience of ethnicity is exaggerated nationally because of the concentration of media outlets in Toronto as well.

These regional concentrations have clear political and social consequences. To the extent that provincial and municipal services may be available to meet specific ethnic related needs, then concentrations may be used as leverage with political authorities. Studies of ethnic politics and ethnic voting are beyond the scope of this paper, but residential concentrations may clearly play a role in key ridings. In the United States steps are taken to draw or redraw electoral districts to ensure minority groups fair electoral representation. Could, and should, Canada move in the same direction?

The clustering of ethnic groups in Canada's large cities obviously affords a critical mass needed for community development. On the other hand, ethnic concentrations in the cities pose dangers to cultural survival, in that the city is generally seen as a centre for competing attractions of a modern cosmopolitan society, seducing ethnic traditionalists away from their heritage and community. It would thus be valuable to compare ethnic group life outside the major metropolitan areas with that found in these large cities. Mother tongue retention rates are greater in urban areas, due no doubt to the high immigrant proportions (Herberg 1989:111). There exist a number of small-scale case studies of ethnic life in outlying areas, where the critical mass does not exist, which are often fascinating (see for example, a 1988 special issue of *Canadian Ethnic Studies* on ethnicity in Atlantic Canada, 20(3), or studies of Jews in Atlantic Canada and western Canada found in Weinfeld et al. 1981). These diverse works have not been synthesized into an overarching comparative treatment of urban/rural or centre/periphery ethnic life.

There is a substantial tradition of measuring ethnic residential segregation (note that the term 'segregation' reflects the American legacy in which Black residential concentrations were understood to be involuntary, the products of a general pattern of racial segregation) in Canadian urban areas, using primarily measures such as indices of residential dissimilarity and Gini coefficients, to yield 'objective' measures of concentration. Overall, levels of ethnic segregation in Canadian cities remain high (Kralt 1986a, b) and do not show a consistent pattern of decline over time, as might be expected according to certain forms of assimilationist theory (Balakrishnan 1982; Breton et al. 1990:94–8). Herberg finds a similar pattern of constancy between 1951 and 1981 for non-British and non-French groups, using a different measure of ethnic concentration over five CMA's (1989:138).

There is a problem of interpreting such objective measures. Whether one looks, using 1981 census data, at Gini coefficients for Montreal or Toronto (Kralt 1986 a, b), or indices of dissimilarity for Toronto (Breton et al.), or indices of relative concentration for five CMAs (Herberg 1989), one finds puzzling patterns. Some European groups score high (with Jews usually highest), others score low. Visible minority groups, specifically Asian and Black groups, are often less concentrated that certain European groups. (Because of the pre-existing English-French segregation, Gini coefficients for minority groups in Montreal tend to be higher than those for Toronto.) How do we make sense of the fact that in 1981 Toronto, Hungarians and Blacks, Chinese and Greeks, have equivalent indices of segregation, with the Portuguese almost twice as segregated as Ukrainians?

These observed concentrations are not only immigrant enclaves, of Chinatown or Little Italy. Even more puzzling is the case for third-generation residents of Toronto, who seem on average to be *more* or comparably segregated than the first generation (Breton et al. 1990:101). For Hungarians, Yugoslavs (sic), Portuguese and Chinese, segregation increases with generation; the reverse is the case for Italians and Ukrainians.

Using these measures it is difficult to make a case for segregation as reflecting discrimination, since one would therefore expect to find higher levels of concentration for non whites. Yet substantial evidence exists that some groups, notably Blacks, do face discrimination in housing markets in Toronto (Henry 1989; Economic Council of Canada 1991).

Moreover, economic class differences themselves cannot account for observed patterns. High income groups such as Jews, are the most segregated, and other studies have found that economic class alone does not explain observed patterns (Balakrishnan 1982; Darroch & Marston 1971; Richmond & Kalbach 1980). There seems to be some independent ethnic factor at work, perhaps voluntaristic or perhaps simply inertia. It is also possible that using objective measures based on census tracts may be misrepresenting the subjective realities as experienced by people.

Torontonians in general report that their 'present' neighbourhood is far less likely to be ethnically concordant than their previous neighbourhood, or the neighbourhood in which they grew up: 16.9 per cent to 32.6 per cent to 66.6 per cent (Kalbach 1990:111). Reitz notes generational declines in a three-item index of residential segregation which combined an objective and subjective measure (1980:131). Weinfeld found a similar pattern using an index which included a stated preference for ethnic residential concentration (1981).

It is possible that our measures are not capturing the current realities of urban ethnic life. Indeed the patterns of these indices suggests a stochastic residential system with a great deal of noise. Moderate Gini coefficients reported for Blacks in Toronto or Montreal may not be capturing the dynamics of poverty and racism found in some areas of concentration such as Jane-Finch or Côte des Neiges.

What are the links between physical proximity, as defined in ethnic areas or neighbourhoods, and ethno-cultural survival? Much of our thinking here dates back to the image of ethnic neighbourhoods inhabited largely by immigrants, surrounded by the bakery, grocery, and ethnic clubs and associations. Yet in an early article Etzioni (1959) argued that with developments of modern communication and transportation, the requirement of actual proximity was lessened, that is, ethnic communities could persist despite greater dispersion. This factor was found for Halifax Jews two decades ago (Gillis & Whitehead 1971), but the generalizability of this case is unclear.

The voluntary re-creation of second- and third-generation 'gilded ghettos' by Jews, who also demonstrate comparatively high levels of communal solidarity and cultural retention, suggest there still may well be an important role for residential clustering (Forest Hills, Thornhill in Toronto, Côte St Luc/Hampstead, or Dollard in Montreal) past the immigrant generation. This is also suggested by some of the high Gini coefficients for a number of older ethnic groups, cited above.

Further research is needed on the link between ethnic residential concentrations and actual measures of ethnic cultural retention, and ethnic politics. The study of ethnic residential segregation must no longer focus on statistical patterns of white European groups, which are of minimal policy relevance. The literature is missing the ethnic/urban action. Indices of dissimilarity for third-generation Hungarians do not reveal the real ethno-racial dynamics going on in Canadian cities. Qualitative studies of specific ethnic neighbourhoods – White or otherwise – should be undertaken. There is a well-developed American tradition of qualitative studies of such communities, beginning with Gans' now classic *The Urban Villagers* and continuing into the present (cf. Rieder 1985). One can suggest that in some American cases the identity of White urban ethnics is nurtured in neighbourhood opposition (Bensonhurst, South Boston) to non-White groups. In-depth Canadian qualitative research on the texture of urban neighbourhoods began with Crestwood Heights (Seeley et al. 1956). This approach to urban ethnicity builds upon and extends the contradiction whereby personal assimilation does not negate the existence of continuing ethnic residential communities, pointed out by Darroch (1981) and Darroch and Marston (1984) but not addressed by other researchers.

But the future of urban ethnicity in Canada hinges more on the fate of visible minority groups, within the context of poverty, racism, and real or perceived danger. Links between residential concentrations and school racial integration, with attendant issues of 'White flight,' may also emerge. Thus we need a better understanding of the meaning of neighbourhoods, whether in suburbs, ethnic enclaves, or the inner city, for both White and visible minority Canadians. And statistical studies might begin to emulate American research by computing measures along dichotomous lines, such as visible minority/White.

ETHNIC ORGANIZATIONS AND INSTITUTIONAL COMPLETENESS

For some time there has been a growing recognition that the voluntary associations of the ethnic polity may play an important role in the perpetuation of ethnic life, particularly for middle-class leaders. The idea of institutional completeness emerged first as a construct related to the process of immigrant integration (Breton 1964. For additional research dealing with institutional completeness see the paper by Buchignani in this volume). Related to the idea of the organized life of an ethnic community is the role of the ethnic press and media.

The basic finding which emerges from the research is that ethnic organizations and media operate almost completely for and through immigrant members of ethnic communities, and their direct impact on lives of Canadian ethnics is minimal, particularly after the first generation. This pattern is at variance with the seemingly increased salience of ethnic organizations and communal leaders in the public, political sphere, and what may be called the emergence of American style ethnic politics in the Canadian political system, certainly by the late 1980s (Stasiulis & Abu Laban 1990).

In this sense ethnic organizations emerge as types of pressure groups on the mainstream political system, similar to other such actors. It is beyond the scope of this paper to assess whether these ethnic leaders are generals without (non-immigrant) troops. Of course similar questions of representativity and constituency can be posed to most of the roster of interest groups and interest group leaders active in the political process. Nor can we focus on the detailed workings of ethnic polities and possible links with ethnic identity (Breton 1991).

Many ethnic Torontonians are unfamiliar with any ethnic organizations. While Jews score highest in familiarity with 94 per cent, next come Ukrainians and Portuguese at 70 per cent and 67 per cent respectively, with four other groups clustering around the 50 per cent mark. Far fewer are in fact members of at least one such organization, ranging from 63 per cent for Jews and 51 per cent for Ukrainians to 9 per cent for Germans and 12 per cent for West Indians (Breton et al. 1990:229). The perceived efficacy of these organizations may be low. Less than half the Torontonians indicated they would turn to a an ethnic organizations in cases of discrimination, ranging from 44 per cent for Jews to 19 per cent for West Indians.

Looking at the four White European groups in Toronto, one notes in addition a substantial generational decline in participation in ethnic group functions (with the exception of Jews) as well as a decline in the obligation to support group needs and causes, again with the exception of Jews (Isajiw 1990:78.). Again we should note that there are significant numbers, though not majorities, among the second and third generation who are prepared to support such causes. This pattern in generational decline for both organizational involvement and reading the ethnic press in Toronto has been well documented (Weinfeld 1981b).

The issue of the extent to which support for group causes actually might translate into active participation regarding concrete events remains to be fully established. One case study focused on the mobilization of the Ukrainian and Jewish communities in Canada concerning the issue of prosecution of alleged Nazi war criminals in Canada. This event triggered a substantial degree of mobilization of the Ukrainian community, and received substantial media coverage in both the general and Ukrainian press over a two-year period. Yet a survey of Canadians in western Canada, including 143 (predominantly Canadian-born) respondents of Ukrainian origin, found almost negligible familiarity with the Deschenes commission report and attendant issues (Troper & Weinfeld 1988:313). The finding is relevant given the relatively strong position of Ukrainian Canadians on other measures of communal cohesion.

Studies of the ethnic media also would seem to confirm this general pattern. There has been a substantial increase in numbers of ethnic newspapers, perhaps aided through government support, from 155 in 1965 to 251 in 1981 (cited in Herberg 1989:236). This increase has been matched by large increases between 1966 and 1981 in the hours per week of ethnic radio and television available in Ontario in either ethnic languages or in English (Herberg 1989:231, 233). Yet this increase may reflect the input of substantial post-war migrations. If we look at consumption of broadcast and print media patterns we see a massive decline for those of later generation. Black and Leithner found 85–90 per cent of the Canadian-born ethnics almost never read the non-official language media written in ethnic languages (1987). This of course reflects declining competence in the ethnic language, as well as declining interest in ethnic affairs. Other studies of Toronto ethnic media including English-language print and electronic media, found similar patterns of decline for four European ethnic groups (Breton et al. 1990).

It is debatable whether the ethnic media can or ought to shift resources and emphasis away from ethnic languages and its immigrant constituency, to English and French, in the hope of securing the interest of later generations. Clearly such a move might add to the difficulties faced by ethnic languages, assuming the NOL press is one of the main-stays of ethnic languages. There is no easy solution. One can find even reverse scenarios. The Yiddish press is on its very last legs in Canada, and Jewish print media operate almost entirely in English and French. Yet *The Canadian Jewish News* has recently added a column in Yiddish as a gesture of solidarity with an ethnic language in trouble.

There is another way in which the ethnic community operates to integrate the life of its members, and that is in the economic sphere. The chapter cannot address the complex issue of discrimination and the various socio-economic inequalities faced by minority Canadians (see Li 1988 for data and an interpretation). But note that in some cases the ethnic community may serve as an economic resource for minority/ immigrant communities. One study of the Jewish 'sub-economy' of Montreal suggested that interactions in this economic network were not correlated with economic penalties, though the reasons for the persist-ence of the phenomenon into second and third generations were unclear (Weinfeld 1988). Research on ethnic labour market concentrations in Toronto yielded mixed results. While newer immigrant groups may have suffered negative outcomes, other groups may experience, depend-ing on circumstance, positive outcomes as well (Reitz 1990: ch. 4).

It is important to stress that generational decline in participation in organized communal life, or consumption of the ethnic media, does not detract from two key points: the first is that these organizations may play an important role in the process of immigrant adaptation and integra-tion. Updated research on this integrating function of ethnic organiza-tions is lacking. But ethnic organizations, clubs, and associations offer a buffer against too rapid change, and a link with traditional supports. They both socialize the immigrant into the new society while also preserving links to the past. However, some evidence suggests that for some groups, there may be a generalized negative correlation between attachment to an in-group and general political participation; a type of trade-off as suggested in the introduction to this paper. This was found for Southern Europeans and Chinese in Toronto (Reitz 1980:228).

Second, those Canadians of any generation who find ethnic organiza-tional participation satisfying are simply choosing an option available in a free and democratic society. Constituencies of interest groups of all kinds vary in size. Government subsidies for ethnic communal organiza-tions and activities, which are relatively small amounts, are no more and no less valid than subsidies for other activities for other interest groups, from hikers to opera lovers.

Research is needed in the following areas:
- We need more case studies of ethnic organizations in operation, specifically regarding relations between ethnic leaders and rank-and-file members. Detailed research is also needed on the ways in which organizational participation is understood by actors as related to other components of ethnic identity.
- Research is needed on the degree to which old country events affect Canadian ethno-cultural identities, among both immigrants and the later generations. Much of this will also relate to coverage of some events in the mainstream media. One study found that Montreal Jews found news from the Middle East of greatest interest, compared to domestic or other news (Weinfeld & Eaton 1979:47). Another study has contended that media reporting of international events contributes to negative stereotyping of Arabs (Antonius 1986).
- Ethnic schools and educational programs can be seen as a crucial type of ethnic organizational activity related to socialization. Little is known in general about the long-term impact of ethnic schooling on the general ethnic identification of Canadians. Survey research on American Jews has discovered that the home environment plays a far greater role in transmitting Jewish identity than does schooling alone (Bock 1976). Moreover, for Jewish schooling to be effective it is estimated that a minimum threshold of 3000 total hours would be required (Himmelfarb 1977). Little is known about Canadian ethnic groups in this regard.

ETHNIC SELF-IDENTIFICATION, ETHNIC CULTURE,
AND THE ETHNO-CULTURAL REPERTOIRE

What's in a name? Specifically, the labels people choose to describe themselves can tell us something about how they perceive themselves, or at least how they feel they are perceived by others.

The census itself has loosened its grip, allowing for the selection of multiple ancestries, chosen by 17.2 per cent of the population in 1986. This is a conservative figure, since mixed British origins such as English-Irish are considered as 'British' single origin. In the 1980 US census, some 37 per cent of those responding chose a multiple ancestry; 46 per cent did so in the US 1979 Current Population Survey. Moreover, 8.9 per cent had no response and 5.4 per cent selected American or US in the 1980 census (Lieberson & Waters 1987:28–50).

Not surprisingly, far fewer Canadians would voluntarily identify themselves as, or select, a specific ethnic identity than might appear from census data. This was true for a sample of university students from Atlantic Canada (Edwards & Doucette 1987), a sample of western Canadian adults (Mackie 1978) and a sample of Calgary university students from a 'White ethnic' origin group (Mackie & Brinkerhoff 1984), samples in Winnipeg and Edmonton (Dreidger et al. 1982), and national samples (O'Bryan et al. 1975; Berry et al. 1977). A high result would be about 50 per cent claiming a whole or partial ethnic identity.

Levels of ethnic identification in Toronto, as well as support for the idea of cultural pluralism, were found to be relatively higher than corresponding ethnic related behaviours, for Jews, Slavs, and Italians in 1970 (Weinfeld 1981b). In other words, ethnic self-identification may be a relatively painless and costless way of signing on to a 'motherhood' proposition of the value of ethnic or cultural diversity.

Indeed, many studies and public opinion surveys have found even among the general or non-ethnic population, high support for the value of cultural diversity (Berry et al. 1977; Weinfeld 1981b) despite the emerging critique of multicultural policy reflected by the Spicer Report and other observers (Bibby 1989).

However we interpret the salience of various measures of ethnic self-identification or self-labelling, the proportions who do so decline with increasing generation, along assimilationist, predictable lines (Breton et al. 1990; Driedger 1989:160–2; Reitz 1980:131; Weinfeld 1981b). But here, too, we might note that something is making a minority of ethnic Canadians cling to an ethnic label. Reitz identifies the concepts of ethnic 'persisters and revivers.' (1980:133–5). Thus there is even a small minority – about 20 per cent of third-generation high identifiers – of Canadians whose ethnic commitments might seem to be *greater* than those of their parents. Reitz suggests a possible levelling off in the rate of decline in ethnic identity by the third generation. Among third-generation high identifiers he finds that 75 per cent are likely to be revivers rather than persisters. But the point to remember is that the proportion of third-generation high identifiers itself is small.

Reitz also explores directly the question of parental attachment and commitment to the ethnic group as an explanatory variable for children's outcomes, through an index of parental commitment (1980:133–4). All things being equal, Reitz finds what one would suspect, that the higher the level of parental commitment the higher that of respondents themselves.

In fact, family background may well be the single most important variable which may explain adult ethnic identification. It is parents who choose whether or not to educate and socialize their children into the ethnic community, through the family environment, schools, youth groups, summer camps, and so on. These socializing factors must counteract the assimilationist tugs of the broader environment. It is methodologically complex to disentangle the effects of family background, measured comprehensively, from those of other socializing agents; in any event, such systematic quantitative research for Canadian ethnic identity has been very rare.

Perhaps our instruments, our measures, must be more subtle. Names, both surnames and given names, play a clear role in processes of ethnic identification and perception, which deserve further study (Isaacs 1975). More research is needed on the elements of what can be called the ethno-cultural repertoire. The term denotes a collection of characteristics and actions which are constitute the content of the ethnic dimensions of a person's normal, routine life. Such elements, like speech patterns, body language, and lifestyle preferences (ethnic food, names, customs and rituals, consumption patterns, home decoration and artifacts, recreational choices, music and clothing), require more intensive study. It is more likely that ethnicity for the Canadian-born and later generations plays a role in the affective, life-cycle interstices of life, rather than as a cultural blueprint which determines major patterns of daily behaviour. Available evidence does indeed suggest that consumption of ethnic foods and retention of ethnic customs tend to erode less rapidly than other aspects of ethnicity (Breton et al. 1990). Many of these items of the ethno-cultural repertoire, such as ethnic foods and ethnic music, have been well integrated into 'mainstream' Canadian culture.

Research is needed on how such seemingly ritualistic aspects of ethnicity, though infrequent, may contribute to a sense of ethnic identity. Driedger (1989:143–8) has outlined several other factors, such as territory, historical symbols, and ideology, important to an understanding of ethnicity and its possible persistence. Historical symbols can play a role. Little is known about the degree of ethnic knowledge about the homeland or history among Canadian ethnics.

How many third-generation ethnics can locate their homeland, or home province or town, on a map? And is this important? What impact, if any, do historical and/or homeland events have on second and third generation ethnics? One study found a relatively low level of historical knowledge about the Holocaust among a sample of young adult Jews in Montreal (Sigal & Weinfeld 1989:130–1), though the Holocaust has emerged as a central theme of communal expressions of Jewish identification. Theoretically, homeland news events presented through the media can have a reinforcing impact on identity, counteracting the natural socio-demographic drift. Similarly, domestic developments which may affect the perceived status of the group in Canada – prejudice, discrimination, or possible conflicts of interest over certain public policy issues – can also counteract such assimilationist forces.

There is another major domain in which ethnic culture plays a role, namely as a predictor or shaper of values, attitudes, and related behaviours in a variety of personal and private domains. Consider a range of variables having to do with relations with the elderly, courtship, marriage formation and dissolution, sexual attitudes and practices, childrearing, relations of parents with children and between spouses, and attitudes to the extended family. Some child-rearing differences were found among ten nations, net of social class (Lambert et al. 1979). It is thus not surprising that immigrant ethnic cultures might reflect such national differences in attitudes and behaviours, and indeed this is recorded anecdotally by journalists and social workers.

Many of these issues, which remain underresearched in Canada, are fraught with controversy. The debate contrasting cultural differences with cultural deficits (a more normative assessment), or whether behavioural differences are due to social structural–including racist – or cultural factors, are examples.

Traditionally, Canadian research on matters such as the ethnic family has generally focused on studies of extended kin and intergenerational relations, relying on benign or exotic case studies (Ishwaran 1980). Much work on ethnic families has been descriptive and ethnographic, and focused specifically on the travails of immigrant families involved in the process of adjustment to life in Canada (see several studies of Asian family life in Ujimoto & Hirabayahsi 1980). One unusually systematic study demonstrated generational declines in familistic behaviours among Canadian Japanese (Maykovich 1980).

It is well beyond the scope of this paper to enter into research areas which intersect ethnic cultures with areas of psychology, psychiatry, mental health. There is a Canadian tradition of investigating such socio-psychological outcomes, using psychometric scales and other measures (Berry & Wilde 1972; Berry et al. 1987; Gardner & Kalin 1981; Greenglass 1972). One study reported fairly similar responses to value questions by Anglo-Celtic and Anglophone 'other ethnic' Canadians, though the latter group is not broken down by specific ethnic group and generational status (Berry et al. 1977:57).

The easiest differences to describe are those with a demographic component (Halli et al. 1990). But again observed differences in demographic indicators may or may not reflect normative cultural influences, or social structural forces (Burch 1990). Much of this existing Canadian demographic research suffers in its reliance on 1981 data and underanalysis of non-European groups. Many of the more sensitive public policy issues deal with visible minority groups. For example, there exists essentially no scientific literature on the Black family in Canada, compared to the voluminous literature on the topic which exists in the United States (for a review see Jaynes & Williams 1989:ch. 10).

From the available literature it remains unclear whether any observed differences in these domains will survive into later generations, assuming increased levels of acculturation. Consider the emerging area of study, the ethnic elderly (*Canadian Ethnic Studies* 1983; Driedger & Chappell 1987; Payne & Strain 1990). Clearly ethnic differences are most salient among the *immigrant* generations, and questions as to optimal quality of care must recognize ethnic variations and needs. But at least one study has demonstrated no significant variation in social support of the elderly for English, French, Ukrainian, and German Canadians, largely Canadian-born groups. This suggests a possible process of assimilation in relation to familial obligations (Payne & Strain 1990), supporting the findings of Maykovich (1980) regarding three generations of Japanese Canadians.

Ethnic and ethno-religious cultures may affect values in other domains. One is political, including attitudes to authoritarianism. tolerance, and left-right cleavages. Other value differences might be found in areas such as achievement orientation, self-esteem, and educational attainment. Some studies of educational achievement suggest that differences exist between Chinese-born and Canadian-born Chinese, tentatively supportive of an assimilationist perspective (Lee 1990; Leung & Foster 1985).

Research is needed on the following topics:

- How widespread are elements of an ethno-cultural repertoire among Canadian ethnic groups, particularly past the immigrant generation. The changing of ethnic names is a phenomenon which deserves greater study. What meaning do such elements actually have in the lives of Canadians? Intensive ethnographic studies in settings such as ethnic churches, social clubs, and restaurants would prove highly useful.
- What is the impact of the international and domestic context on ethnic identity? Do ethnic Canadians follow homeland news events particu-

larly closely? And the bottom line: what do they actually do about such developments, if anything? Does mobilization extend beyond the foreign-born, stoking the fires of identity of later generations?

- To what extent do differences in attitudes and values, in areas dealing with the family, interpersonal relations, socio-politics, and psycho-social functioning, exist among ethnic groups in Canada? Do these differences decline with succeeding generations? And are they related to what we can usefully call ethnic cultures?

CONCLUSION

For many Canadians, the retention of ethnic identities and ties is now seen as problematic. The new critique of multiculturalism consists of two strands. The first is that diversity may be contributing to national and political disunity. There is little empirical research extant which might be brought to bear on this question. Reitz found a negative correlation between ethnic in-group attachment and political participation, controlling for generation, and more pronounced for his Southern European and Chinese respondents (1980:227–8). Multicultural organizations generally adopt positions sympathetic to Canadian unity, support for French and native rights, and tolerance for all minorities; little is known about the hold of these views among the more ethnically attached rank and file. Some researchers have posited a relation described as the 'multicultural assumption' in which positive own group evaluation translates into a generalized tolerance (Berry et al. 1977:248; see the sections on 'security' in the paper by Kalin and Berry in this volume for evidence supportive of this assumption).

In another form of the divisiveness argument we have the fear that ethnic ties might also lead to the importation of Old World conflicts with their passion and often bloody manifestations onto Canadian soil, possible involving a conflict with the Canadian 'national interest.' The internment of Japanese Canadians during the Second World War is only the most extreme example of the general possibility; the recent Gulf War raised similar fears, fuelled by racist incidents, among Canadian Arabs and Jews. Given the decline of ethnic organizational participation and identity among the later generations, one can hypothesize that such mobilization outside the immigrant generation is likely to be low.

The second strand is the claim that there are deep cultural and value differences which may make the successful integration of recent immi-grant ethnic groups very difficult. Not all elements of an ethno-cultural repertoire, particularly as certain beliefs and values are translated into actions, may be seen as acceptable. For some Canadians, for a series of complex reasons, some ethno-cultural symbols such as the turban and the chador are more threatening than others. In the broad sense there is no support for this apprehension concerning the cultures of Canada's newer, visible minority groups. For example many of such immigrants and their children – male and female – from allegedly traditional societies boast above average levels of educational attainment, notably in fields related to science and technology.

But of course *some* components of traditional ethnic cultures may well be out of place in the liberal democratic society of Canada. We do try to take gender equality seriously, and we do not permit the murder of authors of allegedly blasphemous books. The notion of a 'moral contract,' in which immigrants agree to uphold the Canadian Charter of Rights and Freedoms and the host society agrees to respect immigrant cultures and help in integration has entered public debate (Economic Council of Canada 1991). What is needed is systematic research to investigate the actual, as opposed to alleged, prevalence of supposed opposing values among Canadian ethnic groups, and the degree to which they may lead to socially and legally unacceptable actions (child abuse and spouse abuse are one such area). Such research would be more controversial than much ethnic research in the past.

A final point. There is also a tendency of late in the popular media to present cultural diversity in its problematic socio-psychological aspects, with regard to the cultural travails of the second generation, caught between the traditionalist demands of immigrant parents and the seductive temptations of the new society.

It is not clear whether such a claim is supported by findings in the mental health literature, and whether such youngsters display more impaired functioning than do other control groups. In fact what seems likely is that for refugee children, factors such as the specific group, social class, circumstances of flight, age, as well as policies in receiving countries may all play a role (Beiser et al. 1988). Difficulties of immigrant adjustment may or may not persist for the long term and intergenerationally. Acculturative stress has been developed as a concept to describe stressors originating in the acculturating experience of various types of Canadian groups. The outcomes, positive or negative, of such processes of acculturation may indeed vary by the effect of intervening variables (Berry & Kim 1987; Berry et al. 1987). Certainly, clinical studies and journalistic accounts are no substitute for scientific research with representative samples. One such study of Canadian-born offspring of Jewish Holocaust survivors found little evidence of impaired psycho-social functioning (Sigal & Weinfeld 1990).

But in any case intergenerational tensions are old hat to any immigration experience. The children and grandchildren survive. We have little systemic sociological research on the true scope of such intergenerational turmoil, and whether it differs from that which is historically found in all immigrant families.

By most accepted definitions and measures, ethno-cultural assimilation is proceeding, notwithstanding the rhetoric of multiculturalism, and is more pronounced among the later generations in Canada. Two broad issues emerge which should be central to future research in this area:

- It is possible that because of reliance on these definitions and measures, analysts may be missing processes of 'transformation' of ethnic identities and cultures, rather than assimilation or dilution (transformation is used here in the sense of Cohen 1988). Ethnicity may be less pronounced yet still salient, expressed in new transformationist modalities. Of course, one person's transformationist is another's wishful thinker.
- It remains unclear as to whether the experiences of visible minority Canadian groups will parallel those of the White ethnic groups. Racism and racial discrimination, which can persist well after acculturation has occurred, immigration trends, and alleged cultural differences may all play a significant role.

REFERENCES

Alba, Richard C. (1990). *Ethnic identity: The transformation of white America*. New Haven: Yale University Press

Alpalhao, J.A., and DaRosa, V.M.P. (1978). *Les Portugais du Québec*. Ottawa: Éditions de l'Université d'Ottawa

Antonius, Rachad (1986). L'information internationale et les groupes ethniques: Le cas des Arabes. *Canadian Ethnic Studies, 18*(2):115–29

Balakrishnan, T.R. (1982). Changing patterns of ethnic residential segregation in the metropolitan areas of Canada. *Canadian Review of Sociology and Anthropology, 19*:1:92–110

Beiser, Morton et al. (1988). *After the door has been opened: Mental health issues affecting immigrants and refugees in Canada*. Report of the Canadian Task Force on Mental Health Issues Affecting Immigrants and Refugees. Ottawa: Supply and Services Canada

Berry, J.W., Kalin, R., and Taylor, D.M. (1977). *Multiculturalism and ethnic attitudes in Canada*. Ottawa: Minster of Supply and Services

Berry, J.W., and Kim, U. (1987). Acculturation and mental health. In P. Dasen, J.W. Berry, and N. Sartorius (eds), *Cross-cultural psychology and health: Towards applications* (pp 207–36). London: Sage

Berry, J.W., Kim, U., Minde, T., and Mok, D. (1987). Comparative studies of acculturative stress. *International Migration Review*, 21(3):491–511

Berry J.W., and Wilde, G.J.S. (eds) (1972). *Social psychology: The Canadian context*. Toronto: McClelland & Stewart

Bibby, Reginald (1990). *Mosaic madness*. Toronto: Stoddart

Black, Jerome, and Leithner, Christian (1987). Patterns of ethnic media consumption: A comparative examination of ethnic groupings in Toronto *Canadian Ethnic Studies*, 19(1):21–41

Bock, Geoffrey (1976). The Jewish schooling of American Jews: A study of noncognitive effects. Unpublished doctoral dissertation, Harvard University

Breton, R., Isajiw, W.W., Kalbach, W.E., and Reitz, G.J. (1990). *Ethnic identity and equality: Varieties of experience in a Canadian city*. Toronto: University of Toronto Press

Breton, Raymond (1964).'Institutional completeness of ethnic communities and the personal relations of immigrants. *American Journal of Sociology 70*(2): 193–205

– (1991). *The governance of ethnic communities: Political structures and processes in Canada*. New York: Greenwood

Buckner, Taylor (1987). Attitudes towards minorities: Four year results and analysis. In Frank Chalk (ed.), *The review of antisemitism in Canada* (pp 8–18). Montreal: League for Human Rights of B'nai Brith

Burch, Thomas K. (1990). Family structure and ethnicity. In S.H. Halli, F. Trovato, and L. Driedger (eds), *Ethnic demography: Canadian immigrant, racial and cultural variations* (pp 199–212). Ottawa: Carleton University Press

Canadian Ethnic Studies (1983). Volume on ethnicity and aging, 15(3)

Canadian Institute of Public Opinion (1983). Gallup Report. 2 June

Cohen, Steven M. (1988). *American assimilation or Jewish revival?* Bloomington: Indiana University Press

Danesi, Marcel (1985). Ethnic language and acculturation: 'The case of Italian Canadians.' *Canadian Ethnic Studies*, 17(1):48–103

Darroch, Gordon (1981). Urban ethnicity in Canada: Personal assimilation and political communities. *Canadian Review of Sociology and Anthropology*, 18(1):93–9

– and Marston, Wilfred (1984). Patterns of urban ethnicity: Towards a revised ecological model. In Noel Iverson (ed.), *Urbanism and Urbanization* (pp 127–62). Leiden: E.J. Brill

De Vries, John (ed.) (1987). *Ethnic Canada: Identities and inequalities*. Toronto: Copp Clark Pitman

– (1988). The integration of ethno-cultural communities into Canadian society: A selected bibliography. Ottawa: Policy and Research, Multiculturalism

Driedger, Leo (1989). *The ethnic factor: Identity in diversity*. Toronto: McGraw-Hill Ryerson

– (1990). Language and ethnicity: Canadian aspects. In Peter S. Li (ed.), *Race and Ethnic Relations in Canada* (pp 231–50). Toronto: Oxford University Press

– , and Chappell, Neena (1987). *Aging and ethnicity*. Toronto: Butterworths

– , and Hengstenberg, Peter (1986). Non-official multilingualism: Factors affecting German language competence, use, and maintenance in Canada. *Canadian Ethnic Studies, 18*(3):90–109

Dreidger, L., Thakar, C., and Currie, R. (1982). Ethnic identification: Variations in regional and national preferences. *Canadian Ethnic Studies, 14*(3):57–68

Economic Council of Canada (1991). New faces in the crowd: Economic and social aspects of immigration. Ottawa: Supply and Services Canada

Edwards, John, and Doucette, Lori (1987). Ethnic salience, identity, and symbolic ethnicity. *Canadian Ethnic Studies, 19*(1):52–62

Etzioni, Amitai (1959). The ghetto: A re-evaluation. *Social Forces*, March, 255–62

Gans, Herbert (1962). *Urban villagers*. New York: Free Press

Gardner R., and Kalin, R. (1981). *A Canadian social psychology of ethnic relations*. Toronto: Methuen

Gillis, A. Ronald, and Whitehead, Paul D. (1971). 'Halifax Jews': A community within a community. In Jean Leonard Elliott (ed.), *Immigrant groups* (pp 84–94). Scarborough: Prentice-Hall

Glazer, Nathan, and Moynihan, Daniel P. (eds) (1975). *Ethnicity: Theory and experience*. Cambridge: Harvard University Press

Goldstein, Jay, and Segall, Alexander. 1985. Ethnic intermarriage and ethnic identity. *Canadian Ethnic Studies, 18*(3):60–71

Greeley, Andrew (1974). *Ethnicity in the United States: A preliminary reconnaissance*. New York: John Wiley

Greenglass, Esther (1972). A comparison of maternal communication between immigrant Italian and second generation Italian women living in Canada. In J.W. Berry and G.J.S. Wilde (eds), *Social psychology: The Canadian context* (pp 335–44). Toronto: McClelland and Stewart

Hakuta, Kenji (1986). *Mirror of language: The debate on bilingualism*. New York: Basic Books

Halli, Shiva S., Trovato, Frank, and Driedger, Leo (eds) (1990). *Ethnic demography: Canadian immigrant, racial and cultural variations* Ottawa: Carleton University Press

Henry, Frances (1989). Housing and racial discrimination in Canada: A preliminary assessment of current initiatives and information. Mimeo. Ottawa: Policy and Research, Multiculturalism and Citizenship. August

Herberg, Edward N. (1989). *Ethnic groups in Canada: Adaptations and transitions.* Scarborough, ON: Nelson

Himmelfarb, Harold (1977). The non-linear impact of schooling: Comparing different types and amounts of Jewish education. *Sociology of education.* Pp 114–29

Ioannou, T. (1983). *La communauté grecque de Québec.* Quebec: Institut québécois de recherche sur la culture

Isaacs, Harold (1975. *The idols of the tribe, group identity and political change.* New York: Harper & Row

Isajiw, Wsevolod W. (1990). Ethnic identity retention. In R. Breton et al. (eds), *Ethnic identity and equality* (pp 34–91). Toronto: University of Toronto Press

Ishwaran K. (ed.) (1980). *Canadian families: Ethnic variations.* Toronto: McGraw-Hill Ryerson

Jaynes, Gerald D., and Williams, Robin (1989). *A common destiny: Blacks and American society.* Washington: National Academy Press

Juteau, Danielle (1991). The sociology of ethnic relations in Quebec: History and discourse. Toronto: Ethnicity Core Area, Department of Sociology, University of Toronto, January

Kalbach, Warren (1990). Ethnic residential segregation and its significance for the individual in an urban setting. In R. Breton et al. (eds), *Ethnic identity and equality* (pp 92–134). Toronto: University of Toronto Press

Kalbach, Warren, and McVey, Wayne (1979). *The demographic bases of Canadian society.* Toronto: McGraw-Hill Ryerson

Kralt, John (1986a). Atlas of residential concentration for the Census Metropolitan Area of Montreal. Multiculturalism Canada. Ottawa: Minister of Supply and Services

– (1986b). Atlas of residential concentration for the Census Metropolitan Area of Toronto. Multiculturalism Canada. Ottawa: Minister of Supply and Services,

– , and Pendakur, Ravi (1991). Ethnicity, immigration and language transfer. Ottawa: Multiculturalism Sector, Multiculturalism and Citizenship. 22 Apr.

Lambert, Wallace, Hamers, Josiane, and Frasure-Smith, Nancy (1979). *Child-rearing values: A cross national study.* New York: Praeger

– and Taylor, Donald (1984). Language in the education of ethnic minority children in Canada. In Ronald Samuda, John W. Berry, and Michel Laferrière (eds), *Multiculturalism in Canada: Social and educational perspectives* (pp 201–15). Toronto: Allyn and Bacon

Lasry, Jean Claude (1982). Une disapora francophone au Québec: Les juifs sépharades. *Questions de culture*, 2:113–38

Lee, Judy M.Y. (1990). Culture, identity and education: An exploration of cultural influences in academic achievement. Unpublished master's thesis, McGill University

Leung, Julian J., and Foster, Stephen (1985). Cultural differences in attitudes towards teaching and learning: Chinese-Canadian and non-Chinese Canadian children. *Canadian Ethnic Studies*, 17(1):90–7

Li, Peter S. (1988). *Ethnic inequality in a class society.* Toronto: Wall and Thompson

Lieberson, Stanley, and Waters, Mary (1987). *From many strands: Ethnic and racial groups in contemporary America.* New York: Russell Sage Foundation

Mackie, Marlene (1978). Ethnicity and nationality: How much do they matter to western Canadians? *Canadian Ethnic Studies*, 10:118–29

– and Brinkerhoff, M. (1984). Measuring ethnic salience. *Canadian Ethnic Studies*, 16:114–31

Mallea, John R. (1984). Cultural diversity in Canadian education: A review of contemporary developments. In Ronald Samuda, John W. Berry, and Michel Laferrière (eds), *Multiculturalism in Canada: Social and educational perspectives* (pp 78–100). Toronto: Allyn and Bacon

Maykovich, Minako (1980). Acculturation versus familism in three generations of Japanese Canadians. In K. Ishwaran (ed.), *Canadian families: Ethnic variations* (pp 65–83). Toronto: McGraw-Hill Ryerson

O'Bryan, K.G., Reitz, J.G., and Kuplowska, O. (1975). Non official languages: A study in Caandian multiculturalism. Ottawa: Minister of Supply and Services

Painchaud C., and Poulin, R. (1983). *Les italiens au Québec.* Hull: Asticou/Critiques

Payne, Barbara J., and Strain, Laurel A. (1990). Family social support in later life: Ethnic variations. *Canadian Ethnic Studies*, 22(2):99–110

Pendakur, Ravi (1990). Speaking in tongues: Heritage language maintenance and transfer in Canada. Ottawa: Multiculturalism and Citizenship Canada. November

Reitz, Jeffrey G. (1980). *The survival of ethnic groups.* Toronto: McGraw-Hill

– (1985). Language and ethnic community survival. In R. Bienvenue, and J. Goldstein (eds), *Ethnicity and ethnic relations in Canada* (pp 105–23). Toronto: Butterworths

– (1990). Ethnic concentrations in labour markets and their implications for ethnic inequality. In R. Breton et al. (eds), *Ethnic identity and equality* (pp 135–95). Toronto: University of Toronto Press

Richmond, Anthony G., and Kalbach, Warren E. (1980). *Factors in the adjustment of immigrants and their descendants: A census analytical study.* Statistics Canada. Ottawa: Minister of Supply and Services

Rieder, Jonathan (1985). *Canarsie: The Jews and Italians of Brooklyn against liberalism.* Cambridge: Harvard University Press

Seeley, John R., Sim, R. Alexander, and Loosely, Elizabeth W. (1956). *Crestwood Heights.* Toronto: University of Toronto Press

Sigal, John, and Weinfeld, Morton (1989). *Trauma and rebirth: Integenerational effects of the holocaust.* New York: Praeger

Stasiulis, Daiva, and Abu Laban, Yasmeen (1990). Ethnic minorities and the politics of limited inclusion in Canada. In Alain Gagnon and James Richardson (eds), *Canadian politics* (pp 580–608). Peterborough: Broadview Press

Troper, Harold, and Weinfeld, Morton (1988). *Old wounds: Jews, Ukrainians and the hunt for Nazi war criminals in Canada.* Markham, ON: Penguin

Ujimoto, K. Victor, and Hirabayashi, Gordon (eds) (1980). *Visible minorities and multiculturalism: Asians in Canada* Toronto: Butterworths

Weinfeld, Morton (1981a). Intermarriage: Agony and adaptation. In M. Weinfeld, W. Shaffir, and I. Cotler (eds), *The Canadian Jewish mosaic* (pp 365–82). Rexdale, ON; John Wiley

– (1981b). Myth and reality in the Canadian mosaic: Affective ethnicity. *Canadian Ethnic Studies, 13*(3):80–100

– (1984). Le milieu juif contemporain du Québec. In Pierre Anctil and Gary Caldwell (eds) *Juifs et réalités juives au Québec* (pp 53–80). Québec: Institut Québécois de recherche sur la culture

– (1988). The Jewish sub-economy of Montreal. In L. Tepperman and J. Curtis (eds), *Readings in sociology* (pp 324–33). Toronto: McGraw-Hill Ryerson

– , and Eaton, William W. (1979). The Jewish community of Montreal. Montreal: Jewish Community Research Institute.

AUGIE FLERAS

Media and Minorities in a Post-Multicultural Society: Overview and Appraisal

Canada is virtually alone among the handful of nation-states that has capitalized on multicultural principles as an official framework for sorting out ethnoracial diversity. Countries such as Australia (Foster & Seitz 1989; Richmond 1991) and New Zealand to some extent (Fleras 1984; Pearson 1991) have been no less enterprising in reordering society along pluralist lines. Yet none have ventured as far as Canada in formalizing a multicultural agenda, in the process validating its claim as the world's first and only official multicultural society. This commitment to diversity has been strengthened in recent years with passage of the Multiculturalism Act in 1988, the Charter of Rights and Freedoms in 1985, and the Employment Equity Act in 1986. Proclamation of a federal department of Multiculturalism and Citizenship in April 1991 lends further credence to Canada's credentials.

These initiatives in 'managing diversity' continue to attract worldwide attention and global acclaim. But such accolades gloss over certain discrepancies between rhetoric and reality (Cummins & Danesi 1990). Criticism by academics (Bibby 1990) and journalists (*The Economist* 1991) has proliferated, with many pouncing on official multiculturalism as irrelevant, wasteful, divisive, counterproductive, expedient, naive, decorative, and misplaced (Fleras & Elliott 1991). Failure by major institutions to 'mainstream' diversity have made them particularly vulnerable targets. Few, however, with the possible exception of urban policing, have attracted as much criticism and concern as the mass media.

As repeatedly observed in the literature and research, media treatment of aboriginal and racial minorities in Canada is mixed at best, and deplorable at worst.[1] The mass media have been reproached by scholars and activists for unbalanced, biased, and inaccurate coverage of racial minorities, many of whom continue to be insulted, stereotyped, and caricaturized – when not actually ignored by the media (Spoonley & Hirsch 1990). Media institutions have come under scrutiny for disregarding minority representation and meaningful input, thus robbing the media of credibility as a progressive social force. The cumulative impact of such discriminatory behaviour is unmistakably clear: The media are accused of acting irresponsibly towards minorities in a society where multicultural principles prevail, but do not always translate into practice. Unless improvements in the level of representation and involvement are forthcoming, it is argued, the rupture in media-minority relations will squander Canada's multicultural potential.

Admittedly, significant strides in media integration of racial minorities have not gone unnoticed (Karim 1989). But much existing research continues to underestimate the challenges of restructuring media-minority relations (Wyckham 1983). In trying to tarnish the media for wrongdoings, both real and perceived, many studies tend to downplay the commercial logic underpinning media dynamics. The constructed character of media reality is also ignored, as are deeply entrenched media values and corporate commitments. Reluctance to confront these sometimes knotty issues has made it relatively easy to criticize the mass media. But the promotion of solutions for mutual benefit is another story. The calibre of studies may improve with growing perception of the mass media as a 'contested site' for control among competing sectors. Nevertheless, the struggle to enhance minority access, equity, and representation is likely to be a prolonged affair even with more sophisticated analysis (MacGregor 1989).

This study examines and analyzes the nature, scope, and status of social science research and scholarly literature on media-minority relations since 1971. It provides an overview of the studies during the past 20 years, assesses and evaluates the relevant research and literature, furnishes a critique of the shortcomings, and makes recommendations for future lines of inquiry. Several questions are central as organizing principles: What is the problem in media-minority relations? Who is responsible? Why? With what impact and effects? What can be done to ameliorate the condition? Answers to these questions underscore the effect of media negligence and mistreatment. But many studies have been equally negligent in ignoring the media as institutions with distinctive agendas and organizational priorities. Refusal to insert a 'media dimension' into this research can only lead to further delays in securing a multicultural balance between media goals and minority aspirations.

OVERVIEW: PAST AND PRESENT

As might be expected, the relationship between the media and minorities is complex and elusive. It is also fraught with ambiguity and stress as Canada undergoes a period of turmoil and change at social, demographic, and political levels. The media in Canada convey information (both deliberate and inadvertent) about ethnoracial minorities – that is, who they are; what they want; why; how they propose to achieve their goals; and with what consequence for Canadian society. Research interests have settled in around the question of media responsibility in reflecting and reinforcing diversity in Canada.

How, then, do we begin to assess and evaluate the existing research in this area? What assumptions guide studies and conclusions? What are the concepts and theories employed by scholars? What methods do they rely on for data collection? How accurate and representative is the coverage of media-minority relations? Answers to these questions are, frankly, subjective. Nevertheless certain commonalities are evident in how the literature has dealt with media acceptance (or lack thereof) of minorities. They also provide a convenient point of departure for sorting out issues in media-minority relations.

Coverage of the Literature

One may have expected expansive coverage of media-minority relations in the literature. The politics and profile of the 'new' mosaic would have demanded as much. But coverage of media and minorities has been erratic in terms of output and quality. A cursory examination of major Canadian journals dealing with ethnic and racial minorities supports this assertion. Since its inception in 1971, *Canadian Ethnic Studies* has devoted several articles to this topic. Prominent among these is a study by Dorothy Zolf (1989), who compared and contrasted multiculturalism and broadcasting policy in four countries, including Canada. Another study resulted in Doreen Indra's (1981) analysis of print mistreatment of minority women in Vancouver presses between 1905 and 1976. Also of note were several studies on the ethnic media and immigrant adaptation by Jerome Black and Christian Leithner (1987, 1988) preceded by an earlier publication by Lawrence Lam (1980).

Other journals are mixed in their coverage. The periodical *Currents*, produced by the Urban Alliance on Race Relations, has published several lively (but short) pieces on media-minority relations. An entire issue in 1986 was devoted to media coverage of minorities, including those already cited by Ginzberg and DuCharme. Additional articles dealt with media treatment of aboriginal peoples as well as of Arabs and Islam.

The periodical *multiculturalism/multiculturalisme* has occasionally attended to media-minority relations. Several articles have appeared including one by Grace Anderson's (1983) on the functions of ethnic press. Another is by Suwanda Sugunasiri (1983) in a critique of mainstream bias (by omission or commission), coupled with proposals for improvement. In a special issue on multiculturalism and media in 1981, Baha Abu-Laban (1981) commented on media responsibility to enhance Canada's multicultural mix by dealing with the concerns of minority groups. Wilson Head (1981) critically examined visible minority groups in Canada's mass media, and followed this up with a plea for improvement through education.

The *Canadian Journal of Communication* has also ventured into this domain (see Raboy 1988). Of some note was a study by Enn Raudsepp (1985) on the characteristics of the Aboriginal press in Canada. A vibrant Aboriginal press is critical, according to Raudsepp, considering the marginal status of Aboriginal peoples in the mainstream press (with a heavy reliance on conflict-deviance situations). It also constitutes a culture-free space for Aboriginal peoples to reclaim identities and to explore lived-in experiences.

Government publications have provided a useful source of information (Report, *Reflections* 1988; *National Proceedings* 1988). In a study commissioned by the Department of Multiculturalism and Citizenship, Karim H. Karim (1989) examined press perception of multiculturalism and race relations by way of a content analysis of five major Canadian dailies (*Globe and Mail*, *Le Devoir*, Ottawa *Citizen*, Montreal *Star*, Winnipeg *Free Press*). His primary findings revealed a certain bias that included:

(a) a steady rise in newspaper coverage of multicultural issues (both positive and negative) from 1980 to 1988, in addition to greater use of the term itself as the 1980s drew to a close.

(b) With the exception of the Montreal *Star*, the media displayed a critical attitude to multiculturalism, preferring to see it as an obstacle to nation-building, as well as an irritant in forging national identity and unity. The press also took a dim view of politicians and ethnic brokers who manipulated multiculturalism for political purposes.

(c) Multiculturalism was associated with 'inverse' discrimination ('tribalization or ghettoization'), and few made an effort to link multiculturalism with race relations and employment equity. Most were oblivious to government anti-racist campaigns and efforts to remove discriminatory barriers through programs in institutional accommodation.

For Karim, the Canadian public has been shortchanged by media waffling over multiculturalism and race relations. Recommendations for improvement lay in greater awareness of multiculturalism in terms of race relations, social justice, improved intercultural understanding, removal of discriminatory barriers, and intergroup conflict reduction.

Elsewhere, coverage on media-minority relations is sparse. Singer (1983, 1986, 1991) has included a section in his readers/texts on media and minorities. Regrettably, Singer's (1986) study of minorities and advertising industry is drawn primarily from American material. Others such as Lorimer and McNulty (1987, 1991) and Vipond (1989) have been less generous in their coverage. Films and documentaries are more difficult to assess; they also are outside the scope of this paper. However, the recent production by Carleton University's School of Journalism entitled 'Colour of the Spots' furnishes useful insights into select aspects of media-minority relations. Unfortunately both the panelists and audience members were put in a position of defining problems and promulgating solutions in an utopian manner.

Perspectives on Research: Ethnic Media versus Race Relations

Perspectives on media-minority research reveal an interesting pattern involving two distinct traditions. The study of *ethnic media* departs in content and style from *race relations* perspective. Unlike the race relations approach with its focus on institutional accommodation and racial discrimination, the ethnic media studies are concerned essentially with the process of immigrant adaptation. Methods of data collection are varied: race relations studies veer towards content analysis as the preferred method, whereas ethnic media analyses employ conventional survey and statistical methods.

Ethnic media studies fall into four major categories. First, with respect to integration and immigrant adaptation, ethnic media are disclaimed as largely inconsequential in one way or the other as sources of assistance or information about Canada. Lam's (1980) investigation of Chinese print consumption in Toronto falls into this category. Second, ethnic media are believed to facilitate the integration of immigrants into society by serving as a buffer and agents of socialization. Black and Leithner (1987) provide lukewarm support for this hypothesis in their analysis from a 1983 metro Toronto survey. Despite a decline in ethnic media consumption over time, they point out, the integration of minorities into Canada's political process is not seriously disrupted. Third, ethnic media promote particularism, thus deterring immigrant transition into society through reinforcement of group specific patterns and ethnocultural values. Kim and Kim (1989), for example, argue that ethnic newspapers (Korean papers in Canada in this case) may isolate the ethnic community socially and culturally, by fostering heritage culture values and links with the home country. Black and Leithner (1988) refute this position on the basis of findings that reveal modest increases in ethnic political involvement. Fourth, ethnic media may discharge a number of concurrent positive functions (Surlin & Romanov 1985). Ethnic (heritage language) papers create safe havens for ethnic cultures to flourish, while simultaneously fostering newcomer adaptation to the new cultural environment.

Race Relations and the Media

The volume of publications on media-race relations has not been impressive, either in numbers or quality. Still it is possible to discern recurrent patterns from this relationship. Foremost here is the treatment of racial minorities as invisible, in terms of race-role stereotyping, as a social problem, and as adornments (Fleras 1991). Even a cursory examination of these thematic issues reveals serious gaps in media-minority relations.

Minorities as Invisible
The sweep of literature from 1971 to the present acknowledges the exclusion of racial and aboriginal minorities from media circles (Elkin 1971; Owaisi & Bangash 1977; PEAC Report 1982; Thornicroft 1983; Niemi & Salgado 1989). Canada's racial and Aboriginal diversity is poorly reflected in the advertising, programming, and newscasting sector of the popular media. Racial minorities are reduced to invisible status through 'underrepresentation' in programming, staffing, and decision-making (CRTC 1986). When presented, people of colour often are confined to largely stereotypical roles involving the themes of charity, tourism, or entertainment, but rarely in serious contexts or high-status roles. In surely a scathing indictment if there ever was one, the trade magazine *Marketing* even praised certain types of South African 'mixed' beer advertising as more enlightened than Canada's 'lily-white' images (Editorial 1990).

Numerous studies have confirmed what many regard as obvious. A study by Robert MacGregor (1989) of visible minority women in *Maclean's* magazine over a thirty-year period concluded that women of colour remained largely invisible judging by the number of appearances in ads and articles. Most were also restricted to limited set of roles as well as a narrow range of goods and services – an observation replicated nearly a decade earlier in a study by Doreen Indra (1981) of minority women depictions in the Vancouver presses. Even substantial representation in the media may be misleading, others argue, if the minority presence is slotted into a relatively small number of narrowly defined programs (Spears & Seydegart 1990).

No less disturbing is the absence of racial minorities in creative positions. Minorities are excluded from roles related to producer, director, editor, or screenwriter; fewer still are destined to attain the upper levels of management where key decision-making occurs. The consequences of such exclusion are cause for concern. Instead of empowerment on the basis of their experiences, minority realities are refracted through the prism of a White-controlled media (Richardson 1990; Laurier LaPierre, *Globe and Mail*, 16 May 1990). For women of colour, the situation is more perilous. They are doubly jeopardized by 'pale male' ideologies that devalue women's contributions, distort their experiences, limit their options, and undermine self-confidence and sense of belonging to Canada (Indra 1981; Wilson & Gutierrez 1985). The net impact of media 'whitewashing' (especially in advertising and newscasting) contributes towards the invisibility of minorities in society. The perpetuation of Canada's 'white face' also 'denies their existence, devalues their contribution to society, and trivializes their aspirations to participate, as fully-fledged members ...' (Niemi & Salgado 1989:28). In these types of situations, one might conclude, what is *not* included by the media is as important as what is.

Minorities as Stereotypes

Minorities have long complained of stereotyping by the mass media. Historically, people of colour were portrayed in a manner that did not offend prevailing prejudices and mainstream attitudes. Images of racial minorities were steeped in unfounded generalizations that veered towards the comical or grotesque. For example, media stereotypes of Aboriginal peoples dwelt on the themes of 'the noble savage,' the 'savage Indian,' or the 'drunken Native.' Other racial minorities were labelled as drop-outs, pimps, and drug pushers, while still others have been typecast as mathematical or scientific geniuses. Liberties taken with minority depictions in consumer advertising were especially flagrant. In an industry geared towards image and appeal, the rule of homogeneity and conservatism prevailed: advertisers wanted their products sanitized and stripped of controversy for fear of lost revenue (Hastings 1991; Cuff 1991).

Mass media stereotyping has shown only marginal improvement (Karim 1989). The ratings game excludes any complex depiction of minorities at odds with prevailing stereotypes. Race-role images continue to be reinforced, perpetuated, and even legitimized through media dissemination and selective coverage. News about minorities is not randomly selected, but reflects majority expectations about minority status, role, and contribution to society. Minorities are role-typed with certain products or services, presumably on the basis of research that isolates a desired target group, then links it with an intended audience as part of a marketing/advertising strategy (MacGregor 1989; Wyckham 1983). Racial minorities are often cast into slots that reflect a 'natural' propinquity for the product in question. Who better to sell foreign airlines, quality chambermaid service in hotels, or high cut gym shoes? The cumulative effect is 'narrow' casting of the worse type. Minorities are paired with exotic and tropical areas, portrayed as famine victims (usually children) in underdeveloped countries, enlisted as congenial boosters for athletics and sporting goods, or ghettoized in certain marketing segments related to 'rap' or 'hip hop.' Through stereotypes, in other words, minorities are put down, put in their place, or put up as props for the edification of the mass audience.

Minorities as Social Problem

Racial minorities are frequently singled out by the media as a 'social problem,' or as 'having problems' in need of political attention or scarce national resources (Satzewich 1990). They are taken to task by the media for making demands that may imperil Canada's unity or national prosperity. Consider the case of Canada's Aboriginal peoples when they are depicted as: (a) a threat to Canada's territorial integrity (the Lubicon blockade in 1988 or the Oka Mohawk confrontations in the summer of 1990) or to national interests (the Innu protest of the NATO presence in Labrador), (b) a risk to Canada's social order (the violence between factions at the Akwesasne Reserve), (c) an economic liability (the costs associated with massive land claims settlement or recent proposals to constitutionally entrench inherent self-governing rights), and (d) a crisis throughout the criminal justice system (ranging from Donald Marshall case to policing shootings of Aboriginal victims).

The combined impact of this negative reporting paints a villainous picture of Canada's first peoples (*Toronto Star*, 17 April, 1991). Time and again they come across as 'troublesome constituents' whose demands for self-determination and right to inherent self-government constitute an anathema to Canada's liberal-democratic tradition. Elsewhere, racial minorities both foreign- and native-born are targets of negative reporting (DuCharme 1986). This negativity is drawn in part from content, as well as from the positioning and layout of the story, length of article and size of type, content of headlines and kickers (phrases immediately after the headline), use of newspeak or inflammatory language, use of quotes, statistics, and racial orgins. Media reporting of refugees is normally couched in terms of illegal entry and associated costs of processing and integration into Canada. Immigrants are routinely cast as potential troublemakers who steal jobs from Canadians, engage in illegal activities such as drugs or smuggling, and imperil Canada's unity and identity. Worse still, they offer little in return for Canada's largesse.

Minorities as Adornment

Racial minorities are normally portrayed by the media as irrelevant to society at large (MacGregor 1989). This decorative effect is achieved by casting minorities as entertainment with which to amuse or divert the audience. John Haslett Cuff, the media critic for the *Globe and Mail* (21 August 1990), concluded that Blacks on television are locked into roles as as villains or victims; alternately as buffoons or folksy sitcom types. Only rarely do they appear as heroes, overtly sexual beings, or perceptive critics of society. Popular magazines such as *National Geographic* are likewise susceptible to charges of trivializing minority experiences with glossy decriptions of the exotic and colourful rather than the exploititive and unequal (Raub 1988).

Advertising must also share the blame in transforming minorities into ornaments for display. Their presence and impact may be diffused by casting them as children or as subservient adults. They may be viewed only as part of a crowd, or as 'walking away from the camera' – an observation noted by the jazz pianist Oscar Peterson in describing the presence of Black musicians on beer commercials (Allen 1991). The narrow casting of minorities as idle or decorative is distortive. It also has the potential to desensitize the audience by making it more callous and indifferent towards minority experiences in a predominantly White society.[2]

Evidence from the past twenty years has confirmed what ethnoracial minorities have long protested. If the media represent a mirror that reflects an image of society, we still have a long way to go in achieving a multicultural 'looking glass self' (Desbarats 1987–8:23). The media possess at best a love-hate mindset towards minorities – 'attraction' when convenient to sell copy or advertise consumer goods, 'avoidance' when denial or distortion is preferred. Few will dispute the anomalies that pervade media-minority relations. Minorities are known to be both underrepresented and misrepresented by an industry seemingly impervious to change (Wolfe 1991). Mass media treatment of racial minorities has been accused of slanted coverage, ranging from the unfair and inadequate (Singer 1983) to allegations of outright racism and corporate betrayal (DuCharme 1986). Despite improvements, media portrayals of diversity border on the negligent or irrelevant, in the process rendering minorities 'invisible' (Report, *Equality Now!* 1984). But the literature has been less successful in articulating the reasons behind this discrepancy. Nor have proposed solutions to the problem received much in the way of research attention. The absence of a theoretical framework for understanding media-minority relations is equally regrettable.

ASSESSMENT AND APPRAISAL

Underlying Assumptions: Racism in the Media

Media mistreatment of racial minorities is routinely acknowledged by the literature even if its precise nature remains unclear. What is less explicit are the reasons behind this negligence. Why are racial minorities not reflected to any significant degree in consumer advertising, on television programming, and in news accounts? Neglect of minorities in the media may arise from a variety of reasons: from hard-boiled business decisions reflecting market forces, on down to a lack of cultural awareness and deep-seated prejudices. Certain working assumptions about racial minorities may also inhibit progressive action. People of colour are infrequently used in the advertising of beauty care and personal hygiene, so entrenched is the image of 'whiteness' as the preferred standard of beauty (Bledsloe 1989). Rarely are they advertised in association with high-price or luxury items. Reluctance among advertisers is further fueled by anxieties over a White boycott of minority-related products – not to mention a perceived loss of sophistication and exclusiveness despite a lack of evidence to this effect (PEAC 1982).

The questions are clearly before us. Does media mistreatment of minorities imply the presence of personal prejudice or overt discrimination? Or does it reflect a preference to act out of self-interest and within market place dictates – especially during economic recessions and periods of corporate restructuring? Is it racism, or are media personnel unsure of how to deal with diversity without a whiff of paternalism? Do advertising moguls fear marketing mistakes that could attract negative product publicity; worse still, incite a consumer boycott (*Toronto Star*, 19 May 1990)? Are minorities themselves unwilling to enter media professions because of low status associated with such employment (Khan 1989)? Answers to these questions are critical, but often begin with the assumption that media-minority relations are driven by racism and discrimination – at times deliberate, at other times inadvertent. Such an accusation needs further exploration.

'Politely Now': Media Racism in Canada

The literature and research on media-minority relations appear to share a common assumption. Minority exclusion and misrepresentation stem from conscious and unconscious expressions of racism (and sexism) by mainly white management. How reliable is this conclusion? One rarely encounters blatant expressions of discrimination or explicit racial slurs in the mass media. Overt hostility and open discrimination are neither acceptable nor legal. Various human rights codes and the Charter of Rights and Freedoms prohibit discriminatory behaviour of any kind on the basis of race, colour, or national origin. Granted, there is reporting that verges on the openly racist. The *Toronto Sun* newspaper, for example, has been singled out for coverage that allegedly conveys 'biased, inaccurate, and unbalanced portrayals of visible minorities' (Ginzberg 1986). Race-tagging – the identification of person by race even if irrelevant to the story (Spoonley & Hirsch 1990) – remains a problem in some circles. The English-speaking press continues to be accused of smearing Quebec's independence plans through unwarranted criticism of Quebec's response to the Oka crisis (McKenzie 1991), combined with excessive zeal in pursuing other less-flattering racial incidents (Picard 1991).

Polite forms of discrimination are certainly in evidence, and may be reflected in refusal to hire or promote racial minorities in the workplace for one reason or another. The decision is not overtly discriminatory, but phrased in a manner consistent with abstract principles of justice, equality, or fair play ('we treat everybody alike') (Dovidio et al. 1989).

Subtle racism may be in effect when media routinely accept the government's position in conflict situations as restrained and responsible. By contrast, assertive minority groups tend to be discredited as illegitimate, deviant, unrepresentative, highly factionalized, and prone to violence. Thoughtful discussion about minority issues is dissipated by media obsession with events and incidents rather than with the big picture (causes and context). Polite put-downs (ranging from disbelief to sarcasm or ridicule) are not necessarily accidental, but may constitute a discriminatory bias that is both pervasive yet discrete. In short, imbalances in media-minority relations are chronic; they reflect and reinforce expressions of power or structure at systemic and institutional levels.

Systemic Discrimination

Discrimination is often institutionalized within the mass media. Under institutional discrimination, rules and procedures are deliberately invoked to deny fair, just, and equitable treatment. This exclusion need not be explicit or deliberate (Fulford 1986), but becomes systemic when embedded and institutionalized. Discrimination is systemic through organizational procedures and policies that adversely effect minority chances. No one sets out to flagrantly violate the rights of others. But those in positions of authority may inadvertently contribute to the problem by invoking seemingly neutral rules, standards, and expectations. For example, the exclusion of minorities from advertising is discriminatory in consequence (if not in intent) when employment opportunities are restricted on largely spurious grounds such as minimum weight or height qualifications (Niemi & Salgado 1989). Applying equal standards to unequal situations is no less systemic since such actions freeze the status quo and reinforce the prevailing distribution of power. In brief, systemic discrimination does not spring from malicious motives as much as from tacitly accepted frameworks that extol majority priorities at minority expense.

How do the media discriminate systemically? Earlier I implied a 'shallows and rapids' treatment of racial minorities by the mass media. In general, Third World minorities are ignored or rendered irrelevant by mainstream presses. Otherwise coverage is activated by the context of crisis or calamity, involving natural catastrophes, civil wars, and colourful insurgents. Violence and mayhem do occur, of course, but the absence of balanced coverage results in blinkered portrayals of who they are and what collectively they want. This distortion may not be deliberately engineered. Rather, the misrepresentation is systemic in light of media preoccupation with readership and advertising revenues. The flamboyant and sensational are highlighted to satisfy audience needs and sell copy, without much regard for its effects on racial minorities. The mass media may not be aware of its discriminatory impact, arguing that they are reporting only what is news. Nevertheless, the resulting outcome paints an unflattering portrayal of indigenous peoples or racial minorities as 'not quite human' and less worthy of our sympathy or foreign aid (Elliott & Fleras 1991).

Research Methods

Research in the area of media-race relations has relied on a limited number of methods. Many of the findings to date originate from a data collection method known as content analysis. The core of content analysis entails analyzing the content of certain information by counting the number of incidents/objects that occur over time or across space according to a predetermined set of categories. MacGregor's (1989) longitudinal study of visible minority women in *Maclean's* over a thirty-year period is one instructive example of this genre.

Content analysis approaches are subject to criticism of reliability and replicability. These methodological difficulties are compounded when items are taken out of context, isolated for statistical purposes, and divorced from any sense of history, interaction, or significance (Wyckham 1983). In the case of advertising, Wyckham continues, the creative aspect of putting together an ad campaign are all but ignored. Only the finished commercial product is included, as is the frequency occurrences of minorities as they appear over time or across a number of media outlets. Any concept of the decision-making process behind the characterization of the product/service is all but ignored, as is the targetting of the market niche and the role of advertising in the marketing strategy. As a result, a reliance on content analysis makes it difficult to disentangle consequences from intent or projections. Nor is there any way of determining whether responses are representative of the audience. Not unexpectedly, advertisers have not shown much enthusiasm for conclusions based on content analysis, given its subjectivity and lack of validity or replication (Wyckham 1983).

CRITICISM AND RECONCEPTUALIZATION

Public images of racial minorities are conceivably influenced by the mass media. Such an admission reinforces the need to acknowledge the rationale behind media logic, objectives, content, and styles. The mass media not only codify and shape perceptions of reality. They also constitute a constructed reality in that the media have been created for a specific purpose. This constructed character imposes restrictions and constraints on what the media may or may not do. Foremost among these constraints is the commercial logic that no longer exempt even public broadcasting from financial considerations. In looking to secure as large an audience as possible for revenue purposes, both public and private media are predominantly business ventures whose bottom lines are profit and accountability to shareholders. The corporatist nature of the media puts an additional premium on upholding the logic of bureaucratic rationality and control, often at the expense of conventional social values (Weber 1947; Hummel 1988).

Putting the media back into media-minority relations reinforces a key conviction: media dynamics cannot be divorced from the political and economic context that creates, sustains, and modifies media-minority relations (Taras 1991). As well, the media constitute organizational forces in their own right, with a corresponding assemblage of symbols, meanings, and aesthetics. Acknowledging the media as a social force within a broader context is pivotal in exposing the 'unspoken assumptions' governing media dynamics. What is the nature of this 'hidden agenda' and how does this affect – however inadvertently – media perception of racial minorities?

Media Logic: Newscasting, Programming, and Advertising

Both print and electronic news are a case in point. What eventually becomes the news is not something intrinsic out there, with clearly marked labels that everybody can agree upon. Nor is news a random reaction to disparate events by detached professionals (Clarke 1981). News is a socially constructed process, shaped in part by a collective set of intrinsic values and created through the interplay of uneven forces (Satzewich 1990; Taras 1991). A pervasive bias in newsmaking stems from an interplay between private ownership and profit imperative, coupled with the various biases inherent within the news process (including coverage, news collection, reporting, news sources, editorial gatekeeping, presentation) (Herman & Chomsky 1988). Increasingly intense competition for the consumer dollar encourages the repackaging of news as entertainment with an informative slant ('infotainment'). The net result (that is, news that is 'print to fit') ressembles a 'residue' that says more about media priorities than reality itself.

Television programming is likewise constrained by inherent limitations. Despite the illusion of diversity, television programming conforms to a remarkably formulaic process. Under the slogan of 'safe, simple, and familiar,' TV content is sanitized and bleached for fear of disturbing the consuming public. Televison characters are typecast within a restricted span of roles consistent with public expectations lest they interfere with the undisturbed flow of advertising messages (Cuff 1990). The cumulative effect of television programming results in the perpetuation of a 'boxed-in reality.' It is not so much that television programming transcends reality. More to the point, reality is 'bracketed' to conform with the practical constraints of a 26-inch screen, a half-hour time slot for resolution of plot and problems, and a story line filled with unblemished characters of implausible virtue and free-spending habits. The audience in general is poorly served by the distortions of a boxed-in reality. Minorities are doubly jeopardized by media propensity to *homogenize* ('whitewash') pluralistic experiences for majority consumption (Wolfe 1991).

Nowhere is the one-sidedness of the media more evident than in the realm of advertising. Advertising is central to media processes. Media dynamics revolve around providing an outlet for advertising, in the main by attracting as wide an audience as possible for maximizing product sales. To secure the allegiance of the buying public, advertising conforms to an underlying code that seeks to: (a) attract viewer attention; (b) arouse interest; (c) target an audience; (d) manipulate images; (e) neutralize reservations; and (f) create conviction through positive reinforcement. The advertising media capitalizes on consumerist fantasies as one way of massaging the message for more. But media messages generally exclude minorities from such definitions, in effect relegating diversity to the periphery.

This negative portrayal of racial minorities is consistent with media logic, operations, and objectives. The media are involved in the construction of reality through the processes of socialization, legitimation, and agenda-setting. The media also constitute a *constructed* reality, composed of diverse forces, internal and external constraints, and personalities. The combined impact of these imperatives leads to a one-sided coverage of minority issues. More disturbing still, it also invokes charges of 'propaganda.'

Media-Minority Relations as Propaganda

The nature of media-minority relations can be critically explored by reference to the concept of *propaganda*. Propaganda can be defined expansively or narrowly, but we prefer to see it as a communication process in which behaviour is influenced through symbolic manipulation of emotions and attitudes (Qualter 1991). In taking this perspective, I do not equate propaganda with blatant brainwashing or crude displays of formal state censorship in a totalitarian regime. Nor do I subscribe to the notion that propaganda constitutes a deliberate attempt at blinkered information. Propaganda as discourse may reflect unconscious processes or unintended outcomes in the same way that systemic discrimination is based not on intent but on the negative consequences of even well-meaning rules, equal standards, or uniform procedures (Fleras & Elliott 1991). Yet even unintended consequences are anything but inconsequential. As outcome or process, propaganda may lead to the exclusion of alternative points of view; reduction of dissent and disagreement; manufacture of consensus and consent; compliance with the dominant ideologies; and definition of outer limits of permissibility in society.

The impact of the media as a system of propaganda is subtle and oblique. This very unobtrusiveness transform the media into a powerful agent of domination and control (Herman & Chomsky 1988). The media fix the premises of public dialogue by defining the outer perimeters of debate, thus massaging audience perceptions of what is normal or necessary. Media images about normalcy or acceptibility are absorbed without much awareness of the indoctrination process. Spirited discussion and lively dissension may be encouraged, but only within the parameters that constitute an elite consensus. The fundamental premises upon which our society is founded – the virtues of materialistic progress and competitive individualism – are rarely scrutinized. Also unexamined are the tacit assumptions underlying the interpretation of reality from 'pale' male perceptions. The dynamics of propaganda, therefore, provide a vantage point for analyzing media treatment of racial minorities whose powerlessness make them a convenient target for massaging the masses.

FUTURE DIRECTIONS

Responding to the Crisis: 'Two Steps Forward ...'

That prejudice and discrimination persist in certain quarters of Canada is surely beyond doubt or dispute at this stage of our history. The proliferation of discriminatory acts and persistence of systemic bias is well documented in the literature (Henry & Tator 1985; McKague 1991). The media are no different in this sense. The marginality of minorities is reflected, reinforced, and amplified by the media. Minorities are routinely 'sidestreamed' by media politics, in effect minimizing levels of involvement and decision-making. But recognition of a problem is one thing; to initiate meaningful changes may be something altogether different, and the research in this area indicates that much remains to be done.

What do racial and aboriginal minorities expect of the mass media? In a society where the media claim to represent and to be representative of public interest, minorities are determined to stake out some degree of control over the 'who,' 'why,' 'what,' and 'how' of media-minority relations. Responsible coverage of minority interests and concerns is predicated on the need to curb (a) selective and sensationalistic accounts, (b) images and words that demean and malign, (c) portrayals that are biased and unbalanced while lacking any sense of context, and (d) stereotyping which invokes hatred and fear (Rees 1986a, b). This demand for self-determination is proposed for all levels of operation, from hiring and programming to decision-making and agenda-setting.

Changes are already in progress (*Currents* 1987; Raboy 1988). A new Broadcasting Act has has come out in favour of 'cultural expression' by expanding air time for ethnoracial minorities. As well, the CRTC has made it known that broadcasters will be evaluated on the basis of employment equity hiring when licences come up for renewal (*Kitchener-Waterloo Record*, 3 September 1992). Passage of the Multiculturalism Act in 1988 has obligated all government departments and Crown agencies to improve access, equity, and the representation of minorities. This mainstreaming is applied throughout the organization (in terms of hiring, promotion, and training), and externally through delivery of culturally sensitive services (Secretary of State 1988). Rules are in place to deter abusive representations that expose individuals to hatred on the basis of race or ethnicity, as well as age, gender, religion, or disability. Additional reforms include sensitivity training for program and production staff, language guidelines to reduce race-role stereotypes, and monitoring on-air representation of racial minorities.

The expansion of the 'third media' (including ethnic presses and non-English, non-French broadcast programs) is a prime example of minority inroads (Taborsky et al. 1986). More than 200 ethnic periodicals were accounted for in 1980 with a readership of over 2 million (Black & Leithner 1987). At present there are 2000 hours a week of third language programming divided among eight multilingual radio stations, CFMT

Toronto – the world's only full time commercial television station to feature multicultural programming, eight TV stations with some language programs, sixty radio stations that offer ethnic programming, three pay and specialty services, and community-based programs on cable television (Report, *National Proceedings* 1988). Reforms are also evident in the private sector where Toronto's CITY-TV station and on-air programming elsewhere are tackling multicultural issues (*Toronto Star,* 19 May 1990). In yet another success story, the Northern Native Broadcast Access Program has facilitated the broadcasting of culturally relevant/language specific programming throughout many parts of northern Canada (Minore & Hill 1990). Conferral of Aboriginal control over aboriginal media has had the empowering potential of any program that evolves from the experiences of those directly affected.

To sum up, the existing literature is guarded about a proposed reordering of media-minority relations – at one end, there is cautious optimism; at the other, outright despair. Yet media efforts to improve race relations are as likely to be greeted with derision or scepticism rather than with support and encouragement. Positive portrayals and inclusive programming may be dismissed as window-dressing, condescending, tokenistic, and unrealistic in terms of audience aspirations. Bewildered and taken aback by criticism for their efforts, the media have moved cautiously, much too cautiously, in many eyes, in accommodating diversity.

Proposals for the Future

Advances in the study of media-minority relations have been duly noted by taking stock of the current literature and research. Studies to date have emphasized descriptive accounts that rarely delve into causes, impacts, and solutions. Media-minority relations are rarely anchored in the contexts of inequality and power, media dynamics, organizational change, and minority experiences. Recommendations and proposals for future research are based on those grounds.

1 Research on media and minorities in a multicultural Canada has been erratic at best, non-existent at worst. Many of the studies originate in Toronto with the result they may be of limited application outside of major urban centres. A cross-section of Canada's minority (ethnic, racial, and aboriginal) sectors is included in the literature, although the coverage of any single group is too thin for solid conclusions. The studies themselves tend to be highly descriptive and ad hoc, with

little or no attention to theory-building, model construction, or practical application. Discussions of media-minority relations tend to be framed in the discourse of psychology or prejudice, and only infrequently in terms of power, group dynamics, and resource allocation.

2 With race relations at the forefront of Canada's post-multicultural surge, media-minority relations are shifting toward issues of social equality, equal opportunity, occupational stratification, institutional accommodation, and employment equity. Further research will need to determine whether 'mainstreaming' the media can bring about fundamental change, or merely reinforce a business-as-usual syndrome. More research must also capitalize on the experiences of those directly affected by media mismanagement, rather than rely exclusively on the perspectives of academics or media apologists. As nation-building continues apace, more attention must be devoted to the role of the media in the ongoing reconstruction of Canadian society along post-multicultural lines.

3 Research on media-minority relations has concentrated on criticizing media mistreatment of minorities. Additional research is required to explain why this state of affairs is tolerated, and what can be done to accelerate changes already in progress. The prospect for engineering change can be daunting enough under the best of circumstances. In an industry reknowned for its conservatism and penchant for the tried and formulaic, the media are unlikely to move away from formats that proved successful in the past. In other words, studies for redefining media-minorities relations must start from a key premise: The media are predisposed to action and reform – but only when consistent with commercial interests, political realities, and inner logic.

4 Future investigation must take into account the media component of media-minority relations. Research in this field could profit from envisaging the media as a 'contested site' involving a tension between opposing ideologies and competing groups for control of the agenda. The forces for control and containment are as real as those of resistance or reform, and neither is likely to dominate for extended periods of time. That knowledge alone should sensitize future studies to the realities of media logic.

5 Much of what passes for media mistreatment of minorities is based on perception of the media as a powerful tool of socialization with tyrannical powers to destroy, seduce, and exploit. But many have discarded the 'magic bullet' perspective on media impacts (Tate & Mc-

Connell 1991), preferring a more complex relationship both indirect and diffuse, and difficult to disentangle from related socialization agencies (Troyna 1984). Intervening variables prevail, including age, gender, socioeconomic status, income and educational levels, personal needs and personality characteristics, context of interaction, and degree of social embeddedness and integration (Brannigan 1991). In other words, the complex nature of media-minority relations is beyond the simplistic causal connection implicit in content analysis methods.

SUMMARY AND CONCLUSION

Canada is undergoing a period of profound upheaval at demographic, social, and political levels. Traditional myths and conventional practices are slowly crumbling under the onslaught of new realities, but many remain firmly entrenched as vested interests balk at discarding the tried and true. New visions are gaining credence as they filter into our national consciousness. Yet many new ideas are lacking the singularity of purpose to displace traditional paradigms. This interplay between the old and new can be disruptive, especially when buffetted by competing worldviews and evolving agendas.

In a seemingly progressive society such as Canada the media have lagged behind in mainstreaming diversity. This criticism applies across the board – from workforce composition and employment opportunities on the one hand, to media portrayals of minorities on the other. Minorities tend to be treated poorly, if at all, with depictions either unflattering or wooden. Media mishandling of minorities is compounded by a pervasive racism, both muted and polite as well as institutional and systemic. The perils of propaganda in massaging the masses are no less a hindrance in forging what is multiculturally fair, just, and equitable.

The mass media play an influential role in terms of defining what is normal or desirable. This is accomplished in large part by specifying a cultural framework that provides a reference point for acceptance or rejection. In serving as a primary channel of communication, the mass media have the potential to articulate a powerful statement about the legitimacy of diversity in a post-multicultural world. Yet they are equally likely to defend the economic, political, and social agenda of monoculturalism. At the core of this redefinition process is power. Media-minority relations will remain 'contested' until the issue of power is resolved, in terms of who owns it, who has access to it, and whose values will dominate? It is conjectural whether or not the media can establish a culturally-sensitive and racially-based approach for managing diversity. Recent reforms suggest the potential for progress. They also reveal how the slow and erratic pace of reform is nothing to boast about.

NOTES

1 A note of caution before proceeding. First, the term 'ethnoracial' minority is employed in a broader sense to include both racial and ethnic groups, as well as Aboriginal peoples. In one sense this inclusiveness is purely for analytic convenience. Aboriginal peoples most emphatically reject themselves as another minority group, and much of the current politics in redefining aboriginal-state relations are based on distancing aboriginal 'nations' from immigrants and their descendents (Elliott & Fleras 1991). For my purposes Aboriginal and ethnoracial (ethnic and racial) minorities are classified together on the grounds they as a group occupy a relatively powerless position in society. A similar assessment applies to women, but women as minorities are addressed only in passing, notwithstanding references to women of colour. For various reasons, not the least of which reflected space constraints, the relationship between the French-speaking and English-speaking media is omitted. Second, a study of this nature is selective in what it may or may not include. Films, radio, and computer technologies are ignored for the most part, whereas mass news media (both print and electronic), television programming, and advertising (especially print) are accorded intensive treatment. This decision is more than a personal preference; it reflects an imbalanced slant in coverage by the existing literature.

2 Other minority groups in Canada have also criticized media for lapses in judgment. The misrepresentation and underrepresentation of women in the media has attracted attention when we take into account the literature and research devoted to this area (Wyckham 1983; Media Watch 1986; MacGregor 1989). The film *(Still) Killing Us Softly* (1979, 1987) is perhaps the most articulate of indictments against advertising and its disparagement of women. Women continue to be cast as inferior and subordinate, unlike men who are portrayed as dominant and superior with access to power, resources, decision-making opportunities and high status (despite a greater range of male images that extend beyond the 'sturdy oak' model). They are defined as low status domestic servants, as excessively concerned with nurturing and self-sacrifice, as dependent on male definitions of beauty, as decorative sex objects who crave male attention or degradation, preoccupied with youth, fitness, and attractiveness to the exclusion of personal

or career growth, and as superwomen who juggle dual careers between the kitchen and the boardroom. It is not the use of these stereotypes per se that is worrisome, according to Wyckham (1983). Rather it is the circulation of negative stereotypes whose cumulative effect serves to reinforce the myth that biology is not only destiny, but also an index of personality, life chances, and self-worth.

REFERENCES

Ali Khan, Azhar (1989). Summary of presentation. In O.P. Dwivedi, Ronald D'Costa, C. Lloyd Stanford, and Elliot Tepper (eds), *Canadian 2000: Race relations and public policy*. Dept. of Political Studies, University of Guelph, Guelph, ON

Abu-Laban, Baha (1981). Multiculturalism and Canadian television: A critical review. *Multiculturalism*, 5(1):3–7

Allen, Dianne (1991). What's wrong with these pictures? *Toronto Star* 5 January

Anderson, Grace M. (1983). The functions of the ethnic press. *Multiculturalism*, 8(1):29–30

Bibby, Reginald (1990). *Mosaic madness: The potential and poverty of Canadian life*. Toronto: Stoddart

Black, Jerome, and Leithner, Christian (1987). Patterns of ethnic media consumption: A comparative examination of ethnic groupings in Toronto. *Canadian Ethnic Studies*, 19(1):21–39

– (1988) Immigrants and political involvement in Canada: The role of the ethnic media. *Canadian Ethnic Studies*, 20(1):1–20

Bledsloe, Geraldine (1989). The media: Minorities still fighting for their fair share. *Rhythm and Business Magazine*, March/April, 14–18

Brannigan, Augustine (1991). Is pornography criminogenic? The career of a moral problem. In Benjamin Singer (ed.), *Communications in Canadian society* (pp 322–43). Scarborough: Nelson

Cardozo, L. Andrew (1986). Multiculturalism as an urban policy: An area in need of development. *Multiculturalism/Multiculturalisme*, 11(2):10–13

Clarke, Debra (1981). Second-hand news: Production and reproduction at a major Ontario television station. In Liora Salter (ed.), *Communication studies in Canada* (pp 20–51). Toronto: Butterworths

CRTC (1986). *Sex-role stereotyping in the broadcast media: A report on industry self-regulation*. CRTC. Ottawa

Cohen, Phil, and Gardner, Carl (eds) (1982). *It ain't half racist, mum: Fighting racism in the media*. London: Comedia Publishing

Cuff, John Haslett (1990). Beyond tokenism but a far cry from ideal. *Globe and Mail*, 21 Aug.

– (1991). Civil wars that nobody wins. *Globe and Mail*, 8 Nov., C-3

Cummins, Jim, and Danesi, Marcel (1990). *Heritage languages: The development and denial of Canada's linguistic resources*. Toronto: Garamond/Our Schools-Our Selves Education Foundation

Currents (1987). Minority broadcasting. Report of the Task Force on Broadcasting Policy. *Currents*, 4(2):15–16

Department of Education (1989). *Media literacy: Resource guide (intermediate and senior divisions)*. Toronto: Ministry of Education

Desbarats, Peter (1987/8). The impact of the media on race relations (excerpts of a speech by Peter Desbarats, Dean of Graduate School of Journalism at University of Western Ontario). *Currents*, 4(4):23

Dovidio, John F., Mann, Jeffrey, and Gaertner, Samuel L. (1989) Resistance to affirmative action: The implications of aversive racism. In F.A. Blanchard and F.J. Crosby (eds), *Affirmative action in perspective* (pp 83–102). New York: Springer-Verlag

DuCharme, Michele (1986). The coverage of Canadian immigration policy in the *Globe and Mail* (1980–5). *Currents*, Spring, 6–11

Economist (1991). Survey of Canada. 19 June. Reprinted in *Globe and Mail*, 19 July 1991

Editorial (1990). Canada has a coat of many colors. *Marketing*, 11 June

Elliott, Jean Leonard, and Fleras, Augie (1991). *Unequal relations: An introduction to race and ethnic dynamics in Canada*. Scarborough, ON: Prentice-Hall

Elkin, Frederick (1971). The employment of visible minority groups in mass media advertising. Report submitted to Human Rights Commission in Ontario

Fleras, Augie (1984). Monoculturalism, multiculturalism, and biculturalism. The politics of Maori policy in New Zealand. *Plural Societies*, 15:52–75

– (1991). Racial minorities and the mass media in a multicultural society. In Benjamin D. Singer (ed.), *Communication in Canadian society* (pp 344–67). Toronto: Nelson

– , and Elliott, Jean Leonard (1991). *Multiculturalism in Canada: The challenges of diversity*. Scarborough: Nelson

Foster, Lois, and Seitz, Anne (1989). The politicization of language issues in 'multicultural' societies: Some Australian and Canadian comparisons. *Canadian Ethnic Studies*, 21(3):55–73

Fulford, Robert (1986). Minority opinion. *Currents* (originally in *Saturday Night*, Apr. 1986), 26

Ginzberg, Effie (1986). Power without responsibility: The press we don't deserve. A content analysis of the *Toronto Sun*. *Currents*, Spring, 1–5

Granzberg, Gary (1989). Portrayal of visible minorities by Manitoba television: A summary of findings. *Currents*, 5:25

Hastings, Deborah (1991). Networks standards 'Written in Sand' *Globe and Mail*, 18 Nov.

Head, Wilson (1981). A critical examination of visible minority groups in Canadian mass media. *Multiculturalism*, 5(1):8–12

Henry, Frances, and Carol Tator (1985). Racism in Canada: Social myths and strategies for change. In Rita M. Bienvenue and Jay E. Goldstein (eds), *Ethnicity and ethnic relations in Canada* (2nd ed.) (pp 321–35). Toronto: Butterworths

Herman, Edward S., and Chomsky, Noam (1988). *Manufacturing consent: The political economy of the mass media*. New York: Pantheon Books

Hummel, Ralph P. (1988). *The bureaucratic experience* (3rd ed.). New York: St Martin's Press

Indra, Doreen (1981). The invisible mosaic: Women, ethnicity and the Vancouver press. *Canadian Ethnic Press*, 13(1):63–74

Karim, Karim H. (1989). Perceptions about multiculturalism: A content analysis of newspapers, academic papers, ethnocultural organizations, briefs, attitude surveys, and ministerial correspondence. Policy and Research, Multiculturalism Sector, Multiculturalism and Citizenship. Ottawa

Khan, Azar Ali (1989). Summary of Presentation. In O.P. Dwivedi et al. (eds), *Canada 2000: Race relations and public policy*. Guelph, ON: Dept of Political Studies, University of Guelph

Kim, Ki Su, and Gon Kim, Young (1989). Who reads an ethnic language newspaper, and why? *Multiculturalism/Multiculturalisme*, 12(1):28–30

Kitchener-Waterloo Record (1992). CRTC urges broadcasters to hire minorities. 3 Sept.

Lam, Lawrence (1980). The role of ethnic media for immigrants: A case study of Chinese immigrants and their media in Toronto. *Canadian Ethnic Studies*, 12(1):74–90

Lorimer, Rowland, and McNulty, Jean (1987). *Mass communication in Canada*. Toronto: McClelland & Stewart

MCF Media Conference (1990). Sharing the message: Multiculturalism in the media. Pre-conference notes from the Multicultural Communications Foundations, Grant MacEwen Community College, Edmonton, AB

MacLean, Eleanor (1981). *Between the lines: How to detect bias and propaganda in the press and everyday life*. Montreal: Black Rose Books

MacGregor, Robert M. (1989). The distorted mirror: Images of visible minority women in Canadian print advertising. *Atlantis*, 15(1):137–43

McKague, Ormand (1991). *Racism in Canada*. Saskatoon: Fifth House Publishing

McKenzie, Robert (1991). Anglo media accused of smearing Quebec. *Toronto Star*, 16 Mar.

Media Watch (1987). *Adjusting the image: Women and Canadian broadcasting*. Report of a National Conference on Canadian Broadcasting Policy held in Ottawa, 20–2 Mar.

Minore, J.B., and Hill, M.E. (1990). Native language broadcasting: An experiment in empowerment. *Canadian Journal of Native Studies, 10*(1):97–119

National Proceedings (1988). The role and function of the media in depiction & promotion of visible minorities in the media and society at large. Proceedings of the National Symposium on Progress Toward Equality. Compiled and edited by Aziz Khaki. Vancouver: 16–18 Sept.

Niemi, Fo, and Salgado, Mario (1989). Minorities in billboard advertisements in Montreal's subway stations. *Currents, 5*(3):27–8

Owaisi, L., and Bangash, Z. (1977). Visible minorities in mass media advertising. Report submitted to the executive of the Canadian Consultative Council on Multiculturalism, Ottawa

PEAC (1982). The role of non-whites in English-language television advertising in Canada. A report commissioned by the Secretary of State, Multicultural Directorate. Ottawa

Pearson, David (1991). Biculturalism and multiculturalism in comparison. In Paul Spoonley et al. (eds), *Nga take: Ethnic relations and racism in Aotearoa/New Zealand* (pp 194–214). Palmerston North, NZ: Dunmore Press

Picard, André (1991). Talking of bias, who's the target? *Globe and Mail*, 15 Nov.

Qualter, Terence H. (1991). Propaganda in Canadian society. In Benjamin D. Singer (ed.), *Communications in Canadian society* (pp 200–12). Scarborough, ON: Nelson

Raboy, Marc (1988). Two steps forward, three steps back: Canadian broadcasting policy from Caplan-Sauvageau to Bill C-136. *Canadian Journal of Communication, 14*(1):70–5

Raub, Wendy (1988). The *National Geographic* portrayal of urban ethnicity. *Journal of Urban History, 14*(3):321–44

Raudsepp, Enn (1985). Emergent media: The Native press in Canada. *Canadian Journal of Communication, 11*(2):193–209

Reports (1984). *Equality now!* Report of the Special Committee on Visible Minorities in Canadian Society. Bob Daudlin, MP, Chairman. Published under authority of the Speaker of the House of Commons by the Queen's Printer for Canada

– (1988). *Reflections from the electronic mirror.* Report of a National Forum on Multiculturalism and Broadcasting. Hosted by the Canadian Multiculturalism Council on behalf of the Minister of State for Multiculturalism. Toronto, 13–14 May. Minister of Supply and Services, Canada

Rees, Tim (1986a). Racism in the press. *Currents*, Spring, 1

– (1986b). Racism in the UK media. *Currents*, Spring, 1

Richardson, Boyce (1990). Media define when Natives are worth covering. *Toronto Star*, 12 Sept.

Richmond, Anthony (1991). Immigration and multiculturalism in Canada and Australia: The contradictions and crises of the 1980s. *International Journal of Canadian Studies, 3*(Spring):87–109

Satzewich, Vic (1990). The social construction in Canada of race relations in Britain: The 1958 disturbances. *Plural Societies, 20*(3):13–30

Secretary of State (1988). *A matter of balance*. Ottawa: Department of the Secretary of State

Singer, Benjamin D. (1983). Minorities and the media. In Benjamin D. Singer (ed.), *Communications in Canadian society*. Don Mills, ON: Addison-Wesley

– (1986). *Advertising and society*. Don Mills: Addison-Wesley

– (ed.) (1991). *Communications in Canadian Society*. Scarborough: Nelson

Spears, George, and Seydegart, Kasia (1990). *Societal diversity in TV Ontario programming*. Ontario Educational Communications Authority, Toronto. Printed in *Currents, 7*(1):19–20

Spoonley, Paul, and Hirsch, Walter (1990). *Between the lines: Racism and the New Zealand media*. Auckland: Heinemann Reed

Sugunasiri, Suwanda (1983). Media and multiculturalism. *Multiculturalism, 7*(1):17–23

Surlin, Stuart H., and Romanov, Walter I. (1985). The uses and gratification of heritage language newspapers and general Canadian mass media by five heritage language groups. *Multiculturalism/Multiculturalisme, 8*(2):21–7

Taborsky, Vaclav et al. (1986). *Mosaic in media. Selected works of ethnic journalists and writers*. Canadian Ethnic Journalists' and Writers' Club

Taras, David (1991). *The newsmakers: The media's influence on Canadian politics*. Scarborough, ON: Nelson

Tate, Eugene D., and McConnell, Kathleen (1991). The mass media and violence. In Benjamin Singer (ed.), *Communications in Canadian society* (pp 299–321). Scarborough, ON: Nelson

Thornicroft, R. (1983). *Multicultural research survey summary*. Np

Troyna, Barry (1984). Media and race relations. In E. Ellis Cashmore (ed.), *Dictionary of race and tehnic relations* (pp 157–60). London: Routledge and Kegan Paul

Vipond, Mary (1989). *The mass media in Canada*. Toronto: Lorimer

Weber, Max (1947). *A theory of social and economic organization*. New York: Oxford University Press

Wilson, Clint C., and Gutierrez, Felix (1985). *Minorities and the media: Diversity and the end of mass culture*. Beverly Hills, CA: Sage

Wolfe, Morris (1991). Cross current. *Globe and Mail*, 12 Nov.

Wyckham, Robert G. (1983). Female stereotyping in advertising. Discussion Paper 83-010-02. Faculty of Business Administration. Simon Fraser University, Burnaby, BC

Zolf, Dorothy (1989). Comparisons of multicultural broadcasting in Canada and four other countries. *Canadian Ethnic Studies, 21*:13–26

RUDOLF KALIN AND J.W. BERRY

Ethnic and Multicultural Attitudes

This paper provides an overview of ethnic and multicultural attitudes from a social-psychological perspective. We take the position that individuals and their attitudes are important elements in multicultural societies for four reasons. First, it is individuals who act (aggress and attack) and react (resist and engage in backlash) to other persons, and to groups; thus individuals are one locus of ethnic and race relations. Second, there are limits to the social changes that can be brought about by legal or institutional means, limits that reside in psychological phenomena. It is known that attitudes and behaviours can be shifted, but not beyond certain personal limits. Third, individual attitudes provide a necessary support base for multicultural policies and programs. We consider that these, to be successful, should have broad and general support in the population. When they are at variance with widely held attitudes, there are likely to be reactions against them. From this perspective, it becomes imperative to know about and to understand relevant attitudes. Fourth, with a knowledge of individual attitudes it becomes possible to track over time, and even to forecast, relative degrees of harmony and conflict in society. Moreover, by examining various social and demographic correlates of these attitudes, and their distribution in the population, we may be able to pinpoint specific areas of potential difficulties, and be in a position to take preventive measures.

Our emphasis in reviewing the available materials is upon national studies of ethnic and multicultural attitudes, carried out predominantly by social psychologists and sociologists, but also by political scientists and economists. The studies reviewed in the present paper pertain primarily to Canada outside Quebec. The paper by Bourhis in this volume reviews studies conducted in Quebec.

We define *attitude* as a person's organized set of beliefs, evaluations, and predispositions to act favourably or unfavourably in regard to a particular social object. In this paper, these social objects are multiculturalism, immigration, and ethnic groups. We also consider the related issues of identity, prejudice, and stereotypes, and the various determinants and correlates of these attitudes.

MULTICULTURALISM BELIEFS AND ATTITUDES

Multiculturalism means different things to different people. This situation presents a difficulty for those wishing to assess attitudes, for if the attitude object is not clearly specified, the resulting research and interpretation will be muddled. A major distinction has been made between 'multiculturalism as fact,' and 'multiculturalism as policy' (Berry & Kalin 1989). In the former can be included such phenomena as the actual cultural diversity in the Canadian population and in the latter the various multiculturalism policies.

Much of the information reviewed in this section derives from a national survey carried out in 1974 (Berry, Kalin & Taylor 1977) with a sample of 1849 respondents. Analyses of a more recent survey (1991) on many of the same issues are in progress, and are not yet available for inclusion in this chapter.

Perception of Multiculturalism

In the 1974 national survey (Berry et al. 1977), the cultural maintenance aspect of the federal multiculturalism policy was incorporated into a policy perception question with three options: assimilation (i.e., encourage immigrants to give up their customs); permissive integration (allow them to maintain their customs); and supportive integration (encourage them to maintain their customs). Nationally, the perceptions were 13.4 per cent for the first (assimilation) option, and 60.1 per cent and 26.5 per cent for the two integration options respectively. Thus, even early in the life of the policy, it was clear to the vast majority of respondents that it was not one of assimilation, but did involve some degree of cultural maintenance.

Multicultural Ideology

In the Berry et al. (1977) national survey, the construct of *multicultural ideology* was proposed and assessed. Statements supporting integration (own cultural maintenance and sharing this with others) were given positive weight. Items supporting assimilation and segregation were scored negatively. Overall, national support was moderately positive.

Since this initial study, some of the original questions (but not the whole scale) have been used in various public opinion polls. For example, the question 'It would be good to see all ethnic groups in Canada retain their cultures' received a 64 per cent endorsement in the 1974 national survey (Berry et al. 1977), and 58 per cent in a 1979 Decima survey (Decima 1980). Another item, 'It is best for Canada if all immigrants forget their cultural background as soon as possible,' was disagreed with by 64 per cent of respondents in the Berry et al. (1977) survey, by 68 per cent in the 1979 Decima survey, by 75 per cent in the 1985 Environics Survey, and by 68 per cent in the 1989 Environics Survey. These rather consistent results suggest moderate and continuing support for cultural maintenance aspects of the policy.

When considering the scale as a whole, approximately twice as many respondents accepted a multicultural ideology as opposed it (63.9 per cent vs 32.2 per cent). A similar ratio was recently obtained (1991) in a *Globe & Mail* and CBC News poll (63 per cent vs 31 per cent) by asking respondents to choose between two statements, one indicating that diversity is one thing they like about Canada, and the other that diversity causes problems.

While accepting the idea of multiculturalism and approving the retention of heritage identities, there is also a suggestion that Canadians are not willing to accept newcomers totally unchanged. In the Berry et al. (1977) national survey, more people agreed than disagreed with the statement that 'Canada would be a better place if ethnic groups would keep their own way of life alive' (47 per cent agreed vs 36 per cent disagreed), but in later Environics surveys the trend reversed: in Environics 1985, 42 per cent agreed and 36 per cent disagreed, while in Environics 1989 only 36 per cent agreed and 59 per cent disagreed.

There is a suggestion in these findings that Canadians expect some accommodation to the Canadian way of life by those who come to this country. Several further questions asked in various surveys point to the same conclusion. In Berry et al. (1977), one question was: 'People who come to Canada should change their behaviours to be more like us.' Results showed that 50 per cent agreed with this statement and in the Decima 1979 survey, 48 per cent agreed. The idea of accommodation was captured in several other survey questions. To the question: 'Ethnic groups should try as much as possible to blend into Canadian society and not form a separate unit,' in both Environics (1985, 1989) surveys, 81 per cent of respondents agreed with this statement. In the Fletcher (1989) survey 63 per cent agreed with the statement: 'People who come to live in Canada should try harder to be more like other Canadians.' Fletcher (1989) also asked: 'While it is all well and good to celebrate one's heritage it is more important for new immigrants to learn what it is to be Canadian than to cling to their old ways.' Seventy-five per cent of respondents expressed agreement with this statement.

While the responses to these opinion statements could possibly be interpreted as a reluctance on the part of Canadians to accept and embrace multiculturalism fully, they are consistent with the interpretation that while Canadians accept multiculturalism in the sense of accepting the retention of ethnic identity and heritage, they also expect newcomers to this country to accommodate to the Canadian way of life. In Berry's (1984) terminology this mode of adaptation to a host society is called *integration*.

Another approach to assessing the notion that Canada should be culturally plural has been taken by Bibby (1987). He has asked respondents whether they prefer to have Canada as a 'mosaic' or as a 'melting pot' (after giving brief sketches of the meaning of these two terms). The 1985 results indicated a strong preference for the 'mosaic' (56 per cent) over the 'melting pot' (27 per cent), with 13 per cent having no preference and 4 per cent giving some other response. Most recently, (*Maclean's* 1990) 68 per cent of respondents endorsed Canada's multicultural approach to ethnic diversity. We may conclude that Canadian attitudes are clearly not assimilationist; rather they support some degree of cultural maintenance by ethnic groups along with some degree of sharing with, and accommodation to, the larger society.

Multiculturalism Component Attitudes

The 1971 federal policy initiated a number of programs. In Berry et al. (1977) there were six questions that inquired about attitudes toward programs implementing the cultural maintenance aspects of the policy. Overall, support was moderately positive; however, the more 'public' programs (such as radio and TV programs in heritage languages, or teaching them in regular school classes), were viewed moderately negatively. Community cultural centres, ethnic histories, and folk festivals, though, were all well supported.

Perceived Consequences of Multiculturalism

What people believe will result from pursuing a course of multiculturalism was assessed by Berry et al. (1977) using five questions. Overall,
findings indicated a moderately positive perception of the consequences
of multiculturalism. For example, 61.9 per cent agreed that 'Canada will
be richer in culture,' while 53.7 per cent disagreed that 'our Canadian
way of life will be destroyed.' In some contrast to these rather positive
views about the consequences of multiculturalism, there was division in
response to the item 'social harmony will improve in Canada,' with 39.1
per cent agreeing, 35.7 per cent disagreeing, and 25.2 per cent providing
a mid-response.

IMMIGRATION BELIEFS AND ATTITUDES

Immigration and Multiculturalism

The relationship between immigration and multiculturalism deserves
some attention before attitudes in this domain are analyzed. On the one
hand, it is clear that immigration traditionally has been the source of
ethnic diversity. Immigration continues to supply ethnic communities
with new members who may reinforce and keep alive cultural traditions.
In this sense immigration and multiculturalism are closely related. They
may also be related in the minds of Canadians who think primarily of
immigrants when the topic of multiculturalism is raised. On the other
hand, multiculturalism is theoretically independent of immigration. It is
possible that various ethnic groups would continue to maintain their
distinctiveness for generations even in the absence of further immigration. In this sense multiculturalism can exist without immigration.
Because immigration continues, however, and consists increasingly of
immigrants from nontraditional sources, study of attitudes towards
immigrants and immigration is important in the context of examining
multicultural and ethnic attitudes.

General Immigration Attitudes

Immigration is not a simple attitude object. Concern with immigration
may involve the desired level of the Canadian population (maintenance,
or growth). It may also be concerned with types of immigrants (e.g.,

regarding ethnic or racial origin). In the literature on immigration attitudes these issues have sometimes been confused. For example, a decline in support for a larger population might be interpreted as evidence of intolerance towards ethnic diversity. Tienhaara (1974) analyzed public opinion surveys asking Canadians whether they would like to see Canada have a much larger population. A steady decline was observed in Canadians wanting a larger population between 1945 and 1973. The Economic Council of Canada (1991a, 1991b) extended this analysis up to 1983 and found a further slight decline to a possible levelling off. Whether this decline is related only to concerns about size of population or also to its ethnic composition is unclear from these survey results.

When opinion surveys are directly concerned with beliefs about levels of immigration, as opposed to population in general, the views of Canadians do not necessarily become clearer. On the basis of a national survey of attitudes and perceptions of some dimensions of refugee and immigration policy, Angus Reid (1989) reported a growing consensus among Canadians that immigration levels are increasing. Focus groups, studied in conjunction with the national survey, revealed that the basis for this belief was primarily a perception that visible minorities were increasing. Evaluative reactions to the perceived increase were divided. Approximately as many Canadians favoured the increase as opposed it. The Economic Council of Canada (1991a, 1991b) conducted extensive studies on immigration in order to make recommendations regarding appropriate levels of future immigration, and concluded with cautious optimism about the degree of tolerance of Canadians regarding immigration in general.

General immigration attitudes have also been studied by asking Canadians about the perceived (positive, neutral, or negative) consequences of immigration. On the basis of several surveys (Berry et al. 1977; Filson 1983; Angus Reid 1989) it seems most appropriate to describe Canadians as divided in these attitudes. Similar numbers of Canadians see positive and negative consequences.

Attitudes Towards Types of Immigrants

Several surveys suggest that Canadians favour certain types of immigrants over others. Open immigration without selection is generally rejected by Canadians according to the surveys by Berry et al. (1977) and Angus Reid (1989). Among the most acceptable immigrants are those that have relatives in Canada and those with high levels of education and/or job skills (Berry et al. 1977; Angus Reid, 1989). Some concern is raised from survey results regarding the acceptability of visible minorities. Berry et al. (1977) and Filson (1983) discovered a preference order for immigrants that is not dissimilar to the ethnic hierarchy discussed in the next section of this chapter.

In addition to the division among Canadians regarding immigration, there are also some apparent contradictions. The national survey by Berry et al. (1977) asked respondents to indicate their intention to be friends with, and to have a business or professional relationship with, immigrants or majority Canadians (English or French, depending on the respondent) said to be in high- or low-status occupations. Majority Canadians were uniformly preferred over immigrants, regardless of type of relationship. Respondents also expressed a relatively lower willingness to seek the services of immigrants in high- (e.g., teacher or dentist) as compared with low-status (e.g., plumber or shoemaker) occupations. In a different part of the survey, respondents had expressed a preference for high- as opposed to low-status immigrants. These two results suggest a contradiction in attitudes, and indicate that Canadians are ambivalent about high-status immigrants. This ambivalence may well cause considerable hardship for immigrants, particularly those of higher status. A similar contradiction and ambivalence in attitudes had earlier been observed by Jones and Lambert (1965).

ETHNIC ATTITUDES

The 1974 national survey (Berry et al. 1977) examined attitudes towards eight ethnic groups in Canada (English, French, Jewish, Ukrainian, Italian, Chinese Canadians, and Canadian Indians) and towards 'Immigrants in General.' Ratings on a number of evaluative adjective scales (e.g., 'hardworking,' 'important,' 'likeable') revealed a definite hierarchy or preference, in the order listed above (most accepted listed first). Other groups mentioned by respondents received evaluations ranging from Scottish Canadians (which were positive, similar to English Canadians and French Canadians), to Portuguese, Spanish, Greek, Black, and to East Indian Canadians (which were negative, similar to Chinese Canadians and Canadian Indians). This ethnic attitude hierarchy is comparable to the historical evidence (Palmer 1975), to social distance ratings (Mackie 1974), and to prestige ratings (Pineo 1977).

Attitudes towards Native Canadians have received some special attention (e.g., Filson 1983; Ponting 1984; Indian and Northern Affairs

1980, 1984; Angus Reid 1990). In general, Native Canadians collectively are viewed somewhat positively, particularly in regard to their cultural and environmental qualities; there is also a sense of shared responsibility to improve their economic plight. However, interpersonally (as noted above) relatively negative attitudes are in evidence.

Attitudes of English and French Canadians towards each other have also received special attention (e.g., Lambert & Curtis 1982; Bibby 1987). In the Berry et al. (1977) survey there was substantial positive mutual regard found between these two groups. Trends are difficult to assess. However, Bibby (1987) provides some evidence that between 1975 and 1985, English Canadians think less frequently that 'French Canadians have too much power in national life.'

Other specific groups have also been the object of study (see, e.g., Dion 1985). In particular, attitudes towards East Indian Canadians, Blacks and Orientals have been tracked by Bibby (1987), who finds that respondents are increasingly 'at ease' with members of these groups.

In Toronto (Breton et al. 1990), respondents of 'majority Canadian' background were asked their attitudes towards various ethnic groups, using acceptance as 'neighbours' and as 'close relatives by marriage' as indicators. Generally, acceptance as neighbours was high (ranging from 92 per cent for German Canadians, to 83 per cent for Chinese Canadians, with a drop to 67 per cent for West Indian Canadians). Acceptance as relatives was generally lower, ranging from 87 per cent for German and Ukrainian Canadians, 84 per cent for Italian Canadians, 77 per cent for Jewish Canadians, 68 per cent for Portuguese Canadians, 65 per cent for Chinese Canadians, and 49 per cent for West Indian Canadians. Despite the absence of East Indians/South Asian Canadians as attitude objects in the study by Breton et al. (1990), a rough comparison can be made with the various national survey results. The similarity in the hierarchy is very clear, suggesting a degree of stability for the ethnic attitudes of majority Canadians over time.

ACCULTURATION ATTITUDES

Most studies of ethnic attitudes in Canada are of those held by dominant groups towards specific ethnic or racial groups. Another approach has been to assess the attitudes of persons who are members of these latter groups towards various kinds of relationships with their own group and the dominant society. These preferences have been termed acculturation attitudes (Berry, Kim, Power, Young & Bujaki 1989). When two issues are considered (the degree to which cultural and identity maintenance are desired, and the degree to which contact with people of other cultures is sought), four general attitudes are defined. When desire for cultural maintenance is low, combined with a preference for contact with others, the attitude is called *assimilation*. When the opposite pattern is present (high cultural and identity maintenance and low contact with other groups) then the attitude is *separation*. When there is a preference for both own group cultural maintenance and other group contact and participation, the *integration* attitude is defined. Finally, when there is minimal interest or possibility of either (low cultural maintenance and other group contact), there is the attitude of *marginalization*.

Scales to assess these four attitudes have been developed and employed with a variety of acculturating groups in Canada (Native and immigrant groups, and French Canadians living outside Quebec). Results of these studies (Berry et al. 1989) indicate a widespread preference for integration, but there are important levels of support for separation and assimilation among some individuals in some groups; marginalization is least preferred by all groups in these studies. Individual differences on these attitudes are associated with generational status (first generation less assimilationist than second and later generations), and length of residence. There are also variations in acculturation attitudes by actual degree of contact and participation by acculturating individuals in the larger society, and by level of schooling (longer residence, more contact, and higher education are associated with increasing assimilation and decreasing separation preferences).

With respect to the adaptation being made by acculturating individuals to life in Canada, integration attitudes are most commonly associated with better mental health and personal satisfaction, while feelings of being marginalized are associated with relatively poor adaptation (Berry, Kim, Minde & Mok 1977). These acculturation attitudes then are useful indicators not only of the character of intergroup relations in Canada, but also of the quality of these relations for ethnic and immigrant peoples.

Prejudice

Prejudice can be defined as a strong antipathy towards a particular ethnic or racial group. Important manifestations of prejudice are *ethnocentrism, racism,* and *discrimination*.

Ethnocentrism. This notion refers to the tendency to make 'we-they' distinctions, accompanied by a relatively positive evaluation of 'we,' and a negative evaluation of 'they,' and the tendency to judge others by the standards and values of one's own group.

Ethnocentrism can be assessed using a scale of the same name, and by examining the pattern of relative own-group/other-group attitudes. Both were used by Berry et al. (1977). The general scale produced an overall mean that was moderately tolerant (non-ethnocentric). The pattern of own- and other-group attitudes (from the 1974 survey; see Berry & Kalin 1979) has revealed that the five most numerous groups (Angloceltic, French, German, Italian, and Ukrainian Canadians) evaluate their own group highly, and relatively more highly than other groups, but this generally positive evaluation and this own–other difference are highest for French Canadians, lowest for German Canadians, and intermediate for English, Italian, and Ukrainian Canadians.

Racism. When prejudice is specifically directed at racial groups (in Canada, usually those of non-European background, sometimes termed 'visible minorities'), the concept of racism is used. In Berry et al. (1977), there was no general racism scale employed; however, one item in the ethnocentrism scale referred to 'coloured people,' and (as reported earlier) some visible minority groups were included in those towards which specific attitudes were expressed. The one race-related item received a response in a distinctly non-racist direction. However, as we have seen, in the same study West Indian, Chinese, 'Negro,' and East Indian Canadians, as well as Canadian Indians were all in the lowest range of the attitude hierarchy (although Japanese Canadians were viewed more positively).

Secondary analyses of national surveys conducted in 1968, 1973, 1978, and 1983 were carried out by Lambert and Curtis (1984), focusing on the issue of interracial marriages. The same issue has been examined by Bibby (1987). Both studies report a decline in opposition to such marriages over time. For example, in the latter study, opposition to White-Black marriage went from 43 per cent in 1975 to 37 per cent in 1980, to 28 per cent in 1985.

A national survey in 1989 by Fletcher was concerned with issues related to the Charter of Rights. Some questions were directed towards racial prejudice and related issues (e.g., immigrants, cultural maintenance). There were five distinct samples: a national representative sample, one of legislators, one of lawyers, one of government executives, and one of police. With respect to the importance of 'making special efforts to protect ethnic and racial minorities' there were wide differences in the 'very important' response (50 per cent nationally, and ranging from 63 per cent for legislators to 27 per cent for police). To the statement 'Just as is true of a fine race horse, some breeds of people are just naturally better than others,' 12 per cent of the national sample agreed, but only 5 per cent of executives, while 23 per cent of police agreed. However, there was a high level of acceptance for all samples (over 90 per cent) of the idea that 'It's better for people of different races to live and work together.'

A survey of white respondents in Toronto was carried by Henry (1978) using 150 questions referring to race in general and to particular racial groups (ie, Blacks, Indo-Pakistanis), as well as to immigrants. Of these questions, 57 were factor-analyzed, and a standard score was produced from the single factor. Using this standard score, Henry created four groups: 15.8 per cent were labelled 'very racist' (standard score greater than –1.0); 35.2 per cent were 'somewhat racist' (standard score between -1.0 and 0); 30.2% were 'somewhat tolerant' (score between 0 and +1.0), and 18.8 per cent were 'very tolerant' (score greater than 1.0). From this distribution, Henry considered that 51 per cent of the sample was racist. However, the procedures involved in the factor analysis, score standardization, and making categories out of a continuous dimension led inevitably to this arbitrary conclusion.

Discrimination. When general prejudice and specific ethnic attitudes are acted upon leading to differential treatment, *discrimination* is the result. Discrimination is important to examine, in addition to attitudes, since not all attitudes manifest themselves in overt behaviour (norms and laws may affect their expression); conversely, not all differential treatment is based on an underlying attitude, since other factors (e.g., economic self-interest) may determine the act. Discrimination in the form of a preference for interactions with majority Canadians versus immigrants was found in the national survey by Berry et al. (1977), as noted in the earlier section on attitudes towards immigrants.

Experimental studies, using mock employment-suitability decisions based upon résumes and variously accented recorded interviews (Kalin & Rayko 1978; Kalin, Rayko & Love 1980) also reveal discrimination. In one study, foreign-accented job-seekers were rated as relatively more suitable for a low-status job (plant cleaner), but relatively less suitable for high-status jobs (industrial mechanic and foreman). In another study, four different foreign accents were used. Results indicated that English- and German-accented persons were rated as suitable for high-status jobs, while West Indian- and South Asian-accented persons were rated as more suitable for the low-status job.

Two field studies of discrimination have been carried out by Henry (Henry & Ginzberg 1985; Henry 1990) using actors posing as job applicants for jobs advertised in Toronto newspapers. In both studies, there were two conditions: a telephone approach and an in-person job application. In the telephone condition, White Canadians (non-accented), White immigrants (accented), West Indians, and Indo-Pakistanis (both accented) made phone enquiries. For the in-person study, matched pairs of job applicants (one Black and one White) were sent to apply for the positions. In the study by Henry and Ginzberg (1985), there was evidence of substantial job discrimination against non-Whites in both conditions. However, in the study by Henry (1990), Black in-person applicants received the same number of job offers as Whites, but there was evidence that Whites were treated better (more politely, etc.) during the interview. In the telephone condition, however, the 1990 results still exhibited evidence of discrimination, with White Canadians being told that the job was open more than were White immigrants, West Indians, or Indo-Pakistanis.

Perception of Prejudice. People's views about prejudice in others have also been examined nationally and regionally. Bibby (1987) reports that prejudice and discrimination against cultural and racial groups are thought to be present by a majority of Canadians. In 1985, 11 per cent said it exists and is getting worse, 20 per cent said it exists but is getting better, and 28 per cent said it exists but it is not changing; 9 per cent said it does not exist but was a problem in the past, and 32 per cent said it has never been a problem.

In Toronto, Breton et al. (1990) found that members of seven ethnic and racial groups perceived the extent of prejudice and discrimination (as judged by their acceptance as neighbours and as relatives) to be relatively good: for most groups the majority of respondents indicated they were accepted very or somewhat easily in both relationships. However, this varied from a high (for 'as neighbours') of over 90 per cent for German and Ukrainian Canadians, 78 per cent for Jewish Canadians, and 58 per cent for West Indian Canadians. For acceptance 'as relatives,' the perceptions were generally lower, ranging from over 80 per cent for German, Italian, and Ukrainian Canadians, 78 per cent for Portuguese, 57 per cent for Chinese, 42 per cent for Jewish, and 35 per cent for West Indian Canadians.

ETHNIC STEREOTYPES

The area of ethnic stereotypes has been extensively researched by Canadian social psychologists and sociologists. This literature has been reviewed by Taylor (1981; Taylor & Lalonde 1987). The first extensive use of the term stereotype as referring to 'pictures in our head' about other people is attributed to Lippmann (1922). From the beginning, the term was used in a pejorative sense as indicative of inferior thought processes. Throughout most of the history of the term, American social scientists have suggested that stereotypes are motivated by prejudice, that they lack validity, and that they represent exceptionless generalizations. Only relatively recently have American social psychologists acknowledged that stereotypes may be relatively inevitable and normal aspects of cognitive functioning (Hamilton 1981). Whereas earlier definitions of stereotypes maintained that they were 'false,' 'rigid,' and 'oversimplified' generalizations, more recent ones correspond to their actual measurement more closely by stating that they are consensual beliefs held by one group about the attributes of another (Taylor 1981; and Taylor & Lalonde 1987).

The completely negative view of stereotypes has been challenged by Canadian researchers. Mackie (1973, 1974) has questioned the common assumption that stereotypes are inevitably false. She compared the stereotypes of Alberta Indians, Hutterites, and Ukrainians with publicly available social indicators and found a substantial correspondence between what stereotypes suggested and what was actually true. Her studies support the idea that stereotypes may contain at least a 'kernel of truth.' Gardner and his coworkers (Gardner, Wonnacott & Taylor 1969; Gardner, Taylor & Feenstra 1970) have empirically examined the common view that stereotypes inevitably indicate prejudice. They demonstrated that stereotypes, as consensual beliefs about traits associated with a group, are independent of evaluative reactions, that is, attitudes towards the group. Such studies demonstrate that individuals who endorse stereotypes about a group may have negative, positive, or neutral attitudes towards that group.

An interesting question arises as to why the negative connotations of stereotypes developed in the United States were questioned in Canada. Taylor and Lalonde (1987) have argued that stereotypes are likely considered to be socially undesirable in a society that values cultural homogeneity, as does, for example, one that has a melting-pot ideology. In such a society group differences are considered to be a source of conflict and are therefore discouraged in fact or in social discourse. In a multicultural society, on the other hand, cultural diversity is encouraged and stereotypes may become an important vehicle for recognizing ethnic distinctiveness and expressing ethnic pride. Such a view of stereotypes does *not* mean that *all* stereotypes are appropriate or that stereotyping is *always* acceptable. Stereotypes that convey racism, or insistence on stereotyping in the face of contradictory information is inappropriate in a multicultural as well as an assimilationist society.

ETHNIC IDENTITY

The Nature and Scope of Ethnic Identity

Diversity of ethnic origin does not necessarily make a country multicultural. To the extent that there is large-scale assimilation, having diverse origins may not be a significant social or psychological fact. In order to examine whether ethnic origin is psychologically and socially significant, the ethnic identity[1] of Canadians has to be examined. Driedger (1989) has given the following definition: 'Ethnic identity is a positive personal attitude and attachment to a group with whom the individual believes he has a common ancestry based on shared characteristics and shared socio-cultural experiences (p 162).' As is the case with other attitudes, ethnic identity can vary from being positive to neutral to negative. From this consideration, it follows that ethnic identity does not coincide entirely with ethnic origin. Ethnic identity is a possible measure of the involvement in, and commitment of Canadians to, multiculturalism. If ethnic identity is strong and widespread, then most Canadians will have a stake in multiculturalism. If, on the other hand, ethnic identity is weak on the average, and significant to only relatively few Canadians, public interest in, and support for, multiculturalism may be weak. We may even expect some opposition, if a large number of Canadians feel that multiculturalism does not apply to them and therefore feel left out.

A distinction can be made between *behavioural* and *symbolic* ethnic identity. Behavioural ethnic identity consists of outward expressions, such as being able to speak a heritage language and use it frequently, choosing best friends primarily from one's own group, practising endogamy, and belonging to ethnic and/or religious organizations of one's group. Driedger's (1975, 1976) Ethnic Cultural Identity index is a good measure of behavioural ethnic identity. Symbolic ethnic identity consists of knowledge of and pride in one's ethnic origin. This may or may not be accompanied by behavioural expression of this identity. The symbolic and behavioural aspects of identity are involved in the conceptualization and assessment of acculturation attitudes discussed in an earlier section.

Symbolic ethnic identity (Gans 1979) is primarily psychological and not behavioural. Although behavioural and symbolic ethnic identity may be empirically related, in the sense that a person with a strong symbolic identity is also likely to have a strong behavioural identity, the two are conceptually distinct. It may be possible to have a behavioural ethnic identity without an accompanying symbolic identity, and vice versa. The independence of these two types of identity yields a typology that is very similar to that proposed by Roberts and Clifton (1990), although it should be recognized that identity refers to the level of the individual, whereas the various types of multiculturalism outlined by Roberts and Clifton refer to the group or collective level. Having both a behavioural and symbolic identity is similar to what these authors have called institutionalized multiculturalism. Having a behavioural, but not a symbolic ethnic identity, resembles ritualistic multiculturalism, and having a strong symbolic, but weak behavioural ethnic identity, is akin to symbolic multiculturalism. Having neither identity means assimilation.

In addition to the distinction between behavioural and symbolic ethnic identity, it is also useful to emphasize that identity varies among individuals according to valence (from positive to neutral to negative) and in terms of salience (importance of ethnic as opposed to other aspects of a person's self-definition).

Behavioural Ethnic Identity

Several studies have shown that behavioural ethnic identity is strong and vigorous in some segments of Canadian society. A study by O'Bryan, Reitz & Kuplowska (1976) of ten ethnic groups in five Canadian metropolitan areas, found that 50 per cent of the sample was fluent in a non-official heritage language and that 55 per cent of the sample made daily use of such a language. Anderson and Driedger (1980) conducted a large number of interviews during 1969 to 1971 in 18 ethno-religious block settlements in Saskatchewan. Ethnic identity, in terms of several behavioural indices, was very high in all groups, but particularly so among Hutterites, Ukrainians, Poles, and Mennonites. There were also variations among different groups in the strength of ethnic identity.

In a large survey conducted during 1978–9 in Toronto, Breton et al. (1990) found evidence of strong ethnic expression, although the usual generation effect was found, that is, ethnic identity declined over generations. Strength of ethnic identity varied substantially among groups, with Jews maintaining strong identity and Germans only weak. In addition to demonstrating behavioural ethnic identity measured in traditional ways, Breton et al. also found substantial ethnic residential grouping and occupational ethnic concentration.

In the studies just reviewed, ethnicity was part of a deliberate sampling strategy and it may, therefore, not be too surprising that strong ethnic identity was found among respondents. Driedger (1975) conducted a study with a more general sample of 1560 undergraduates at the University of Manitoba. Behavioural ethnic identity in this sample was substantially lower than in the study of block settlements, and there were also substantial variations. Strongest identity was found among students of French and Jewish, and the weakest identity among those of British and Scandinavian origin.

It can be concluded from these studies, that behavioural ethnic identity, particularly among some groups of 'other ethnic' origin, is quite strong in anglophone Canada. It also has to be remembered, however, that there are substantial variations by group in the strength and mode of expression of ethnic identity.

Symbolic Ethnic Identity

Several different kinds of questions have been employed in different studies to assess symbolic ethnic identity. Respondents can be provided with response alternatives, as in the Berry et al. (1977) survey: 'Do you think of yourself as a Canadian, ethnic origin-hyphen-Canadian (e.g., Italian-Canadian), or ethnic origin (e.g. Italian), etc.'? In the total sample, 59 per cent identified as 'Canadian.' But there were substantial variations in ethnic identity according to ethnic origin. Among respondents of Angloceltic origin, 80 per cent identified as 'Canadian,' the most frequent response among those of French origin was 'French Canadian,' (44 per cent) followed by 'Canadien' (26 per cent), followed by Québécois (22 per cent). Among Canadians of 'other ethnic' origin, 59 per cent identified as 'Canadian,' 28 per cent as hyphenated Canadians, and 5 per cent in terms of their ethnic origin without a hyphen.[2]

In the study by O'Bryan et al. (1976) 35 per cent identified as 'Canadian,' 45 per cent had a dual identity, consisting either of 'hyphenated Canadian' or a 'Canadian of other ethnic origin,' and 17 per cent identified with an ethnic only label (e.g., Chinese). In a study of a large sample of Canadians, Boyd et al. (1981) discovered that 86 per cent identified as 'Canadian.' Frideres and Goldenberg (1977) studied ethnic identity in a sample of University of Calgary students. In their investigation, 67 per cent identified as 'Canadian,' 12 per cent responded with a hyphenated identity, and 11 per cent gave an ethnic-only response.

When respondents are given identity alternatives from which to select, it may well be possible that investigators suggest an appropriate response to respondents. In order to overcome this problem, Mackie (1978) asked a sample of adults from Calgary the following question: 'Canada is made up of many people who have come from all over the world, like the Irish, Italian, Norwegian, Chinese, etc. Do you identify with any of these people? If so, which one?' Thirty-two per cent in this sample gave an ethnic-only response (e.g., Italian), less than 1 per cent gave a hyphenated response, but a substantial majority of 67 per cent gave a response of 'none.' Mackie (1978) assessed ethnic identity in a second way. She asked respondents to provide 20 statements to the question 'Who am I?.' If ethnicity is salient to an individual's sense of self it should appear in one of the statements. However, results showed that only 3 per cent mentioned ethnic origin. Other factors, for example, religion with 18 per cent, and being Canadian with 10 per cent, were much more frequently mentioned.

In commenting on these results, Driedger, Thacker, and Currie (1982) wondered whether respondents might have missed the 'etc.' in Mackie's first question, and not finding their ethnic group among any of those mentioned responded with none. Driedger et al. (1982) therefore proposed that an open-ended question would be a more suitable way to assess people's identity. They conducted studies in Winnipeg and Edmonton where they asked respondents 'How would you define your ethnicity?' The three responses were then coded into one of three categories: 'Canadian,' 'hyphenated Canadian,' and 'ethnic.' In Winnipeg, 30 per cent identified as 'Canadian,' 10 per cent gave a hyphenated response, and 50 per cent gave an 'ethnic' response. In Edmonton 49 per cent identified as 'Canadian,' 8 per cent gave a hyphenated response, and 37 per cent responded with an ethnic-group only. Driedger reasoned that in western Canada ethnicity plays a greater role than in the east and he felt that the higher ethnic or hyphenated response as compared with the national sample by Berry et al. (1977) was primarily a result of difference in the region of respondents.

Mackie and Brinkerhoff (1984) completed a comprehensive study comparing different methods of soliciting ethnic-identity responses and also measuring ethnic salience and concluded that in their sample of Calgary residents of primarily European origin, ethnic identity had low salience. Mackie and Brinkerhoff (1988) conducted a comparative study of Canadian and American students. They expected ethnic identity to be more salient in the Canadian sample because of the 'mosaic' orientation, as opposed to the 'melting-pot' ideology of the United States. Results did not follow these expectations. The salience of ethnic identity was equally low in both countries.

A study assessing both behavioural and symbolic identity was reported by Weinfeld (1981). Using data from a 1970 survey of Toronto household heads, he examined the ethnic identification of Slavic, Jewish, and Italian respondents who were either immigrants or Canadian-born. Ethnic self-identification (as opposed to identifying as 'Canadian') was high among this sample (e.g., 80 per cent of Slavic immigrants had an ethnic identity vs only 20 per cent with a Canadian identity). Weinfeld also noted, however, that behavioural ethnic identity lagged behind symbolic (which he called 'affective') and followed more of an 'assimilationist' vs a 'survivalist' pattern.

A number of conclusions are possible on the basis of these studies. Although symbolic ethnic identity is probably a key to understanding the individual's attachment to their ethnic heritage, its measurement is far from clear. How investigators choose to assess symbolic ethnic identity probably has a large impact on results obtained. It is also clear that as ethnic identity may vary by region, and certain population characteristics, the precise nature of the sample used influences the results obtained. Age of respondent and generational status is also likely to be important. It appears that those studies that used younger Canadians (who were also university students) received a higher percentage of respondents who chose 'Canadian.' However, despite these cautions, a majority of anglophone Canadians identify as 'Canadian,' as opposed to having some sort of ethnic identity. This conclusion is warranted on the basis of those studies that employed general, or national, as opposed to primarily 'other ethnic' samples. For the general anglophone population, therefore, ethnic identity appears to have low salience.

This latter conclusion seems to contradict studies of behavioural ethnic identity, on the basis of which we concluded that there are strong and vibrant ethnic communities where substantial proportions of members continue to show outward expression of ethnic identity. This contradiction is more a matter of appearance than substance. Both conclusions are possible. Clearly for some Canadians ethnic heritage is very important, both behaviourally and symbolically. For others it is not important and they feel that being Canadian does not require an additional heritage identity. To understand the possible response of Canadians to multiculturalism as a model for the country and as public policy, it would be useful to know precisely for what proportion of Canadians ethnic heritage is salient and important, and for how many an identity of 'Canadian' is meaningful and sufficient without an additional heritage identity. Unfortunately, because of the small number of studies and their methodological differences a precise answer is not possible. A reasonably educated guess, however, can be attempted. Based particularly on the studies that used national or general samples, it seems reasonable to suggest that in anglophone Canada (and excluding 'French Canadian' from consideration) an ethnic identity is of any substantial significance for only a third or less of the Canadian population. For at least two-thirds of Canadians a national 'Canadian' identity predominates and ethnic heritage may at best have some occasional symbolic or behavioural significance.

These conclusions challenge those who suggest that multiculturalism may well be an artifact or a fiction (Lupul 1984; Porter 1979). The vitality of certain ethnic communities and the strong behavioural expression of many individuals has to be accepted as positive evidence of ethnic diversity that goes beyond statistical origin categories. On the other hand, the assertions of those who say that 'multiculturalism is for all Canadians,' or that 'everyone in Canada is ethnic' are also suspect. The relatively low salience of ethnic identity and the preference for a 'Canadian' identity in a majority of Canadians is not likely to lead to a resounding endorsement of these assertions. Individuals for whom ethnic identity has relatively low salience may display a relative lack of enthusiasm for, and involvement in, multiculturalism.

DETERMINANTS AND CORRELATES OF ATTITUDES

Throughout this review, we have reported findings as they pertain generally to the Canadian population. In this section we address the presence of group and individual differences in attitudes.

Socioeconomic Status

A common finding for many attitudes is that those higher in status (particularly those with higher educational attainment) have more open, tolerant, or liberal views. In the 1974 national survey (Berry et al. 1977), this general relationship was very much in evidence. For example, endorsement of Multicultural Ideology increased in a linear fashion over the educational range, from primary through secondary to university education. The same pattern was also evident for attitudes towards one non-Native visible minority group (Chinese Canadians). However, there was no significant variation for Canadian Indians. Using income and occupational status the same pattern was found.

The meaning of these variations is open to some dispute. One can interpret them at face value (better-educated people are more tolerant); or one can seek alternative explanations such as better-educated people can see through the intent of the question, or they know it is not acceptable to express intolerance in contemporary society.

Some detailed analyses have provided insight into these relationships. For example, Buchanan (1987) surveying anglophone New Brunswickers' attitudes towards French Canadians and bilingualism found that it is not just the amount of education, but the type: those who had been educated in the technical stream had significantly more negative attitudes than those with more academic schooling. Buchanan also found some evidence for non-linearity of these attitudes with education.

Ethnicity

Beyond the ethnocentric tendency to view one's own group relatively positively, there is some evidence that ethnicity may be more generally related to social attitudes. In the Berry et al. (1977) survey, many attitudes (e.g., Multicultural Ideology, Perceived Consequences of Multiculturalism, and of Immigration) were viewed significantly less positively by French-Canadian than by Angloceltic respondents; those of 'other ethnic' origins frequently revealed similar attitudes to those of Anglocelts. Similar differences were found by Lambert and Curtis (1982, 1984). Several explanations have been offered for the differences between the attitudes of Canadians of Angloceltic and French origins regarding immigration and multiculturalism. One of these maintains that French Canadians have long been threatened as a linguistic minority. The somewhat less favourable multicultural and immigration attitudes of French as compared with Angloceltic Canadians can be understood as a response to this perceived threat (Berry et al. 1977; Bourhis 1987, this volume).

The less favourable attitudes held by French as compared with English Canadians does not extend to racial attitudes, however. Lambert and Curtis (1984) reported greater tolerance among Québécois than

Angloceltic respondents with regard to attitudes involving racial issues (specifically on the issue of interracial marriage). It is possible that the perceived threat mentioned above is engendered primarily by cultural, but not racial, differences.

Community Size

Community size was also found to be related to immigration attitudes in the survey reported by Berry et al. (1977) as well as the extensive analysis of opinion surveys by the Economic Council of Canada (1991b). The general finding is that the larger the community size, the more positive are immigration and multiculturalism attitudes. Respondents from larger cities tend to have more favourable immigration attitudes than respondents from rural areas.

Social Ecology

One of the more complex issues in understanding the distribution of attitudes is their relationship to familiarity or contact with other groups (Amir 1969). On the one hand it is believed that 'familiarity breeds contempt'; on the other, knowledge is supposed to yield understanding and possibly acceptance. In the Berry et al. (1977) survey, ratings were obtained of how familiar a particular ethnic group was to the respondent (rating 'well known to me') and their evaluation of the group (i.e., ethnic attitude). In a further analysis of the data, Kalin and Berry (1982) examined the question of contact within census tracts (essentially neighbourhoods). An analysis of rated familiarity with the actual presence of a given ethnic group showed that ethnicity is being signalled accurately, as evidenced by the significant correlations between percentage ethnic-group presence and ratings (by non-members) of the ethnic group on how well known they were. The same kind of question is possible with evaluative ratings: are non-members more or less positive in their attitudes as a function of the percentage presence of a particular ethnic group in their neighbourhood? Early studies in the United States (of Whites' attitudes towards Blacks) suggests that there is an 'ideal ratio' to achieve positive attitudes, but beyond this proportion there is a 'tipping point' where attitudes become more negative.

The results of Kalin and Berry (1982) indicate a positive relationship between the presence of a group and attitudes towards that group for the groups in their study (German, Italian, Ukrainian, and French Canadians evaluated by non-members; French Canadians evaluated by Anglocelts outside Quebec; French Canadians evaluated by others outside Quebec; and English Canadians evaluated by French Canadians inside Quebec). The one exception is the evaluation of Canadian Indians by others; here there is a negative relationship. Kalin and Berry (1982) concluded that contact probably enhances positive attitudes, at least in residential neighbourhoods where contact is generally voluntary and at roughly equal status. However, in no case was percentage composition higher than 20 per cent, and so the possibility of a 'tipping point' above that figure remains untested. Moreover, all the groups (except one) were of European origin; and the one non-European group (Canadian Indians) were viewed more negatively as their proportion increased. It is not known whether this different relationship is due to race or some other factor. Hence, it is not possible to generalize this single exception to other racially distinctive groups in Canada.

Security

The 'multicultural assumption' (Berry et al. 1977:224) is the idea that when people feel secure in their own cultural identity, they will be in a position to accept the identities of those who differ from them. This point of view is expressed in the 1971 Multiculturalism Policy statement: 'National unity, if it is to mean anything in the deeply personal sense, must be founded in confidence in one's own individual identity; out of this can grow respect for that of others and a willingness to share ideas, attitudes and assumptions.' The relationship between confidence in one's identity and tolerance was assessed (Berry et al. 1977) by creating two 'security' scales: cultural security and economic security. It was hypothesized that the more one feels that multiculturalism and immigration threaten the identity of one's ethnic group, and one's economic prospects, the more intolerant one would be. Results have strongly supported this prediction, both in the survey results themselves, and in subsequent studies. For example, Taylor et al. (1979) found in community samples in Montreal, Kingston, and Edmonton that those who were insecure held less positive attitudes towards multiculturalism and towards one selected ethnic group (Italian Canadians). Cameron and Berry (1990) found feelings of cultural and economic security to be related to more positive attitudes towards immigrants and refugees, and Berry and Bourcier (1989) found that both aspects of security also predicted positive attitudes towards official bilingualism and towards French Canadians in eastern Ontario.

One aspect of economic security relates to unemployment. Since some of the concerns about immigration pertain to possible unemployment being a consequence, investigations have examined the relationships between actual unemployment level and immigration attitudes. The Economic Council of Canada (1991b) found that when unemployment rates were high, respondents were less inclined to support high volumes of immigration. This result was observed in both anglophone and francophone samples. A different conclusion was reached by Schissel et al. (1989), who performed secondary analyses on the data employed originally by Berry et al. (1977). Schissel et al. (1989) obtained information on unemployment rates in a number of cities where the 1974 national survey data had been collected. They came to the rather strong conclusions that immigration attitudes do not have economic roots, because they found only very weak relationships between unemployment levels and immigration attitudes. Their conclusion must be treated with some caution, however, because they had only a very small number of respondents in some of the cities. Since the analysis by the Economic Council of Canada (1991b) is based on a greater number of respondents, in a greater variety of settings, the conclusion reached by the Council, that higher unemployment rates lead to reluctance to accept immigrants, must probably be given more credence.

PROFILE OF ETHNIC AND MULTICULTURAL ATTITUDES

Given the large amount of information provided on ethnic and multicultural attitudes, it is useful to provide a summary. One way to accomplish this summary is to contrast what these attitudes do *not* indicate with what they *do*. Canadians are *not* strongly *assimilationist with regard to others*. They do not think encouraging immigrants to give up their heritage customs should be government policy. On the contrary, they support the principle of multiculturalism, at least in a permissive form. That is, they believe that ethnocultural groups should have the freedom to retain their heritage ways and they see cultural diversity as an asset.

Canadians are *not* strongly *racist* or *xenophobic*. Only small minorities advocate subordination, social distance, or hatred of visible minorities. Such minorities may, of course, voice their concerns in a way that is disproportionate to their presence in Canada. There is the disturbing finding, however, that visible minorities, particularly South Asians, appear near the bottom of attitudinal preference hierarchies.

At the other extreme, Canadians are *not* supportive of *unrestricted multiculturalism*, but insist on some definite limits. They are not in favour of a completely open immigration policy. They prefer a policy that is selective and based primarily on economic considerations. They are concerned about ghettoization, separatism, and unwillingness by ethnic groups to make a commitment to this country. They expect immigrants and established ethnic groups to accommodate to Canada. It is difficult, at this time, to specify precisely the limits of tolerance for diversity, on the one hand, and the expectation for accommodation, on the other. Some guesses are possible, however. Quite acceptable are the retention of symbolic ethnic identity, the retention of heritage customs in the private domain, and the display of cultural symbols on certain appropriate public occasions (folk festivals, special radio and television stations, commercial establishments, etc.). Probably unacceptable are heritage customs that conflict with Canadian laws and go against strongly held Canadian values. This is an area where further research can inform us of the limits of multiculturalism.

The conclusion that Canadians expect ethnic groups to accommodate to Canadian society seems at variance with the earlier statement that they are not strongly assimilationist with regard to others. The apparent contradiction is removed through the concept of *integration* (Berry 1984) which consists of retention of heritage culture, coupled with accommodation to the host society.

We reached the conclusion earlier that Canadians are not assimilationist with regard to others. A large majority of them, however, seem to be *assimilationist with regard to themselves*. This conclusion is based on the preference for a 'Canadian' as opposed to an 'ethnic' identity, and the low salience of ethnicity, as compared with other aspects of the self. This predominant tendency towards personal assimilation suggests that multiculturalism is not a very important issue for most Canadians, although it may become more important if many of those who consider themselves 'Canadians' and not 'ethnic' feel left out of the multiculturalism policy.

EVALUATION OF MULTICULTURALISM ATTITUDE RESEARCH

The present review of attitudes related to multiculturalism has identified a number of gaps and inadequacies. There are only a few comprehensive studies in the form of national surveys and most of these are available only through limited circulation. It would be useful to have a national data bank for the purpose of collecting and making available to researchers data sets from large-scale surveys. Although some data banks exist (e.g., at the Institute for Social Research at York University), they usually contain only data sets that have been made public. Surveys completed by private companies would have to be purchased by the data bank.

Of the studies reviewed in this paper, those conducted with respondents from specific ethnic groups and with a relatively strong ethnic attachment predominate. Such studies are, of course, useful because they inform us about ethnic identity and cultural maintenance among Canadians of 'other ethnic' origin. It has to be borne in mind, however, that these investigations deal with special segments of the population and therefore cannot be used to make inferences about the whole population. This becomes an issue when trying to assess the *active* and *interested*, as opposed to the *passive* and *permissive* support for multiculturalism. Active support is much more likely among those committed to an ethnic identity. The support in a general population, where ethnic commitment is lower, is more likely to be passive and permissive.

Besides the scarcity of studies, there is also a dearth of well-developed and established measures of ethnic, racial, and multicultural attitudes. There are few questions that are consistently asked so that tracking of attitudes over time becomes possible. A problem that applies to opinion surveys in general also applies to surveys in the area under review. Attitudes are often measured through single or small sets of questions. The development of valid scales, composed of a number of related items, to measure key attitudes would be a great asset.

Most surveys on ethnic attitudes also suffer from a lack of a theoretical orientation. They tend to be descriptive and do not concern themselves with possible explanations for variations in attitudes. Although economic and cultural insecurities have often been mentioned as likely precursors of intolerance, there has been little systematic effort to measure these variables and to establish their theoretical significance.

NOTES

1 The present review focuses on studies of ethnic identity of adult Canadians through surveys. There is considerable literature on the development of ethnic identity in children, including ethnic-identity conflict. For a review of these studies in the Canadian as well as the international context, see Aboud (1988).
2 It should be noted in this context that there must have been some misunderstanding of the results of Berry et al. (1977), Driedger et al. (1982), and Driedger (1989) about the precise meaning of the response categories. What Berry et al. (1977) labelled 'other ethnic' was an ethnic-hyphen-Cana-

dian identity (e.g.. Polish-Canadian). Driedger interpreted that as an ethnic-only (e.g., Polish) identity. Consequently the figures reported by Driedger et al. (1982) and Driedger (1989) are at variance with what was actually found by Berry et al. (1977).

REFERENCES

Aboud, F.E. (1988). *Children and prejudice*. Oxford: Blackwell
Amir, Y. (1969). Contact hypothesis in ethnic relations. *Psychological Bulletin,*
  71:319–42
Anderson, A.B., and Driedger, L. (1980). The survival of ethnolinguistic minorities: Canadian and comparative research. In Howard Giles et al. (eds), *Language and ethnic relations* (pp 67–85). New York: Pergamon Press
Angus Reid Associates (1989). *Attitudes and perceptions of selected dimensions of
  refugee and immigration policy in Canada*. Final Report to Employment and Im-
  migration Canada
Angus Reid Group (1990). *Canadians views and attitudes regarding issues associated
  with Aboriginal peoples*. Vancouver
Berry, J.W. (1984). Multicultural policy in Canada: A social psychological
  analysis. *Canadian Journal of Behaviourial Science, 16*:353–70.
Berry, J.W., and Bourcier, D. (1989). Attitudes towards official bilingualism in
  Eastern Ontario. Paper presented to Canadian Psychological Association,
  Halifax
Berry, J.W., and Kalin, R. (1979). Reciprocity of interethnic attitudes in a
  multicultural society. *International Journal of Intercultural Relations, 3*:99–
  112.
– (1989). *Design specifications for major attitude and opinion leader survey research
  on multiculturalism*. Final Report to Ministry of Multiculturalism and Citizenship, Ottawa.
Berry, J.W., Kalin, R., and Taylor, D.M. (1977). *Multiculturalism and ethnic
  attitudes in Canada*. Ottawa: Ministry of Supply and Services
Berry, J.W., Kim, U., Minde, T. and Mok, D. (1987). Comparative studies of
  acculturative stress. *International Migration Review, 21*:491–511
Berry, J.W., Kim, U., Power, S., Young, M., and Bujaki, M. (1989). Acculturation
  attitudes in plural societies. *Applied Psychology, 38*:185–206
Bibby, R. (1987). Bilingualism and multiculturalism: A national reading. In L.
  Driedger (ed.), *Ethnic Canada: Identities and inequalities* (pp 158–69). Toronto:
  Copp Clark Pitman
Bourhis, R.Y. (1987). Social psychology and heritage language research: A
  retrospective view and future trends for Canada. In J. Cummins (ed.), *Heri-*

tage language research in Canada: Research perspectives. Ottawa: Secretary of State, Multiculturalism

Boyd, M., Goyder, J., Jones, F.E., McRoberts, H.A., Pineo, P., and Porter J. (1981). Status attainment in Canada: Findings of the Canadian mobility study. *Canadian Review of Sociology and Anthropology, 18*:657–73

Breton, R., Isajiw, W., Kalbach, W., and Reitz, J. (1990). *Ethnic identity and equality*. Toronto: University of Toronto Press

Buchanan, A.G. (1987). Education and ethnic attitudes: Some observations on anglophones in New Brunswick. *Canadian Ethnic Studies, 19*:110–16

Cameron, J., and Berry, J.W. (1990). Intergroup attitudes: Self-esteem and threats to identity. Paper presented to Canadian Psychological Association, Ottawa

Decima Research Ltd. (1980) *Report # 2161*. Submitted to Ministry of State for Multiculturalism, Ottawa

Dion, K.L. (1985). Social distance norms in Canada: Effects of stimulus characteristics and dogmatism. *International Journal of Psychology, 20*:743–49

Driedger, L. (1975). In search of cultural identity factors: A comparison of ethnic minority students in Manitoba. *Canadian Review of Sociology and Anthropology, 12*:150–62

– (1976). Ethnic self-identity: A comparison of ingroup evaluations. *Sociometry, 39*:131–41

– (1989). *The ethnic factor: Identity in diversity*. Toronto: McGraw-Hill Ryerson

Driedger, L., Thacker, C., and Currie, R. (1982). Ethnic identification: Variations in regional and national preferences. *Canadian Ethnic Studies, 14*(3):57–68

Economic Council of Canada (1991a). *New faces in the crowd: Economic and social impacts of immigration*. Ottawa: Economic Council of Canada

– (1991b). *Economic and social impacts of immigration*. Ottawa: Economic Council of Canada

Environics Research Group (1985). The dynamics of 'New Multiculturalism.' Toronto: Unpublished report

– (1989). *Focus Canada Report*, 1989–92 edition

Filson, G. (1983). Class and ethnic differences in Canadians' attitudes to native people's rights and immigration. *Canadian Review of Sociology and Anthropology. 20*(4):454–82

Fletcher, J. (1989). *Results of the survey on racial prejudice*. Dept of Political Science, University of Toronto

Frideres, J.S., and Goldenberg, S. (1977). Hyphenated Canadians: Comparative analysis of ethnic regional and national identification of Western Canadian university students. *Journal of Ethnic Studies, 5*:91–100

Gans, H.J. (1979). Symbolic ethnicity: The future of ethnic groups and culture in America. *Ethnic and Racial Studies, 2*:1–20

Gardner, R.C., Taylor, D.M., and Feenstra, H.J. (1970). Ethnic stereotypes: Attitudes or beliefs? *Canadian Journal of Psychology,* 24:321–34

Gardner, R.C., Wonnacott, E.J., and Taylor, D.M. (1968). Ethnic stereotypes: A factor analytic investigation. *Canadian Journal of Psychology,* 22:35–44

Globe & Mail and CBC News (1991). National poll results. *Globe & Mail,* 5 Nov.

Hamilton, D.L. (1981). Illusory correlation as a basis for stereotyping. In D.L. Hamilton (ed.), *Cognitive processes in stereotyping and intergroup behaviour.* Hillsdale, NJ: Erlbaum

Henry, F. (1978). *The dynamics of racism in Toronto.* Toronto: York University

– (1990). *Who gets the work in 1989?* Report for Economic Council of Canada, Ottawa

Henry, F., and Ginzberg, E. (1985). *Who gets the work? A test of racial discrimination in employment.* Report to Urban Alliance on Race Relations, Toronto

Indian and Northern Affairs (1980). *An overview of some recent research on attitudes in Canada towards Indian people.* Ottawa: Dept of Indian and Northern Affairs

– (1984). *Images of Indians held by non-Indians: A review of current Canadian research.* Ottawa: Dept of Indian and Northern Affairs

Jones, F.E., and Lambert, W.E. (1965). Occupational rank and attitudes toward immigrants. *Public Opinion Quarterly,* 29:137–44

Kalin, R., and Berry, J.W. (1982). The social ecology of ethnic attitudes in Canada. *Canadian Journal of Behavioural Science,* 14:97–109

Kalin, R., and Rayko, D.S. (1978). Discrimination in evaluative judgements against foreign accented job candidates. *Psychological Reports,* 43:1203–9

Kalin, R., Rayko, D.S. and Love, N. (1980). The perception and evaluation of job candidates with four different ethnic accents. In H. Giles, W.P. Robinson and P. Smith (eds), *Language: Social psyhcological perspectives.* Oxford: Pergamon

Lambert, R.D., and Curtis, J.E. (1982). The French and English Canadian language communities and multicultural attitudes. *Canadian Ethnic Studies,* 14:43–58

– (1984). Québécois' and English Canadians' opposition to racial and religious intermarriage, 1968–1983. *Canadian Ethnic Studies,* 16:30–46

Lippman, W. (1922). *Public opinion.* New York: Harcourt, Brace & World

Lupul, M. (1984). On being analytically or scientifically ethnic. *Canadian Ethnic Studies,* 16(2):116–17

Mackie, M. (1973). Arriving at 'truth' by definition: The case of stereotype inaccuracy. *Social Problems,* 20(4):431–47

– (1974). Ethnic stereotypes and prejudice: Alberta Indians, Hutterites, and Ukrainians. *Canadian Ethnic Studies,* 6(1–2):39–52

– (1978). Ethnicity and nationality: How much do they matter to Western Canadians? *Canadian Ethnic Studies*, 10:118–29

Mackie, M., and Brinkerhoff, M.B. (1984). Measuring ethnic salience. *Canadian Ethnic Studies*, 16(1):114–31

– (1988). Ethnic identification: Both sides of the border. *Canadian Ethnic Studies*, 20(2):101–13

Maclean's (1990). 2 Jan.

O'Bryan, K.G., Reitz, J.G., and Kuplowska, O.M. (1976). *Non-official languages: A study in Canadian multiculturalism*. Ottawa: Supply and Services Canada

Palmer, H. (1975). *Immigration and the rise of multiculturalism*. Toronto: Copp Clark

Pineo, P. (1977). The social standing of ethnic and racial groupings. *Canadian Review of Sociology and Anthropology*, 14:147–57

Ponting, J.R. (1984). Conflict and change in Indian/non-Indian relations in Canada. Comparison of 1976 and 1979 national attitude surveys. *Canadian Journal of Sociology*, 9:137–58

Porter, J. (1979). *The measure of Canadian society*. Toronto: Gage

Roberts, L.W., and Clifton, R.A. (1990). Multiculturalism in Canada: A social perspective. In Peter S. Li (ed.), *Race and ethnic relations in Canada* (pp 120–47). Toronto: Oxford University Press

Schissel, B., Wanner, R., and Frideres, J.S. (1989). Social and economic context and attitudes toward immigrants in Canadian cities. *International Migration Review*. 23:289–307

Taylor, D.M. (1981). Stereotypes and intergroup relations. In R.C. Gardner and R. Kalin (eds), *A Canadian social psychology of ethnic relations* (pp 151–71). Toronto: Methuen

Taylor, D.M., and Lalonde, R.N. (1987). Ethnic stereotypes: A psychological analysis. In L. Driedger (ed.), *Ethnic Canada: Identities and inequalities* (pp 347–73). Toronto: Copp, Clark, Pitman

Tienhaara, N. (1974). *Population and immigrants: What do Canadians want?* Report R-36, Dept of Manpower and Immigration. Government of Canada: Information Canada

Weinfeld, M. (1981). Myth and reality in the Canadian mosaic: 'Affective ethnicity.' *Canadian Ethnic Studies*, 13(3):80–100

RICHARD Y. BOURHIS

Ethnic and Language Attitudes in Quebec

In Quebec, ethnic attitudes are not only intricately bound up with attitudes about language but are also related to language laws which have profoundly changed the balance of power existing between francophone, anglophone, and allophone communities. The Quebec situation is one in which it is difficult to study attitudes about ethnicity and language without also considering the inter-group and public-policy context in which such attitudes have been shaped and maintained.

Even with a French mother-tongue population of 5.4 million people, the francophone majority in Quebec accounts for no more than 2 per cent of the predominantly English-speaking population of North America. The 1986 Canadian census showed that francophone minorities living outside Quebec were concentrated in Ontario with 475,600 Franco-Ontarians (5 per cent of the provincial population) and New Brunswick with 234,000 Acadians (34 per cent of the provincial population). Another 240,000 francophones are dispersed in the other provinces of Canada. In a recent analysis of the 1991 census, de Vries (1994) noted that the high anglicization rate of francophone minorities in the Prairie provinces, British Columbia, and the Maritime provinces other than New Brunswick is such that the continued existence of these linguistic communities is in doubt. The provision of French-language services to francophone minorities has also met some resistance on the part of some Anglo-Canadians intolerant of French minorities outside Quebec (Berry & Bourcier 1989; Bourhis 1994; Canada 1990; Sloan 1990).

In view of the above trends, Quebec francophones see their province as the last territorial enclave in which a distinctively French society can survive within the North American setting. Successive Quebec governments have been suspicious of the federal government's multiculturalism policy, since this vision of a multicultural society undermines the place of francophones as one of Canada's two founding nations. Instead, Quebec francophones have strongly supported language-planning measures designed to enshrine the status of French as the official language of Quebec society (Bourhis 1984c; Bourhis & Lepicq 1993; Levine 1990). In contrast, Quebec anglophones have resisted such measures, seeing them as demoting anglophones from the status of an Anglo-Canadian dominant group to the position of a linguistic minority within Quebec (Caldwell 1984; Legault 1992; Taylor 1986).

In Quebec it has become customary to use the term 'allophones' to describe individuals who have neither French nor English as a mother tongue regardless of whether such individuals are first-, second-, or third-generation immigrants to Quebec. The term 'heritage language group' is the equivalent term often used in Anglo-Canada. The term 'immigrant' refers to first-generation newcomers to Quebec not born in Canada. Though Quebec allophone and immigrant groups have traditionally adopted English as the language of upward mobility in the province, recent demolinguistic and voting patterns suggest that immigrants and allophones are gradually adopting French as the language of economic and social integration within Quebec society.

The first part of this paper deals with some of the key demolinguistic and ethnocultural aspects of the Quebec population. These basic features of Quebec's demographic profile are necessary in order to understand current relations between the province's linguistic and ethnocultural communities. Furthermore, it is difficult to understand current multicultural issues in Quebec without also discussing the ethnic and linguistic conflicts that have long characterized relations between the francophone and anglophone communities of the province. Consequently, the second part of this paper deals with key language-policy issues which have both reflected and changed relations between francophones and anglophones in the province. The third part of the article focuses on Quebec's allophone and ethnocultural communities as they have been affected by French/English tensions and by recent immigration policies initiated by the Quebec government.

DEMOLINGUISTIC PROFILE OF QUEBEC'S ETHNOLINGUISTIC
COMMUNITIES

According to the Canadian census, the total population of Quebec was 6,454,490 in 1986. Of this population, 78 per cent is made up of individuals whose ethnic background is French (over 5 million), while 6 per cent is made up of individuals whose ethnic origin is British (380,265). The major ethnic groups in Quebec other than those of French and British background are the following: Italian (2.5 per cent), Jewish (1.3 per cent), Greek (0.7 per cent), West Indian (0.6 per cent), Portuguese (0.5 per cent), German (0.4 per cent), and Chinese (0.4 per cent). Other increasingly important visible minority groups in Quebec are the Haitians (0.2 per cent) and Vietnamese (0.2 per cent). Taken together, ethnic group members other than French, British, and Aboriginals made up 10.6 per cent of the Quebec population in 1986. Though Quebec's 48,548 Aboriginals make up 0.8 per cent of the Quebec population, this group cannot be discussed further here due to space limitations. For recent analyses of Aboriginal groups in Quebec see Maurais (1992) and Taylor and Wright (1989).

The more usual depiction of the Quebec population is that based on the mother tongue of its inhabitants. Results from the 1986 Canadian census showed that French mother-tongue speakers made up close to 82 per cent of the Quebec population while anglophones constituted 11 per cent and allophones made up 6 per cent of the population. The major allophone groups in Quebec are made up of individuals who declared the following languages as their mother tongue: Italian (1.8 per cent), Greek (0.6 per cent), Spanish (0.4 per cent), Portuguese (0.4 per cent), Cantonese (0.3 per cent), and Arabic (0.2 per cent). It is noteworthy that Quebec allophones make up only 14 per cent of the total number of Canadians who declared in the 1986 census that their mother tongue was a language other than English or French.

The Montreal metropolitan region is the major urban centre of Quebec with a population of 2.9 million, of which 68 per cent are French mother-tongue speakers (1.9 million; 1986 census). Montreal is also a multilingual city with English mother-tongue speakers (15 per cent of the population) and allophones (12 per cent of the population (Termotte & Gauvreau 1988). The territorial concentration of Montreal's language groups is such that in western sectors of Montreal, anglophones constitute the majority while francophones form the majority in eastern sectors of the city (Blanc 1986). Ethnolinguistic and ethnocultural groups such as Italians, Greeks, Jews, Chinese, West Indians, and Haitians also have a tendency to be concentrated in specific sectors of Montreal (Balakrishnan & Kralt 1987). However, the other urban centres of the province (Québec, Trois-Rivières, Sherbrooke) are linguistically quite homogeneous, with the French mother-tongue concentration ranging from 89.6 per cent to

97.3 per cent of the population. The less urbanized regions of the province are also predominently francophone, with 92.5 per cent of the population declaring French as their mother tongue.

When considering the 1986 census data on the dispersion of first-generation immigrants who settled in Quebec, one notes that 87 per cent of Quebec immigrants settled in the Montreal metropolitan region, thus constituting 16 per cent of the total Montreal population. The concentration of immigrant groups in urban centres has become the rule rather than the exception in most cities of North America. However, the proportion of Quebec immigrants settling in Montreal is greater than that recorded for the proportion of Ontario immigrants settling in Toronto (59 per cent; Paillé 1991). Allophone and ethnocultural communities concentrate in Montreal mainly because the city offers better economic opportunities and allows such groups to maintain ethnolinguistic networks which provide the social and cultural supports needed to adjust more readily within the majority setting (Blanc 1986). The concentration of ethnocultural communities within Montreal has meant that it is the Montreal rather than the Quebec population as a whole that has had to adjust to the realities of multilingualism and ethnic pluralism. The concentration of both anglophone and allophone groups in the Montreal metropolitan area is a factor which has contributed to ethnic and linguistic tensions in the region (Latouche 1989).

Given the importance of language issues in Quebec society it has become customary to use knowledge of French and English as an important index of the linguistic integration of both the anglophone and allophone communities of the province. The proportion of French/English bilinguals in Quebec has risen steadily from 1971 to 1981 to 1986. As can be seen in Figure 1, the increase in bilingualism was most marked among both the anglophone and allophone mother-tongue communities while bilingualism among francophones also increased during this period. Overall, French/English bilinguals are concentrated in the Montreal region relative to the Quebec population as a whole.

In the Montreal region, the proportion of anglophones who reported knowledge of both French and English rose from 35 per cent in 1971 to 54 per cent in 1986. Though these figures show that a substantial proportion of Quebec anglophones did learn French, these proportions also reflect the effect of the emmigration of a large number of Quebec anglophones during this period, many of whom were economically mobile unilinguals dissatisfied with Quebec language and fiscal policies (Caldwell 1984, 1994).

FIGURE 1
Knowledge of French and English (in per cent) as a function of the mother tongue of
respondents (French, English, other) in Montreal (1971–86). Based on Statistics Canada
data (1971, 1981, 1986) with permission of the Conseil de la langue française (CLF 1991).

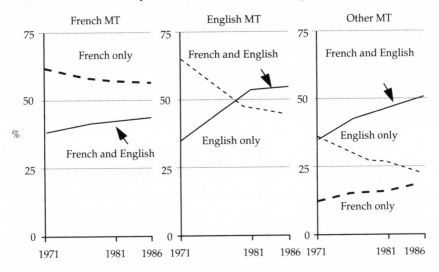

Francophones concerned with the survival of French in Quebec are
especially sensitive to the fact that the proportion of French mother-
tongue unilinguals has decreased in the Montreal region from 62 per
cent in 1970 to 56 per cent in 1986. It is also noted that the proportion of
francophone bilinguals in Montreal has risen from 38 per cent in 1970 to
44 per cent in 1986. Given the key role of Montreal in the Quebec economy, many francophones feel that it is in Montreal that the fate of the
French language in Quebec will be determined (Levine 1990). It is the
necessity of using French to communicate with the francophone unilingual majority which has legitimized language laws designed to increase
the status of French relative to English in Quebec. It is argued that if the
majority of Montreal francophones become bilingual, then the rationale
for using French will give way to the advantage of using English as the
sole language of business and upward mobility within the city.

As can be seen in Figure 1, the proportion of Montreal allophones
who declared knowledge of both French and English did increase from
35 per cent in 1971 to 50 per cent in 1986. Language shift observed
among Quebec allophones has tended to favour the knowledge of
French more than English recently. While knowledge of 'only English'

dropped from 36 per cent in 1971 to 22 per cent in 1986, a reverse pattern was obtained for knowledge of 'only French,' which increased from 13 per cent to 17 per cent among Quebec allophones. While Quebec language laws promulgated since the 1970s help account for gains observed for the French language, English retains its attraction as the language of business and geographical mobility for many Quebec allophones. However, French/English bilingualism has supplanted English unilingualism as the preferred mode of linguistic integration among Quebec allophones. As will be seen in the next two sections, there is evidence that the longer-term effects of Quebec language laws and immigration policies will further enhance the usefulness of French as the language of economic and social integration for both the anglophone and allophone minorities of Quebec.

Sociolinguistic research has shown that language use at home tends to be the last bastion of minority language use for most linguistic minorities in Canada (Bourhis 1987; de Vries 1994). Mother-tongue language use at home constitutes an important index of language maintenance for both official and heritage language groups in Canada (Breton, Reitz & Valentine 1980). Herberg (1989) has also shown that heritage language use at home contributes to the cultural maintenance of ethnic groups. Results from the 1986 Canadian census have shown that heritage language maintenance is much stronger among Quebec allophones than it is among heritage language groups who have settled outside Quebec (Paillé 1991). For instance, whereas 67.7 per cent of allophones who settled in Quebec report they still use their heritage language as their only language of the home, only 47.6 per cent of such groups outside Quebec still report using their heritage tongue as the only language at the home. This difference in heritage language maintenance is even more pronounced in the case of second-generation allophone groups in Quebec (62.6 per cent) relative to second generation heritage-language groups (34 per cent) in Anglo-Canada. Note that the stronger rate of heritage-language maintenance observed in Quebec is obtained even though the absolute number of heritage-language group speakers found in Quebec is smaller than that found in Ontario and British Columbia (Paillé 1991).

This fundamental difference between Quebec and the rest of Canada as regards heritage language maintenance can be partly explained by the fact that, in Quebec, the drawing power of English as the language of business and upward mobility must compete with French not only as the language of the francophone majority but also as the official language of the province (Baillargeon & Benjamin 1990). For Quebec allophones, these competing language forces increase the attractiveness of maintaining both their heritage language and their ancestral culture in the province. Quebec allophones also see the benefit of becoming proficient in both French and English. The dynamics of these competing linguistic pressures have been confirmed in a study of the differential heritage language maintenance rates of Italians and Portuguese settled in Quebec compared to those settled in Ontario (Da Rosa & Poulin, 1986).

ETHNIC RELATIONS BETWEEN FRANCOPHONES AND ANGLOPHONES IN QUEBEC

An overview of ethnic relations between francophones and anglophones in Quebec contributes to a better understanding of multiculturalism issues for three main reasons. First, demographically, the French and the English are the main source of diversity in Canada. Multiculturalism issues are thus embedded within this basic bicultural aspect of Quebec and Canadian society. Second, English-French relations constitute the major arena for intercultural relations in Canada. The nature of these relations has necessarily affected the dynamics of intergroup relations between the two official-language groups and the various heritage language communities across the country. Given the breadth and depth of research devoted to French/English relations in Quebec, it is clear that this research tradition can serve as a guideline for pursuing the study of heritage groups and multicultural issues in the country. Third, it is in Quebec that French/English rivalries have been most intense and consequently have had the greatest impact on the integration strategies of allophone and ethnocultural communities. Thus, a proper overview of multiculturalism issues in Quebec is impossible without first addressing key features of French/English tensions in the province.

The social changes brought about by the 'Quiet Revolution' made a growing number of Quebec francophones more aware of the threat posed to the French language by its co-existence with English as the language of business and upward mobility in North America (Coleman 1984). But relative to its rural and religious past, the modernization of Quebec society also meant that the French language had perhaps become the last symbol of Québécois francophone distinctiveness in an increasingly materialistic and consumer-oriented society (Bourhis & Lepicq 1993). With the French language emerging as the last bastion of Québécois francophone identity it was perhaps inevitable that successive Quebec governments should find it necessary to intervene in the linguistic domain through language-planning action (Bourhis 1984c; Levine 1990).

Four major factors help account for language-planning efforts in Quebec during the 1960s and 1970s (D'Anglejan 1984; Laporte 1984). First, the demographic decline of francophones in the rest of Canada meant that Quebec was seen as the last enclave in which a French-speaking society could maintain itself as a majority culture on the continent. The legacy of anti-French laws in Anglo-Canada, the isolation of francophone communities across the country, and the need to know English for economic survival in North America contributed to the massive anglicization of French-Canadian minorities outside Quebec (Breton et al. 1980; Bourhis 1984a). Even the Official Languages Act of 1969, declaring English and French the two official languages of Canada, was seen as 'too little, too late' as a way of stemming the tide of French Canadian assimilation to English in the anglophone provinces (Mackey 1983).

The second factor was the demographic changes occurring within Quebec itself. By the mid-1970s demographers had confirmed the decline in the Quebec birthrate from one of the highest to one of the lowest in the western world (Lachapelle & Henripin 1980). This dramatic decline of the birthrate meant that Quebec francophones could no longer rely on the so-called 'revanche des berceaux' to maintain their demographic strength within Quebec (Caldwell & Fournier 1987). Without a sustained francophone Québécois birthrate, reliance on immigration and the assimilation of immigrants to the francophone linguistic community rather than to the anglophone one became important issues for many francophones who were concerned about the numerical decline of their linguistic group within the province (Termotte & Gauvreau 1988).

Third, the freedom of language choice in Quebec schools meant that the majority of immigrants chose English- rather than French-medium schools for their children (Maurais 1989). Over the years a majority of second-generation immigrants assimilated to the English rather than the French linguistic milieu in Quebec (Mallea 1984). Thus, in the view of many francophones, freedom of language choice for immigrants in Quebec schools meant that the projected long-term demographic growth in Quebec favoured the anglophone rather than the francophone linguistic community (D'Anglejan 1984).

The fourth factor which prompted language legislation was the awareness of anglophone domination of business and economic activity in the province. The Report of the Royal Commission on Bilingualism and Biculturalism (Canada 1969) had shown that, even with equal education and qualifications, francophones were discriminated against by anglophones in Quebec industries and business firms. Furthermore, the results of the Gendron Commission (Quebec 1972) showed that English, not French, was the language of upward social mobility in the Quebec work world.

Taken together, these factors did not augur well for the long-term prospects of the French language in Quebec. Between 1969 and 1977 successive Quebec governments promulgated three different language laws designed to address basic features of each language problem enumerated above (Bill 63, Bill 22, and Bill 101). The most recent of these laws, known as the Charter of the French language (Bill 101), was adopted in 1977 as the first legislative act of the pro-sovereignty Parti Québécois government and promulgated French as the official language of Quebec (Maurais 1987). While Bill 101 recognized the right of Aboriginals to use their own language in all domains including the language of schooling (Maurais 1992), Bill 101 was essentially designed to enhance the status of French relative to English in Quebec (Caldwell 1984).

Bill 101 guaranteed the rights of every Quebecer to receive communications in French when dealing with civil administration, semi-public agencies, and business firms, including the right by all customers to be informed and served in French. The law also ensured the right of all workers to work in French and not to be dismissed or demoted for the sole reason that they were monolingual in French. Unlike earlier language legislation, Bill 101 also outlined both incentives and sanctions to catalyze the adoption of French as the language of work in Quebec business firms and industry. Business firms with more than 50 employees were requested to obtain a francization certificate which attested that they had the necessary infrastructure to use French as the language of work within their organization (Daoust 1984; Bouchard 1991).

Bill 101 also guaranteed English schooling to all present and future Quebec anglophone pupils. All immigrant children already in English schools by the time the bill was passed along with all their current and future siblings were also guaranteed access to English schooling. However, the law made it clear that all subsequent international immigrants to Quebec would have to send their children to French primary and secondary schools. The law did not affect freedom of language choice at the primary- and secondary-school levels for parents wishing to enrol their children in fee-paying private schools. Furthermore, freedom of language choice was guaranteed to all post-secondary students who can choose to attend either French or English medium colleges (CEGEPs) and universities in Quebec.

The immediate reaction of francophones to Bill 101 was quite positive, since the law was seen as being effective in securing the future of the French language majority within Quebec society (Bourhis 1984a; Levine 1990; Maurais 1987). Anglophone reactions to Bill 101 were largely negative, since the law was seen as an attack on the traditional status of the English-speaking community in the province (Legault 1992; Taylor 1986). Bill 101 forced many anglophones to see themselves as minority-group members rather than as dominant-group individuals (Jackson 1982; Caldwell 1984). In the immediate aftermath of Bill 101, anglo-phones were most concerned about the erosion of their demographic base resulting from the fact that most new immigrants to Quebec would now have to send their children to French rather than English primary and secondary schools (Mallea 1984). Bill 101 has had its intended impact on the linguistic enrolment of the primary and secondary school system. In the Montreal metropolitan region allophone enrolment in the French primary and secondary school system increased from 37 per cent in 1980 to 75 per cent in 1990 (CLF 1992). The English mother-tongue enrolment in the French school system also increased somewhat during this period, rising from 16 per cent in 1980 to 19 per cent in 1990. This shift in favour of enrolment in the French school system is a direct result of the Bill 101 legislation and has had a negative impact on the demographic base of the English school system.

While most business firms did comply with the Quebec government francization requirements (Daoust 1984; Maurais 1987), a number of large anglophone businesses covertly or overtly moved their base of operation from Quebec to other parts of Canada, especially Ontario and the western provinces (Miller 1984). A recent analysis of the francization certificate records compiled by the Office de la Langue Française has shown that businesses and corporations whose ownership was anglo-phone have been the slowest in obtaining their francization certificates relative to businesses owned by francophones and allophones interests (Bouchard 1991). However, Bill 101 has contributed to improving the status and use of French as the language of work in Quebec business firms and industries (Béland 1991).

Following the election of the pro-sovereignty Parti Québécois in 1976, many anglophone individuals dissatisfied with Quebec's language and fiscal policies emigrated to Ontario and other provinces of Canada. Census results showed a decline of 12 per cent in Quebec's English-speaking population between 1971 and 1981. This exodus of 120,000 English mother-tongue speakers occurred among the more economically mobile elements of the anglophone community, a good number of whom were unilingual English (Caldwell 1984). Of the Quebec anglophones who stayed, many mobilized as group members to defend their status as the English-speaking minority of Quebec (Legault 1992). By 1982 this mobilization culminated in the creation of an anglophone pressure group, known as Alliance Quebec, whose aim was to promote the interests of English Canadians in Quebec (Caldwell 1984). Interestingly, while Bill 101 was essentially aimed at enshrining French as one of the most valued dimensions of Québécois francophone identity, the demotion of English implied in the law may have served to raise the English language as a much more highly prized symbol of Quebec anglophone identity (Bourhis & Lepicq 1993; Caldwell 1994). To this day Alliance Quebec has along with the Equality party lobbied and pressured the Quebec government to maintain and improve its services to the English speaking minority in the province (Legault 1992).

A number of studies conducted following the adoption of Bill 101 showed that the law did have some impact on patterns of French-English language use in the province and was influential in altering the relative prestige of these two languages in the Quebec setting. A 1977 sociolinguistic survey showed that, attitudinally at least, both Montreal francophone and anglophone students reported using French in public settings such as stores and restaurants more frequently a few months after Bill 101 than before its promulgation (Bourhis 1983). These results suggested that measures for promoting French usage in Quebec were already producing their desired effects shortly after the adoption of the law. This was corroborated in a major telephone survey carried out in 1979 by the Conseil de la Langue Française. This Quebec-wide survey showed that 70 per cent of the francophone sample and 87 per cent of the anglophone sample were of the opinion that French was more frequently used in commercial and public service transactions in 1979 than five years earlier, prior to the promulgation of Bill 101 (Bouchard & Beauchamps 1980). These trends were confirmed ten years later in a field experiment by the Conseil de la Langue Française which showed that in 60 per cent to 90 per cent of cases, francophone clients were successful in receiving services in French while shopping in stores situated within downtown Montreal (Monnier 1989). However, the study showed that the possibility for a francophone to be served in French declined to 50 per cent in western sectors of Montreal, where anglophones remain the majority.

Did the Quebec francophone emancipation movement of the last 20 years have an impact on the ethnic attitudes of anglophones and francophones? In their now classic study, Lambert, Hodgson, Gardner, and Fillenbaum (1960) examined the evaluative reactions of anglophone and francophone undergraduate students towards French and English speakers, using the matched guise technique. In this technique, listeners were made to believe they were rating eight different persons while in fact they were rating four male bilingual speakers each reading the same passage of prose twice, once in English and once in French. Results showed that anglophone listeners rated speakers with an evaluative bias in favour of their owngroup since on seven items, including both status (e.g., intelligence, competence) and solidarity traits (e.g., likeable, kind, dependable), they rated the English speakers more favourably than the French speakers. In contrast, francophone listeners not only rated the English speakers more favourably than the French speakers on both status and solidarity traits, but they did so on as many as ten of the fourteen personality items used in the study. These results were interpreted as reflecting a form of *owngroup denigration* on the part of francophones who had internalized the negative views anglophones had of them as low-status group members within Quebec society. The experimental situation confronted the francophone respondents with a comparison of French and English speakers on the very language dimension which most vividly symbolized the status disadvantage of the francophone community relative to the dominant anglophone minority in Quebec. Given that the study focused on the language dimension, it was perhaps not surprising to find francophone listeners acknowledging their status disadvantage relative to the anglophone speakers used in the study. However, this interpretation does not help explain why francophone subjects downgraded their owngroup speakers even on traits related to the solidarity dimension, which had little to do with the status differentials which existed between the two linguistic communities.

In an exact replication of the Lambert et al. (1960) study, Genesee and Holobow (1989) examined whether stereotypes of anglophone and francophone speakers had changed almost three decades later. It was expected that the improved status position achieved by the Quebec francophone majority during the 1970s and 1980s along with language-planning laws in favour of French would have a favourable effect on the stereotypes of Quebec francophones. As in the original study, anglophone undergraduates displayed an evaluative bias in favour of their own group since they rated the English guises more favourably than the

French guises on both status and solidarity traits. Results also showed that francophone undergraduates now upgraded their evaluation of the French guises on solidarity traits, revealing a more favourable Québécois ethnolinguistic identity. However, Genesee and Holobow's (1989) results revealed that *both* anglophone *and* francophone undergraduates continued to downgrade the French guises relative to the English guises on status traits. These recent results mirror more closely the general findings obtained in a large number of language attitude studies elsewhere in the world, which shows that the ingroup language is evaluated more favourably on solidarity dimensions, while the outgroup language is upgraded on status traits *if* the outgroup language is dominant (Bourhis 1982; Ryan & Giles 1982). Though English is not institutionally dominant relative to French in Quebec, it remains that English is the high-status language of upward mobility in North America.

Bill 101 stipulated that all consumers of goods and services in Quebec have a right to be informed and served in French. The effectiveness of this feature of Bill 101 was investigated in studies of client/clerk encounters. Two large-scale matched guise studies were conducted: one in Montreal and the other in Quebec City (Genesee & Bourhis 1982, 1988). Over 1200 francophone and anglophone students were asked to listen to recorded dialogues in which clients using French and English in various combinations were served by clerks also using various language combinations. It was found that listeners' evaluations of the speakers were most influenced by the situational norm. That is, that the customer is always right and the clerk should respond in the language in which he is addressed by the customer whether this be French or English. In both studies the clerk was downgraded for violating the situational norm, not only by anglophone but also by francophone listeners. Interestingly, it was Montreal anglophone bilinguals from French immersion schools who were *least* tolerant towards a francophone clerk who failed to converge to English when serving an anglophone client. Having made a personal effort to learn French, it seemed that anglophone bilinguals were particularly intolerant with francophones who did not make a similar effort to learn English and use it appropriately in client/clerk encounters. These results provide evidence that Montreal anglophones who learn French do not necessarily gain more tolerant attitudes towards language use in bicultural encounters with traditionally lower-status francophone interlocutors. In contrast, results obtained in Quebec City showed that francophone bilinguals having made a personal effort to learn English were no more disapproving of anglophone clerks who failed to converge to French with francophone clients than were French or English unilingual listeners. The studies also showed that, despite recent efforts to increase the status of French in Quebec, English still enjoyed a great deal of prestige as the language of business transactions not only in Montreal but even in Quebec City, where 96 per cent of the population is francophone. Anecdotal observations of French/English language use in Montreal work settings also attest to the prestige of English relative to French (Heller 1988).

Further evidence reflecting the enduring prestige of English relative to French was obtained in a series of Montreal field studies conducted in 1977 and 1979 (Bourhis 1984b). These studies monitored the actual language behaviour of francophone and anglophone respondents (N=380) on the streets and campuses of central Montreal. In a face-to-face variation of the matched guise technique, a perfectly bilingual female confederate asked pedestrians to provide directions to the nearest metro station. The plea for directions was voiced in either fluent French or fluent English by the bilingual confederate. Results showed a 93 per cent rate of convergence to English by francophone pedestrians responding to the plea for directions voiced in English by the White 'anglophone' confederate. Under equivalent conditions, anglophones converged to French with the White 'francophone' confederate in 71 per cent of the cases. In these studies even a few words voiced in the other's language, such as a greeting or a leave-taking utterance, were coded as a converging response.

Two Montreal follow-up field studies were conducted under exactly the same conditions in 1991 (N=540): one with a white bilingual confederate and the other with a Black bilingual confederate (Moise & Bourhis 1994). In both of these studies the Black and White female confederates were perfectly bilingual while the second language competence of the respondents was also controlled. In an exact replication of the 1977–9 results, anglophones converged to French with the White 'francophone' confederate in 71 per cent of the cases. Results obtained with francophone pedestrians showed a slight drop in the rate of convergence to English (84 per cent) in response to the plea for directions voiced in English by the White 'anglophone' confederate. Patterns of convergence obtained with the Black interlocutor closely mirrored those obtained with the White confederate. While 87 per cent of the francophone pedestrians converged to English in their response to the English plea voiced by the Black experimenter, only 67 per cent of the anglophones converged to French when responding to the plea voiced in French by the Black interlocutor. Francophone consistence in converging to English attests to the status of English in Quebec and reflects a basically accommodative orientation among francophones towards anglophones' linguistic needs regardless of skin colour. Anglophone rates of convergence to French have remained stable during the 1977 to 1991 period despite sustained language-planning efforts to increase the status of French relative to English. That 30 per cent of Montreal anglophones still maintain English when responding to a plea voiced in French reflects the enduring position of anglophones as high-status group members whose personal language choices need not be constrained by the linguistic needs of the francophone majority. Indeed, the president of Alliance Quebec, Reed Scowen, recently urged Quebec anglophones to adopt English-language maintenance as a collective ethnic affirmation strategy when dealing with individual Quebec francophones (Scowen 1991).

Taken together, the results of the matched guise and language-use studies show that members of the anglophone community not only enjoy much status as a collectivity but also behave psychologically as members of an elite minority group in Quebec (Sachdev & Bourhis 1990, 1991). This interpretation concurs with recent analyses of the collective strategies adopted by anglophones as an elite group within the Quebec intergroup setting (Legault 1992). Quebec anglophones remain the best-endowed linguistic minority in Canada. To this day Quebec anglophones enjoy their own autonomous state-funded English medium school system, which ranges from kindergarten through primary, secondary, and university education (Mallea 1984). Moreover, in Montreal and across the province, anglophone individuals can receive most federal, provincial, and municipal, commercial, and financial services in English. These English-language services reinforce a work environment in which English remains the language of upward mobility in business, industrial, and financial establishments. A law passed in 1986 (Bill 142) also guarantees all anglophones full rights to English-language services in important domains such as health care and social services. The adoption of the health reform Bill 120 in 1991 also guarantees that Quebec anglophones are fully represented within regional health and hospital boards across the province. Furthermore, given the demographic concentration of Quebec anglophones within the western region of Montreal, it remains quite possible for individual anglophones to live much of their daily life solely through the medium of English. Despite anglophone opposition to the passage of Bill 178 banning the use of English on outside commercial signs, the president of Alliance Quebec recently asserted: 'The time has come to pass a clear message to English-speaking people outside the province: life is good in Quebec, and they can live here in English if they want to' (Scowen 1991:115).

Given the status of English as the language of upward mobility within North America, it may yet take many years for French to be seen as having a prestige position equivalent to that of English even within a majority French setting such as Quebec. Indeed, in a survey of linguistic attitudes conducted in 1983 with senior secondary school and CEGEP students, Sénéchal (1987) found that 52 per cent of francophone students in the study (N=402) felt that the future of the French language in Quebec was threatened, while 44 per cent felt that it was inevitable that English remain as the main language of business and finance in the province. In contrast, 77 per cent of the anglophone students surveyed in the study (N=361) felt that the future of French in Quebec was assured, though 40 per cent concurred that it was inevitable that English remain as the main language of business and finance in the province. Interestingly, the majority (60 per cent) of allophone students surveyed in the study (N=809) also felt that the future of French in Quebec was assured, though this group of respondents also concurred (47 per cent) that English would remain as the principal language of business and finance in Quebec.

The greatest challenge to francophones in Quebec remains their uneasy status relationship with English speakers within the province. Language-planning has had a favourable impact on the use of French as the language of Quebec society including the work world. However, given that English is the language of business in North America, it seems obvious that the economic and social mobility of francophones within and beyond the Quebec border still depends on bilingual competence. Despite impressive gains by francophones in socioeconomic status and increased control over their own economy (Vaillancourt 1992), it remains that important sectors of the province's economy are still controlled by anglophone interests be they Quebec- Canadian-, or American-based. Quebec's further integration within the North American economic market has been enshrined through the Canada–US free-trade agreement signed in January 1989 and should maintain if not accentuate the presence of English on the Quebec economic and cultural market (Bourhis & Lepicq 1993).

Recent demographic projections for the year 2000 suggest that the Quebec French mother-tongue population is likely to drop slightly in absolute terms owing to a combination of factors including a low birthrate and an aging population (Termotte & Gauvreau 1988). For the same period the study predicts that the emigration of anglophones to Anglo-Canada and their low birthrate would likely result in the gradual erosion of the anglophone group from 11 per cent to 10 per cent of the Quebec population. Combined, the above demographic trends are not favourable for Quebec anglophones. Though aligned with the dominant Anglo-American culture of the continent, Quebec anglophones constitute a unique case: they represent the most demographically weak English-speaking community in North America. The president of Alliance Quebec has warned that if Quebec anglophones themselves do not take measures to improve their demographic base in Quebec, they may lose key components of the institutional support they presently enjoy because of the lack of demand resulting from the demographic decline of their community (Scowen 1991).

Francophones feel threatened demographically as a minority in North America while anglophones feel threatened demographically as a minority in Quebec. Neither francophones nor anglophones can count on increased birthrates to substantially improve their respective demographic position in the province. Likewise, given the difficult economic situation in Quebec, neither anglophones nor francophones can count on attracting immigration from other Canadian provinces to improve the strength of their respective linguistic communities within the province. By default, Quebec allophones and international immigrants remain the only realistic means of improving the relative demographic position of francophones and anglophones in the province. Both the anglophone minority and the francophone majority depend on the linguistic assimilation of immigrants to boost their respective collective position within the province. However, allophone and immigrant groups have their own linguistic and cultural goals as distinctive collective entities within the Quebec setting. It is to these ethnolinguistic and ethnocultural communities that the last section of this paper is devoted.

QUEBEC'S ALLOPHONE AND ETHNOCULTURAL COMMUNITIES

Unlike the situation in the other Canadian provinces (Kalin & Berry, this volume), Quebec allophone and ethnocultural communities have long been in the interesting position of deciding whether to seek integration within the anglophone or francophone host communities. The gradual equalization of the 'drawing power' of the English and French language in Quebec during the last two decades has also made the option of maintaining the heritage language and culture more attractive for allophone and ethnocultural communities. However, growing linguistic tensions between the francophone and anglophone communities have put added pressure on allophone and ethnocultural minorities to openly 'take sides' in the Quebec linguistic debate. Quebec's growing reliance on immigration to maintain its demographic strength and to revitalize its economy has situated allophones and ethnocultural communities at the centre of the Quebec debate on what constitutes the 'Québécois' identity.

'Québécois' identity has long been synonymous with French mother-tongue background, Québécois French ancestry, and identification with Québécois culture and traditions. However, the francization of Quebec immigrants originating from diverse ethnocultural backgrounds implies that knowing French may eventually be a sufficient condition for becoming a true 'Québécois' (Breton 1988). Tensions arising from this redefinition of who *should be* and who *can be* a true 'Québécois' have been at the core of a growing debate in Quebec society (Helly 1992; Labelle 1990; Latouche 1989). At one pole, civic nationalists uphold that immigrants and members of cultural communities can be considered 'Québécois' as long as they learn French and participate in all their civic duties and responsibilities (e.g., pay taxes, obey civil and criminal laws). Under this definition, immigrants and members of cultural communities need not identify or participate in Québécois culture and political aspirations as these are matters of private individual choice beyond the reach of the state as stipulated in the Quebec Charter of Human Rights and Freedoms. Towards the other pole of the continuum are those that expect immigrant groups and cultural communities to not only learn French and participate in all the civic duties of a Quebec citizen but also expect such groups to espouse as 'their own' the fundamental values of the true 'Québécois' in important domains of activities including cultural and political orientation (e.g., defence of the French language and culture, Quebec sovereignty). At the end of the continuum are ethnic nationalists who would find it difficult to accept as true 'Québécois,' immigrants and members of cultural communities who do not have French as a mother tongue, have no Québécois French ancestry and lack identification with 'Québécois' culture and political aspirations. Tensions arising from these competing definitions of who is a true 'Québécois' are at the root of an ongoing debate concerning the 'integration strategies' of immigrants within the francophone and anglophone host communities who themselves must adjust to the realities of a multiethnic and multicultural society (Helly 1992; Langlais Laplante, & Levy 1990).

This section provides a preliminary analysis of the integration patterns of Quebec allophone and ethnocultural communities. Using published demolinguistic and census data, the first part of the section provides a broad outline of how allophone groups have sought to integrate linguistically and culturally among Quebec's francophone and anglophone host communities. The integration strategies of ethnolinguistic and ethnocultural minorities are not independent of government policies regarding both the immigration and integration of immigrant populations. Given that Helly (this volume) recently provided a detailed overview of such policies implemented in the Quebec setting, only a brief mention of recent policy orientations needs to be made here.

The second part of this section will be devoted to an overview of selected published studies dealing with the ethnic and multicultural attitudes held not only by members of allophone and ethnocultural minorities but also by members of the francophone and anglophone host communities. The dearth of ethnic attitude research in Quebec does not allow a systematic breakdown of how Quebec's diverse ethnic groups perceive their linguistic and cultural integration within Quebec society. The conclusion drawn from this overview is that much more empirical research is needed to understand better the complex and dynamic nature of interethnic relations in Quebec.

Linguistic Integration of Allophone Communities

It was shown earlier that allophones who settled in Quebec are more likely to maintain their heritage language as the language of the home than allophones settled in the other parts of Canada. However, recent trends also show that the proportion of allophones who declared a knowledge of French (including only French as well as French and English) has increased from 47 per cent in 1971 to 66 per cent in 1986. It was also seen that Bill 101 is having much of its intended effect in increasing the proportion of allophone groups enrolled in the French primary and secondary school system across Quebec (from 39 per cent in 1980 to 75 per cent in 1990). However, given the mandatory nature of enrolment in French primary schools, enshrined in Bill 101, such figures do not reveal much about allophones' true orientations as regards their desire to integrate linguistically in the French or English segments of Quebec society. A somewhat more revealing measure of allophone linguistic preferences can be obtained by considering enrolment in collegiate schooling where freedom of choice between French or English CEGEPs is in effect.

As may be expected, francophone (95 per cent) and anglophone (92 per cent) student enrolment in their respective mother-tongue CEGEPs remained quite high during the last decade (CLF 1992). However, allophone enrolment in French CEGEPs increased from 15 per cent in 1980 to 23 per cent in 1986 and to as much as 41 per cent in 1990. The 1990 figures reflect the fact that 73 per cent of the allophones schooled in the French secondary school system did decide to remain in the French system at the collegiate CEGEP level. Conversely, 24 per cent of the allophones schooled in the French secondary school system did switch to English CEGEPs despite the academic risks involved in pursuing collegiate studies in a language other than the one used for studies at the secondary school level. Of the allophones schooled in the English secondary school system less than 1 per cent are known to switch to French for their collegiate studies at the CEGEP level (CLF 1992).

Access to university education remains an option for only a minority of the post-secondary student population. Based on 1988 Quebec university figures, recent calculations have shown that whereas anglophones have a 34 per cent chance of graduating with a bachelor's degree, allophones have a 20 per cent chance, while this probability drops to 18 per cent for francophones (CLF 1991). Given the role of university education in promoting improved access to desirable positions in the work world, students in Quebec are careful in choosing both the language and the specific university they seek to attend as undergraduates. Universities also play a key role in fostering the reproduction of the sociocultural values of the linguistic communities they serve. Thus, whether students choose to attend a French- or English-language university can be used as an indirect measure of the linguistic and cultural orientation of Quebec francophone, anglophone, and allophone students.

Government figures show that a steady 6 per cent minority of French mother-tongue students chose to attend English language universities in the 1984 to 1990 period (CLF 1992). Likewise only a minority of 7 per cent to 8 per cent of English mother-tongue undergraduates chose to attend French-language universities during this period. Though these figures show that the vast majority of both French and English mother-tongue undergraduates choose to attend their owngroup language universities, it remains that in absolute terms, more francophone undergraduates attended English-language universities than anglophones attended francophone universities during this period.

During the 1984 to 1990 period, more allophone undergraduates choose to attend English-language universities (58 per cent) than

francophone universities (42 per cent; CLF 1992). The patterns of enrolment in Quebec universities show that English universities exert much
drawing power in attracting both allophone and francophone students
while keeping its traditionally anglophone clientele. However, chrono-
logically, the impact of Bill 101 on university enrolment has not yet had
a chance to manifest itself. Given the increase in the proportion of
allophones enrolled in French CEGEPs observed up to 1990, it is likely
that more allophones will choose to attend French-language universities
in the 1990s.

Other indirect measures of the linguistic and cultural orientation of
allophone groups in Quebec can be obtained using mass-media data.
Two of these are the readership of French and English Montreal daily
newspapers and the viewers of French and English television channels.
In Montreal the number of French-language daily newspaper copies has
increased from 259,700 in 1960 to 462,900 in 1990. In contrast, the number
of English-language newspaper copies printed in Montreal has dropped
substantially from 246,200 in 1960 to 147,300 in 1990 (CLF 1992). The
comparable patterns for Quebec as a whole show that while 31 per cent
of daily newspaper copies were printed in English in 1960, this figure
dropped to only 16 per cent in 1990. However, the drawing power of the
last English-language daily newspaper in Montreal (*The Gazette*) remains
strong in 1990, given that its readership is made up not only of anglophones (57.5 per cent) but also of allophone (23.7 per cent) and francophone (18.8 per cent) readers. Taken together the three French language
dailies in Montreal have a readership made up of mostly francophone
readers (87 per cent) while the anglophone (6.4 per cent) and allophone
(6.6 per cent) readership remains marginal. The popularity of the English
press among Montreal allophone readers does suggest a degree of
identification with anglophone perspectives on news events in Quebec,
Canada, and the world.

The linguistic and cultural orientations of Quebec's ethnolinguistic
groups can also be reflected in their television-viewing habits. In Quebec,
viewers can choose to watch TV channels that are francophone, English-
Canadian, American, or multilingual (Tele Latino, Tele Italiano, Chinavi-
sion, etc). Combining data obtained during the 1987–9 period, results
show that Montreal francophones reported watching mainly French-
language stations (83.7 per cent) while they divided the remaining of
their TV viewing time between English-Canadian (8 per cent) and
American (6.4 per cent) TV channels (CLF 1991). Thus, francophones
devoted 14 per cent of their TV viewing time to English-language sta-

tions. In contrast, Montreal anglophones reported only marginal interest in French-language TV viewing (4.8 per cent), while most of their attention was devoted to English-Canadian (52.8 per cent) and American (37.5 per cent) TV stations (CLF 1991).

Montreal allophones emerged with TV viewing patterns which were somewhat more diversified than those of anglophones. Allophones devoted the majority of their TV-viewing time to English-Canadian (41.1 per cent) and American (23.2 per cent) TV channels for a total English-language viewing time of 64 per cent. However, unlike anglophones, allophones did show interest in French-language TV programming since they devoted 27.5 per cent of their viewing time to French stations (CLF 1991). As one would expect, allophones also reported devoting 5.8 per cent of their viewing time to multilingual TV stations which share their programming time among the heritage language groups of the Montreal area.

Taken together, the above higher-education and mass-media ethnolinguistic patterns suggest that allophone communities have a more open orientation towards the Quebec French language majority than does the longer-established anglophone community. However, it remains that to this day, allophones are more attracted to English Canadian and Anglo-American cultural and educational offerings than they are to Québécois French offerings in these domains.

Awareness of allophone linguistic and cultural orientations has prompted the provincial government to be more attentive to the linguistic skills of immigrants recently settled in Quebec. Recent analyses showed that the proportion of immigrants declaring *no* knowledge of either French or English jumped from 11 per cent in the 1981–6 period to 42.5 per cent in the 1986–90 period (CLF 1992). Conversely, the proportion of immigrants who declared knowing French only dropped from 37 per cent in the 1981–6 period to 18.2 per cent in the 1986–90 period. Immigrants declaring knowledge of both French and English also dropped from 29 per cent in 1981–86 to only 14.3 per cent in the 1986–90 period. These dramatic shifts in the linguistic composition of Quebec immigrants have created increased pressures on the capacity of Quebec society to properly accommodate first-generation immigrants in the francophone community. Given that 87 per cent of immigrants to Quebec settle in Montreal, it is municipal services along with French schools serving the Montreal population that have had to adapt most quickly to the changing demolinguistic characteristics of recently arrived immigrants (Pagé 1988).

In December 1990, the Ministère des Communautés Culturelles et de l'Immigration tabled a major policy document on immigration which focused on the need to devote more effort on the francization and social integration of Quebec immigrants (MCCI 1990). In proposing to increase the proportion of French-speaking immigrants settling in the province, the policy states: 'Because prior knowledge of French facilitates integration into the French-speaking community, eliminates the cost involved in learning a new language, and improves the probability of retaining immigrant populations, Quebec's objective is to increase the number of French-speaking immigrants to 40 per cent in 1994.' (MCCI 1990:11). This modest goal should be achieved given that French only and French-English bilinguals constituted 32 per cent of immigrants settled in Quebec during the 1986–90 period.

The policy program clearly recognizes that increasing immigration to Quebec must be coupled with a more energetic plan to facilitate the linguistic integration of non-French-speaking immigrants within francophone society. The concrete 'Action Plan' proposed in spring 1991 (MCCI 1991) called for an increase from 40 per cent to 60 per cent of non-French-speaking immigrants to be made eligible for French-language courses offered in the COFI program by 1994. The COFI program pays immigrants a salary while they learn French and can also offer daycare services for parents learning French in the program. The COFI also offers part-time French courses for immigrants already employed in the workforce. However, Helly (this volume) notes that the demand for French courses in the COFI still exceeds the supply, while COFI teachers remain in a precarious employment position within the program. These shortcomings along with others limit the effectiveness of this program in promoting the linguistic integration of immigrants.

The 'Let's Build Quebec Together' policy statement (MCCI 1990) does not propose substantial government involvement favouring institutional support for the maintenance of heritage languages and cultures in the province. As such, the policy remains distinct from Canada's original multiculturalism policy (Berry 1984, 1991). Though the policy makes it clear that immigrants must learn French as the language of integration with the host majority, it recognizes the value of cultural pluralism and offers modest financial support for the promotion of heritage cultures and languages (teaching and mass media) while funds are also allocated for programs designed to improve relations between ethnocultural groups and the host community (MCCI 1991).

Ethnic Attitudes in Quebec: Francophones, Anglophones, and Allophones

Results of the Berry, Kalin & Taylor (1977) multiculturalism survey conducted with Canadian respondents (N=1825) showed that whereas heritage language groups and Anglo-Celts (anglophones of British descent; henceforth English Canadians) were mildly supportive of multiculturalism ideology, francophones sampled across Canada were less favourably disposed towards this federal policy. Another important facet of attitudes towards multiculturalism is the perceived consequences of the policy on the cultural diversity, social harmony, and unity of Canada. The combined scores for these items showed that English-Canadian and heritage groups were more positive about the consequences of this policy for Canadian society than were French-Canadian respondents. A further breakdown of the responses showed that French Canadians, more than English Canadians and heritage groups, felt that multiculturalism policies could make French Canadians weaker as a voice in Canada. English Canadians and French Canadians who felt economically and culturally insecure were more negatively disposed towards multiculturalism and had unfavourable behavioural intentions towards its programs. It was noteworthy that French Canadians in the survey felt much less economically and culturally secure than English Canadians and thus, on the whole, emerged to be less tolerant towards multiculturalism and its programs than English Canadians (Berry et al. 1977; Bourhis 1987).

As regards the teaching of heritage languages within school hours, results of the Berry et al. (1977) survey showed that heritage language groups were as opposed to such level of support as were English-Canadian respondents while Quebec francophones were most opposed to such measures (Bourhis 1987). Francophones were more opposed to paying taxes for multiculturalism programs compared to English Canadians and heritage groups, who were mildly opposed to such taxes. Finally, results obtained on the the ethnocentrism scale used in the Berry et al. (1977) survey showed that English-Canadian and 'other ethnic' respondents in the study were less ethnocentric than French-Canadian respondents.

There is a debate concerning explanations for the claim that Quebec francophones are more prejudiced, less tolerant of immigrants and less supportive of multicultural ideology than anglophones and 'other ethnic' Canadians. To the degree that Quebec francophones form an 'ethnic class' they are portrayed as feeling culturally threatened by the presence of immigrants and unassimilated ethnic groups in Quebec (Cappon, 1978; Murphy 1981). Conversely, English Canadians in general are portrayed as not feeling so threatened collectively since they are members of the dominant group politically and economically in Canada. In contrast, Guindon (1978) suggests that the so-called xenophobic character of the Québécois is a myth and a cultural stereotype which 'can only serve political legitimations, which is precisely what they are used for' (p 243).

Lambert and Curtis (1983) proposed that Quebec francophones may be less tolerant towards specific immigrants who are non-French-speaking and who are thus perceived as a specific threat to the survival of French in Quebec. To test this hypothesis Lambert and Curtis (1983) analyzed data collected in 1977 from English-Canadian and Quebec francophone respondents (N=3288). While controlling for level of education and income, English-Canadian and francophone Québécois responses were contrasted on a broad range of ethnic attitudes including rejection of minority cultures, denial of immigrant's contribution, rejection of English-speaking immigrants, rejection of Italians, rejection of non-Whites and preference for limited immigration. As in the Berry et al. (1977) survey, results in this study showed that the higher the education and income of both the English-Canadian and Quebec francophones, the more tolerant and accepting of immigrants and minority cultures were the respondents. However, differences between English-Canadians and Quebec francophones emerged even when controlling for level of income and education. Cultural anxieties about specific groups of immigrants emerged for both the francophone and English Canadian respondents. Quebec francophones were more opposed to immigration overall and to further immigration from Britain, the U.S., and Italy than were English Canadians. Francophones were also more in favour of the cultural assimilation of immigrants and less convinced of the value of contributions made by immigrants to the host community than were English Canadians. However, English Canadians were more likely to object to further immigration from the West Indies, India, and Pakistan than were Quebec francophones. English Canadians emerged with greater racial concerns than Quebec francophones, especially as regards the presence of visible minority immigrants (Lambert & Curtis 1983).

Recently, Bolduc and Fortin (1990) proposed that Quebec francophone attitudes towards immigration and multiculturalism could be explained not only by using the usual measures of education and occupational status but also by considering that such attitudes are indeed linked to the belief that immigration poses a threat for the survival of the French language in Quebec. Bolduc and Fortin analyzed results of a previous telephone survey conducted in 1987 with the following three groups of Quebec residents: 365 French mother-tongue respondents; 70 English mother-tongue respondents, and 33 allophone respondents.

Unlike earlier studies contrasting Quebec francophones with anglophones from all parts of Canada, results showed that Quebec francophones and Quebec anglophones had similar attitudes towards immigration on most questionnaire items except those dealing with the French language and the item on multiculturalism. Half the francophone and anglophone sample was positive about the impact of immigration on the Quebec economy and employment levels while the other half of each group felt negative about the effects of immigration. Quebec francophones and anglophones agreed that factors such as the country of origin, race, and colour as well as religious background were not the most important criteria for the selection of immigrants to Quebec. Both groups were equally divided between those who felt that Quebec should receive fewer immigrants and those who felt that the current immigration rate should be maintained.

However, anglophones were more positively disposed than francophones towards the idea that Quebec should become a multicultural society with a greater role assigned to different ethnic and racial groups. On the French-language issue, francophones felt that prior knowledge of French was a more important basis for selecting immigrants to Quebec than did anglophones. Also, francophones were more likely to feel that immigrants had a negative impact on the French language in Quebec than did anglophones. More important, results showed that francophones felt that immigration constituted a greater threat to the French language in Quebec than did anglophones.

Bolduc and Fortin tested the basic notion that francophones may be less favourably disposed towards multiculturalism mainly because they are more likely to perceive immigration as a threat to their own language than do anglophones. When the authors statistically controlled for feelings of threat to the French language associated with immigration, they found that Montreal francophones did not differ from Quebec anglophones in their attitudes towards multiculturalism in Quebec. In a further analysis the authors showed that francophone and anglophone differences in attitudes towards immigration and multiculturalism were due mostly to divergence of opinions between the two groups regarding immigration as a threat to the future of French in Quebec (55 per cent of the variance). It was concluded that francophone ambivalence regarding the multicultural ideology and immigration issues is more related to concerns about the survival of the French language in Quebec than to an underlying xenophobic orientation particular to francophones as a group.

Finally, Bolduc and Fortin contrasted the attitudes of Quebec allophones with those of francophones and anglophones. As expected, allophone respondents more readily recognized the positive impact of immigration on the Quebec economy than did both the francophone and anglophone respondents. As with francophones and anglophones, allophones agreed that factors such as the country of origin, race, and colour as well as religious background were not the most important criteria for the selection of immigrants to Quebec. Allophones were as positive about Quebec becoming multicultural as were anglophones and shared anglophone views that immigration did not threaten the French language in Quebec. However, allophones joined francophones in the view that knowledge of French was an important criterion for selecting immigrants to Quebec, a view not shared by Quebec anglophones. Taken together, these patterns of results show that allophones have their own distinctive views on Quebec immigration which tend to situate them between francophones and anglophones on a number of issues. As yet, no large-scale study of attitudes towards multiculturalism and ethnicity has been specifically designed for allophones, francophones, and anglophones in the Quebec setting. Given Quebec's growing reliance on international immigration to bolster its demographic base it is clear that a broad survey of Quebec's ethnocultural communities and its host communities is necessary. It is only in the last decade that more focused attention has been paid to specific allophone and ethnocultural communities in Quebec (Caldwell 1983; Juteau-Lee 1983; Langlais et al. 1990; Pagé 1988).

A program of research on the ethnic attitudes and integration strategies of Quebec allophone and ethnocultural communities has been under way at McGill University since the mid-1980s. The research involves small samples of first-generation Quebec immigrants including Greeks, Jews, South Americans, Vietnamese, East Indians, and Haitians. Taken together research findings from this series of studies provide a preliminary portrait of the ethnic attitudes and integration strategies of some of Quebec's cultural communities (Moghaddam 1988, 1992). This paper closes with a brief overview of some of the main findings obtained in this recent series of studies.

The McGill group first examined the strength of motivation towards heritage culture maintenance among Quebec ethnolinguistic communities. The overall finding is that Quebec ethnolinguistic communities are positively motivated towards heritage language and culture maintenance. The strongest support for heritage culture maintenance was obtained among 'non-visible' groups such as Greeks (Lambert, Mermigis & Taylor 1986) and Jews (Taylor, Moghaddam & Tchoryk-Pelletier 1990). However, the following visible minority groups were less interested in heritage culture retention: immigrants from India (Moghaddam, Taylor & Lalonde 1989); immigrants from Haiti; immigrants from South American countries; and immigrants from Vietnam (Taylor et al. 1990). Moghaddam and Taylor (1987) interpreted the moderate endorsement of heritage culture maintenance among visible minority groups as a form of psychological ambivalence reflecting the experience of prejudice and discrimination. In a study of East Indian immigrant women in Montreal, Moghaddam, Ditto and Taylor (1990) found that higher psychological stress was experienced by women who abandoned their traditional cultures in order to assimilate into mainstream society. In part, this stress was also attributed to increased exposure to discrimination due to increased interaction with anglophone and francophone majority group members within the host society.

As noted earlier, one feature of the Quebec setting is that even though immigrants experience the drawing power of the Anglo-American setting as elsewhere in Canada, they are also exposed to the influence of another majority force, which is the French language and culture in Quebec. One result of these competing forces is that immigrant communities are more likely to maintain their heritage language in Quebec than elsewhere in Canada. Another measure of this phenomenon was recently documented in the study conducted by Moghaddam (1992) dealing with the *cultural maintenance* of first-generation immigrants in Quebec. Moghaddam (1992) proposed that conceiving assimilation and cultural retention as being opposite poles of a single dimension was too simplistic for the Quebec setting. Assimilation was conceptualized as an individualistic mobility strategy in which the immigrant abandons the heritage group and attempts to join the majority group. In contrast, culture retention implies a more collectivist strategy involving cooperation between members of the ethnic collectivity and the maintenance of the culture of origin.

In his study, Moghaddam (1992) measured assimilation and culture retention as two independent dimensions among a combined group of visible minority groups in Montreal (N=413). The majority of respondents in the study (51 per cent) emerged as high on culture maintenance and low on assimilation. This group scored highest on a self esteem scale suggesting that culture retention without assimilation to the host community is a strong orientation among first-generation immigrants to Quebec. The neutralizing drawing power of English and French in Quebec seemed reflected by the fact that only 13 per cent of the respondents emerged as low on culture maintenance and high on assimilation. Another 17 per cent of the respondents were both high on culture maintenance and high on assimilation. Finally, the 19 per cent of respondents who were both weak in culture maintenance and desire to assimilate were not the 'marginal' types described by Berry (1984) but rather were more like 'rugged individualists' determined to make it on their own regardless of ethnolinguistic background.

Moghaddam et al. (1991) also explored the social identity of students attending a French medium college (CEGEP) in Montreal. Quebec francophones (N=150) and five samples of first-generation immigrant groups (N=30 each) participated in this study: European francophones (Belgian, Swiss, French), Jews, Latin Americans, Haitians and South East Asians. Immigrant-group students were asked the extent to which they perceived themselves as 'foreigners,' 'immigrants' and 'Québécois' as well as the extent to which they believed that Quebec francophone students perceived them as belonging to each of these categories. The Quebec francophone students were also asked the extent to which they perceived the five groups as 'foreigners,' 'immigrants,' and 'Québécois.'

The rank order of the groups in terms of perceiving themselves as 'Québécois' from most to least was as follows: (1) European francophones, (2) South Americans and Asians, (3) Haitians and Jews. The rank order of the groups in terms of how the Quebec francophone students perceived them from most to least Québécois was: (1) European francophones and Jews, (2) South American, Asians, and Haitians. Thus the largest discrepancy between immigrant group perceptions and Quebec francophone perception emerged in the case of the Jewish group. Furthermore, the European francophones assumed themselves to be more accepted by the Quebec francophones than they actually were, while the Haitians perceived themselves to be even less accepted than they actually were. The Haitians assumed that the Quebec francophones perceived them less as Québécois and more as 'foreigners' and as 'immigrants' than the Quebec francophones actually saw them. Given that both European francophones and Haitian immigrants share French as a common language with the Quebec francophones, it seems that the visible-minority status of Haitians played a role in these perceptions. In contrast, European francophones feel more confident in being accepted given the historical role of French culture in Quebec.

Stereotypes can have a strong impact on the integration strategies of first-generation immigrants. In an analysis of other features of the Moghaddam et al. (1991) study, Tchoryk-Pelletier (1989) had the Quebec francophone college students rate European francophones, Jews, Latin Americans, South East Asians, and Haitians on a series of traits including hard-working, intelligent, trustworthy, likeable, clannish, and aggressive. The following patterns are those reflecting ratings above or below the average score obtained for the combined ratings of all the target groups. Quebec francophones had positive stereotypes towards European francophones rating them as being above average on trustworthiness, likeability, and successfulness at school. Though Jews were perceived as hard-working, they were rated less trustworthy, likeable, and sincere than average. As regards visible minority groups, results showed that Quebec francophones had very positive stereotypes towards Asians while they had negative ones towards Haitians. Asians were perceived as hard-working, intelligent, trustworthy, respectful of school regulations, and successful at school. In contrast, Haitians were seen as aggressive, clannish, and less hard-working, less intelligent, and less trustworthy as a group. Haitians were also rated less respectful of school regulations and less successful in school. Latin Americans were perceived as more aggressive than average, less hard-working and respectful of school regulations than average.

A social distance item was also constructed so respondents could rate the desirability of working with each target group as a colleague on a school project (Tchoryk-Pelletier 1989). The following patterns are those reflecting ratings above or below the average score obtained from all respondents for the combined ratings of all the target groups. First, Quebec francophones as well as members of each immigrant group who took part in the study rated a member of their own ethnic group as one of their most preferred colleagues for the school project. This pattern of preference for members of the ingroup rather than for members of the outgroup is in line with most studies of intergroup attitudes and behaviours and reflects a basic bias in favour of the ingroup relative to outgroups (Berry & Kalin 1979; Messick & Mackie 1989; Tajfel 1981).

The social distance ratings of outgroup others revealed what may well be a consensually shared status hierarchy of ethnic groups in Montreal.

European francophones and Quebec francophones were the types of individuals most often selected as colleagues by all groups except Haitians and Latin Americans. In turn, Haitians and Jews were less likely to be selected than average by respondents from all the ethnic groups who took part in the study. Haitians and South Americans were the only groups to select only members of their owngroup as preferred colleagues. These social distance results agree with stereotype ratings and show that immigrant groups themselves tend to share some of the views endorsed by the majority culture, especially as regards the 'desirability' of being associated with European francophones and the 'less desirable' option of associating with Haitians and Jews.

The above patterns of stereotypes were reflected in feelings of discrimination experienced by the different groups in the study (Tchoryk-Pelletier 1989). Though personal experiences of being the victim of discrimination at school were generally quite low, Jews, Latin Americans and Haitians were above average in reporting feelings of having been discriminated against. Moghaddam and Taylor (1987) have found that visible minority groups such as Haitians and Asians do report high levels of personal discrimination. This trend is also reflected in studies of discrimination in rental housing in Montreal. For instance, in their interview study with Montreal landlords, Hilton, Potvin, and Sachdev (1989) found that francophone landlords were quite positive about renting to ingroup members (Quebec francophones), were generally neutral about renting to Quebec anglophones, slightly negative about renting to Italians and Asians, and strongly negative about renting to Haitians.

Stereotypes and discrimination against immigrant and other minority groups are a reality in most urban centres of Canada and the world (Berry et al. 1977; Herberg 1989). However, the dysfunctional aspects of prejudice and discrimination are such that it is important to sustain research efforts to better understand these phenomena and to combat them (Messick & Mackie 1989; Sachdev & Bourhis 1991; Tajfel 1981). Research efforts in this field have just begun in Quebec and must be increased given the reality of ethnic pluralism in the province (Bourhis & Guimond 1992; Bourhis & Gagnon 1993).

CONCLUSION

Quebec's growing reliance on international immigration to maintain its demographic and economic base has brought to the fore the issue of who is and who can be a 'true Québécois.' As seen earlier, the question of what constitutes the 'Québécois identity' is the topic of ongoing debate between civic nationalists and ethnic nationalists (Breton 1988; Helly 1992). At the core of this debate are the linguistic and cultural integration strategies of Quebec immigrant and cultural communities within Quebec society. Thus, research on issues related to pluralism, multiculturalism, and intergroup relations is as pertinent in Quebec as it is in Canada.

This overview of interethnic relations in Quebec demonstrates that the fate of immigrant and ethnocultural communities is inevitably linked with that of the francophone and anglophone communities of the province. Therefore, multiculturalism research in Quebec can no longer afford to focus strictly on heritage groups to the exclusion of their relationship with francophone and anglophone host communities. The next decade of multiculturalism research must be broadened to include not only the study of heritage groups per se but also their relationship with francophones and anglophones in Quebec. This recommendation reflects current theory and research on the dynamics of inter-group relations which stresses the interdependence of ethnolinguistic groups in multiethnic and multilingual settings.

The overview of inter-group relations in Quebec has also brought to the fore the necessity of studying interethnic relations between members of contrasting immigrant and ethnocultural groups who must often compete and collaborate with each other, especially in urban settings. Collaboration, competition, and conflicts between visible and non-visible heritage groups, especially in the school setting, the work place, and the rental housing sector is worthy of much closer attention and should be granted priority for multiculturalism research.

More social psychological research is needed on the causes, mechanisms, and functions of stereotyping, prejudice, and discrimination which often characterize relations between anglophone and francophone host communities as well as ethnocultural and allophone groups in Quebec. The nature, function, and prevalence of prejudice and discrimination in the police force, social services, the work world, and rental housing needs to be studied and better understood. Prejudice and discrimination between contrasting members of minorities must also be studied in their own right because ethnic relations between visible and non-visible heritage group communities have an impact on the climate of intergroup relations between host communities and heritage groups.

NOTE

The author wishes to thank the following institutions for their generous help in providing documents and research reports which were invaluable in writing this article: le Ministère des Communautés culturelles et de l'immigration; le Conseil de la langue française; l'Office de la langue française; l'Institut québécois de recherche sur la culture. The author would also like to thank the following individuals for their very helpful comments on earlier versions of this paper: John Berry, Denise Helly, Rudy Kalin, Jacques Maurais, Fathali Moghaddam, Céline Moise, Kenneth McRae, Michel Paillé, and Itesh Sachdev. Comments and criticisms concerning this paper should be addressed to: Richard Y. Bourhis, Département de psychologie, Université du Québec à Montréal, CP 8888, Succ. A, Montréal, Québec, Canada H3C 3P8.

REFERENCES

Baillargeon, M., and Benjamin, C. (1990). *Caractéristiques linguistiques de la population immigrée recensée au Québec en 1986.* Montréal: Ministere des communautes culturelles et de l'immigration
Balakrishnan, T.R., and Kralt, J. (1987). Segregation of visible minorities in Montreal, Toronto and Vancouver. In L. Driedger (ed.), *Ethnic Canada* (pp 138–57. Toronto: Copp Clark Pitman
Béland, P. (1991). *L'usage du français au travail: Situation et tendances.* Québec: Conseil de la langue française
Berry, J.W. (1984). Multicultural policy in Canada: A Social Psychological analysis. *Canadian Journal of Behavioural Science,* 16:353–70
– (1989). *Attitudes towards official bilingualism in Eastern Ontario.* Paper presented to Canadian Psychological Association Annual Meeting, Halifax
– (1991). *Sociopsychological costs and benefits of multiculturalism.* Economic Council of Canada, Working Paper No. 24
– , and Bourcier, D. (1989). Attitudes towards official bilingualism in eastern Ontario. Paper presented to Canadian Psychological Association, Halifax
– , and Kalin R. (1979). Reciprocity of inter-ethnic attitudes in a multicultural society. *International Journal of Intercultural Relations,* 3:99–112
Berry, J.W., Kalin, R., and Taylor, D. (1977). *Multiculturalism and ethnic attitudes in Canada.* Ottawa: Ministry of Supply and Services
Blanc, B. (1986). Problématique de la localisation des nouveaux immigrants à Montréal. *Canadian Ethnic Studies,* 18:89–108
Bolduc, D. and Fortin, P. (1990). Les francophones sont-ils plus 'xénophobes'

que les anglophones au Québec? Une analyse quantitative exploratoire. *Canadian Ethnic Studies*, 22:54–77

Bouchard, P. (1991). *Les enjeux de la francisation des entreprises au Québec 1977–1984.* Montréal: Office de la langue française

– , and Beauchamps, P. (1980). *Le Français, langue des commerces et des services publics.* Québec: Gouvernement du Québec, Office de la langue française

Bourhis, R. (1982). Language policies and language attitudes: Le monde de la Francophonie. In E.B. Ryan and H. Giles (eds), *Attitudes towards language variation* (pp 34–62). London: Edward Arnold

– (1983). Language attitudes and self-reports of French-English language use in Quebec. *Journal of Multilingual and Multicultural Development*, 4:163–79

– (1984a). The charter of the French language and cross-cultural communication in Montreal. In R.Y. Bourhis (ed.), *Conflict and Language Planning in Quebec* (pp 174–204). Clevedon, Eng.: Multilingual Matters

– (1984b). Cross-cultural communication in Montreal: Two field studies since Bill 101. *International Journal of the Sociology of Language*, 46:33–47

– (1984c). Language policies in multilingual settings. In R. Bourhis (ed.), *Conflict and language planning in Quebec* (pp 1–28). Clevedon, Eng.: Multilingual Matters

– (1987). Social psychology and heritage language research: A retrospective view and future trends for Canada. In J. Cummins (ed.), *Heritage language research in Canada: Research Perspectives* (pp 13–44). Ottawa: Secretary of State, Multiculturalism

– (1994). Introduction and overview of language events in Canada. *International Journal of the Sociology of Language*, 106. Thematic issue: French-English language issues in Canada. Issue Editor: Richard Y. Bourhis (forthcoming)

Bourhis, R.Y., and Gagnon, A. (1993). Préjugés, discrimination et relations intergroupes. In R. Vallerand (ed.), *Introduction à la psychologie sociale contemporaine* (pp 707–74). Boucherville, Québec: Gaetan Morin

Bourhis, R.Y., and Guimond, S. (1992). La psychologie sociale des préjugés et de la discrimination entre groupes sociaux. *Revue québécoise de psychologie, 13* (Numéro thématique: Préjugés et discrimination/logie

Bourhis, R.Y., and Lepicq, D. (1993). Quebec French and language issues in Quebec. In R. Posner and J.N. Green (eds), *Trends in romance linguistics and philology*, Volume 5: *Bilingualism and linguistic conflict in romance* (pp 345–81). The Hague and Berlin: Mouton de Gruyter

Breton, R. (1988). From ethnic to civic nationalism: English Canada and Quebec. *Ethnic and Racial Studies, 11*:85–102

Breton, R., Reitz, J., and Valentine, V. (1980). *Cultural boundaries and the cohesion of Canada.* Montreal: The Institute for Research on Public Policy

Caldwell, G. (1983). *Les études ethniques au Québec: Bilan et perspectives*. Québec: Institut québécois de recherche sur la culture
– (1984). Anglo-Quebec: Demographic realities and options for the future. In R.Y. Bourhis (ed.), *Conflict and Language Planning in Quebec* (pp 205–21). Clevedon, Eng.: Multilingual Matters
– (1994). English Quebec: Demographic and cultural reproduction. In R.Y. Bourhis (ed.), French-English language issues in Canada. *International Journal of the Sociology of Language, 106* (forthcoming)
– , and Fournier, D. (1987). The Quebec question: A matter of population. *Canadian Journal of Sociology, 12*:16–41
Canada (1969). *Royal Commission on Bilingualism and Biculturalism, Book III: The work world*. Ottawa: The Queen's Printer
– (1990). *Commissioner of Official Languages Annual Report*. Ottawa: Ministry of Supplies and Services
Cappon, P. (1978). Nationalism and inter-ethnic and linguistic conflict in Quebec. In L. Drieger (ed.), *The Canadian Ethnic Mosaic: A quest for identity* (pp 327–39). Toronto: McClelland & Stewart
CLF (1991). *Indicateurs de la situation linguistique au Québec*. Québec: Conseil de la langue française
– (1992). *Indicateurs de la situation linguistique au Québec: Édition 1992*. Québec: Conseil de la langue française
Coleman, W. (1984). *The independence movement in Quebec: 1945–1980*. Toronto: University of Toronto Press
D'Anglejan, A. (1984). Language planning in Quebec: An historical overview and future trends. In R. Bourhis (ed.), *Conflict and language planning in Quebec* (pp 29–52). Clevedon, Eng.: Multilingual Matters
Daoust, D. (1984). Francization and terminology change in Quebec business firms. In R.Y. Bourhis (ed.), *Conflict and language planning in Quebec* (pp 81–113). Clevedon, Eng.: Multilingual Matters
Da Rosa, V., and Poulin, R. (1986). Espaces ethniques et question linguistique au Québec: à propos des communautés italienne et portugaise. *Canadian Ethnic Studies, 18*:144–50
de Vries, J. (1994). Canada's official language communities: An overview of the current demolinguistic situation. In R.Y. Bourhis (ed.), French-English language issues in Canada. *International Journal of the Sociology of Language, 106* (forthcoming)
Genesee, F., and Bourhis, R.Y. (1982). The social psychological significance of code-switching in cross-cultural communication. *Journal of Language and Social Psychology 1*:1–27
– (1988). Evaluative reactions to language choice strategies: The role of socio-structural factors. *Language and Communication 8*:229–50

Genesee, F., and Holobow, N. (1989). Change and stability in intergroup perceptions. *Journal of Language and Social Psychology*, 8:17–38

Guindon, H. (1978). The modernization of Quebec and the legitimacy of the Canadian state. In D. Glenday, H. Guindon and A. Turowetz (eds), *Modernization and the Canadian State* (pp 212–46). Toronto: Macmillan

Heller, M. (1988). Strategic ambiguity: Code-switching in the management of conflict. In M. Heller (ed.), *Codeswitching* (pp 77–96). The Hague and Berlin: Mouton de Gruyter

Helly, D. (1992). *L'Immigration pourquoi faire?* Québec: Institut québécois de recherche sur la culture

Herberg, E. (1989). *Ethnic Groups in Canada: Adaptations and transitions.* Scarborough: Nelson

Hilton, T., Potvin, L., and Sachdev, I. (1989). Ethnic relations in rental housing: A social psychological approach. *Canadian Journal of Behavioural Science*, 21:121–31

Jackson, J. (1982). The language question in Quebec: On collective and individual rights. In G. Caldwell and E. Waddell (eds), *The English of Quebec: From majority to minority status* (pp 363–77). Québec: Institut québécois de recherche sur la culture

Juteau-Lee, D. (1983). Présentation: Les autres ethniques. *Sociologie et société*, 15:3–8. (Numéro thématique)

Labelle, M. (1990). Immigration, culture et question nationale. *Cahiers de recherche sociologique*, 4:143–51

Lachapelle, A., and Henripin, J. (1980). *La situation démolinguistique au Canada.* Montréal: Institut de recherches politiques

Lambert, R. and Curtis, J. (1983). Opposition to multiculturalism among Québécois and English-Canadians. *Canadian Review of Sociology and Anthropology*, 20:193–206

Lambert, W.E., Hodgson, J., Gardner, R., and Fillenbaum, S. (1960). Evaluational reactions to spoken languages. *Journal of Abnormal and Social Psychology*, 60:44–51

Lambert, W.E., Mermigis, L., and Taylor, D. (1986). Greek Canadians' attitudes toward own group and other Canadian ethnic groups: A test of multiculturalism. *Canadian Journal of Behavioural Science*, 18:35–51

Langlais, J., Laplante, P. and Levy, J. (Eds.) (1990). *Le Québec de demain et les communautés culturelles.* Montréal: Editions du Méridien

Laporte, P. (1984). Status of language planning in Quebec: An evaluation. In R.Y. Bourhis (ed.), *Conflict and Language Planning in Quebec* (pp 53–80). Clevedon, Eng.: Multilingual Matters

Latouche, D. (1989). Le pluralisme ethnique et l'agenda public au Québec. *Revue Internationale d'action Communautaire*, 21(61):11–26

Legault, J. (1992). *L'invention d'une minorité: Les Anglo-Québécois.* Montréal: Boréal

Levine, M. (1990). *The reconquest of Montreal: Language policy and social change in a bilingual city.* Philadelphia: Temple University Press

Mackey, W. (1983). US language status policy and the Canadian experience. In J. Cobarrubias and J. Fishman (eds), *Progress in Language Planning* (pp 173–206). Berlin and New York: Mouton

Mallea, J. (1984). Minority language education in Quebec and anglophone Canada. In R.Y. Bourhis (ed.), *Conflict and language planning in Quebec* (pp 222–60). Clevedon, Eng.: Multilingual Matters

Maurais, J. (1987). L'expérience québécoise d'aménagement linguistique. In J. Maurais (ed.), *Politique et aménagement linguistique* (pp 359–416). Québec & Paris: Conseil de la langue française & Le Robert

– (1989). Language status planning in Quebec. In C. Lauren and M. Norman (eds), *Special language: From humans thinking to thinking machines* (pp 138–49). Clevedon, Eng. Multilingual Matters. Conseil de la langue française

– (ed.) (1992). *Les langues autochtones au Québec.* Quebec: Le Conseil de la Langue Française

MCCI (1990). *Let's build Quebec together: Vision, a policy statement on immigration and integration.* Montreal: Ministère des communautés culturelles et de l'immigration

– (1991). *Plan d'action gouvernemental en matière d'immigration: 1991–1994.* Montréal: Ministère des Communautés culturelles et de l'immigration

Messick, D., and Mackie, D. (1989). Intergroup relations. *Annual Review of Psychology,* 40:45–81

Miller, R. (1984). The response of business firms to fhe Francization process. In R.Y. Bourhis (ed.), *Conflict and Language Planning in Quebec* (pp 114–29). Clevedon, Eng.: Multilingual Matters

Moghaddam, F. (1988). Individualistic and collective integration strategies among immigrants: Toward a mobility model of cultural integration. In J. Berry and R. Annis (eds.), *Ethnic psychology* (pp 69–79). Lisse: Swets & Zeitlinger

– (1992). Assimilation et multiculturalisme: Le cas des minorités au Québec. *Revue québécoise de psychologie,* 13:140–57

Moghaddam, F., Ditto, B., and Taylor, D. (1990). Attitudes and attributions related to psychological symptomatology in Indian immigrant women. *Journal of Cross-Cultural Psychology,* 21:335–50

Moghaddam, F., and Taylor, D. (1987). The meaning of multiculturalism for visible minority immigrant women. *Canadian Journal of Behavioural Science.* 19:121–36

Moghaddam, F., Taylor, D., and Lalonde, R. (1987). Individualistic and collective integration strategies among Iranians in Canada. *International Journal of Psychology*, 22:301–13

– (1989). Integration strategies and attitudes toward the built environment: A study of Haitian and immigrant women in Montreal. *Canadian Journal of Behavioural Science*, 21:160–73

Moghaddam, F., Taylor, D., Tchoryk-Pelletier, P., and Shapenack, M. (1991). How accurate are we in judging how others perceive us? An assessment of self-perceptions among minority groups in Quebec. Unpublished manuscript, Dept of Psychology, McGill University

Moise, L.C., and Bourhis, R.Y. (1994). Language et ethnicité: Communication interculturelle à Montréal, 1977–1991. *Canadian Ethnic Studies* (forthcoming)

Monnier, D. (1989). *Langue d'accueil et langue de service dans les commerces à Montréal*. Québec: Conseil de la langue française

Murphy, R. (1981). Teachers and the evolving structural context of economic and political attitudes in Quebec society. *Canadian Review of Sociology and Anthropology*, 18:157–82

Pagé, M. (1988). L'éducation interculturelle au Québec: Bilan critique. In F. Ouellet (ed.), *Pluralisme et l'école* (p 271–300). Quebec: Institut québécois de recherche sur la culture

Paillé, M. (1991). Choix linguistique des immigrants dans les trois provinces canadiennes les plus populeuses. *International Journal of Canadian Studies*, 3:185–93

Quebec (1972). *Report of the Commission of Enquiry on the Position of the French Language and on Language Rights in Quebec*. (Gendron Commission) Québec: Editeur Officiel du Québec

Ryan, E. B., and Giles, H. (eds) (1982). *Attitudes towards language variation*. London: Edward Arnold

Sachdev, I., and Bourhis, R.Y. (1990). Language and social identification. In D. Abrams and M. Hogg (eds), *Social identity theory: Constructive and critical advances*. New York: Harvester/Wheatsheaf

– (1991). Power and status differentials in minority and majority group relations. *European Journal of Social Psychology*, 21:1–24

Scowen, R. (1991). *A different vision: The English in Quebec in the 1990s*. Don Mills, ON: Maxwell Macmillan Canada

Sénéchal, G. (1987). *Les allophones et les anglophones inscrits à l'école française: Sondage sur les attitudes et les comportements linguistiques*. Québec: Documentation du Conseil de la langue française

Sloan, T. (1990). Bill 8: Rumbles of discontent. *Language and Society*, 30:21–2

Tajfel, H. (1981). The social psychology of minorities. In H. Tajfel (ed.), *Human groups and social categories* (pp 309–43). Cambridge: Cambridge University Press

Taylor, D. (1986). *La réaction des anglophones face à la Chartre de la langue française.* Montréal: Office de la langue française

Taylor, D., Moghaddam, F., and Tchoryk-Pelletier, P. (1990). Dimensions of heritage culture maintenance in Quebec. Unpublished manuscript, Dept of Psychology, McGill University

Taylor, D., and Sigal, R. (1982). Defining 'Québécois': The role of ethnic heritage, language, and political orientation. *Canadian Ethnic Studies, 14*:59–70

Taylor, D., and Wright, S. (1989). Language attitudes in a multilingual northern community. *The Canadian Journal of Native Studies, 9*:85–119

Tchoryk-Pelletier, P. (1989). *L'adaptation des minorités ethniques.* Montréal: CEGEP de Saint-Laurent

Termotte, P., and Gauvreau, D. (1988). *La situation démolinguistique au Québec.* Québec: Conseil de la Langue Française

Vaillancourt, F. (1992). *Langue et statut économique au Québec 1980–1985.* Quebec: Conseil de la langue française

ENOCH PADOLSKY

Canadian Ethnic Minority Literature in English

INTRODUCTION

Any survey of Canadian ethnic minority literature and of its critical reception has to begin by recognizing that a major demographic shift has occurred and is continuing to occur in Canadian literary output in English. Twenty or thirty years ago literature in English Canada consisted primarily of writings by British-Canadian writers and a few individuals from a small number of Canadian ethnic minority groups (e.g., Icelandic, Jewish, Ukrainian). Today, Canadian literature reflects a much broader proportion of a changing Canadian society and both the number of writers and the group experiences represented have expanded dramatically. Not surprisingly, this increasing diversity is having an impact on the way Canadian literature is perceived, and a number of critical, theoretical, and institutional issues have arisen because of it. At the moment these issues are in the process of being absorbed into a literary critical scene which also reflects other kinds of theoretical and critical challenges (e.g., feminism, post-colonialism, new historicism) and though changes in Canadian literary scholarship with regard to ethnic minority writing are clearly in the wind, the resolution of these new issues still lies in the future.

Before looking into these issues, however, I would like to outline briefly the literary situation – the general situation of the creative works being published (production) and the scholarly and critical responses to them (reception). The need to consider both aspects (production and reception) in such a review derives from the integral connection between the two areas in the functioning of the 'institution' of Canadian literature, in its broadest sense. The situation of the writers, the types of publications, the history of canonical inclusion (or exclusion), and the conceptualization of minority writers/texts within the literary institution generally cannot be separated from evaluation of scholarly activities and theoretical/critical approaches adopted towards the texts, and from questions such as who the scholars are, what they choose to do, and how they are supported.

I LITERARY AND CRITICAL OVERVIEW

To provide a complete list of Canadian ethnic minority writers (with related scholarly work and criticism) would be to put together a bibliography and not a survey. Indeed, even to list the Canadian groups from which these writers arise would be too long for this overview. What follows is thus highly selective, leaving out many writers and groups. Further, as is usual in any critical activity, the factors I have chosen to single out may be said to reflect the implied critical perspective that I bring to the subject. The general outline provided in this first section, therefore, underlies and correlates with the critical evaluative sketch in the second part on the current situation of Canadian ethnic minority writing and criticism.

The Question of Language

It is important to note at the outset that restricting an overview such as this one to minority writing in English alone is in significant ways artificial and distorting. Ethnic minority literature in languages other than English (or French) has existed in Canada for many years. The list of such literary productions should undoubtedly begin with the long tradition of Canadian Aboriginal oral literature, a body of material of increasing significance to current Aboriginal writers. German language writing has been documented to the eighteenth century (Tötösy 1989) and substantial collections have been noted for Canadian literary texts in 'Croatian, Czech, Estonian, German, Hungarian, Icelandic, Latvian, Polish, Russian, Slovak, Ukrainian and Yiddish' (Young 1982:105). To these should be added texts by writers more recently arrived in Canada (or from groups who have only begun to find expression) in languages such as Spanish, Chinese, Urdu, Hindi, and Punjabi (see Dimić 1989:573).

Yet these literary productions have largely been overlooked in Canadian criticism, in spite of the fact that they represent a substantial body of interesting literary material, and present both an experiential record central to the Canadian experience of the writers, the groups, and the country as a whole, and a basis of comparison with official-language minority and majority writing. Only a small number of these 'non-official language' writers have been translated into English and unfortunately, very little research and criticism has been published on them, especially in English. As noted below, however, some scholarly documentation and criticism is beginning to appear, if on a limited scale. I have tried to keep this body of literary material in mind here, even if the bulk of my comments derive from minority literature written and/or published in English. At the same time I am very much aware of the critical gap that I and other critics face in excluding, by default, most Canadian non-official language writing from the discussion. Canadian minority writing also occurs in French, of course, but I have included it only occasionally in this study, even when translated into English, since it will be dealt with elsewhere in this book.

Historical Perspective

Minority writing has been a factor long enough in Canadian literature for questions of generational continuity and other aspects of literary history to arise. In the larger social/literary context, early minority writers who succeeded in entering the Canadian literary scene can be said to have opened the way to others. The success in the 1920s and 1930s of writers such as Laura Salverson, Frederick Philip Grove, and A.M. Klein established the possibility of a minority perspective within Canadian literature and it is around these authors that the beginnings of scholarly research and criticism on Canadian minority writing can be traced. One can also refer to a continuity over generations for writers from a number of different groups. In Jewish-Canadian writing, for example, a poetry tradition can be traced from A.M. Klein to Irving Layton, Miriam Waddington, Leonard Cohen, and Seymour Mayne. And in prose, Mordecai Richler, Adele Wiseman, and Henry Kreisel are followed by writers such as Matt Cohen and J.J. Steinfeld.

Similar patterns can be noted in Icelandic-Canadian writers (from Laura Salverson to W.D. Valgardson, David Arnason, and Kristjana Gunnars), Hungarian-Canadian writers (John Marlyn to Gabriel Szohner and Stephen Vizinczey), Ukrainian-Canadian writers (Illia Kiriak and Vera Lysenko to Maara Haas, George Ryga, Andrew Suknaski, Ted Galay, and Janice Kulyk Keefer), or Mennonite-Canadian writers (Rudy Wiebe to Armin Wiebe, Patrick Friesen, Sandra Birdsell, Di Brandt,

Audrey Poetker, and David Waltner-Toews). A similar case could be made for a number of other groups as well. In many of these groups, it should be noted, writing in Canada in languages other than English (Yiddish, Icelandic, Hungarian, Ukrainian, German, etc.) often precedes or parallels these generational patterns and forms part of them. Little research has been done on these generational literary factors.

New Minority Voices

In the post-Second World War period, and especially from the late 1970s onwards, the number of Canadian minority writers increased dramatically, along with the range of groups represented. Italian-Canadian writing, for example, only began to make an impact with the publication of Pier Giorgio Di Cicco's anthology *Roman Candles* in 1978. Since then the number of Italian-Canadian writers has grown to include (among the better-known names): Mary Di Michele, Frank Paci, Mary Melfi, Antonio D'Alfonso, Marco Micone, Nino Ricci, C.D. Minni, Caterina Edwards, and Vittorio Rossi. A great many other European groups have also followed this post-war writing pattern, though not necessarily with the same impact as the larger Italian-Canadian group. Examples include Czech-Canadians Josef Škvorecký and Jan Drabek, Hungarian-Canadians George Jonas and Stephen Vizinczey, Dutch-Canadians Aritha Van Herk, Maria Jacobs, and Hugh Cook, Greek-Canadian Katherine Vlassie, German-Canadians Henry Beissel and Walter Bauer, and Finnish-Canadian Nancy Mattson. In the same period, non-European voices also began to be published in English more extensively than before. Latin American-Canadian writers can be exemplified by Chileans such as Jorge Etcheverry, Nain Nomez, and José Leandro Urbina or Argentinians such as Pablo Urbanyi. Arab-Canadian writers include Emily Nasrallah and Marwan Hassan; West Indian-Canadian writers include Austin Clarke, Marlene Nourbese Philip, Dionne Brand, Sam Selvon, Neil Bissoondath, and Cyril Dabydeen; East Asian-Canadian writers include Michael Ondaatje, Rienzi Crusz, Bharati Mukherjee, Uma Parameswaren, Rohinton Mistry, M.G. Vassanji, W.A. Shaheen and Nazneen Sadiq. Other Asian-Canadian voices to enter the literary field in recent years include Japanese-Canadian Joy Kogawa and Chinese-Canadians Sky Lee, Paul Yee, Jim Wong-Chu, and Yuen Chung Yip (Charles Jang).

In addition, writers from other long-established segments of Canadian society have begun to have a new literary impact: examples include Black Maritime writers such as Maxine Tynes and George Elliott Clarke and the large and growing group of Aboriginal writers in Canada: Lee Maracle, Jeannette Armstrong, Maria Campbell, Daniel David Moses, Tom King, Ruby Slipperjack, Tomson Highway, Beatrice Culleton and others. This brief list of groups and writers representing only a small sample of who has been published in recent years marks the increasing range and diversity of Canadian minority literature and poses at least two important questions: to what degree has Canadian criticism responded to these developments?; how has Canadian criticism altered its perspective of Canadian literature and of minority writing? I will try to assess both these questions later in this paper.

Production Characteristics

Minority writers can be found in almost all forms and genres within Canadian literature: poetry, drama, short story, novel, essay. Similarly, minority writers cover a wide range of regions, of styles (realism to postmodernism), and of thematic, political, and literary concerns. They are interested in 'ethnic minority' issues in varying ways and to varying degrees. Canadian ethnic minority writers, like other Canadian writers, are just as likely to be concerned with whatever writers everywhere address: personal questions, social issues (feminism, the environment, class, etc.), questions of identity or theology, questions of form and genre, the role of the writer, and so on. It is important to note this thematic and artistic diversity, in looking at the corpus, so as not to make (as some critics have) a priori limiting assumptions about what minority writing is as opposed to majority writing. Perhaps one noticeable factor in terms of production is that though some minority writers have been published by mainstream Canadian publishers such as Macmillan, Oxford, Penguin, Anansi, or McClelland & Stewart, most have been published by either regional or group-specific presses: NeWest, Turnstone, Ragweed, Cormorant, Guernica, TSAR, Williams-Wallace, Mosaic, Pemmican, Theytus, and many other even smaller presses. The implications of this factor will be examined later. A second very noticeable production factor is the sheer number of anthologies. Since 1971, anthologies have appeared for a broad range of individual Canadian ethnic minority groups (Italian-Canadian, Polish-Canadian, Dutch-Canadian, Chilean-Canadian, and so on), for various combined ethnic groupings (Black-Canadian, Caribbean-Canadian, Asian-Canadian, Arab-Canadian, Canadian Native, etc.), and in general collections of minority writing (e.g., Hutcheon & Richmond 1990) or in special issues of some journals (e.g., *Canadian Fiction Magazine* 1976, 1980; *Descant* 1987; *Prairie Fire* 1984; *The Canadian Journal of Native Studies* 1985; and *The Toronto South Asian Review* 1983, 1986). This notable trend to anthologize also deserves comment.

Scholarly (Institutional) Activities

Assessing the scholarly and critical activities surrounding Canadian ethnic minority literature needs to be done in relation to Canadian literary criticism generally and, in particular, in relation to the critical terms of reference used in the assessment of the dominant majority literary culture in Canada. A handy starting point, therefore, might be Robert Lecker's recent assessment of 'the canonization of Canadian literature' and the list of 'canon objects associated with the Canadian literature industry' (1990a:658) that are employed by Lecker and Frank Davey in their discussion in that same volume of *Critical Inquiry*. (Interestingly, neither critic takes minority writing much into account in this 'canonical' discussion of the Canadian canon, a tendency repeated in most of the contributions to Lecker's edited collection of essays [1991] on the same topic.) Yet the list of 'canon objects' can usefully be applied to the case of Canadian ethnic minority writing as well. The result is a comparable way of assessing the canonical situation of that body of literature and the scholarly activities associated with it. What, then, is this canonical situation?

Beginning with *funding*, it can be noted that SSHRCC, the Secretary of State for Multiculturalism, the Canada Council, other governmental agencies, universities, and organizations have all provided support both for writers and for scholarly activities related to them. Minority writers have been appointed writers in residence, have won various *awards* including Governor General's awards (e.g., Salverson, Grove, Klein, Richler, Ondaatje, Škvorecký, Ricci), or have been recognized in other ways. A number of *conferences* have been held on the writing of different ethnic minority groups (e.g., Italian-Canadian, Mennonite-Canadian, Canadian Native, Urdu language and literature). These conferences have helped to raise issues (literary and otherwise) relevant to these specific groups, increased the sense of group affiliation and group problems, fostered recognition of the writers in the larger Canadian community, and brought into consideration issues of the larger Canadian context. Other conferences have focused on intercultural and minority/majority issues. Examples include the Edmonton 'Identifications' Conference in 1982, the

Ottawa Conference on Language, Culture and Literary Identity in Canada in 1984, and the Edmonton Conference on Literatures of Lesser Diffusion in 1988. (For published versions, see Balan 1982, Bumsted 1987, and Pivato 1989.) These conferences brought together scholars and writers with different ethnic perspectives and from different parts of Canada. The resulting discussions provided a more general context (theoretical, social, literary) for individual writer/group experiences and allowed larger patterns and shared concerns to be exposed. In addition, other conferences in recent years have been focussed in part on ethnicity and minority literature (e.g., Association of Canadian Teachers of English [ACUTE], Association for Canadian and Quebec Literatures [ACQL], literary sections of the Canadian Ethnic Studies Association [CESA]).

The list of institutional 'products' in the ethnic minority literary critical field is again broad and difficult to cover here. *Anthologies* can be mentioned and, as noted earlier, are quite widespread. A number of *bibliographies* focused on ethnic minority writing have also been published in recent years. The most comprehensive is that of Miska (1990), an updated version of his useful 1980 work. This bibliography covers '5500 references' to '65 nationality groups in more than 70 languages' (vii) and is thus a particularly valuable source of information on other language minority writers and critics. Unfortunately, it is also severely limited in that its coverage is restricted (with the exception of Canadian Natives) to the immigrant generation of minority writers. Useful group bibliographies also exist for some individual groups (e.g., Inuit), in some of the literary histories or group critical books listed below, and, for some of the more established non-official language groups (e.g., Ukrainian-Canadian). Of special note are the bibliographical essays produced under the general editorship of Michael Batts for Multiculturalism Canada in 1988 on Hispanic, Black, Urdu, Hungarian, Polish, Italian, and South Asian-Canadian writers (see also Batts 1991). Another useful source is the literature section of *Canadian Ethnic Studies* bibliographies, which regularly update the initial bibliographical studies (on various groups) done in that journal in 1969 and 1970. In addition, extensive bibliographical entries on individual minority writers who have made their way into the 'central' Canadian canon (e.g., Richler, Ondaatje, Cohen, Grove) can be found in mainstream Canadian bibliographies such as *The Annotated Bibliography of Canada's Major Authors* (Lecker & David 1979–). The large body of less recognized minority writers, however, is represented only to a very limited extent in these general bibliographies.

Literary histories exist for some ethnic minority literatures written in languages other than English or French (e.g., Ukrainian, Hungarian), in the essays that accompany some of the Multiculturalism bibliographies referred to above, and in some of the critical group studies listed below. Brief literary histories of minority writing published in English or of Canadian ethnic minority writing in general can also be found in a number of overview essays or survey articles. In this category might be cited a number of the articles in Balan (1982) and Vassanji (1985), the Palmer and Rasporich entry in *The Canadian Encyclopedia* (1985), some of the Multiculturalism bibliographies once again, essays in special journal issues (e.g., Pivato 1989), the 'Arts and Cultures' section of Volume IV of the Bilingualism and Biculturalism Report (1969), and other scattered articles. General Canadian literary histories (e.g., Klinck & New [1965–90], Keith [1985]) have tended to include only a small selection of Canadian minority writers, have tended to treat these within 'mainstream' categories only (region, genre, form, theoretical trends, etc.), and have ignored or given much less weight to other writers who do not fit the categories, or, of course, who write in other languages (cf. Pivato 1985; Batts 1987). Though there is somewhat more recognition of the presence and impact of ethnicity in the recent essays in Volume 4 (1990) of Klinck and New (see especially the essays by Ricou, Jackel, Hutcheon, Stratford, and Cameron) and in recent articles by Sutherland (1985) and New (1990), the fundamental marginalization of minority writers cannot be said to have changed, and their presence has neither altered the literary historical categories nor fostered their particular concerns. As yet, no book-length literary history of Canadian ethnic minority literature has been written.

The importance of *translations* as a scholarly category for ethnic minority writing should also be noted. As mentioned earlier, the bulk of other language minority writing is still untranslated and mostly unknown to the broader Canadian readership (cf. Young 1982). The number of writers and texts in English translation is growing, however, and this factor alone promises to challenge a number of accepted Canadian literary categories and ultimately to transform the broader perception of the corpus of minority writing. Stratford's discussion of translation (1990) referred to above, for example, focuses on English and French but ends by noting briefly the impact of other languages in this area. The awarding of the 1984 Governor General's Award for Škvorecký's novel *The Engineer of Human Souls* (written in Czech and translated into English) is another important sign of this changing attitude to the place of translations in the canon. Other translations of note include special issues of journals (e.g., *Canadian Fiction Magazine* 1976, 1980), translated anthologies (including Canadian Native writers) and translated works of individual writers (in addition to Škvorecký) such as George Faludy, Waclaw Iwaniuk, Walter Bauer, Rochel Korn, Illia Kiriak, Maria Ardizzi, Yuen Chung Yip, Marco Micone, Emile Ollivier, and Dany Laferrière. To date no bibliography dedicated to translations of Canadian ethnic minority writing has been put together, though many items are listed in Miska (1990) and the other bibliographical sources mentioned above.

Interviews with minority writers have been published in magazines and journals of all types, in general and regional collections of Canadian writers, and in a few collections devoted specifically to minority writers. These interviews are particularly useful since biographical information on many minority writers is often difficult to come by. *Essays* by minority writers are also available in magazines and journals, in general Canadian collections (especially canonical minority writers) in regional collections, or occasionally even on an individual basis (e.g., Grove, Klein, Richler, Wiebe, Škvorecký). These essays cover a wide variety of topics and provide a broad cultural context for critical treatment of the writers and of other general issues.

Finally, *biographies, films,* and *reference guides* should be mentioned as additional institutional forms of scholarly activity related to minority writing. In all these categories, primarily canonized writers (e.g., Grove, Klein, Layton) have been the subject. One highly important institutional development in the field of ethnic minority literature has been the appearance of *journals* that specialize in the literature of particular ethnic groups or where literary study on a group basis is frequent. Examples include *The Toronto South Asian Review* (which has provided an important forum for a very broad range of writers and critics), *Italian Canadiana, Urdu Canada, The Canadian Journal of Native Studies,* and the *Journal of Mennonite Studies.* In addition, there have been special issues of 'mainstream' or other Canadian journals devoted to specific groups of writers or to ethnic minority writing generally (e.g., *Canadian Literature* 1985, 1990, *Canadian Ethnic Studies* 1982, *Canadian Review of Comparative Literature* 1989, and *Prairie Fire* 1984). Together with the group-specific journals, a number of *publishing houses* specializing in or with particular interests in minority literature have also appeared in recent years (e.g., Williams-Wallace, Guernica, TSAR, Pemmican, Theytus, etc.). As noted earlier, these publishers have provided an important outlet for minority writers who might otherwise not have been published by mainstream

Canadian presses. They have also published a disproportionate number of the bibliographies, anthologies, and collections of critical essays.

It would be highly desirable in this overview of scholarly and institutional activity related to Canadian minority writing to be able to provide an assessment of the *teaching* and curricular development of minority texts in Canadian universities. Unfortunately, little critical attention has been devoted to the study of Canadian university curricula generally, not to mention the specific cases of English (and other language) departments, and the more detailed areas of Canadian literature or Canadian minority texts. Broader analyses, of the type done by Price (1984) on Native studies, for example, are simply not available on minority literature. All I can offer here is my own admittedly limited impression that the teaching of minority texts, especially those not yet entered into the canon, has been relatively rare in the past but is now beginning to occur more frequently, though not in proportion to what is available.

Some new authors, particularly where they can be correlated with regional topics (e.g., Prairie writers), 'new canonical' critical trends (e.g., Kogawa and feminism or post-colonialism), or form studies (Birdsell, Valgardson, and the short story) have been added to a number of courses. This development is, of course, to be welcomed, for as noted earlier, minority writers, like other writers, encompass many different factors and deserve to be studied in many different contexts. At the same time, the number of courses devoted to minority writing as such, or where minority writers form a significant part of the course content is undoubtedly still small. Similarly, my impression is that the number of *theses* devoted to non-canonical minority writers is also relatively small, though perhaps growing in recent years, especially in feminist and post-colonial studies. It is extremely difficult to generalize in this area since no comprehensive study of the relevant data has been completed. I will be returning to these issues in the second part of this paper.

Criticism

Critical *books* or *collections* of articles have appeared on a number of *individual* minority writers but the list is relatively short and confined primarily to those minority writers accepted into the canon. Examples include Grove, Richler, Klein, Cohen, Layton, Clarke, Wiebe, Ondaatje, and Škvorecký. It is difficult to generalize about these studies, since the critics' interests tend to reflect date of writing, theoretical assumptions, academic situation, and other contingencies. As a whole, however, these critical books provide a fascinating map of dominant Canadian critical attitudes and assumptions and help to explain why and how these particular minority writers have been accepted into the canon. As such, they provide a basis for studying important issues regarding the literary institution in Canada and the place of ethnic minority writing within it. In addition, some recent book-length studies (e.g., Brown 1989 on Clarke) document the rising challenge of new minority voices and provide alternative perspectives on minority Canadian experience and the canon of Canadian literature. To my knowledge, no evaluative study of this question has yet been undertaken on this corpus.

Critical books and collections of articles (including the conference proceedings mentioned earlier) have also been published on a number of *groups* of writers. These collections, perhaps because of their community focus, have primarily been written or put together by scholars from within the particular groups, have departed more markedly from dominant critical assumptions, and have been more concerned with internal group dynamics and the bases of group cohesion, as well as with relations to the larger Canadian literary/social scene. Good examples are the Italian-Canadian collections by Pivato (1985) and Minni and Ciampolini (1990), the critical anthology on German-speaking writers by Riedel (1984), the collection on Urdu language and literature in Canada by Shaheen, Nasim, and Mirza (1988), and the South Asian-Canadian critical anthology by Vassanji (1985). In contrast, the books or collections on Canadian Native writers, in spite of the presence of a number of Native critics (e.g., King), still seem to be dominated by out-group critics (see, for example, the volumes by Petrone 1990, McGrath 1984, King, Calver & Hoy 1987, and the special issue of *Canadian Literature* 1990). The perspective of these books tends to reflect the sympathetic views of the outsider or the centrality of categories and questions relevant to majority ethnicity (e.g., 'the image of the Indian' in English-Canadian writing). See below for further discussion. The book by Greenstein (1989) on Jewish-Canadian literature is almost alone as an example of a single critic's book-length analysis of Canadian writers from one ethnic grouping, and is impressive as well in its attempt to incorporate into the analysis the author's perspectives on both Jewish historical and intellectual traditions and modern critical and theoretical trends.

A number of books, collections of articles, or conference proceedings have also been published on various aspects of minority writing in general. The Balan (1982), *Canadian Ethnic Studies* special issue (1982), *Canadian Literature* supplement (Bumsted 1987), and Pivato (1989) collections, for example, contain articles on writers from a number of different ethnic groups, including some writing in languages other than English. These collections also include general papers on literary history (Batts 1987) or on different theoretical issues (e.g., Kreisel 1982; Dimić 1989; Loriggio 1989; Padolsky 1989). In addition, Dahlie's book (1986) on Canadian exile literature treats a number of minority writers in a broader Canadian context, Craig's book (1987) examines 'racial attitudes' in English-Canadian fiction, including a number of minority writers, and Mukherjee's book (1988) provides a challenging 'oppositional' perspective on 'Third World' writers in Canada, and on universalist and ideological assumptions within the dominant Canadian literary critical establishment. Finally, Itwaru's recent study (1990) of Canadian immigrant writing analyzes an unusual (and interesting) combination of writers (minority and majority) in the context of multiculturalism, national mythmaking and the 'invention of Canada.'

Articles and book reviews on individual minority writers have also appeared in a broad range of journals, magazines, newspapers, and review outlets. It is difficult to evaluate the range, approach, and coverage of these articles since comprehensive bibliographies in the field, as noted earlier, are not available and no general studies have been done. My impression, based on available bibliographies and my own sampling of the journals, is that established (and 'accepted') minority writers have attracted the bulk of critical attention. Further, book reviews are far more numerous and more widely distributed than articles. The Miska (1990) entries on Italian-Canadian writers, for example, reveal a considerable number of reviews but very few critical articles, even on important writers like Frank Paci, Mary Di Michele, or Pier Giorgio Di Cicco. At the same time, articles by critics interested in current critical approaches (e.g., post-colonialism, post-modernism, feminism) are beginning to appear, making the writers they treat more visible than has been the case. A figure of note in this respect is Japanese-Canadian writer Joy Kogawa, who has attracted more than a dozen critical articles of this sort. A number of articles have also appeared on groups of writers (see the literary histories section above for examples) or on a comparative (e.g., post-colonial) basis. These articles broaden the literary, social, and historical context in which individual minority writers have been considered and tend to treat a wider range of writers than those in the canon. The number and coverage of these articles, however, remain limited, and research opportunities for these kinds of comparative and group studies remain high.

Individual articles on issues related to ethnic minority literature in general have also appeared in journals, collections of articles, books with primarily other focuses, and introductions. Though small in number as yet, these articles are important since (together with the generalist books listed earlier) they help to define the nature and corpus of Canadian minority writing, to raise the issues which relate to this writing, and to suggest theoretical and critical frameworks for approaching the field. Early examples include Mandel's study (1977) of psychological doubleness and the 'ethnic voice' in Canadian writing, Kreisel's assessment (1982) of the 'Ethnic Writer in Canada,' and Blodgett's study (1982) of 'fictions of ethnicity.' In a similar vein, Kroetsch (1985) has examined a 'grammar' of ethnicity in selected writers and Palmer (1987, 1989, 1991) has looked for dominant patterns in minority writing that might be characterized as 'ethnic voice.' From another perspective, Pivato (1985) has assessed the dominant Canadian perception of minority writing, Padolsky (1986–7, 1989, 1990, 1991) has attempted to establish an interdisciplinary, pluralistic and comparative framework for minority writing, Kroller (1989) has assessed the place of minority writers in a comparative Canadian context, Karrer and Lutz (1990) have looked at minority writing in a North American context, and Hutcheon (1988, 1991) has examined minority writers in the context of multiculturalism, feminism, and postmodernism. Loriggio (1987, 1989), Dimić (1989), Godard (1990), and Blodgett (1990) have tried to relate various aspects of minority literature to a number of different European theoretical perspectives. One noticeable feature is that a number of these general articles have appeared in international journals or in books published outside of Canada. The significance of this fact (see discussion of this point in the second part below) can be related to the intercultural aspects of minority writing as well as to the importance of issues of Canadian multiculturalism and pluralism in an international context.

II CRITICAL EVALUATION

Questions of the Canon and Other Critical Issues

The survey of the literature, scholarly activities, and critical research covered in the first part of this paper raised as an underlying issue the question of the 'canon' within the institution of Canadian literature. This question arises because Canadian ethnic minority literature is perceived by many writers and critics to be in an unequal situation relative to

Canadian majority literature, of not being sufficiently represented in canonical areas, or of not being perceived in appropriate ways. As such, canonical issues in literature are closely connected to social and instrumental questions and practices in other domains – economic, political, social. Analyses of canonical issues for ethnic minority literature thus form part of the evaluation of Canadian social attitudes and practices related to the policy of multiculturalism and to other issues regarding Canada's pluralistic society. Just as a feminist perspective on Canadian literature might question whether female authors have been published, distributed, read, taught, recognized, and interpreted on the basis of gender equality and from unbiased or appropriate perspectives, so an ethnic minority perspective might ask whether ethnic minority writers are being published in sufficient numbers, by the same presses as majority writers, with the same distribution practices; whether they are being supported and recognized in relation to their abilities; whether they are being taught in Canadian universities to an appropriate degree and in appropriate ways; whether students are being encouraged to carry out research on them; whether scholars are writing on them (and in appropriate ways); whether these scholars are being given access to established journals, are being funded and rewarded in normal ways, and so on. As my phrasing suggests, these questions all foreground the issue of what is 'appropriate' and raise, among other things, problems such as the universality of standards in literature and the desirability or inevitability of having canons.

These are not just questions of personal preference. Some minority writers (and critics), for example, might 'prefer' to be judged strictly as 'writers' (or critics) without regard for the possibility of inherent biases on the basis of ethnicity or minority status. Yet the assumption of or preference for universality unfortunately does not preclude the possibility that, in social terms, biases on the basis of ethnicity and minority status (gender or other grounds) may be very much in play. The commentary which follows attempts to evaluate this situation though my analysis is again less thorough than I might wish, since evidence on these institutional issues has not been systematically collected and analyzed in the critical literature.

At the very least, however, the first part of this paper alone would suggest that ethnicity and minority status are and have been salient factors in the establishment and maintenance of a dominant canon in Canadian literature. It therefore seems relevant to consider the degree to which minority writing has been affected by canonical exclusion, ways in which it has been included, and whether the canonical situation of minority writing/criticism is now changing. The survey of the literature above has shown that some minority writers have been published and recognized for many years in Canada, that generational literary traditions have even succeeded in being established for some groups, that many new writers (and groups) are achieving voice, that some minority writers writing and publishing in other languages are now being translated and recognized, that critical/institutional canon-supporting scholarly activity is being carried out in a great many areas (such as bibliographies, anthologies, conferences, articles, books, journals), and that the impact of minority writing and its criticism within the canon has been increasing in recent years.

At the same time, careful analysis of the details of these developments casts some doubt on the nature of the inroads made by minority texts and writers into the Canadian canon. As suggested above, many minority writers are still being published, individually or in anthologies, in group-specific journals or by group-run, small, or regional presses. The same is true for a great many of the works of scholarship and criticism on them. (Thus, for example, three of the critical books referred to earlier – Pivato, Mukherjee, and Itwaru – were written by minority critics and published by minority-oriented presses – Guernica, Williams-Wallace, and TSAR.) If it is true, as Barbara Herrnstein Smith (1983) argues, that publications, anthologies, critiques, and other institutional 'products' help to produce literary value and may be taken (as Knowles 1991 does for Canadian drama) as indicators of canonical inclusion, it is equally true that this is primarily the case for 'mainstream' institutional production. In this sense, it is legitimate to ask, for example, whether the proliferation of minority anthologies noted earlier signifies canonical value or whether it marks the difficulty individual minority writers have in getting published other than in group anthologies. Further, production conditions on the margins, which is where much minority writing and criticism can be found, tend to entail 'marginal' problems: distribution of texts is often difficult, reviews are fewer and less prominent, libraries are less likely to carry texts, publishing houses are less able to reprint them, teachers less likely to teach them, students to write theses on them, critics less likely to find them, write on them, and be published.

I am aware that some minority writers have overcome these problems and that many new and even some established Canadian majority writers share these difficulties. But the situation for minority writers is on the whole noticeably worse in that control of the main production and

reception institutions (journals, publishing houses, university departments, libraries, awards committees, learned societies) still rests with
those who reflect the dominant discourse of the traditional canon in
Canadian literature (cf. the essays in Lecker 1991). Even assuming a
universal generosity and openness to new ideas, topics and forms on the
part of this gatekeeping establishment, it is difficult not to conclude that
there is some impact for minority writing and criticism, whether in the
difficulty in being published, in attracting peer attention, or in how texts
may be perceived and treated. To quote Lorris Elliott on Canadian Black
writing (1988:4–5): 'Despite the outbursts of literary activity by Blacks in
Canada in the 1970s, comparatively little of the work produced has been
published by recognised Canadian publishers or in recognised journals
... so that the question arises of possible discrimination by Canadian
publishers against Black writers ... [Furthermore] library holdings of
Black Canadian literature are so poor ... that there is apparently no place
in the classification systems employed under which such literature might
be distinguished. This makes it very difficult for those ... that have
expressed a desire for information on Black writing in Canada to obtain
the necessary works for their curricula.' Comprehensive study of
systemic factors such as these has not been carried out but additional
evidence for this reading of the situation of minority writing (and
criticism) can be found, to list just a few more examples, in statements
such as that of Bharati Mukherjee in her introduction to *Darkness*, in the
controversy over minority writing at the PEN conference in Toronto in
1989 (see Philip 1990), in the analyses of literary history (Batts 1987),
established literary frameworks (Pivato 1985; Padolsky 1986–7), canons
(Knowles 1991), and discussions of Mukherjee (1988) and Itwaru (1990).

A second significant area in the critical evaluation of Canadian ethnic
minority literature is the situation of minority writers and minority
topics that *have* been included within the canon. Again, there is not much
published analysis in this area but some generalizations could probably
be made (with appropriate reservations). The list of established minority
writers is relatively short, and an incommensurate percentage of criticism has addressed this short list. Furthermore, much of the criticism of
canonized minority writers has treated them in relation to 'mainstream'
categories: Grove and Wiebe as Prairie writers, Klein and Layton as
modernist poets, Ondaatje and Cohen as post-modern writers. Other
minority writers seem to function within the canon as 'token' immigrant
or 'ethnic' writers (e.g., Laura Salverson, John Marlyn, Adele Wiseman),
and often within the framework of a 'mainstream' view or thesis of

Canadian literature (e.g., 'survival,' Atwood 1972; the 'mainstream,' Sutherland 1985).

What this means is that much of the criticism of minority writing has tended to generalize or universalize the writing, looking at characteristics that derive from or relate to the dominant cultural mythology. As Woodcock put it, writing on Mordecai Richler in 1971 (and this approach is still undoubtedly widely shared), the importance of the Jewish contribution to Canadian literature is that Jewish writers 'have revealed with a peculiar force and sensitivity the tensions that are characteristic of Canadian life and particularly Canadian urban life. This, it seems evident, is because the themes of which they treat with such a complex heritage of experience, the themes of isolation and division, are also the themes from which it is difficult for any writer in Canada to escape' (20–1). Or as Arun Mukherjee stated in her broader analysis of Western criticism and Third World writers: 'Western critics have been so busy proving the universality of texts that they have no time for dealing with the specificity of these texts' (1988:13). As a result, group-specific issues and social community concerns (discrimination, racism, social inequality, and other issues of ethnicity, class and gender) have until recently tended to be ignored or downplayed in criticism of minority writers. Klein's poems on French Canada or poetic art are 'mainstream' and important; his poems on 'Jewish' themes are much less likely, I suspect, to be taught in a Canadian university classroom.

A further consequence of this perspective is that writers who fit the dominant ideological mythology (and do not challenge it) tend to be accepted more easily into the critical environment than those who do not. This, too, Mukherjee (1988) has argued with reference to Ondaatje and Bissoondath. Further, when some 'ethnic' writers fill the function within the critical framework as 'tokens' of themes such as 'the immigrant experience,' writers from other groups or even from the same group tend to be regarded as further tokens of the same theme and are much less likely to be welcomed. Who needs 17 other Mennonite-Canadian writers when there is Rudy Wiebe? This too, of course, is a form of avoidance of the 'specificity of texts' but it is undoubtedly a factor in the critical reception of many new minority writers.

Finally, there is the case of Canadian Native writers, topics, and criticism. As I noted earlier, mainstream presses and critics seem to be more inclined to publish anthologies and critical studies on Canadian Native topics than in the case of non-Native minority groups. Paradoxically, however, this seemingly contradictory phenomenon of growing (dominant) canonical interest in and sympathy for Native writing actually constitutes a special case of the problem of absorption into dominant categories discussed above. The problem – the core issue in the 'appropriation debate' – is who will speak for Canadian Native peoples and how. As Emma LaRoque (1975:8) put it: 'One of the most severe problems the Native person is faced with today is that he is defined outside himself.' Or as Lenore Keeshig-Tobias (1988) put it even more passionately: 'Who knows best how to present the Native perspective? ... Well, today it seems, there's a host of professionals dealing with the printed word (editors, publishers, producers, directors, writers, story-tellers, journalists), all non-Native, who have taken over the work of the missionaries and the Indian agent. They now know best how to present the Native perspective, never dreaming, of course, it is basically their own perspective ...'

Finally, I would like to assess probable future directions in research on Canadian ethnic minority writing and some problem areas that may lie ahead. In recent years, as the overview in the first part of this paper has shown, new critical approaches and new theoretical developments have led to an increase of critical attention to both established and newer minority writers. The conferences, collections of articles, and books discussed above suggest that future criticism of Canadian minority literature will increasingly reflect these new theoretical developments and the growing critical interest in post-colonial, post-modern, and feminist perspectives. Older critical approaches such as Atwood's discussion of immigrant writers (1972) or Woodcock's discussion of Richler (1971) quoted above are likely to be replaced by approaches such as Mukherjee's discussion of South Asian-Canadian writers or Green-stein's discussion of Jewish-Canadian writers. Yet this does not necessarily mean that criticism of Canadian minority literature will enter fully and appropriately into the literary institution in the near future. At the moment, critics of minority writing are still relatively few, and tend to have minority backgrounds themselves. Further, the new approaches raise a number of new problems as well.

If new perspectives have challenged (to some extent) the traditional canon in Canadian literature, they have also brought with them new sets of privileged assumptions and interests which may or may not fit the cases of all minority writers. An interest in post-modern writing, for example, raises certain minority writers (such as Cohen, Ondaatje, and Gunnars) to critical centrality. But what then happens (critically) to those minority writers who choose (perhaps from a desire for closer communal ties to a traditional community readership; cf. Valgardson 1979) to continue working within a realist tradition of writing? Does the rise of feminism and post-modernism explain the new interest in Gunnars or Di Michele and the relative lack of interest in Valgardson or Di Cicco? What happens when whole groups of minority writers do not illustrate topics of current critical interest? Linda Hutcheon, for example, notes (1991) that Italian-Canadian writers, unlike the other writers she addresses, do not make use of the post-modern irony that is her focus. Will this mean critical oblivion for these kinds of writers?

Second, there is the problem of adaptation to the Canadian context. The theoretical models and feminist or post-colonial focuses currently gaining favour in Canadian criticism have for the most part been developed in European, American, or other international contexts. For this reason they no doubt bring to bear on Canadian topics a considerable freshness of analysis and explanatory power. At the same time, they no doubt also require adaptation and development within Canadian experience. Unless the definitions, concepts, and critical frameworks underlying these approaches are adapted in the light of 'local' Canadian experience, the same problems of distortion, 'appropriation,' and exclusion found in the older canonical approaches are likely to reappear. It is thus not just legitimate but essential to ask whether the new literary critical models are being applied with a full awareness of the complexity and diversity of Canadian minority writing and its various literary traditions, whether these models are taking into account the large body of Canadian work available in other disciplines on the social, psychological, and historical contexts of minority ethnicity in Canada, or whether these models being applied top-down, in a distant, ethnocentric, or purely formal way. Are, for example, gender or post-colonial studies on Canadian minority writers taking into account the impact of ethnicity in the Canadian (as opposed to other countries) context for both male and female writers from diverse cultural backgrounds and from groups with different historical and social experiences? The answers to questions such as these are not yet clear but they may very well determine the future place of minority writing in Canadian literature and the nature of the research on it in the years to come.

The need to adapt critical approaches to the specificity of the Canadian context does not, however, mean excluding broader cross-cultural or international perspectives. As a final point in this section, therefore, I would like to return to the intercultural, international, and multilinguistic aspects of Canadian minority writing. Canadian minority writing, whether in English or in other languages, derives from and relates to diverse and specific literary, linguistic, and social histories and traditions. This diversity is manifested within the history and geography of Canadian group experience. As one example, it is worth recalling that many minority literatures (Native, Italian, Arab, Jewish, Black) exist in Canada in both official languages and other languages and/or dialects as well.

In addition, for many non-Native minority writers, this diversity is reflected internationally, since the complex world of the old ethnicity, current relations with ancestral homelands (where applicable), and other intercultural and intertextual factors all form part of the current cultural environment for these Canadian writers. This intercultural complexity helps explain the internationalization (Germany, Italy, Scandinavia, Japan, United States) of Canadian literature (and indeed of Canadian studies) and is reflected in the international publications on Canadian minority writing noted in part one. What these factors add up to is a reminder that critical work on Canadian minority writing needs to consider both Canadian and old ethnicity contexts and that the salience and specificity of each context needs to be evaluated in the individual cases being examined. The critical reception of writers such as Škvorecký, Mistry, Ricci, and others suggests that to some extent this is beginning to happen and that some 'internationally' connected Canadian writing is being recognized (though this may not be the general situation) as long as it is available in English. But considerably more critical study needs to be devoted to these intercultural, 'transcultural,' and multilinguistic issues in Canadian minority writing. The case for research into non-English Canadian writing is particularly clear. As the Miska bibliography (1990) indicates, some research on Canadian literature written in the non-official languages does exist, but it is doubtful that it is being widely read or taken into account in Canadian literature.

At the same time, my impression is that too much of this research reflects only the particular linguistic and cultural contexts of the individual groups being studied and that not enough attention is being given to comparative questions, to Canadian writing in other languages or even to the 'mainstream' (i.e. English and French) literary cultures. The difficulty here is, of course, the barrier of language, but there are also attitudinal barriers that need to be addressed. Researchers in all language groupings need to be more aware of the potential relevance of work being done in the different groups, given the shared commonality of minority experience (literary and social) in the broader Canadian context. On the other hand, the idea that Canadian literature can only be written in English or French, that 'a Syrian writing about Mount Royal in Arabic is creating Arabic literature; a Syrian writing about Mount Royal in English or French is creating Canadian literature' (quoted in Pivato 1985:29) – has to give way to a broader, more pluralistic view of Canadian literature. Neither assimilation (denying the specificity of diverse Canadian literary and social experiences) nor ghettoization (denying the relationships and commonalities of those experiences) seem to me to be suitable research attitudes within Canadian literature. Research strategies and policies based on such limiting attitudes seem particularly inappropriate for Canadian minority writing and criticism. Needless to say, the importance of translation (in as many directions as possible, and for criticism as well as for primary texts) cannot be stressed too much as a means of changing these attitudes.

Research Needs and Policy Implications

By way of conclusion, I would like to summarize the research needs outlined in the sections above, and, to encourage discussion of what can be done to improve the situation of minority writing and criticism, to suggest some of the policy implications that seem to arise. As noted at the outset, Canadian minority writers are a growing presence within Canadian literature and scholarly activities, institutional support, and basic critical research have begun to reflect this fact. Nevertheless, as a group, they are not yet an established part of the Canadian canon, and there seem to be a number of obstacles that need to be overcome before they will be able to receive critical and institutional attention in ways that seem appropriate in the pluralistic society that Canada has become. New critical trends and approaches have opened up the Canadian canon in recent years, but minority writing and the Canadian context have not been seminal to these developments and adjustments no doubt need to be made. At the same time, insufficient attention has been given to comparative (including minority-majority) approaches, intercultural factors, and non-official language writing. Many individual minority writers are still not being published by mainstream presses, and much essential scholarly and critical work remains to be done. These include:
- more critical analyses of all kinds (articles, books, conferences) for the many outstanding minority writers who have as yet attracted little critical attention, for groups of writers, and for the field as a whole;
- bibliographical work at the individual, group, and general levels, particularly for second-plus generations of minority writers;

- literary histories for many groups, for texts in both official and non-official languages, and for the field as a whole;
- theoretical adaptation and integration of new critical frameworks for Canadian ethnic minority writing;
- the inclusion of more minority writers into university curricula, in undergraduate, graduate, and thesis areas;
- additional study of the institutional aspects of Canadian literature in order to evaluate better the situation of minority writing and criticism;
- more comparative (majority-minority; minority-minority; Canadian-international), interdisciplinary, and intercultural study; and
- more translation, dissemination, and cross-linguistic study of both non-official and official minority writing and criticism.

As far as *policy implications* are concerned, one corollary of this analysis is that it seems to justify, as a counterbalance to the inherent institutional biases against which minority writing and criticism operate, continuation of existing policies of governmental support (for minority writers, presses, journals, conferences, research projects) in order to supplement production and reception of minority literature within mainstream literary institutions, help legitimize that literature, and strengthen the case for its inclusion in appropriate ways within the canon. The assumptions here, of course (perhaps big assumptions), are that this governmental support is not itself affected by inherent dominant biases (or political pressures) and that such support functions effectively to counterbalance rather than isolate minority writing and criticism. Ideally, of course, Canadian ethnic minority literature simply needs to be fully integrated in every way into the institution of Canadian literature.

Specific policy implications that follow from the research and institutional needs listed above may be summarized as follows:

- there is a continued need for support for minority writers by funding agencies as a means of legitimizing, publishing, and encouraging critical recognition;
- there is also a continued need for support for the scholarly, institutional, and critical work that needs to be carried out on Canadian minority writing;
- there must be a re-examination of the governmental understanding and implementation of multicultural policy to (a) reflect majority ethnicity in a pluralistic framework and (b) to work towards integrating the cultural aspects of Canadian minority ethnicity within existing institutional structures from which they have been excluded;
- implementation of policy initiatives in the literary area (perhaps on

the model of already existing 'chairs of ethnic studies') that would encourage the Canadianization of research and curricula in university language and literature departments and related institutional activities (e.g., journals), the natural homes (because of linguistic and cultural knowledge) of much of the needed research on Canadian non-official language writing and criticism; and
– there must be institutional encouragement of interdisciplinary, multidisciplinary, and intercultural forms of scholarly, institutional, and critical activity in the field of Canadian ethnic minority literature.

REFERENCES

Atwood, M. (1972). *Survival*. Toronto: Anansi
Balan, J. (ed.) (1982). *Identifications: Ethnicity and the writer in Canada*. Edmonton: Canadian Institute of Ukrainian Studies, University of Alberta
Batts, M. (1987). Literary history and national identity. In J.M. Bumsted (ed.), A/Part: Papers from the 1984 Ottawa conference on Language, Culture and Literary Identity in Canada (pp 104–10). *Canadian Literature*. Supplement No. 1
– (1991). 'Pilot' bibliographies of Canadian ethnic literature (German, Hungarian, Italian, Polish, Spanish). *Canadian Ethnic Studies*, 23(1):97–103
Blodgett, E.D. (1982). *Configurations: Essays on Canadian literatures*. Toronto: ECW Press
– (1990). Ethnic writing in Canadian literature as paratext. *Signature*, 3:13–27
Brown, L.W. (1989). *El Dorado and paradise: Canada and the Caribbean in Austin Clarke's fiction*. Parkersburg, IA: Caribbean Books
Bumsted, J.M. (ed.) (1987). A/Part: Papers from the 1984 Ottawa Conference on Language, Culture and Literary Identity in Canada. *Canadian Literature*. Supplement No. 1
Craig, T. (1987). *Racial attitudes in English-Canadian fiction 1905–1980*. Waterloo: Wilfrid Laurier University Press
Dahlie, H. (1986). *Varieties of exile: The Canadian experience*. Vancouver: UBC Press
Davey, F. (1990). Critical response I, Canadian canons. *Critical Inquiry*, 16(3): 672–81
Dimić, M.V. (1989). Canadian literatures of lesser diffusion: Observations from a systemic standpoint. *Canadian Review of Comparative Literature*, 16(3–4): 565–74
Elliott, L. (1988). *Literary writing by Blacks in Canada: A preliminary survey*. M. Batts (ed.). Ottawa: Multiculturalism and Citizenship Canada

Godard, B. (1990). The discourse of the other: Canadian literature and the question of ethnicity. *The Massachusetts Review, 31*(1–2):153–84

Greenstein, M. (1989). *Third solitudes: Tradition and discontinuity in Jewish-Canadian literature.* Kingston: McGill-Queen's University Press

Hutcheon, L. (1988). *The Canadian postmodern: A study of contemporary English-Canadian fiction.* Toronto: Oxford University Press

– (1991). *Splitting images: Contemporary Canadian ironies.* Toronto: Oxford University Press

– , and Richmond, M. (eds) (1990). *Other solitudes: Canadian multicultural fictions.* Toronto: Oxford University Press

Itwaru, A.H. (1990). *The invention of Canada: Literary text and the immigrant imagination.* Toronto: TSAR

Karrer, W. & Lutz, H. (eds). (1990). *Minority literatures in North America: Contemporary perspectives.* Frankfurt: Peter Lang

Keeshig-Tobias, L. (1988). Introduction. *The Magazine to Re-establish the Trickster,* (1):2–3

Keith, W.J. (1985). *Canadian literature in English.* London: Longman

King, T., Calver, C., and Hoy, H. (eds) (1987). *The native in literature: Canadian and comparative perspectives.* Toronto: ECW Press

Klinck, C.F., and New, W.H. (eds) (1965–1990). *Literary history of Canada.* 2nd edition. Toronto: University of Toronto Press

Knowles, R.P. (1991). Voices (off): Deconstructing the modern English-Canadian dramatic canon. In R. Lecker (ed.), *Canadian canons: Essays in literary value* (pp 91–111). Toronto: University of Toronto Press

Kreisel, H. (1982). The 'ethnic' writer in Canada. In J. Balan (ed.), *Identifications: Ethnicity and the writer in Canada* (pp 1–13). Edmonton: Canadian Institute of Ukrainian Studies, University of Alberta

Kroetsch, R. (1985). The grammar of silence: Narrative patterns in ethnic writing. *Canadian Literature, 106*:65–74

Kroller, E-M. (1989). The cultural contribution of the 'other' ethnic groups: A new challenge to comparative Canadian literature. In D. Riemenschneider (ed.), *Critical approaches to the new literatures in English.* Essen, Germany: Blaue Eule

LaRoque, E. (1975). *Defeathering the Indian.* Agincourt, ON: Book Society

Lecker, R. (1990a). The canonization of Canadian literature: An inquiry into value. *Critical Inquiry, 16*(3):656–71

– (1990b). Critical response II, Canadian canons. *Critical Inquiry, 16*(3):682–89

– (ed.) (1991). *Canadian canons: Essays in literary value.* Toronto: University of Toronto Press

– , and David, J. (eds) (1979–). *The annotated bibliography of Canada's major authors.* Toronto: ECW Press

Loriggio, F. (1987). The question of the corpus: Ethnicity and Canadian litera-
ture. In J. Moss (ed.), *Future indicative: Literary theory and Canadian literature*
(pp 53–68). Ottawa: University of Ottawa Press
– (1989). History, literary history, and ethnic literature. *Canadian Review of
Comparative Literature, 16*(3–4):575–99
McGrath, R. (1984). *Canadian Inuit literature: The development of a tradition.*
Ottawa: National Museums of Canada
Mandel, E. (1977). The ethnic voice in Canadian writing. In W. Isajiw (ed.),
Identities: The impact of ethnicity on Canadian society (pp 57–68). Toronto: Peter
Martin
Minni, C.D., and Ciampolini, A.F. (eds) (1990). *Writers in transition: The proceed-
ings of the first national conference of Italian-Canadian writers.* Montreal: Guer-
nica
Miska, J. (1990). *Ethnic and Native Canadian literature: A bibliography.* Toronto:
University of Toronto Press
Mukherjee, A. (1988). *Towards an aesthetic of opposition: Essays on literature,
criticism and cultural imperialism.* Stratford, ON: Williams-Wallace
Mukherjee, B. (1985). Introduction. *Darkness.* Markham, ON: Penguin
New, W.H. (1990). Studies of English Canadian literature. *International Journal of
Canadian Studies, 1–2*:97–114
Padolsky, E. (1986–7). The place of Italian-Canadian writing. *Journal of Canadian
Studies, 21*(4):138–52
– (1989). Canadian minority writing and acculturation options. *Canadian Review
of Comparative Literature, 16*(3–4):600–18
– (1990). Establishing the two-way street: Literary criticism and ethnic studies.
Canadian Ethnic Studies, 22(1):22–37
– (1991). Cultural diversity and Canadian literature: A pluralistic approach to
majority and minority writing in Canada. *International Journal of Canadian
Studies, 3*:111–28
Palmer, T. (1987). Ethnic response to the Canadian prairies, 1900–1950: A
literary perspective on perceptions of the physical and social environment.
Prairie Forum, 12(1):49–74
– (1989). The fictionalization of the vertical mosaic: The immigrant, success,
and national mythology. *Canadian Review of Comparative Literature, 16*(3–4):
619–55
– (1991). Mythologizing the journey to and from otherness: Some features of
the ethnic voice in Canadian literature. In V.G. Lerda (ed.), *From 'melting pot'
to multiculturalism: The evolution of ethnic relations in the United States and
Canada* (pp 91–113). Rome: Bulzoni
– , and Rasporich, B. (1985). Ethnic literature. *The Canadian encyclopedia.* Edmonton: Hurtig. I:595–8

Petrone, P. (1990). *Native literature in Canada: From the oral tradition to the present.* Toronto: Oxford University Press

Philip, M.N. (1990). Publish & be damned. *Fuse Magazine, 13*(6):40–2

Pivato, J. (ed.) (1985). *Contrasts: Comparative essays on Italian-Canadian writing.* Montreal: Guernica

– (ed.) (1989). Literatures of lesser diffusion. [Special issue]. *Canadian Review of Comparative Literature, 16*(3–4)

Price, J. (1984). A critical analysis of graduate theses in Native studies. *Canadian Journal of Native Studies, 4*(1):139–46

Report of the Royal commission on Bilingualism and Biculturalism. (1969). Vol. 4. The cultural contribution of the other ethnic groups. Ottawa: Queen's Printer

Riedel, W.E. (1984). *The old world and the new: Literary perspectives of German-speaking Canadians.* Toronto: University of Toronto Press

Shaheen, W.A., Nasim, A., and Mirza, I. (eds) (1988). *Across continents: A review of Urdu language and literature in Canada.* Ottawa: National Federation of Pakistani Canadians

Smith, B.H. (1983). Contingencies of value. *Critical Inquiry, 10*:1–35

Stratford, P. (1990). Translation. In C.F. Klinck and W.H. New (eds), *Literary history of Canada.* Second edition. Vol. IV:97–107. Toronto: University of Toronto Press

Sutherland, R. (1985). The mainstream of Canadian literature. In M.G. Vassanji (ed.), *A meeting of streams: South Asian Canadian literature* (pp 69–77). Toronto: TSAR

Tötösy de Zepetnek, S. (1989). Literary works by German-speaking Canadians and their critical appraisal. *Canadian Review of Comparative Literature, 16*(3–4): 669–86

Valgardson, W.D. (1979). Personal gods. *Essays in Canadian Writing, 16*:179–86

Vassanji, M.G. (ed.) (1985). *A meeting of streams: South Asian Canadian literature.* Toronto: TSAR

Woodcock, G. (1971). *Mordecai Richler.* Toronto: McClelland & Stewart

Young, J. (1982). The unheard voices: Ideological or literary identification of Canada's ethnic writers. In J. Balan (ed.), *Identifications: Ethnicity and the writer in Canada* (pp 104–15). Edmonton: Canadian Institute of Ukrainian Studies, University of Alberta

SHERRY SIMON ET DAVID LEAHY

La recherche au Québec portant sur l'écriture ethnique

ENGLISH ABSTRACT

The emergence of an ethnic voice in Quebec literature is a relatively recent phenomenon. While writers of various cultural origins have been writing within the Quebec context for many years, it was only in the 1980s that there came into critical existence a category designating authors of immigrant or culturally diverse origins. The important Montreal Jewish writers of the 1940s and 1950s (Cohen, Richler, Klein, Layton) wrote in English and considered themselves part of a larger Canadian writing context; writers like Alice Parizeau, Naïm Kattan, Michel Salomon and Jean Basile who wrote in French, were not necessarily given special consideration as immigrant writers.

We can actually put a date on the moment when this situation began to change. In 1983 a number of publications began to consider the existence of an 'ethnic' or 'immigrant' voice in Quebec literature: *Les études ethniques au Québec* by Gary Caldwell set the stage by reconverting the term 'ethnic' away from its previous sociological use to designate French Canadians and used it instead to apply to the populations other than French-Canadian in Quebec. *Quêtes*, a volume of texts by Italo-Québécois authors was published by Fulvio Caccia and Antonio d'Alfonso the same year; Régine Robin published her *Québécoite* in 1983 and a dossier devoted to 'minority writing' appeared in the magazine *Spirale*. In addition, the important magazine *Vice Versa*, whose pages have become the clearest expression of the ideology of 'transculture,' was first published in 1983. (Jean Jonassaint's journal *Dérives* could be seen as an important precursor of the magazine.) Marco Micone's play *Gens du silence* and the 'Interculturelles' readings organized by the Union des écrivains québécois both took place in 1982.

The difficulties of finding appropriate terms to categorize these writers (and the communities from which they emerge) points, however, to the malaise which informs the idea of an ethnic corpus within Quebec literature. Such terms as 'pluriethnique,' 'immigrante,' 'migrante,' 'minoritaire,' 'mineure,' 'transculturel,' 'métissé' have been proposed to suggest new paradigms of literary identity, or to speak of writing which refuses identity, living on the periphery, the 'entre-deux,' the 'hors-lieu' of nomination. Our postmodern fascination with, and distrust of, categories of difference throws suspicion on ethnicity, just as it does on gender, race, and nationality.

Quebec literary critics have resisted, in fact, the division of the literary corpus along 'national' lines. Two important recent studies, Pierre Nepveu's *Écologie du réel* and Simon Harel's *Voleur du parcours*, rather seek new ways of conceptualizing literary affiliation and alterity in a 'post-national' context. Devoting a substantial chapter to writers of non-Québécois origin (Marilù Mallet, Anne-Marie Alonzo, Marco Micone, Régine Robin, Antonio D'Alfonso, Mona Latif-Ghattas, and others), Nepveu chooses to characterize this writing as 'migrante' (in movement), and to declare its affinities with the central tradition of Quebec writing. Simon Harel chooses to explore novels by Jacques Godbout, Jacques Poulin, Nicole Brossard, and Jacques Ferron, in order to define the structure of 'alteration' and 'cosmopolitanism' which underlies them. Rather than confining writers to the determinism of origin, these studies seek to define the thematic and formal levels at which their work questions paradigms of cultural identity. In this sense, the issues of ethnic writing can be seen as encompassing all of Quebec literature.

In recent years, interest in the cultural diversity of Quebec literature has become increasingly institutionalized, in the form of research groups, course offerings and seminars. Some of these projects include the 'Montréal imaginaire' research group at the Université de Montréal, a *Dictionary of Immigrant Writers* (by Anne Vassal) to be published by the Institut Québécois de recherche sur la culture, a research group on 'Écrivaines migrantes' and on 'Discours du pluralisme culturel' at Concordia University.

Once the 'archaeological' work of finding and identifying writers of diverse cultural origins in Quebec has been completed (there is some of the same drive to rediscover lost writers here as there is in feminist writing), it is likely that the category of ethnic writing will be of limited critical fruitfulness. A purely sociological identification of origins is of little literary relevance. Instead, whether it be through the analytical prism of language, of gender, of postmodernism, or of architectures of social space, these works will lend themselves to the same paradigms of critical analysis as other works of Quebec literature.

La réflexion sur la littérature ethnique[1] du Québec s'insère dans une problématique et une histoire fort différentes de celles qui prédominent au Canada anglais. Alors que dans la littérature anglocanadienne il existe une assez longue tradition de littérature immigrante, semblable à celle des États-Unis, l'apparition au sein de la littérature québécoise d'auteures et d'auteurs d'origines culturelles diverses est relativement neuve. À l'image d'une société soudainement consciente de son caractère pluriel, la littérature québécoise s'est trouvée confrontée durant les années 80 à une redéfinition de ce que signifie l'écriture 'd'ici'; il s'est créé une reconnaissance du caractère pluriel de la culture québécoise.

Mais comment définir cette pluralité? Comment la souhaiter? Un premier fait s'impose: impossible de parler de la pluralité culturelle sans interroger la notion même de l'identité culturelle, de l'ensemble des représentations, des institutions, et des affiliations qui en constituent le fondement. On se rend compte que la pluralité culturelle n'est pas la juxtaposition ou l'amoncellement d'unités culturelles autonomes et closes; la pluralité culturelle n'est pas l'*inter*-culturel – l'ouverture tolérante d'une collectivité cohérente et unifiée à une autre. Du fait même l'ethnicité n'est pas l'envers rassurant ou le miroir minoritaire du national. Toute 'unité' identitaire, le national comme l'ethnique, est soumis à ce qu'on peut appeler l'épreuve de la culture, la reconnaissance du caractère mouvement, de plus en plus hybride des références et des symboles. L'émergence des voix 'minoritaires,' dans le domaine littéraire comme ailleurs, s'accompagne donc inévitablement d'une réflexion générale sur l'identité culturelle sous tous ses aspects, celle du centre autant que celle des marges.

UN PHÉNOMÈNE SOCIO-CULTUREL NOUVEAU

Les analystes sont d'accord pour affirmer que l'apparition sur la scène littéraire au cours des années 80 d'un certain nombre d'auteurs d'ori-gines culturelles diverses constitue un fait nouveau dans l'évolution de l'institution littéraire (Godbout 1986, par exemple). Ceci ne veut pas dire évidemment qu'il n'existait avant 1980 aucun écrit d'auteurs non-cana-diens français au Québec. La nouveauté consiste en la *reconnaissance* de la part de la critique de la pluralité culturelle de l'écriture québécoise.

Alors que Montréal a été le foyer d'une importante production littéraire juive durant les années 50, 60 et 70, par exemple, nous savons que ces écrivains (Klein, Cohen, Richler, etc.) ont choisi l'anglais comme langue d'expression et se sont affiliés à la littérature canadienne-anglaise, voire anglo-américaine. Les frontières des affiliations culturelles ne sont pourtant pas immuables: il n'est pas inconcevable qu'à un moment donné, ces romans – en traduction française – ne soient annexés par une littérature québécoise, encore une fois subissant la reconfiguration de ces contours.[2] Il existait également avant les années 80 déjà des appels à la transformation de la perception de l'espace culturel québécois: mentionnons le travail de Jean Jonassaint et la revue *Dérives*, Bertrand et Morin, *Le Territoire imaginaire de la culture* (1979), et également certaines études de type thématique et comparatiste: Victor Teboul, *Mythes et images du Juif au Québec* (1977), Max Dorsinville, *Caliban without Prospero: Essay on Quebec and Black Literature* (1974) et *Le Miracle et la métamorphose: Essai sur les littératures du Québec et d'Haïti* (1970). Toutefois, ces expressions n'ont pas atteint le stade du consensus avant les années 80. Quand Max Dorsinville parle en 1972, par exemple, du rapport entre les écrivains haïtiens et les écrivains québécois, c'est pour souligner le *parallèlisme* dans le rapport au 'pays.' Il s'agit toutefois de deux littératures distinctes (Dorsinville 1972).

La prise de conscience à laquelle nous faisons référence date essentiellement du début des années 1980. En effet l'année 1983 fait figure d'année clé dans l'évolution de la critique: paraissent en cette année *Les études ethniques au Québec* de Gary Caldwell (1983), *Quêtes*, textes d'auteurs italo-québécois de Fulvio Caccia et Antonio d'Alfonso (1983) ainsi qu'un premier dossier consacré à l'écriture minoritaire dans la revue *Spirale*. La revue *Vice versa*, dont les pages serviront de lieu privilégié à l'expression des débats autour de la 'transculture,' voit le jour en 1983. N'oublions pas la manifestation (considérée par la presse comme un demi-échec) des 'Interculturelles' organisé par l'UNEQ en mars 1982. Et la mise sur pied d'un très important chantier de recherche sur les minorités ethnoculturelles du Québec à l'Institut québécois de recherche sur la culture.

De par l'existence de la revue *Vice versa* et les activités d'animation culturelle qu'elle organise, ainsi que la maison d'édition Guernica (dirigée par Antonio d'Alfonso) et le succès des oeuvres de théâtre de Marco Micone, la communauté italo-québécoise acquiert une visibilité particulière dans ce contexte. Bien que très active sur le plan littéraire, la communauté haïtienne s'impose moins en tant que groupe sur la scène culturelle québécoise. Toutefois, les oeuvres de Gérard Etienne, de Dany

Laferrière, de Jean Jonassaint, d'Émile Ollivier sont abondamment commentées dans la presse. *La parole métèque,* revue féministe, fondée en 1987 et prenant en quelque sorte la relève de la défunte *Vie en rose,* fait parler des écrivaines de toutes origines, et notamment les femmes d'origines maghrébine, libanaise et égyptienne.

Au cours des dernières années, l'intérêt pour les auteures et auteurs d'origines culturelles diverses est allé en s'accentuant et a pris des formes institutionnelles inédites. Parmi les activités associées au 'chantier' traitant des communautés ethno-culturelles par l'Institut québécois de recherche sur la culture, Pierre Anctil a consacré un travail important aux écrivains juifs de Montréal (1984). Un projet actuellement en cours (dirigé par Denise Helly et Anne Vassal) vise à la préparation d'un dictionnaire auteures et des auteurs immigrants au Québec et à l'analyse d'un corpus de romans d'auteurs immigrés du Tiers Monde au Québec et ayant traité la question de la différence culturelle dans une de leurs oeuvres fictionnelles.

L'important projet de recherche, 'Montréal imaginaire,' qui se poursuit depuis 1988 à l'Université de Montréal, a touché de diverses manières des nouvelles perceptions de la littérature québécoise. Une série de conférences 'Autrement, le Québec,' tenue en 1988–9 et publiée dans la revue *Paragraphes,* comprend des contributions de Régine Robin 'À propos de la notion kafkaienne de "littérature mineure": quelques questions posées à la littérature québécoise' et de Pierre Nepveu, 'Qu'est-ce que la transculture?' qui chacune à sa façon interroge l'évolution de l'identité de la littérature québécoise. Pour Régine Robin, les 'transformations linguistiques, lexicales, même syntaxiques, une hybridité culturelle affirmée, de nouveaux types d'écriture' résulteront sans doute de l'intégration des écritures immigrantes à la littérature québécoise (p 9). Pour Pierre Nepveu, il est essentiel d'éviter que la 'transculture' ne devienne synonyme de confusion, essentiel de revendiquer plutôt 'la réappropriation d'une québécité elle-même transculturelle' (p 27).

Il ne faut pas sous-estimer, à mon avis, l'importance symbolique d'une autre publication du Groupe de recherche Montréal imaginaire. Il s'agit de *Montréal, l'invention juive,* Actes du colloque tenu le 2 mars 1990 (1991). Des textes de Régine Robin, Robert Melançon, Esther Trépanier, Pierre Nepveu, Sherry Simon et David Solway parlent de l'évolution de l'identité juive montréalaise dans la littérature et les arts plastiques. Cette publication (et le colloque qui est à son origine) témoigne d'un bouleversement radical dans les frontières du travail intellectuel québécois. Les Juifs et autres groupes minoritaires ne font plus exclusivement partie du champ de recherche anglophone; l'appropriation de l'espace montréalais dans sa totalité par la recherche francophone littéraire implique une redistribution importante des tâches. Plusieurs chapitres de l'important volume *Promenades littéraires dans Montréal* (1989) traduisent cette sensibilité nouvelle, faisant du paysage urbain un tissu cosmopolite et plurilingue. 'Voix de Montréal' est le titre choisi par Pierre L'Hérault pour le cours qu'il enseigne à l'Université Concordia, consacré en grande partie aux écritures minoritaires. La ville cosmopolite, expression par excellence de l'hétérogénéité culturelle, devient ainsi un objet privilégié de la recherche.

La bibliographie préparée par Benoît Melançon dans le cadre du projet 'Montréal imaginaire' porte très précisément sur le lien entre la littérature des communautés culturelles et l'espace culturel montréalais (*La littérature montréalaise des communautés culturelles* 1990) Il s'agit là d'un premier effort de synthèse de la recherche portant sur la littérature des communautés culturelles. Signalons la parution de deux ouvrages importants de critique qui ont pour objet le cosmopolitisme et la pluralité de la littérature québécoise: les études de Pierre Nepveu, *L'Écologie du réel* (1988) et Simon Harel, *Voleur de parcours* (1989), qui toutes deux inaugurent de façon éclatante un mouvement de révisionnisme critique qui cherche à lire 'autrement,' dans un contexte cosmopolite et post-national, le texte québécois.*Voleurs de parcours* de Simon Harel ne traite pas directement d'un corpus d'écrits minoritaires. Pourtant, sa problématique 'cosmopolite' rejoint directement notre propos. Son projet consiste à relire certaines oeuvres de la modernité québécoise dans la perspective d'en dégager le questionnement identitaire. En cela, son livre rejoint celui de Pierre Nepveu *L'Écologie du réel*, où Nepveu impose 'l'écriture migrante' au centre même de la tradition québécoise.

Autres signes de la place grandissante qu'occupent les écrivains d'origines culturelles diverses dans l'espace institutionnel: dans le dossier *Spécial Québec* paru dans le *Magazine littéraire* en octobre 1986, une attention particulière est accordée à Anne-Marie Alonzo et à Marco Micone. Un article de fond souligne le caractère cosmopolite de la culture montréalaise (Clément Trudel, 'Une ville cosmopolite') *Lettres québécoises* a consacré dans son numéro d'été 1992 un dossier préparé par Jean Jonassaint aux écrivains immigrants. Un recueil consacré aux récentes tendances de la littérature québécoise consacre un article sur cinq à la question de l'hétérogénéité culturelle (Simon, dans *L'âge de la prose* 1992). Deux anthologies récentes sont *Québec kaleidoscope, Fictions. PAJE Editeur* (1991) et *Lectures plurielles: Coexistence et cultures* (Collectif sous la direction de Norma Lopez-Therrien. Logiques\Écoles 1991). Un numéro spécial du magazine *Lettres québécoises* sous la direction de Jean Jonassaint a été consacré aux écrivains immigrants (été 1992).

QUESTIONS CONCEPTUELLES: ÉCRITURE MINORITAIRE ET CULTURE QUÉBÉCOISE

Peut-on parler, par conséquent, d'une littérature 'ethnique' du Québec? Peu d'analyses l'ont fait. À cela il y a plusieurs raisons d'ordre différent. S'il est évident que certains écrivains choisissent d'exploiter la thématique de la rencontre culturelle, il n'existe évidemment aucun rapport de cause à effet entre l'origine socio-culturelle de l'auteur et la portée de son écriture. À cela il faut ajouter que le contexte intellectuel des années 80 est largement méfiant des certitudes identitaires. Se rejoignent dans une même 'dérive identitaire' (L'Hérault 1991) les discours issus du 'post-nationalisme' (Nepveu), de la sensibilité féministe et de la diversité ethno-culturelle. Les années 80 se présentent comme une période de 'révisionnisme' plutôt que d'affrontements identitaires. Il s'amorce vers la fin des années 80 une série de relectures de la littérature québécoise (Nepveu, Harel) qui mettent en question les schémas unitaires et nationalistes qui avaient caractérisé le travail de certains critiques précédents. Les revues *Vice versa* et *La parole métèque* s'efforcent chacune d'être le lieu d'un débat très large sur les enjeux sociaux de la pluralité culturelle, mettant toutefois l'accent sur la littérature. *Identités nationales*, recueil de Benesty-Sroka (1990) en fait preuve également. Bref, l'effort critique pour caractériser l'écriture minoritaire évite en général une caractérisation sociologique de l'écrivaine ou l'écrivain.

Ces considérations expliquent qu'il s'est présenté un certain embarras terminologique dans le traitement de ce mouvement de pluralisation. Comment rendre compte de la 'différence' qui s'installe dans la littérature québécoise? De nombreux termes voient le jour qui jouissent d'une faveur plus ou moins grande: littérature ethnique, pluriethnique, immigrante, migrante, minoritaire, mineure, transculturelle, métissée; écriture des communautés culturelles, de la périphérie, de la dérive, de l'entre-deux et du hors-lieu. En effet, la critique est soucieuse dans l'ensemble de souligner les *convergences* entre les écritures issues des communautés culturelles et les autres, de manière à reconnaître et à mettre en question la pertinence de la question de l'origine.

Le terme ethnique, à cause surtout de ses affiliations sociologiques, est donc vite écarté de la discussion littéraire. Terme dont les fortunes ont été très variables à l'intérieur de la sociologie québécoise (désignant d'abord à partir des travaux d'Everett Hughes dans les années 30 et 40 jusqu'aux années 60 les Canadiens-français, ensuite tous les habitants du Québec à l'exception des Canadiens-français, voir Caldwell) l'ethnicité suppose un ensemble de traits cohérents à saveur anachronique. 'Comment concilier cette notion anachronique avec la déterritorialité, l'interchangeabilité, la mutation technologique, la libre circulation des cultures et des identités mass-médiatisées qu'appelle la modernité? Depuis les migrations massives, quelque chose a changé pour les groupes habitués à vivre depuis des siècles sur leur lopin de terre: le rapport au territoire' (Caccia 1985:11). Définir l'écrivain(e) par son origine ethnique, c'est supposer qu'il/elle participe à une identité pleine, la contrepartie symétrique de l'identité pleine majoritaire. On peut aussi définir l'ethnicité, comme dans la tradition inaugurée par Everett Hughes à partir d'une volonté d'appartenance (est ethnique celui qui désire affirmer son appartenance au groupe). Toutefois, il est clair que les écrivains en tant que groupe sont très peu désireux de se faire identifier exclusivement à partir d'une origine spécifique (voir les discussions, par exemple, dans *Vice versa* 'Ecrire la différence,' 1984). La spécificité culturelle de l'origine devient une matière privilégiée à exploiter, oui, mais elle ne détermine en rien le caractère de l'écriture. L'écriture n'est pas l'expression d'une identité pré-existante, pré-discursive; elle est au contraire le dévoilement et le travail des difficultés identitaires.

Pour caractériser ces écritures qui mettent en question les certitudes de l'identitaire, Caccia propose (à la suite de Deleuze et Guattari, qui ont lancé le terme dans leur *Kafka: Pour une littérature mineure* 1975) la notion de 'devenir minoritaire':

Si l'on considère la catégorie du *minoritaire* comme étant la condition objective, historique d'un groupe ou d'un individu ,dominé, par rapport à une 'majorité' dominante, le *devenir minoritaire* lui, suppose un dépassement, une assomption capable de mettre en crise la culture dans l''écartèlement' (Jabès) dont elle est justement le noeud, la caution. Ce travail est loin d'être l'apanage de la seule 'minorité.' Tous ceux qui choisissent de travailler autrement la langue, la culture participent à cette dynamique évitant ainsi l'écueil du ghetto et sa propension à sécréter 'du mineur,' des formes 'mineures.' Car c'est le *devenir minoritaire* et non le *mineur* qui détient la force de négation et de révolte qui empêche la majorité d'écraser la minorité. C'est dans la mesure où il s'arrache du mineur et du ressentiment qu'il engendre que le minoritaire peut s'identifier à toutes les minorités. Situation propice à l'innovation surtout lorsqu'elle se conjugue, comme c'est le cas ici, avec une autre minorité.' (Caccia, 1985:13)

Alexis Nouss offre un prolongement tout à fait pertinent de cette notion de 'mineur' dans son analyse de Ferron (1991) et Pierre L'Hérault développe également une pensée du mineur par rapport à Ferron (1989).

Dès 1984 Caccia n'hésite pas à associer ethnicité et postmodernité. C'est par des nouvelles représentations de l'ethnicité, explique-t-il, que les cultures minoritaires peuvent entrer en concurrence avec les cultures mass-médiatisées, afin de les déstabiliser.

Marco Micone pour sa part introduit la notion de *culture immigrée*, refusant la spécificité des origines en faveur d'une seule réalité immigrante reposant sur trois axes: le vécu au pays de l'exode, l'expérience de l'émigration-immigration et le vécu au pays d'accueil. 'J'écris pour raconter l'émigration du point de vue de ceux qui l'ont subie' (1985b:114).

C'est également sous le signe de *l'hétérogène* que s'est posée la question de la pluralité littéraire. Le groupe de recherche à l'Université Concordia se propose dans *Fictions de l'identitaire au Québec* une 'analytique de l'identitaire.' Dans sa contribution, Pierre L'Hérault trace une cartographie de l'hétérogène, réseau de termes et de discussions qui constituent une nouvelle trame dans le texte québécois. Pour L'Hérault, cette problématisation de l'identitaire n'est pas un fait extérieur à la culture québécoise mais au contraire y est bien enracinée. Ainsi expose-t-il les éléments communs qui soutiennent – et malgré un support idéologique différent – les questionnements identitaires chez François Charron, chez Régine Robin et chez France Théoret.

Poursuivant le projet d'une *analytique* de l'identitaire, S. Simon et Robert Schwartzwald explorent dans ce même recueil les fondements conceptuels de certains discours identitaires. Schwartzwald analyse la manière dont le *topos* de l'homosexualité a été utilisé par certains critiques culturels, tandis que Simon explore l'évolution de la conceptualisation de l'espace culturel québécois, en particulier à travers la notion de l'ethnicité. Si un critique littéraire comme Jean-Charles Falardeau pouvait encore concevoir un rapport unitaire entre culture, ethnie et littérature, si un courant critique québécois au cours des années 70 s'est évertué à découvrir la spécificité de la littérature québécoise, la critique contemporaine reconnaît la pluralité constitutive du champ culturel, nécessairement traversé par des lignes de tension diverses.

Pour sa part, Pierre Nepveu choisit de parler 'd'*écritures migrantes.*' Le chapitre qu'il consacre aux oeuvres de Anne-Marie Alonzo, Robert Berrouet-Oriol, Fulvio Caccia, Antonio D'Alfonso, Joel DesRosiers, Gérard Étienne, Nadia Ghalem, Jean Jonassaint, Naïm Kattan, Dany Laferrière, Mona Latif-ghattas, Nadin Latif, Marilù Mallet, Marco Micone, Vera Pollack et Régine Robin (oeuvres parues au cours des années 80) est significatif à plus d'un titre. Il s'agit du premier traitement collectif consacré à cette écriture au sein d'un ouvrage critique sur la littérature québécoise. Pour Nepveu 'l'imaginaire migrant se donne essentiellement comme brouillé, écartelé entre des contradictions impossibles à résoudre' (p 199). 'En fait ce sont les catégories mêmes du proche et du lointain, du familier et de l'étranger, du semblable et du différent qui se trouvent confondues' (p 200). Il souligne toutefois les convergences entre les problématiques de l'écriture migrante et la littérature québécoise dans son ensemble, qui s'est 'largement définie, depuis les années soixante, sous le signe de l'exil (psychique, fictif), du manque, du pays absent ou inachevé et, du milieu même de cette négativité, s'est constituée en imaginaire migrant, pluriel, souvent cosmopolite' (p 201). S'agit-il là simplement de l'expression d'un cliché 'postmoderne'? Nepveu s'en inquiète, tout en constatant l'inévitabilité de la contradiction dans laquelle nous vivons, à la fois dans le drame et l'euphorie de la confusion des signes.

Comment nommer la réalité plurielle de la littérature québécoise sans tomber dans un relativisme débridé? Comment traiter de cette question *littéraire*, mais sociale aussi, sans se perdre dans l'esthétisme? Voilà autant de questions qui ne peuvent pas recevoir de réponse simple. Dans une intervention polémique, Daniel Latouche reproche aux théoriciens de *Vice Versa* d'avoir transformé un débat de société en jeu esthétisé (1990).

On comprend, donc, toute la difficulté qu'il peut y avoir à nommer une réalité encore très diffuse et qui questionne de manière directe la conceptualisation de l'institution littéraire, voire, de la société québécoise.

LES PERSPECTIVES CRITIQUES

Les approches thématiques: le récit de l'immigration

Peu d'études ont jusqu'ici été consacrées au récit d'immigration au Québec. Plusieurs projets sont actuellement en cours et des parutions au cours des années à venir viendront combler ce manque.

La question de la langue

Vu l'importance de la langue comme outil critique pour la littérature québécoise, il n'est pas étonnant que la littérature minoritaire ait été abordée sous cet angle. Fulvio Caccia a analysé avec une grande perspicacité à la fois la question du choix de la langue française pour les écrivains italophones ('L'Ecrivain italophone et son rapport à la langue,' 'Les poètes italo-montréalais: Sous le signe du Phénix') et le rapport à l'altérité qui s'y exprime. Caccia utilise les quatre niveaux de langue proposés par Henri Gobard pour caractériser le rapport complexe de l'écrivain d'origine italienne aux langues: le dialecte italien serait la langue vernaculaire, l'anglais la langue véhiculaire, le français la langue référentiaire, l'italien la langue mythique. Pour Caccia et pour Bertrand qui le suivra, la notion d'un usage intensif de la langue comme langue d'écriture (notion empruntée à Deleuze) serait la voie ouverte aux créateurs italiens. Le texte capital de Deleuze et Guattari sur la 'langue mineure, la langue déterritorialisée' (dans *Kafka*) ressort comme un leitmotif chez plusieurs critiques des années 80. Les écrits de Régine Robin, qui précisent davantage le rapport de Kafka à la langue, ont également été des sources importantes pour Caccia et les autres critiques de la littérature minoritaire.

C'est par le biais de la langue que Caccia établit le rapport 'en miroir' de l'immigrant et du colonisé québécois. Étant tous deux dans un rapport de désaisissement par rapport à la langue, ils pourront exploiter – chacun de manière différente – cette faiblesse pour en faire une force. Voilà le défi transculturel. C'est dans un court texte paru dans *Le Devoir* que Caccia (avec Lamberto Tassinari) donne le plus grand développement à son idée: la nouvelle 'lingua franca' de la modernité québécoise émergera de la rencontre entre deux langues historiquement caractérisées par la faiblesse: la langue aliénée du Québec colonialisé et la langue fragile des écritures immigrantes.

En se confrontant à d'autres langues, en se laissant volontairement traverser par elles, le français acquiert ainsi les vertus d'une langue *forte* qui préside à la circulation et à la transformation des autres cultures. C'est l'assomption de sa faiblesse qui retourne ici en force, nommant le réel sans l'interpréter, s'assumant dans son miroitement infini, dans ses fractures, ses accents détournés, dans sa liberté totale. (1986)

Pierre Bertrand fait écho à cet article dans 'La langue et l'écriture' (1990) où il conclut: 'Les immigrants ne font que mener à sa pleine lumière un problème qui se pose d'abord chez le Québecois "de souche," comme on dit. Comment écrire en québécois? ... Le québécois est une langue marginale, anormale, *anomale*. Mais ceci ne constitue pas un défaut ... La pauvreté du québécois, qui, comme toute pauvreté, peut se manifester par une étrange richesse, fait de celui-ci une langue d'emblée accueillante.' Voir aussi Tassinari sur la force faible de la nouvelle société transculturelle (1989).

C'est par le biais de la langue que S. Simon aborde également quelques écrits minoritaires (1983). Elle insiste sur le travail de la langue chez Fennario, Micone, Robin et Jonassaint, travail qui milite contre une conception 'naturaliste' de la langue littéraire et qui expose les rapports de pouvoir charriés par les codes linguistiques. Elle insiste sur la portée idéologique du caractère volontairement fracturé du texte chez Robin et Jonassaint.

La réflexion de Micone sur la langue est fondée dans l'expérience du manque qui est l'expérience immigrante. Ses premières interventions racontent la difficile maîtrise du français ('Le travail sur la langue,' 1983–4) et le choix délibéré de faire résonner une langue hybride, un 'langage imaginé,' populaire. Il mettra davantage l'accent par la suite sur l'existence d'une 'culture d'immigré,' commune à tous les immigrants et devant être prise en compte par la culture d'accueil. Il s'agit d'un ensemble d'éléments qui font de l'expérience de l'immigré une expérience dynamique.

Le seul espoir qui nous reste, c'est de transformer cette société d'accueil pendant le processus d'assimilation. Car nous n'avons pas le choix, si nous voulons un espoir, un but: s'assimiler dans un Québec pétrifié, c'est à la fois mourir et ne rien apporter: l'autre piège, c'est la marginalisation, la ghettoisation. (Micone dans Lefebvre, *Le Devoir* 1986, cité par P. L'Hérault)

Architectures de l'espace culturel

Robert Berrouet-Oriol, dans deux articles parus dans *Vice-versa* (1986), salue dans *Manhattan Blues* de Jean-Claude Charles (paru en France) et *Comment faire l'amour avec un nègre sans se fatiguer* de Dany Laferrière, deux ouvrages qui effectuent une 'rupture avec les modèles dominants de la littérature haïtienne, qui ont longtemps privilégié l'écriture indigéniste ou "engagée." Ces ruptures donnent à voir, en leurs ressemblances et différences, l'inscription non conventionnelle de deux jeunes auteurs dans l'insularité je-ville; je-nègre dans la nuit; je-marginal en devenir transculturel; je-nègre\femelle-blanche; je-sujet écrivant, rupture avec un certain imaginaire du pays profond.' Berrouet-Oriol, comme de nombreux autres critiques, traite le livre de Laferrière avec respect et distance, reconnaissant là à la fois quelque chose de nouveau et 'un précieux cliché de la modernité ... en terre-Québec' (p 58) S. Simon souligne également le caractère paradoxal du texte de Laferrière. L'hétérogénéité des références culturelles font de ce texte un véritable ramassis hybride; en même temps l'utilisation complice de certains codes culturels interpellent directement le lecteur (masculin) québécois (*Vice Versa* 1986).

L'accueil enthousiaste donné par le public québécois au roman de Dany Laferrière ne suffit pas, de l'avis de certains, pour conclure à l'ouverture du public québécois à autrui. On entend de temps en temps des dénonciations fracassantes au sujet du 'non-accueil' d'un livre ou un autre (Berrrouet-Oriol à propos du livre *Le pouvoir des mots* de Jean Jonassaint; Heinz Weinmann au sujet du livre *Le voleur de parcours* de Simon Harel). Toutefois, on entend également l'avis contraire: 'Il n'est pas exclu que nous assisterons, au cours des prochaines années, à un repositionnement du champ littéraire québécois travaillé par l'écriture migrante et l'écriture métisse. Aussi, il importe d'accorder la meilleure attention à l'émergence d'écritures qui, labourées ici et ailleurs, seront celles des sujets migrants, de l'imaginaire migrant, des parcours migrants, celles de l'errance, de *l'errance en soi*, de la non-identification' (Harel 1989:21). Jean Jonassaint écrit (*Lettres québécoises*): 'il y a manifestement une mutation incroyable qui s'opère dans le milieu littéraire québécois depuis les années 1970. Une réelle ouverture sur le monde, et dans l'espace romanesque, et dans le champ éditorial' (1986:80).

À sa parution en 1983, le roman de Régine Robin, *La Québécoite*, a reçu un accueil plutôt silencieux. (Mais soulignons l'intérêt tout particulier dans ce contexte d'un article de Madeleine Gagnon dans la revue *Possibles* 1983.) Signe du temps, ce roman reçoit de la part de la critique actuelle un intérêt intense. Son roman est devenu une exploration emblématique des signes proliférants de la culture. Comme le roman de Dany Laferrière, *Comment faire l'amour* – mais d'une manière très différente – *la Québécoite* propose une lecture privilégiée de l'espace culturel montréalais. On peut prévoir que l'avalanche de publications consacrées à Montréal l'année prochaine (1992, le 350e anniversaire de la fondation de Montréal) donnera une très grande place à l'analyse de ce roman.

RECHERCHES À VENIR

Identification du corpus 'pluriethnique'

Pour mesurer la très grande diversité des origines socio-culturelles des auteures et auteurs québécois, il est sans doute important d'en faire un recensement empirique. Ces recherches sont actuellement en cours, mais l'utilisation de marqueurs sociologiques pose problème. Veut-on identifier les auteurs 'immigrants,' des auteurs originaires des communautés culturelles ou plutôt des textes qui explorent la problématique de la pluralité culturelle? Au-delà de l'intérêt purement informatif qu'une énumération des auteurs immigrants peut représenter, il est peu pertinent à l'analyse littéraire de savoir que Jacques Folch-Ribas est d'origine catalane, que Michel van Schendel est né en Belgique, que Jean Basile est d'origine russe – du moment où le texte ne porte aucune trace d'un travail à partir de ces identités. Entre l'immigrant de langue française, venu au Québec par choix dans les années 50, le réfugié chilien ou l'écrivain italo-québécois né et élevé au Québec, il n'y a pas de commune mesure. La catégorie de 'l'écrivain immigrant' sera d'utilité limitée.

Perspectives critiques

La recherche doit être axée autour de perspectives critiques. Pourquoi s'intéresse-t-on à l'écriture des auteures et auteurs d'origines diverses? C'est en définissant des *axes critiques* (thématiques, identitaires, poétiques) que la problématique trouvera sa pertinence. En d'autres mots, la dimension sociale de cette écriture doit se révéler à partir d'analyses poétiques et conceptuelles.

Dans sa présentation du numéro de la revue *Paragraphes* consacré à 'Autrement, le Québec' (1989), André Brochu signale le retour dans les années 80 d'un souci de redéfinir, encore une fois, le 'nous' québécois. Le très grand intérêt actuellement accordé à l'écriture minoritaire et à toutes les expressions de l'hétérogénéité culturelle témoigne de ce mouvement. Ainsi, c'est moins 'la littérature ethnique' comme telle qui doit être un champ privilégié de recherche que les conceptions d'identité culturelle que véhicule le texte littéraire. Ceci dit, les écritures 'minoritaires' constituent un terrain particulièrement riche dans ce contexte, puisqu'elles choisissent souvent d'explorer et de travailler, sous divers angles, la question des appartenances culturelles.

Les questions qui me semblent centrales pour la recherche à venir sont les suivantes:

– *Qu'est-ce que le pluralisme culturel? Comment le texte littéraire questionne-t-il les frontières de l'identité culturelle?*

Cette question suppose une recherche à la fois conceptuelle et textuelle, sur un corpus très varié de textes. Il n'est pas suffisant de déclarer que les frontières identitaires sont en plein mouvement; il faut préciser les formes et les configurations qu'assume la pluralité culturelle. Le pluralisme n'est pas le cumul d'identités pleines mais plutôt la formation (toujours en mouvement) de formes identitaires nouvelles.

Plusieurs voies d'approche sont possibles. Il y a bien entendu l'exploration thématique de l'altérité, telle qu'elle a été amorcée dans une perspective plutôt classique par Laurent Mailhot, par exemple, dans le volet 'Autres regards' de son recueil *Ouvrir le livre* ou à partir de matrices théoriques postmodernes et 'post-nationales' par Simon Harel et Pierre Nepveu. Dans le premier cas le rapport à l'Autre est étudiée sans que la *structure* de l'altérité soit elle-même mise en question; dans le second c'est la conceptualisation même de l'altérité qui est objet d'étude. Il y aurait également des approches axées sur les aspects formels du texte: le plurilinguisme et l'imaginaire des langues dans le roman québécois, la nature et la cohérence des références. Autour de quels référents, allusions, attributs, la culture (du propre, de l'étranger) se présente-t-elle? Quels objets culturels sont valorisés et sous quelle forme la communauté est-elle imaginée?

– *Comment définir le contexte historique et discursif qui donne lieu au Québec à une formulation nouvelle de la problématique de la pluralité?*

Nous avons maintenant suffisamment de recul chronologique pour pouvoir revenir avec profit sur les premières années de la décennie 1980. Il s'agit d'analyser la réception critique de l'écriture minoritaire dans le contexte post-référendaire de la société québécoise, en rapport particulièrement aux discours politiques et conceptuels (par exemple, le féminisme). Comment se modifie la représentation de soi identitaire? Il s'agit ici d'études 'interdiscursives' qui étudieraient en parallèle des discours de différents champs: cinéma, politique, littérature.

En effet, pour comprendre la complexité des enjeux qui s'expriment dans la transformation de la représentation de l'espace culturel, il nous semble essentiel d'adopter une démarche interdiscursive. C'est dans la confrontation de diverses configurations discursives que l'on peut nuancer des positions et saisir les diverses matrices idéologiques qui soutiennent les discours sur la pluralité culturelle. C'est ainsi qu'en restant attentifs à la mise en garde de Pierre Nepveu: 'il est essentiel d'éviter que la 'transculture' devienne synonyme de confusion et soit toujours défini comme un mode qui vient d'ailleurs. Il faut une 'réappropriation d'une québécité elle-même transculturelle' (Nepveu 1989: 27), on peut prévoir que la problématique de l'écriture ethnique deviendra de plus en plus celle de la littérature québécoise dans son ensemble.

NOTES

1 Ce terme a été choisi faute d'un meilleur. Faut-il parler de littérature ethnique, minoritaire, immigrante, migrante, mineure? L'embarras terminologique témoigne des difficultés conceptuelles qui surviennent lorsqu'on veut isoler un corpus d'écrits issus des 'communautés culturelles.'

2 Nous n'abordons pas dans ce rapport le regard actuellement porté sur les écrivain-e-s anglophones dans le contexte québécois. Malgré les efforts de certains analystes de considérer sous une seule perspective les minorités anglophones et allophones du Québec (c'est la démarche de Caldwell, par exemple, 1983), ce point de vue ne tient pas compte de l'expérience historique et du pouvoir institutionnel très différente des deux groupes.

BIBLIOGRAPHIE

Cette bibliographie a été préparée par David Leahy. Il s'agit d'une bibliographie sélective.

Générale

Alavo, Y. (1988). Médias et minorités: L'égalité d'abord. *La Parole métèque,* (5):6–7

Alsène, E. (1988). Le syndrome de la corde à linge. (Dossier: Le Québec des différences: Culture d'ici). *Possibles, 12*(3):101–8

Anctil, P. (1981). Communautés culturelles et communautés québécoises: de quelle intégration s'agit-il? *Jonathan, 1*(2)

– (1984). Double majorité et multiplicité ethnoculturelle à Montréal. *Recherches sociographiques, 25*(3):441–56

Aw, E.R. (1990). Femmes africaines et traditions dans l'espace canadien. *La Parole Métèque,* (13–14):24–5

Balthazar, L. (1989). Pour un multiculturalisme québécois. *L'Action nationale,* 79(8):942–53

Bariteau, C., et Genest, S. (1987). Axes majeurs et développements récents de l'anthropologie au Québec. *Anthropologie et sociétés, 11*(3):117–42

Baum, G. (1991). Le pluralisme ethnique au Québec. *Relations,* (570):117–19

Beaucage, P. (1990) Fragments de miroirs: l'identité ethnique, parole et travail. (Dossier: Culture/Cultures). *Possibles, 14*(3):13–28

Benesty-Sroka, G. (1990). *Identités nationales. Interviews.* Montréal: La pleine lune

Berdugo-Cohen, M., Cohen, Y., et Lévy, J.J. (1987). *Juifs Marocains à Montréal. Témoignages d'une immigration moderne.* Montréal: Éditions VLB

Bertrand, C., et Morin, M. (1979). *Le territoire imaginaire de la culture*. Montréal: Hurtubise HMH

Bertrand, P. (1985). Note sur la 'différence': Écrire la différence? (1). (Dossier: Écrire la différence: actes du colloque sur la littérature des minorités). *Vice Versa*, 2(3):23

– (1986). Transmigrations. *Vice Versa*, (16):28–9

– (1987). Le voyage immobile. Le Québec de l'an 2000 face au défi de la transculture. *Vice Versa* (22–3):8–9

– (1988). Le Québec multiethnique. (Dossier: Le Québec des différences: Culture d'ici). *Possibles*, 12(3):67–74

Boulanger, N. (1991). Ces jeunes qui viennent d'ailleurs. *ZIP*, 5(7):32–3

Caccia, F. (1984). Ethnicité comme post-modernité. *Vice Versa*,

– (1985). Langues et minorité. (Dossier: Écrire la différence: actes du colloque sur la littérature des minorités). *Vice Versa*, 2(3):10–11

– (1986). L'Altra Riva. *Vice Versa*, (16):44–5

– , et Tassinari, L. (1985). Minorité et territoire. Entretien avec Félix Guattari. *Vice Versa*, 2(4):4

Caldwell, G. (1982). Identité ethno-culturelle au Québec. *Le Devoir*. 12 mars, p 22

– (1983). *Les études ethniques au Québec*. Québec: Institut québécois de recherche sur la culture

– (1988). Immigration et la nécessité d'une culture publique commune. *L'Action nationale*, 78(8):705–11

Cambron, M. (1990). L'impossible contrat polémique. (Dossier: Culture/Cultures). *Possibles*, 14(3):39–53

Cohen, Y., et Lévy, J.J. (1988). Du soleil à la liberté/itinéraire. (Dossier: Le Québec des différences: Culture d'ici). *Possibles*, 12(3):119–28

Collectif (1983). Dossier: Minorités du Québec. *Conjonctures*, (4):67–144

– (1984). Dossier: L'Amérique inavouable. *Possibles*, 8(4)

– (1985). Dossier: Écrire la différence: actes du colloque sur la littérature des minorités. *Vice Versa*, 2(3)

– (1986). Dossier: Hommage aux communautés culturelles du Québec. *Forces*, (73)

– (1987). Dossier: Le renouveau féministe est une dénonciation de l'indifférence des femmes nées ici vis-à-vis des femmes immigrants. *La Parole métèque*, 2(4)

– (1987). Dossier: Les 'ethniques' et les médias. *Humanitas*, (17)

– (1987). Dossier: Les créateurs ethniques et leur place dans la cité. *Humanitas*, (20–1)

– (1988). Dossier: Le Québec et l'autre. *Conjonctures*, (10–11)

– (1989). Dossier: Villes cosmopolites et sociétés pluriculturelles. *Revue internationale d'action communautaire*, (21/61)

- (1989). Dossier: Cultures en exil. *Conjonctures*, (12)
- (1989). Dossier: Nonobstant la langue. *Vice Versa*, (27)
- (1990). Dossier: 'Droits, libertés, justices.' *Médium*, (36):7–31
Delgado, P. (1988). Pour un Québec non raciste. (Dossier: Le Québec des différences: Culture d'ici). *Possibles*, 12(3):111–18
DePasquale, D. (1986). Les Emigrés de l'intérieur. *Vice Versa*, (13–14):30
de Saint-Maurice, F. (1991). Resterons-nous français? *Nuit blanche*, (43):28
Elbaz, M. (1983). La Question ethnique dans la sociologie québécoise: Critique et questions. *Anthropologie et Sociétés*, 7(2):77–84
François, N. (1983). *Bibliographie des thèses et des mémoires sur les communautés culturelles et l'immigration au Québec*. Montréal: Ministère des Communautés culturelles et immigration du Québec
Gagnon, G. (1988). Plaidoyer pour la convergence culturelle. (Dossier: Le Québec des différences: Culture d'ici). *12(3):37–44*
- (1990). Entre le zombie et le fanatique: Finkielkraut, Rioux, Ricard. (Dossier: Culture/Cultures). *Possibles*, 14(3):29–37
Godbout, J. (1986). Special Québec 1986. *Magazine littéraire*, (234):94–5
Harvey, F. (1988–9). Groupes ethniques: enjeu de la lutte linguistique au Québec. *Journal of Canadian Studies*, 23(4):37–43
Harvey, J. (1988). Racisme, ethnocentrisme, xénophobie et immigration. *L'Action nationale*, 78(5):323–38
Jean, M. (1986). Notes sur le regard de l'autre. *Dérives*, (52):45–50
Jonassaint, J. (1985). Pour Patrick Straram. (Dossier: Écrire la différence: actes du colloque sur la littérature des minorités). *Vice Versa*, 2(3):12–13
Labelle, M. et al. (1987). *Histoires d'immigrées*. Montréal: Boréal
Lamonde, Y., et Caldwell, G. (1988). Les contraintes, les possibles. (Dossier: Le Québec des différences: Culture d'ici). *Possibles*, 12(3):45–51
Lamore, J. (1987). Transculturation: naissance d'un mot. *Vice Versa*, (21):18–19
Langlais, J., et Rome, D. (1986). *Les Juifs et les Québécois français, 200 ans d'histoire commune*. Montréal: Éditions Fides Collection Essais
Larue, M. (éd.). (1990). (Dossier: Culture/Cultures). *Possibles*, 14(3):7–133
Lévesque, C. (1990). L'autre pays, le pays de l'autre. (Dossier: Culture/ Cultures). *Possibles*, 14(3):115–33
Lévesque, R. (1982). Le Québec et la culture immigrée. *Le Devoir*, 27 mai, p 17
Marcil, C. (1981). Les communautés noires au Québec. *Education Québec*, 11:(6):18–26
Meintel, D. (1989). Les Québécois vus par les jeunes d'origine immigrée. *Revue internationale d'action communautaire*, (21/61):81–94
Melançon, B. (1988). A la recherche du Montréal yiddish. *Vice Versa*, (24): 12–13

Ménard, J., et Gironnay, S. (1990). Perles d'Haiti: ces Québécoises font une brillante carrière. *Châtelaine*, *31*(5):48–50, 52

Michaud, G. (1988). 'On ne meurt pas de mourir.' Réflexions sur le Sujet-Nation. *Études françaises*, *23*(3)

Micone, M. (1985). La culture immigrée: ou l'identité des gens du silence. (Dossier: Écrire la différence: actes du colloque sur la littérature des minorités.). *Vice Versa*, *2*(3):13–14

– (1987). Démarginaliser les jeunes allophones. Dans Collective. *L'Avenir du français au Québec*. Montréal: Québec/Amérique 41–6

– (1990). De l'assimilation à la culture immigrée. *Possibles*, *14*(3):55–64

Morin, M. (1989). L'autre Amérique. *Vice Versa*, (27):7–11

Ollivier, É. (1990). Le visible et le troisième millénaire. *Possibles*, *14*(2):89–95

Pagé, L. (1987). Le respect des minorités n'est pas incompatible avec le respect de nous-mêmes; allocution. *L'Action nationale*, *76*(6):518–19

Pagé, M. (1988). Pourquoi l'éducation interculturelle? (Dossier: Le Québec des différences: Culture d'içi). *Possibles*, *12*(3):77–89

Ricard, F. (1989). Marcel Rioux entre la culture et les cultures. *Liberté*, *31*(2):3–13

Ricard, R. (1977). Le multiculturalisme, un 'non-sens'? *Relations*, (37):70–3

Rioux, M. (1988) Les frusques de la semaine et l'habit du dimanche. (Dossier: Le Québec des différences: Culture d'ici). *Possibles*, *12*(3):27–36

Rocher, F., & Guay, J.-H. (1990). La culture au pluriel. *Possibles*, *14*(3):65–75

Rome, D, Nefsky, J., et Obermeir, P. (1981). *Les Juifs au Québec: Bibliographie rétrospective annotée*. Québec: Institut québécois de recherche sur la culture

Roy, A. (1985). *Paul Tana: Café Italia, Montréal*. *Spirale*, (56) [Compte rendu du film: *Café Italia, Montréal*]

Royal Society of Canada (1989). *Colloque: nationalisme et diversité culturelle au Québec*, (4):60, 62ff.

Salvatore, F. (1985). Le métissage: le défi d'avenir du Québec. (Dossier: Écrire la différence: actes du colloque sur la littérature des minorités). *Vice Versa*, *2*(3):19–20

Simard, J.-J. (1990). La culture québécoise: question de nous. *Cahiers de recherche sociologique*, (14):131–41

Simon, S. (1985). Présentation: Des différences. (Dossier: Écrire la différence: actes du colloque sur la littérature des minorités.). *Vice Versa*, *2*(3):9–10

– (1987). [Compte rendu: *Histoires d'immigrés* Labelle et al.] *Spirale*, (71)

– (1990). Géométries de la culture: fragments. *Possibles*, *14*(3):109–14

Tassinari, L. (1989). La ville continue: Montréal et l'expérience transculturelle de [la revue]. *Vice Versa*, (21):57–62

Teboul, V. (1977). *Mythes et images du Juif au Québec*. Montréal: Éditions de La grave

Tehanni, A. (1990). Montréal, Algérie. *Possibles, 14*(2):133–9

Thibault, A. et al . (1988). (Dossier: Le Québec des différences: culture d'ici). *Possibles, 12*(3):7–132

– (1990). Le spécifique et l'universel dans la culture québécoise. (Dossier: Culture/Cultures). *Possibles, 14*(3):87–95

Tremblay, M.-A. (1990). Crise de l'identité culturelle des francophones québécois. bibliog. *Action nationale, 80*(5):654–83

Trudel, C. (1986). Montréal la cosmopolite. *Magazine littéraire*, (234):95–6

van Schendel, N. (1987). Identité en devenir et relations ethniques: cadre théorique d'analyse. *Apprentissage et socialisation ... en piste, 10*(2):87–97

– (1989). Nationalité, langue et transculture. *Vice Versa*, (27):22–5

– (1990). *Vice Versa* à l'endroit ou réponse à une critique esthétisante. *Vice Versa*, (28):45–6

Critique littéraire

Allard, J, Simard, S., et Robert, L. (1985). Dossier: Naïm Kattan. *Voix et images, 11*(1):6–54

Anctil, P. (1984). Les écrivains juifs de Montréal. Dans G. Caldwell et P. Anctil (eds), *Juifs et réalités juives au Québec*. Québec: IQRC, pp 195–252

Beaudoin, R. (1986). Les mouches du plafond. *Liberté*, (165):126–31. [Compte rendu: Laferrière et autres]

Beaudoin, Réjean (1989). *Lettres québécoises*. [Compte rendu: *l'Écologie du réel*]

Berrouet-Oriol, R.(1986). Négrophile, schizophrénie ou les avatars de l'errance urbaine. *Vice Versa*, (13–14):58–9

– (1987). L'effet d'exil. *Vice Versa*, (17):20–1

Bertrand, P. (1990). La langue et l'écriture. *Vice Versa*, (28):50–2

Blouin, J. (1984 juillet). Le silence parle italien. *L'Actualité*, (9):68–73

Bourassa, A. (1984–5). Le Théatre des Italiens. *Lettres québécoises*, (36): 39–41

Caccia, F. (1983–1984). Marco Micone: Le travail sur la langue. *Vice Versa, 1*(3):4–5

– (1985). Les poètes italo-montréalais, sous le signe du Phénix. *Canadian Literature*, (106):19–28

– (1985). *Sous le signe du Phénix: Interviews avec des créateurs italo-québécois*. Montréal: Guernica

– , et D'Alfonso, A. (1983). *Quêtes: textes d'auteurs italo-québécois*. Montréal: Éditions Guernica

Collectif. (1983). Dossier: Les minorités au Québec. *Spirale*, (39):7–10

– (1986). Québec 1986. *Magazine littéraire*, (234):92–128

D'Alfonso, A. (1983). Bribes sur l'italianité. *Spirale*, (39):10

- (1985). Je suis duel. (Dossier: Écrire la différence: Actes du colloque sur la littérature des minorités). *Vice Versa*, 2(3):21

Desaulniers, R. (fév-mars 1984). Entretien sur *Quêtes*, recueil de textes d'auteurs italo-québécois. *Vice Versa*, 1(4):22–3

Dorsinville, M. (1970). *Le Miracle et la métamorphose. Essai sur les littératures du Québec et d'Haiti*. Montréal: Éditions du jour

- (1972). Pays, parole et négritude. *Canadian Literature*, (51):55–64

- (1974). *Caliban without Prospero. Essay on Quebec and Black literature*. Erin, ON: Press Porcepic

Fortin, A. (1990). Ici, l'autre: Simon Harel vient de lancer *Le voleur de parcours*. *Nuit blanche*, (39):10–11. [Compte rendu]

Frédéric, M. (1991). L'écriture mutante dans *la Québécoite* de Régine Robin. *Voix et Images*, (48):493–502

Gagnon, F. (1990). L'épreuve de l'hôte. *Liberté*, (189):74–7. [Compte rendu: *Le voleur de parcours*]

Gagnon, M. (1983). Histoire-fiction. *Possibles*, 8(1)149–59. [Essai sur *La Québécoise* de Régine Robin]

Gauvin, L. (1984). De Sao Paulo à Montréal: circuits littéraires. *Possibles*, 8(4): 119–31

Giroux, R. (1989). Situation de la littérature québécoise depuis 1980 à la lumière des éditeurs (de livres et de périodiques) qui la régissent. *Moebius*, (41): 127–35

- (1991). [Compte rendu de *Le voleur de parcours* de S. Harel] *Lettres québécoises*, (61):44–5

Harel, S. (1989). *Le voleur de parcours: Identité et cosmopolitisme dans la littérature québécoise contemporaine*. Préface de René Major. Longueuil: le Préambule, Collection L'univers des discours

Horguelin, T. (1989). Le conflit insoluble de la modernité. *Spirale*, (87):8. [Compte rendu: *l'Écologie du réel*]

Jonassaint, J. (1986). *Le pouvoir des mots, les maux du pouvoir: Des romanciers haïtiens de l'exil*. Paris, Montréal, Arcantère: PUM

- (ed.) (1992) Dossier: Écrivains immigrants. *Lettres québécoises*

- , et Racette, A. (1986). L'avenir du roman québécois serait-il métis? *Lettres québécoises*, (41):79–80

La Rue, M., en collaboration avec Chassay, J.-F. (1989). *Promenades littéraires dans Montréal*. Québec/Amérique

La Rue, M. (1988). Préface à *Déja l'agonie*. Montréal: L'Hexagone

L'Hérault, P. (1985). Le métissage culturel. (Dossier: Écrire la différence: actes du colloque sur la littérature des minorités). *Vice Versa*, 2(3):15–16

– (1986). Opérer un déplacement de perspectives. Dans F. Léger et L. Savoie (eds), *Didactique en question: Le point vue de 22 spécialistes en français langue seconde*. Beloeil: Éditions la lignée 93–7

– (1987). Langue commune: lieu de parcours transculturels. *Bulletin de l'ACLA. Actes 18e Colloque annuel. 'Linguistique appliquée à l'aménagement linguistique,'* 9(2):89–98

– (1989). *Volkswagen Blues: Traverser les identités*. *Voix et Images*, (43):28–42

– (1990, mai). Ferron l'incertain: du même au mixte. Actes du Colloque de l'ACFAS. Québec: Québec

– (1991). Pour une cartographie de l'hétérogène: dérives identitaires des années 1980. Dans S. Simon et al., *Fictions de l'identitaire au Québec*. Montréal: XYZ

Longfellow, B. (1986). L'Écriture féministe de *Journal inachevé* (Marilù Mallet) et *Strass Café*. *Dérives*, (52):101–16

Mailhot, Laurent (1992). *Ouvrir le livre*. Montreal: L'Hexagone

Marcotte, H. (1990). Interview. Dany Laferrière. 'Je suis né comme écrivain à Montréal.' *Québec français*, (79):80–1

Melançon, B. (1988). A la recherche du Montréal yiddish. *Vice Versa*, (24):12–13

– (1989). *Liberté*, (183):138–46. [Compte rendu: *l'Écologie du réel* de P. Nepveu]

– (1990, mars). *La Littérature montréalaise des communautés culturelles. Prolégomènes et bibliographie*. Montréal: Université de Montréal, Groupe de Recherche Montréal Imaginaire

– (1991). La littérature montréalaise et les ghettos. *Voix et Images*, (48):482–92

Micone, M. (1985a). La culture immigrée ou l'identité des gens du silence. (Dossier: Écrire la différence: actes du colloque sur la littérature des minorités.). *Vice Versa*, 2(3):13–14

– (1985b). Écrire la culture immigrée. *Écrits du Canada français*, (55):114–19

– (1989). Un pouvoir à partager. *Jeu*, (50):83

Montréal, l'invention juive. Actes du colloque tenu le 2 mars 1990 (1991). Montréal: Université de Montréal, Montréal imaginaire

Nepveu, P. (1988). *L'Écologie du réel. Mort et naissance de la littérature québécoise contemporaine*. Montréal: Boréal, Collection Papiers collés, 197–210

– (1989). Qu'est-ce que la transculture? (Dossier: Autrement, le Québec: Conférences 1988–1989.). *Paragraphes*, (2):15–31

Nouss, A. (1991). Faiseur de contes: Jacques Ferron portrait d'une écriture en mineur. Dans S. Simon et al., *Fictions de l'identitaire au Québec*. Montréal: XYZ

Ollivier, É. (1990). Québécois de toutes souches, bonjour! *Vice Versa*, (28):47–8

Robin, R. (1985). La différence quand même. (Dossier: Écrire la différence: actes du colloque sur la littérature des minorités). *Vice versa*, 2(3):17–19

– (1988). Ce serait un roman ... ou Montréal comme hors-lieu. *Vice Versa*, (24):23–4

- (1989). À propos de la notion kafkaïenne de 'littérature mineure': quelques questions posées à la littérature québécoise. (Dossier: Autrement, le Québec: Conférences 1988–9). *Paragraphes*, (2):5–14
- (1989). La langue entre l'idéologie et l'utopie. *Vice Versa*, (27):28–32
Roy, C. (1986). Écrire la différence? (3). Du pareil au même. *Vice Versa*, 2(5): 15–16
Schwartzwald, R. (1991). (Homo)sexualité et problématique identitaire. Dans S. Simon et al., *Fictions de l'identitaire au Québec*. Montréal: XYZ
Simon, S. (1983). Écriture et minorités au Québec (dossier) *Spirale*, (39):7
- (1984). Écrire la différence: La perspective minoritaire. *Recherches sociographiques*, 25(3):457–65
- (1985) Speaking with authority: The theatre of Marco Micone. *Canadian Literature*, (106):57–64
- (1987). Cherchez le politique dans le roman en vous fatiguant. *Vice Versa*, (17):21, 32
- (1990a) Entre les langues: écriture juive contemporaine à Montréal. *Montréal l'invention juive*. Actes du colloque, groupe de recherche Montréal imaginaire. Université de Montréal 87–102
- (1990b). The Geopolitics of sex, or signs of culture in the Quebec novel (sur Dany Laferrière). *Essays in Canadian Writing*, (40):44–9
- (1991). Espaces incertains de la culture. Dans S. Simon et al., *Fictions de l'identitaire au Québec*. Montréal: XYZ
- (1992) Le roman des années 80: la culture en question. Dans L. Gauvin (ed.), *L'âge de la prose*. Montréal: VLB Editeur et Rome: Bulzoni Editore, Rome
Sirois, A. (1982). L'Étranger de race et d'ethnie dans le roman québécois. *Recherches Sociographiques*, 23(1–2):187–204
Thibault, M. (1989, déc). L'odyssée de Marilù Mallet. *Châtelaine*, 30(12):141–6
Vassal, A., et Helly, D. (à paraître). *Dictionnaire des écrivains immigrés au Québec*. Montréal: Institut québécois de recherche sur la culture
Whitfield, A. (1989). Pour une littérature post-québécoise. *Lettres québécoises*, (53):45–6. [Compte rendu: *L'Écologie du réel* de P. Nepveu]
- (1990). Littérature et identité nationale. *Lettres québécoises*, (59):45–6. [Compte rendu: *Le voleur de parcours* de S. Harel]

RICHARD CLÉMENT

Acquiring French as a Second Language in Canada: Towards a Research Agenda[1]

I was told by a very middle-class parent, of the Westmount Rhodesian variety, who was one of the more vocal advocates of French immersion that 'we want our children to learn their language. We don't want our children to associate with them.' (Bain 1991:17).

Bruce Bain's account of the initial meetings leading to implementation of the St-Lambert French immersion program in the early 1960s detracts only slightly from the perspective proposed by other authors (e.g., Swain & Lapkin 1982; Genesee 1987). Indeed, most agree that the St-Lambert project was instigated by parents who thought that the political situation was changing in Quebec and that it might be useful for their children to know the French language. Although issues of national unity, cultural enrichment, and cross-cultural rapprochement were at stake, Bain proposes that the interest in acquisition of French coincided with chauvinistic beliefs which, in his view, would perpetuate the existence of the two solitudes across Canada. Fundamental to this argument is the matter of the goals served by the promotion of French as a second language (FSL), and, by extension, individual bilingualism.

What are these goals? There seems to be quite a gap between the zeitgeist of the Trudeau era and the current ideology represented, for example, by the results of the Spicer Commission. The fact is that questioning the value of ethnic diversity is not a purely Canadian phenomenon. A cover story in a recent issue of *Time* (Gray 1991) was titled 'Whose America? A Growing Emphasis on the U.S.'s "Multicultural" Heritage Exalts Racial and Ethnic Pride at the Expense of Social Cohesion'(p 8). In a twin article, historian Arthur Schlesinger (1991) proposes that 'The eruption of ethnicity is, I believe, a rather superficial enthusiasm stirred by romantic ideologues on the one hand and by unscrupulous con men on the other: self-appointed spokesmen whose claim to represent their minority groups is carelessly accepted by the media' (p 14). Contrasting views are, however, proposed by opponents of the English-only movement aimed at reducing cultural and linguistic diversity (Cummins 1991; Padilla et al. 1991).

Compounding the confusion created by this political unrest is the limited understanding of what FSL acquisition is about. An overwhelming majority of studies have been devoted to the linguistic outcomes of FSL programs (e.g., for review, Genesee, 1987; Lambert & Tucker 1972; Swain & Lapkin 1982). With few exceptions related to cognitive (e.g. Cummins 1983; Hamers & Blanc 1989) and social aspects (Gardner 1985; Gardner & Clément 1990), little conceptual and empirical attention has been aimed at understanding the processes behind the acquisition or teaching of FSL. This is surprising in view of the fact that over half of Canadian school children are enrolled in second-language courses (Statistics Canada 1990). It is also a source of concern given that our knowledge of FSL acquisition, limited as it is, should be our main resource for implementing and managing heritage language programs, an issue rapidly coming to the forefront in the Canadian societal agenda.

The review that follows is not exhaustive. The imposed length of this chapter prohibits such an attempt. Rather, in view of the preceding discussion, I will focus on the social aspects of FSL, emphasizing processes, within the objective of proposing desirable research developments. To organize the material at hand (not to segregate the issues), individual and contextual factors will be discussed in separate sections.

INDIVIDUAL DIFFERENCES

The study of individual social characteristics has evolved from concepts and measures designed to focus on individual differences to concepts underlining the relevance of social aspects. Central to the concerns of researchers investigating social psychological aspects is the role of motivation. Motivation is proposed as the prime social psychological determinant, not only of French proficiency but also of a family of behaviours associated with the acquisition, use and maintenance of FSL (see Gardner 1985; Gardner & Clément 1990). Early research on the social foundations of motivation was inspired by the work of Mowrer (1950) according to whom, first-language acquisition is influenced by one's identification with the first-language models, usually parents. On that basis, Gardner and Lambert (1959) argued that a strong motivational basis for learning the second language might be the individual's desire to identify with valued members of the other community, a tendency later identified as reflecting an integrative motive (Gardner & Smythe 1975).

The influence of the integrative motive on French language achievement has been well documented. The results of the cross-national survey of FSL conducted by Gardner and his collaborators shows that in spite of local variations, affective predispositions towards French, francophones, and the French class are related to FSL achievement (see Gardner 1985). Furthermore learning French requires persistent efforts from the student, efforts which may be short-lived, particularly when French courses are optional (cf. Lewis & Shapson 1989). Clément, Smythe, and Gardner (1978) showed that, compared with other variables, such as French achievement and linguistic aptitude, attitudes and motivation were consistently better predictors of a student's decision to persist or drop out of a French course.

Another related phenomenon which has attracted attention is classroom behaviour. Do students who are more active in the French classroom also show more *integrativeness*? The results reported by Naiman, Fröhlich, Stern, and Todesco (1978) and Gliksman, Gardner, and Smythe (1982) suggest that this is the case. Taken together these results and the preceding one therefore provide some evidence that attitudes and motivation are not only directly related to competence but also to behaviours which may be instrumental to the development of French proficiency.

A recent elaboration of this trend of research has been to consider the problem of second-language retention. From the review proposed by Vechter, Lapkin, and Argue (1990) and other work in the area (e.g., Gardner, Moorcroft & Metford 1989), it seems that three factors are related to second-language retention: the degree of knowledge of the second language, the opportunity to use the second language, and cognitive factors related to memory retrieval. In the final analysis, however, all three factors have as a common determinant the willingness to seek and/or avail oneself of opportunities to use French which, as illustrated above, is to a large extent dependent upon the individual's attitudes and motivation.

The research on attitudes and motivation reported so far has established their role in the acquisition of FSL by Canadians. Most studies were conducted in the field with the absence of control implied in such research. Even though more refined statistical techniques such as causal modelling have recently been applied to the phenomenon (e.g., Clément & Kruidenier 1985; Gardner & Lalonde 1983) the basic evidence is correlational, with the result that causal inference remains hazardous. Better controlled research therefore appears to be in order.

Another methodological problem concerns evaluation of French proficiency. Contrasting with the research oriented towards more pedagogical issues (e.g., Harley 1986; Harley, Allen, Cummins & Swain 1990), research dealing with attitudes and motivation has typically used global measures of proficiency – mostly of passive skills. Refinement of these tools would establish with more precision the locus of impact of attitudinal dispositions.

Besides these methodological issues, the importance of the attitude and motivation literature is to a large extent related to the expectation that changing attitudes may lead to increased proficiency, which in turn may lead to increased contact with the second-language group, and to more positive attitudes. Of course, matters are not that simple. In an annotated bibliography of about 600 articles on inter-ethnic contact, Desrochers and Clément (1979) report few that are directly relevant to the matter of second-language attitudes and motivation. This is rather surprising in the context of Canadian FSL education presumably being aimed at promoting greater cross-cultural understanding.

The few studies that have assessed the results of cross-cultural contacts with francophones have reported mixed results. For example, Hanna and Smith (1979) conclude from their study of a bilingual exchange program that 'generalized positive/negative attitudes toward the other language group are not of great significance to exchange participants' (p 52). Other studies report different results when considering factors which may mediate the effect of contact. For example, Clément, Gardner, and Smythe (1977a) have compared the attitude change of students participating in a three-day excursion to Quebec City to that of a similar group of individuals who chose not to do so. The excursion group was further divided into those who reported having had a high frequency of contact with francophones and those who reported a low frequency of contact. The results show that it is those who had a more positive attitude who availed themselves of more contact. Also, after accounting for initial differences in attitudes, it is the high contact group that showed the most positive changes in attitudes. Furthermore, the low contact group returned home with a less pronounced motivation to learn French than that of those students who had not participated in the excursion. This and similar studies (e.g., Desrochers & Gardner 1981) buttress the conclusion that the link between the acquisition of FSL and harmonious anglophone-francophone relationships is complex and requires more empirical attention than it has so far received. Among key issues is that of the factors which mediate the positive outcome of contact, be it from the point of view of inter-group attitudes or of influencing motivation to learn French.

The interest in cross-cultural contact has given rise to two extensions of the social-psychological framework described in the preceding pages. The first elaboration concerns the role of anxiety or (inversely) self-confidence about using the second language. Reporting on FSL data, Gardner (1979) notes that for anglophones living in a setting where contact with francophones is available, anxiety about using French is a better predictor of performance than attitudes or motivation. Similar results obtained with francophones learning English as a second language led Clément (Clément 1986; Clément, Gardner & Smythe 1977b, 1980; Clément & Kruidenier 1985) to propose a sequential model whereby attitudes would orient the individual to seek or avoid contact with members of the second-language group and, if that contact were available, its frequency and quality would determine self-confidence. In such situations, it is the latter factor which would be the prime determinant of proficiency in the second language.

The development of language confidence would therefore rest upon characteristics of contact with members of the second language-speaking group. But apart from relatively elementary work identifying frequency and aspects of quality such as intimacy, cooperativeness, and equality, little is known about how a positive outcome is achieved (Wrightsman 1972: Ch. 11). Some conceptualizations have called in social network analysis (e.g., Prujiner, Deshaies, Hamers, Blanc, Clément & Landry 1984) to fill this void. To date, little empirical research is, however, available.

The second elaboration of the approach originally proposed by Gardner and Lambert (1972) concerns the role of orientations to FSL acquisition. Orientations correspond to the reasons invoked by the individual for learning French. Two main orientations were proposed originally: (1) an integrative orientation – corresponding to learning French to identify with valued members of the corresponding group, and (2) an instrumental orientation corresponding to pragmatic reasons such as school or job-related achievements.

While Gardner and Lambert (1972) did leave the door open for additional orientations to be active, much literature on this topic has made exclusive use of the integrative and instrumental orientations, at times opposing them as two poles of a continuum or confounding their operational definition. Clément and Kruidenier (1983) argued that the confusion and controversy which ensued (cf. Gardner 1980; Oller & Perkins 1978) was in part due to a failure to allow for the possibility of multiple orientations to emerge, depending on the setting. Their results show that among eight groups of students (francophones and anglophones learning English/French or Spanish as a second language in a unicultural or multicultural milieu), four general orientations emerged: all groups were characterized as learning their respective second language for friendship, travel, instrumental, and travel reasons. Furthermore, some additional orientations emerged as a result of the relative familiarity of the target language group, namely identification and integration orientations.

The Clément and Kruidenier (1983) study also raised the issue of the particular socio-political context of learning, a matter dealt with in the next section. Of immediate concern, however, are the effects of contact and opportunity for use on individual social psychological processes. One reason for the increased interest in this phenomenon may be evolving political and social conditions which have made, notably, French and English groups more salient to one another. Political decisions regarding national bilingualism increased media coverage and exposure and facilitated travel opportunities are factors which have made francophones 'present' to the anglophone population even in areas where French is not spoken. Contrasting with the rapid evolution of the means and opportunity for contact, little is known about the parameters which determine its consequences. Further research should also take into consideration the fact that much contact is indirect, mediated by electronic or other means, the effect of which remains unknown.

CONTEXTUAL FACTORS

The effect of contact and concomitant language confidence on French proficiency introduces the perspective of contextual effects on the teaching and learning of French. Whereas individual differences have had their place for some time within social psychological studies of FSL, interest in contextual effects is more recent (but see Lambert, Havelka & Crosby 1958, for an exception). The discussion that follows will consider, separately, academic and social contexts of acquisition. It would be expected that the individual differences described in the previous section would operate in conjunction and in interaction with the learning context. That issue is, however, in itself, underresearched.

Academic Contexts

When attempting to review academic interventions one is struck by the wide variance in structure, pedagogical approach, and aims of the programs.[2] Canadian FSL programs can be classified according to their length, point of entry, and intensity. Thus, early total immersion involves the exclusive use of French by the teacher upon entry at the kindergarten level and the gradual introduction of English language for some subjects starting in Grade 3. The increase in amount of English varies from program to program but does not usually exceed 60 per cent until Grade 11. In the case of late immersion, elementary grade years are spent in 'core' French program involving 10–15 per cent instruction in French, followed by one or two years (Grades 7–8) with 80–5 per cent instruction in French and a follow-up period (Grades 9–11) with 20–40 per cent instruction in French. Other formulae involve starts in Grades 4 or 5 (middle-immersion) and less intensive use of French in the early grades (partial immersion).

These various educational approaches have been widely and intensely evaluated, not only in Canada, particularly in comparison with the achievement of students involved in core French programs and with that of native francophones. Some aspects of these programs will be evaluated in greater detail below. It is, however, useful to note at the outset two results which have been obtained repeatedly. First, when comparing same-age students, and notwithstanding the factors described below, achievement in French seems to be directly related to the amount of French instruction received. That is, total immersion students do better than partial immersion students who, in turn, do better than core French students. That is not to say, however, that core French should be treated as a *parent pauvre* of French instruction (see Stern 1982). The adoption of a program should follow the goals set by an institution.

The second recurrent result is that anglophone students schooled in French do not suffer any backlog in English-language arts once these are introduced in the curriculum around grades 3 or 4. Parkin, Morrison, and Watkin (1987), however, note that this may have been due to the fact that immersion students may come from families where literacy is developed and modelled by parents and older siblings. This may not always be the case as immersion programs become less 'elitist' in terms of the population they attract, clearly an issue that requires continuous monitoring.

Three issues remain comparatively contentious when assessing the effects of immersion. They are the levels of French proficiency achieved by the students, the cognitive impact of these programs and their attitudinal/motivational impact.

French Proficiency

The question of level of French proficiency is crucial because of the implied or explicit goal of most immersion programs to produce individuals who have a functional knowledge of French. On that matter, the research evidence is mixed and the evaluation of results is further plagued by the variety of research instruments that are used. It has generally been found that only total immersion students fare as well as native French-Canadian speakers on measures of reading and oral comprehension (Lambert & Tucker 1972; Genesee 1987; Swain & Lapkin 1982). Quite different results are obtained for some aspects of production skills. Whereas immersion graduates appear to be able to maintain a coherent and appropriate verbal interaction, their knowledge of grammatical aspects appears to be limited (Cummins & Swain, 1986). The linguistic analyses conducted by Spilka (1976), Adiv (1980), Pawley (1985), and Pellerin and Hammerly (1986) suggest that immersion students show deficits in the area of lexical availability, syntax and verb choices. Furthermore, Hammerly (1989a, 1989b) claims that these errors are characteristic of an immersion classroom pidginized variety of French which has become fossilized, unalterable.

Whereas most researchers recognize the problem, the proposed explanations and solutions vary. It seems that development of language ability in the immersion classroom does not follow the development in subject-matter competence. From the little we know about what happens in the immersion classroom (e.g., Genesee 1987; Swain & Lapkin 1986), students' usage of French is mostly reactive and limited in terms of discursive amplitude. Furthermore, Allen, Swain, Harley, and Cummins (1990) in their observational study of eight immersion classes report that only 19 per cent of the errors made by students when speaking French were corrected by their teacher, and then only inconsistently and ambiguously. Lambert (1974) and Swain and Lapkin (1986) attribute these production problems to the lack of opportunity for contact with native speakers of French. In that respect, Genesee, Holobow, Lambert, and Chartrand (1989) report more encouraging results obtained by involving anglophone students in an otherwise French school in Quebec. The issue of language production is crucial because it determines to some extent the manner and outcome of inter-group contacts. Anecdotal evidence suggests that in bilingual settings, the anglophone who 'understands-every-thing-but-will-not-speak-French' is not better evaluated than his unilingual counterpart.

Another issue which arose in connection with French achievement is that of the relative efficiency of different programs, particularly early and late immersion. This issue also became entangled with that of the presumed existence of a *best age* to learn a second language. Arguments in favour of an early start for learning a second language were based on neurological evidence (Lenneberg 1967; Penfield & Roberts 1959) to the effect that brain plasticity is reduced with the onset of puberty. Consequently, early immersion should be preferable to late immersion. The biological basis of the critical period hypothesis is also usually supplemented with other reasons: there is much less time to devote to L2 acquisition in the secondary grades than in the primary grades; it is a good idea to introduce the notion of cultural plurality at an early age; language learning is the principal task of primary education. Thus, the answer to the maturational question becomes clouded with other considerations of a pedagogical or organizational nature.

Whereas advocates of a biologically-determined sensitive period have succeeded in showing the complex role of neurological organizations, they have also demonstrated the great plasticity of the human brain. The functions of destroyed or atrophied regions may be taken over by other regions. It is thus difficult to show that maturation of certain areas is directly responsible for particular behavioural phenomena. Furthermore, too many factors intervene, such as family environment, education, and pedagogical approaches to allow for an adequate test of the hypothesis. Within the context of optimizing French acquisition it may be more profitable to ask how best to teach students from different age groups. This would be more in line with results obtained to date.

In tests of the relative achievement of early and late immersion students (see Genesee 1987; Harley 1986), the former group usually achieves better than the latter. There are, however, studies that report minimal differences (Harley 1986) or no difference (Genesee 1981; Shapson & Day 1982). The results obtained by Wesche, Morrison, Ready, and Pawley (1990) further suggest that none of the differences endure when, having graduated, early and late immersion students find themselves in the university setting. These are striking results given the difference in exposure to French (1400 hours for 2 years' late immersion vs 5000 hours for early immersion). Older students may simply be more efficient language learners, bringing to the task a greater degree of cognitive maturity and literacy.

Very little is known about these differences, which are contrary to the original sensitive period hypothesis. Reinforcing the case for an early start, however, is the fact that younger children may not have yet formed prejudices against members of the target group or developed self-consciousness about making mistakes in public. Indeed, research is needed on how younger and older learners differ in terms of skills, strategies, and attitudes, particularly on how these differences interface with the pedagogical approaches used. For example, in spite of the current popularity of the communication (or experiential) approach to learning second languages, adults may appreciate an explicit understanding of the rules which govern the system they are attempting to master.

Cognitive Aspects

Although the cognitive aspects pertaining to FSL acquisition are usually represented as individual characteristics, it is useful to discuss them within the contextual aspects because their effects are shown mostly in academic settings. Furthermore, as will be shown later, their origin and development are hypothetically linked to their social context. The two questions that I would like to raise are related respectively to the cognitive benefits accruing from the acquisition of a second language and to the suitability of French immersion for every child.

The matter of the cognitive benefits one may obtain by learning a second language has a relatively long history within this domain of research. Whereas early statements spoke against bilingual education (see Darcy 1953; Peal & Lambert 1962), more recent and better controlled research has tended to show that bilinguals have greater mental flexibility and greater facility in concept formation (Peal & Lambert 1962), greater ability at verbal originality and verbal divergence tests (Cummins & Gulutsan 1974) and better performance in rule discovery tasks (Bain 1975), to name but a few issues. While results such as these have been obtained in Canada and all over the world (see Hamers & Blanc 1989), much less is known about the specific nature of the bilingual's advantage, nor is it entirely clear how this advantage, also labelled *additive bilingualism*, comes to be developed.

Lambert and Tucker (1972) had suggested that children involved in a bilingual program were more likely to develop *incipient contrastive linguistics* which would result eventually in greater metalinguistic awareness – a capacity to distinguish a symbolic system from its referent and functions that would be at the basis of their greater cognitive capacity. In fact, Bialystok and Ryan (1985) have suggested that metalinguistic awareness corresponds to two independent types of competence: the capacity to analyze structures that give access to representations and the capacity to exercise cognitive control over representations (i.e. structure them in time and space). To my knowledge, there is only one study that has attempted to address the issue, that conducted by Cummins (1978) on Irish-English bilinguals in Ireland. Confirmatory results were obtained, but since this issue is a fundamental claim of bilingual education it is in dire need of more research directed at the components and cognitive functions of metalinguistic awareness.

The development of metalinguistic awareness would constitute an important achievement of bilingual children. Cummins' (1979) analysis would, however, suggest conditions under which such an outcome could not be attained. He suggests that in order for a cognitive deficit (*subtractive bilingualism*) to be avoided, a first *threshold* of first-language development must be attained by the child raised bilingually. Positive cognitive outcomes would only accrue if, in addition, a second-language competence threshold is attained. Between the two thresholds, cognitive deficits are avoided and the child develops an intermediate level of bilingualism with competence in the first language.

The empirical evidence bearing on this issue is rather tenuous, although the results reported by Swain and Lapkin (1991) tend to confirm the role played by a definition of the upper threshold as first-language literacy. One difficulty here is obviously to define what the thresholds are for a given child involved in a given program. This is a crucial preliminary step if one is to conduct a true test of this approach.

Together with the threshold hypothesis, Cummins (1979) proposes the *interdependence hypothesis*, according to which the level of competence in the second language is a function of competence in the first language. As discussed earlier, there is some empirical evidence concerning the interdependence hypothesis, starting with Cummins' reanalysis of previous results (see Cummins and Swain 1986). In a more recent study by Harley, Cummins, Swain, and Allen (1990) it is further suggested that the interdependence may concern skills that are of a context-reduced academic type. Furthermore, other evidence (see Feuerverger 1989;

Swain & Lapkin 1991) suggests that the effect may be bidirectional, that is, from the second to the first language.

A question directly related to the threshold and interdependence issues, with immediate implications for children in bilingual programs, is that of the suitability of immersion for all children. In a controversy that developed some years ago, Trites (1981) contended that students showing a developmental lag in the maturation of temporal lobe regions may be unfit for French immersion. A number of researchers have questioned his results (e.g., Cummins 1979) and in a series of better controlled studies, Bruck (1982) showed that these disadvantaged students fared no worse than similar students placed in the regular core French program. In fact, they may have had an advantage learning French through an immersion approach as opposed to the more stringent rule and vocabulary learning approach of core French programs.

Still, as underlined by Wiss (1989), there may be children who do not have the linguistic maturity to benefit from immersion from the early kindergarten years. In terms of the threshold hypothesis, these children may not have yet attained, for a variety of reasons, the first threshold of first language development. A first research task here would be to develop assessment instruments permitting a more precise identification of such cases.

Socio-Cultural Aspects

Besides the issue of the cognitive dimension of academic programs, there is that of their social and cultural consequences. No matter how varied the aims of bilingual education are in Canada, they always comprise as a goal some aspect of attitude change and/or greater cultural understanding.

It seems evident at the outset that students involved in immersion programs and their parents have more positive attitudes towards learning French, bilingualism, and French Canadians than students enroled in the regular French program (see Genesee 1987; Ouellet 1990). It seems, furthermore, that graduates of immersion are more satisfied with their French-language training and that they envisage more positively the possibility of living in a French environment and becoming fully bilingual than students from the regular French program (see Cziko, Lambert, Sidoti & Tucker 1980). It is not clear, however if these differences are due to the immersion experience itself or if they were present at the outset. The more positive attitudes of the parents may be communicated to children long before they enter school. It does seem clear, however, that whatever attitudinal outcome there is to immersion programs, it is not related to level of French achievement (Gardner 1985).

As far as identity is concerned, while identifying themselves as English Canadians, immersion students find French Canadians and English Canadians to be more similar to each other and themselves, more similar to French Canadians than students in the regular program (see Cziko, Lambert & Gutter 1980). These effects have been noted as early as Grade 1 (Genesee, Tucker & Lambert 1978).

When the evolution of students is assessed through longitudinal research, the few studies available suggest that the initial difference between immersion and non-immersion students disappears in the senior elementary years. (Genesee, Morin & Allister 1974; Lambert & Tucker 1972). Genesee (1987) attributes this disappearance to the lack of direct contact between immersion students and native speakers of French. Furthermore, in research using a diary approach, it has been found that whereas immersion students made more reactive use of French than regular program students, they were not different in the extent to which they actively sought occasions to use French – a problem underlined earlier when reviewing in-class behaviour.

Corollary evidence on the effects of contact is also available from studies of special intensive programs. Clément (1979) conducted two parallel studies in which Yukon high school students were either involved in a two-week immersion program in Quebec or lived for eight days with a French family in Quebec. When compared to their respective control groups, the immersion students showed a decrease in French-use anxiety, whereas the residence group showed an increase in positive attitudes towards French-Canadians. These results, together with those reported by Gardner, Ginsberg, and Smythe (1976) and Stennett and Earl (1982), suggest that variations in pedagogical approach may affect attitudes differentially and independently from French achievement.

The picture of the FSL student that emerges from the scant empirical evidence is that of a socially well-motivated individual originating from a supportive milieu whose positive predispositions are not maintained throughout their schooling years and who will not usually volunteer to use French outside of school. Wesche et al. (1990) also find that this pattern is present when the immersion graduates reach university. Immersion graduates look positively upon their experience, but it seems to have little tangible consequence in terms of inter-group interactions unless the learning context involves, in one way or another, an intensification of the curricular requirements and greater personal involvement. In fact, it appears that they are less tolerant of francophones who do not speak English when the norms dictate it than core French students (Genesee & Bourhis 1982, 1988). These conclusions are tentative, however, and, given the importance of the issue more research is needed to pinpoint precisely the social consequences of bilingual schooling and the role which direct contact and pedagogical approaches have towards more positive outcomes.

Social Contexts

When evaluating factors which are likely to influence immersion graduate's usage of French outside the classroom, Genesee, Rogers, and Holobow (1983) found that an important correlate was the extent to which these students perceived that French Canadians supported their efforts. Similarly, Cleghorn and Genesee (1984) conducted an ethnographic study of an immersion school in Montreal. Their findings show little informal interaction between francophone immersion teachers and other anglophone teachers. Furthermore, meetings were conducted in English, as it was the language of administrators: patterns of language usage reminiscent of when English was the dominant language in Quebec. What these two studies show is that the outcomes of learning French in the classroom should be expected to reflect wider societal conditions and tensions. In fact, it seems evident, when dealing with the inconsistencies of the world-wide literature on bilingualism (e.g., Hamers & Blanc 1989), that the wider social context in which a second-language is learned has an effect on the level of competence achieved by the learner as well as on the cognitive and affective outcomes of second-language acquisition.

A recurrent but underresearched theme in the corresponding theorizing is that positive outcomes of second-language acquisition will be achieved only to the extent that the individual's first language and culture is well established and valued (Clément 1984; Cummins & Swain 1986; Hamers & Blanc 1989; Landry & Allard 1990). This is an amplified restatement of the cognitive interdependence hypothesis described earlier. It is not only argued that cognitive benefits will accrue if the first language is mastered but also that cultural outcomes in the sense of sharing two cultural identities will occur only if the first language and identity are established (Clément 1984) and that both cultural and cognitive outcomes will result from a socially bound developmental process originating in the early childhood environment (Hamers & Blanc 1989).

Prujiner (Prujiner et al. 1984; cf. Hamers & Blanc 1983:Ch. 7) together with a multidisciplinary team attempted to map out the different dimensions of the social context on the acquisition of a second language. The related conceptualizations which evolved from that collective effort (e.g., Clément 1984; Hamers & Blanc 1983 1989; Landry & Allard 1990) stress the importance of at least two levels which may be influential. The first level is structural and concerns the relative demographic, social status, and institutional standing of the first- and-second language groups, aspects which Giles, Bourhis, and Taylor (1977) have taken to be determinants of the ethnolinguistic vitalities of the communities involved.

The second level corresponds to that of the individual's communication network (Rogers & Kincaid 1981): irrespective of the structural (objective) linguistic composition of a community, an individual's actual linguistic milieu is composed of those people with whom he or she interacts. This raises the possibility that members of a closely knit minority language group may actually live in the sheltered environment of their own language community. This possibility would occur particularly in cases where the different members of a community covered, as a group, most of the functions required of community life (e.g., as merchants, service workers, professionals) developed *institutional completeness*, and, at the same time, had little opportunity for group membership change.

The interface between the wider structural context and the language networks raises interesting possibilities concerning the outcome of second-language acquisition for various status groups. For example, Cummins (1976, 1984) proposes that the positive cognitive outcomes of bilingualism would occur for children whose first language and culture is strong enough not to be replaced when learning the second language. Conversely, Clément (1980) predicts that a high level of competence in the second language coupled with a minority status would result in the loss of the first identity (i.e. cultural and linguistic assimilation). This may not occur, however, if the minority individual is 'shielded' by a dense proximal network. Under these circumstances, conditions may develop to create an additive bilingualism setting in an otherwise subtractive environment, which could explain the long-term survival of some minority groups and, as well, the superior achievement of some of their members, supported as they are by a cohesive first-language network.

But what does this have to do with learning French as a second language? In most of Canada, French is a minority-group language. The positive results reported concerning the cognitive development of anglophone students are, therefore, not surprising. From a social-psychological point of view, Gardner (1985:Ch. 6) reports that actual parental encouragement and perceived parental encouragement are consistently correlated with motivation. Gardner and Lalonde (1983) also report a positive association between students' perception of the importance given to the language course objectives by the school administrator and an integrative motive. Thus, it appears that while community influence is operative, the context of the acquisition of French in most of Canada supports positive outcomes.

It may be entirely different in Quebec. The early studies reported by Lambert and Tucker (1972) described a situation very similar to that in the rest of Canada. The evolution of language legislation in that province coupled with the changing political climate (cf. Bourhis & Lepicq 1993) may have *created* a new minority with the Québec anglophones. Fear of assimilation (Clément 1980; Taylor, Ménard & Rheault 1977) may indeed be the reason for the avoidance of contact described by Genesee. If this is the case, anglophone students of French in Quebec are in the paradoxical situation of avoiding contact to preserve their identity, but in so doing, never to achieve mastery of the active skills of their second language. For theoretical reasons as well as for applications, it is urgent that research be done towards developing a solution to this dilemma.

The problematic situation in Quebec is likely to endure, given stronger legislation in favour of French, on the one hand, and on the other, the increasing number of minority group citizens (Paillé 1989) and the increasing density of the population in finite geographical territory. For example, Taylor (1990) and Taylor and Wright (1989) have described the situation of northern Quebec Inuit for whom for historical reasons the preferred second language is English and not French, a tendency contrary to that province's socio-political agenda. D'Anglejan, Renaud, Arseneault, and Lortie (1981) have also described the difficulties related to the acquisition of French by recently arrived immigrants placed in the Centre d'orientation et de formation des immigrants (COFI) of the Québec government. In addition to poor socio-economic conditions, the seclusion and discrimination by host francophones may curtail their attempts to make active use of the language. In cases where immigrants are readily integrated, because learning French places them in a situation of subtractive bilingualism, English may become a preferred medium – again an issue warranting research.

To conclude this section on the social context, it appears that, contrary to what the plethora of research reports on academic interventions would lead us to think, the acquisition of French (or any language for that matter) is intimately linked to its social context. The social context and not the pedagogical curriculum may therefore be the critical determinant of the cognitive and social outcomes. This calls for a serious reorientation of the funding efforts of Canadian agencies interested in national harmony; more attention to the linguistic-social immersion rather than school immersion may be worthwhile.

CONCLUSION: MOVING TOWARDS A RESEARCH AGENDA

I have tried, as I reviewed the specific issues, to describe what would be important avenues for future research. In conclusion, I would like to outline three more general guidelines. First, I was struck by the conceptual seclusion of education-based research from other disciplines concerned with language issues. In spite of a strong emphasis on socially related determinants in the former approach (e.g., Genesee 1987; Harley et al. 1990), little or no reference is made to social psychological approaches (e.g., Gardner 1985; Giles & Byrne 1982; Clément & Kruidenier 1985), cross-cultural psychology (Berry 1990) or intercultural communication (e.g., Giles & Robinson 1990; Kim & Gudykunst 1988) and the converse is also true (but for an exception see Hamers & Blanc 1989). My first general recommendation is, therefore, for more 'cross-disciplinary' research ventures in this domain.

My second remark concerns the scope and goals of research in this area. For obvious political and accountability reasons much of the impressive amount of research done on FSL has been geared towards insuring its credibility, promotion, and/or survival under the scrutiny of educational agencies. Much of the research, conducted at considerable cost to the Canadian public, redundantly shows the same results, with minor permutations of locus, grade level and pedagogical formula. But since the original studies (e.g., Lambert & Tucker 1972), the research which has had a significant impact on the field has not necessarily been that which has confirmed outcomes. Rather, considering the results of the research on the production limits of immersion graduates, on the relative efficacy of older learners and on the nature of student-teacher classroom interaction (Harley et al. 1990), it is those studies which have shown limitations that have advanced knowledge by destroying myths, imposing new points of view, and promoting further research. My recommendation is, therefore, for more critical and formative research.

My last remark is a rejoinder to my introduction. It concerns my continued ignorance of the goal of teaching and learning FSL, or rather, the apparent absence of any commitment to promote, evaluate, and revise programs according to designated and defined socially relevant goals. For example, I have suggested elsewhere (Clément 1980, 1984) that the ultimate impact of second-language fluency and relevant contextual dimensions could influence individuals' ethnolinguistic identity. Borrowing from Berry (1990), the latter could be further construed as *integration* (simultaneous identification with two groups), *assimilation* (identification with the second language group), *separation* (exclusive identification with the first-language group) and *deculturation* (identification with none of the groups). When Canadians (Berry, Kalin & Taylor 1977), Americans (Lambert & Taylor 1988) and the French (Lambert, Moghaddam, Sorin & Sorin 1990) are asked about the desirability of heritage culture maintenance, the response is generally positive (but see Lambert et al. 1990) – in favour of integration.

Contrasting with the above, when respondents are asked to what ethnolinguistic group they feel they belong in different situations, the answer is generally in favour of the first language group (i.e. separation) for both majority and minority francophones and anglophones (see Clément & Noels 1992). A reversal in favour of the exclusive identification with the second language group (i.e. assimilation) is found for those minority individuals using their second language most often (Clément, Gauthier & Noels 1991). All respondents therefore report an opposition between the two linguistic identities and a personal choice which coincides with their dominant-language usage.

Taken together, the above results show a global endorsement of a multicultural ideology that would be conducive to the continued promotion and acceptance of French culture. At the same time they suggest that centring such enterprise on FSL acquisition alone may not be the best answer. The fundamental question of the nature of the process, if any, relating the acquisition of French by individuals and increased social harmony remains to be researched.

NOTES

1 Completion of this paper was facilitated by a grant from the Social Sciences and Humanities Research Council of Canada. The author is grateful to Elena Mihu for her help in researching and assembling the reference material used in this paper as well as to Sharon Lapkin for her comments on an earlier draft. Correspondence should be addressed to the author, School of Psychology, University of Ottawa, 125 Université, Ottawa K1N 6N5.

2 A number of book-length reviews have been written on FSL programs in
   Canada (e.g., Cummins & Swain 1986; Lambert & Tucker 1972; Genesee
   1987; Swain & Lapkin 1982). My intention in the following is to focus on a
   few of the issues which apparently have given rise to interest and/or
   controversy.

REFERENCES

Adiv, E. (1980). An analysis of second language performance in two types of
   immersion programs. *Bulletin of the Canadian Association of Applied Linguistics*,
   2(2):139–52
Allen, P., Swain, M., Harley, B., and Cummins, J. (1990). Aspects of classroom
   treatment: Toward a more comprehensive view of second language education. In B. Harley, P. Allen, J. Cummins, & M. Swain (eds), *The development of
   second language proficiency* (pp 57–81). Cambridge: Cambridge University
   Press
Bain, B. (1975). Toward an integration of Piaget and Vygotsky: Bilingual considerations. *Linguistics*, 16:5–20
– (1991). What price naiveté? *The ATA Magazine*, 47(4):15–18
Berry, J.W. (1990). Psychology of acculturation. In J. Berman (ed.), *Nebraska
   Symposium on Motivation*, Vol. 37 (pp 201–34). Lincoln: University of Nebraska Press
Berry, J. W., Kalin, R., and Taylor, D.M. (1977). *Attitudes à l'égard du multicultur-
   alisme et des groupes ethniques au Canada*. Ottawa: Ministère des Approvision-
   nements et Services du Canada
Bialystok, E., and Ryan, E. B. (1985). A metacognitve framework for the devel-
   opment of first language and second language skills. In D.L. Forrest-Pressley,
   G.E. MacKinnon, & T.G. Waller (eds), *Meta-cognition, cognition, and human
   performance.* (pp 217–52). New York: Academic Press
Bourhis, R.Y., and Lepicq, D. (1993). Quebec French and language issues in
   Quebec. In R. Posner & J.N. Green (eds), *Trends in romance linguistics and
   philology:* Volume 5: *Bilingualism and linguistic conflict in romance* (pp 157–92).
   The Hague and Berlin: Mouton de Gruyter
Bruck, M. (1982). Language disabled children: Performance in an additive
   bilingual education program. *Applied Psycholinguistics*, 3:45–60
Cleghorn, A., and Genesee, F. (1984). Languages in contact: An ethnographic
   study of interaction in an immersion school. *TESOL Quarterly*, 18:595–625
Clément, R. (1980). Ethnicity, contact and communicative competence in a
   second language. In H. Giles, W.P. Robinson, and P.M. Smith (eds), *Lan-*

guage: Social psychological perspectives (pp 147–54). Oxford, NY: Pergamon Press

– (1984). Aspects socio-psychologiques de la communication inter-ethnique et de l'identité sociale. *Recherches Sociologiques, 15*:293–312

– (1986). Second language proficiency and acculturation: An investigation of the effects of language status and individual characteristics. *Journal of Language and Social Psychology, 5*:271–90

Clément, R., Gardner, R.C., and Smythe, P.C. (1977a). Inter-ethnic contact: Attitudinal consequences. *Canadian Journal of Behavioural Science, 12*:293–302

– (1977b). Motivational variables in second language acquisition: A study of Francophones learning English. *Canadian Journal of Behavioural Science, 9*:123–33

Clément, R., Gauthier, R., and Noels, K. (in press). Choix langagiers en milieu minoritaire: Attitudes et identité concomitantes. *Canadian Journal of Behavioural Science*

Clément, R., and Kruidenier, B.G. (1983). Orientations in second language acquisition: I. The effects of ethnicity, milieu, and target language on their emergence. *Language Learning, 33*:273–91

– (1985). Aptitude, attitude and motivation in second language proficiency: A test of Clément's model. *Journal of Language and Social Psychology, 4*:21–37

Clément, R., and Noels, K. (1992). Langue, statut et acculturation: une étude d'individus et de groupes en contact. In M. Lavallée, F. Ouellet, and F. Larose (eds), *Identité, culture et changement social: Actes du 3ième colloque de l'ARIC* (pp 315–26). Paris: L'Harmattan

– (1991). Towards a situated approach to ethnolinguistic identity: The effects of status on individuals and groups. *Journal of Language and Social Psychology*

Clément, R., Smythe, P.C., and Gardner, R.C. (1978). Persistence in second language study: Motivational considerations. *Canadian Modern Language Review, 34*:688–94

Cummins, J. (1976). The influence of bilingualisn on cognitive growth: A synthesis of research findings and explanatory hypotheses. *Working Papers on Bilingualism, 9*:1–43

– (1978). Bilingualism and the development of meta-linguistic awareness. *Journal of Cross-Cultural Psychology, 9*:131–49

– (1979). Lingusitic interdependence and the educational development of bilingual children. *Review of Educational Research, 49*:222–51

– (1983). Language proficiency, biliteracy and French immersion. *Canadian Journal of Education, 8*(2):117–38

– (1984). Bilingualism and Cognitive Functioning. In S. Shapson amd V. D'Oyley (eds), *Bilingual and Multicultural Education (Multilingual Matters; 15)*, Clevedon, Eng.: Multilingual Matters

- (1991). Forked tongue: The politics of bilingual education: A critique. *The Canadian Modern Language Review*, 47(4):786–93

Cummins, J., and Gulutsan, M. (1974). Some effects of bilingualism on cognitive functioning. In S. Carey (ed.), *Bilingualism, Biculturalism and Education*. Edmonton: University of Alberta Printing Dept

Cummins, J., and Swain, M. (1986). *Bilingualism in Education*. New York: Longman

Cziko, G.A., Lambert, W.E., and Gutter, J. (1980). The impact of immersion-in-a-foreign-language on pupils' social attitudes. *Working Papers on Bilingualism*, 19:13–28

Cziko, G.A., Lambert, W.E., Sidoti, N., & Tucker, G.R. (1980). Graduates of early immersion: Retrospective views of grade 11 students and their parents. In R.N. St.Clair and H. Giles (eds.), *The Social and Psychological Contexts of Language* (pp 131–92). Hillsdale, NJ: Erlbaum

d'Anglejan, A., Renaud, C., Arsenault, R.H., and Lortie, A.M. (1981).*Difficultés d'apprentissage de la langue seconde chez l'immigrant adulte en situation scolaire: Une étude dans le contexte québécois*. Québec: Centre international de recherche sur le bilinguisme

Darcy, N.T. (1953). A review of the literature on the effects of bilingualism upon the measurement of intelligence. *Journal of Genetic Psychology*, 82:21–57

Desrochers, A., and Clément, R. (1979). *The social psychology of inter-ethnic contact and cross-cultural communication: An annotated bibliography*. Québec: International Centre for Research on Bilingualism, Laval University

Desrochers, A., and Gardner, R.C. (1981). *Second language acquisition: An investigation of a bicultural excursion experience*. Quebec: International Centre for Research on Bilingualism, Laval University

Feuerverger, G. (1989). Jewish-Canadian ethnic identity and non-native language learning: A social-psychological study. *Journal of Multilingual and Multicultural Education*, 10(4):327–57

Gardner, R.C. (1979). Social psychologoical aspects of second language acquisition. In H. Giles and R. St. Clair (eds), *Language and Social Psychology* (pp 193–220). Oxford: Basil Blackwell

- (1980). On the validity of affective variables in second language acquisition: Conceptual, contextual and statistical considerations. *Language Learning*, 30:255–70

- (1985). *Social psychology and second langauge learning: The role of attitudes and motivation*. London: Arnold

Gardner, R.C., and Clément, R. (1990). Social psychological perspectives on second language acquisition. In H. Giles and W.P. Robinson (eds), *Handbook of Language and Social Psychology* (pp 495–517). Chichester, Eng.: John Wiley & Sons

Gardner, R.C., Ginsberg, R.C., and Smythe, P.C. (1976). Attitude and motivation in second-language learning: Course related changes. *Canadian Modern Language Review, 32*:243–6

Gardner, R.C., & Lalonde, R.N. (1983). The socio-educational model of second language acquisition: An investigation using LISREL causal modelling. *Journal of Language and Social Psychology, 2*:1–15

Gardner, R.C., and Lambert, W.E. (1959). Motivational variables in second language acquisition. *Canadian Journal of Psychology, 13*:266–72

– (1972). *Attitudes and motivation in second language learning.* Rowley, MA: Newbury House

Gardner, R.C., Moorcroft, R., and Metford, J. (1989). Second language learning in an immersion programme: Factors influencing acqustion and retention. *Journal of Language and Social Psychology, 8*:287–305

Gardner, R.C., and Smythe, P.C. (1975). Second language acquisition: A social psychological approach. *Research Bulletin No. 332*, Dept of Psychology, University of Western Ontario, London, Canada

Genesee, F. (1981). A comparison of early and late second language learning. *Canadian Journal of Behavioural Sciences, 13*:115–28

– (1987). *Learning through two languages.* Cambridge, MA: Newburg House

Genesee, F., and Bourhis, R.Y. (1982) The social psychological of code-switching in cross-cultural communication. *Journal of Language and Social Psychology, 1*:1–28

– (1988) Evaluative reactions to language choice strategies: Francophones and Anglophones in Québec City. *Language Sciences, 8*:229–50

Genesee, F., Holobow, N.E., Lambert, W.E., and Chartrand, L. (1989). Three elementary school alternatives for learning through a second language. *Modern Language Journal, 73*(2):250–63

Genesee, F., Morin, S., and Allister, T. (1974). *Evaluation of the 1973–74 pilot grade 7 French immersion class: June 1974.* Montreal: Protestant School Board of Greater Montreal, (mimeo)

Genesee, F., Tucker, G.R., and Lambert, W.E. (1978). The development of ethnic identity and ethnic role-taking skills in children from different school settings. *International Journal of Psychology, 13*:39–57

Giles, H., Bourhis, R.Y., and Taylor, D.M. (1977). Towards a theory of language in ethnic group relations. In H. Giles (ed.), *Language, ethnicity and intergroup relations* (pp 307–48). New York: Academic Press

Giles, H., and Byrne, J.L. (1982). An intergroup approach to second language acquisition. *Journal of Multilingual and Multicultural Development, 1*:17–40

Giles, H., and Robinson, W.P. (eds) (1990). *Handbook of language and social psychology.* London: John Wiley & Sons

Gliksman, L., Gardner, R.C., and Smythe, P.C. (1982). The role of the integrative motive on students' participation in the French classroom. *Canadian Modern Language Review*, 38:625–47

Gray, P. (1991, July). Whose America? *Time*, pp 8–13

Hamers, J. F., and Blanc, M.H.A. (1989). *Bilinguality and Bilingualism*. Cambridge, Eng.: Cambridge University Press

– (1983). *Bilingualité et bilinguisme*. Brussels: Mardaga. Série Psychgologie et Sciences Humaines

Hammerly, H. (1989a). French immersion (does it work?) and the development of the Bilingual Proficiency Report. *Canadian Modern Language Review*, 45(3):567–78

– (1989b). *French immersion: Myths and reality*. Calgary: Detselig Enterprises

Hanna, G., and Smith, A.H. (1979). Evaluating summer bilingual exchanges: A progress report. *Working Papers on Bilingualism*, 19:29–58

Harley, B. (1986). *Age in second language acquisition*. Clevedon, Avon, Eng.: Multilingual Matters

Harley, B., Allen, P., Cummins, J., and Swain, M. (eds) (1990). *The development of second language proficiency*. Cambridge, Eng.: Cambridge University Press

Harley, B., Cummins, J., Swain, M., and Allen, P. (1990). Introduction. In B. Harley, P. Allen, J. Cummins, and M. Swain (eds), *The Development of Second Language Proficiency* (pp 1–6). Cambridge, Eng.: Cambridge University Press

Kim, Y.Y., and Gudykunst, W.B. (eds) (1988). *Theories in intercultural communication*. Newbury Park: SAGE Publications

Lambert, W.E. (1974). Culture and language as factors in learning and education. In F.E. Aboud and R.D. Meade (eds), *Cultural Factors in Learning and Education*. Bellingham, WA: Fifth Western Washington Symposium on Learning

Lambert, W.E., Havelka, J., and Crosby, C. (1958). The influence of language acquisition contexts on bilingualism. *Journal of Abnormal and Social Psychology*, 60:44–51

Lambert, W.E., Moghaddam, F.M., Sorin, J., and Sorin, S. (1990). Assimilation vs multiculturalism: Views from a community in France. *Sociological Forum*, 5(3):387–411

Lambert, W.E., and Taylor, D.M. (1988). Assimilation versus multiculturalism: The views of urban Americans. *Sociological Forum*, 3(1):72–88

Lambert, W.E., and Tucker, G.R. (1972). *Bilingual education of children: The St Lambert experiment*. Rowley, MA: Newbury House

Landry, R., and Allard, R. (1990). Contact des langues et developpement bilingue: Un modèle macroscopique. *Canadian Modern Language Review*, 46:527–53

Lenneberg, E. (1967). *Biological foundations of language*. New York: Wiley

Lewis, C., and Shapson, S. M. (1989). Secondary French immersion: A study of students who leave the program. *The Canadian Modern Language Journal*, 45(3):539–78

Mowrer, O.H. (1950). On the psychology of 'talking birds': A contribution to language and personality theory. In O.H. Mowrer (ed.), *Learning theory and personality dynamics: Selected papers* (pp 668–726). New York: Ronald Press

Naiman, N., Frohlich, M., Stern, H.H., and Todesco, A. (1978). The good language learner. *Research in Education Series No. 7*. Toronto: Ontario Institute for Studies in Education

Oller, J.W., and Perkins, K. (1978). Intelligence and language proficiency as sources of variance in self-reported affective variables. *Language Learning*, 28:85–97

Ouellet, M. (1990). *Synthèse historique de l'immersion française au Canada suivie d'une bibliographie sélective et analytique*. Québec: Centre international de recherche sur l'aménagement linguistique. Publication B-175

Padilla, A.M., Lindholm, K.J., Chen, A., Duran, R., Hakuta, K., Lambert, W., and Tucker, G.R. (1991). The English-only movement: Myths, reality, and implications for psychology. *American Psychologist*, 46(2):120–30

Paillé, M. (1989). *Nouvelles tendances démolinguistiques dans l'île de Montréal 1981–1996*. Québec: Conseil de la langue française

Parkin, M., Morrison, F., and Watkin, G. (1987). *French immersion research relevant to decisions in Ontario*. Toronto: Queen's Printer for Ontario

Pawley, C. (1985). How bilingual are French immersion students? *Canadian Modern Language Review*, 41(5):865–76

Peal, E., and Lambert, W. E. (1962). The relation of bilingualism to intelligence. *Psychological Monographs*, 76:1–23

Pellerin, M., and Hammerly, H. (1986). L'expression orale après treize ans d'immersion française. *Canadian Modern Language Review*, 42(3):592–606

Penfield, W.P. and Roberts, L.R. (1959). *Speech and Brain Mechanism*. London: Oxford University Press

Prujiner, A., Deshaies, D., Hamers, J.M., Blanc, M., Clément, R., and Landry, R. (1984). *Variation du comportement langagier lorsque deux langues sont en contact*. Québec, CIRB, Série G, no. 5

Rogers, E.M., and Kincaid, D.L. (1981). *Communication networks: Toward a new paradigm for research*. New York: Free Press

Schlesinger, A. (1991, July). The cult of ethnicity, good and bad. *Time*, p 14

Shapson, S., and Day, E. M. (1982). A comparison study of three late immersion programs. *Alberta Journal of Educational Research*, 28:135–48

Spilka, I. (1976). Assessment of second-language performance in immersion programs. *Canadian Modern Language Review*, 32:543–61

Stennet, R.G., and Earl, L.M. (1982). *Elementary French program evaluation: The effect of succesive increases in instructional time.* Research Report, London, ON: Board of Education for the City of London

Stern, H.H. (1982). *Issues in early core French: A selective and preliminary review of the literature 1975–1981.* Research report no. 163. Toronto: Board of Education for the City of Toronto

Swain, M., and Lapkin, S. (1982). *Evaluating bilingual education: A Canadian case study.* Clevedon, Eng.: Multilingual Matters

– (1986). Immersion French in secondary schools: 'The goods' and 'the bads.' *Contact,* 5(3):2–9

– (1991). Heritage language children in an English-French bilingual program. *The Canadian Modern Language Review,* 47(4):635–41

Taylor, D.M. (1990). *Carving a new Inuit identity: The role of language in the education of Inuit children in Arctic Quebec.* Commissioned by Katvik School Board

Taylor, D.M., Ménard, R., and Rheault, E. (1977). Threats to ethnic identity and second language learning. In H. Giles (ed.), *Language, ethnicity and intergroup relations* (pp 99–118). London: Academic Press

Taylor, D.M., and Wright, S.C. (1989). Language attitudes in a multilingual northern community. *The Canadian Journal of Native Studies,* 9(1):85–119

Trites, R. (1981). *Primary French immersion: Disabilities and predictions of success.* Toronto: OISE Press

Vechter, A., Lapkin, S., and Argue, V. (1990). Second language retention: A summary of the issues. *Canadian Modern Language Review,* 46(2):289–303

Wesche, M.B., Morrison, F., Ready, D., and Pawley, C. (1990). French Immersion: Postsecondary consequences for individuals and universities. *Canadian Modern Language Review,* 46(3):430–51

Wiss, C. (1989). Early French immersion programs may not be suitable for every child. *Canadian Modern Language Review,* 45(3):517–29

Wrightsman, L.S. (1972). *Social psychology in the seventies.* Belmont, CA: Wadsworth Publishing Company

JIM CUMMINS

Heritage Language Learning
and Teaching

Although heritage language[1] teaching has been conducted by ethnocultural community groups in Canada throughout most of this century, it is only during the past 15 years that federal and provincial governments have provided direct funding to support such teaching. The allocation of 'taxpayers' money,' however modestly, to encourage the maintenance of 'non-official' languages and cultures represented a radical departure from previous assimilationist policies.

While ongoing demographic changes constitute an obvious political reality that underlies the response of governments to what has pejoratively been termed 'ethnic demands,' several more substantive rationales have also emerged in both national and provincial policy debates. Specifically, heritage language promotion has been justified as integral to any genuine policy of 'multiculturalism' since culture and language are so closely intertwined. It has also been argued that language maintenance promotes overall cognitive development and aspects of academic achievement among students from heritage language backgrounds. Finally, it has been suggested that heritage languages are significant national resources with respect to Canada's economic and diplomatic role in an increasingly interdependent world.

This paper focuses on the research basis for these claims. While most of the Canadian research that has been carried out focuses on the individual and societal factors that influence heritage language development, and the cognitive and academic correlates of such development, some research is also relevant for the broader issues of the relationship between heritage language promotion and multiculturalism policy generally and the potential economic and diplomatic benefits of investments in heritage language teaching. I will first sketch the policy background to these issues and outline the current status of heritage language provision across the country in order to provide a context for understanding the research that has been conducted.

POLICY CONTEXT AND CURRENT PROVISION

Federal policy with respect to heritage language teaching takes place within the context of Canada's national policy of multiculturalism, proclaimed by then Prime Minister Trudeau in October 1971. One outcome of this policy was the commissioning of the Non-Official Languages Study (O'Bryan, Reitz & Kuplowska 1976), which found substantial support among ethnocultural communities across the country for heritage language teaching within the public school system. A parallel study, the Majority Attitudes Study (Berry, Kalin & Taylor 1977), found some lukewarm support for the policy of multiculturalism among anglophone and francophone Canadians but significant opposition to the use of public monies to support the teaching of heritage languages.

Despite the ambivalence of many anglophone and francophone Canadians, the federal government initiated the Cultural Enrichment Program in 1977. This program provided some very modest support (approximately 10 per cent of the operating costs of supplementary schools, usually conducted on Saturday mornings) directly to ethnocultural communities for the teaching of heritage languages. This support was eliminated in 1990 (as part of a more general fiscal belt-tightening), but the federal government emphasized that it was simply changing priorities for heritage language support rather than diminishing its commitment to heritage languages. The major federal initiative in this area in recent years has been the proposed establishment of the National Heritage Languages Institute in Edmonton, Alberta. Although Parliament has allocated approximately six million dollars, no action has been taken by the federal government to establish the Institute at this time.

Because education is under provincial jurisdiction, the federal government cannot provide support directly to school systems for the teaching of heritage languages. Most provincial governments, however, operate programs designed to encourage the teaching of heritage languages. The most extensive of these provincial programs has been Ontario's Heritage Language Program (HLP). Announced in the spring of 1977, the HLP provides funding to school systems for 2½ hours per week of heritage language instruction. School systems are mandated to implement a program in response to a request from community groups who can supply a minimum of 25 students interested in studying a particular language. Currently, more than 60 languages are taught to more than 120,000 students in the HLP. A central aspect of the HLP is that the instruction must take place outside the regular five-hour school day. This allows for three basic options, namely, on weekends, after the regular school day, or integrated into a school day extended by half an hour. This latter option has been highly controversial within the Toronto Board of Education, occasioning a teacher work-to-rule for several months during the early 1980s (see Berryman 1986; Cummins & Danesi 1990, for more detailed accounts of these controversies).

In Quebec, the Programme d'Enseignement des Langues d'Origine (PELO) was also introduced in 1977. This program was established on generally similar lines to the Ontario HLP but on a considerably smaller scale. In 1989–90 14 languages were taught to 5886 students in the program. The Quebec government initially took responsibility for the development of programs of study and curriculum guides at the elementary level for Greek, Italian, Portuguese, and Spanish. Subsequently, the Ministry of Education delegated the responsibility to school boards which wished to offer courses in other languages. While it is possible for school boards to offer the language within the regular school day, this happens only rarely, most courses being offered for 30 minutes daily during the lunch break or before or after school (see d'Anglejan & De Koninck 1990; McAndrew 1991, for more detailed descriptions).

In Manitoba, Saskatchewan, and Alberta, provincial governments are generally very supportive of heritage language teaching, partly because of the relatively high proportion of the populations of these provinces that are of ethnocultural backgrounds and partly because, unlike Ontario, there has been relatively little controversy surrounding the teaching of heritage languages. In these three provinces, bilingual programs involving 50 per cent of the instruction through a heritage language are in operation, although the numbers of students involved are relatively small. The two most common languages taught in these bilingual programs are Ukrainian and German, although in Edmonton programs involving Hebrew, Yiddish, Chinese (Mandarin), Arabic, and Polish are also in operation. A variety of heritage languages are also taught as subjects within the school systems and by community groups with financial support from the provincial governments.

In British Columbia, one Russian-English bilingual program was started in 1983 and continues to operate in school district no. 9 at Castlegar. Beynon and Toohey (1991) estimate that there were about 17,000 students enrolled in community language schools in British Columbia in 1988–9. While policy-makers in the province for many years resisted pressure from ethnocultural communities to support heritage language teaching, the government has recently developed a policy framework that would support implementation of heritage language teaching should school districts choose to become involved in the area.

In the Atlantic provinces, approximately 1500 students were enrolled in heritage language supplementary school programs as of 1986–7. These programs received financial assistance from the federal government. No provincial government heritage language support programs are in place in these provinces.

RESEARCH FINDINGS

The review of research findings in this section is confined to research carried out in the Canadian context. For reviews of the international research literature, the reader is referred to Hakuta (1986) and Skutnabb-Kangas (1984). A previous review of the Canadian heritage language literature (Cummins 1983) surveyed the evaluation studies carried out prior to 1983 in some depth and thus the major focus of this review is on more recent studies. In addition to Cummins (1983), heritage language provision and research is documented in Cummins (1984, 1991a), and in Cummins and Danesi (1990). In reviewing the evaluation research, selected evaluations carried out prior to 1983 will be examined since few more recent evaluations are available. The research will be organized into four broad categories: (a) surveys of attitudes/experiences, (b) program evaluations, (c) studies of heritage language development in the home and preschool, and (d) studies that focus on correlates of heritage language development in school.

Survey Research

Survey research has tended to depict a relatively positive picture of heritage language programs across Canada. Keyser and Brown (1981), for example, reported a high degree of satisfaction with the program offered by the Metropolitan Separate School Board in Toronto on the part of both parents and school staffs. Almost eleven thousand parents responded to the questionnaire (representing more than 18,000 students in the program). Parents considered that the program had increased communication between family members (80 per cent), provided a deeper appreciation of family heritage (81 per cent), and improved performance in subject areas in the regular program (59 per cent). School principals were similarly positive about the impact of the heritage language program (HLP) in their schools, 61 per cent indicating that it had a positive effect and only 6 per cent a negative effect. Despite the overall positive orientation to the program revealed in the survey, the authors note that a small proportion of regular program teachers perceive the HLP as time-consuming and disruptive (see Cummins 1983, for a more extensive review).

A survey carried out by the Toronto Board of Education (Larter & Cheng 1986) showed that 88 per cent of respondents (569 out of 644) who included principals, teachers, heritage language instructors, and parents of children in integrated/extended day schools felt that children should learn their heritage language for the following major reasons: to improve communications with relatives; to enhance pride in heritage; to maintain and revitalize culture and religion; and because languages are best learned when young. While this report paints a generally positive picture of the integrated/extended day program in the Toronto board, it should be placed in the context of the fact that just two years prior to the report, negative feelings among regular program teachers about the proposal to institute heritage language teaching within an extended school day resulted in a six-month work-to-rule by the teachers.

A national survey of school boards carried out by the Canadian Education Association (1991) indicated that 'satisfaction with the heritage language programs runs high in almost every school board surveyed' (pp 47–8). Among the advantages cited by teachers, parents and students were the following: positive attitude and pride in one's self and one's background; better integration of the child into school and society; increased acceptance and tolerance of other peoples and cultures; increased cognitive and affective development; facility in learning other languages; increased job opportunities; stronger links between parent and school; and ability to meet community needs.

Disadvantages cited by boards of education were far fewer than advantages. According to the Canadian Education Association report, most boards mentioned primarily administrative difficulties connected to scheduling, classroom space, and class size, as well as shortages of appropriate teaching materials in the target language. A limitation of this survey is that the questionnaires were presumably completed most often by heritage language program coordinators in the different boards (the report does not specify who provided the data) and thus an overly positive picture of the program may have been presented.

In summary, the three surveys reviewed above suggest that heritage language programs tend to be viewed positively by both parents and school staff. This conclusion should be treated cautiously, however, in view of the fact that at times of political controversy in relation to the teaching of heritage languages (e.g., 1983–4 in Metropolitan Toronto - see Cummins & Danesi 1990) a substantial number of regular program teachers have expressed strong negative attitudes about the educational wisdom of teaching heritage languages. In addition, the Majority Attitudes Study (Berry et al. 1977) and the fourth OISE survey of public attitudes in Ontario (Livingston & Hart 1983) both indicated considerable public ambivalence in regard to government-supported heritage language teaching.

Evaluation Research

The evaluation research data are reviewed in Cummins (1983) and in the Appendix to Cummins and Danesi (1990). Cummins and Danesi drew the following conclusion on the basis of these evaluations: 'Virtually all the evaluations reviewed, whether of enrichment or transition programs, show clearly that time spent with the minority language as the medium of instruction results in no academic loss to students' progress in the majority language. In some cases, in fact, students who received less English instruction performed significantly better in English academic skills than comparison groups in all-English programs' (1990:133). Two examples will illustrate these patterns. The first example is of an 'enrichment' program (Fishman 1976) designed to promote bilingualism and biliteracy while the second is a 'transition' program intended to facilitate students' integration into the regular English-medium program.

Edmonton Public School Board English-Ukrainian Program
In September 1973, the Edmonton Public School Board (EPSB) introduced the English-Ukrainian bilingual program at the kindergarten level. In kindergarten 100 per cent of the instructional time was in Ukrainian, after which instructional time was divided equally between English and Ukrainian. Mathematics, English language arts, and science were taught in English, while social studies, physical education, Ukrainian language arts, art, and music were taught in Ukrainian.

More than three-quarters of the students came from homes in which one or both parents could speak Ukrainian and only about 10 per cent of the students had no Ukrainian ancestry. However, only about 15 per cent of the students were fluent in Ukrainian on entry to school. Unlike typical students in French immersion programs, the bilingual students were representative of the EPSB system in terms of both ability level and parental socioeconomic status. For example, their Grade 1 score (averaged over five years from 1974 to 1978) on the Metropolitan Readiness Test was only one point above the EPSB mean, and less than 50 per cent of the parents had post-secondary education (Edmonton Public Schools 1980).

In the first year of the evaluation, control students were chosen from among students in regular unilingual English program classes across the EPSB system whose parents had the same socioeconomic level and knowledge of Ukrainian as the program parents. In subsequent years control students were randomly chosen from the same schools as students in the bilingual program. The selection was stratified on the basis of gender, school, and ability level.

No consistent pattern of differences emerged in comparisons of English and mathematics skills between program and control students in the early grades. However, at the Grade 5 level (the last year of the evaluation) the first cohort of bilingual program students performed significantly better than control students in mathematics and on both decoding and comprehension subtests of the standardized reading test that was administered.

The evaluation carried out by the EPSB also examined the issue of whether the program was equally appropriate for students of different ability levels. This was done by dividing students into high, medium, and low ability levels and testing for program-by-ability interaction effects in a two-way analysis of variance design. No evidence of interaction effects was found, indicating that low-ability students had no more difficulty in the bilingual program than they would have had in the regular program.

A study was carried out with Grade 1 and 3 students in order to investigate bilingual children's metalinguistic development. The study (Cummins & Mulcahy 1978) revealed that students who were relatively fluent in Ukrainian because their parents used it consistently at home were significantly better able to detect ambiguities in English sentence structure than either equivalent unilingual English-speaking children not in the program or children in the program who came from predominantly English-speaking homes.

The EPSB evaluation also reported that students' Ukrainian skills developed in accord with program expectations and that students also developed an appreciation for and knowledge about Ukrainian culture. In addition, a large majority of the parents and program personnel were pleased with the program, thought the students were happy, and wanted the program to be continued to higher grade levels.

Toronto Board Italian Kindergarten Transition Program

In the early 1970s the Toronto Board of Education implemented an experimental transition program which allowed the curriculum to be presented in the child's first language (Italian) during the two introductory kindergarten years of schooling (i.e. ages 4–5, 5–6). The original proposal (Grande 1975) had recommended that literacy skills be introduced in the child's first language but this was rejected by the board because the Ontario Education Act prohibited the use of languages other than English or French as a medium of instruction except on a temporary basis to ease students' integration into the school system. Because of this legal restriction, promotion of Italian skills was not an objective of the program.

Almost all students in the program were born in Canada and had learned Italian (or dialect) as a first language. Seventy-nine percent of the parents spoke Italian extensively with their children, but only 53 per cent of the children still spoke Italian as the main language at home. Only 7 per cent of children who had older siblings were spoken to in Italian by these siblings. Thus, at the start of the program some children used more English than Italian, whereas others spoke no English at all.

In the classroom standard Italian, dialect, and English were all used quite freely with frequent spontaneous switching of languages by students and teacher. The proportion of English use increased consistently during the junior kindergarten (JK) year and by the senior kindergarten (SK) year 'Italian was used only occasionally in activities involving the whole class, but more often with a few individuals who still used their mother tongue' (Shapson & Purbhoo 1977:489).

The evaluation of the transition program involved observations of verbal participation in the classroom, tests of language comprehension, teacher assessments of student progress, and parent questionnaires. Comparisons were made with students in regular kindergarten classes from two other schools whose students had language backgrounds similar to those of the program students. There is little reason to suspect initial pre-treatment differences between program and comparison students since virtually all parents who were offered the transition option in the program school accepted it and the enrolment justified two transition classes.

Classroom observations showed that a significantly larger proportion of students in the transition classes participated in class discussions (59 per cent v 43 per cent), and contributed both spontaneously (45 per cent v 28 per cent) and in response to questions (41 per cent v 28 per cent). Shapson and Purbhoo suggest that 'Increased participation in class discussions may be considered a signal that the child feels comfortable and important in school. It might be viewed as an indicator of self-concept' (p 490). No group differences in English (or Italian) language comprehension as measured by the Peabody Picture Vocabulary Test were found in either JK or SK. Teachers' ratings of overall academic performacne revealed more positive comments for the transition students in SK. Shapson and Purbhoo caution, however, that this result may be due to differences in teachers' styles of reporting.

It was also reported that 'while parents from the comparison group expressed as great an interest in their children's education, the transition group parents attended more school functions, participated more in classroom events and talked regularly with the teacher' (1977:493). Shapson and Purbhoo attribute this greater involvement to the obvious fact that a common language makes communication easier.

In summary, the program objectives were clearly met in that participation by students and their parents in the educational process was facilitated by the incorporation of Italian as a medium of instruction.

The findings of one other longitudinal evaluation (Genesee, Tucker, & Lambert 1978; Genesee & Lambert 1980) are worth briefly noting in that they demonstrate that trilingual education involving a heritage language together with the two official languages is also feasible. Genesee and Lambert concluded on the basis of their evaluation of a Hebrew, French, English trilingual program in Montreal that these Hebrew day schools 'were able (1) to achieve the goals of regular school programs with regard to native language development and academic achievement, (2) to maintain important religious, cultural and linguistic traditions, and (3) at the same time, to develop the children's competence in a language of local importance' (p 25).

The evaluations reviewed above and in Cummins (1983) have focused on the effects of bilingual instruction on the individual student. Berryman (1986), by contrast, has carried out a case study that explored the effects of an integrated/extended day model of heritage language provision on the school system as a whole. He concluded that while such programs may generate short-term tensions within individual schools, they have more potential to legitimate heritage language provision as a valid educational enterprise than alternative models (e.g., weekend or after-school programs).

Heritage Language Development in the Home and Preschool

Several studies show that the use of a minority language in the home is not, in itself, a handicap to children's academic progress. For example, the Cummins and Mulcahy (1978) study reviewed above reported that students who used Ukrainian consistently at home were better able to detect ambiguities in English sentence structure than either monolingual English students or those who came from Ukrainian ethnic backgrounds but who used English mainly in the home. In a study conducted in Montreal among Italian background children, Bhatnagar (1980) reported that students who used both Italian and an official Canadian language (ie, English or French) in the home were performing better in English or French of both the spoken and written variety than those who used English or French all the time. He concluded that 'language retention ... should lead to higher academic adjustment, better facility in the host language, and better social relations of immigrant children' (1980: 155).

This conclusion is consistent with the results of a longitudinal study that followed 20 Portuguese-background students in Toronto from the Junior Kindergarten (JK) (age 4) through Grade 1 (age 6) levels (Cummins 1991c). The data indicated that the language shift process was already well-underway even at the JK level, despite the fact that parents and grandparents used Portuguese predominantly with them in the home. The process escalates during the early school years such that by the end of Grade 1, only two (out of 14) children were rated as more conversationally fluent in Portuguese than in English and only three were rated as equally proficient in English and Portuguese. In other words, the acquisition of English conversational fluency is not a problem for the vast majority of children but maintenance of the first language beyond a superficial level is a relatively rare phenomenon.

A second finding of this study was that both literate and conversational skills in children's L1 were significantly related to the development of literate and conversational skills in L2. In fact, the same developmental process appears to underlie growth in both languages in the sense that children who performed well in Portuguese literacy-related tasks at the JK, SK, and Grade 1 levels also tended to perform well in English literacy-related tasks at these grade levels. English reading skills at the Grade 1 level were almost as strongly predicted by Portuguese as by English measures of conversational and pre-literate skills.

This pattern has important implications for the education of bilingual students in the early years of schooling. It is still common practice in many school systems to discourage parents from promoting their children's L1 in the home and to assume that English (or French) language preschool would be more educationally appropriate than provision of preschool experiences in the child's home language. The fallacy of these assumptions can be seen by comparing the reading performance in English of children who were maintaining their Portuguese proficiency as compared to those who were losing their proficiency. The mean scores in Grade 1 Reading Vocabulary and Comprehension for those with higher ratings of Portuguese Conversational Proficiency at the Grade 1 level (N=6, scores 3–5) were 24.67 (Vocabulary) and 23.50 (Comprehension) compared to 16.62 and 15.75 for those with relatively low levels (N=8, scores 1 and 2). In other words, there is approximately one standard deviation difference in performance in favour of those who are maintaining their L1 skills. This is not a direct causal relationship since, as suggested above, both Portuguese and English oral proficiency, reading attainment and conceptual growth appear to be reflective of a more general developmental process. However, the positive relationship between Portuguese proficiency and English reading attainment does illustrate how misguided the assumptions of some educators are with respect to this issue.

Chumak-Horbatsch (1984) has similarly pointed to the difficulties of promoting languages in the home even when parents are committed to using the heritage language consistently with their children. In a study of parent and preschool child interaction in homes where parents had an explicit policy of speaking only Ukrainian with their children, Chumak-Horbatsch noted that children were frequently exposed to English in the environment (e.g., shopping trips) and in the home (e.g., when mothers answered the phone) and the status differential between the languages was already becoming apparent to children.

The experience of one heritage language preschool has been documented. This was a program initiated by the Inter-Cultural Association of Greater Victoria in cooperation with the Hindu Parishad and the Sikh Temple. The program was intended for Punjabi-speaking families with preschoolers (MacNamee & White 1985). Sessions took place Mondays and Wednesdays for two hours of the afternoon in a local church hall used as a meeting place by the Hindu Parishad. While the children attended a preschool program supervised by a preschool teacher and members of the local Punjabi-speaking community, the adults (mostly grandparents) got together for English-as-a-second-language (ESL) instruction taught by an ESL teacher.

MacNamee and White note that the initial goal of the preschool had been to help the children take first steps in using English while stimulating and reinforcing their command of their first language. However, they found that children who already had some preschool experience did not need any help with English but had to be encouraged to use Punjabi. The children's initial unwillingness to use the home language or to discuss Indian themes also extended to an attitude of rejection towards the older people when they contributed traditional songs and stories. This attitude gradually shifted as the program continued, although it did not disappear entirely:

By the third week, we noticed that the language balance was gradually shifting with a lot more Punjabi being used by the children in the preschool space - in play interaction, in spontaneous presentation of song and rhyme, and so on. It was found important to take a direct interest in the children's linguistic accomplishment, for with a little encouragement they provided Punjabi words for a wealth of items. That the previous preschool experiences these children have had - enriching though they may undoubtedly have been in many respects - did not come across as being supportive of a bilingual/bicultural lifestyle is suggested by an exchange that occurred during play. Two children are talking in Punjabi. A third child interjects (in English): 'No Punjabi in the school!' (1985:21)

At this point the preschool teacher talked with them about how not everybody can speak two languages and how lucky they are that they can. As a result of this type of encouragement the children became more eager to talk about their language and culture.

MacNamee and White go on to discuss the fact that in successful bilingual or multilingual situations languages are maintained because they have distinct contexts and ranges of functions. A preschool program focussing on heritage language development can help establish a distinct context for the heritage language by associating it with the home envi-

ronment and the ethnic community where it will not be in direct competition with the much more powerful English language. Such a program

can make truly bilingual/bicultural lifestyles possible for the young by demonstrating that two languages can be learned in tandem, with the development of
one contributing to the development of the other. In this way, preschool education, however alien it may be to the cultural tradition of an ethnic community
such as the one involved in our programme, can be a valuable supplement to the
family's efforts to implant and develop language and culture in the young child.
(p 22)

The preschool program can provide a structure whereby the ethnic
community can encourage parents to interact with their children in ways
that are likely to promote later school success (e.g., conversation, children's books, films, and educational events in the heritage language).
MacNamee and White stress, however, that the ethnic community itself
must be in charge of the program. They suggest that a proliferation of
ethnic preschools in Canada is neither unreasonable nor unworkable and
is, in fact, a rational response on the part of communities and educators
to the 'astounding' evidence that 'children whose language and culture
are only developing can, following preschool experiences in majority-
culture settings, already be rejecting their own families' language and
culture' (p 23).

This conclusion is clearly consistent with those of the Cummins
(1991c) study of language shift among Portuguese-background children.
It also reinforces the arguments of Wong Fillmore (1991) in the United
States context that preschool provision in children's home language is
crucial for continued communication between parents and children in
that language during the early school and adolescent years.

Correlates of Heritage Language Development in School

A large number of studies carried out since the early 1960s suggest that
far from being a negative force in children's personal and academic
development, bilingualism is positively related to aspects of both
cognitive and academic progress. Specifically, children who have
continued to develop their two languages are reported to exhibit a
greater sensitivity to linguistic meanings and greater flexibility in their
thinking than in the case of monolingual students (see Lambert 1990 for
a review).

A recent study carried out by Danesi, Cicogna, Gaspari, and Mene-chella (1990) illustrates this pattern. Two groups of 100 randomly chosen Italian-background children were compared on aspects of English language skills: one group that had studied Italian as a heritage language and a second group that had not. Significant differences were found in English spelling skills in favour of those who had studied Italian.

Two studies also suggest that development of heritage language proficiency can positively influence the learning of additional languages (Swain & Lapkin 1991). Both studies were conducted in a large Metropolitan Toronto school board that offers French as a second language for 20 minutes a day from Grades 1 through 4 followed by the option of a French-English bilingual program from Grades 5 through 8. Students also have the option of participating in a heritage language program from kindergarten through Grade 8.

The first study (Bild & Swain 1989) reported that Grade 8 students from heritage language backgrounds performed better than an English-background group on a variety of grammatical measures of French but not on measures of lexical knowledge. A significant positive correlation between the number of years in heritage language classes and indices of French proficiency was also noted in this study.

The second study (Swain, Lapkin, Rowen & Hart 1991) involved more than 300 Grade 8 students in the same bilingual program. Swain et al. compared four groups of students on various measures of French proficiency: those who had no knowledge of a heritage language (HL); those with some knowledge but no literacy skills in the HL; those with HL literacy skills but who mentioned no active use of HL literacy; and finally those who understand and use the HL in the written mode. The first group had parents with higher educational and occupational status than the other three groups, who did not differ in this regard.

Highly significant differences in favour of those students with HL literacy skills were found on both written and oral measures of French. There was also a trend for students from Romance language backgrounds to perform better in oral aspects of French, but the effect of this variable was considerably less than the effect of literacy in the heritage language. The authors conclude that there is transfer of knowledge and learning processes across languages and development of first-language literacy entails concrete benefits for students' acquisition of subsequent languages.

The interdependence of literacy-related skills across languages was also investigated in four studies carried out in the Toronto context with

Japanese-, Vietnamese-, and Portuguese-background students. Cummins, Swain, Nakajima, Handscombe, Green, and Tran (1984) set out explicitly to test the hypothesis that cognitive/academic aspects of L1 and L2 are interdependent in two studies involving 91 Japanese and 45 Vietnamese-background students. The Japanese students were the children of temporary residents who were in Canada for business or professional reasons, whereas the Vietnamese sample consisted of refugee students. The Japanese students attended a Saturday Japanese school which aimed to help students keep up with the curriculum in Japan in order to ease scholastic reintegration when they returned (often after as much as 5–6 years of residence abroad). Students were selected from Grades 2–3 and 5–6 (Canadian grades) in order to allow the effects of length of residence (LOR) to be separated from age of arrival (AOA). Thus, a Grade 2 student with two years LOR has an AOA of about five years whereas the AOA for a Grade 6 student with two years LOR is about nine years. All the Vietnamese sample were recent arrivals (LOR 5–22 months) and ranged in age between nine and seventeen years. Thus, all the sample had received at least some education in Vietnamese prior to immigration to Canada.

The dependent variables for the Japanese group consisted of five English decontextualized verbal academic measures (two reading measures from the Grade 2 Gates McGinitie reading tests and three oral language tasks) and contextualized measures derived from ratings of student interviews (administered to a subsample, N=59). Students were also interviewed in Japanese and were administered a Japanese standardized diagnostic reading measure.

A factor analysis of English measures in the Japanese study revealed three factors: (1) a grammatical competence factor, (2) an interactional style factor related to the amount of elaboration and detail volunteered by students in the interview, and (3) a decontextualized or verbal academic competence factor. Regression analyses of these three factor scores on L2 exposure (i.e., LOR) and personal attribute variables (e.g., parent ratings of student personality traits) showed a strong relationship between LOR and all three dimensions. The proportion of explained variance ranged from .26 for the English grammatical factor to .17 for the verbal academic factor with the interactional style factor in an intermediate position (R square = .21). A block of variables representing L1 cognitive/academic attributes of the students (e.g. Japanese reading T-score, AOA in Canada) was entered next into the equation. This block added only 3 per cent and 6 per cent to the explained variance for L2 grammatical competence and interactional style but 18 per cent to explained variance for the L2 verbal academic factor. Next, a block representing Japanese interactional style and parental ratings of their children's extraversion-introversion was added. This block accounted for only 4 per cent and 2 per cent increment to explained variance for L2 grammatical competence and verbal academic abilities but 17 per cent increment for the English interactional style factor. In other words, variables related to students' L1 cognitive and literacy skills contributed significantly to the development of L2 cognitive and literacy skills, while interactional style dimensions in L1 and L2 were closely related to personality attributes of the students. In contrast to the role individual attributes of the students played in the development of these aspects of L2 proficiency, grammatical proficiency in L2 was most significantly influenced by variables related to the amount of L2 input students received (i.e., LOR).

The major variable predicting Japanese academic proficiency was age on arrival. The older a student was when s/he immigrated to Canada, the more likely to perform well on the Japanese measures.

The interdependence hypothesis was also supported in the Vietnamese study, where performance on a Vietnamese antonyms measure together with students' age accounted for 61 per cent of the variance in an English antonyms measure. Probably due to the restricted range for LOR among the Vietnamese sample, LOR accounted for only 6 per cent of the variance in the English antonyms measure when entered first into the regression equation.

A more recent study of 273 Grades 2–8 Japanese students in Toronto (Cummins & Nakajima 1987) reported findings consistent with those of the previous study. English and Japanese standardized measures of reading were administered to the sample together with assessments of writing skills in both languages. LOR accounted for 35 per cent of the variance in English reading scores with the verbal academic block (Japanese reading, AOA, and age) accounting for an additional 20 per cent. Minimal variance was accounted for by these variables on measures of English writing (e.g., holistic ratings of writing quality and spelling errors). It was possible to examine the relationship between English and Japanese writing measures for a subsample (N=70). A number of Japanese writing variables related significantly to overall quality of English writing and to English spelling. Among the strongest relationships was that between Japanese spelling (Katakana) and English spelling. This relationship was independent of more general cognitive/academic variables such as Japanese reading proficiency and age.

The interdependence hypothesis was also supported in a study of 191 Grade 7 Portuguese-background students in Toronto. It was found that measures of students' discourse proficiency (i.e. judgments regarding coherence and cohesiveness of text) in Portuguese and English were strongly interrelated (r=.54, p<.001, N=65). The English discourse measure loaded on a Portuguese proficiency dimension in a principal components analysis carried out on the data (Cummins, Lopes & King 1987; Cummins, Harley, Swain & Allen 1990).

In this study, a number of predictors related significantly to indices of Portuguese proficiency. As summarized by Cummins et al.:

With respect to the formal measures of Portuguese proficiency, amount of exposure, both formal exposure in heritage language classes and the informal exposure involved in visits to Portugal, amount of Portuguese television watched, use made of other forms of Portuguese media (e.g. radio, reading books, writing letters), and going to mass in Portuguese, appeared to play a major role in predicting different aspects of proficiency, particularly oral grammatical proficiency. (1990:125)

It is significant that in this study there was minimal variation in students' oral fluency in English but considerable variation in indices of both academic and conversational Portuguese proficiency. Virtually all students exhibited English conversational abilities that were close to indistinguishible from those of native speakers of English, but there was clear evidence of loss of Portuguese language skills among a substantial number of students. Very large differences on Portuguese language measures (particularly on grammatical indices) were found when students' proficiency was compared to that of a sample of monolingual students in the Azores.

Finally, a recent study (De Koninck & d'Anglejan 1991) conducted in Quebec compared the oral and written production of allophone and francophone students at both elementary and secondary levels. It was possible to distinguish certain features of the allophones' productions that reflected the use of second language learning strategies (e.g., use of non-specific vocabulary).

CONCLUSION

A considerable amount of research on heritage language development has been carried out in the Canadian context. This research shows clearly that bilingual and even trilingual programs that use a heritage language as a medium of instruction are feasible. As in the case of French-English bilingual programs for both majority and minority students, less instruction through the societal majority language (i.e. English outside of Quebec) does not result in lower levels of academic performance in that language. This pattern has been attributed to the interdependence of cognitive and academic abilities across languages (e.g., Cummins 1983).

A moderate relationship of cognitive and academic abilities across languages was also observed in studies involving students from Japanese, Vietnamese, and Portuguese backgrounds. These studies also highlighted the rapidity of first-language loss among minority students. This language shift process appears particularly strong with students who arrive in Canada at relatively young ages (prior to 8) or who are born in Canada.

This pattern is consistent with the claim of respondents in the Non-Official Languages study (O'Bryan et al. 1976) that support from the school is required if heritage languages are to be maintained even at a minimal level across generations. The extent to which typical programs involving less than three hours per week can succeed in promoting maintenance has not been answered by the research, although several studies show significant correlations between attendance at heritage language classes and proficiency in the language. Attainment of literacy in the heritage language also appears to entail advantages with respect to the learning of additional languages and the development of metalinguistic awareness.

These data suggest that the misgivings that some educators have with respect to the educational wisdom of heritage language teaching have little basis in reality. There is no evidence of any negative effect of heritage language development on proficiency in the official languages; in fact, the trends in the research are all in the opposite direction, suggesting that the development of literacy in the heritage language may enhance aspects of students' academic performance in the two official languages.

A number of other issues related to the intersection of heritage language provision and multicultural education that have not been subject to formal research to this point should be raised. The question of how effective heritage language teaching is in reversing language loss has not been answered; nor do we know what levels of proficiency formal heritage language teaching (whether in public or supplementary schools) is capable of developing. These would appear to be urgent issues to investigate if heritage languages are seriously viewed as human resources that have significance for both domestic policy (multiculturalism) and international relations.

A second issue concerns the relationship between heritage language provision and anti-racist education. A major goal of multicultural policy is to promote equity for students from diverse backgrounds and among the multicultural initiatives in school boards have been attempts to involve parents from ethnocultural backgrounds more actively in the life of the school and attempts to reduce bias in standardized psychological and achievement testing. Neither of these forms of initiative is likely to be particularly successful when school staffs remain monolingual and monocultural. It has been suggested (Cummins 1991b) that a broadened conception of heritage language provision might be capable of addressing these equity issues more adequately than is presently the case. This proposal is for the creation of a new category of 'community language specialist' in the public schools. The mandate of these professionals would be (a) to teach heritage languages or tutor children in first language literacy skills, (b) to assist in assessing children's level of functioning in their home language either as an adjunct to psychological or speech/language assessment in English or as an aid to initial placement of students, and (c) to undertake school-community liaison with respect to visiting families, translation of materials to be sent home, interpretation at parent-teacher meetings, and orientation of new students and parents. The presence on school staffs of people with knowledge of particular communities and their languages would represent an important resource to enable the entire school to fulfil its educational mandate. This type of provision is necessary if heritage language development is to become a legitimate part of children's educational experience and form part of a broader anti-racist program focused on educational equity.

NOTES

1 The term 'heritage language' usually refers to all languages other than the Aboriginal languages of First Nations peoples and the 'official' Canadian languages (English and French). A variety of other terms have been used in Canada to refer to heritage languages: for example, 'ethnic,' 'minority,' 'ancestral,' 'third,' and 'non-official' have all been used at different times and in different provinces. The term used in Quebec is 'langues d'origine.' The term 'community languages' used commonly in Australia, Britain, and

New Zealand is rarely used in the Canadian context. A number of Canadian proponents of heritage language teaching have expressed misgivings about the term because 'heritage' connotes learning about past traditions rather than acquiring language skills that have significance for children's overall educational and personal development. In the Toronto Board of Education the term 'modern languages' is used partly in an attempt to defuse the strong emotional reactions that the term 'heritage languages' evokes.

REFERENCES

Benyon, J., and K. Toohey. (1991). Heritage language education in British Columbia. *Canadian Modern Language Review,* 47(4):606–16
Berry, J.W., Kalin, R. and Taylor, D.M. (1977). *Multiculturalism and ethnic attitudes in Canada.* Ottawa: Ministry of Supply and Services Canada
Berryman, J. (1986). Implementation of Ontario's Heritage Languages Program: A case study of the extended school day model. Unpublished doctoral dissertation, University of Toronto
Bhatnagar, J. (1980). Linguistic behaviour and adjustment of immigrant children in French and English schools in Montreal. *International Review of Applied Psychology,* 29:141–59.
Bild, E.R., and Swain, M. (1989). Minority language students in a French immersion programme: Their French proficiency. *Journal of Multilingual and Multicultural Development,* 10(3):255–74
Canadian Education Association. (1991). *Heritage language programs in Canadian school boards.* Toronto: Canadian Education Association
Chumak-Horbatsch, R. (1984). Language in the Ukrainian home: Its use in ten Toronto families attempting to preserve their mother tongue. Doctoral dissertation, University of Toronto
Cummins, J. (1983). *Heritage language education: A literature review.* Toronto: Ministry of Education, Ontario
– (1984). *Heritage languages in Canada: Research perspectives.* Ottawa: Multiculturalism Canada
– (ed.) (1991a). Heritage languages (Special Issue). *The Canadian Modern Language Review,* 47(4)
– (1991b). Introduction. *The Canadian Modern Language Review,* 47(4):601–5
– (1991c). The development of bilingual proficiency from home to school: A longitudinal study of Portuguese-speaking children. *Journal of Education,* 173:85–98

– , and Danesi, M. (1990). *Heritage languages: The development and denial of Canada's linguistic resources.* Toronto: Our Schools Our Selves/Garamond

Cummins, J., and Mulcahy, R. (1978). Orientation to language in Ukrainian-English bilingual children. *Child Development,* 49:1239–42

Cummins, J., Harley, B., Swain, M., and Allen, P. (1990). Social and individual factors in the development of bilingual proficiency. In B. Harley, P. Allen, J. Cummins, and M. Swain (eds) *The development of second language proficiency* (pp 119–33). Cambridge, Eng.: Cambridge University Press

Cummins, J., Lopes, J., and King, M.L. (1987). The language use patterns, language attitudes, and bilingual proficiency of Portuguese Canadian children in Toronto. In B. Harley, P. Allen, J. Cummins, and Swain, M. *The development of bilingual proficiency.* Volume 3. *Social context and age.* Final report submitted to the Social Sciences and Humanities Research Council. Modern Language Centre, Ontario Institute for Studies in Education

Cummins, J., and Nakajima, K. (1987). Age of arrival, length of residence, and interdependence of literacy skills among Japanese immigrant students. In B. Harley, P. Allen, J. Cummins, and M. Swain, *The development of bilingual proficiency. Volume 3. Social context and age.* Final report submitted to the Social Sciences and Humanities Research Council. Modern Language Centre, Ontario Institute for Studies in Education

Cummins, J., Swain, M., Nakajima, K., Handscombe, J., Green, D., and Tran, C. (1984). Linguistic interdependence among Japanese and Vietnamese immigrant students. In C. Rivera (ed.), *Communicative competence approaches to language proficiency assessment. Research and application* (pp 60–81). Clevedon, Avon, Eng.: Multilingual Matters

Danesi, M., Cicogna, C., Gaspari, A., and Menechella, G. (1990). Lo studio di una seconda lingua in un contesto scolastico-formale. Risultati di una ricerca statistica. *Rassegna Italiana di Linguistica Applicata,* 22: 205–25

d'Anglejan, A., and De Koninck, Z. (1990). Educational policy for a culturally plural Quebec. In V. D'Oyley and S. Shapson (eds), *Innovative multicultural teaching* (pp 151–66). Toronto: Kagan and Woo

De Koninck, Z., and d'Anglejan, A. (1991). Une étude de productions orales et écrites d'élèves allophones et d'élèves francophones frequentant des écoles pluriethniques de Montréal. Unpublished manuscript, Université Laval

Edmonton Public Schools (1980). *Summary of the evaluations of the bilingual English-Ukrainian and bilingual English-French program.* Edmonton: Edmonton Public School Board

Fishman, J. (1976). Bilingual education: What and why? In J.E. Alatis and K. Twaddell (eds), *English as a second language in bilingual education* (pp 263–72). Washington, DC: TESOL

Genesee, F., and Lambert, W.E. (1980). Trilingual education for the majority
group child. Unpublished research report, McGill University
Genesee, F., Tucker, G.R., and Lambert, W.E. (1978). An experiment in trilin-
gual education: Report 3. *Canadian Modern Language Review*, 34:621–43
Grande, A. (1975). A transition program for young immigrant children. In A.
Wolfgang (ed.), *Education of immigrant students* (pp 35–45). Toronto: OISE
Hakuta, K. (1986). *Mirror of language: the debate on bilingualism*. New York: Basic
Books
Keyser, R., and Brown, J. (1981). *Heritage language survey results*. Research
Department, Metropolitan Separate School Board, Toronto
Lambert, W. (1990). Persistent issues in bilingualism. In Harley, B., Allen, P.,
Cummins, J., and Swain, M. *The development of second language proficiency* (pp
201–18). Cambridge, Eng.: Cambridge University Press
Larter, S., and Cheng, D. (1986). *Teaching heritage languages and cultures in an
integrated/extended day*. Research Report #181. Toronto: Toronto Board of
Education
Livingston, D.W., and Hart, D.J. (1983). *Public attitudes towards education in
Ontario 1982: Fourth OISE survey*. Toronto: OISE
MacNamee, T., and White, H. (1985). Heritage language in the preschool.
Language and Society, 15:20–3
McAndrew, M. (1991). L'enseignement des langues d'origine à l'école publique
en Ontario et au Québec: Politiques et enjeu. *The Canadian Modern Language
Review*, 47(4):617–34
O'Bryan, K.G., Reitz, J., and Kuplowska, O. (1976) *The non-official languages
study*. Ottawa: Supply and Services Canada
Shapson, S., and Purbhoo, M. (1977). A transition program for Italian children.
Canadian Modern Language Journal, 33:486–96
Skutnabb-Kangas, T. (1984). *Bilingualism or not: The education of minorities*.
Clevedon, Avon, Eng.: Multilingual Matters
Swain, M., and Lapkin, S. (1991). Heritage language children in an English-
French bilingual program. *Canadian Modern Language Review*, 47(4):635–41
Swain, M. Lapkin, S., Rowen, N., and Hart, D. (1991). The role of mother
tongue literacy in third language learning. In S.P. Norris and L.M. Phillips
(eds), *Foundations of literacy policy in Canada* (pp 185–206). Calgary: Detselig
Enterprises
Wong Fillmore, L. (1991). A question for early-childhood programs: English
first or families first? *Education Week*, 19 June 1991

PETER J. GAMLIN, DAGMAR BERNDORFF,

ANNA MITSOPULOS, AND KLIA DEMETRIOU

Multicultural Education in Canada from a Global Perspective

OVERVIEW

This paper considers Canadian research on Multicultural Education (ME) over the past two decades. An extensive search of the Canadian Educational Index (CEI), the Educational Resources Information Center (ERIC), and Dissertation Abstracts International (DAI) generated materials for the literature review. Although the primary concern of the paper was to examine ME research in Canada, secondary objectives included a review of ME policy and programs. Research in the field of English as a Second Language (ESL) is considered in relation to the more general field of ME. The considerable space allocated to conceptual analysis in this paper was deemed necessary since there is a relative paucity of research and theoretical guidance specific to the field of ME. Recommendations are provided to scholars, suggesting promising new directions for both basic and applied research.

INTRODUCTION

A few comments will serve to root the phrase 'multicultural education' in a conceptual context that has been endorsed by every major scholar in the field. First and foremost, education *for* a multicultural, pluralistic society provides ME for everyone, an ideal that emphasizes 'unity over diversity,' putting commonality ahead of difference, underlining the belief in equality of opportunity and equity of outcome for all people, respect for human dignity, and the conviction that no single pattern of living will be valued above another. On this view, to be different is not to be inferior (Kallen 1956); 'a difference is not a deficit.' To be different presents a challenge and an opportunity to find the ways and means for establishing a 'partnership' or partnerships between others who may also be 'different' and/or with the 'others' who may constitute the mainstream 'other(s)' in the society.

This view of multicultural education (ME) presents a dilemma, namely, how to balance minority culture distinctions with national unity concerns. On the one hand, there is a pull away from multiculturalism in the clamour of the mainstream of peoples for efforts to be directed towards social cohesion and national identity. On the other hand, we have multiculturalism, which seems to be propelled by two dominant forces perceived as a kind of 'brake' to national unity: one is directed at global multiculturalism, a universalism that is internationalist in its orientation, affirming that individuals from all cultures are viewed as sharing and holding in common certain values and concerns; the other force is directed towards the necessity for some degree of autonomy or 'distinctiveness' for minority groups within the mainstream of society. In both cases, there is a common de-emphasis on the need for a unidimensional focus on national identity as the pre-eminent overarching concern.[1]

UNITY IN DIVERSITY

Before we can give serious thought to research on multicultural education (ME) in Canada it is useful to further consider the issues raised above and to do so from a cross-cultural, global perspective. Multicultural policy seems somewhat at odds with mainstream opinion. For example, if the dominant opinion prevails that multiculturalism acts as a 'brake' on national unity, then the mainstream will not give full support to a policy valuing difference and/or global commonality perspectives. Newcomers will be asked to become 'Canadian,' under the assumption that by joining the mainstream, national unity and social cohesion will result. But there is ample evidence that this assumption is flawed. It seems clear that while many members of minority groups in the United States and Canada, especially in second and third generations, have shed a good deal of their cultural distinctiveness, their associations with other minority groups are minimal, as are their contacts with the dominant society. We need only mention the racial riots in Halifax, New York, and Washington. This state of affairs would seem to underlie the demands by especially 'visible minority' groups (more contemporary language would refer to 'persons of colour') for strong anti-racist legislation. This kind of perspective has led to the rejection of the assimilationist or

melting pot paradigm and the adoption of anti-racist legislation. Ultimately, this perspective has led to the conclusion that while the invitation to join the mainstream may be appealing, in practice it is prejudice,
stereotyping, and in general discriminatory attitudes that hold sway,
thereby preventing access to the mainstream societal process.

Considering the foregoing comments, an effective multicultural policy
must therefore be developed to address not only mainstream concerns of
national unity, but also to respond to the reality of racism and prejudice.
Indeed, existing multicultural policy and legislation including anti-racist
legislation may be perceived to create further disunity in that the current
emphasis is on maintaining cultural distinctiveness and/or on embrac-
ing commonality by focusing on universalism to resolve discriminatory
and prejudicial attitudes.

In order to develop a more comprehensive approach to multiculturalism in response to the concerns raised above, we need to consider exactly
what is appealing about the melting pot ideal since this turns out to be
one of the central sticking points in the piece. The key idea is that as
newcomers are exposed to 'resident' nationals both will be transformed;
a totally new blend, culturally and biologically, is achieved. This contin-
ual process of evolution would be driven by an appeal to the need for
national unity and social cohesion, as seen above. Perhaps unintentional-
ly, however, proponents of the melting pot ideal have adopted, at least
implicitly, a point of view that would define and anticipate an idealized
outcome for this so-called evolutionary process. The paradigm model
has come to be known as the Anglo-Core Culture Conformity (ACCC)
ideal. Indeed, when one speaks of assimilation in Canada it is generally
in reference to this ideal. Obviously to anticipate an idealized outcome
for the 'evolutionary' process is to defeat the very meaning of transformation. This may in fact be the central problem, because while ME may
result in cultural groups having deeper understanding of their cultural
heritages and those of others, and while prejudices are minimized and
the appreciation of all differences maximized, the central problem will
remain: some groups will be disenfranchised with respect to social stratification. Various groups will continue to get different access to society's
socioeconomic resources. In other words, some cultural groups wind up
on top of the heap, others in the middle, and others at the bottom.

As we redress this imbalance, we have begun to make a case for
multiculturalism, which translates in the above analysis to making a case
for the transformative process itself, unencumbered by preconceived
notions, including ACCC ideals. This is, of course, making a case for the

democratic process. According to Tesconi (1990), the multicultural argument essentially takes the older position on Cultural Pluralism (Kallen 1956).[2] The core of this argument is that 'one's group must be free to bring its contributions, its strengths, its values, etc., to a larger democratic process. If the group is not permitted to do this, because of Anglo-conformity or melting pot demands, then democracy does not exist' (Tesconi 1990:33).

On this last point, a solution to the 'multicultural dilemma' should be found in the democratic process. In respect to 'unity' in diversity issues, access to democratic institutions and process seem to provide a level playing field upon which the various forces for evolutionary change could play themselves out. But clearly the 'playing field' has been tilted and politicized to the point where even James Banks, who has written widely in support of cultural pluralism and multicultural education, warns us that 'if carried to its logical extreme, the cultural pluralism argument can be used to justify racism, cultural genocide, and other cultural practices which are antithetical to a democratic society' (Banks 1981:229).

THE GLOBAL RESPONSE

The global influence on ME is clearly reflected in approaches taken in the United Kingdom. James Lynch (1989), for example, has devoted an entire chapter to human rights issues, which he believes should constitute the core of the ME curriculum. Outlining the history of human rights legislation beginning with the Universal Declaration of Human Rights, presented to the General Assembly of the United Nations in December 1948, Lynch details the subsequent response to this declaration at various national levels. Since its 30 articles cover freedom of thought, expression, religion, and assembly, and include passages on discrimination, torture, unfair detention, rights to life, a home, work, education, and health, it is perhaps not surprising that 'policing' that body of laws has never been a high priority for governments. Canada has done perhaps more than any other nation to formally incorporate many aspects of the original Declaration. Canada has both a Human Rights Act, passed in 1977, and a Charter of Rights and Freedoms, dating from 1982 and attached to its constitution. Section 27 of the Charter specifically supports the preservation and enhancement of the multicultural heritage of Canadians. There is also a more recent Multiculturalism Act (12 July 1988, Bill C-93), which aims to give full legislative expression to the racial and cultural diversity of Canada, to provide for a race relations strategy, to engage the public in overcoming prejudice and discrimination, and institutions in securing equality, regardless of race, colour, age, religion, or sex. There are extensive structural facilities at national and provincial levels for the enforcement of all these provisions. The United States also has civil rights legislation and a Commission at the national level, with other organs at state and sometimes county levels. Countries such as the United Kingdom have legislation against racial and gender discrimination but not yet against religious intolerance or discrimination. As Lynch (1989) notes:

human rights represent the only universally recognized codes for the regulation of human behaviour across the levels and dimensions of the global multicultural curriculum; human rights go beyond cultural diversity to the domain of common humanity, common values and common entitlements. In this respect they reinforce the sense of similarity, of human unity, and attitudes of reciprocity and solidarity, which are at the heart of a global multicultural curriculum. They diminish rather than enhance social category salience. They alone embrace and comprehend all cultural diversity, including moral diversity, and extend it. They are normative statements about human life. They derive from the very existence of that life, they apply everywhere and to everyone, and are, thus, the only universal body of moral guidance on the relationships of individuals, groups and nations, and internally within nations. (p. 72)

This is a ringing statement indeed, and would be totally convincing as the basis upon which to build an ME curriculum as well as to conduct research on ME, except for an earlier caveat: the fundamental dilemma for ME that was introduced above. The human rights approach might be perceived to weaken national boundaries and social cohesion within those boundaries, and is therefore left open to critique based on national unity issues. Nevertheless, this approach is an important step towards rationalizing the democratic process, so as to offer a playing field that provides common purchase for everyone. Unfortunately, while the recourse to universal principles governing human conduct, realized principally in human rights legislation of one kind or another, may ameliorate stereotypic and prejudicial perceptions, both across and within diverse ethnic and mainstream groups, the hard fact remains that this position will be perceived by many as a direct challenge to the preservation of national boundaries. We must resolve this dilemma if we are to develop convincing ME curricular activities as well as strategies for research. Some suggestions in this direction are made below, but first we shall consider the Australian and Canadian positions on multicultural policy and ME programming.

THE AUSTRALIAN RESPONSE

The Australian approach to ME was selected for separate comment because of the extraordinary effort that has been devoted to exploring many of the issues raised above. Furthermore, there are many similarities between Canada and Australia in respect to indigenous as well as non-indigenous populations and to resultant demands in various degrees by different cultural groups for 'distinct society' status.

The most recent document dealing with policy issues in ME was prepared by the National Advisory and Co-Ordinating Committee on Multicultural Education (NACCME). The report was titled *Education in and for a Multicultural Society: Strategies and Issues for Policy Making* (May 1987). To quote from NACCME: 'Pluralism requires not just an acceptance of and request for differences and other points of view, but also of learning how to cope and manage value conflicts and tension' (p 23). We will learn to do this in the NACCME view through intercultural understanding and recourse to universal human values: ' Within Australian society, there are binding values which form the basis of commonality in a pluralistic society, and which can lead to a more equitable multicultural curriculum. Tolerance, impartiality, respect, integrity and honesty are among the more obvious values which both permit and yet ultimately circumscribe cultural plurality. Indeed such values, if consciously held and pursued, *will resolve the apparent paradox of a pluralistic common culture*' (p 31). This is the hope and the promise.

Although it is clear on the NACCME framework that intercultural understanding is the key and that universal values and human rights is the motor, it is not so clear that good will, respect for the national boundary, and social cohesion will be the outcome. More radical developments may ensue.

Spurred on by the spirit of internationalism and universal human rights, supported by a truly democratic ethos, there is nothing to prevent a radical and 'evolutionary' process from emerging. This is one aspect of the ME dilemma because on this account the primary value and overarching concern in intercultural education is for the *global community*, which could conceivably and on occasion take precedence over the maintenance and preservation of national boundaries.[3]

As far as minority culture boundaries are concerned, we simply have no idea what effect the focus on intercultural education will have on the maintenance of those boundaries. Increased intercultural understanding and greater sensitivity to the global community may also weaken minority culture boundaries. Alternatively, minority culture boundaries may be maintained to co-exist with a greater appreciation of global community priorities. Social cohesion within national boundaries then would receive diminished attention. There is no research or theoretical position that would predict differentially between these possible outcomes. But it would seem plausible and borne out by recent events at Oka, Quebec, that those cultural groups striving to right perceived injustice, particularly in respect to social stratification, may very well seek recourse in a global forum and through an institution such as the United Nations.

THE CANADIAN RESPONSE

In order to establish a context for Canadian research on ME, it is not only necessary to pull out the central issues as we have done above, but also to consider global curricular responses to ethnic diversity. A useful framework is provided by Lynch (1989:35–43). Following a brief presentation of this work, a review of Canadian approaches to research on ME is introduced along with conclusions and recommendations for further ME research and curricular development.

Referring to Figure 1, adapted from Lynch (1989:42), the reader will note that while the early global approaches to ME were aimed primarily at achieving cognitive (knowledge and content) outcomes, more recent approaches consider different kinds of ME curriculum models that attempt to integrate cognitive and affective domains. Therefore, while the early 'additive' approaches made no attempt to tackle racial and ethnic stereotypes along with prejudicial values, later approaches not only attempt to come to grips with these issues, they do so across the mainstream curriculum. Early approaches may have resulted in the strengthening of 'the "them" and "us" perception of both or all groups, reinforcing status differential, exacerbating poor self-image and emphasizing difference and therefore category distinctions between students of perceived different kinds' (Lynch 1989:36). According to Lynch, the folkloric ME response also emphasized difference and the exotic with the consequence that difference was once again accentuated. The permeative phase redressed this situation somewhat by introducing appropriate

FIGURE 1

Curricular responses to cultural diversity: A phase typology

Historical phase	Approach label	Defined cause	Identified mediator	Preferred intervention	Effects
1	ethnic studies	poor self-image	socio-economic & racial experience	additive curriculum	unknown
2	folkloric multicultural	curricular neglect	curriulum	curriculur 'sprinkling'	some cognitive
3	permeative multicultural	schooling	schools	holistic policies	some cognitive
4	anti-racist	structure of society	racism	radical political change (revolution)	counter-productive
5	group work	educational strategies	classroom approaches	group work	both cognitive & affective
6	prejudice reduction	school & society	both	holistic policy & practice	same as above

Adapted from Lynch 1989

content along with teaching materials and methods. And importantly, attention was given to similarity and commonality as well as to difference, even though in the main the balance was tipped towards difference.

In the mid-1980s, in a few countries such as the United Kingdom and Canada, the anti-racist phase began as a 'manifestly political attempt to exert influence for major change in schooling as a means of combating the structural and systemic racism, seen as endemic in market economies' (Lynch 1989:37). Lynch contends that the early phase of anti-racist education, at least in the United Kingdom, resulted in 'a massive reaction by powerful majority groups in society, by all possible means, including public ridicule of the excesses and aberrations of the movement' (ibid.:38). This phase also coincided with what Lynch describes as educational 'apartheid,' 'including strident demands for separate schools on religious and sexist grounds and an outpouring of middle-class children from the state into the private school system' (ibid.:38). Within the British context, anti-racist educational approaches were condemned by minority groups 'as palliatives in the service of dominant groups in society' (ibid.).

While the reaction in Canada to an anti-racist policy and program does not appear to be as strident as Lynch describes for the United Kingdom, nevertheless the response to ME policy and curriculum is currently the subject of extensive debate, both within minority cultural group communities, as well as in the mainstream press. Considering the unity in diversity, 'multicultural dilemma' issue raised above and the context of the Canadian debate today around sovereignty association, distinct society concerns, and massive changes in the global community, it is little wonder that ME policy is under considerable scrutiny. Perhaps this is the ideal socio-political climate in Canada to popularize the kinds of development Lynch sees for ME approaches described in his fifth and sixth phases. The emphasis here is on the need to personalize ME approaches; to develop individual, 'empathic' responses to minority cultural group similarity and commonality, thereby achieving a better balance with difference orientations. From this point of view, ME program and policy must be integrated with all other curriculum areas. And finally, if ethnocultural and 'visible minority' groups are to view ME approaches as other than 'palliatives in the service of dominant groups,' links must be made to social stratification issues and the economy in general.

The perspective here is not simple, since the primary objective in this approach to ME is again to stress intercultural understanding, to help individuals develop and appreciate commonalities of one kind or another, commonalities that will bridge real cultural group differences: to wring out unity from diversity, *and to see the benefit to this approach.*

It is clear that an approach to research on ME requires a framework emphasizing the need for individuals to develop a strong sense of self-identity on various levels: the ethnic group level; the national level; and the global level. In the development of a strong sense of 'who am I,' ethnic group identification, or ethnic identity, is the primary building block.[4] According to Lewin (1948), 'identifying with one's culture and people is important because a person's self-definition is enhanced through the ethnic reference group with which he or she identifies' (cited in Akoodie 1984). When an individual values his or her ethnicity, feelings of belonging and a sense of support exist within the individual, ultimately enhancing his or her self-esteem, and providing him or her with the willingness to work in a cohesive society (Christian et al. 1976). Without this foundation, the results are feelings of insecurity, inferiority, discomfort, and marginality, all of which affect self-concept (Lipton 1963; Akoodie 1984; Berry 1989).

While identifying with one's own ethnic group is important, it does not singularly contribute to national unity. The assumption that fostering a secure ethnic identity leads to a greater acceptance of people of diverse cultural and racial groups underlies some of the materials written about ME (Aboud 1987; Genessee, Tucker & Lambert 1978; Lambert, 1984; Rotheram & Phinney 1987). This assumption needs to be addressed in future research (see, e.g., Demetriou 1992). Although the valuing of self-identity is important, it is not sufficient on its own. A strong ethnic identity does not necessarily imply that one has knowledge of cultural issues, has achieved reduction in prejudicial thought, and has the skills necessary to interact cross-culturally. We suggest that a comprehensive approach to ME must convey this type of knowledge and foster these types of skills. The need for social cohesion requires becoming competent not only in the context of one's own ethnic group, but also across cultural contexts. This kind of multicultural competence contributes to national cohesion by allowing individuals to relate to members of other groups. Therefore, research on ME will need to evaluate programs designed to help individuals acquire multiple group memberships or multiple identities; that is, to wear different hats in different circumstances, and to do so within the democratic ethos tradition. There is evidence to indicate that minority children may, in fact, develop a bicultural identity; that is, they acquire the norms of both dominant and minority cultures which are integrated and available to be used according to the situational context by 'switching' between the two sets of values, attitudes, and languages (Ramirez & Castenada 1974; Wolfgang & Josefowitz 1978; Mitsopulos 1989; Noels & Clément 1991).[5] However, according to Noels & Clément, 'This is not to say that an individual's identity is subject to haphazard alterations as the context changes, but rather that the expression of ethnic identity may be constrained by socially-prescribed rules and norms governing interactions for different socially-defined situations' (p 4) (for discussion see Alexander & Wiley 1981; Jackson 1988).[6]

The benefits associated with bicultural identity are suggested by research showing that students with this kind of competence fare better than their monocultural counterparts. Such students demonstrate greater role flexibility, flexibility in cognitive style, adaptability, creativity, high self-esteem, greater understanding, and higher achievement than others (Akoodie, 1980, 1984; Christian et al. 1976; Cross 1982; Ramirez 1983). Further studies are required to describe more fully the relationship between bicultural competence and these variables.

In summary, ME curricular activities and evaluative research would centre on the individual, demonstrating the appropriateness of *simultaneous* identification with a number of different constituencies (individual, cultural group, national, and global). This is a pragmatic approach to ME, showing how social cohesion can be achieved within multiple contexts. The major objective in this approach would be to help individuals learn to set priorities (which hat to wear under which circumstances) taking into account current legislation and human rights concepts. This approach requires a holistic view, considering both global and national concerns. Obviously, 'critical thinking,' flexibility, and creativity would be central components in this kind of ME activity.

HISTORICAL OVERVIEW: TWENTY YEARS OF ME POLICY
AND PROGRAMS IN CANADA

A brief consideration of multicultural policy and approaches to ME, taking into account the Canadian sociocultural matrix over the past two decades, will contextualize the results of our review of research on ME in Canada presented below.

To recapitulate Lynch's historical outline, it is possible to distinguish at least four phases of ME 'policy' development in Canada. The first phase, in the early 1970s, was focused primarily on introducing 'song and dance,' life-style activities as a minor aspect of the total curricular approach. The second phase, in the mid and late 1970s, was focused on language retention issues and realized in heritage language program development and English as a Second Language (ESL) activities that were in the main 'additive' components to the larger curricular effort. A third phase, in the early and mid 1980s, considered broader issues turning around equity concepts, stressing not only equality of opportunity but the requirement that there also be equality of outcome, that is, success. A fourth phase, beginning in the early 1980s and extending to the present, put increasing emphasis on race relations. For example, Ontario adopted a Race Relations Policy in 1983 to compliment the multicultural policy (see McLeod 1984).

Race relations has received considerable attention in Ontario. For example, in 1986, as a result of involvement by the Ontario Human Rights Commission, a provincial conference was organized to consider ME policy in the province. Subsequently in 1987, a follow-up report, *The Development of a Policy on Race and Ethnocultural Equity*, was produced by the Provincial Advisory Committee on Race Relations. The report strongly endorsed the need for anti-racist education while downplaying the importance of more traditional ME approaches. Nevertheless, the Ontario Ministry of Education (June 1989) has apparently opted for taking the 'broader' ME perspective as reflected in the document: *Changing Perspectives: A Resource Guide for Race and Ethnocultural Equity-Junior Kindergarten-Grade 12/OACs.*

Given the evolving nature of ME concepts, it is perhaps not surprising that implementation of ME policy in Canada is varied, spotty, and lacks cohesion (see below). McLeod (1981) provides a useful typology of these various approaches. The three categories of approach are (1) ethnic specific, (2) problem-oriented, and (3) cultural/intercultural. The first approach emphasizes specific ethno-cultural perspectives such as Black heritage programs or heritage language programs. The second approach is problem-oriented around concerns such as anti-racism, the kinds of services offered to newcomers such as interpreter programs, health services, as well as a broad range of problems associated with intercultural communication. The third category of approach is most closely identified with intercultural understanding, including human relations, cultural sharing, Native rights, bilingualism, and human rights.

Currently there may be some evidence for a fourth category of approach that is specific to ESL progamming. Scholarly opinion suggests that ESL programs should be integrated in ME programs so that students struggling to learn English will be exposed to various multicultural issues particularly from a more global perspective. Research in Canada and the United States 'has demonstrated that the social distance and attitudes of one group toward another can be successfully changed through certain language education models to produce less distance and more positive attitudes' (Padilla et al. 1991). Researchers such as Patricia Wakefield (1988) agree that 'although the necessity remains for providing quality programs to teach children English, there is a broader responsibility for educators to use cultural diversity as a resource to enrich the lives and broaden the perspectives of all children. Knowledge of one's own cultural heritage and appreciation of the many linguistic and cultural heritages around us will surely result in the emergence of a truly Canadian identity' (p viii).

According to Handscombe (1989), to ensure successful integration the school is required to indicate clearly to students how much they and their cultural group contribute to the intellectual and social life of the school as a whole. ESL programs should include this type of material as part of the curriculum. A Quebec study by Lambert (1987) involving

English-speaking students at various grade levels in public schools who were being educated in French immersion programs suggested that attitudes can cluster into higher order, generalized orientations that encompass not only tolerance for another group, but also knowledge of, appreciation for, and interest in people from that group.

According to Martin-Jones (1989), 'the way forward in the teaching/learning of ESL will undoubtedly continue to be in the direction of mainstreaming.' Martin-Jones also believes that every effort should now be made to ensure that the experience of minority children in mainstream classrooms in the 1990s is very different from the 'sink or swim' model of the 1950s and 1960s. Future research should include integration of ESL in ME programs.

The variety of approaches to ME in Canada is understandable given that the provinces have sole jurisdiction over education, while culture is an area of open jurisdiction. Furthermore, with respect to policy initiatives, multiculturalism is always to be viewed within the context of official bilingualism. For example, the Multiculturalism Act of July 1988 specifically states: 'It is hereby declared to be the policy of the Government of Canada to: (j) advance multiculturalism throughout Canada in harmony with the national commitment to the official languages of Canada.'

Given the variety of approaches to multicultural policy and program initiatives, it is little wonder that the field of ME lacks cohesion. The situation is further muddied when multicultural policy is unevenly applied. To take the situation in Ontario as an example once again, although the Ontario government has adopted both multicultural and race relations policies, the Ontario Ministry of Education, in spite of encouraging some 125 local Boards of Education to adopt policies, has not yet adopted an overtly stated ME policy. And, perhaps we should not be surprised to learn that only 40 boards have adopted a specific policy with respect to multiculturalism (Mock & Masemann 1987).

Boards of Education faced with an ethnically diverse population (e.g., there are more than 80 ethnocultural groups in the Toronto area) have primarily taken a comprehensive approach to setting multicultural policy. For example, in 1988 the Board of Education for the City of Scarborough (in Metropolitan Toronto) established its 'Race Relations, Ethnic Relations, and Multicultural Policy.' The Board 'condemns and does not tolerate any expression of racial or cultural bias by its trustees, staff or students'; the Board 'reaffirms its commitment to develop and promote racial harmony among its students, staff, and the community, and to provide education that is anti-racist and multicultural'; the Board 'will continue to develop curricular and co-curricular programs that provide opportunities for students to acquire positive attitudes toward racial, cultural, and religious diversity;' the Board 'will attempt to ensure that schools in their day-to-day operations, and co-curricular activities identify and eliminate those policies and practices which, while not intentionally discriminatory, have a discriminatory effect'; the Board 'recognizes that in order to ensure equal access and opportunity for achievement of their full potential, students from racial and cultural minority groups may require special considerations with respect to (a) reception, (b) assessment, (c) placement, (d) programming, (e) monitoring, (f) meaningful communication with parents/guardians.' The Board also commits itself 'to support multicultural clubs when requested by students and/or staff, to provide opportunities for students in all schools to participate in multicultural leadership camps, and to further strengthen leadership programs.'

It may be that the comprehensiveness of this kind of multicultural policy statement leads to the diversity of ME approaches found within and between various Boards of Education. Consequently, ME lacks cohesiveness, presenting problems for policy development and program implementation.

This brief survey of multicultural policy and practice in Canada begins to establish a connection with Lynch's historical outline (see Figure 1). Anti-racist education approaches are beginning to be incorporated into ME curricular activities in Canada. As well, increasing attention is being given to issues of discrimination and prejudice reduction. The caveat here, of course, is that relatively few Boards of Education have a specific policy on multiculturalism and/or race relations.

To anticipate the next section somewhat, it is precisely because the field of ME is not cohesive that we need to put significant effort into the kind of critical analysis provided in this paper. Only in this way will we begin to provide the necessary theoretical guidance to do significant research on ME.

ME RESEARCH IN CANADA

An exhaustive review of the Canadian Education Index (CEI), the Educational Resources Information Center (ERIC), and Dissertation Abstracts International was undertaken in order to examine what has been written in the past 20 years in the field of ME in Canada. This research was difficult because of the numerous headings and changes in headings under which materials were recorded during this period. For example, the following ten headings represent transitions within ME in Canada:

- anti-racist education
- biculturalism
- cultural differences
- ethnic groups
- intercultural education
- multicultural education
- multiculturalism
- native peoples
- race relations
- racial discrimination.

Despite the fact that much general information has been written on the topic, the literature search indicates that research in education for a pluralistic society, particularly as it pertains directly to program evaluation, is relatively scarce. This finding concurs with Tator and Henry's (1991) findings, which indicate a Canadian-wide shortage of research evaluating existing programs in ME. The materials considering the topic of multicultural education are predominantly descriptive and cover some 23 topics ranging from Aboriginal education and in-service teacher education to legislation and philosophy. The available research material, mainly in the more general area of social psychology, may have implications for programming, but does not specifically deal with program development or evaluation. Other branches of research that have a bearing on ME fall under the following categories:

- research on issues of ethnic identity (e.g., Aboud 1987; Berry 1989; Demetriou 1992; Driedger 1975, 1989; Lambert 1987; Mitsopulos 1989; Noels & Clément 1991)
- social psychology (e.g., Eiseman 1986; Haughton 1986; Issar 1988; Pierre-Jacques 1986; Wong, Derlega & Colson 1988)
- demographic information (e.g., Chen 1987; Paquette 1990)
- teacher education (e.g., Abdallah-Pretceille 1988; Myles & Ratzlaff 1988; Mock & Masemann 1987)
- methodology (e.g., Anisef 1986; Johnson & Johnson-Lee 1988)
- bibliographic materials (e.g., Martynowych 1979; Mock 1984; Multiculturalism Directorate 1981)
- ESL (e.g., Cummins 1989; Handscombe 1989; Martin-Jones 1989; Padoliak 1988; Staab 1991).

A few key references for ME program and policy development as well as program evaluation are the following: Arthur, Avril, Étienne, and Turcotte (1988); Council of Ministers of Education (1986); D'Oyley and Shapson (1986); Findlater (1987); Gagnon-Heynemen (1988); Herbert (1989); Hitner, Starr Associates (1985); Jack (1989); Lessard and Crespo (1989); Lingard (1988); Megalokonomos (1984); Melenchuk (1987); Mylopoulos (1985); Tator and Henry (1991).[7]

Although the literature review was extensive, it was limited in certain ways. One limitation is that Canadian scholars often publish their work in international journals; however, a thorough search of these journals would have been beyond the scope of this paper. Also, some research may have been conducted at the school board level and may not be accessible through the various data bases or through survey reports like that of Tator and Henry (1991). The multiplicity of headings under which ME information is categorized further complicated the literature review and may have led to an inadvertent omission of some ME research articles. Finally, the search of the CEI, ERIC, and Dissertation Abstracts International generated very few articles directed to ME in Quebec. In order to provide a more complete picture of the research on ME in Canada we have borrowed from a review of French-language literature prepared by Denise Helly (see paper in this volume).

CONCLUSIONS

In this paper we have shown that although there is globe-setting multi-cultural policy in place at national and regional levels in Canada, there is not yet a coherent framework of ME theory and practice that will provide significant guidance to either researchers or practitioners in the field. We reached this conclusion in the course of reviewing research on ME in Canada from a global perspective. We discovered that there is no cohesive body of research that easily coalesces to yield a domain of inquiry focused on ME. Our review showed a conceptual underpinning to ME that is less than coherent. We have attempted to capture the essence of this kind of theoretical unease in our discussion of what we have termed the 'multicultural dilemma.' In an effort to bring together both research and theory, we have chosen to put a face on ME that emphasizes the importance of self-esteem and identity together with the various skills associated with bicultural competence, particularly the ability to function successfully in multiple contexts of mainstream activities. Currently, it seems that the field of ME is comprised of two major blocks of activities, one involving program or curriculum development largely uninformed by research, the other represented by a wide diversity of social science research, such as on self-esteem/identity issues, which at best relate tangentially to ME. We suggest that these major areas of activity need to be linked. To this end, we recommend the following:
– Efforts must be directed at identifying accurate levels of participation

of ethnic and racial minorities in elementary and secondary education across Canada. These demographics are essential to developing a rationale that would suggest that ME is appropriate *for* a multicultural, pluralistic society, *for everyone* in society.

- On this last point, Canadians must continue to debate the substantive issues related to living in a multi-ethnic society. For example, with the sociocultural reality of French Canada and the increasing efforts of Native Canadians to achieve distinct society status or at least the recognition of their 'inherent rights,' together with a variety of other claims for regional 'distinctiveness,' to what extent are New Canadians expected to accommodate to these 'realities,' acknowledging the status quo as it were? Will 'citizenship' requirements include recognition of the special or preferred status of these groups? Stated differently, Canadians must decide to what extent human rights and the democratic ethos, including partnership and equal stakeholder concepts, will take precedence, if at all, over the preferred status of established sociocultural groups in Canada. The approach to ME described in this paper is relatively neutral in the debate. The primary educational objectives in this approach consider the skills that are necessary to function in an optimal capacity in different sociocultural groups and mainstream institutions. Whether access to these groups and institutions should be automatic and mandated through human rights and anti-racist legislation or whether access should be 'negotiated' is a matter for debate by Canadians.

- Thoughtful attention needs to be given to describing approaches to ME that focus on the skills that will facilitate the functioning of individuals in multiple contexts.

- National unity must be considered a fundamental component and topic of ME. The 'multicultural dilemma,' identified in this chapter as the dual emphasis on internationalism and cross-cultural similarity, along with the emphasis on difference across ethnic and racial communities, has tended to de-emphasize the importance of social cohesion at the national level.

- Basic research from social and educational psychology as well as from other learned disciplines must inform the development of ME program development and evaluation. Particular emphasis should be given in research to the relations between self-esteem, identity, and the relevance of situations (contexts) as these variables relate to the ability of individuals to identify with (relate to) national as well as local issues.

A primary concern in this work should be the processes that enable individuals to establish multiple group affiliations and memberships across local, regional, and national contexts.

- With reference to the above, research should explore the relation between growth in intercultural understanding and successful functioning in multiple group settings.

- ME program development and evaluation should be holistic, integrating a variety of special needs services, such as ESL and mainstream educational objectives. Since ME programming *for* a pluralistic society is for every student, second-language learning, including FSL, should be fully integrated into ME activities.

- Research on ME at elementary and secondary levels should be published in the formal literature or at least indexed with a national agency. Most of the work in ME is published informally by local agencies or institutions such as Boards of Education and consequently remains largely inaccessible.

- Alternative approaches to ME must be encouraged at both research and practice levels. Particularly important is the need to make explicit the theoretical perspective of basic research studies as well as the theoretical basis for 'action research' approaches and program development.

NOTES

Corespondence should be addressed to the first author, Department of Aplied Psychology, Ontario Institute for Studies in Education, 252 Bloor St W, Toronto, ON M5S 1V6.

1 One aspect of the dilemma has been put succinctly by Young Pai (1990): 'A central problem of cultural pluralism is how minority groups can maintain enough separation from the dominant cultures to perpetuate and develop their own ethnic traditions without, at the same time, interfering with the execution of their standard responsibilities to the American society of which they are also members. That is, how can cultural diversity and unity be maintained simultaneously, particularly when conflicts arise between the society at large and these sub-units?' (pp 16–17). Even more succinctly, Tesconi (1990) puts the central question this way: 'How does a nation with no one clear cultural standard, no one race, no one history, no one ethnic stock, and with numerous languages, continue to exist as one?' (p 29).

2 Tesconi (1990:38–40) suggests that there are five common assumptions underlying Cultural Pluralism and Multicultural Education ideological constructs. These are: (1) 'that an individual's membership in, and attachment to, primary ethnic or cultural group life, and the socially encouraged involvement in it, promote those characteristics in a person usually associated with a healthy personality type – self-esteem, sense of belonging, respect for others, purposefulness, and critical thinking' (p 38). (2) 'that a personality characterized by tolerance of, and openness to, different others – necessary to a truly democratic society – is dependent upon the opportunity of individuals to encounter and interact with a variety of culturally different others' (p 38). (3) 'that no one way of life can be said to be better than any other and that to be humane a society must afford room for many competing and oftentimes conflicting ways of life' (p 39). (4) 'that it is valuable to have many ways of life in competition, and that such competition leads to a balance or equilibrium in the social order' (p 40). (5) 'that loyalty to a larger society – a nation – is a function of, and dependent on, socially sanctioned loyalties rooted in a multiplicity of diverse ethnic and cultural groups. It is this assumption which leads cultural pluralists and multiculturalists to the notion that a society will be rich, unified, healthy, and nourished to a fuller life, to the extent that it is fashioned out of genuine human groupings' (p 40).

3 This is not far-fetched. More than ever, people, ideas, commodities, money, and information are moving freely across national frontiers. As this occurs several significant questions arise: Is a unified world culture emerging? If so, how will this affect the autonomy of existing cultures? Will they be supplanted by a unified culture, or can they maintain distinct identities? In fact, there are already 'third cultures,' for example, international law, the financial markets, and mass media conglomerates. These elements transcend national boundaries.

4 In studying the ethnic identity of children, research has primarily focused on children's understanding of their membership in an ethnic group and their identification with that group. For example, early American research concentrated on Black children's racial awareness, racial identification, and racial preference (Clark & Clark 1947). Recent studies have looked at the process of identity formation in specific minority groups, such as Blacks (Cross 1978) and Asian-Americans (Fox & Jordan 1973); self-identification or labelling in young children or adults (Giles, Taylor, & Bourhis 1977); and ethnic behaviour patterns as an aspect of identity (Rotheram & Phinney 1987). Still other research has studied the effect of structural assimilation,

particularly intermarriage, on ethnic identity (Alba 1985); and cultural awareness and ethnic identity among children of interethnic marriages (Snyder, Lopez & Padilla 1982).

Research on the ethnic identity of adolescents and adults has, in many respects, paralleled research on children, but in more sophisticated language and with more age-appropriate measures. Both American and Canadian research on ethnic identity have examined ethnocultural factors as indicators of ethnic identity. These have included religion, endogamy, ingroup friends, language use, ethnic organizations, and ethnic media use (e.g., Sanua 1965; Driedger 1973; Breton 1964; Segalman 1967).

Canadian research on ethnic identity has primarily focused on adult populations, generally overlooking children and adolescents. Such research has examined the salience of ethnic identity in undergraduate students (Driedger 1975; Mackie & Brinkerhoff 1984; Shamai 1986) and adolescents (Mitsopulos 1989); and the importance of ethnicity to adult Canadians (Frideres & Goldenberg 1982).

5 The following studies pertaining to research with children indicate the influence of sociocultural factors on the development of ethnic identity and bicultural identity. The overall message to be gained from these findings is that the attitudes of grade-school children remain quite malleable and that ME programs could be developed to counteract racial prejudice in children. A study by Genesee, Tucker, and Lambert (1978) investigated the influence of variations in type of school setting on the development of role-taking skills and ethnic identity. The results indicated that children who were exposed to a second-language environment identified with their native-language reference group later and less consistently than children in the native-language programs. The second-language children identified more with the second-language group. These results demonstrate the influence of sociocultural factors on the development of ethnic identity and ethnic role-taking skills.

There has been considerable research examining children's peer preferences in integrated, multi-ethnic settings. A study conducted by Singleton and Asher (1979) indicated that children gave rather positive ratings to cross-race classmates and that race accounted for much less of the variance in children's ratings than did sex. These findings suggest that children who are exposed to a multicultural environment tend to accept cultural differences and perhaps focus on similarities.

6 Although young children make generalizations about groups, they do not necessarily extend their beliefs over time and across situations (Ramsey 1987). For example, Porter (1971) found that some children who made nega-

tive comments about cross-racial people in interviews were observed shortly afterwards playing with their cross-racial classmates (cited in Ramsey
1987). Finkelstein and Haskins (1983) also provide support for this hypothesis. Kindergarten children were observed during classroom instruction
and during recess on school playgrounds. Both Black and White children
showed same-colour preferences in social behaviour, but this tendency was
not stable over situations. The children selected same-colour peers to
interact with more frequently during recess than during classroom instruction. Children's global categorizations and rigid expectations about cross-
racial people seem to be more easily overcome by immediate experiences
than are adult's attitudes (Ramsey 1987). Katz and Zalk (1978) compared
the relative efficacy of four short-term intervention techniques for modify-
ing negative racial attitudes. Results revealed a significant short-term
reduction in prejudice in all experimental groups.

7 For a more complete reference list contact the principle author.

REFERENCES

Abdallah-Pretceille, M. (1988). Quelques points d'appui pour une formation
   des enseignants dans une perspective interculturelle. Dans F. Ouellet (ed.),
   Pluralisme et école (pp 495–510). Québec: Institut québécois de recherche sur la
   culture
Aboud, F.E. (1987). The development of ethnic self-identification and attitudes.
   In J.S. Phinney and M.J. Rotheram (eds), *Children's ethnic socialization* (pp
   32–55). California: Sage Publications
Akoodie, M.A. (1980). Immigrant students: A comparative assessment of ethnic
   identity, self-concept, and locus of control among West Indian, East Indian,
   and Canadian students. Unpublished PH D thesis, University of Toronto
– (1984). Identity and self-concept in immigrant children. In R.J. Samuda, J.W.
   Berry, and M. Laferrière (eds), *Multiculturalism in Canada: Social and educational perspectives* (pp 253–65). Toronto: Allyn & Bacon
Alba, R.D. (1985). The twilight of ethnicity among Americans of European
   ancestry: The case of Italians. *Ethnic and Racial Studies*, 8(1):134–58
Alexander, C.N., and Wiley, M.G. (1981). Situated activity and identity formation. In M. Rosenberg and R. Turner (eds), *Social psychology: Sociological
   perspectives*. New York: Basic Books
Anisef, P. (1986). *Models and methodologies appropriate to the study of outcomes of
   schooling in Ontario's multicultural society*. Toronto: Ontario Ministry of Education

Arthur, M., Avril, A., Étienne, P., et Turcotte, P. (1988). *L'intervention intercultu-relle*. Ébauche d'un projet de Recherche-Action-Formation mené auprès d'adolescents en contexte pluri-ethnique, Montréal

Banks, J. (1981). Cultural pluralism and the schools. In J.M. Rich (ed.), *Innovations in education*. Boston: Allyn & Bacon

Berry, J.W. (1989). Psychology of acculturation. In J. Betman (ed.), Cross-cultural perspectives (pp 201–34). Lincoln: University of Nebraska Press

Breton, R. (1964). Institutional completeness of ethnic communities and the personal relations of immigrants. *American Journal of Sociology, 70*:193–205

Chen, M. (1987). *The every secondary student survey* (Research report No. 191). Toronto: Toronto Board of Education

Christian, J., Gadfield, N.J., Giles, H., and Taylor, D.M. (1976). The multidimensional and dynamic nature of ethnic identity. *International Journal of Psychology, 11*:281–91

Clark, K.B., and Clark, M.P. (1947). Racial identification and preference in Negro children. In T.M. Newcomb and E.L. Hartley (eds), *Readings in social psychology* (pp 169–78). New York: Holt, Rinehart & Winston

Council of Ministers of Education (1986). *Multicultural education policies in Canada*. Report presented to the OECD's Centre for Educational Research and Innovation, Toronto

Cross, W. (1978). The Thomas and Cross models of psychological nigrescence: A literature review. *Journal of Black Psychology, 4*:13–31

– (1982). Black families and black identity development. *Journal of Comparative Family Studies, 12*:19–50

Cummins, J. (1989). Heritage language teaching and the ESL student: Fact and fiction. In J.H. Esling (ed.), *Multicultural education and policy: ESL in the 1990s*. Toronto: Ontario Institute for Studies in Education

Demetriou, K. (1992). *Ethnic identity and self-esteem among Greek-Canadian adolescents*. Unpublished master's thesis. University of Toronto

D'Oyley, V., and Shapson, S. (1986, April). *Research on multiculturalism in the curriculum from a Canadian perspective*. Paper presented at the annual meeting of the American Educational Research Association, San Francisco, CA (ERIC Document Reproduction Service No. ED 293 753)

Drieger, L. (1973). Impelled group migration: Minority struggle to maintain institutional completeness. *International Migration Review, 7*:257–69

– (1975). In search of cultural identity factors: A comparison of ethnic students. *Canadian Review of Sociology and Anthropology, 12*:150–62

– (1989). *The ethnic factor: Identity in diversity*. Toronto: McGraw-Hill Ryerson

Eiseman, T.O. (1986). Research report: Caribbean students in Montreal schools. *McGill Journal of Education, 21*:163–8

Findlater, S. (1987). *Rapport synthèse des politiques et des orientations concernant le multiculturalisme, l'éducation interculturelle et l'éducation antiraciste dans les dix provinces du Canada*. Québec: Commission des droits de la personne du Québec

Finkelstein, N.W., and Haskins, R. (1983). Kindergarten children prefer same-color peers. *Child Development, 54*:502–8

Fox, D.J., and Jordon, V.B. (1973). Racial preference and identification of Black American Chinese, and White children. *Genetic Psychology Monographs, 88*:229–86

Frideres, J., and Goldenberg, S. (1982). Ethnic identity: Myth and reality in western Canada. *International Journal of Intercultural Relations, 6*(2):137–51

Gagnon-Heyneman, D. (1988). *Instrument de travail en éducation interculturelle et sur le multiculturalisme canadien*. Recherche en cours. Montréal: Université du Québec à Montréal

Genesee, F., Tucker, G.R., and Lambert, W.E. (1978). The development of ethnic identity and ethnic role taking skills in children from different school settings. *International Journal of Psychology, 13*(1):39–57

Giles, H., Taylor, D.M., and Bourhis, R.Y. (1977). Dimensions of Welsh identity. *European Journal of Social Psychology, 7*:29–39

Handscombe, J. (1989). Mainstreaming: Who needs it? In J.H. Esling (ed.), *Multicultural education and policy: ESL in the 1990s*. Toronto: Ontario Institute for Studies in Education

Haughton, H.S. (1986, December). *Reproducing visible-minority exclusion from the Ontario school curriculum: An ethnography of educational processes*. Paper presented at the Annual Conference of the Ontario Educational Research Council, Toronto (ERIC Document Reproduction Service No. ED 284 809)

Herbert, Y.M. (1989). Teachers collaborate and dialogue in a curriculum implementation project. *Multiculturalism, 12*(1):3–8

Hitner, Starr Associates. (1985). *Race relations program review*. Toronto: Toronto Board of Education

Issar, N. (1988). *A comparison of values of East Indian, East Indian Canadian, and European adolescents*. Unpublished doctoral dissertation, University of Toronto

Jack, D. (1989). Improving students' ethnic attitudes: A grade 3 multicultural education program. *Multiculturalism, 12*(2):14–16

Jackson, J.M. (1988). *Social psychology, past and present: An integrative orientation*. Hillsdale, NJ: Lawrence & Erlbaum

Johnson, N.A., and Johnson-Lee, B.A. (1988). Ethnographic research in education: Strategies for reappraisal. *McGill Journal of Education, 23*:231–41

Kallen, H. (1956). *Cultural pluralism and the American idea*. Philadelphia: University of Pennsylvania Press

Katz, P.A., and Zalk, S.R. (1978). Modification of children's racial attitudes. *Development Psychology, 14*(5):447–61

Lambert, W.E. (1984). Cross-cultural perspectives on children's development of an identity. *Teachers' College Record, 85*(3):349–63

– (1987). The effects of bilingual and bicultural experiences on children's attitudes and social perspectives. In P. Homel, M. Palij, and D. Aaronson (eds), *Childhood bilingualism: Aspects of linguistics, cognitive, and social development* (pp 197–221). Hillsdale, NJ: Erlbaum

– , Mermigis, L., and Taylor, O.M. (1986). Greek Canadians' attitudes toward own group and other Canadian groups: A test of the multiculturalism hypothesis. *Canadian Journal of Behavioural Science, 18*:35–51

Lessard, C., et Crespo, M. (1989). L'éducation multiculturelle au Canada: Politiques et pratiques. Dans D. Ray et D. Poonwassie (éds), *Tomorrow can be better*. Toronto: Nito Garland

Lingard, J. (1988). *Multicultural education in Saskatchewan: Perception, implementation and relevance* (Report No. 178). Regina, SK: Saskatchewan School Trustees' Association

Lipton, A. (1963). Cultural heritage and the relationship to self-esteem. *Journal of Educational Sociology, 36*:211–12

Lynch, J. (1989). *Multicultural education in a global society*. New York: Falmer Press

Mackie, M., and Brinkerhoff, M.B. (1984). Measuring ethnic salience. *Canadian Ethnic Studies, 16*(1):114–31

McLeod, K.A. (1981). Multiculturalism and multicultural education. In *Canadian Society for the Study of Education. Eighth Yearbook*

– (ed.) (1984). *Multicultural early childhood education*. Toronto: OISE Press

Martin-Jones, M. (1989). Language education in the context of linguistic diversity: Differing orientations in educational policy making in Britain. In J.H. Esling (ed.), *Multicultural education and policy: ESL in the 1990s* (pp 36–58). Toronto: Ontario Institute for Studies in Education

Martynowych, O.T. (1979). *A selective preliminary bibliography of Canadian reference materials pertaining to education within a multicultural context*. Winnipeg, MB: Department of the Secretary of State (ERIC Document Reproduction Service No. ED 221 608)

Megalokonomos, T. (1984). *Evaluation of Eastern Ontario Multiracial, Multicultural Leadership Programme* (Report No. 84:11). Ottawa, ON: Ottawa Board of Education, Research Centre

Melenchuk, A.S. (1987). *The effects of a cross-cultural training program on the attitudes of eighth graders toward Prairie Indians* (SSTA Research Centre report No. 149). Regina, SK: Saskatchewan School Trustees' Association

Mitsopulos, A. (1989). *Ethnic identity among second generation Greek-Canadian adolescents.* Unpublished master's thesis. University of Toronto

Mock, K.R. (1984). *Multicultural early childhood education bibliography and resource list.* Ontario

– and, Masemann, V.L. (1987). *Multicultural teacher education in Canada: A directory of programs and practitioners.* Presented at the 3rd National Conference of the Canadian Council for Multicultural and Intercultural Education

Multiculturalism Directorate (1981). *Publications supported by the multiculturalism directorate.* Ottawa, ON: Department of the Secretary of State (ERIC Document Reproduction Service No. ED 213 791)

Myles, D.W., and Ratzlaff, H.C. (1988). Teachers' bias towards visible ethnic minority groups in special education referrals. BC *Journal of Special Education,* 23,:231–41

Mylopoulos, C. (1985). Trends in multicultural programming. *Canadian Library Journal, 42*(1):23–5

Noels, K.A., and Clément, R. (1991). Ethnolinguistic identity and second language competence: A situated approach. Paper presented at the 4th International Conference on Language and Social Psychology, University of California, Santa Barbara

Padilla, A.M., Lindholm, K.J., Chen, A., Duran, R., Hakuta, K., Lambert, W., and Tucker, G.R. (1991). The English-only movement: Myths, reality, and implications for psychology. *American Psychologist, 46*(2):120–30

Padoliak, E. (1988). Canadian materials for ESL: Where are they? TESL *Talk, 18*(1):148–61

Pai, Y. (1990). Cultural pluralism, democracy and multicultural education. In B.B. Cassara (ed.), *Adult education in a multicultural society.* New York: Routledge

Paquette, J. (1990). Beyond the multicultural mystique: The politics and promise of educational participation data by ethnicity and language use. *Canadian Journal of Education, 15*:450–4

Pierre-Jacques, C. (1986). L'école québécoise et les familles haïtiennes. *Revue des Sciences de l'Éducation, 12*:120–7

Porter, J.D.R. (1971). *Black child, white child: The development of racial attitudes.* Cambridge, MA: Harvard University

Ramirez, M. (1983). *Psychology of the Americas: Mestizo perspectives on personality and mental health.* New York: Academic Press

– , and Castenada, A. (1974). *Cultural democracy, bicognitive development, and education.* New York: Academic Press

Ramsey, P.G. (1987). Young children's thinking about ethnic differences. In J.S.

Phinney, and M.J. Rotheram (eds), *Children's ethnic socialization*. California: Sage Publications

Rotheram, M.J., and Phinney, J.S. (1987). Introduction: Definitions and perspectives in the study of children's ethnic socialization. In J.S. Phinney and M.J. Rotheram (eds), *Children's ethnic socialization* (pp 32–55). California: Sage Publications

Sanua, V.D. (1965). A study of the adolescents attending Jewish community centers in New York. *Journal of Jewish Communal Service*, 41:402–24

Segalman, R. (1967). Jewish identity scales: A report. *Jewish Social Studies*, 29:92–111

Shamai, S. (1986). Ethnic national identity among Jewish students in Toronto. Unpublished PHD dissertation, University of Toronto

Singleton, L.C., and Asher, S.R. (1979). Racial integration and children's peer preferences: An investigation of developmental and cohort differences. *Child Development*, 50:936–41

Snyder, N., Lopez, C.M., and Padilla, A.M. (1982). Ethnic identity and cultural awareness among offspring of Mexican interethnic marriages. *Journal of Early Adolescence*, 2(3):277–82

Staab, C. (1991). Classroom organization: Thematic centers revisited. *Language Arts*, 68(2):108–13

Tator, C., and Henry, F. (1991). *Multicultural education: Translating policy into practice*. Carol Tator and Frances Henry Equal Opportunity Consultants, Toronto

Tesconi, C.A. (1990). Multiculturalism in education: The importance of meaning. In B.B. Cassara (ed.), *Adult education in a multicultural society*. New York: Routledge

Wakefield, P. (1988). Dedication. In J.H. Esling (ed.), *Multicultural education and policy: ESL in the 1990s* (pp vii–ix). Toronto: Ontario Institute for Studies in Education

Wolfgang, A., and Josefowitz, N. (1978). Chinese immigrant value changes and value differences compared to Canadian students. *Canadian Ethnic Studies*, 10:130–5

Wong, P.T., Derlega, V.J., and Colson, W. (1988). The effects of race on expectancies and performance. *Canadian Journal of Behavioural Science*, 20:29–39

BRIAN J. O'NEILL AND SHANKAR A. YELAJA

Multiculturalism in Postsecondary Education: 1970–91

One of the most pressing questions facing the university is how to foster an environment in which individuals from an increasingly diverse society can enjoy the freedom to study, teach or conduct research without fear of discrimination, and in which one does not compromise freedom of inquiry and expression. (Dickson 1992:1).

This conundrum was the focus of a symposium held at Queen's University for university presidents considering how they could promote 'a learning environment which recognizes and respects the dignity of all persons' (Berry, Joneja, Robillard & Sinnott, 1992). What guidance in responding to this question is provided by research on multicultural issues in Canadian postsecondary educational institutions? This paper identifies areas in which investigations have been conducted and provides an overview of findings. It critically analyzes the quality of this body of research and proposes an agenda for future inquiry.

Canadian institutions are under increasing pressure to respond to ethnic and racial differences with fairness and sensitivity. This change in social values is expressed in both federal and provincial legislation. The Canadian Charter of Rights and Freedoms and federal and provincial human rights codes recognize and protect the rights of minority groups to equal treatment (Naidoo & Edwards 1991). The Canadian Employment Equity Act (1986) mandates fair employment practices with respect to minorities. In addition, the Canadian Multiculturalism Act (1988) supports the retention of ethnic minorities' cultural distinctiveness while facilitating their integration into society. These statutes are forcing organizations which serve the public to examine the impact of their policies and structures on members of ethnocultural minority groups.

Universities and community colleges are particularly targeted for reform because participation in higher education by members of minority groups is seen as a path towards social and economic equity with other Canadians (Anisef, Bertrand, Hortian & James 1985). Faculty and student organizations recommend policy and program changes which will facilitate the participation of members of underrepresented groups ('Employment Equity' 1990; Ontario Federation of Students 1991). They call for involvement of members of ethnocultural communities in institutional decision-making, active recruitment and support of minority students, and inclusion of racial and cultural concerns in curricula and research activities. These critics also advocate the adoption of personnel policies which will increase minority representation on faculties and staffs. Assuming continuing growth in the ethnic and racial diversity of the Canadian population and future political and social support for multicultural policies and programs, these challenges cannot be ignored. Response is rendered particularly difficult by the complexity of the country's system of higher education.

Harry Arthurs (1992), former president of York University in Toronto, has articulated the complexity of seeking to maintain 'academic freedom' while countering discrimination within postsecondary educational institutions. He contends that universities are not necessarily less prejudiced than the societies in which they are located. Arthurs argues that policy changes alone are insufficient to eliminate discrimination since universities are political environments in which diverse interests compete for resources. In his view 'Racism is a social and economic, a political and cultural phenomenon. It has to be confronted by social and economic, political and cultural strategies' (Arthurs 1992:4). For such tactics to succeed, it is necessary to have within the university

a student body and a faculty and staff complement which reflect the diversity of Canadian society, which extend opportunity and respect to all talented people, which honestly take the measure of how race – like class and gender – can debilitate and disentitle, which are prepared to pay the price of equity, which speak out against discrimination, and which maintain the maturity and integrity to distinguish substance from symbolism and high standards from good intentions. (Arthurs 1992:4–5)

In order to increase the participation of members of racial and ethnic minorities, Arthurs recommends changes in approaches to selecting and supporting students and in recruiting and promoting faculty. He cites barriers to undertaking such initiatives: lack of financial resources, anxiety engendered by encounters with persons whose appearance, customs, and values are unfamiliar, fear of change itself, and the presence of racists on campus.

Women and ethnocultural minorities face similar barriers to participation in postsecondary education. Often, traditional academic criteria have been used to prevent members of both groups from achieving success within the system (Hanen 1992). Feminist educators have called for structural changes which will eliminate inequality in access and results (Gaskell & McLaren 1987b). They advocate revised standards, modified curriculum content, and innovative teaching methods. In the same way that proponents of multicultural change argue that the educational system reflects the dominant culture, feminists hold that mainstream curricula exhibit a male slant which neglects women's values (Gaskell & McLaren 1987a). The efforts of feminist scholars and educators to gain recognition of women's issues in academia provide a useful paradigm for understanding racial and ethnic minorities' drive for change in postsecondary education.

ETHNOCULTURAL DIVERSITY AND MULTICULTURALISM

Canada has always been racially and culturally diverse. Aboriginal peoples, the earliest inhabitants of the land, have a variety of cultures and languages. Initial colonization was carried out by members of distinct ethnic groups from the British Isles and France. Historically, the majority of immigrants to Canada were of various European backgrounds (Badets 1989). However, recently there has been a dramatic increase in immigration from other sources, particularly Asia and South America. The greatest increases were in those who speak Chinese, Spanish, Punjabi, and Arabic (Fraser 1992).

'Multiculturalism' refers to 'a society that is characterized by ethnic or cultural heterogeneity ... to an ideal of equality and mutual respect among a population's ethnic or cultural groups; and ... to government policy proclaimed by the [Canadian] federal government in 1971 and subsequently by a number of provinces' (Burnet 1988:1401). The goals of the Canadian Multiculturalism Act (1988) are to help ethnic groups maintain their cultural traditions, to reduce barriers to minorities' full participation in society, and to encourage understanding between diverse ethnocultural groups (Bibby 1991). Approximately half the funds distributed under the act support language training and services which help immigrants integrate into Canadian society, while another quarter backs programs to reduce discrimination (Goar 1991).

Multiculturalism has proved to be a controversial social policy. Early indications were that Canadians supported the concept of multicultural-ism, although the degree of support varied across the country (Berry, Kalin & Taylor 1977). Recently, however, opposition to the policy has surfaced. The Citizens' Forum on Canada's Future found some citizens concerned about the policy's effect on national unity ('The Forum,' 1991). These apprehensions may be in reaction to increased immigration from non-European sources ('Misgivings,' 1991). Claude Corbo (1992), Rector of the University of Quebec at Montreal, has expressed anxiety that support for immigrants' traditions and languages may impede newcom-ers' assimilation into Quebec society and ultimately dilute francophone culture. However, Gerry Weiner (1992), the federal Minister of Multicul-turalism and Citizenship, believes that multiculturalism strengthens, rather than weakens, national unity. He argues that since multicultural-ism bolsters the equality of all Canadians and encourages participation of minorities in social institutions, it enhances the allegiance of immi-grants to the communities in which they live. These contentions are supported by recent polls (see Kalin & Berry, this volume) which indicate that the majority of Canadians continue to support multicultural policy (Simeon 1991) and believe that racial diversity is an asset (Mitchell 1991). Bibby (1991) holds that the multiculturalism policy has succeeded in achieving its first two goals in that it 'has heightened our awareness of cultural diversity and contributed to more just and fair conditions for cultural minorities' (p A22). However, he argues that the policy has failed to achieve its third goal, 'to promote interaction among all cultural groups in the interests of national unity' (ibid.), a default which may explain concerns about declining national unity.

CANADIAN POSTSECONDARY EDUCATION

This paper examines research on the policies and programs of univer-sities and community colleges. Universities focus on education in the arts and sciences, the professions, and research. In 1990 over 500,000 full-time students (Laver 1991:28) were registered in Canada's 89 degree-granting universities and colleges (Lewis & Benedict 1991:12). In contrast to universities, community colleges concentrate on technical training for careers in human services, industry, and commerce. According to Statis-tics Canada, the full-time community college enrolment was 320,000 in

1985 (Parliament 1986:12) and there were 111 community colleges as of 1990 (Association of Canadian Community Colleges 1990). Participation in postsecondary education has increased dramatically since 1961 (Mori & Burke 1990:32). This is reflected in the level of educational achievement of the population. In 1986, 20 per cent of Canadians had obtained a degree or diploma and 20 per cent had partially completed programs. Rates of enrolment and retention of postsecondary students vary considerably across the provinces and are related to social and economic factors (Anisef et al. 1985). Variations in participation in postsecondary education may also be due to the availability of educational institutions. For instance, the Atlantic provinces have relatively fewer community colleges than Ontario and Quebec, which have extensive systems (Anisef et al. 1985; Association of Canadian Community Colleges 1990).

Most provinces lack a comprehensive policy regarding multicultural issues in education (McLeod 1981). There is a lack of information about the use of quotas to boost the number of minority students and faculty in universities and community colleges. However, numerous programs have been instituted in postsecondary institutions to meet the special needs of the diverse population. The 1987 report of the Canadian Council of Ministers of Education describes initiatives to recruit students from ethnocultural minority groups, studies of immigrants' training needs, and programs which help students upgrade their skills in order to gain university admission. It also documents programs which assist immigrants with foreign qualifications to move into the teaching, nursing, and social work professions in Canada.

Canadian legal education has responded to ethnic and racial diversity by establishing programs for members of underrepresented minorities (*Information Book* 1991; Mazer 1989). Most law schools have flexible admission criteria which consider the circumstances of disadvantaged students such as Natives and ethnic minorities. For example, the University of Saskatchewan offers a unique program which prepares Native students for application to law schools across the country; the University of Windsor selects law students based on their potential contribution to society and the profession rather than on minimum academic criteria; the law school of Dalhousie University has a program geared for Native and Black students (Clark 1992).

Quebec uses postsecondary education to facilitate the integration of ethnic minorities into its francophone culture. The University of Quebec has adopted a multicultural perspective, and is developing courses and research projects which focus on cultural diversity (Corbo 1992; Larose

1990). Many of the province's community colleges have programs which focus on French language skills and understanding of cultural differences (Association of Canadian Community Colleges 1990). For instance, Peggy Tchoryck-Pelletier (1989) of Cégep de Saint-Laurent has conducted research on the integration of members of ethnic minorities.

Recently, new programs have developed to meet the needs of Native peoples. The Saskatchewan Indian Federated College and a Native studies program at Trent University have been instituted. Native social work education programs exist across the country (Castellano, Stalwick & Wien 1986; Task Force 1991). There are also special programs to promote Native access to health sciences at the University of Toronto, and nursing at Lakehead University. In addition, many community colleges offer technical, business, health, and social service courses geared to Native communities (Association of Canadian Community Colleges 1990).

Overall, the response to multiculturalism by postsecondary education varies by region and type of program. Professional faculties are particularly sensitive to the need for change because of service demands from minority clients and patients. Schools are experimenting with different models of education. Two major approaches are facilitation of minority participation in mainstream programs and development of separate, parallel programs for specific groups such as Native peoples. The response of francophone schools in Quebec is complicated by the provincial goal of integrating immigrants into francophone culture, while newcomers have the option of attending anglophone postsecondary institutions.

REVIEW PROCEDURES

The goal of this paper is to evaluate major studies regarding multicultural postsecondary education conducted during the past 21 years. Reports were accessed through ERIC (1970–1991), the data bases of the Educational Resources Information Centre, the *Canadian Education Index* (1965– 1991), the *Microlog Index: Canadian Government Publications and Reports* (1979–1990), and the library collection of the Ontario Institute for Studies in Education. The authors acquired additional documents through personal contacts and attendance at conferences.

The review is limited to studies regarding multicultural issues in Canadian postsecondary education. Thus, it includes inquiries which examined aboriginal and francophone issues in a multicultural context but does not include studies which focus exclusively on aboriginal or francophone concerns.

EVALUATION OF RESEARCH

There is a lack of research on multicultural issues in Canadian higher education, and where inquiry has been undertaken, it has often been methodologically flawed. This review includes 25 studies which deal with multicultural issues in postsecondary education. Seven of these studies are national in scope, while eight are provincial. The remainder concentrate on institutions in particular cities, most frequently Toronto. The inquiries address a variety of issues: student motivation, learning needs, participation and achievement of members of diverse ethnocultural groups, systemic discrimination, and professional education. Only James (1990) concentrated on a particular ethnic group, African-Canadians. Racism emerges most consistently as a significant concern within postsecondary institutions. Social work appears to be the one discipline with a particular focus on multicultural issues, since seven of the studies focus on some aspect of training for social services.

Many of the studies reviewed lack a theory base. Anisef, Okihiro, and James (1982), Player and Ralph (1990), and Richmond (1986) are exceptions. These investigators used variations of social class theory to analyze their data. Levin and Dennison (1986) used an organizational change model and James (1990) had a phenomenological orientation. The absence of a theoretical framework makes it difficult to determine the significance of much of the data.

Canadian researchers have most frequently used qualitative and comparative approaches to explore multicultural issues in higher education. Typically investigators employed non-systematic data collection methods. The majority of the studies used a combination of questionnaires and semi-structured interviews to elicit descriptive data from purposively selected respondents. Only the studies by Denis (1978) and Richmond (1986) had rigorous quantitative designs. There were no longitudinal studies. The result of this pattern is a lack of statistical data which could be used to assess needs and evaluate effectiveness.

It appears that research on multiculturalism in postsecondary education is in the exploratory stage. The topics studied are diverse and the institutions in which research has been conducted are unique. The techniques used are relatively unsophisticated and there is a lack of replication, leading to problems in generalizing the findings. However, despite the weak research designs, there is a similar pattern in the findings of many studies, which suggests the inquiries have a degree of validity. For these reasons, the findings of most of the studies should be judiciously applied in other settings.

RESEARCH CONTENT AND FINDINGS

Because of the diversity in theoretical perspectives and methodologies within this body of research, this section presents studies categorized according to their main focus. It provides an overview of issues examined, research strategies employed, and summaries of findings. It also identifies major strengths and weaknesses in the body of research.

Institutional Responses

Investigations of postsecondary institutions' responses to multiculturalism centre on native issues, racism, minority access, and curriculum content. Universities across the country have carried out studies to identify changes needed in their institutional responses to ethnic and racial diversity. For instance, Dalhousie University (Clark 1992), the University of Quebec at Montreal (Corbo 1992), Queen's University (Berry et al. 1991), the University of Western Ontario, and the University of Winnipeg (Hanen 1992) have each examined issues in their internal environments regarding multiculturalism. However, findings of schools' internal studies are not easily accessible since these reports are not circulated widely. The studies summarized below suggest the major issues concerning multiculturalism within postsecondary educational institutions. The Commission of Inquiry on Canadian University Education undertook an assessment of the performance of institutions of higher education (Smith 1991). The Commission held public hearings across the country and received over 450 submissions (p 7). A large number of witnesses and briefs called for the inclusion of knowledge from non-European sources in curricula. The Commission recommended that 'in order to ensure reasonable balance and choice, universities should continue to encourage many different individual experiments in curricular organization (as is now happening) and share the results widely' (p 74). It also identified the relative absence of Native peoples in universities and advocated continuing federal support for programs which enhance Aboriginal participation in higher education. The Commission called for establishment of transition programs in universities and development of 'university-equivalent programs' near Native communities (p 99). Although not referring to disadvantaged ethnocultural groups specifically, the Commission recognized that socioeconomic and cultural factors may create barriers to university attendance. It recommended the creation of outreach programs at the secondary school level to encourage selected students to continue their studies.

The Association of Canadian Community Colleges (1990) surveyed non-university postsecondary institutions regarding their policies and programs with respect to multiculturalism. Questionnaires were distributed to 131 colleges across the country. The instrument collected data about the ethnocultural characteristics of the communities in which the colleges were located and the characteristics of the student population. It also probed for information regarding policies and programs which focus on ethnocultural groups. The report provides a list of Native and multicultural programs in colleges and detailed descriptions of five of them. Data indicate the largest group of special programs were responses to the needs of Aboriginal peoples. Most of these programs were offered by colleges in Northern communities. In contrast, programs in colleges in larger urban areas focus on diverse racial and cultural groups. Although many colleges have developed innovative programs, the majority lack policies and programs related to ethnocultural issues. It appears that anglophone colleges have tended to develop programs in cooperation with minority communities, while francophone colleges have focused on responding to the diversity within their student bodies.

At the level of the individual institution, Ramcharan, Chacko, and Baker (1991) surveyed racial minority students at the University of Windsor in order to determine the effect of discrimination on them. They used strategic random sampling to ensure the sample (n=100) was representative of the racial and national background of the non-White student population. Visa students comprised 58 per cent of the respondents. The researchers conducted structured interviews focusing on demographic data, perceptions regarding university personnel, discrimination, student relationships, and other problems. In considering the findings of this study, it is important to keep in mind that they reflect the perspective of a sample of minority respondents, largely visa students, whose views may be significantly different than those of permanent residents and White students. The results indicated that 15 per cent of the sample perceived discrimination, primarily verbal harassment, on campus, and 41 per cent identified similar events in the community. Discrimination among non-White students was identified by 18 per cent of respondents. A majority felt that university staff were more concerned with the needs of White students than those of visible minorities and that the university had not taken enough action to reduce prejudice. They advocated educational and legislative approaches to counter racism. Interestingly, racism was less of a priority than financial and academic issues and cultural differences. Although interracial friendships were common, minority students found the campus atmosphere uncomfortable. The authors recommended programs to reduce racist attitudes of students and university personnel, and development of a generic course on multiculturalism for all students.

An example of a study conducted by a university of its own needs in adapting to multiculturalism is that conducted by Rossi and Wayne (1990) at the University of Toronto. The researchers used availability sampling as a method of selecting respondents. This is an adequate method for exploratory studies in which the goal is to maximize the amount of data gathered (Seaberg 1988). Rossi and Wayne solicited written submissions from faculty, staff, and students of the university and met with individuals and groups. They also conferred with informants at York and Harvard universities and the University of Michigan. Although Rossi and Wayne found little evidence of overt, individual discrimination, they did uncover concerns about pervasive systemic discrimination, particularly with respect to Black faculty, staff, and students. Respondents expressed concern regarding the selection and promotion of racial minority faculty and support staff, and lack of support for minority students. They also identified bias in curriculum content and teaching methods. The researchers found that professional faculties, particularly social work, medicine and management studies, were taking the most significant initiatives towards incorporating multicultural issues into their programs. Rossi and Wayne recommended development of policies to counter discrimination and increase the representation of racial minorities on faculty, changes in teaching methods and approaches, and improved support services for minority students. They also advocated the collection of data on the ethnicity of students in order to identify under-represented groups.

Fallis, Keetch, and Podziemski (1990) studied the attitudes of community college students towards multiculturalism. They surveyed a sample (n=375) of students in business, technical and health programs at Georgian College in Barrie, Ontario. The majority of the respondents were of British heritage. Fallis et al. found that students had mixed reactions to ethnocultural diversity. Respondents recognized the contributions made by newcomers, claimed to disregard the ethnocultural background of their employers, and supported multicultural education. However, a significant minority felt that newcomers cause racial problems and deprive them of jobs. They advocated tighter immigration controls and assimilation of newcomers. The authors concluded that the study points to the continuing need for multicultural education.

In summary, the data on institutional issues indicates that there is a need for innovation in policies and programs to make schools more receptive to the needs of racial and cultural minorities. Community colleges and professional schools are experimenting with special programs, particularly focused on the needs of Natives. Recognition of, and response to, these issues varies widely across the country.

Access and Participation

The Special Committee on Participation of Visible Minorities in Canadian Society (1984) was mandated by the federal government to examine racial discrimination in Canadian society. The Committee carried out a comprehensive assessment, receiving input from hundreds of groups from across the country. The data indicated that 'visible minorities' are subject to 'discrimination, non-acceptance, low expectations by teachers, and lack of respect for and recognition of the learners' past experience' (p 133). The Committee recommended that educational institutions become more accessible and sensitive to racial minority students.

Despite the importance of the issue, studies of educational accessibility have given little attention to ethnicity. The study conducted by Anisef, Okihiro, and James (1982) is one of the few investigations which assess the impact of ethnicity on access to higher education. With a primary focus on Ontario universities, the authors traced the development of policies regarding postsecondary education, reviewed factors affecting university attendance, and analyzed 1971 and 1976 Ontario census data. Writing from a social stratification perspective, Anisef et al. concluded that the most significant factor associated with access to university is social class status. Except for Natives, who were significantly underrepresented, the participation of members of ethnic minority groups was proportional to their presence in the Ontario population. However, a limitation of this study is that since it was based on data regarding students' mother-tongues, it does not identify the participation rates of racial and ethnocultural minorities who speak English.

Based on a review of 1981 data, Anisef (1984 cited in Anisef et al. 1985) determined that the participation of non-English speaking mother-tongue minorities in postsecondary education in Ontario increased between 1971 and 1981. In contrast, fewer Native men sought higher education during that period. The rate of participation of minorities in non-university postsecondary education exceeded that of those with English as their mother-tongue.

The term 'allophones' is often used in Quebec to refer to people whose mother tongue is neither English or French. In contrast to the situation in Ontario, although allophones comprised 13 per cent of the 1988 Quebec population, they accounted for only 6.8 per cent of student enrolment in the province's universities, primarily in Montreal's anglophone schools (Larose 1990). The University of Quebec has attempted to attract minority students through forging links with ethnic communities and providing orientation programs and supports for ethnic students. During the 1980s there was a significant increase in enrolment of allophone students in francophone community colleges, and a small expansion in French language universities (see Bourhis, this volume).

Another study which touched on the accessibility of postsecondary education to minorities was that of Levin and Dennison (1989). They surveyed administrators, faculty, support staff, and students in 14 community colleges across Canada with respect to all facets of the institutions' functioning. The findings were that colleges experienced pressure to provide special programs for minority groups rather than accommodating them within their general programs. Although respondents identified the need for changes in student support services, curricula, and organizational structures in order to meet the needs of minority students, few program changes had been implemented. The investigators concluded that accessibility to community colleges decreased during the 1980s and that their programs were not as responsive to the needs of the population as had been envisaged when the community college system was instituted.

Mazer and Peeris (1990) gathered information on access to legal education for minorities. They found a general lack of data regarding the ethnic and racial backgrounds of university students. However, they were able to establish that between 1973 and 1989, the Native Law Centre of the University of Saskatchewan facilitated the graduation of 118 Native persons from law programs (p 9). In reviewing statistics from the 1986 Canadian census, they concluded that aboriginal Canadians and visible minorities are severely underrepresented in the legal profession.

To recapitulate, the data available suggest a high rate of participation by members of most ethnic minority groups. The striking exception is Native Canadians, who are significantly underrepresented. There is a lack of data as to the participation of members of other racial minorities. Research focused specifically on participation rates of racial and cultural minorities and on barriers encountered by these groups is needed.

Ethnicity and Educational Goals

One of the factors which determines participation in postsecondary education is the motivation of members of various ethnic groups for attaining higher education. Two studies are relevant to this issue. Denis (1978) explored the relationship between ethnicity and educational goals. She collected information from a random sample (n=1318) of English speaking first-year community college and university students in Toronto and Montreal by means of a questionnaire regarding ethnic background and educational objectives. Denis found that educational aspirations were related to ethnic background as well as gender. The sons of Canadian-born parents had lower aspirations than other men. Foreign-born respondents who did not speak English at home were more likely to pursue a community college diploma than a university degree. The findings have limited application to the current Canadian population, which includes many persons of Asian and African ancestry, since they are based on data from respondents of European backgrounds only. Another limitation of this study was that it did not control for the effects of social class differences.

James (1990) also looked at the relationship between educational goals and minority status. He explored the career aspirations of Black youth and their expectations of success. James conducted in-depth open-ended interviews of 60 young people between the ages of 17 and 24. He found the young people had high expectations of education and career success. Although the respondents identified discrimination as a significant obstacle, they saw attainment of higher education as a means to counter its impact. Despite viewing schools as inherently racist, the respondents believed they could overcome this barrier by working harder than other students.

Overall, these studies suggest that members of ethnocultural minorities are highly motivated to pursue higher education. The question is whether they are able to implement their goals successfully.

Achievement

The ethnic minority population presents a mixed picture with respect to educational achievement. According to the 1986 Canadian census, people whose mother tongue is neither English or French have a higher rate of university education than other groups (Baril & Mori 1991). As well, a large proportion have obtained community college diplomas or have partially completed postsecondary programs. However, the highest proportion of persons with less than high school education is also found within ethnic minority groups. This may be accounted for by the large number of older immigrants who came to Canada without a high level of education. Within Quebec, allophones are less successful than anglophones, but more successful than francophones (Bourhis, this volume). Research into these phenomena is warranted to determine if there are barriers to members of certain groups and to assess the educational needs of older allophones.

Richmond (1986) investigated the relationship between ethnic background and educational achievement. He used telephone interviews of a random sample (n=3522) of adults in Metropolitan Toronto to gather information about respondents' ethnicity and educational achievement as well as demographic, social, and economic factors in family backgrounds. The sample was stratified by ethnogenerational categories and gender. Richmond found that persons with ethnic minority backgrounds were more successful educationally than respondents with British or American ancestry. He noted that this may be due in part to Canadian immigration policies which favour the admission of highly qualified immigrants. Thus recent newcomers from non-European countries have a higher educational level than earlier European immigrants and their sponsored relatives. A limitation of this study is that it did not provide detailed data regarding non-British and non-American immigrants which would have allowed analysis of the achievement of various cultural and racial minorities. Richmond calls for longitudinal studies of the influence of cultural factors on motivation for higher education.

To recap, these data suggest that members of ethnic minorities are successful in achieving higher education. However, there is a lack of findings regarding educational levels among specific cultural and racial groups. It may be that high performance by members of certain minorities masks difficulties encountered by members of other backgrounds. There is a need for investigation into the educational achievement of members of various racial and cultural groups in order to identify barriers to success.

Educational Needs

There has been little investigation of the educational requirements of multicultural populations. Hynes (1988) conducted a needs assessment of underserved ethnic and racial groups in Toronto on behalf of George Brown College. In addition to reviewing demographic data regarding the ethnocultural characteristics of the population, the investigator gathered data by means of questionnaires and interviews of respondents from the college, other educational programs, social agencies, the federal and provincial governments, and minority communities. The data indicated needs in the areas of policy development, staff training, recruitment and support of students from diverse backgrounds, and curriculum content. With respect to the specific training needs, the study revealed needs for upgrading the technical skills of staff in social agencies which serve minorities, assisting immigrants with foreign training to qualify for practice in Canada, improving the language and skills of minorities with less than Grade nine education, and facilitating ethnic minority students in applying their bicultural experience and language abilities in helping their communities. The findings were used to formulate recommendations in response to these issues.

Professional Education

The Committee for Intercultural/Interracial Education in Professional Schools (1991) conducted a study of multiculturalism in Ontario professional schools. One hundred and ninety-five faculty and administrators participated in workshops held in eight locations across the province. Data were gathered by questionnaires and group discussions. The findings suggested that community colleges offer the majority of courses related to multicultural issues and that most of these courses are optional. Barriers to teaching and research regarding multiculturalism included shortage of resources, lack of time and resistance from faculty. A major concern of respondents was the underrepresentation of racial minorities among administrators and students, particularly in education, law, and medicine. They identified concerns regarding restrictive admission criteria, lack of support for minority students, and culturally-biased evaluation methods. The respondents recommended the development of policies and programs to respond to these issues.

Medical Education

There is a lack of systematic investigation of the educational response of individual professions in Canada to racial and cultural diversity. Only one study was found relating to medical education. Hennen and Blackman (1990) conducted a survey to determine the training regarding multicultural issues provided in the five undergraduate medical education programs and five family residency programs in the province of Ontario. They gathered data regarding current programs as well as desirable changes by means of questionnaires administered to program directors and by interviews with directors and students. Hennen and Blackman found that there were no mandatory courses regarding multiculturalism. Two schools offered electives which could include content on minority issues. Respondents recommended integration of multicultural issues throughout the curriculum, provision of information to faculty regarding ethnocultural diversity, and the use of medical settings in ethnic minority communities in the experiential training of students. The data suggested that barriers to the inclusion of multicultural content were lack of interest by teachers and students and difficulty in incorporating more content into already crowded curricula.

Social Service Education

National, provincial, and local studies have been conducted regarding multiculturalism in social service education programs. The Task Force on Multicultural and Multiracial Issues in Social Work Education of the Canadian Association of Schools of Social Work (1991) gathered information from all university social work education programs across the country. O'Neill and Yelaja (1991) focused on schools of social work in Ontario. The Carleton University school of social work explored issues related to race and ethnicity in its own program (*Priority Assessment* 1990). Laskin, Malmo, and Shaw (1980) compared social service education programs at the university, polytechnic, and community college levels in Metropolitan Toronto. In each of these studies, data were collected by means of questionnaires and interviews of faculty, students, and community members.

A similar pattern of issues emerged in each of these studies. Schools recognized that some ethnocultural minority communities have educational and service needs which differ from those of the dominant cultural groups. Although there was a consensus on the need to prepare students to be effective in working with clients from racial and cultural backgrounds different than their own, programs were not organized to achieve this goal. There were programs for specific minorities such as Natives and francophones outside Quebec but none which have integrated a multicultural ideology into their core program. There was some feeling among immigrant and Aboriginal communities that specialized community college training better meets their needs than do mainstream social work programs (Task Force 1991).

Systemic discrimination, particularly with respect to racial minorities, emerged as a major concern. Despite the lack of data regarding the ethnic and racial backgrounds of administrators, faculty, and students, there was a perception that minorities are not adequately represented. There was a lack of initiatives to attract and maintain faculty and students from diverse groups. Minority students were concerned about the racist climate they encountered within schools.

Respondents stressed the need to incorporate issues related to racial and ethnic diversity throughout all aspects of social work training. Although most schools included some content on ethnocultural diversity in their programs, there was no consistency regarding content or teaching methods. With few exceptions, students were not required to take courses related to multicultural issues. The majority of schools had field placements in social agencies which serve minorities, but there was little emphasis on using them for developing cross-cultural intervention skills. Respondents advocated broadening the curriculum to include knowledge about the ethnocultural diversity of Canada, the special needs of minorities, and anti-racism. The data suggested faculty need additional training in order to implement these changes.

In summary, the preparation of workers for service to minority clients has a low priority in social service education programs. There is no systematic approach to the training of students to work with ethnic and racial minority clients in either universities or community colleges. Although there is widespread recognition of the need to deal with multicultural and multiracial issues in social work education, it appears that there has been little progress since Laskin et al. (1980) did their study.

Teaching Methods in Social Services

Two studies examined approaches to incorporating ethnocultural diversity in human services training programs. Player and Ralph (1990) evaluated the inclusion of race issues in a core course at the Carleton University school of social work. The authors found that White students needed to explore their own feelings and values regarding racism and to develop skills in working with people of diverse backgrounds. They concluded that non-White students need to express their anger about discrimination and to learn how to use this to stimulate change. Player and Ralph recommended experiential teaching methods and involvement of racially mixed teams of instructors and speakers from minority communities.

Blum (1990) studied issues in the provision of training in social services to students from diverse ethnocultural backgrounds. The investigator interviewed Native, immigrant, and foreign students in university and community college programs in Manitoba. She found that students from the dominant culture had a particular need for knowledge and skills related to diversity, while students from ethnocultural minority groups had the need to learn about professional helping skills. Blum determined that the presence of ethnic diversity among students contributed to their understanding of cultural differences. She emphasized the need for attention to issues related to immigration and the impact of the dominant culture on minority values and institutions.

In brief, the available research suggests that experiential approaches are most effective in sensitizing students to ethnocultural diversity. Students from different backgrounds have distinct learning needs. A heterogeneous mix of students and teachers enhances learning for members of all groups.

STRENGTHS AND WEAKNESSES

Several strengths are evident in the existing body of research on multiculturalism in higher education. The diversity in topics and settings available for study provides a fertile field for investigators to pursue their scholarly interests. Qualitative designs, which predominate in the existing body of research, are appropriate and useful for understanding new and complex issues about which little is known (Epstein 1988). This aptly describes the situation with respect to the incorporation of multiculturalism into higher education.

Research on multiculturalism in postsecondary education has a number of deficits. The major weakness is the small size of the existing body of research in the area. Basic data about the participation of ethnocultural minorities in higher education, curriculum content, teaching methods, and program effectiveness are missing. There has been no assessment of the social, political and financial costs and benefits of responding to ethnocultural diversity. The methodological soundness of some of the studies is questionable in that much of the work has been conducted without the use of a theoretical framework or systematic data collection methods.

To some extent, these deficiencies are due to the low level of interest in research on higher education in general (Smith 1991), and with respect to racial and cultural diversity in particular. If multicultural issues were given higher priority on the research agenda, undoubtably the area would be investigated more thoroughly and effectively.

CONCLUSION

Research on multiculturalism in Canadian postsecondary education supports Chief Justice Brian Dickson's answer to the question he raised regarding how universities might develop 'an environment in which all feel that they are truly free to participate as fully as they desire' (Dickson 1992:6). He believes that reform can be achieved by measures which will discourage discrimination while preserving openness to all ideas within universities:

While we must live up to our responsibility to foster institutional equity – that is, to adjust the structure of the university so as to foster equality of opportunity – we must also recognize that a commitment to freedom of inquiry and freedom of speech means that we must seek to avoid imposing any one conception of the perfect curriculum or of the range of issues that is appropriate to talk about in a university setting (Dickson 1992:22).

Justice Dickson urged postsecondary institutions to carry out their legislated responsibilities by fully implementing policies and programs which protect minorities against discrimination on campus. However, he argued that prohibitions against discrimination by themselves will not be sufficient to accommodate members of diverse groups while protecting academic freedom. He urged universities 'to effect change not by dictating acceptable forms of speech but through the recruitment of talent from minority groups and the integration of faculty members with diverse backgrounds and perspectives' (Dickson 1992:24). The existing body of research on multiculturalism in postsecondary education provides guidance to educators pursuing this goal. However, in order to fully achieve the integration of racial and ethnic minorities within universities and community colleges, further research in the area is needed.

REFERENCES

Anisef, P., Bertrand, M., Hortian, U., and James, C. (1985). *Accessibility to post-secondary education in Canada: A review of the literature*. Ottawa: Dept of the Secretary of State of Canada, Education Support Branch

Anisef, P., Okihiro, N., and James, C. (1982). *Losers and winners: The pursuit of equality and social justice in higher education*. Toronto: Butterworths

Arthurs, H.W. (1992). Keynote panel remarks. In J.W. Berry et al. (eds), *National symposium on institutional strategies for race and ethnic relations at Canadian universities*. Kingston: Queen's University

Association of Canadian Community Colleges (1990). *Serving the needs of a changing community: A survey report on multiracialism and multiculturalism in Canada's community colleges and technical institutes*. Toronto: Association of Canadian Community Colleges

Badets, J. (1989, Autumn). Canada's immigrant population. *Canadian Social Trends*, 2–6

Baril, A., and Mori, G.A. (1991, Spring). Educational attainment of linguistic groups in Canada. *Canadian Social Trends*, 17–18

Berry, J.W. et al. (1991). *Towards diversity and equity at Queen's* (Report of the Principal's Advisory Committee on Race Relations). *Queen's University Gazette*, 23:11

Berry, J.W., Joneja, M., Robillard, M., and Sinnott, J. (eds) (1992). *National symposium on institutional strategies for race and ethnic relations at Canadian universities*. Kingston: Queen's University

Berry, J.W., Kalin, R., and Taylor, D.M. (1977). *Multiculturalism and ethnic attitudes in Canada*. Ottawa: Supply and Services Canada

Bibby, R. (1991, 10 October). Multiculturalism needs a helping hand. *Globe and Mail*, A22

Blum, E. (1990). The education and training of professionals and paraprofessionals involved in settlement and integration. In S.A. Yelaja (ed.), *Proceedings of the Settlement and Integration of New Immigrants to Canada Conference* (pp

83–101). Waterloo: Wilfrid Laurier University, Faculty of Social Work and Centre for Social Welfare Studies

Burnet, J. (1988). Multiculturalism. In J.H. March (ed.), *The Canadian encyclopedia* (2nd ed., Vol. 3, p 1401). Edmonton: Hurtig

Castellano, M.B., Stalwick, H., and Wien, F. (1986). Native social work education in Canada. *Canadian Social Work Review*, 3:166–84

Clark, H.C. (1992). Keynote panel remarks. In J.W. Berry et al. (eds), *National symposium on institutional strategies for race and ethnic relations at Canadian universities*. Kingston: Queen's University

Committee for Intercultural/Interracial Education in Professional Schools. (1991). *Professional requirements in an intercultural, interracial society*. Available from CIIEPS, c/o Faculty of Nursing, 50 St George St, Room 87, Toronto, ON, M5S 1A1

Corbo, C. (1992). Les universités face à la diversité culturelle: Éléments de statégie institutionnelle. In J.W. Berry et al. (eds), *National symposium on institutional strategies for race and ethnic relations at Canadian universities*. Kingston: Queen's University

Denis, A.B. (1978). The relationship between ethnicity and educational aspirations of post-secondary students in Toronto and Montreal. In M.L. Kovacs (ed.), *Ethnic Canadians: Culture and education* (pp 231–42). Regina: Canadian Plains Studies Research Center

Dickson, B. (1992). Freedoms and responsibilities in the universities' response to a multicultural society. In J.W. Berry et al. (eds), *National symposium on institutional strategies for race and ethnic relations at Canadian universities*. Kingston: Queen's University

'Employment equity for academics in the designated groups: Visible minorities, the disabled and native peoples' (1990, November). *OCUFA Forum Supplement*. Pp 1–4

Epstein, I. (1988). Quantitative and qualitative methods. In R.M. Grinnell, Jr. (ed.), *Social work research and evaluation* (3rd ed. pp 185–98). Itasca, IL: F.E. Peacock

Fallis, F., Keetch, S., and Podziemski, T. (1990). *Student attitudes and characteristics related to multiculturalism: Survey results*. Barrie, ON: Georgian College

Fraser, G. (1992, 16 Sept.). Official mother tongues slip. *Globe and Mail*, A1

The forum: A report to the people from the Citizens' Forum on Canada's Future (1991, 29 June). *Globe and Mail*, A7–A10

Gaskell, J., and McLaren, A. (1987a). Introduction to part three: The nature of curriculum: Whose knowledge? In J. Gaskell and A. McLaren (eds), *Women and education: A Canadian perspective* (pp 193–201). Calgary: Detselig Enterprises

– (1987b). Introduction to part two: Unequal access to knowledge. In J. Gaskell
  and A. McLaren (eds), *Women and education: A Canadian perspective* (pp 105–
  15). Calgary: Detselig Enterprises

Goar, C. (1991, 31 August). One final appeal for multiculturalism. *Toronto Star*,
  D5

Hanen, M.P. (1992). From monologue to dialogue on race and ethnic relations:
  Creating a climate for institutional change. Panel presentation. In J.W. Berry
  et al. (eds), *National symposium on institutional strategies for race and ethnic
  relations at Canadian universities*. Kingston: Queen's University

Hennen, B.K.E., and Blackman, N. J. (1990). *The teaching of multicultural aspects
  of health care in Ontario undergraduate medical schools and in Ontario family
  medicine residency programs: Evaluation report and conference proceedings.*
  London: University of Western Ontario, Faculty of Medicine

Hynes, M. (1988). *Access to potential: A two-way street: An educational and training
  needs assessment of Metro Toronto's diverse racial and cultural communities.*
  Toronto: George Brown College

Information Book (Canadian ed.) (1991). Newtown, PA: Law School Admission
  Services

James, C. (1990). *Making it: Black youth, racism and career aspirations in a big city.*
  Oakville, ON: Mosaic

Larose, Y. (1990, December). L'université du Québec et les communautés
  culturelles: Le temps d'agir. Réseau, 23–4

Laskin, B., Malmo, G., and Shaw, E. (1980). *Research study III: The response of
  social service educational programs to ethnic groups.* Unpublished MSW research
  report, University of Toronto, Faculty of Social Work

Laver, R. (1991, 21 Oct.). Modern times are tougher times. *Maclean's* 28–9

Levin, J.S., and Dennison, J.D. (1989). *Responsiveness and renewal in Canada's
  community colleges: A study of change in organizations.* Vancouver: Kwantlen
  College & University of British Columbia. ERIC Document Reproduction
  Service No. ED 308–919

Lewis, R., and Benedict, M. (1991, 21 Oct.). A measure of excellence. *Maclean's*
  12–13

McLeod, K. (1981). Multiculturalism and multicultural education: Policy and
  practice. In D. Dorotich (ed.), *Education and Canadian multiculturalism:
  Some problems and some solutions* (pp 12–26). Saskatoon: Canadian Society
  for the Study of Education ERIC Document Reproduction Service No. ED 223
  738

Mazer, B. (1989). Access to legal education and the profession in Canada. In N.
  Kibble, R. Dhavan, and W. Twining (eds), *Access to legal education and the legal
  profession* (pp 114–31). London: Butterworths

Mazer, B.M., and Peeris, M.S. (1990). *Access to legal education in Canada: Databook 1990.* Windsor, ON: University of Windsor, Faculty of Law

Misgivings about Canada's multiculturalism policy (1991, 5 Aug.). *Globe and Mail,* A10

Mitchell, A. (1991, 5 Nov.). 63% like multiracial Canada. *Globe and Mail,* A1, A2

Mori, G., and Burke, B. (1990, Summer). Changes in educational attainment. *Canadian Social Trends:* 32–3

Naidoo, J.C., and Edwards, R.G. (1991). Combatting racism involving visible minorities: A review of relevant research and policy development. *Canadian Social Work Review,* 8:211–36

O'Neill, B.J., and Yelaja, S.A. (1991). Multicultural issues in social work education. *Canadian Social Work Review,* 8:168–89

Ontario Federation of Students (1991, Jan.). *Whitewashed: Institutional racism in Ontario post-secondary education.* Available from Ontario Federation of Students, 643 Yonge St., Toronto, ON, M4Y 1Z9

Parliament, J. (1986, Winter). Community colleges: An alternative to universities. *Canadian Social Trends:*10–13

Player, C., and Ralph, D. (1990, June). Feminist, anti-racist social work education: A case study. Paper presented at the annual meeting of the Canadian Association of Schools of Social Work, Victoria, BC

Priority assessment: Race, ethnicity and aboriginal issues and strategies for addressing these (1990). Ottawa: Carleton University School of Social Work

Ramcharan, S., Chacko, J., and Baker, R. (1991). *An attitudinal study of visible minority students at the University of Windsor.* Windsor, ON: University of Windsor

Richmond, A.H. (1986). Ethnogenerational variation in educational achievement. *Canadian Ethnic Studies,* 18(3):75–89

Rossi, M., and Wayne, J. (1990). Report of the presidential advisors on ethnocultural groups and visible minorities at the University of Toronto. Unpublished report

Seaberg, J.R. (1988). Utilizing sampling procedures. In R.M. Grinnell, Jr. (ed.), *Social work research and evaluation* (3rd ed. pp 240–57). Itasca, IL: F.E. Peacock

Simeon, R. (1991, 30 Apr.). Now the good news: We have a lot in common. *Globe and Mail,* A15

Smith, S. (1991). *Report: Commission of Inquiry on Canadian University Education.* Ottawa: Association of Universities and Colleges of Canada

Special Committee on Participation of Visible Minorities in Canadian Society (1984). *Equality now: Report of the Special Committee on Visible Minorities in Canadian Society.* Hull, PQ: Supply and Services Canada

Task Force on Multicultural and Multiracial Issues in Social Work Education

(1991). *Social work education at the crossroads: The challenge of diversity*. Ottawa: Canadian Association of Schools of Social Work

Tchoryck-Pelletier, P. (1989). *L'adaptation des minorités ethniques*. Ville St Laurent, PQ: Cégep de Saint-Laurent

Weiner, G. (1992). Banquet address. In J.W. Berry et al. (eds), *National symposium on institutional strategies for race and ethnic relations at Canadian universities*. Kingston: Queen's University

IZA LAPONCE

The State of Bibliographic Control of Publications in the Field of Multiculturalism

References and bibliographies for whom: undergraduates, graduates, academic researchers, or members of the public at large? Librarians preparing guides to resources or evaluating collections always struggle with this question. Typically we evade it and try to satisfy everybody. That catholicity appears in the typical introductory guides, often called 'START HERE' that university libraries offer to their users: if you research a particular aspect of ethnicity but know little about it – 'start' with an encyclopedia article, progress to a general bibliography, then go to specialized bibliographies or periodical indexes.

I have adopted this familiar format in the presentation of a 'Start Here' guide (see Appendix), where the basic and the esoteric find their place. The entries in that compilation start with encyclopedias and reach machine-readable files through print bibliographies.

Most of the works in the Appendix have been already described by Dorothy Ryder (Ryder 1981) or K. Nilsen (Nilsen 1992). I will not duplicate their work. Instead I will make an overall evaluation of the bibliographic control of materials on ethnicity, point out deficiencies. and suggest remedies.

In preparing the Appendix, I was guided by Jean Burnet's definition of multiculturalism as referring to ' a society that is characterized by ethnic or cultural heterogeneity'; referring as well to 'the policy proclaimed by the federal government in 1971 and subsequently by a number of provinces' (Burnet 1988). We are thus dealing with a very broad field of literature which includes the study of ethnic, racial and religious groups, their relations and conflicts, immigration history and policy, acculturation, demography, culture, and education policy.

A quick reading of the Appendix might give the impression that the field is well covered and the information well controlled. A more attentive analysis will show that the situation is not all that satisfactory. Let us judge the adequacy of bibliographic coverage by three criteria: *coverage, updatedness,* and *retrievability.* By retrievability, I mean the possibility of finding what one wants and what is listed but more or less hidden. For instance suppose someone were working on the acculturation of women of low socioeconomic strata belonging to so-called visible minorities. That researcher would not want to examine all the publications on social class, or on Chinese, Japanese, Blacks, South Asians, Cambodians, Laotians, Vietnamese, Native peoples, women, minorities, racial relations, refugees, and acculturation. He or she would want to link the concepts of 'acculturation' and 'women' to a given ethnic group, and within that group to limit the search to concepts such as 'poverty' or 'social class' or 'socio-economic status.' A most complete and up to date bibliography is useless should it fail such test of retrievability.

Basic References

Let us consider first the category *Handbooks, Dictionaries, and Directories.* No serious problem here at present, but, very likely, a serious lacuna in a few years time.

The various volumes of the *Handbook of North American Indians* are very dated and (that is the cost of meticulous scholarship) their publication is very slow. That datedness restricts the use of an otherwise excellent bibliography, but in as much as the volumes are a compilation of ethnological studies of Native peoples of specific areas and specific cultures and are not focused on present conditions, being old is not a mortal sin. The indexing of each volume is excellent for a print product.

The Canadian Encyclopedia is current and its coverage is good. There are separate entries for specific ethnic and religious groups and articles on such topics as multiculturalism, and immigration. But the future of that publication is very much in doubt. In a few years time it will be outdated. That is serious because, unlike the *Handbook of North American Indians, The Canadian Encyclopedia* focuses on present conditions.

In short, the assessment of the most basic sources in our *Start Here* category is: good at present but problematic usefulness in the not too distant future.

Statistics

The statistics and census section needs few comments. Canada conducts decennial censuses and smaller ones every five years. Various specialized statistical products on ethnicity and language groups are published in print and machine-readable formats. Obviously the machine-readable publications are more useful for the sophisticated researcher since they permit the manipulation of data to suit specific needs.

Bibliographies

Bibliographies listed in this category are monographic publications which list selected books, periodical articles, research reports, dissertations, government publications and any other literature germane to a specific topic. Some are no more than an alphabetic list of works, with a rudimentary subject index, others offer a classified list of literature, with no subject index at all; still others are highly sophisticated research tools that have an excellent subject approach to the materials they list and permit a quick and specific retrieval of information. Taken as a whole, the bibliographies dealing with Canadian ethnic studies are moderately good in their coverage but, with few exceptions, they fail the 'up to date' and the 'retrievability' tests.

Of the 22 bibliographies which deal with ethnic groups *in general*, 13 were published before 1985 and most of them offer access to the data only by name of specific ethnic groups or by very broad subject categories such 'immigration.' Miska's *Ethnic and Native Canadian Literature: A Bibliography* stands out as an exception. It is current, its entries are classified by ethnic groups, and the indexes permit retrieval by title of the work or by name of the author.

The *specialized* bibliographies are not any better than the general ones in terms of accessibility. They provide an uneven coverage and they too are often very dated (see Table 1).

Of the 53 bibliographies devoted to specific ethnic groups, 36 were published before 1985, 17 published in 1985 or later. Of all the groups, the Native Indians are the best served, with 20 titles listed. That last statistic, however, should not be read with too much satisfaction since some of the best bibliographies pertaining to the Native peoples, those with good indexes for useful retrieval, are now in the outdated category (notably Abler 1974, Smith 1983 & Whiteside 1973).

TABLE 1

Specialized bibliographies, by subject and year of publication

Name of ethnic group*	Years of publication
French	1972, 1981, 1982, 1983, 1987, 1991
English	1985, 1987, 1987, 1991
Germans	1982
Scottish	
Italians	1988
Irish	
Ukrainians	1981
Chinese	
Dutch	
Jewish	1981
Polish	1958, 1978
Blacks	1970, 1985, 1988
North American Indians	1973, 1974, 1975, 1976, 1976, 1976, 1979, 1982, 1983, 1983, 1984, 1984, 1984, 1986, 1986, 1986, 1989, 1990, 1990, 1990
Metis	1973, 1980, 1986, 1990
Inuit	1973, 1986, 1990
Others	
Asians	1989
Czechs/Slovaks	1976
Doukhobors	1972
East Indians	1971, 1977
Filipinos	1977
Hungarians	1977, 1987
Japanese	1975
Mennonites	1989
Portuguese	1969
Romanians	1980
Serbs	1976
Slovenes	1981

* First 15 entries are those of the census

To fill the gap created by these outdated bibliographies, one could use the annual bibliography of *Canadian Ethnic Studies*, but here we meet a retrievability problem. The literature in a *CES* bibliography is listed alphabetically, by author, and arranged in very broad categories. That forces the user to hunt for specific items in the hope of locating something of interest. A more efficient method of updating old bibliographies calls for the use of indexing and abstracting services such as the *Sociological Abstracts* or *America: History and Life*. These indexes are discussed in the next section.

Indexes and Abstracts

As just indicated, *Indexes and Abstracts* are useful for updating the monographic bibliographies. They are also the first tool used to locate the latest published journal articles (most indexes do not list books). It must be pointed out that not all the titles in this sections are truly indexes in the narrow sense of the term, some (such as *Canadiana* and *Bibliographie du Québec*) have been included here for reasons of convenience, because they share some of the features of indexes: frequency of publication, a predetermined body of literature, an indexing of materials by means of a predictable controlled retrieval vocabulary, and a variety of retrieval possibilities.

All, except the *Canadian Public Administration: Bibliography*, are published at least annually, most are issued several times a year and cumulated annually.

The Appendix lists 23 major titles which always include material of interest to the Canadian ethnic scholar. Eleven of these publications are Canadian. Let us first deal with the latter.

Canada's national bibliography, *Canadiana*, is the register of the nation's published intellectual creativity. It lists books, some 'grey' literature, federal and provincial government publications, reports, dissertations, theses, audio and visual materials that have been published (or produced), in Canada or abroad, by Canadians or pertaining to Canada. It is published in microfiche format. In addition, in the last ten years, the National Library has provided Canadian libraries an online access to a merged file of *Canadiana*, the *Canadian Institute for Historical Microreproductions Microfiche Catalogue*, *Canadian Theses*, *Retrospective Bibliography*, and *Cataloguing in Process* (CIP). One of the best features of this file is its reasonable cost, well within the means of most libraries. One of its greatest weaknesses is its present data management system (DOBIS,) which does not support Boolean free-searching. The same file is available through CAN/OLE, which does permit Boolean searching, but at much higher cost. *Canadiana*'s main drawbacks are the incompleteness of its coverage of 'grey literature' (reports, research papers, etc.) and the time lag between the time of publication and the time of listing. Even the CIP is behind time. It also misses roughly 64 per cent of the literature of interest to Canadian social scientists.[1]

La Bibliographie du Québec is Quebec's equivalent of *Canadiana*. It is published in paper format, with an online access available through the UTLAS Catalogue Support System (CATSS).

The old *Canadian News Index, Canadian Magazine Index,* and *Canadian Business Periodicals Index,* amalgamated into the *Canadian Index* (paper format) in 1993, are also available on CD-ROM under the name of *Canadian Business and Current Affairs.* They have a strong business focus, which might be useful for those examining ethnicity and commerce or business but is of limited use to most students of ethnicity because it hardly goes beyond indexing newspapers and a few academic magazines.

The Canadian Periodical Index (CPI), has a much broader coverage, reaching back in time to 1920 and offering, for the 1920–60 period, the only means of locating articles written in Canada at that time. It indexes the major Canadian social science and humanities journals, although it sometimes takes years before a newly created journal is picked up for indexing. It is not, unfortunately, a reference tool primarily intended for the academic researcher. From the very beginning, it was designed to serve a wider public, including schools and public libraries. Because of this policy, it often fails to pick up important Canadian academic publications. In addition, it does not index journals published outside Canada and for that reason misses a great proportion of the scientific journal literature. The CPI is available for online at-distance searching through InfoGlobe, and in a CD-ROM format. Unfortunately, as yet the search software used leaves much to be desired.

Point de repère is Quebec's equivalent of the *Canadian Periodical Index.* Its coverage is multidisciplinary, with strong emphasis on the humanities and social sciences. The paper version is published ten times a year and cumulated annually. There is also a microfiche edition. Electronically it is searchable from 1980 through SDM (Services documentaires multimedia).

Government publications are among the most difficult and time-consuming material to locate. Their indexing is far from satisfactory, in part because of the nature of publications that range from the flimsy and the ephemeral to regular reports with no distinctive titles, and to book-like publications. The monographic items pose little problem. They can be catalogued by a library as books, and easily located by users. But what of the thousands of other items published each year – those with no titles, those that in fact have titles and are quite distinct but are buried under the name of a series or are listed under the complicated name of a bureau or commission?

An added confusion comes from the fact that not all government publications are listed in *Government of Canada Publications* catalogue. Only the items for sale by the Canadian Communication Group Publishing are listed. Publications issued by Statistics Canada have their own catalogue, as do those of almost all other government departments. Why this confusion? The materials listed in the *Government of Canada Publications* exist in machine-readable form for the purpose of paper publication. It would be surprising if the same was not true of the Statistics Canada and other departmental catalogues. It should be no great undertaking to combine the departmental publications catalogues with those of *Canadiana* and the Government of Canada Publications and, having merged their files, to make them available in a CD-ROM format, or on magnetic tapes.

The *Canadian Education Index* includes materials on ethnicity, notably articles written by Canadian educators (in Canadian journals) dealing with the political socialization of immigrant children, language teaching, children's adjustment problems, education policy vis-à-vis native peoples, and so on. The index is available for electronic at-distance online searching through BRS, it may also be purchased on tape for local mounting and online retrieval, or it may be purchased on CD-ROM from Micromedia. Because of the flaws in the software, the CD-ROM version, at present is the least useful.

Canadian Public Administration Bibliography is an irregularly updated, ongoing printed bibliography. It lists books, research reports, articles, and other types of publications dealing with the Canadian public service, public administration, and public policy. It covers all sorts of literature dealing with language policy, English-French relations, ethnicity, and racial relations.

The Index to Canadian Legal Periodical Literature covers legal periodical articles published in Canada. It is particularly important for locating literature pertaining to civil rights and ethnicity, native rights, the Constitution, and political rights. At present it is available only in printed format.

Directory of Statistics in Canada is published in paper format and is also available on magnetic tape for local library mounting. It lists not only the publications of Statistics Canada, but also those of the other federal departments, provincial governments, and documents published by various Canadian research institutes and research bodies. Its subject indexing is detailed and specific. Bibliographic information is enhanced by long and detailed abstracts fully searchable in the electronic format. Libraries may also purchase a companion microfiche set of the full contents of the publications listed in the Index.

The former *Canadian News Index*, now part of the *Canadian Index*, is indispensable for locating news stories in the leading Canadian newspapers. Because of its broad subject headings, this index is difficult to use in paper form. The electronic formats enhance its value. Libraries can acquire it on magnetic tape for local mounting, or in CD-ROM format as part of *Canadian Business and Current Affairs*. It can also be searched at-distance through DIALOG.

In the 1960s, foreign indexing services, mostly American, began to pick up the more prestigious Canadian academic journals. None of these services has a comprehensive coverage, but together they have become an indispensable supplement to the Canadian indexes.

For instance, social psychology and political sociology articles are well covered in *Psychological Abstracts* and *Sociological Abstracts*. One can easily locate there studies published not only in the major Canadian, but also in foreign journals. In libraries that have these indexes in electronic format, complicated searches, covering the 1974–93 period can be done in a few minutes. The electronic format of the *MLA Bibliography* offers the same service in the field of Canadian literature. While the electronic version of *Linguistics and Language Behavior Abstracts: LLBA*, available through BRS and DIALOG, and also on CD-ROM is essential for anyone working in the field of language teaching, language acquisition, and language behaviour.

The American equivalent of the *Canadian Education Index* is called *ERIC* (Educational Resources Information Center). This is one of the largest and most sophisticated of computerized bibliographic retrieval databases. In the last few years it has been listing more and more Canadian materials, and has become an excellent starting place for finding literature on ethnicity and education.

Special mention should be made of a bibliography, which unfortunately, in recent years, had been allowed to lag behind in its publication schedule, but which has now resumed its regular appearance. *The International Bibliography of Social and Cultural Anthropology*, published annually, is available in paper format only. It is among the most important research tools for anyone working on any aspect of ethnic studies, including Canadian ethnic studies. The resuscitated bibliography unfortunately no longer offers its formerly excellent subject indexing. This makes retrieval much more difficult.

One of my favourite indexes is *America: History and Life*. Contrary to its title, it covers both Canada and the United States. Its primary focus is historical, but it also provides good coverage of social, cultural, economic, religious, and political subjects. It is one of the few indexing services that lists not only articles and books, but in the case of books of collective scholarship, also lists individual chapters and offers an abstract for each entry. In paper form, it is published quarterly, indexed annually, and has a cumulated author and subject index every five years. The subject indexing is excellent for a paper edition. The data base is available for online searching through BRS and DIALOG, as well as in CD-ROM format.

Theses

The bibliographic control of Canadian theses and dissertations is unsatisfactory. *Canadiana* and *Canadian Theses* list these materials, but do so very poorly in comparison to the Americans, who have an excellent bibliographic control of their doctoral dissertations, (though not of their Masters' theses). *Dissertation Abstracts International* at one time included a large number of Canadian dissertations, but today includes only those whose authors pay for inclusion. *Canadian Theses* is a microfiche product which lists MA and doctoral dissertations done either in Canada or abroad and pertaining to Canada. The index is cumbersome to use and the amount of information inadequate. The listing is slow, often with delays of two to three years.

Summary

In summary, the indexes listed in the Appendix pass the tests of currency. As for the test of coverage, they all fail individually but pass as a group, a group that must include both the Canadian and the foreign publications. No library in Canada could support Canadian ethnic studies solely with either the Canadian or the foreign indexing services. Both are needed, yet together they do not provide comprehensive listing of the existing materials. As for the test of retrievability it is generally satisfactory because of the recent conversion of many of these indexes to electronic formats.

Additional Comments

There remains one type of publication that is almost impossible to locate, in the field of ethnicity as in other fields of Canadian studies: the articles published in festschriften, the papers presented at conferences, and the studies commissioned on specific topics. Only a few of these contributions are reprints. Most of them are original works. This type of publication is quite common in Canada. (Indeed, I suppose the chapters of this very volume will fall into that category.) There is practically no control on this kind of material. A few items are picked up by *America: History and Life,* and the *Index to Social Sciences and Humanities Proceedings,* but most are simply lost.

Overall Evaluation and Suggested Remedies

At present, retrieving material in the field of Canadian ethnic studies, as indeed in all Canadian studies fields, is like fishing at random. One knows there are lots of fish out there, but where? If one has prior knowledge of the location, one may find what one searches for, but in the absence of that knowledge, finding it will be a matter of luck.

Improving the scope and coverage of ethnic bibliographies is up to the academic community. It would be nice to have more specialized bibliographies, but the improvements urgently needed concern the other two dimensions of our evaluation: those of time lag and retrievability. In these two domains, the computer is likely to be our saviour.

Traditional library services are rapidly being transformed by the changing needs of the academic research community and the opportunities afforded by the new information technologies. Besides the printed form, information is now made available in a variety of new formats: video, audio, microform, floppy discs, and electronic.

Much has been written about the imminent demise of printed journals and books. Rogers and Hurt wrote recently that 'scholarly journals are obsolete as primary vehicle for scholarly communication'(Rogers & Hurt 1990). Personally, I consider this unlikely. True, there are now journals that exist in an electronic format only, and the use of electronic networks, bulletin boards and electronic mail is steadily increasing, but printed journals are not disappearing. On the contrary, as Rogers and Hurt themselves point out, in 1988 alone, 5000 *new* journals were published. But the more print there will be, the more urgent will be the need to abstract and index that print electronically.

Before the 1970s, paper format was the only practical way to publish bibliographic information. Microfiche was the next alternative. It lowered the cost of publishing considerably and rendered possible continuous cumulations and updates. The format however remained unpleasant. Users never developed a liking for it. By contrast, the successor to the microfiche, the electronic format, became popular almost immediately. Libraries now offer several ways of searching materials electronically: *locally* by accessing the library files that have been put in machine-readable formats, by buying and mounting commercial files on the library's mainframe computer, by searching materials stored on floppy discs or on CD-ROMs, and *at-distance* by accessing the databases of commercial vendors through companies such as BRS or DIALOG.

In the last three years, since the UBC Library made its various online catalogues accessible to the public, I have noticed an unprecedented enthusiasm for the new technology. I'm sure that our experience mirrors that of all other large Canadian academic libraries. Users find the interactive searching so successful that they are willing to acquire the skills to use it.

Institutions and private scholars with access to computers are compiling bibliographic files. In the last ten years, for instance, UBC Library has encouraged librarians to compile their own bibliographic databases. These files are now made available for public access. Examples are *Vancouver Centennial Bibliography*, which contains over 18,000 items; *BC Local History Bibliography*; *Canadian Childhood Bibliography* (a large database of over 16,000 publications very useful for both educators and researchers working on multiculturalism); *British Columbia Theses Catalogue*, and the *Canadian Politics Bibliography*, which lists more than 28,000 items.

The success of the electronic media over its predecessor is due mostly to its vast superiority on the criteria of retrievability. It enables searches by author's name, by subject, by words in titles or in abstracts, and additionally it enables one to link terms to restrict or enlarge a search. Now, at last, finding the works pertinent to the study of acculturation among low income, visible minority women becomes possible, provided of course that the database be comprehensive enough. Technically the problem of retrievability has been solved, and so has the problem of datedness. So we are back to the problem of comprehensiveness.

In a recent editorial in *The Canadian Library Journal*, Michael Mayer (1990) points out that we are undergoing a revolution comparable to that which took us from oral tradition to written word. We are in the process of fundamentally changing the storage and transmission of knowledge. With this conversion, slowly but surely, the role of librarians and libraries is changing. The costs of the new technology are staggering. Not counting the hardware, the software, programming, and storage, it may easily cost tens of thousands of dollars to create even a modest-sized database, let alone one the size, breadth, and sophistication of *Sociological* or *Psychological Abstracts*, *ERIC*, or *America: History and Life*. The cost of generating files, however, is only the beginning. To make them available to libraries for at-distance searching, powerful time-sharing computers which permit access by a large number of simultaneous users have to be purchased and maintained, fast and sophisticated printers must be provided to deliver off-line prints, customer service department and document delivery services must be created. Costly satellite communication channels and telephone links have to be maintained. Skilled, highly paid professionals have to be employed.

To ensure commercial viability, charges for using such services must be high. A commercial host offering online databases is obviously going to mount only the files which will have a large demand. Only information deemed to have a potentially wide appeal will be disseminated electronically. In the field of science, this may not be a problem since the entire world is a potential market. Mathematics, physics, chemistry, medicine all have universal appeal, but Canadian ethnic studies? Thus far, the only Canadian databases available commercially are those aimed at business people, lawyers, and educators/high school/public library users. Furthermore, whatever is available at-distance can be reached only at a cost that the researcher is rarely willing to pay. To illustrate these costs, consider a somewhat complicated search that lasts about 15 minutes and retrieves 100 citations. Add three citations displayed online to make sure that one she is getting the desired material. Add the cost of the librarian's time (1 hour at $60.00), add communications costs of and exchange charges since all but the librarian's salary must be paid in American currency. The total cost will range roughly from $80.00 if one searches the *Canadian Business and Current Affairs* database on CAN/OLE to $150.00 if one searches the *Dissertation Abstracts* on DIALOG. The economics of using the same databases in a CD-ROM format are obvious. For a set subscription rate (on the average $2000.00US), the database can be used constantly at no additional cost. This is particularly attractive to library patrons.

Mayer estimates that 65 per cent of bibliographic database suppliers have their head offices in the United States, and that this proportion is growing. More seriously, the field of electronic publishing ownership has fallen to large conglomerate corporations. I have no philosophical quarrels with multinational firms as long as they serve my needs, but in the field of Canadian ethnic studies they do not. That being the case, what can be done?

The solution might be in a joint effort by Canadian academia – research libraries, professional associations such as the Canadian Studies Association, the Bibliographic Society of Canada, and the Royal Society of Canada – as well as research-granting bodies such as the Canada Council and the Social Sciences Federation of Canada; they might get together and do what the National Library might have done but failed to do. We need to cooperate beyond the domain of ethnic studies. We need to create a vastly expanded *Canadiana* database that would fill the gaps of coverage identified and would offer its electronic service to Canadian libraries at a fraction of the commercial cost. This is quite possible. Such an enterprise could be based in any of the large library systems that already have sophisticated computer and software systems. The geographical location of such a centre is immaterial. For academic purposes the telecommunications network already exists. *Internet* will be vastly expanded and improved in the next few years, and since the American part of it is government-funded, the cost of using the Canadian segment will remain reasonable. The basic technical infrastructure exists. We need only create an organization.

Such an organization could be patterned on the Inter-University Consortium for Political and Social Research (ICPSR).[2] and the Colorado Alliance of Research Libraries (CARL)[3] models. The organization envisaged here would collect and administer ethnic and other bibliographies pertaining to Canada. The non-commercial data files meeting the Consortium's standards of quality control would be mounted for online access if they were ongoing projects. For the files that were finished or terminated, the consortium would develop the appropriate software and distribute the files to its members in an integrated data base, preferably in CD-ROM format. The SSHRCC might require that the bibliographies it funds be put in an electronic format and deposited at that Consortium. There are probably hundreds, if not thousands, of interesting Canadian files.

Obviously the Consortium should have editorial discretion to accept only those files it judges to be of sufficient quality, a quality to be determined by peer review. The governing council of the Consortium should include academics, librarians, and technicians. Member institutions would pay an annual subscription fee and receive the bibliographies free of charge, while non-members would be charged for whatever they acquired. The Consortium might need a grant at the start of its operation but should eventually operate as a cost recovering institution.

In addition to providing access to data already compiled, the Consortium should also initiate a cooperative on-going indexing project of Canadian 'grey literature,' journal articles and essays in collectively published works. Here CARL's *UnCover* might serve as a rough model, but our database would include more than journal articles. Our Consortium might be linked with a document delivery service. If CARL could create such a cooperative database with only eight Colorado libraries, surely Canada could do as well. And, of course, we would want to cooperate with the American Research Libraries Group (RLG) and the American Council of Learned Societies (ACLS) who have established 'a task force to investigate the creation of a multidisciplinary bibliography in history and related studies' (Porro 1992).

Among the databases that would hopefully be included in a future Canadian Electronic Bibliographies Consortium should be a Canadian cultural and social anthropology project. Nothing of the sort exists at the moment. Such a datafile should include literature on cultural and social anthropology of Canadian native peoples as well as other ethnic groups. It should be retrospective, listing books, journal articles, reports, working papers, government publications, theses and dissertations, and chapters in collectively published works. It should include materials published in Canada as well as abroad. I have no doubt that there would be a large academic market for such a file, not only in Canada but abroad, particularly in the United States.

CONCLUSION

The other chapters in this volume suggest, very generally, that the field of multicultural studies in Canada is in relatively good health, that Canada is an example to the rest of the world. The same cannot unfortunately be said of the bibliographic control of the field. I do not wish to leave the impression that the situation is catastrophic. It is not. This survey identified excellent publications. But the coverage is far from systematic. We are in danger of not making a rapid enough transition from print to the electronic age. We must ensure that we do not become dependent on foreign sources that will satisfy our research needs only partially. A collective enterprise is necessary, one that calls for the collaboration of governments, libraries and academics on a national scale. We need to create a Canadian electronic library consortium. Why not start with the field of multiethnic and multicultural studies?

NOTES

1 A bibliography of about 5000 items compiled for a 1992 survey of research on multiculturalism (Laponce 1992) included the following types of entries: books, pamphlets, and theses, 31.5 per cent; journal articles, 44 per cent; chapters in collective works, 24.5 per cent.

2 The ICPSR was founded as a partnership between the University of Michigan Survey Research Center and 21 universities. Its mission was to collect and disseminate machine-readable *numeric* social science data. In 1962, when it was becoming increasingly clear that important numeric data were being produced and then 'lost' – either because no one knew of their existence or because card files on which the data was stored got lost, damaged, or thrown out – American social scientists became concerned to preserve such valuable research tools. What each individual researcher could not do, could be done by a collective. The institution was financed essentially by membership fees, foundation grants, and grants from the University of Michigan. Since then, membership has expanded to over 330 universities all over the world. It has become 'a central repository and dissemination service for machine-readable social science data' where scholars deposit their data (ICPSR 1990:3) This date is 'cleaned' by the Consortium, put in standard machine-readable format, and made available to members together with code books, free of charge.

3 It is symptomatic of the present lack of communication that Batts' electronic bibliography of German, Italian, Polish, and Spanish literatures (Batts 1991) became known to me only from reading *Ethnic Studies*, although we are both at the same university and both in the process of building machine-readable files in related areas.

REFERENCES

Batts, M.S. (1991). 'Pilot' bibliographies of Canadian ethnic literature (German, Hungarian, Italian, Polish, Spanish) *Canadian Ethnic Studies*, 23(1):97–103
Burnet, J. (1988). Multiculturalism. In *Canadian encyclopedia*. Vol. 3, p 1401. 2nd ed. Edmonton: Hurtig Publishers
Inter-university Consortium for Political and Social Research (1990). *Guide to resources and services, 1989–1990*. Ann Arbor, MI, The Consortium
Laponce, Iza (1992). *Mosaican: A data base of research on Canada's multicultural society*. Ottawa: Multiculturalism and Citizenship Canada
Mayer, M. (1990). Transformation of librarianship; Editorial. *Canadian Library Journal*, 47(4):233–5
Nilsen, K. (ed.) (1992). *Guide to basic reference materials for Canadian libraries*. 8th ed. Toronto: Published for the Faculty of Library and Information Science by University of Toronto Press

Porro, J. (1992). *RLG and ACLS sponsor task force on multidisciplinary bibliography* (E-mail personal communication 6 Mar. 1992

Rogers, S.J., and Hurt, C.S. (1990). How scholarly communication should work in the 21st century. *College & Research Libraries, 51*(1):5–6, 8

Ryder, D.E. (1981). *Canadian reference sources; a selective guide.* 2nd ed. Ottawa: Canadian Library Association

APPENDIX

START HERE: Guide to reference materials on multiculturalism in Canada

I BOOKS on this subject may be searched: online or in a subject micro-
catalogue, or in a library's subject card catalogue under specific headings. If a library is using the Library of Congress or National Library
subject headings, one might start with:

Ontario – Emigration and immigration
Canada – Emigration and immigration
Canada – English-French relations
Canada – Foreign population
Canada – Population – Ethnic groups
Chinese Canadians – Ontario
Greek Canadians – Quebec
Ethnic attitudes
Ethnic groups – Education
Ethnic press – Manitoba – Winnipeg
Ethnic relations
Ethnicity – Canada – Bibliography
Minorities – Canada
Social work with minorities – B.C. – Vancouver
Linguistic minorities

II HANDBOOKS, DICTIONARIES, DIRECTORIES, ETC.

Bogusis, R. *Checklist of Canadian ethnic serials.* Ottawa, Newspaper
    Division, Public Services Branch, 1981. 381 p.
Canadian encyclopedia. 2d ed. Edmonton, Hurtig Publishers, 1988. 4 v.
Canada. Multiculturalism Directorate. *The Canadian family tree: Canada's*

peoples. Rev. and updated ed. Don Mills, Ont., Corpus Information
   Services, 1979. 250 p.
Handbook of North American Indians. W.C. Sturtevand, general editor.
   Washington, D.C., U.S. Superintendent of Documents, 1978– . See
   especially v. 4, 5, 7, 15.
Markotic, V. and B. Hromadiuk. *Ethnic directory of Canada.* 2d ed.
   Calgary, Western Publishers, 1983. 123 p.
Tanner, H.H. *Atlas of Great Lakes Indian history.* Norman, Newberry
   Library, University of Oklahoma Press, 1987. 224 p.
Waldman, C. *Atlas of the North American Indian.* New York, Facts on
   File, 1985. 276 p.

III STATISTICS

The 1986 Census Canada is the latest published census. The following
parts may prove to be useful:

   93–154 – Profile of ethnic groups
   93–102–103 – Language
   93–155 – Profile of immigrant population
   93–109 – Ethnicity, immigration, citizenship
   93–153 – Language retention and transfer
   93–157 – Canadians and their occupations (occupations by ethnic
      origin and mother tongue)

Machine readable data files

Canada 1986 Census. Ottawa, Statistics Canada, Electronic Data Dissemi-
   nation Division, Data Dissemination Division, 1991–. 1 computer
   laser optical disk.
Demography short form files (1986 census of Canada). Ottawa, Statistics
   Canada, 1986. 1 computer tape reel + documentation [CdBk]. Contains aggregate data on demography.
Families public use microdata file (1986 census of Canada). Ottawa, Statistics
   Canada, 1986. 1 computer tape reel + documentation [CdBk]. Contains a wide range of statistical data on the population of Canada.
   Data are based on a sample of 67,000 families, and 36,000 non-family
   persons representing approximately 1% of all families and non-
   family persons in Canada. Users can return to the base unit of the
   census enabling them to group data to suit their own requirements.

Households short form files (1986 census of Canada). Ottawa, Statistics Canada, 1986. 1 computer tape reel + documentations [CdBk]. Contains aggregate household data.

Mother tongue short form file (1986 census of Canada). Ottawa, Statistics Canada, 1986. 1 computer tape reel + documentation [CdBk]. Contains aggregate data for mother tongue.

Ethno-cultural long form files (1986 census of Canada). Ottawa, Statistics Canada, 1986. 1 computer tape + documentation [CdBk]. Contains aggregate ethno-cultural data.

Language long form files (1986 census of Canada). Ottawa, Statistics Canada, 1986. 1 computer tape + documentation [CdBk]. Contains aggregate language data.

Households long form files (1986 census of Canada). Ottawa, Statistics Canada, 1986. 1 computer tape + documentation [CdBk]. Contains aggregate household data.

Individual file (1986 census of Canada). Ottawa, Statistics of Canada, 1986. 1 computer tape reel + documentation [CdBk]. Contains a wide range of statistical data on the population of Canada, the provinces and most metropolitan areas. Data are based on a sample of 500,000 individuals, representing approximately 2% of the population.

Other statistical sources

Bourbeau, R. *Canada, a linguistic profile / Le Canada, un profil linguistique.* Ottawa, Statistics Canada, 1989. 37, 37p.

Historical statistics of Canada. F. H. Leacy, editor. 2nd ed. Ottawa, Statistics Canada, 1983. 800 p.

Immigration statistics / Statistiques d'immigration. 1946/55– . Ottawa, Immigration and Demographic Policy Group, Employment and Immigration Canada, 1955– . (annual)

Indian register population by sex and residence / Population du régistre des Indiens selon le sexe et la residence. Ottawa, Registration, Revenues and Band Governance Indian and Inuit Program, Dept. of Indian Affairs and Northern Development, 197– . (annual) Title changes frequently

Lachapelle, R. and L. M. Dallaire. *Demolinguistic profiles of minority official language communities / Profils démolinguistiques des communautés minoritaires de langue officielle.* Ottawa, Promotion of Official Languages Branch, Dept. of the Secretary of State of Canada, 1990. 13 parts; each part covers one province or territory, and one part summarizing the national picture.

Language retention and transfer / Retention et transfert linguistiques.
Ottawa, Statistics Canada, 1989. 1989. 1 v. (various pagings).
Laroque, G.Y. and R.P. Gauvin. *1986 census highlights on registered
Indians: Annotated tables / Points saillants du recensement de 1986 sur les
Indiens inscrits.* Ottawa, Quantitative Analysis and Socio-demo-
graphic Research, Indian and Northern Affairs, Canada, 1989. 31 p.
Loh, S. *Registered Indian household and family projections 1986–2011 /
Projections de la population indienne inscrite, 1986–2011.* Ottawa, Statis-
tics Canada, 1990. 53 p.
Multicultural Canada: a graphic overview / Un Canada multiculturel.
Ottawa, Multiculturalism and Citizenship Canada, 1990. 81, [41],
[41], 81 p.
Statistiques culturelles du Québec, 1971–1982. Québec, Institut québécois
de la recherche sur la culture, 1985. 1 v. (various pagings)
White, P. M. *Ethnic diversity in Canada / Diversite ethnique au Canada.*
Ottawa, Statistics Canada, 1990. 48, 50p.

IV BIBLIOGRAPHIES This literature may consists of journal articles,
reports, essays in collected works, government publications, or dissertations which are often not listed in the library's catalogue.

GENERAL

Berry, J.W. and G.J.S. Wilde. *Social psychology of Canada: An annotated
bibliography.* Kingston, Queen's University, 1971. 96 p.
Burnet, Jean R. *Multiculturalism in Canada.* Ottawa, Dept. of the Secre-
tary of State of Canada, 1988. 26 p., 29 p.
Canada. Dept. of Citizenship and Immigration. *Citizenship, immigration
and ethnic groups in Canada: A bibliography ... 1920–1958.* Ottawa, The
Department, 1960. 190 p.
– *Citizenship, immigration and ethnic groups in Canada: A bibliography,
1959–68.* Ottawa, The Department, 1962–1969. 3 v.
Canada. Dept. of the Secretary of State. Library. *A Selected bibliography of
current readings on ethnic groups with special relevance to Canada.*
Ottawa, The Department, 1970. 8 l.
– Library. *Canadian ethnic groups bibliography.* 2d ed. Ottawa, Secretary
of the State, 1985. 96 l.
– Research and Planning Branch. *Selected bibliography on francophone
minorities in Canada / Bibiographie choisie sur les minorités francophones
au Canada.* Ottawa, The Branch, 1972. 2 v.

Canada. Office of the Commissioner of Official Languages. *Annotated bibliography of the official languages of Canada*. Ottawa, The Office, 1991. 53 p.

Canadian ethnic studies: Bibliography / Etudes ethniques du Canada: Bibliographie. 1969–1976. Calgary, Alta., University of Calgary.
Ceased as a separate publication, but included now on an annual basis in the *Canadian Ethnic Studies* journal.

Desrochers, A.M. *The social psychology of inter-ethnic contact and cross-cultural communication: An annotated bibliography*. Quebec, International Center for Research on Bilingualism, 1979. 261 p.

Gregorovich, A. *Canadian ethnic groups: A selected bibliography of ethnocultural groups in Canada and the Province of Ontario*. Toronto, Ontario Dept. of the Provincial Secretary and Citizenship, 1971. 208 p.

Jackson, R. 'Development of the multicultural policy in Canada: A bibliography.' *Canadian Library Journal* v.33 (3), 1976, pp 237–43.

Mahler, Gregory, comp. *Contemporary Canadian politics: An annotated bibliography, 1970–1987*. New York, Greenwood Press, 1988. 400 p.

Mallea, J. R. and E.C. Shea. *Multiculturalism and education: A selected bibliography*. Toronto, Ontario Institute for Studies in Education and Ontario Ministry of Culture and Recreation, 1979. 290 p.

Miska, John. *Ethnic and native Canadian literature: A bibliography*. Toronto, University of Toronto Press, 1990. 445 p.

Mazur, Carol and Sheila Pepper. *Women in Canada: A bibliography, 1965–1982*. 3rd ed. Toronto, Press, 1984. 377 p.

Publications supported by the Multiculturalism Directorate, Government of Canada. Ottawa, Dept. of the Secretary of State, Multiculturalism Directorate, 1981–1987. 3 v.

Reid, Darrel R. *Bibliography of Canadian and comparative federalism, 1980–1985*. Kingston (Ont), Queen's University, Institue of Intergovernmental Relations, 1987. 492 p.

– *Bibliography of Canadian and comparative federalism, 1986*. Kingston (Ont), Queen's University, Institue of Intergovernmental Relations, 1988. 105 p.

Thibault, C. *Bibliographia canadiana*. Don Mills, Ont., Longman Canada, 1973. 795 p.

Supplemented and updated by Aubin, Paul.
Bibliographie de l'histoire du Quebec et du Canada, 1946–1980. Quebec, Institut quebecois de la recherche sur la culture, 1981– . 5 v.

REGIONAL

Western Canada

Arora, V. *The Saskatchewan bibliography.* Regina, Saskatchewan Provincial Library, 1980. 787 p.

Artibise, A.F.J. *Western Canada since 1870: A select bibliography and guide.* Vancouver, University of British Columbia Press, 1978. 294 p.

British Columbia Centennial Committee. *Ethnic groups in British Columbia: A selected bibliography* ... Victoria, 1957.

Duff, W. *Indians of British Columbia: Selected bibliography.* Vancouver, University of British Columbia, 1986. 3v. in 1.

Hackett, C. *A bibliography of Manitoba local history: A guide to local and regional histories.* 2d ed. Winnipeg, Manitoba Historical Society, 1989. 156 p.

Hale, L. *Vancouver centennial bibliography.* Vancouver, Vancouver Historical Society, 1986. 4 v.

Krótki, Joanna E. *Local histories of Alberta: An annotated bibliography.* 2d ed. Edmonton, Dept. of Slavic and East European Studies, University of Alberta, 1983. 430 p.

Liddell, P.G. *A Bibliography of the Germans in British Columbia.* Vancouver, CAUTG, 1982. 89 p.

Madill, D. *Select annotated bibliography on British Columbia Indian policy and land claims.* Ottawa, Treaties and Historical Research Centre, Research Branch, Corporate Policy, Dept. of Indian and Northern Affairs, 1982. 27 p.

Strathern, G. M. *Alberta, 1954–1979: A provincial bibliography.* Edmonton, University of Alberta, 1982. 745 p.

Central Canada

Bishop, Olga. *Bibliography of Ontario history 1867–1976: Cultural economic, political, social.* Toronto, Univerity of Toronto Press, 1980. 2 v. See v.1, pp. 473–515: Also check index in v.2 for more specific topics.

Dworaczek, M. *Minority groups in Metropolitan Toronto.* Toronto, Ontario Ministry of Labour, Research Library, 1973. 57 p.

– *Supplement.* Toronto, Ontario Ministry of Labour, 1975. 48 p.

Helms, J. *The Indians of subarctic: A critical bibliography.* Bloomington, Univerity of Indiana University Press, 1976. 91 p.

Helms, J. and R. Kurtz. *Subarctic Athapaskan bibliography.* Iowa City, Dept. of Anthropology, University of Iowa, 1984. 515 p.

Gérvais, Gaetan. *The Bibliography of Ontario history / La biliographie d'histoire Ontarienne 1976–1986.* Toronto, Dundurn Press, 1989. 695 p. See particularly pp. 253–281.

Lambert, R.D. *The sociology of contemporary Quebec nationalism: An annotated bibliography and review.* New York, Garland Publishing Inc., 1981.

Moulary-Ouerghi, Josiane and C. Villemaine. *Referendum québécois: Bibliographie.* Montreal, Editions Bergeron, 1983. 276 p.

O'Donnell, B. *Printed sources for the study of English-speaking Quebec: An annotated bibliography of works printed before 1980.* Lennoxville, P.Q., Bishop's University, 1985. 298 p.

Rome, D. [et al.] *Les juifs du Québec: Bibliographie rétrospective annotée.* Québec, Institut québécois de recherche sur la culture, 1981. 317 p.

Senécal, A. *Quebec studies: A selected, annotated bibliography.* Burlington, Vt., Information Center on Canada, 1982. 215 p.

Atlantic Canada

Morrison, James H. *Common heritage: An annotated bibliography of ethnic groups in Nova Scotia.* Halifax, N.S., International Education Centre, Saint Mary's University, 1984. 130 p.

SPECIFIC ETHNIC GROUPS

Blacks

Anderson, W.W. *Caribbean orientations: A bibliography of resource materials on the Caribbean experience in Canada.* Toronto, Williams-Wallace, 1985. 238 p.

Blizzard, H. *West Indians in Canada: A selective annotated bibliography.* Guelph, The Library University of Guelph, 1970. 41 l.

Govia, Francine and Helen Lewis. *Blacks in Canada in search of the promise: A bibliographical guide to the history of Blacks in Canada.* Edmonton, Harambee Centres Canada, 1988. 102 p.

Asians

Buchignani, N. 'A review of the historical and sociological literature on East Indians in Canada.' *Canadian ethnic studies* v.9(1) 1977, pp. 86–108.

Indra, Doreen Marie. *Southeast Asian refugee settlement in Canada: A research bibliography*. Ottawa, Canadian Asian Studies Association, Carleton University, 1984. 29 l.

Iwaasa, D.B. *The Japanese Canadians: A bibliography*. [s.l] Iwaasa, 1975. 27 l.

Jain, S.K. 'East Indians in Canada.' *Research Group for European Migration Problems. Bulletin*, supplement 9, June 1971, pp. 3–16.

Kim Hyung-Chan. *Asian American studies: An annotated bibliography and research guide*. New York, Greenwood Press, 1989. 584 p.

Saito, S. *Filipinos overseas: A bibliography*. New York, Center for Migration Studies, 1977. 156 p.

Europeans

Anderson, G.M. *Selected bibliography on Portuguese immigration*. Toronto [n.p.] 1969. 8 p.

Brye, D.L. *European immigration and ethnicity in the United States and Canada: A historical bibliography*. Santa Barbara, Calif., ABC-Clio Information Services, 1983. 458 p.

Dwyer, J.D. *Slovenes in the United States and Canada: A bibliography*. Minneapolis, Immigration History Research Center, University of Minnesota, 1981. 196 p.

Gakovich, R. P. and M. M. Radovich *Serbs in the United States and Canada: A comprehensive bibliography*. Minneapolis, Immigration History Research Center, University of Minniapolis, 1976. 129 p.

Jarabek, E. *Czechs and Slovaks in North America: A bibliography*. New York, Czechoslovak Society of Arts & Sciences in America, 1976. 448 p.

Krisztinkovich, Maria. *A Doukhobor bibliography*. Vancouver, University of British Columbia Library, 1968–1972. 3 v. & Suppl.

Miska, John P. *Canadian studies on Hungarians, 1886–1986: An annotated bibliography of primary and secondary sources*. Regina, Canadian Plains Research Center, 1987. 245 p.

Myroniuk, H. and C. Worobec. *Ukrainians in North America: A select bibliography*. Toronto, Multicultural History Society of Ontario, 1981. 236 p.

Redekop, Calvin W. *Bibliography of Mennonities in Waterloo county and Ontario*. 2d ed. Waterloo, Ont., Institute of Anabaptist and Mennonite Studies, Conrad Grebel College, 1989. 19 p.

Sokolyszyn, A. and V. Wertsman. *Ukrainians in Canada and the United States: A guide to information sources*. Detroit, Mich., Gale Research Co., 1981. 236 p.

Sturino, F. *Italian-Canadians studies: A select bibliography*. Toronto, Mariano E. Elia Chair in Italian-Canadian Studies, York University, 1988. 100 p.

Szeplaki, J. *Hungarians in the United states and Canada: A bibliography*. Minneapolis, Immigration History Research Center, University of Minnesota, 1977. 113 p.

Turek, V. *Polonica Canadiana: A bibliography list of the Canadian Polish imprints, 1848–1957*. Toronto, Polish Alliance Press, 1958. 138 p.

Wertsman, V. *The Romanians in America and Canada: A guide to information sources*. Detroit, Mich., Gale Research Co., 1980. 164 p.

Zolobka, V. *Polonica Canadiana, a bibiographical list of the Candian Polish imprints, 1958–1970, with supplement 1848–1957*. Toronto, Polish Allaince Press, 1978. 414 p.

Native peoples

Abler, T. and S. Weaver. *A Canadian Indian bibliography, 1960–1970*. Toronto, University of Toronto Press, 1974. 732 p.

Bramstedt, W.C. *North American Indians in towns and cities*. Monticello, Ill., Vance bibliographies, 1979. 74 p.

Brooks, I.R. *Native education in Canada and the United States: A bibliography*. Calgary, Office of Educational Development, Indian Students University Program Services, University of Calgary, 1976. 298 p.

Clements, W.M. and F.C. Malpezzi. *Native American folklore, 1879–1979: An annotaed bibliography*. Athens, Ohio, Swallow Press, 1984. 247 p.

Friesen, J.W. and T. Lusty. *The Metis in Canada: An annotated bibliography*. Toronto, OISE Press, 1980. 99 p.

Fritz, L. *Native law bibliography*. 2d ed. Saskatoon, University of Saskatchewan, Native Law Centre, 1990. 167 p.

Horn, C. and C.T. Griffith. *Native North Americans: Crime, conflict and criminal justice: A research bibliography*. 4th ed. Burnaby, B.C., Northern Justice Society, 1989. 275 p.

Krech, S. *Native Canadian anthropology and history: A selected bibliography*. Winnipeg, University of Winnipeg, 1986. 214 p.

Madill, D. *Select annotated bibliography on Metis history and claims*. Ottawa, Treaties and Historical Research Centre, Indian and Northern Affairs Canada, 1983. 45 p.

Meiklejohn, C. and D.A. Rokala. *The Native people of Canada: An annotaed bibliography of population biology, health and illness*. Ottawa, National Museums of Canada, 1986. 564 p.

Murdock, G.P. *Ethnographic bibliography of North America*. New Haven, Conn., Human Relations Area Files Press, 1975. 5 v.
Supplemented by:
Martin, M. M. *Ethnographic bibliography of North America: 4th edition supplement 1973–1987*. New Haven, Conn., Human Relations Area Files, 1990. 3 v.
Native peoples: Resources pertaining to Indians, Inuit, and Metis. 4th ed. Winnipeg, Native Education and Training, 1990. 263 p.
Peters, E. J. *Aboriginal self government in Canada: A bibliography 1986*. Kingston (Ont.), Institute of Intergovernmental Studies, 1986. 112 p.
Roy, B.K. *The rights of indigenous peoples in international law: An annotates bibliography*. Saskatoon, University of Saskatchewan Native Law Centre, 1985. 97 p.
– *Supplement* Saskatoon, Univerity of Saskatchewan Native Law Centre, 1986. 33 p.
Smith, D.L. *Indians of the United States and Canada: A bibliography*. Santa Barbara, Calif., ABC-Clio Inc., 1974–1983. 2 v.
Whiteside, D. *Aboriginal peoples: A selected bibliography concerning Canada's first people*. Ottawa, National Indian Brotherhood, 1973. 345 p.

V   INDEXES AND ABSTRACTS

America: history and life. 1964– . Santa Barbara, ABC-Clio.
  (quarterly, subject and author indexes cumulate annually, and every 5 years). Available for at-distance online searching through DIALOG or KNOWLEDGE INDEX. Also available in CD-ROM format
Arts and humanities citation index. 1976– . Philadelphia, Institute for Scientific Information (semi-annual, cumulates annually). Available for at-distance online searching through BRS, DIALOG
Bibliographic index. v.1– ; 1938– . New York, H.W. Wilson. (annual). Available for at-distance online searching through WILSONLINE. Also available in CD-ROM format
Bibliographie du Québec. v.1– ; 1968– . Montreal, Bibliothèque nationale du Québec, 1970– (Annual). Available for at-distance online searching through CATSS (UTLAS)
Canadian business and current affairs. Toronto, Micromedia. Available for at-distance online searching through CAN/OLE, DIALOG, QL. Also availabe in CD-ROM format.
Canadian education index. 1965– . Ottawa, Canadian Council for Research in Education. (semi-annual, cumulates annually). Available

in CD-ROM format and in magnetic tape for onsite mainframe mounting.

Canadian index. v. 1–; 1993–. Toronto, Micromedia (monthly, cumulates annually). CD-ROM version called *Canadian Business and Current Affairs.*

Canadian news index. v.1–16: 1977–1992. Toronto, Micromedia. (Monthly, cumulated annually). Since 1993 continued by *Canadian index,* but separate news index available on magnetic tape. Available for at-distance online searching.

Canadian periodical index. 1920– . Toronto, InfoGlobe. (monthly with annual cumulations). Cumulations: 1920–1937; 1938–1947; 1948–1959. From 1960–, cumulations are annual. Available for at-distance online searching through InfoGlobe. Soon to be available in CD-ROM format.

Canadian public administration: Bibliography / Administration publique canadienne: Bibliographie. v.1– ; 1972– . Toronto, Institute of Public Administration of Canada. (irregular)

Canadiana; Canada's national bibliography. 1950– . Ottawa, National Library, 1951– (Annual, with periodic cumulations on microfiche). Available for at-distance searching through DOBIS and CAN/OLE

Directory of statistics in Canda. v.1–; 1985–. Toronto, Micromedia, 1986–. (annual) Previous title: *Canadian statistics index.* Available on magnetic tape for local library mounting.

ERIC. 1966– . Washington, D.C., Educational Resources Information Center, 1966– (Monthly, with annual cumulations) Made up of two separate indexes: *Resources in education* (RIE) and *Current index to journals in education* (CIJE). Available for online searching through DIALOG, BRS, KNOWLEDGE Also available on magnetic tape and CD-ROM formats

Government of Canada publications / Publications du gouvernement du Canada. v.1– ; 1927/38– . Ottawa, Supply and Services Canada. (Frequency varies over the years, recently quarterly, with annual indexes). Title varies over the years.

Index to Canadian legal periodical literature. v.1– ; 1963/65– . Montreal, Canadian Association of Law Libraries. (quarterly, with annual cumulations. Also cumulates every 5 years)

Index to social sciences and humanities proceedings. v.1– ; 1979– . Philadephia, Institute for Scientific Information. (quarterly, with annual cumulation)

International bibliography of social and cultural anthropology / Bibliographie

internationale d'anthropologie sociale et culturelle. v.1– ; 1955– . London, Routledge. (Annual, but very late in being published)
Linguistics and language behavior abstracts: LLBA. v.1– ; 1967– . La Jolla, Calif., Sociological Abstracts. (Quarterly with annual subject and author indexes). Title varies: 1967–1985 Language and language behavior abstacts. Available for at-distance online searching through BRS and DIALOG.
MLA international bibliography of books and articles on the modern languages and literatures. v.1– ; 1921/25– . New York, Modern Language Association of America. (Annual). Available for at-distance online searching through DIALOG, KNOWLEDGE INDEX and WILSONLINE Also available in CD-ROM format.
Point de repere. v.1– ; Jan/Feb. 1984– ; Montreal, Centrale des bibliotheques, Bibliotheque nationale du Quebec, 1984– (10 times a year, with annual cumulation). Merger of *Periodex* and *Radar.* Available for at-distance searching from SDM as file REPERE
Population index. v.1– ; 1935– . Princeton, N.J., Office of Population Research, Princeton University. (Quarterly, with annual subject cumulation)
Psychological abstracts. v.1– ; 1927– . Arlington, Vir., American Psychological Association Inc. (Monthly, with cumulated annual author and subject indexes. Larger subject and author cumulations exist for the early period). Available for at-distance online searching (as PSYCINFO) for the period 1967 to date, through BRS, DATA-STAR and DIALOG. The PSYCINFO is also available in CD-ROM format.
Social sciences citation index. 1966– . Philadelphia, Institute for Scientific Information. (Issued three times a year, the third issue is the annual cumulation. Also has following cumulations: 1956–65; 1966–70; 1971–75; 1976–80; 1981–85). Available for at-distance online searching through BRS, DATA-STAR, DIALOG. Also available in CD-ROM format. 1966–
Sociological abstracts. v.1– ; 1953– . New York, Sociological Abstracts Inc. (6 issues a year, with a cumulated annual author and subject index). Available for at-distance online searching through BRS, DATA-STAR, KNOWLEDGE INDEX and DIALOG. Also available in CD-ROM format.

VI THESES

National Library of Canada. *Canadian theses.* v.1– ; 1952– . Ottawa, National Library (Annual, with some cumulation. The years

1947/60– 1979/80 are in paper editions. From 1980 the publication is in microfiche)

Dissertation abstracts international. Section A: Humanities and social sciences. v.1– ; 1938– . Ann Arbor, Mich., University Microfilms. (Monthly, with subject and name indexes cumulated annually. There are also major subject and author cumulations available) Title varies: Microfilm abstracts; Dissertations abstracts. Available for at-distance searching through OCLC Online Computer Library (EPIC), BRS, DIALOG and KNOWLEDGE INDEX.

Index